IN ▶▶ THE NEWS

PEARSON

Upper Saddle River, New Jersey   Boston, Massachusetts   Chandler, Arizona   Glenview, Illinois

Letter to the Reader

If someone were to tell you "History happens every day," how would you respond? You might be tempted to say: "History is only in the past. Old places, lost kingdoms, faraway lands . . . stuff like that." But events happening around the world right now will be history some day. Small events may only be part of your own personal history. Larger events may change the course of history in your community, your nation, or the world.

The news of these events comes from everywhere, right? It's on television, it's online, it's in newspapers, it's on the radio; it even comes by word of mouth. You are bombarded from every direction. How you choose to use that information is up to you. You can ignore it, or you could recognize that it is changing the world you live in. Many successful people are those who not only know what is happening around them, but who can also see the possible consequences.

On the following pages, you will encounter some recent events and trends. You will see how the balance of power adjusts and shifts around the world. You will explore some of the major issues in the news today—the world economy, the environment, the stresses of population growth, and ideological conflicts. You will see how change affects individuals and nations in an interconnected world.

Discussion questions throughout the readings have no right or wrong answers. But as you and your classmates discuss possible answers, you will be engaging in the discourse allowed by our democratic system. As you explore and discuss, you may try to answer this question for yourself: How does this affect me?

Consider the words of Thomas Jefferson, *"If a nation expects to be ignorant and free . . . it expects what never was and never will be."*

IN▶▶ THE NEWS

Chip Somodevilla/Getty Images

Peter Macdiarmid/Getty Images

Boston Globe / Getty Images

Cover photos: (TL) Win McNamee/Getty Images; (TR) Nasser Nouri Xinhua News Agency/Newscom (BL) Ryan McGinnis /Getty Images; (BR) PARANJPE/AFP/Newscom

Global Hard Times

The world's economies face recession, job loss, austerity, and protests.

Thousands protest against Spanish austerity measures in Madrid. Several hundred government workers joined the protest after the latest measures to lower Spain's deficit were announced; a 65-billion-euro ($80 billion) austerity package involving tax increases and cuts in unemployment benefits.

Eurozone in Trouble

Making sense of the debt crisis.

Q What is Europe's "sovereign debt crisis"?

A Sovereign debt refers to the money a country has borrowed to pay for expenses, such as salaries, public services, and pensions. Countries borrow by selling bonds. Investors buy the bonds that will be repaid, with interest, over time. If a country's economy is weak, investors will not buy its bonds unless the country pays high interest, which then makes borrowing more costly. Greece, Spain, Portugal, Ireland, and Italy have debt problems.

Q What is the Eurozone?

A The Eurozone includes the 17 European countries that use a common currency, the euro. Some Eurozone countries, such as the United Kingdom, do not use the euro.

Science Photo Library / Alamy

EU Wins Nobel Peace Prize

The Norwegian Nobel Committee awarded the Nobel Peace Prize for 2012 to the European Union (EU). Although some critics questioned the timing of the award, the committee explained its choice. "The EU is currently undergoing grave economic difficulties and considerable social unrest," the committee announced in a statement. "The Norwegian Nobel Committee wishes to focus on what it sees as the EU's most important result; the successful struggle for peace and reconciliation and for democracy and human rights. The stabilizing part played by the EU has helped to transform most of Europe from a continent of war to a continent of peace."

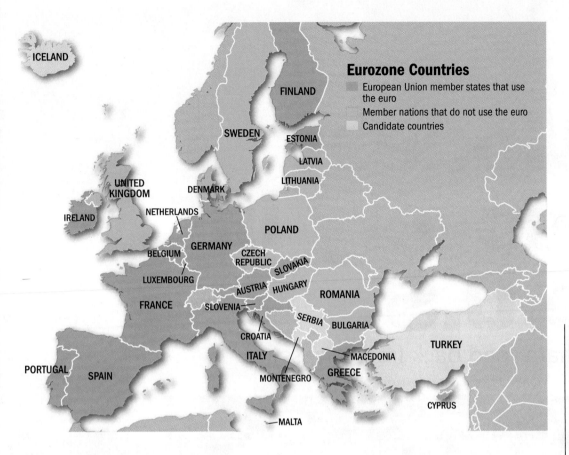

Eurozone Countries

European Union member states that use the euro

Member nations that do not use the euro

Candidate countries

ICELAND

FINLAND

SWEDEN

ESTONIA

LATVIA

LITHUANIA

UNITED KINGDOM

DENMARK

IRELAND

NETHERLANDS

POLAND

BELGIUM

GERMANY

CZECH REPUBLIC

SLOVAKIA

LUXEMBOURG

AUSTRIA

HUNGARY

ROMANIA

FRANCE

SLOVENIA

SERBIA

BULGARIA

CROATIA

TURKEY

ITALY

MACEDONIA

PORTUGAL

SPAIN

MONTENEGRO

GREECE

CYPRUS

MALTA

Q Why did huge protests erupt in Greece?

A During the boom times, Greece borrowed heavily. Then the global economic meltdown battered its economy, leaving it with massive debt. Led by Germany, Europe's strongest economy, negotiators drew up a bailout plan that required Greece to make deep spending cuts. The Greek government agreed. Harsh austerity measures brought layoffs and cuts in services. Facing severe hardships, angry Greeks stormed into the streets in protest.

Q Why is austerity so unpopular?

A Austerity involves deep cuts in government spending in order to reduce borrowing. It brings layoffs, cuts in health care and education, and lower salaries and pensions.

Q How has the debt crisis affected governments in Europe?

A In 2012, voters in France, Greece, Spain, Ireland, Portugal, and the Netherlands rejected leaders who backed austerity in favor of those who promised to increase spending. More spending, they said, would boost growth and spur recovery, allowing countries to repay their debts. The elections showed growing support for political parties on the far right, such as neo-Nazis, and on the far left, such as anti-capitalists.

Q How do Europe's debt problems affect the U.S.?

A In an interconnected world, what happens in Europe has global impact. Europe's economic crisis hurts U.S. trade because Europeans buy fewer U.S.-made goods. European problems cause U.S. stock values to fall. Finally, Europe's problems raised the "contagion fear" of a new credit crisis. Global financial markets are intertwined. U.S. banks, for example, may own French debt. French banks, in turn, may own Italian debt. If Italy defaults, or fails to repay its debts, French banks are hurt, which in turn hurts U.S. banks.

> **Should some eurozone measures be used in the U.S.? Why or why not?**

New Economic Players

A powerful new bloc is emerging onto the world economic stage. Dubbed "The Brics" by economists, the bloc includes five influential, emerging economies: Brazil, Russia, India, China, and South Africa. Together they carry some serious economic muscle. They represent 45 percent of the world's population and about a quarter of all global economic activity. Politically, they are a diverse group, but economically, they have an ambitious goal: To shift the balance of global economic power from the developed world, especially the U.S. and European Union, to the emerging world. If the Brics succeed, they will create a new multipolar world. Their goal is a challenge to developed economies in the West that have long dominated the global economy.

A Modest Recovery in the U.S.

The long, hard road back from recession.

John Moore/Getty Images

Job applicants line up to meet potential employers at a job fair in New York City. Some 400 arrived early for the event, but up to 1,000 people were expected.

For millions of Americans, the story is all too familiar: Working one job for years, they've been laid off and unable to find the same kind of work. If there is a job, it's temporary or doesn't pay as well or is in a different industry.

"I hate being unemployed. I never know if I can pay bills or feed myself or my dog," said one person on an online job search forum. "I don't sleep well and spend most of my time looking for a place to work."

David R. Frazier Photolibrary, Inc. / Alamy

Boom Times

Job seekers have flooded into the oil-rich part of North Dakota. At a time when millions of Americans are jobless, North Dakota boomtowns have jobs to spare. The boom has brought growth and opportunities, but for some, it is a nightmare. "We've been invaded," remarked farmer Dan Kalil. All he sees are oil rigs marring the landscape. The boom has strained the resources of small towns. Roads are jammed with trucks and the housing shortage is so severe that some people live in their cars.

Making a Comeback

The great recession had officially ended by June 2009. By then, it had thrown millions of Americans out of work. Even as a modest recovery crept into gear, the jobless rate remained high.

The recession was longer and deeper than previous downturns. More jobs were lost than in any recession since the early 1980s. Jobs in construction disappeared when the housing market crashed. Jobs in transportation, mining, and utilities also dried up. Hard-pressed towns, cities, and states slashed their budgets and laid off workers. As they cut funding for many programs, still more jobs were lost.

By 2012, unemployment had fallen to about 8 percent but still not to pre-recession levels of 6 percent. Jobs and the economic recovery were hotly debated during the election. At issue was the question: Should the government stimulate the economy by spending to create jobs or should it cut budgets deeply to reduce the national debt?

The recovery was slow and uneven. Large cities and their surrounding areas moved ahead first. Less urbanized areas saw slower gains.

Some industries fared better than others. Green industries, such as companies that manufactured solar panels, benefited from policies that promoted green energy. As Americans focused more on staying healthy, they boosted sales of companies selling health-related products and services. In technology, web-based industries, web games, and the social networking industry made gains. Even the housing market slowly improved, although home prices remained low. Consumers began to spend again, upping demand for goods and services. As businesses recovered, they expanded and hired more workers.

John Darkow/Columbia Daily Tribune

Full Recovery

Some economists predicted that a full recovery might not be reached until 2017 or 2018. Outside shocks like the European debt crisis or a prolonged, steep rise in oil prices could also hurt. Some experts worried that if not enough new jobs were created and the economy remained weak, the U.S. could slip back into recession. Others warned of a lesson learned from the Great Depression that reducing spending could send a recovery back into recession.

Why does the jobless rate remain high?

The Costs of College

A Houston father expects to spend $1.5 million to put his five kids through college. The father can afford that staggering tuition bill. Most Americans cannot. Instead, about two-thirds of American students borrow money for college. Today, students owe more than $1 trillion in loans. Recent grads enter a weak job market. Some work two or three jobs just to pay off interest on their debt.

Is a college degree worth it? Despite the high cost, experts say a college degree is a good investment. Over a lifetime, college grads earn much more than those without a degree. College costs have soared for private and for-profit colleges, and even for state schools that were once more affordable. Since 2008, as states slashed budgets, they cut aid to education. To make up the difference, state schools upped tuition and fees. Advisors urge students to learn about loans and make smart choices about what college to attend before taking on crushing debt.

Obama Wins!

President Obama faces a tough agenda that includes the economy, job creation, and foreign affairs.

President Barak Obama and Vice President Joe Biden defeated Republican Mitt Romney and his running mate, Representative Paul Ryan. Obama now faces the challenge of fulfilling his promises to improve the economy and maintain U.S. leadership in the world.

When Barack Obama took office as President in 2009, the nation was in the worst economic crisis since the Great Depression. As he sought reelection in 2012, his approval rating was near 51 percent—slightly below the historical average.

With many Americans dissatisfied, Republican presidential challenger Mitt Romney went on the offensive. He focused on what he considered Obama's failure to solve the nation's economic problems: "The President has disappointed America because he hasn't led America in the right direction," Romney said. "He took office without the basic qualification that most Americans have and one that was essential to the task at hand. He had almost no experience working in a business."

Romney and his vice presidential running mate Paul Ryan pushed a conservative agenda of slashing taxes and federal spending. Romney promised to use his business expertise and experience as governor of Massachusetts to solve the country's financial woes.

Despite the loss, Romney and the Republican party will continue to press their agenda, though they vow to work across party lines to achieve it. "The Nation, as you know, is at a critical point," said Romney in his concession speech. "At a time like this, we can't risk partisan bickering and political posturing."

During Obama's speech at the Democratic National Convention, he set the agenda for his second term. "I'm asking you to rally around a set of goals for your country. Goals... that will lead to new jobs, more opportunity, and rebuild this economy on a stronger foundation."

Obama won the election with 332 electoral votes to Romney's 206. No president since Franklin D. Roosevelt had won reelection with unemployment so high. One factor in Obama's victory might have been his appeal to the middle class, who had been hit hard by the economic crisis. Also, modest gains in employment rates persuaded some that Obama's plan would work given more time.

Time will tell if Obama succeeds. For many people, his record with the struggling economy will be the measuring stick used to determine his level of success.

Barack Obama (D)

Mitt Romney (R)

SOURCE: CNN

Why is the state of the economy a critical issue for voters?

Steve Helber/Associated Press

Mitt Romney

Born in 1947, Willard Mitt Romney is the son of former Michigan Governor George W. Romney. A devout Mormon, Mitt Romney spent two and a half years as a missionary in France. He returned to Michigan in 1969 and married his high school sweetheart, Ann Davies.

Romney does not consider himself to be a career politician. After earning dual degrees from Harvard Law School and Harvard Business School, he worked as a business consultant for many years. He left private industry to serve as president of the 2002 Olympics and CEO of its organizing committee, which was grappling with charges of corruption. Following this, he was elected governor of Massachusetts. He balanced the state's budget and reformed its healthcare system. As a Presidential candidate, he urged deep cuts in federal spending and reform of Medicare and Social Security. "What's happened here isn't complicated," Romney said. "Washington has been spending too much money."

Election 2012

What were the key issues?

The 2012 election presented the sharpest contrast between two candidates in decades. Here are the issues that stood out.

The Economy

Coming out of an economic crisis, many Americans considered the economy the most important election issue. Discussions over unemployment, college costs, job creation, and taxes prevailed. Obama focused on economic stimulus and working with businesses to create jobs. Romney urged tax reduction and spending cuts.

The enormous national debt and government spending were also key economic issues. The debt was over $16 trillion, an all-time high. Republicans criticized the $5 trillion increase of the debt since Obama took office in 2009. Obama said he wanted to use money saved by withdrawing the U.S. from costly wars to lower the debt. Romney promised changes to Medicare, Social Security, and federal services.

Social Issues

The 2010 Patient Protection and Affordable Care Act (PPACA)—dubbed "ObamaCare" by its opponents—has sparked controversy. The main feature of this law, beginning in 2014, is the requirement that most Americans obtain health insurance. Debates have erupted between advocates of government-mandated health care and those who want the government to leave it to the private sector. Romney vowed to dismantle the plan. With President Obama reelected, the plan will continue.

Other key issues were abortion, gay

Bruce Bennett/Getty Images

Republican Presidential candidate Mitt Romney, left, and President Barack Obama talk to each other during a town hall style debate.

marriage, and immigration. Romney called for an end to abortion while Obama supported abortion rights. Obama backed same-sex marriage while Romney argued that marriage should only involve a man and a woman. Both agreed that immigration reform is necessary.

Foreign Policy

How America deals with other countries is always in flux. Debates focused on relations with key nations such as Israel, Iran, Afghanistan, Russia, and China. Many Republicans feel Obama needs a stronger stance when dealing with other nations. Obama promised to work to end the spread of nuclear weapons to such nations as North Korea and Iran.

Why is it necessary for candidates to debate issues during an election?

$uper PACs

In 2010, the U.S. Supreme Court ruled that the government cannot restrict spending on elections by organizations and individuals. This decision gave birth to Super PACs, groups that pump millions of dollars into campaigns. Much of the money is spent on ads that bash the opposing candidate rather than present the candidate's own view on issues. Although the Court decided this is free speech, some people feel this spending unfairly influences elections.

New and Old

Newcomers will mix with many familiar faces in Washington.

The impact of the 2012 election on American government and politics will continue to reveal itself. In addition to the presidential election, American citizens elected 11 governors and 33 senators. Elections were also held for all 435 seats in the House of Representatives.

New Faces

For governor, there were four Republicans and nine Democrats elected; so there are now 29 Republicans, 20 Democrats, and one Independent sitting in the top state seats.

Party lines in Congress stayed much the same, however. The Senate now has 45 Republicans, 53 Democrats, and two Independents. In the House of Representatives, there are currently 232 Republicans and 201 Democrats. Two House members, both Republicans, resigned in early 2013: Tim Scott of South Carolina and Jo Ann Emerson of Missouri.

Women made the biggest news in this election. The year 2013 will mark the first time that there will be 20 women sitting in the Senate. Of particular note is Rep. Mazie Hirono of Hawaii who will be that state's first female Senator. She is also the first Asian-American woman elected to the Senate and she is the first U.S. Senator born in Japan.

Kentucky made headlines because it elected another Republican member of Congress despite the fact that the majority of Kentuckians are registered Democrats. The coal industry backed Andy Barr over his Democratic opponent. Of the six-member delegation, five are now Republican.

Marco Gracia/Associated Press

Sen. Mazie Hirono (D) of Hawaii is the first Asian-American female elected to that office.

James Crisp/Associated Press

Rep. Andy Barr, Kentucky, is one of five Republicans to represent his mostly Democratic state.

Challenges

Many issues faced President Obama and U.S. leadership entering 2013. The top domestic concern continued to be the economy. Despite signs of recovery, unemployment remained high. Creating jobs and keeping more jobs from leaving the United States remained challenging.

On the world stage, the Middle East continued to be an area of concern. In late 2012, tensions grew between Iran and Israel. Many Americans were concerned that Iran was developing nuclear weapons. Anti-American protests erupted in many Muslim states. As leaders of the most powerful nation in the world, President Obama and the new Congress would have to deal with these issues.

What are the advantages and disadvantages of having more than one political party?

The Platform

A platform is a document that summarizes a political party's goals. The 2012 Democratic Party platform emphasized:

Job creation

Tax cuts

Business regulation

Immigration reform

The environment

Reducing nuclear threats

Same-sex marriage

Expanding trade

Technological innovation

Energy independence

Who's Who?

Leaders on the world stage.

Driving Force

JOHANNES EISELE/AFP/ Getty Images/Newscom

Europe ~ Angela Merkel is Germany's first female chancellor. As leader of Europe's economic powerhouse, Merkel is often called the world's most powerful woman. Merkel has been the driving force behind efforts to deal with Europe's debt crisis. She backed tough austerity measures to curb spending but now faces demands both inside and outside Germany to stimulate struggling economies through spending. Merkel grew up in communist East Germany. She and her conservative Christian Democratic Union will remain in power at least until 2013.

Tyrants Toppled

North Africa ~ Three North African strongmen were toppled during the 2011 Arab Spring. First, Tunisia's Ben Ali was forced from office. Then, massive demonstrations in Egypt pushed Hosni Mubarak from power after 30 years. Finally, Libya's bizarre tyrant, Muammar Qaddafi, was overthrown, captured, and killed by rebels after a nine-month civil war.

AFP Photo/Evaristo/ Getty Images/Newscom

Unlikely Leader

Brazil ~ Dilma Rousseff is the first woman to lead Brazil, Latin America's largest nation. Rousseff was a largely unknown political outsider, but in the 2011 elections, she had the support of Brazil's highly popular outgoing president. Rousseff is determined to further the country's strong economic growth, improve education, reduce crime, and boost Brazil's role on the world stage. In 2012, Brazil hosted Rio Plus 20, the global environmental summit. It will host soccer's World Cup in 2014 and the summer Olympics in 2016.

Ramin Talaie/Bloomberg Getty Images

Presidential Ambition

Rwanda ~ Paul Kagame wants to turn tiny landlocked Rwanda into a high-tech, commercial, and banking hub of central Africa. His model is Singapore, a small city-state in Southeast Asia and one of the world's richest nations. Kagame helped end the horrific 1994 genocide that killed 800,000 Rwandans. He became president in 2000. He has brought economic growth, improved health care, reduced crime, and cracked down on corruption. But he is also an authoritarian leader who has trampled on freedoms and silenced opponents.

ITAR-TASS / Mikhail Klimentyev/Newscom

Return of a President

Russia ~ Vladimir Putin again holds Russia's top job. Voters twice elected Putin president, but he could not legally seek a third term in 2008. Putin made sure his close supporter, Dmitry Medvedev, became president. Medvedev then appointed Putin prime minister. In 2012, Putin ran for president again. Many Russians credit Putin with bringing stability and economic progress. Others blast him for manipulating votes and expanding presidential powers. They condemn his ruthless suppression of Chechen rebels and his attack on neighboring Georgia. Putin will hold office until 2018.

EPA/LYNN BO BO/Newscom

Dissident to Lawmaker

Myanmar/Burma ~ Aung San Suu Kyi paid heavily for opposing Myanmar's military rulers. This champion of democracy spent almost 15 years under house arrest. Pushed by economic sanctions, Myanmar's military finally restored civilian rule. In a 2012 election, Aung San Suu Kyi and her party won seats in parliament. In response, the U.S. and other countries eased sanctions to keep Myanmar on the road to democracy. Shortly after the election, Suu Kyi went to Sweden to accept the Nobel Peace Prize that she had won in 1991.

BULENT KILIC/AFP/Getty Images

Under Pressure

Iran ~ President Mahmoud Ahmadinejad is under pressure from international economic sanctions to curb his country's nuclear program. Ahmadinejad denies Iran has a nuclear weapons program, yet sanctions have increased economic hardships for Iranians. Americans know Ahmadinejad for his violent rants against Israel and the U.S. and for refusing to negotiate on the nuclear issue. At home, Ahmadinejad has tense relations with Ayatollah Ali Khamenei, Iran's most powerful leader. In parliament, hardline supporters of Khameni outnumber backers of Ahmadinejad, whose term expires in 2013.

Kyodo/Newscom

New Face, Old Policies

North Korea ~ Kim Jong Un rose to North Korea's top job after his father died in 2011. In this secretive, isolated country, little is known about Kim. Said to be in his late 20s, Kim Jong Un rules a militarized land and hurls belligerent rants against neighboring South Korea. Like his father, young Kim seeks to bargain his country's nuclear weapons program for badly needed U.S. food aid. Military leaders, North Korea's real power brokers, still call the shots.

The Arab Spring

Popular uprisings lead to change in the Middle East, North Africa.

Libyan and Egyptian protesters demonstrate outside the Arab League headquarters in Cairo, Egypt early in 2011.

M uhammad Bouazizi was furious. The police had seized the fruits and vegetables he sold on the street and damaged his wooden cart. The authorities harassed him constantly, perhaps because he did not pay enough in bribes. Each time, the humiliation and frustration grew.

On December 17, 2010, the 26-year-old street vendor went to complain to a city official, but he was turned away. Bouazizi had had enough.

In protest, he stood outside the government building, doused himself with gasoline, and lit a match. The young man died from his burns 18 days later, in early 2011. By then, his action had sparked anti-government protests across the small North African country of Tunisia. From there, the protests swept around the Arab world—with startling results.

Bouazizi's match had helped ignite what the media would call "Arab Spring."

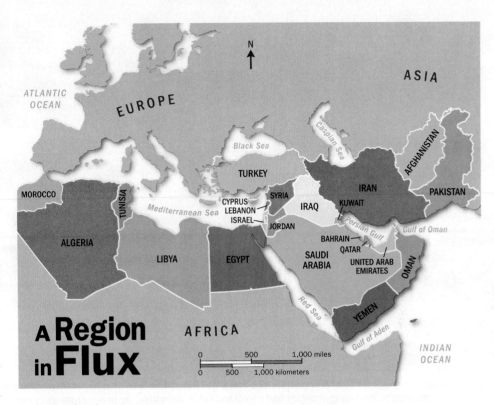

A Region in Flux

Popular Uprisings Topple Dictators

Unrest spread from Tunisia to Egypt, Libya, Yemen, Bahrain, Syria, Algeria, Morocco, and beyond. Despite vast regional, cultural, social, and economic differences, protesters from all of these countries rallied to pro-democracy chants and called for autocratic rulers to step down. Violence broke out as dictators cracked down on protests. Still, a few weeks after Bouazizi's death, Tunisia's president, Zine el Abidine Ben Ali, fled the country after 23 years in power. Hosni Mubarak, Egypt's longtime ruler, was also forced from power after huge demonstrations filled Tahrir Square in central Cairo and erupted elsewhere in the country.

In Egypt, Bahrain, Yemen, and Syria, protestors were beaten, thrown into prison, or killed. After his downfall, Mubarak was convicted of failing to stop the killing of demonstrators.

Protests in Libya led to civil war. With the help of NATO air strikes and surveillance, Libyan rebels toppled and killed the brutal dictator Muammar Gaddafi, who had ruled since 1969.

Why Did Weekly Prayer Produce Mass Demonstrations?

Friday prayers, called *juma*, are special. Muslims gather, usually in a mosque, to pray as a group. Besides prayers, the imam, or spiritual leader, gives a sermon about Islamic teachings and practices. He may also talk about other important matters. During the Arab Spring, spiritual and political matters came together—as they often do in the Muslim world. Protest movements in any Muslim country had a ready-made audience because people were already gathering in mosques. In the past, governments, too, have used Friday to make special announcements.

A Syrian government forces tank patrols the town of Houla, the site of a massacre where more than 100 residents, including women and children, were executed by pro-regime gunmen.

Syria's president, Bashar al-Assad, a member of the non-Muslim Alawi minority, used extreme brutality against protesters in this country where 74 percent of the population is Sunni Muslim. He claimed that a strong hand was needed to keep Syria from splintering into rival groups and to stop terrorists.

By the autumn of 2012, American and international news sources estimated that between 20,000 and 31,000 Syrians had been killed in the conflict, including close to 500 children. Other sources, such as Amnesty International and UNICEF, estimate that over 600 civilians and political prisoners have died in Syrian prisons, while rouhgly 400 children have been arrested and tortured by the government.

Frustrations Fuel Protests

Protesters throughout the region included students, the unemployed, human rights activists, teachers, and many others. Their protests were dubbed a "youthquake" by one observer.

Young and old were frustrated by the lack of opportunity, harsh censorship, police brutality, and corruption at all levels of government.

In the Middle East, almost 65 percent of the people are under the age of 30. Tough economic times have made jobs hard to find for anyone, regardless of their education.

Tunisia's heroic street vendor Muhammad Bouazizi had given up his dream of going to university because he had to support his mother and siblings while earning only $140 a month.

As each government fell, each country set out to shape its own future. In Morocco and elsewhere, governments remained in power, but were under pressure to enact reforms.

This protest movement, which began in late 2010, continued as a powerful idea into late 2012.

| In the struggle for democracy, is violence justified? Explain. |

Facing An Uncertain Future

Rebuilding toppled governments is the hard part.

It took only 18 days to topple long-time Egyptian president Hosni Mubarak, but a year later, tensions remained high.

Early in 2012, a soccer riot erupted in the large city of Port Said. Fans of a winning soccer team attacked rival fans. In the battle that followed, people were trampled or stabbed. More than 70 died. Hundreds were injured. The riot sparked a national outcry—and more street protests—against security forces. Warned of possible violence, officials had failed to prevent it. Would the future bring freedom and stability or lawlessness and chaos?

Free Elections

Egypt, the most populous country in the Middle East, held its first truly free elections. Voters chose members of a new parliament and a president, Mohamed Morsi. Islamist parties won a majority in the

Libyan school children keep busy in a refugee camp in southern Tunisia.

Tweeting a Revolution

As Bouazizi lay dying, a protest campaign erupted on YouTube and Facebook calling for Tunisia's president to resign. The call went viral, propelling protests across the Arab world.
Activists used social media to mobilize people on the street. The Arab Spring

unfolded on Facebook and YouTube and was posted on blogs. Tweets gave up-to-the-minute news of where to protest and how to avoid police barricades. Flash narratives moved obscure events into headlines. In the week before Egypt's Mubarak resigned, tweets rose from 2,300 to 230,000 per day.

Egyptian parliament. The big winner was the Freedom and Justice Party, launched by the long-suppressed Muslim Brotherhood. Non-religious parties failed to win as much popular support and gained fewer seats.

The new government faces daunting tasks. Egyptians want stability and economic growth. Whether or not the government will be able to meet these goals is only one of several unknowns.

Eygpt's powerful military remains suspicious of the new government. The army claimed legislative powers for itself in June, after the Egyptian Supreme Court dissolved the newly-elected parliament. But Morsi reconvened parliament in July as a sign of defiance.

The army has huge economic interests. It runs factories, banks, construction companies, and much more. It is still unclear whether military leaders will be immune from prosecution for corruption, torture, and other abuses that occurred while Mubarak was in power.

Still, many people in Egypt have other concerns. How will Coptic Christians and other religious minorities fare? Will women maintain their rights?

Many young women joined men protesting in countries around the Arab world. The women came from every generation; some wore headscarves, others wore jeans.

"I think it's much easier to bring down a dictator," said one activist, "than to change the patriarchal nature of society."

Transition to Democracy?

In Tunisia, political freedom has not translated into economic security—unemployment among young people remains at 40 percent. Many villages still have no electricity. Educated young people continue to leave the country in a quest for jobs and opportunity.

"We hope for our future," said the head of the elementary school that Muhammad Bouazizi attended. "But hope cannot fill the stomach or educate our children."

Women demonstrate in Bahrain in spite of the government ban on opposition rallies.

AFP PHOTO/MOHAMMED AL-SHAIKH/Getty Images

Some people take a long-term view. "The revolution was not a single event, but the start of an ongoing process," noted one Tunisian.

Libyans are proud of toppling Qaddafi, but tribal differences are still a problem. Armed militias control their own strongholds and torture continues in prisons. "Tomorrow Will Be Better," proclaims a roadside poster. In the face of today's uncertainties, some wonder if that slogan will become true.

Besides the challenge to ensure economic and social justice, gatekeepers for democracy in the Arab world face entrenched groups that once backed the old rulers. Tribal and religious divisions threaten the fragile unity of many countries.

An all-important question is: What role will religion play in politics? Will people opt for a theocratic state like that of Iran or a democracy like that of Turkey?

On the streets of every country in the region, people are focused on jobs, schooling for their children, access to medical care, and the possibility of having better lives.

> **What obstacles do "Arab Spring" countries still face?**

The Technology of Things

Modern technology helps science fiction become science reality.

Cathy Hutchison, of East Taunton, MA, was paralyzed by a stroke 15 years ago. She cannot move a muscle. Yet, in 2012 Cathy lifted a bottle of coffee and sipped from it, using her thoughts to power a robotic arm.

A tiny electrode implanted in Cathy's motor cortex—the part of the brain controlling movement—received signals from Cathy's brain and relayed messages to the robotic arm. This is one example of biotechnology in action. Biotechnology is the manipulation of biological processes through technological means, and it is revolutionizing how humans heal.

The key breakthrough in Cathy's case was the connection—or interface—scientists forged between the brain and a computer. They discovered that the brain, amazingly, still generates signals for hand and arm movement even after years of paralysis. The ability to tap into these signals holds promise for patients who can't move due to stroke or due to spinal chord injuries.

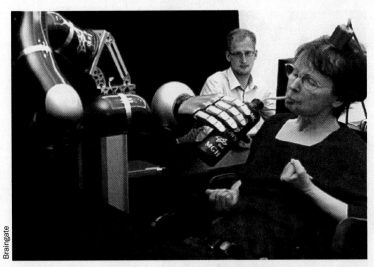

Cathy Hutchison uses thought to power this state-of-the-art robotic arm.

Ethical Issues

Along with the promise of technological advances come ethical issues and concerns. Just because we can do something—create designer body parts or put driverless cars on the road—should we?

Regenerative medicine uses adult stem cells, rather than controversial embryonic stem cells, to help create new organs. However, it's a small step away from regenerative medicine to genetic engineering—

the deliberate modification of an organism's characteristics through changes to its genetic material. Scientists can now "program" patients' white blood cells to attack cancerous and other diseased cells. Yet, the ability to manipulate DNA also raises the issue of parents choosing the sex of their offspring or physical characteristics, like eye or hair color.

The creation of "smart" driverless cars or smart homes and cities bring up vital concerns over our privacy. Google's driverless cars, for instance, rely on data from Google 3D maps, a technology that uses military-quality surveillance images. Or in a city controlled by an Urban Operating System (UOS), there is the fear of being constantly monitored. Some argue that this is an invasion of privacy.

Robot-Propelled

Biotechnology will also help the thousands of Iraq and Afghanistan veterans who have lost legs or arms in combat. These vets, often injured by roadside bombs, need artificial, or prosthetic, limbs.

The Pentagon has invested millions of dollars to help develop prosthetic limbs that move, feel, and respond like flesh and blood ones. Now researchers at the Sandia National Laboratories, the University of New Mexico, and the University of Texas' MD Anderson Cancer Center have discovered a way to fuse patients' nerves to robotic limbs.

Researchers developed a synthetic substance to act as an artificial structure, or scaffold, to support live tissue growth. This substance is flexible, fluid, and porous, allowing nerves to grow and move. It is also super-conductive, so that it can relay thousands of different nerve signals at once.

Right now, the technology works on rats with severed limbs. The rats' own nerve fibers grew through the artificial limbs, fused with and moved them. It may be years before humans can use these ultra life-like limbs, but researchers are determined to, as one said, "give amputees their bodies back."

Designer Body Parts

The same scaffold technique was used to accomplish the world's first transplant of a synthetic organ in 2011.

British and Swedish scientists collaborated to grow an artificial windpipe for a 36-year-old Eritrean man with late-stage tracheal cancer. The man's tumor threatened to block his windpipe. Just two days before this man underwent the transplant, the synthetic windpipe was seeded with stem cells from the patient's own bone marrow.

Stem cells can develop into every type of cell. They soaked into the fake windpipe and recreated the man's own tissue.

With "designer" body parts there is no long wait for donors and no risk of rejection by a patient's immune system. The future challenge is creating more complex, solid organs: kidneys, hearts, lungs, and livers.

Army Pfc Kevin Trimble, 19, adjusts his myoelectric prosthetic. While not exactly robot-propelled, Trimble's new arm is controlled by electric signals from his body.

Medical Mystery

Online gamers took only 10 days to solve a puzzle that scientists have been working on for 10 years.

A gaming team, "Contenders Group," uncovered the molecular structure of a key protein, or protease, that retroviruses use in order to multiply and grow. By learning how this happens, scientists have a better chance of stopping the spread of diseases like HIV/AIDS.

Getting a full picture of protein molecules is notoriously hard. Microscopes show a flat image of what, in reality, could look something more like a tangled knot of spaghetti. Researchers need to be able to see and rotate 3D pictures of these unfolded molecules. This is why a University of Washington biochemist developed the online game *FoldIt,* which enables teams of gamers to compete to unfold chains of amino acids (protein building blocks). Teams win points for finding the most chemically stable shapes.

Center for Game Science.

San Antonio Express-News, Lisa Krantz/AP Photo

AFP PHOTO/Karen BLEIER / Getty Images

The Google self-driving car maeuvers through the streets of Washington, D.C.

Driverless Cars

In the U.S., 40,000 people die in car accidents every year, one every 13 minutes. This spurred Internet search engine giant, Google to pioneer a driverless car. Google's engineers say robot drivers react faster than human ones. Robots don't have "blind spots," but operate with 360-degree perception. And they don't drive while distracted, sleepy, or intoxicated.

Google's driverless cars use multiple sensors, Global Positioning System (GPS) technology, and Artificial Intelligence (AI) software to stay the correct distance away from other vehicles or to enter a busy highway. Several test cars have driven over 250,000 miles. The only two recorded driverless car crashes occurred because of human mistakes and not computer error. .

Nevada was the first state to license driverless cars, but it will be years before unmanned cars take over our highways.

Smart Living

European technology company PlanIt is designing the world's first ever smart city. PlanIt Valley is already under construction in Paredes, Portugal, with 100 million high-tech sensors embedded throughout. These devices, which are common in Formula One racing cars, detect and measure physical properties and feed this data to a central Urban Operating System. The result: A planned city that turns your air conditioner off when you leave the room, guides your car to an empty space, or detects a leak in your sink and dispatches a plumber to fix it.

PlanIT Valley will be more energy efficient and environmentally friendly than most other cities. The first of its planned 150,000 citizens are scheduled to take up residence in 2015.

> **What are the pros and cons of this much technology in everyday life?**

Space Vacation

Would you pay $200,000 to experience five minutes of weightlessness in outer space? So far, 550 wealthy individuals have bought tickets to take a two and a half hour suborbital trip in a Virgin Galactic spaceship. Ticket holders include Stephen Hawking and music star Katy Perry. A venture of Sir Richard Branson, Virgin Galactic will one day take its passengers just over the karman line—the place where space begins.

When the U.S. stopped its manned space shuttle program in 2011, that didn't stop entrepreneurs like Branson and others from reaching for the stars. In only five years, Russia's Orbital Technologies is opening a space hotel 217 miles above the earth where you can stay for five days, traveling 17,500 miles per hour in a low earth orbit. Extras include gourmet food, a special sealed shower, and choice of a vertical or horizontal bed.

Bigelow Aerospace/Splash News/Newscom

This is the design for the world's first intergalactic, inflatable hotel.

FASTER

In 2012, the world's fastest computer was the Japanese "K" supercomputer, which boasts 68,544 Central Processing Units. These CPUs are the computer's "brains," and your computer likely has one or two. The "K" was rated 8.162 petaflops. This means K can perform 8.162 quadrillion floating-point operations per second.

GREENER

Give Harvard scientists a lemon, and they not only make lemonade but also craft a lemon-flavored edible bottle—or wikicell—in which to contain it. Tons of food and drink packaging ends up in landfills. Wikicells, created with biodegradable plastic combined with food particles, can be either peeled off or eaten.

ROOMIER

When the Internet almost ran out of room in 2012, global organization The Internet Society launched a new Internet Protocol. Without the new standard, IPv6, all Internet traffic would simply stop. Now there are 340 trillion trillion trillion addresses. That's enough for everyone in the world to have a billion billion IP addresses for every second of their lives.

STRONGER

Miracle material Graphene is an atomic scale honeycomb lattice of carbon atoms—think atomic chicken wire. It is one of the strongest materials on earth, 200 times stronger than steel. It also stretches like rubber, weighs almost nothing, and conducts heat and electricity better than copper. Graphene charges lithium batteries 10 times faster and gives them 10 times the storage power.

EPA/KIM LUDBROOK/Newscom

How Is the Internet?

National security is so much more than fighting with military might.

The security of the nation depends very heavily on the things that average people see and use every single day - government institutions, travel, money, natural resources and energy, and especially the Internet.

"As Internet usage continues to expand, cyberspace will become increasingly woven into the fabric of everyday life across the globe," says a Department of Defense (DoD) report. "Our reliance on cyberspace stands in stark contrast to the inadequacy of our cybersecurity."

The DoD considers cyberspace to be the next battlefield, one that is peopled by trained computer technicians, and not traditional armed soldiers.

Cyberthreats

Between 2000 and 2010, global Internet usage increased from 360 million to over 2 billion people. People log on to the Internet to do simple personal tasks like shopping, and social networking, or to manage their businesses. Banks use the Internet to transfer vast sums of money. Government agencies, including the DoD and the State Department, use the Internet to gather and store important data. The United States is partnering with other countries to step up cybersecurity efforts against international hackers and terrorists, or cyberthreats.

But cyberthreats are not just international computer geeks trying to hack the mainframe of the DoD. Internet crime and fraud has become big business. Thieves and criminals find ways to gather credit card information and Social Security numbers from people's social networking sites.

Be Prepared for Anything

The Centers for Disease Control (CDC), located in Atlanta, GA, wants Americans to be prepared for anything, even zombies. The Zombie Preparedness campaign is a creative way for the CDC to attract new and younger audiences.

And the campaign has proved to be a success. Materials, which are available for free from the CDC's Web site, include emergency checklists for families and their household pets, directions on how to store supplies, Zombie Preparedness posters, and even a graphic novel titled "Preparedness 101: Zombie Pandemic."

"If you are generally well-equipped to deal with a zombie apocalypse, you will be prepared for a hurricane, pandemic, earthquake, or terrorist attack," said the CDC Director Dr. Ali Kahn. What does it mean to be prepared for the zombie apocalypse or a real disaster? According to the CDC, a disaster kit is a collection of basic items that could be needed by every member of your family. This should include water, food, and medical supplies, enough to last for two weeks.

And according to some experts, finding a chink in the armor of a computer network's security system isn't all that hard. According to a recent New York Times article, "...the more mundane reality is that companies are most often breached by hackers walking down virtual hallways, looking for a single unlocked door. And the proverbial unlocked door can mean entry into the entire data network."

Privacy and Civil Liberties

There is an ongoing debate about how increasing cybersecurity might decrease the free flow of information, all while violating personal freedom and privacy.

While security measures are put in place to protect our society, some argue that they restrict the freedom of individuals. There is currently no clear answer about where the proper checks and balances should be. Internet law is so new and represents such a drastic shift in basic legal assumptions that it is still in the process of development.

According to the Department of Homeland Security, "This free flow of information has proven essential to the rapid evolution and growth of the Internet. Cyberspace must continue to be a forum for free association and free speech."

This statement stands in contrast with how other governments view the Internet. In countries like The People's Republic of China (PRC), information is strictly regulated. The PRC not only blocks website content, but it also monitors the Internet access of individuals.

When should a government enforce strict laws about Internet use?

Bullying

More than one quarter of American students between the ages of 12 and 18 have been bullied in school. Cyber-bullying, harassment through email, IM, text messaging, and social networking is also on the rise. Six percent of all students between the ages of 12 and 18 have reported instances of being bullied online. Bullying incidents include being made fun of or insulted, threatened with harm, being purposely excluded from activities, and being pushed, shoved, tripped, or spit on.

Many states have or are proposing anti-bullying legislation so that bullies can be dealt with appropriately. Legislators claim that bullying interferes with a student's right to a safe place to go to school.

16% are the subject of rumors

28% of students are bullied at school

4% are pushed to do things they did not want to do

6% are threatened with harm

5% are excluded from activites

19% are made fun of, called names, or insulted

7 Billion and Growing

At this rate, the world's population is expected to double every 40 years.

Each day, more than 7 billion people are living, breathing, eating, and sleeping on this planet. And the world's population is still growing. On average, five babies are born and two people die every second.

However, the rate of growth is not the same everywhere. Some nations have lower birth rates and longer average life spans. Such nations are aging—that is, the average age of their population is increasing. In other nations, the birth rate is higher and the average life span lower. Such nations are extremely young.

Countries with older populations—such as the United States, Italy, Japan, Germany, and Sweden—generally enjoy higher standards of living. However, many worry about how to take care of a large senior population. For example, the average American today is expected to live at least until the age of 78.5. This puts an extra burden on programs such as Social Security and Medicare.

In other regions, a large percentage of the population is aged 15 to 29. Such countries face what some call a "youth bulge."

They typically experience high rates of unemployment, underemployment, crime, poverty, and social unrest.

Roughly 65 percent of people living in the Middle East and North Africa are under 30. Millions of young people leaving school have high expectations, but no chance of finding their "dream" job, or perhaps even any job. As a result, many of these people are moving to the cities looking for work, but the competition is fierce.

Cities in these countries can't handle their growing populations. With overcrowding comes an increase in crime and gang-related activity, and greater demand for dwindling resources like clean water. More people are willing to challenge the political status quo because the old system and way of doing things doesn't appear to be working. According to the World Bank, if there is a high youth unemployment rate in developing countries, civil unrest and protests like those seen in the "Arab Spring" of 2011 and 2012 will become more common.

What are some other issues caused by the growing population?

WHERE ARE WE?

TOP 10 MOST POPULATED COUNTRIES

① **China** 1,343,239,923
② **India** 1,205,073,612
③ **United States** 313,847,465
④ **Indonesia** 248,216,193

⑤ **Brazil** 205,716,890
⑥ **Pakistan** 190,291,129
⑦ **Nigeria** 170,123,740
⑧ **Bangladesh** 161,083,804
⑨ **Russia** 138,082,178
⑩ **Japan** 127,368,088

Source: CIA *The World Factbook*

HOW HAVE WE GROWN?

WORLD POPULATION GROWTH FROM 1650–2050

👤 = 200 million people

| 1650 | 1750 | 1850 | 1950 | 2000 | 2012 | 2050 (projected) |

Source: National Geographic Society

COLONIAL AND U.S. POPULATION FROM 1650–2050

green = most densely populated areas

1650	**1750**	**1850**	**1950**	**2000**	**2012**	**2050**
50,400	1,170,800	23,191,876	151,325,798	281,421,906	308,745,538	392,000,000 (projected)

Source: U.S. Census

WHERE ARE WE GOING?

AMERICANS ON THE MOVE The 10 American cities with the greatest percentage of population decline and growth between 2000 and 2010

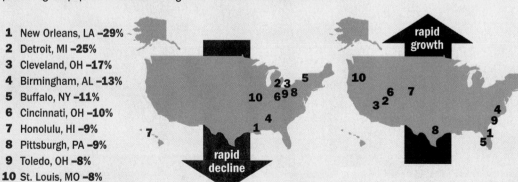

1 New Orleans, LA **–29%**
2 Detroit, MI **–25%**
3 Cleveland, OH **–17%**
4 Birmingham, AL **–13%**
5 Buffalo, NY **–11%**
6 Cincinnati, OH **–10%**
7 Honolulu, HI **–9%**
8 Pittsburgh, PA **–9%**
9 Toledo, OH **–8%**
10 St. Louis, MO **–8%**

rapid decline

rapid growth

1 Palm Coast, FL **+94%**
2 St. George, UT **+53%**
3 Las Vegas area, NV **+42%**
4 Raleigh area, NC **+42%**
5 Cape Coral area, FL **+40%**
6 Provo area, UT **+40%**
7 Greeley, CO **+40%**
8 Austin area, TX **+37%**
9 Myrtle Beach area, SC **+37%**
10 Bend, OR **+37%**

Source: The World Almanac and Book of Facts, 2012

Has the Climate Gone Crazy?

Scientists worry that climate change means more extreme weather.

This arcus cloud is also known as a "shelf cloud." These are usually attached to storm fronts and mean that a thunderstorm is more than likely on its way.

Headlines reported that 2010 was the warmest year ever recorded. Heat waves settled on Asia and Russia causing 15,000 deaths. Droughts struck China, Brazil, and East Africa.

The next year brought more weather extremes. East Africa suffered through one of the driest seasons in 60 years. The U.S. sweltered in its warmest summer ever. Parts of Europe had their warmest spring. North Korea had its coldest winter since 1945. Heavy rains flooded parts of China, Brazil, and Australia.

And 2012 seems to have brought more of the same. Drought dried northeastern Brazil and the midwestern U.S. while heavy rains flooded Ethiopia. Less sea ice covered the Arctic Ocean and less snow than normal fell in Europe and Asia.

Weather patterns may be changing and those changes can have a huge impact. What if the new normal in major food-growing areas makes farmland less productive than the old normal did? Drops in food supplies can pose serious challenges to a growing human population and can also disrupt trade.

What's Causing It?

Most climate scientists agree that temperatures are rising and many also agree that the chief cause is the burning of fossil fuels like coal, oil, and gas. These fuels release chemicals called greenhouse gases (GHGs) into the air. GHGs trap the sun's warmth near Earth's surface.

World leaders have listened to scientists' warnings about climate change. In 1992, representatives from 178 countries met in Brazil to discuss what should be done. They pledged to take steps to cut emission of GHGs.

Those pledges are just *promises*. So far, not very much has been done. Governments have spent large sums to promote cleaner energy and reduced energy use. Yet the results have been minimal. From 1990 to 2008, the world's most developed economies cut their emissions by only about 2 percent.

Some analysts say that these drops only happened because factory manufacturing jobs were moved to other countries. If you take that into account, emissions for the most developed countries actually *increased* 7 percent. Meanwhile, developing countries like China and India have seen their emissions go up even more. It's all about jobs. Countries trying to develop their economies fear that cutting back on emissions will mean slower economic growth, and that means fewer jobs.

Making the problem worse is that leaders worry about putting their country too far in front of other countries. If they move too aggressively to cut emissions, leaders fear that their country's economy will lag while other countries pass it by.

Why is climate change a political issue?

Is the Climate Really Getting Warmer?

Most people agree that the world's climate is getting warmer. However, critics point out that statements about the warmest years on record have flaws. First, records have been kept only fairly recently. A century or so of records is just a fraction of Earth's age. How, then, can we be sure that the temperatures that have been recorded were normal? Second, records are incomplete or may be inaccurate for many of those years. In that case, are comparisons to those records valid? Third, other kinds of data show bigger swings in temperature over a much longer time frame. Some data suggest that the 19th century was on the cool end of this variation. If so, the current rise in temperatures might just be a normal variation.

Boston Globe / Getty Images

Hurricane Sandy Pummels East Coast

Hurricane Sandy hit the East Coast with a vengeance in late October 2012, causing disruptive weather in 19 states, west from New Jersey to Wisconsin and north from the Carolinas to Maine. At its height, the storm stretched for more than 2,000 miles. Its winds and storm surge caused billions of dollars in damage, left millions of people without electricity and heat, and tens of thousands homeless. Communication and public transportation came to a standstill in one of the most densely populated regions of the country. Portions of the Atlantic coastline changed forever.

Sandy is already being called a "superstorm" because her size and makeup was caused by a combination of a late-season hurricane that met up with a winter storm, during the full moon. This is not unheard of, but is still a rare enough occurrence that it has yet to be studied by climate scientists.

Where Will We Get the Energy?

By 2035, the countries of the world will need close to twice as much energy as they did in 2000.

Nearly 85 percent of all the energy used in the world currently comes from three sources: petroleum, oil, ethanol, or other liquids; coal; or natural gas.

These sources of energy produce the greenhouse gases (GHGs) linked to climate change. Liquids—primarily oil—furnish a little over a third of all the world's energy. The good news is that exploration for new oil reserves is constant. The bad news is that some of those sources may be in environmentally sensitive areas. Other reserves have hard-to-get oil. Companies are expected to tap into these sources, but only because the price of oil is expected to rise enough to make it worth their while.

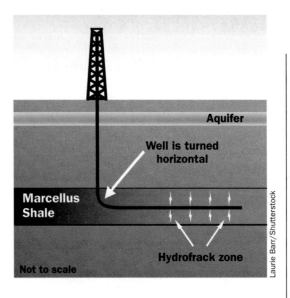

Aquifer

Well is turned horizontal

Marcellus Shale

Hydrofrack zone

Not to scale

Laurie Barr/Shutterstock

What About Gas?

The United States has vast natural gas reserves. Some estimates say that the country has enough gas to last 100 years at current rates of use. That's more than 10 times the amount of its oil reserves.

Of course, gas is a fossil fuel, and burning it does produce GHGs. Still, it's cleaner to obtain than coal. Isn't it?

Much of the country's gas reserves are trapped in the same kind of rock—shale—where some oil is found. Getting this gas out of the ground requires a process called *hydrofracturing*—or *fracking*, for short.

Fracking entails drilling a well into a source of shale gas and pumping water, sand, and chemicals under high pressure into the well. The liquid forces the gas out. Pipelines carry the gas to storage tanks, and the process is complete.

World Energy Use

The U.S. Energy Information Administration has calculated all the energy used around the world in 2008:

Petroleum, oil, ethanol, and other liquids:
34.3%

Coal:
27.5%

Natural gas:
22.6%

Renewables (hydroelectric, solar, wind, and others):
10.2%

Nuclear power:
5.4%

Source: Energy Information Administration, International Energy Outlook, 2011

Wind farms like this one off the coast of the United Kingdom literally harvest wind to create electric power. Wind power consumes no fuel and creates no air pollution. Many of the largest onshore wind farms are located in the United States and the People's Republic of China.

The practice has come under heated debate. Critics say that it uses too much water and that it leaves the water polluted. Some worry about gas entering aquifers, the areas that store underground water. Industry experts say that the likelihood of this happening is small. A draft of a 2011 Environmental Protection Agency (EPA) report linked fracking to the contamination of one aquifer in Wyoming. That report is not final, however, and it came under intense criticism from fracking supporters.

Fracking and the opposition to it are not limited to the United States. Both France and Bulgaria have banned the practice. South Africa placed a temporary halt on fracking, but they recently lifted the ban.

What About Clean Coal?

Coal is another abundant resource in the United States and many other countries. Burning coal releases carbon dioxide into the atmosphere. But some people say that "clean coal" is the answer.

Some coal industry supporters say coal is cleaner today than in the past. Current technology cuts the amount of soot and sulfur dioxide released when burning coal. Environmentalists say that to be *really* clean, coal-fired power plants must pump less carbon dioxide into the air. The most likely answer to that goal is to use what's called carbon capture and storage (CCS). Companies would have to catch carbon dioxide and pump it into the ground. The big problem is that CCS takes a lot of energy to succeed.

Some efforts are being made in this area, though. The United States and the other seven most developed nations agreed to fund projects trying to find CCS solutions. Germany put a CCS power plant online in 2008, but closed it in late 2011. The German plant was small, costly to build, and could not operate profitably without aid from the German government.

Why is the need for energy increasing?

Food Crisis Looms

Drought in the American Midwest leads to food shortages, price hikes around the world.

LARRY W. SMITH/EPA/Newscom

Severe drought conditions that hit corn crops in the American Midwest have led to drastic price increases around the world.

The 2012 drought that hit the Midwest did more than drive prices up at local supermarkets. Some people fear that it may have set off another global food crisis.

A global food crisis occurs when rates of hunger and malnutrition rise sharply. It is usually set off by a shock to either supply of or demand for food and often involves a sudden increase in food prices.

The United States is the largest exporter of corn in the world. When natural disasters such as drought or tornadoes affect corn crops here, the impact is felt worldwide. The United States Department of Agriculture (USDA) predicts that not only will prices continue to go up, but also that the amount of corn exported will drop. Similar shortages in rice and wheat led to the global food crisis of 2008, which fueled political, economic,

and social unrest around the world.

Compared to the average of 16 percent of income that Americans spend, families in less developed countries can spend between 60 and 75 percent of their total budget on food. Any price increase puts them on the brink of disaster. As global climate change causes more extreme weather, floods and droughts may not only lead to more shortages but also more unrest.

Corn is a staple of the American diet for people and for animals. Corn is also used to manufacture everything from penicillin to sugar to glue to ethanol. If corn becomes more expensive, so do many other things.

Congress currently requires that close to 10 percent of the nation's gasoline supply come from corn. Some question the need to feed animals or make fuel out of a dwindling corn supply, especially as prices continue to soar. American cattle ranchers slaughtered cattle to lower this expense. This increased supply temporarily lowered prices at American supermarkets. But it is likely that prices will begin to inch up in 2013.

> **How can the impact of a drought in the United States be felt around the world?**

Meat vs Grain

In countries experiencing rapid economic growth, meat has moved from the side of the dinner plate to the center. People around the world consume more than 284 tons of meat every year and this number is expected to double by 2050. But drought and the resulting grain shortage in the American Midwest have focused more attention on the question of how to best use the world's grain supply. It takes 10 pounds of grain to produce one pound of meat, nearly twice the amount of grain needed to supply the same number of calories in a meat-free diet. Environmentalists, farmers, consumers, vegetarians, and animal rights activists hold a wide range of conflicting opinions on this issue.

The United States and the World

America commands attention as the world's remaining superpower.

Since the end of the Cold War, the U.S. has sought to maintain a stable, democratic world. The State Department takes the lead through its various offices in countries across the globe. Along with U.S. military and aid workers, it promotes the democratic ideals of freedom and tolerance.

Europe and Asia hold a unique place in U.S. foreign relations because of long-standing cultural and historical ties. Many countries in this region also have a political and military alliance with the United States through membership in the North Atlantic Treaty Organization (NATO). The U.S. shares concerns with its allies over the economic woes of Spain, Italy, Portugal and Greece, as well as over Russia's return to a more repressive government. Recently, the European Union has joined the United States in strengthening oil embargoes against Iran in an effort to halt its development of weapons-grade uranium.

South and Central Asia, including countries such as India, Pakistan, and Afghanistan, remain at the center of American interest. Of particular concern is Afghanistan, where the U.S. has been fighting the Taliban since 2001. The U.S. and

U.S. Military Presence in the World

Countries and territories with a U.S. military presence

Source: DoD Base Structure Report Fiscal Year 2010 Baseline and DoD Active Duty Military Personnel Strengths by Regional Area and by Country, Sept. 30, 2010

its NATO allies are committed to helping the country rebuild after years of war. Their goal is to assist the Afghans in establishing a strong economy and a secure, democratic government dedicated to promoting religious tolerance and protecting human rights, especially of women.

Of no less concern is the Middle East where uprisings have toppled dictators in

Petty Officer First Class Sukarno H. Reyes from Oxnard, CA, loads relief supplies onto a helicopter at Banda Aceh airport in the Indonesian province of Aceh.

Egypt, Tunisia, Libya, and Yemen. While a settlement between Palestinians and Israelis remains an objective of U.S. policy, civil war in Syria and Iran's nuclear weapons project threaten to destabilize the already chaotic region. Beyond trade embargoes against Iran, the United States has pressured Syrian strongman Bashar al-Assad to end the bloodshed and step down.

In Africa, the U. S. has contributed to democratic transitions in Cote d'Ivoire, Guinea, and Niger, and supported a successful referendum that led to independence in South Sudan. It has worked with governments across the continent to provide food to drought-stricken regions, to aid refugee populations, and to limit drug and arms smuggling.

In East Asia and the Pacific, tension has arisen among China, Japan, and Taiwan over disputed ownership of islands in the East China Sea. Here, the U.S. has pressed the nations to settle things diplomatically. In another hotspot, North Korea has agreed to suspend its nuclear weapons program and permit inspectors to monitor the situation in exchange for American food aid.

The United States has never lost sight of the importance of Latin America. Through Pathways to Prosperity in the Americas, the U.S. promotes labor rights and environmental protections throughout the region. It also has a national security interest in fighting drug cartels, particularly since drug-driven violence has spilled across the Mexican border into Texas.

> **What are some of the democratic ideals the U.S. seeks to promote around the world?**

Pro-American Support

On the 11th anniversary of the 9/11 attacks on the World Trade Center and the Pentagon, the American consulate in Benghazi, Libya, was stormed by terrorists. Within days after the attack, Libyans were out in force to show their regret for the violence that killed four Americans: The American ambassador, another diplomat, and two State Department security officers. Hundreds of Libyans took to the streets in Benghazi and Tripoli carrying signs with sentiments such as "Sorry People of America This is not the Behavior of Islam and Our Prophet." A campaign started by an American Muslim to gather condolence messages for the family of the American ambassador went viral on the Internet with messages of sympathy being posted by Muslims around the world.

Prentice Hall
AMERICA
HISTORY OF OUR NATION
Civil War to the Present

Authors
James West Davidson
Michael B. Stoff

PEARSON

Boston, Massachusetts • Chandler, Arizona • Glenview, Illinois • Upper Saddle River, New Jersey

THE LANDING OF THE PILGRIMS : 1620 MABELLE L HOLMES

Acknowledgments appear on page 1097, which constitutes an extension of this copyright page.

Copyright © 2014 Pearson Education, Inc. All Rights Reserved. Printed in the United States of America. This publication is protected by copyright, and permission should be obtained from the publisher prior to any prohibited reproduction, storage in a retrieval system, or transmission in any form or by any means, electronic, mechanical, photocopying, recording, or likewise. For information regarding permissions, write to Rights Management & Contracts, One Lake Street, Upper Saddle River, New Jersey 07458.

Pearson, Prentice Hall, Pearson Prentice Hall, and MapMaster are trademarks, in the U.S. and/or other countries, of Pearson Education, Inc., or its affiliates.

"Understanding by Design" is registered as a trademark with the United States Patent and Trademark Office by the Association for Supervision of Curriculum Development (ASCD). ASCD claims exclusive trademark rights in the terms "Understanding by Design" and the abbreviation "UbD".

Pearson Education has incorporated the concepts of the Understanding by Design methodology into this text in consultation with consultant Grant Wiggins, one of the creators of the Understanding by Design methodology. The Association for Supervision of Curriculum Development (ASCD), publisher of the "Understanding by Design Handbook" co-authored by Grant Wiggins, has not authorized, approved or sponsored this work and is in no way affiliated with Pearson or its products.

ISBN-13: 978-0-13-323007-9
ISBN-10: 0-13-323007-4

3 4 5 6 7 8 9 10 V063 17 16 15 14 13

PEARSON

Authors

James West Davidson

Dr. James Davidson is coauthor of *After the Fact: The Art of Historical Detection* and *Nation of Nations: A Narrative History of the American Republic.* Dr. Davidson has taught at both the college and high school levels. He has also consulted on curriculum design for American history courses. Dr. Davidson is an avid canoeist and hiker. His published works on these subjects include *Great Heart,* the true story of a 1903 canoe trip in the Canadian wilderness.

Michael B. Stoff

Dr. Michael Stoff received his Ph.D. from Yale University and teaches history at the University of Texas at Austin. He is the author of *Oil, War, and American Security: The Search for a National Policy on Foreign Oil, 1941-1947,* coauthor of *Nation of Nations: A Narrative History of the American Republic,* and coeditor of *The Manhattan Project: A Documentary Introduction to the Atomic Age.* Dr. Stoff has won numerous grants, fellowships, and teaching awards.

Senior Program Consultants

Albert M. Camarillo

Dr. Albert Camarillo received his Ph.D. in U.S. history from the University of California at Los Angeles. He has been teaching history at Stanford University since 1975. Dr. Camarillo has published six books, including *Chicanos in a Changing Society: From Mexican Pueblos to American Barrios* and *California: A History of Mexican Americans.* His awards for research and writing include a National Endowment for the Humanities Fellowship and a Rockefeller Foundation Fellowship. Dr. Camarillo is the Miriam and Peter Haas Centennial Professor in Public Service.

Diane Hart

Diane Hart is a writer and consultant in history and social studies. She earned bachelor's and master's degrees in history from Stanford University and was a Woodrow Wilson Fellow. As a former teacher at the elementary, secondary, and college levels, Ms. Hart remains deeply involved in social studies education through her active participation in both the National and California Councils for the Social Studies. She has written a number of textbooks for middle school students.

Understanding by Design Consultant

Grant Wiggins

Grant Wiggins, Ed.D., is the President of Authentic Education in Hopewell, New Jersey. He earned his Ed.D. from Harvard University and his B.A. from St. John's College in Annapolis. Dr. Wiggins consults with schools, districts, and state education departments on a variety of reform matters; organizes conferences and workshops; and develops print materials and Web resources on curricular change. He is perhaps best known for being the co-author, with Jay McTighe, of *Understanding by Design* and *The Understanding by Design Handbook*, award-winning materials on curriculum.

Over the past twenty years, Dr. Wiggins has worked on some of the most influential reform initiatives in the country, including Vermont's portfolio system and Ted Sizer's Coalition of Essential Schools. He has established statewide Consortia devoted to assessment reform for the states of North Carolina and New Jersey. Dr. Wiggins is the author of *Educative Assessment* and *Assessing Student Performance*, both published by Jossey-Bass. His many articles have appeared in such journals as *Educational Leadership* and *Phi Delta Kappan*. His work is grounded in 14 years of secondary school teaching and coaching. Dr. Wiggins taught English and electives in philosophy.

Academic Reviewers

William R. Childs, Ph.D.
Associate Professor of History
Ohio State University
Columbus, Ohio

Theodore DeLaney, Ph.D.
Associate Professor of History
Washington and Lee University
Lexington, Virginia

Wanda A. Hendricks, Ph.D.
Associate Professor of History
University of South Carolina
Columbia, South Carolina

Emma Lapsansky, Ph.D.
Professor of History
Haverford College
Haverford, Pennsylvania

Gordon Newby, Ph.D.
Chair, Department of Middle Eastern
 and South Asian Studies
Emory University
Atlanta, Georgia

Judy A. Ridner, Ph.D.
Assistant Professor of History
Muhlenberg College
Allentown, Pennsylvania

Teacher Reviewers

Peggy Althof
Social Studies Facilitation, K–12
D-11 Public Schools
Colorado Springs, Colorado

Lon Van Bronkhorst
K–12 Social Studies Curriculum Supervisor
Grand Rapids Public Schools
Grand Rapids, Michigan

Katherine A. Deforge
Chair, Social Studies Department
Marcellus Central Schools
Marcellus, New York

Roceal N. Duke
District of Columbia Public Schools
Washington, D.C.

Dee Ann Holt
Chair, Social Studies Department
Horace Mann Arts and Science
 Magnet Middle School
Little Rock, Arkansas

Carol Schneider
Curriculum Coordinator
Rock Point Community School
Rock Point, Arizona

Leigh Tanner, Ph.D.
Division of Instructional Support
Pittsburgh Public Schools
Pittsburgh, Pennsylvania

Partnership School Consultants

Melanie Alston
Hackensack Middle School
Hackensack, New Jersey

Matthew Facella
Hackensack Middle School
Hackensack, New Jersey

Karina Koepke
Hackensack Middle School
Hackensack, New Jersey

Richard Yannarelli
Principal
Hackensack Middle School
Hackensack, New Jersey

Content Consultants

Dianna Davis-Horine
Social Studies Consultant
Jacksonville, Florida

Michal Howden
Social Studies Consultant
Zionsville, Indiana

Kathy Lewis-Stewart
Social Studies Consultant
Fort Worth, Texas

Differentiated Instruction Consultants

Donald Deshler, Ph.D
Professor of Special Education (Learning Disabilities)
Director, Center for Research on Learning
University of Kansas
Lawrence, Kansas

Dr. Deshler is the Chair of Prentice Hall's Differentiated Instruction Board. He assembled a distinguished panel of national experts to serve on the board, offering extensive experience in special needs, English language learners, less proficient readers, and gifted and talented students. This team informs Prentice Hall's approach to differentiated instruction and offers guidance on the development of new materials based on this approach.

Anthony S. Bashir, Ph.D.
Coordinator for Academic and Disability Services
Emerson College
Boston, Massachusetts

Cathy Collins Block, Ph.D.
Professor of Curriculum and Instruction
Texas Christian University
Fort Worth, Texas

Anna Uhl Chamot, Ph.D.
Professor of Secondary Education
    ESL and Foreign Language Education
Graduate School of Education and
    Human Development
The George Washington University
Washington, D.C.

Susan Miller, Ph.D.
Professor of Special Education
University of Nevada, Las Vegas
Las Vegas, Nevada

Jennifer Platt, Ed.D.
Associate Dean, College of Education
University of Central Florida
Orlando, Florida

Eric Pyle, Ph.D.
Associate Professor, Geoscience Education
Department of Geology & Environmental Science
James Madison University
Harrisonburg, Virginia

Accuracy Panel

Esther Ratner, Greyherne Information Services

Colleen F. Berg, Greyherne Information Services

Mike Jankowski, M.S. Information Finders

Jane Malcolm, M.L.S. Professional Research
    Services, Tulsa, Oklahoma

Barbara Whitney Petruzzelli, M.L.S.

Amy Booth Raff, M.L.S.

Bernard Rosen, Ph.D.

PBS Videos for *America:* *History of Our Nation* ©2014

PBS educational films deliver rigorous and relevant context through rich media experiences that engage students in exploring curricular concepts and are aligned to the needs of today's teachers and learners. Students and teachers will have access to the videos through the online digital course—both in streaming and downloadable formats.

Ken Burns's *The Civil War*

Unit 5 Civil War and Reunion 476

? **Essential Question:** How was the Civil War a political, economic, and social turning point?

The Civil War: African American soldiers

Table of Contents

The Brooklyn Bridge

Unit 7 A New Role in the World 674

Essential Question: How did a more powerful United States expand its role in the world?

Unit 7 Historian's Apprentice Workshop **760**

Duke Ellington and his band

Table of Contents

D-Day, June 6, 1944

Unit 9 Moving Toward the Future.... 868

Essential Question: How did the United States strive to strengthen democracy at home and to foster democracy abroad?

Unit 9 Historian's Apprentice Workshop

A father and daughter commemorate 9/11

Special Features

Historian's Apprentice Workshop

Answer the Unit Essential Question by analyzing historical documents.

HISTORIAN'S APPRENTICE ACTIVITY PACK

Complete the activity packs to answer essential questions about American history.

Historian's Apprentice Skills for Life

21st Century Learning

Build skills that will help you analyze American history content.

Literature

Experience American history through works of literature.

LIFE AT THE TIME

Learn more about how people lived at different places and times in history.

GEOGRAPHY AND HISTORY

Discover the role geography has played in American history.

Thinking Critically With Images

Special Features *(continued)*

● INFOGRAPHIC

Understand the significance of important historical events and developments.

History *Interactive*

Launch into an interactive adventure to extend your understanding of American history.

Explore the past through the power of technology.

Develop geographic literacy through dynamic map skills instruction. Learn map skills, and interact with every map online and on CD-ROM.

Activate your learning with a suite of tools online and on CD-ROM:
• Interactive Textbook
• Reading and Notetaking Study Guide
• Social Studies Skills Tutor
• Web Resources

Launch into an interactive adventure online—using special graphics in this textbook as jumping-off points—to extend your understanding of American history.

Biography Quest

Search for answers to mysteries about key people in American history.

Links Across Time

Expand your understanding of American history by connecting the past and the present.

MAP MASTER
Skills Activity

Increase your understanding of American history by studying maps.

Special Features (continued)

Illustrated Atlas of American History

Understand your world by comparing maps of the United States today with historical maps.

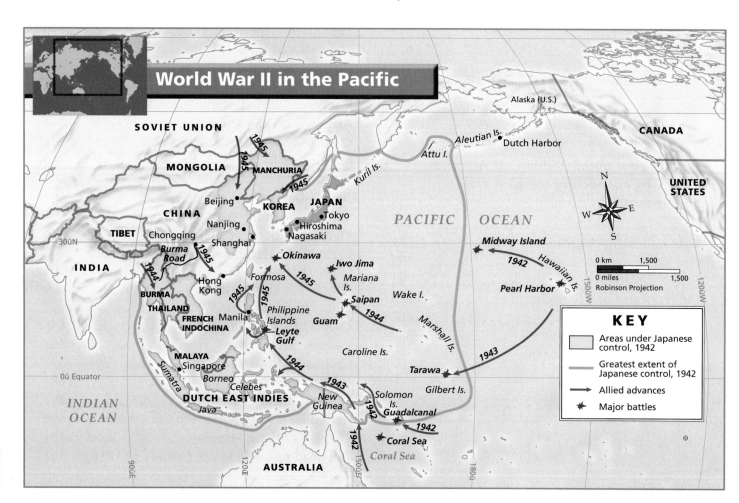

Charts, Graphs, and Diagrams

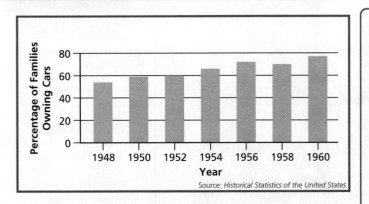

Increase in Car Ownership, 1948–1960

Source: *Historical Statistics of the United States*

Reading Charts
Skills Activity

With the move to the suburbs, people depended more on automobiles. Manufacturers pushed to meet the demands.

(a) **Read a Bar Graph** During which years did automobile ownership remain about the same?

(b) **Identify Causes and Effects** Trace the change in car ownership between 1954 and 1960. List several events (political, social, and economic) that strongly affected the change in ownership at that time.

Special Features *(continued)*

Seward's Folly

Russia offers Alaska.

Will "Billy" Seward trade?

Reading Political Cartoons
Skills Activity

The cartoonist shows a Russian stranger offering to trade "bears, seals, icebergs," and more.

(a) Recognize Points of View What is the cartoonist's opinion about the purchase of Alaska? What symbols does the cartoonist use to make the point?

(b) Apply Information What did people learn about Alaska after 1898? How would you change the cartoon, based on that information?

In-Text Sources

Gain insights by examining documents, eyewitness accounts, and other sources.

Special Features *(continued)*

Ida B. Wells Fights Against Lynching

Antilynching protesters

❝The real purpose of these savage demonstrations is to teach the Negro that in the South he has no rights that the law will enforce. Samuel Hose [a lynching victim] was burned to teach the Negroes that no matter what a white man does to them, they must not resist. . . . The daily press offered reward for [Hose's] capture and . . . incited the people to burn him as soon as caught.**❞**

—Ida B. Wells, "Lynch Law in Georgia," 1899

Reading Primary Sources
Skills Activity

In 1895, journalist Ida B. Wells published an analysis that exposed the truth about the lynching of African Americans.

(a) Interpret a Primary Source According to Wells, why do lynchings occur?

(b) Compare Ida Wells is often classified as a muckraker. How was her work similar to the work of Jacob Riis?

Tools to help you along the way...

Taking Notes

In history, there's a lot to read about and a lot to understand. Taking good notes is one way to help you remember key ideas and to see the big picture. This program has two ways to help you.

You can keep your notes in the *Interactive Reading and Notetaking Study Guide*. Or you can go online to take your notes. Either way, you will be able to record what you are learning. And, by the end of the year, you'll have created a perfect study tool.

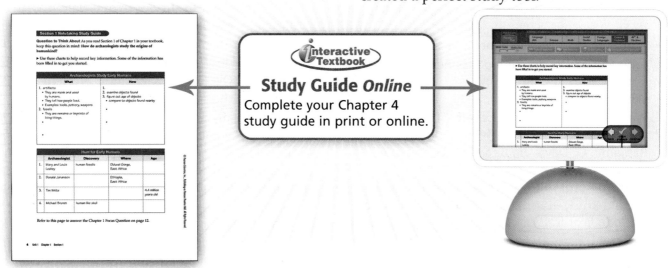

Interactive Textbook

Study Guide *Online*

Complete your Chapter 4 study guide in print or online.

Monitor Your Progress

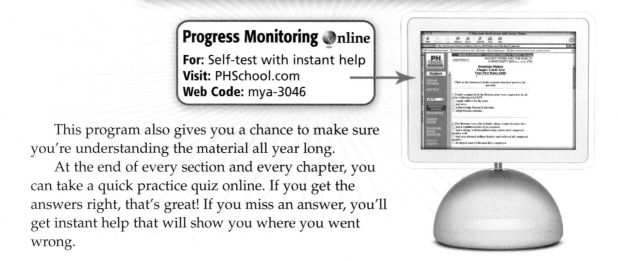

Progress Monitoring **Online**

For: Self-test with instant help
Visit: PHSchool.com
Web Code: mya-3046

This program also gives you a chance to make sure you're understanding the material all year long.

At the end of every section and every chapter, you can take a quick practice quiz online. If you get the answers right, that's great! If you miss an answer, you'll get instant help that will show you where you went wrong.

Historian's Apprentice Toolkit

Introduction: Studying Our Past

The nation was at war with itself, the North fighting against the South. In July 1863, more than 50,000 soldiers had died at a horrible battle in Gettysburg, Pennsylvania. A few months later, President Abraham Lincoln visited Gettysburg to dedicate the battlefield as a cemetery. Lincoln spoke of the soldiers who had given their lives to keep the nation together:

> **The world will little note, nor long remember what we say here, but it can never forget what they did here.**
>
> —Abraham Lincoln, Gettysburg Address

Lincoln was partly right. The world still remembers the soldiers who died during the Civil War. But we also remember what Lincoln said and what he did for the cause of freedom. As you study American history this year, you will be asked to remember all those who came before us—soldiers and Presidents, explorers and inventors, religious leaders and business leaders, the people who wrote our Constitution, and the people who fought to end slavery.

Helping us remember the past is the job of the historian. Historians explore important questions in order to find out how people lived and why they made the decisions they did. Historians also try to understand how history affects our lives today.

On the next few pages, you will learn to think like a historian. You will also get to try out some of the tools historians use. Your Historian's Apprentice Toolkit can make your study of American history easier and more rewarding.

Union soldier

Historical Evidence

Historians use many types of evidence to learn about the past. This evidence can be divided into primary sources and secondary sources.

Primary Sources A primary source is firsthand information about people or events. Primary sources include official documents, such as laws and public speeches, as well as eyewitness accounts, such as diaries, letters, and autobiographies. Primary sources may also include visual evidence, such as news photographs or videotapes.

Another type of primary source is an artifact. This is an item left behind by people in the past. This might take the form of a statue, a tool, or an everyday object.

Primary sources are valuable because they are created at the time when an event occurs. But this does not necessarily make them "true." Primary sources are created by people, and they may reflect the points of view of the people who created them. The person might not have been aware of certain facts, might have been trying to impress someone, or may even have been lying. So primary sources must be evaluated carefully and considered in relation to other sources on the subject.

Secondary Sources Historians also use secondary sources. These are sources created by someone who did not actually witness events. This textbook, for example, is a secondary source. The authors gathered information from many sources to reach an understanding of what happened and why it happened. Then, they wrote their interpretation of the events. Other secondary sources include news articles and biographies.

Types of Historical Sources

Type of Source	Description	Examples

Primary Sources	• Provide direct evidence about an event
	• Have a limited viewpoint
	• May be reliable or unreliable
	• Include objects left behind by people
		• Official documents
		• Letters and diaries
		• Speeches and interviews
		• Autobiographies
		• Photographs
		• Artifacts
		  • Tools and weapons
		  • Statues and other art

Secondary Sources	• Consist of secondhand information about an event • Use primary sources to create a broader picture • May be reliable or unreliable	• History books • Biographies • Encyclopedias and other reference works • Internet Web sites

Using Historical Sources

Everyone who wants to know about history starts by asking questions. You might be familiar with the types of questions found in your textbook or asked by your teacher. But historians ask questions the way a detective would. Each answer is a clue that leads to another question. The questions and answers bring the historian to an understanding of events in the past.

Consider this situation. Patricia was going through some very old books she found in her great-grandmother's trunk in the attic. Between the pages of one book, she found an old letter on thin, yellowing paper. A copy of the letter is shown here at right.

While reading the letter, Patricia asked herself many questions. Some of her questions are shown at right. Trying to find the answers to the questions is the same sort of thinking that historians use to find out about the past.

June 12, 1849

Dear Sean,

Everyone was happy to get your last letter. After surviving such a long, difficult journey, it must have been wonderful to arrive at last in New York.

Things in our village are not as bad as when you left. But many children and old people are still starving, and too many people have no place to live. You were wise to go to America.

Please tell me more about your plans. After traveling for so long, why would you want to begin a new journey? Where is this place called California? And why are you so sure you can get rich there?

I miss you. I only hope I live long enough to join you someday.

Your loving brother,
Michael

Where did Sean come from? Why was the trip so hard?

What has happened to cause these problems?

How does Sean plan to get rich?

Patricia may follow several steps to find the answers to her questions.

- **Start with what is known.** Patricia knows that her ancestors came to the United States from Ireland many years ago. She thinks this letter might explain why.

- **Read and observe.** Patricia can look for further information in primary and secondary sources. She might look at a map to see where Ireland is and how far it is from New York to California.

- **Speculate.** To help get started, Patricia might make some guesses, called hypotheses, about the answers to her questions.

- **Evaluate evidence.** As Patricia finds more information, she will test her hypotheses against the information that turns up. She can always change her hypotheses as she learns more.

- **Draw conclusions.** Patricia states what she believes are the final answers to her questions.

To start her search, though, Patricia will need to practice her skills of reading like a historian and using maps. The information on the following pages will help you review some of these skills.

Read Informational Texts

Reading a magazine, an Internet page, or a textbook is not the same as reading a novel. The purpose of reading nonfiction texts is to acquire new information. On page HT 7, you'll read about some ⊙**Reading Skills** that you'll practice as you read this textbook. Here, we'll focus on a few skills that will help you read nonfiction with a more critical eye.

Analyze the Author's Purpose

Different types of materials are written with different purposes in mind. For example, a textbook is written to teach students information about a subject. The purpose of a technical manual is to teach someone how to use something, such as a computer. A newspaper editorial might be written to persuade the reader to accept a particular point of view. An author's purpose influences how the material is presented. Sometimes, an author states his or her purpose directly. More often, the purpose is only suggested, and you must use clues to identify the author's purpose.

Distinguish Between Facts and Opinions

Active reading enables you to distinguish between facts and opinions when reading informational texts. Facts can be proved or disproved, but opinions reflect someone's own point of view.

Because newspaper editorials usually offer opinions on current events and issues, you should watch for bias and faulty logic when reading them. For example, the newspaper editorial at right shows factual statements in blue and opinions in red. Highly charged words are underlined. They reveal the writer's bias.

More than 5,000 people voted last week in favor of building a new shopping center, but the opposition won out. The margin of victory is irrelevant. Those radical voters who opposed the center are obviously self-serving elitists who do not care about anyone but themselves.

This month's unemployment figure for our area is 10 percent, which represents an increase of about 5 percent over the figure for this time last year. These figures mean that unemployment is worsening. But the people who voted against the mall probably do not care about creating new jobs.

Identify Evidence

Before you accept a writer's conclusion, you need to make sure that the writer has based the conclusion on enough evidence and on the right kind of evidence. A writer may present a series of facts to support a claim, but the facts may not tell the whole story. For example, the writer of the newspaper editorial on the previous page claims that the new shopping center would create more jobs. But what evidence is offered? Is it possible that the shopping center might have put many small local stores out of business? This would decrease employment rather than increase it.

Evaluate Credibility

Whenever you read informational texts, you need to assess the credibility of the writer. In other words, you have to decide whether the writer is believable. This is especially true of sites you may visit on the Internet. All Internet sources are not equally reliable. Here are some questions to ask yourself when evaluating the credibility of a Web site:

☐ Is the Web site created by a respected
organization, a discussion group, or
an individual?

☐ Does the Web site creator include his or her
name as well as credentials and the sources
he or she used to write the material?

☐ Is the information on the site balanced or biased?

☐ Can you verify the information using two other
sources?

☐ Is there a date telling when the Web site was
created or last updated?

Build Vocabulary

One of the most important tools in reading informational texts is to make sure you understand the key vocabulary used by the writer. This textbook helps you with two types of vocabulary—key terms and high-use academic words. Key Terms are words that you need to understand to read about a particular historical event or development. High-use academic words are words that will help you read any textbook.

Key Terms and High-Use Academic Words

Reading Skill

Identify Propositions The study of history often takes you inside important debates over ideas and actions. People propose their ideas and then give reasons to support those ideas. Identifying those propositions will help you to understand the beliefs and experiences of people in an earlier time. One way to identify propositions is to ask yourself what problems people had and how they proposed solving those problems.

Key Terms and People
constitution
executive
economic
depression
Daniel Shays

Government by the States

As the Continental Congress began moving toward independence in 1776, leaders in the individual states began creating governments. Eleven of the 13 states wrote new constitutions to support their governments. A constitution is a document stating the rules under which a government will operate. The other two states—Rhode Island and Connecticut—kept using their colonial charters. However, they removed all references to the British king.

Writing State Constitutions In writing state constitutions, Americans were well aware of the problems that had led to the Revolution. Colonists had been unhappy with governors appointed by the British Crown. Thus, the new constitutions minimized the powers of state governors. Instead, they gave most of the power to state legislatures elected by the people.

204 Chapter 7 Creating the Constitution

① Key social studies terms for each section are introduced in the section opener.

② Notice that they are always shown in blue type within the text narrative. Their definitions are also in blue.

Reading Skill

Identify Propositions The study of history often takes you inside important debates over ideas and actions. People propose their ideas and then give reasons to support those ideas. Identifying those propositions will help you to understand the beliefs and experiences of people in an earlier time. One way to identify propositions is to ask yourself what problems people had and how they proposed solving those problems.

Key Terms and People
constitution
executive
economic
depression
Daniel Shays

Government by the States

As the Continental Congress began moving toward independence in 1776, leaders in the individual states began creating governments. Eleven of the 13 states wrote new constitutions to support their governments. A constitution is a document stating the rules under which a government will operate. The other two states—Rhode Island and Connecticut—kept using their colonial charters. However, they removed all references to the British king.

Writing State Constitutions In writing state constitutions, Americans were well aware of the problems that had led to the Revolution. Colonists had been unhappy with governors appointed by the British Crown. Thus, the new constitutions minimized the powers of state governors. Instead, they gave most of the power to state legislatures elected by the people.

204 Chapter 7 Creating the Constitution

Protecting Rights The Declaration of Independence listed ways that Britain had violated the rights of colonists. To prevent such abuses, states sought to protect individual rights. Virginia was the first state to include a bill of rights in its constitution. Virginia's list included freedom of the press and the right to trial by jury, and it also barred "cruel and unusual punishments." The final clause guaranteed freedom of religion:

❝That religion, or the duty which we owe to our Creator, and the manner of discharging it, can be directed only by reason and conviction, not by force or violence; and therefore all men are equally entitled to the free exercise of religion, according to the dictates of conscience.❞

—Virginia Bill of Rights, 1776

Vocabulary Builder
individual (in duh vɪj oo uhl)
adj. of, for, or by a single person or thing

Protecting Rights
Virginia included a bill of rights in its constitution. The Virginia bill of rights became a model for other states and, later, for the national Constitution. Critical Thinking: *Link Past and Present Which protections in the Virginia bill of*

③ High-use words are underlined in the text and defined in the margin. You can practice these words at Vocabulary Builder Online.

Reading Skills

The History Reading Skills described on this page are important in helping you read and understand the information in this book. Each section teaches a reading skill and gives you a chance to practice the skill as you read. As you learn to use these skills, you will find that you can apply them to other books you read.

Clarify Meaning You can better understand what you read by using summaries and outlines and by taking notes to help identify main ideas and supporting details. **Chapters 21, 22.**

Compare and Contrast When you compare, you examine the similarities between things. When you contrast, you look at the differences. **Chapter 28.**

Use Context Learn to use context clues to help you understand the meaning of unfamiliar words and words with more than one meaning. **Chapters 17, 24.**

Word Analysis Discover how to analyze words to determine their meanings. **Chapter 18.**

Understand Sequence A sequence is the order in which a series of events occurs. Noting the sequence of important events can help you understand and remember the events. **Chapter 15.**

Analyze Cause and Effect Every event in history has causes and creates effects. You will learn how to identify causes, which are what make events happen, and effects, which are what happen as a result of an event. **Chapters 14, 23, 25.**

Draw Conclusions You will learn how to use details from primary and secondary sources to draw conclusions. **Chapters 26, 29.**

Evaluate Information As you read history, it is important to evaluate how writers' support their propositions, or the ideas they put forth. To do so, it is important to know how to identify and explain central issues and frame good research questions. **Chapters 16, 19, 20, 27.**

MAP✴MASTER®

CONTENTS

Go Online PHSchool.com The maps in this textbook can be found online at **PHSchool.com**, along with map-skills practice.

Geography and History

Historical information is not presented only in written sources. Maps are often a key to understanding what happened and why.

Do you remember when Patricia was asking questions about the letter she found? (See page HT 3.) In addition to using primary and secondary sources, Patricia could have used maps to locate Ireland and to trace Sean's route from New York to California.

In order to get the most out of maps as sources, you need to make sure that your geography map skills are strong. On the next few pages, you can review some of the basic tools historians use to understand maps and geography.

The pictures above show two different geographical regions of the United States. The Midwest (above, left) has fertile plains suitable for farming. The rocky coasts of New England (right) are home to a large fishing industry.

Five Themes of Geography

Studying the history and geography of the United States is a huge task. You can make that task easier by thinking of geography in terms of five themes. The five themes below are tools you can use to organize geographic information and to answer questions about the influence of geography and human history.

Location

1 The exact location of a country or city is expressed in terms of longitude and latitude. Relative location defines where a place is in relation to other places. For example, the exact location of the city of Chicago, Illinois, is 42° north (latitude) and 88° west (longitude). Its relative location could be described as "on the shore of Lake Michigan" or "821 miles north of New Orleans."

Place

2 Location answers the question, "Where is it?" Place answers the question, "What is it like there?" You can identify a place by such features as its landforms, its climate, its plants and animals, or the people who live there. Much of the history of the southeastern United States was shaped by the fact that it had a mild climate and fertile land suitable for large-scale farming of crops such as cotton.

Regions

3 Regions are areas that share common features. Regions may be defined by geography or culture. For example, New York is one of the Middle Atlantic states because it is located on the Atlantic Ocean. In colonial days, it was one of the Middle Colonies. And in the early 1800s, New York was one of the "free states" because slavery was banned there.

Movement

4 Much of history has to do with the movement of people, goods, and ideas from place to place. In Patricia's letter, we saw two examples of movement: the movement of immigrants to the United States from other countries and the movement of Americans from the East to the West. Both played a key role in the history and growth of the United States.

Interaction

5 Human-environment interaction has two parts. The first part has to do with the way an environment affects people. For example, people in the desert of the American Southwest developed very different ways of life from those living in the rich farmlands of California. The second part of interaction concerns the way people affect their environment. People mined silver in Nevada and harnessed the power of falling water in North Carolina. In each case, they changed their environment.

Practice Geography Skills

Look at the photographs on page HT 8 and read the caption. How do these pictures illustrate the themes of place, region, and interaction?

Globes

A globe is a model of Earth. It shows the actual shape, size, and location of each landmass and body of water.

Globes divide Earth into lines of latitude and longitude. Latitude measures distance north or south of the Equator, which is an imaginary line around the widest part of Earth. Longitude measures distance east or west of the Prime Meridian, which is an imaginary line running from the North Pole to the South Pole. The diagram below shows how lines of longitude and latitude form a grid pattern on a globe.

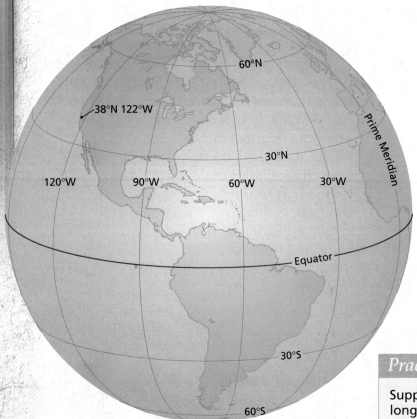

Using lines of latitude and longitude, you can locate any place on Earth. The location of 38° north latitude and 122° west longitude is written as 38° N/122° W. Only one place on Earth has this location: the city of San Francisco, California.

Practice Geography Skills

Suppose that you wanted to plan a long trip. What would be some advantages and disadvantages of using a globe?

Map Projections

Globes are accurate, but they are not easy to carry around, and they are not useful for showing smaller areas of Earth in detail. So mapmakers had to develop methods to show the curved Earth on a flat surface. These methods are known as map projections. All map projections distort Earth in some way. Below are two common types of map projections.

Mercator Projection

In the 1500s, ocean travelers relied on the Mercator projection, named after mapmaker Gerardus Mercator. The Mercator projection accurately shows direction and the shape of Earth's landmasses. However, it distorts distance and size.

Robinson Projection

The Robinson projection shows the correct shape and size of landmasses for most parts of the world. However, it does not show directions as well as a Mercator projection does. It also distorts the size of the North Pole and South Pole.

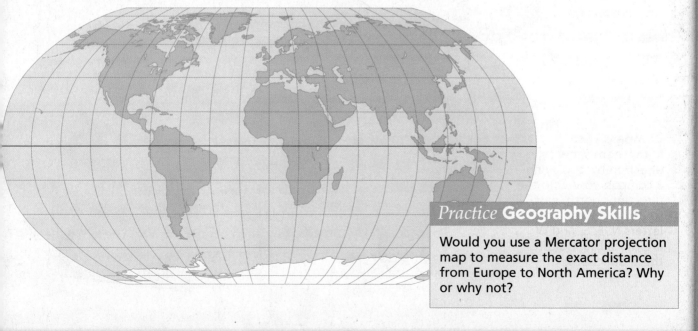

Practice Geography Skills

Would you use a Mercator projection map to measure the exact distance from Europe to North America? Why or why not?

How to Use a Map

Mapmakers provide several clues to help in understanding the information on a map. Maps provide different clues, depending on their purpose or scale. However, most maps have several clues in common.

Locator
Many maps are shown with locator maps or globes. They show where on Earth the area of the map is located.

Title
Maps have titles. The title tells you the subject of the map.

Key
Often a map has a key, or legend. The key shows the meaning of the symbols and colors used on the map.

Compass rose
Many maps show direction by displaying a compass rose with the directions north, east, south, and west. The letters N, E, S, and W are placed to indicate these directions.

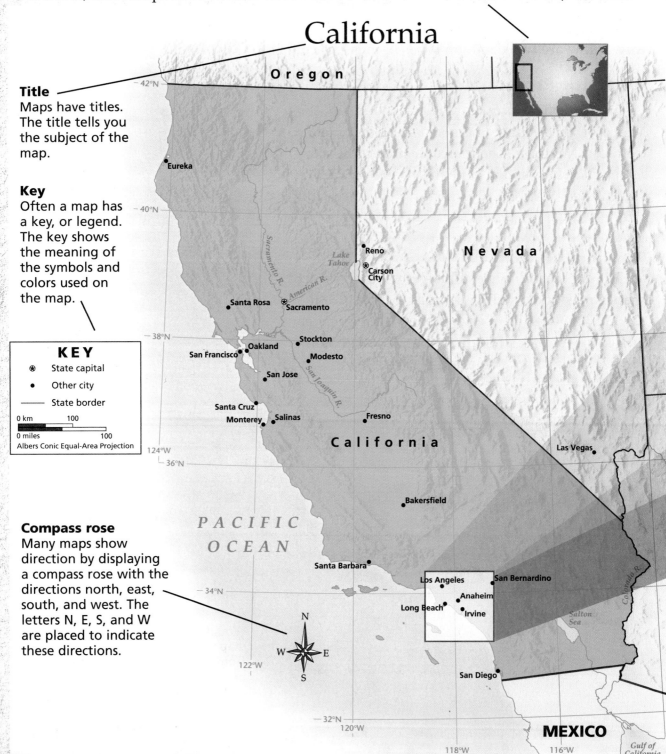

California

KEY
⊗ State capital
• Other city
— State border

0 km 100
0 miles 100
Albers Conic Equal-Area Projection

Maps of Different Scales

Maps are drawn to different scales, depending on their purpose. Here are three maps drawn to very different scales. Keep in mind that maps showing large areas have smaller scales. Maps showing small areas have larger scales.

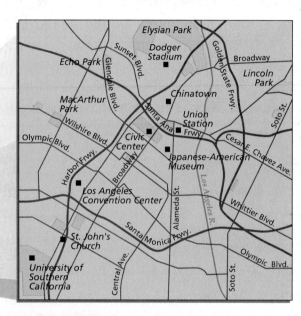

▲ Greater Los Angeles

Find the light gray square on the main map of California (left). This square represents the area shown on the map above. It shows Los Angeles in relation to nearby cities, towns, and the Pacific Ocean. It also shows some features near the city, such as the airport and major roadways.

▲ Downtown Los Angeles

Find the gray square on the map of Greater Los Angeles. This square represents the area shown on the map above. This map moves you closer into the center of Los Angeles. Like a zoom on a computer or a camera, this map shows a smaller area, but in greater detail. It has the largest scale. You can use this map to explore downtown Los Angeles.

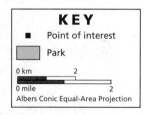

KEY
- ■ Point of interest
- ▨ Park

0 km — 2
0 mile — 2
Albers Conic Equal-Area Projection

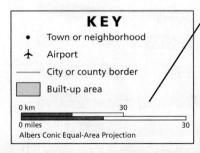

KEY
- • Town or neighborhood
- ✈ Airport
- — City or county border
- ▨ Built-up area

0 km — 30
0 miles — 30
Albers Conic Equal-Area Projection

Scale bar
A scale bar helps you find the actual distances between points shown on the map. Most scale bars show distances in both miles and kilometers.

Practice Geography Skills

- What part of a map explains the colors used on the map?
- How does the scale bar change depending on the scale of the map?

Political Maps

Historians use many different types of maps. On the next four pages, you will see four maps that relate to American history. Each map shows a different area in a different way and for a different purpose.

One of the most familiar types of map is the political map. Political maps show political divisions, such as borders between countries or states. Colors on a political map help make the differences clear. Political maps also show the location of cities. This map shows the United States in 1790, at the time George Washington was President.

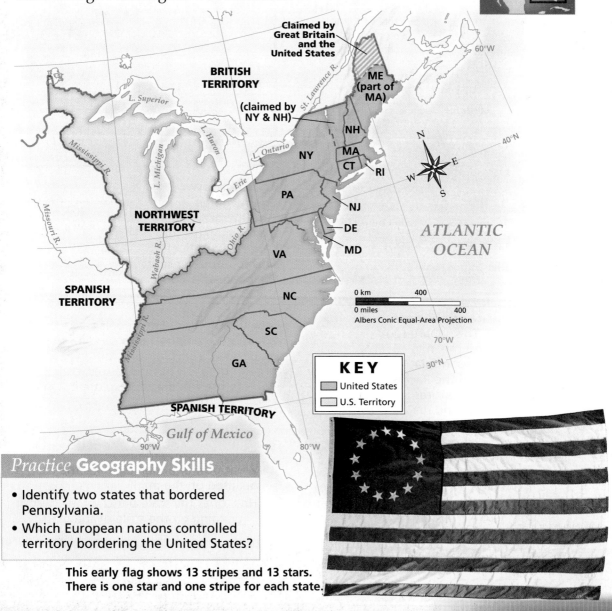

Practice Geography Skills

- Identify two states that bordered Pennsylvania.
- Which European nations controlled territory bordering the United States?

This early flag shows 13 stripes and 13 stars. There is one star and one stripe for each state.

Physical Maps

Physical maps show the major physical features of a region, such as seas, rivers, and mountains. The larger the scale of a physical map, the more detail it can show. For example, the map below shows the rivers that run through the American Southwest. If you compare this map to the physical map in the Atlas at the front of this textbook, you will notice that there are several rivers shown on this map that are not shown on the Atlas map.

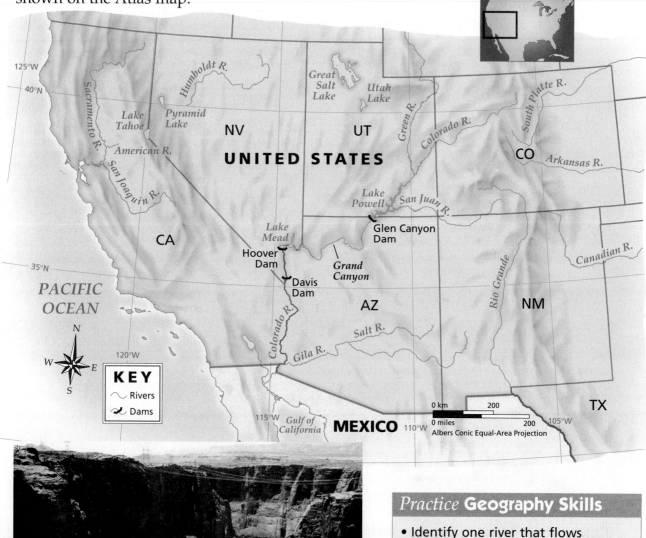

Practice Geography Skills

- Identify one river that flows through New Mexico.
- Describe the path of the Colorado River.

The Colorado River formed the Grand Canyon in Arizona.

Special-Purpose Maps
Battle Maps

In addition to political maps and physical maps, there are different types of special-purpose maps. These range from road maps to weather maps to election maps. Some special-purpose maps use arrows to show the movement of people and goods from place to place. The map below shows the battles and troop movements that led up to the Battle of Gettysburg in July 1863.

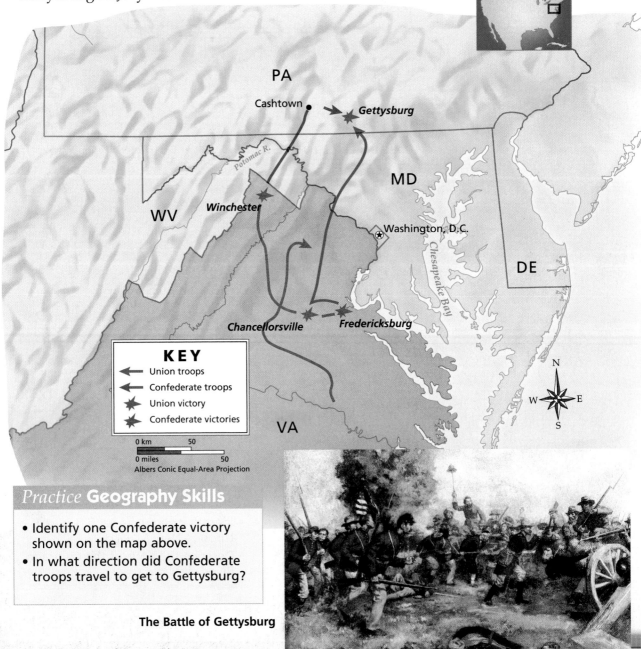

KEY
- ← Union troops
- ← Confederate troops
- ✦ Union victory
- ✦ Confederate victories

0 km 50
0 miles 50
Albers Conic Equal-Area Projection

Practice Geography Skills

- Identify one Confederate victory shown on the map above.
- In what direction did Confederate troops travel to get to Gettysburg?

The Battle of Gettysburg

Election Maps

Have you ever seen a newspaper or watched television during a presidential election? If you have, then you have probably seen an election map. Election maps show all of the states voting in the election. Different colors are used to show which candidates won the vote in which states. The map below shows the election of 1912, when three major candidates were running for President.

KEY
- Theodore Roosevelt
- William Taft
- Woodrow Wilson

Practice Geography Skills

- Which candidate won in California? In Illinois?
- How many states did Taft win?

Cartoon showing Wilson, Taft, and Roosevelt running for President in 1912

Read Visual Information

In this textbook, the information you need to know is presented in written form. Often, however, key information is also summarized in chart form. Charts organize facts and ideas in a visual way that makes them easier to understand.

The next four pages review some of the basic types of visuals you will find in this textbook. Building your ability to analyze visuals will help you get the most out of the information provided.

Timelines

Every chapter in this textbook begins with a timeline. You have used timelines before, but the ones in this book have a few special features. Most of them are made up of two parts:

- **U.S. Events** This is the main part of the timeline. It shows the events that are described in that chapter that took place within the United States.
- **World Events** This part of the timeline shows events that took place in other parts of the world during the same time period. These events are often included because they related to what was going on in the United States.

Timelines make it easier to understand the sequence of events over time. The timelines in this textbook will help you explain how major events are related to one another in time.

> ### Practice Chart Skills
>
> - How many years after gold was discovered in California was gold discovered in Australia?
> - Which world event was probably related to one of the U.S. events?

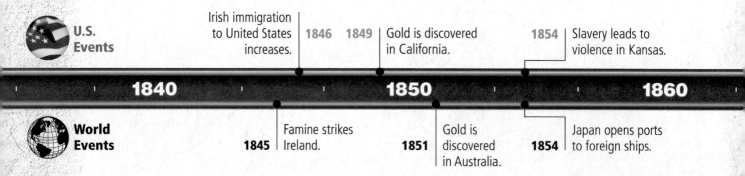

| U.S. Events | | Irish immigration to United States increases. | 1846 | 1849 | Gold is discovered in California. | | 1854 | Slavery leads to violence in Kansas. |

1840   **1850**   **1860**

| World Events | | 1845 | Famine strikes Ireland. | | 1851 | Gold is discovered in Australia. | | 1854 | Japan opens ports to foreign ships. |

Build Chart Skills

Tables

Tables provide a simple way to organize a large amount of information graphically. A table is arranged in a grid pattern. Columns run vertically, from top to bottom. Rows run horizontally, from left to right.

This sample table summarizes some basic facts about four major wars you will learn about this year. The four wars are listed in the column at the far left, at the beginning of each row. The categories of information given about each war are listed at the top of each column.

Tables can be very large. You may have seen computer spreadsheets that include dozens of columns and rows. Yet, all tables follow the same basic grid pattern shown below.

Four American Wars

War	Dates	Opponents	Results
American Revolution	1775–1781	American colonists vs. Britain	• Colonists win. • United States wins independence.
War of 1812	1812–1814	United States vs. Britain	• No clear winner emerges. • Increased sense of national pride felt.
Mexican-American War	1846–1848	United States vs. Mexico	• United States wins. • United States gains new territory in the West.
Civil War	1861–1865	North vs. South	• North wins. • Union is preserved. • Slavery ends.

Practice Chart Skills

- What were the results of the Mexican-American War?
- In which two wars did Americans fight the same opponent?

Pie Charts

Some charts and graphs in this book show statistical information, that is, information based on exact numbers. Pie charts show statistical information in terms of percentages. The circle, or pie, represents 100 percent of a group. Each wedge of the pie represents one subgroup of the whole. The bigger the wedge is, the larger the group. This pie chart shows how the population of southern states was divided in the year 1850, when slavery was still legal in the South.

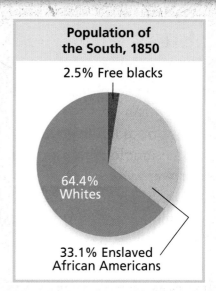

Population of the South, 1850

2.5% Free blacks

64.4% Whites

33.1% Enslaved African Americans

Line Graphs and Bar Graphs

Line graphs and bar graphs show statistical information as it changes over time. The horizontal, or side to side, axis usually tells you the time period covered by the graph. The vertical, or up and down, axis tells you what is being measured. By lining up the points on the graph with the horizontal and vertical axes, you can see how many or how much of something there was at a given time.

On a line graph, the points are connected. On a bar graph, each year is represented by a bar. The line graph (below left) and the bar graph (below right) show the same information: the number of patents, or licenses for new inventions, issued by the U.S. government.

Practice Chart Skills

- What percentage of southern society in 1850 was made up of enslaved African Americans?
- About how many patents were issued in 1860? In 1880?

U.S. Patents, 1860–1900

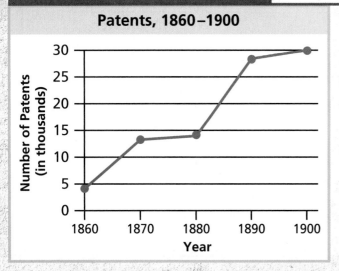

Patents, 1860–1900

Number of Patents (in thousands)

Year

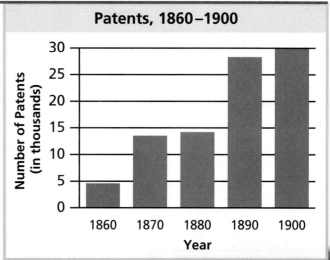

Patents, 1860–1900

Number of Patents (in thousands)

Year

When you are doing research on the Internet, it is important to evaluate the Web sites to determine if the information is valid and objective. The page below is from a Web site about Samuel F.B. Morse.

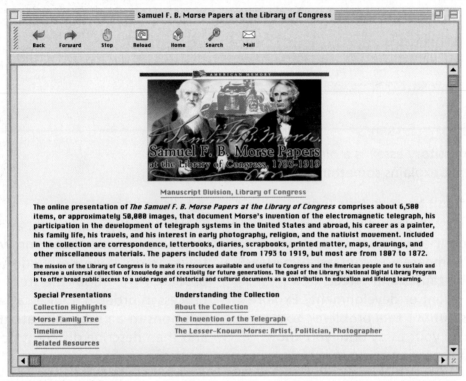

Source: The Library of Congress

Use these steps to learn how to evaluate Internet sources.

- Determine the Web site's purpose. Does the Web site provide information? Is it trying to sell something or to promote a particular point of view?
- Examine the information. Does the site include visuals? Does it include first-person accounts and other primary source materials?
- Compare the information to what you already know. Does the information agree with what you have read in a textbook or in another reliable print source? What other information is provided?
- Evaluate the source. Is the source an established organization? Can you tell who provided the information?

Practice **Internet Skills**

- What is the purpose of this Web site?
- (a) Who is the provider for this site? (b) If you were writing a paper about Samuel F.B. Morse, do you think you could use the information on this Web site? Why or why not?

Write Like a Historian

You have learned how to use historians' tools to learn about the past. The next step is to write about what you have discovered. Historians share their findings in a variety of ways, including expository essays, narratives, research papers, and persuasive essays or speeches. You will have a chance to practice each type through end-of-section and end-of-chapter writing activities.

Expository Essays

An expository essay is a piece of writing that explains something in detail.

❶ Select and Narrow Your Topic

Define exactly what you want your essay to do. Do you want to describe a process? Compare and contrast two ideas? Explain the causes and effects of a historical event or development? Explore possible solutions to a problem? You cannot plan your essay until you know what you are trying to do in it.

❷ Gather Evidence

Create a graphic organizer that identifies details to include in your essay, such as the one shown below.

❸ Write a First Draft

Write a topic sentence, and then organize the essay based on what you are trying to do. If your essay describes a process, write about the steps of the process in order. If your essay explores solutions to a problem, state the problem, and then describe different possible solutions.

❹ Revise and Proofread

Make sure that all the details support your topic sentence.

Problem	Suggested Solutions	Evaluation of Solution
The Articles of Confederation left the nation weak because they did not provide for a central authority.	Leave the Articles alone, and persuade other countries and Americans to respect the new nation.	Not practical—what would make more established governments and local rebels accept a weak authority?
	Get rid of the Articles, and create an entirely new plan.	Possible, but it would be a huge task to start all over again.

If you were writing a problem-solution essay, you might create a chart like this to help you organize your ideas.

Research Papers

Research papers present information that you have found about a topic.

1 Select and Narrow Your Topic

Choose a topic that interests you. Make sure that your topic is not too broad. For example, instead of writing a report on Native Americans, you might write a report about the Cherokees who were forced to move west in 1837 on a journey known as the Trail of Tears.

2 Acquire Information

Locate several sources of information about the topic from the library or on the Internet. Be sure to evaluate the source. Is it reliable? How does the information compare to what you have found in other sources?

For each resource, create a source index card. Then, take notes using an index card for each detail or subtopic. On the card, note which source the information was taken from. Use quotation marks when you copy exact words from a source.

3 Make an Outline

Use an outline to decide how to organize your research paper. Sort your index cards in the same order.

4 Write a First Draft

Write an introduction, a body, and a conclusion. If you are preparing your first draft by hand, leave plenty of space between lines so you can go back and add details that you may have left out.

5 Revise and Proofread

Be sure to include transition words between sentences and paragraphs. Here are some examples:

- To describe a process: *first, next, then*
- To show a contrast: *however, although, despite*
- To point out a reason: *since, because, if*
- To signal a conclusion: *therefore, as a result, so*

Introduction

The Trail of Tears

How would you feel if soldiers came to your home and forced you to move thousands of miles away? This may sound like an impossible nightmare. But that is what happened to the Cherokee people in 1838.

Conclusion

Therefore, the Trail of Tears was a tragedy for the Cherokees and other Native Americans. Sadly, there would be more clashes with settlers in the years to come.

Write Like a Historian

Narrative Essays

History is like a story. It has characters, both leaders and everyday people. It has a setting where events take place. It even has a plot, in which events unfold, conflicts arise, and resolutions occur.

❶ Select and Narrow Your Topic

In this textbook, you will be asked to write narratives about the past. You might be asked to imagine a setting and describe how it affects what is happening. You might be asked to take the point of view of one of history's characters. Or you might be asked to explain the conflict or resolution of a historical situation. First, you must understand what you are being asked to do or who you are asked to be.

❷ Gather Details

Brainstorm a list of details you would like to include in your narrative.

❸ Write a First Draft

Start by writing a simple opening sentence that conveys the main idea of your essay. Continue by writing a colorful story that has interesting details. Write a conclusion that sums up the main points.

❹ Revise and Proofread

Check to make sure you have not begun too many sentences with the word *I*. Replace general words with more colorful ones.

Persuasive Essays

A persuasive essay is a piece of writing that supports a position or opinion.

❶ Select and Narrow Your Topic

Choose a historical topic that has at least two sides or two interpretations. Choose a side. Decide which argument will best persuade your audience to agree with your point of view.

❷ Gather Evidence

Create a chart that states your position at the top, and then lists the pros and cons for your position in two columns below. Predict and address the strongest arguments against your viewpoint.

❸ Write a First Draft

Write a strong thesis statement that clearly states your position. Continue by presenting the strongest arguments in favor of your position and acknowledging and refuting opposing arguments.

❹ Revise and Proofread

Check to make sure you have made a logical argument and that you have not oversimplified the argument.

There are many types of questions in your textbook. Checkpoint Questions help you check your understanding of a small section of your reading. Check Your Progress questions at the end of each section help you practice understandings gained while reading the whole section. Likewise questions at the end of the chapter help you understand content in the chapter.

There is another type of question in this textbook that may be even more important. They are called Essential Questions. You will find them at the beginning of each unit and each chapter. They are also the basis of the Historian's Apprentice Learning System, which appears throughout this book.

Essential questions can really make you think. They don't have a right answer. They often make you think of other questions. But they are important because they get to the heart of the matter. As you think about them, you will come to deep understanding.

▲ The Essential Question for the unit is introduced on the unit opener.

▲ The Historian's Apprentice Activity Pack provides more activities to explore history.

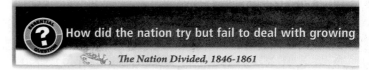

How did the nation try but fail to deal with growing

The Nation Divided, 1846-1861

▲ The Essential Question at the beginning of each chapter helps frame your understanding of the whole chapter.

ACTIVITY

Divide into three groups to build an answer to the unit question: How was the Civil War a political, economic, and social turning point?

One group should use the Think Like a Historian documents to describe the Civil War's political effects. Another group should use the documents to describe the economic effects of the war. The last group should cover the war's social effects. After each group has had time to prepare a presentation, it should report its findings to the rest of the class in the format of a documentary news program.

▲ At the end of every unit you complete an activity that will help you show your understanding.

"Here is not merely a nation, but a teeming nation of nations," wrote poet Walt Whitman. The people of the United States came from all over the world to form a "nation of nations." The history of the United States is the story of how people from many nations and cultures formed one nation with its own heritage and traditions.

A Diverse Nation

From the beginning, the American land was open to the people of the world. Some scientists believe the first people came to North America thousands of years ago by crossing a land bridge that joined Asia to Alaska in North America. Other scientists believe people traveled along coastal routes by boat from Asia. Over thousands of years, groups of people spread throughout North and South America.

Millions of Native Americans were living in the Americas long before Christopher Columbus crossed the Atlantic Ocean from Europe in 1492. Spain sent the first European settlers to the Americas in the 1500s. Other Europeans followed, as did many Africans. By 1775, nearly 3 million people lived in the 13 English colonies on the Atlantic Coast. It was the most densely settled section of North America.

These settlers came to North America for many reasons. Some were looking for farmland at low cost. Others came to escape fierce religious wars in Europe. Most African Americans had been captured in Africa and shipped to the colonies as slaves.

During the 1800s, immigrants continued to arrive. A great famine in Ireland in 1845 sparked a wave of newcomers. Others arrived after a failed revolution in Germany in 1848. In Texas, the Southwest, and California, hundreds of thousands of Mexicans and Native Americans became residents of the United States after the Mexican-American War of 1846–1848. Many Chinese immigrants arrived after gold was discovered in California in 1848.

The Religious Tradition

Many European settlers fled to the colonies in search of religious freedom. At first, most colonies had their own established churches, or churches officially supported by the government. But there were many different religious groups in the colonies and, in time, established churches tolerated those with other beliefs.

After the Revolutionary War, most states did away with established churches. Freedom of religion became one of the fundamental rights in the Constitution of the United States.

The Reforming Spirit

In a democracy, people have the right to speak out to bring about change. During the mid-1800s, many reformers voiced their opinions. They had different goals, but they all hoped to improve the quality of American life.

Religious reformers encouraged people to take personal responsibility for their faith and to lead holy lives. Many held revivals, meetings that stirred a religious spirit in those who attended. Other reformers concentrated on changing the institutions of American society. Some, like Horace Mann, offered ideas for improving education. Through the efforts of Mann and others, many states had created free public elementary schools by the 1850s.

Reformers like Elizabeth Cady Stanton demanded more rights for women. In 1848, she and other feminists met in Seneca Falls, New York. Launching the women's rights movement, they declared, "All men and women are created equal."

Another crusade of the 1800s was the movement to end slavery. Americans known as abolitionists called for an immediate end to slavery. William Lloyd Garrison led the way, founding the *Liberator,* an antislavery newspaper, in 1831. Free African Americans like Frederick Douglass were active in the cause.

Speaking Out Against Slavery Police break up a meeting of abolitionists in Boston in 1860 as Frederick Douglass (center) struggles to finish his speech.

An American Culture

As the young nation developed, American artists and writers began to celebrate the new American culture that was flowering around them.

Ralph Waldo Emerson reflected the optimism and individualism that were typical of the new nation. In his essay "Self-Reliance," Emerson advised his readers to depend on themselves rather than follow others. Henry David Thoreau revealed his own kind of individualism in *Walden,* the story of his solitary life by Walden Pond in Massachusetts.

Perhaps more than anyone else, poet Walt Whitman captured the idealistic spirit of the republic. In *Leaves of Grass,* published in 1855, Whitman describes the people of the nation.

"In all people I see myself, none more and not one
   barleycorn less,
And the good or bad I say of myself I say of them."

—Walt Whitman, "Song of Myself"

Building a Republic

Following the Revolutionary War, Americans began a dramatic political experiment. They decided to create a federal republic. Under this system, voters elect representatives to govern the country.

The plan was especially bold because the United States included many different peoples, spread out over a vast region. A republic that large had never been created. Furthermore, few republics in history had survived for more than a few years.

The English Heritage

Americans did have democratic traditions that they used to guide them. For hundreds of years, the power of English monarchs had been limited by charters, or documents that guaranteed certain rights and privileges to a group of people. Such documents as the Magna Carta, or "great charter," protected English citizens' right to own private property and guaranteed the right to trial by jury.

English settlers brought this tradition of representative government with them. In 1619, the Virginia Colony received a charter that allowed eligible voters to elect a legislature. The Virginia House of Burgesses became the first representative assembly in the Americas.

The 13 colonies were founded at different times and under different circumstances, but eventually, all set up elected legislatures. Representative government became a part of colonial life.

Independence

The colonies' break with England began in the 1760s. Britain had spent large sums of money to protect the colonies during a war with France. Afterward, Parliament decided to control the colonies more closely, particularly to collect taxes. The colonists protested that they did not elect representatives to Parliament. A free people, they argued, could be taxed only by its own legislature.

Parliament refused to back down. During ten years of colonial protests, it imposed harsh measures on the colonies. The colonists responded by sending representatives to a Continental Congress in Philadelphia. In 1776, Congress issued the Declaration of Independence.

Declaring Independence
Delegates sign the Declaration of Independence.

Written by Thomas Jefferson, the Declaration became a landmark in American political thought. It proclaimed that all people were "endowed by their creator with certain unalienable rights," including "life, liberty, and the pursuit of happiness."

After independence, the new nation governed itself under the Articles of Confederation. But the Articles gave most of the power to the states and little to the national government. Congress could not solve crucial economic, political, and foreign policy questions. It could not collect taxes or enforce the laws that it passed.

In the summer of 1787, a special convention met in Philadelphia. Working behind closed doors, it drew up a new Constitution designed to replace the Articles of Confederation. In 1789, the new government went into effect.

A Federal System

The Constitution set up a system of government called federalism. Under federalism, the states and the federal government share the power of governing. The Constitution gives certain powers entirely to the federal government. But all powers that the Constitution does not grant specifically to the federal government are reserved for the individual states.

The Constitution also put in place three separate branches of national government. The executive branch is headed by the President, whose job is to enforce the laws of the land. Congress forms the legislative branch, which makes the laws. The judicial branch, a system of federal courts, decides cases that involve federal law. It also settles disputes between the states.

HISTORIAN'S APPRENTICE ACTIVITY PACK

To further explore the topics in this chapter, complete the activity in the Historian's Apprentice Activity Pack to answer this essential question:

How is the rule of law in the Constitution of the United States rooted in the past?

Separation of Powers

The powers of government are divided, or separated, among three branches of government: the legislative, executive, and judicial branches.

Separation of Powers

Legislative Branch (Congress)	Executive Branch (President) 	Judicial Branch (Supreme Court and Other Federal Courts)
Passes Laws	**Carries Out Laws**	**Interprets Laws**
■ Can override President's veto	■ Proposes laws	■ Can declare laws unconstitutional
■ Approves treaties	■ Can veto laws	■ Can declare executive actions unconstitutional
■ Can impeach and remove President and other high officials	■ Negotiates foreign treaties	
■ Prints and coins money	■ Serves as commander in chief of armed forces	
■ Raises and supports armed forces	■ Appoints federal judges, ambassadors, and other high officials	
■ Can declare war	■ Can grant pardons to federal offenders	
■ Regulates foreign and interstate trade		

Checks and Balances

Legislative Branch (Congress makes laws) 	**Checks on the Executive Branch** ■ Can override President's veto ■ Confirms executive appointments ■ Ratifies treaties ■ Can declare war ■ Appropriates money ■ Can impeach and remove President	**Checks on the Judicial Branch** ■ Creates lower federal courts ■ Can impeach and remove judges ■ Can propose amendments to overrule judicial decisions ■ Approves appointments of federal judges
Executive Branch (President carries out laws)	**Checks on the Legislative Branch** ■ Can propose laws ■ Can veto laws ■ Can call special sessions of Congress ■ Makes appointments ■ Negotiates foreign treaties	**Checks on the Judicial Branch** ■ Appoints federal judges ■ Can grant pardons to federal offenders
Judicial Branch (Supreme Court interprets laws) 	**Check on the Executive Branch** ■ Can declare executive actions unconstitutional	**Check on the Legislative Branch** ■ Can declare acts of Congress unconstitutional

Checks and Balances
To assure that no one branch of government overpowers the other two, the Constitution created a system of checks and balances.

To further strengthen the basic principle of separation of powers, the idea that the powers of government are divided among branches of government, the Constitution also established a system of checks and balances. Under this system, each branch of government can check, or limit, the power of the other two.

A Growing Democracy

Even after the Constitution went into effect, many details of the political system remained to be worked out over time. The Constitution itself may be altered if enough people and enough states agree to a proposed amendment, or change. The process can take months or years to complete. Over the past 200 years, 27 amendments have been adopted.

As the nation gained experience in governing itself, Americans developed new ideas about how a democracy should work. Many states dropped property requirements that limited who was allowed to vote. They permitted all adult white men to vote.

Even so, democracy in the 1800s had serious limits. Women, Native Americans, and most African Americans could not vote.

Even more disturbing was the institution of slavery in the South. Slaves had none of the basic liberties that other Americans cherished. As the nation expanded toward the Pacific Ocean, the debate increased over what a free society should do about slavery.

The Nation Expands

Alexis de Tocqueville, a French visitor to the United States in 1831, was amazed at the bustling activity he saw. "The Americans arrived but yesterday on the territory which they inhabit and they have already changed the whole order of nature for their own advantage."

Colonial Economies

The booming economy of Tocqueville's day was very different from the way Americans made their living during the colonial period. Before the 1800s, most trade involved sending raw materials from colonies to the parent countries in Europe.

In Spain's colonies, for example, silver was mined by Indian laborers and shipped to Europe. The English colonies along the Atlantic Coast sent timber, tobacco, furs, and fish to England. There, manufacturers turned the raw materials into finished products such as ships, hats, and cloth. English merchants then sold the products around the world.

This type of economic system was called **mercantilism.** It was meant to benefit the parent country more than it did the American colonies. To strengthen control over the colonies, England passed laws to regulate colonial trade. Even after independence, most American products were sold abroad.

An Enterprising People

During the 1800s, the economic system changed. American merchants and manufacturers began to sell more products to other Americans, not just to Europe. Encouraging its own industries, the young nation gradually built a strong, independent economy.

The economy grew for several reasons. Americans possessed a bountiful land. It had rich farmland, vast mineral deposits, fine forests, and good waterways for transportation. The population of the United States doubled about every 23 years in the 1800s, due to large families and immigration. Merchants and manufacturers had more customers to whom they could sell American goods.

The Growth of Industry
During the early 1800s, people began working in factories.

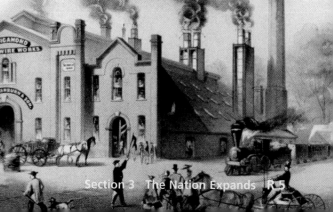

The Journey of Lewis and Clark Shown here with Native American translator Sacagawea and an enslaved African American named York, Lewis and Clark explored lands from the Mississippi River to the Pacific Ocean.

The expanding economy also reflected the democratic character of the nation. In Europe, rigid social divisions made it difficult for anyone to rise out of poverty. However, the situation was different for Americans. Many wanted the opportunity to advance. In the United States, that was possible. Tocqueville noted, "in America most of the rich men were formerly poor," and "any man's son may become the equal of any other man's son."

An Industrial Revolution

The American economy also grew because of a revolution in the way goods were manufactured. Before machines were introduced, most goods were produced by hand. By the late 1700s, steam engines had been developed in England and were used to run machines in English textile mills, spinning cotton thread and weaving it into cloth.

Americans learned how to build similar machines in the early 1800s. New England became the center of a thriving textile industry. The Industrial Revolution led to a new way of producing goods. With the new factory system, workers and machinery were together in one place.

Two Americans, John Fitch and Robert Fulton, put steam engines on boats. Using these steamboats, merchants could ship freight upstream even against strong currents. By the 1840s, engines were also put to work hauling cars along iron rails, or railroads.

Machines had far-reaching effects on farming, too. In 1793, Eli Whitney invented the cotton gin—short for "engine"—a machine that removed seeds from cotton. With a cotton gin, one person could clean as much cotton as it had taken 50 people to clean before. Cotton production in the South spread rapidly. By the 1840s, the South was supplying 60 percent of the world's cotton.

From the Atlantic to the Pacific

As the economy grew, so did the nation itself. Between 1803 and 1853, the United States expanded westward from the Mississippi River to the Pacific Ocean.

President Thomas Jefferson bought the Louisiana Territory from France for $15 million in 1803. Overnight, the Louisiana Purchase doubled the size of the nation. Jefferson had the team of Meriwether Lewis and William Clark explore the vast new lands.

The nation grew again when Texas joined the Union. Since 1821, groups of settlers from the United States had moved to Texas, which was then part of Mexico. As a result of disputes with the Mexican government, Texans declared their independence in 1836 and set up a new nation called the Republic of Texas. Sam Houston became commander of the Texan army. Texas defeated the Mexican army in the war that followed. In 1845, Congress passed a joint resolution **annexing,** or adding, Texas to the United States.

The United States and Britain agreed to divide the Oregon Country in 1846. That same year, the United States went to war with Mexico over the location of the Texas border. Victory in the war gave the United States control of a large new section of territory in the Southwest. The land included the present-day states of California, Nevada, and Utah as well as parts of Arizona, New Mexico, Colorado, and Wyoming.

Many Americans were proud of their country and wanted to expand its borders. By 1853, the United States had fulfilled what many believed was its clear mission, or **Manifest Destiny.** Americans believed they had a right to extend their boundaries to the Pacific Ocean.

Manifest Destiny By 1853 the United States stretched from the Atlantic Ocean to the Pacific Ocean.

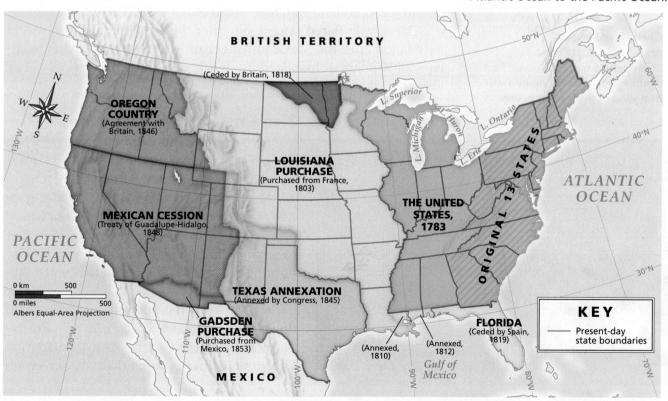

The Union Splits in Two

In 1850, Senator John Calhoun of South Carolina gave his last speech in the Senate. Calhoun warned that "the cords which bind these states together in one common union" were breaking one by one. He predicted that if the disagreements between the North and the South did not end, the Union would fall apart.

Calhoun's warning was prophetic. During the 1850s, a series of dramatic events brought the nation, step by step, to civil war. As Abraham Lincoln said in 1858, "A house divided against itself cannot stand." What most divided that house was the issue of slavery.

Half Slave, Half Free

The issue of slavery had long caused tension between the North and South. Even during the Constitutional Convention of 1787, the question stirred bitter debate.

As settlers moved west during the 1800s, the controversy over slavery continued. Each time a new territory was organized, Congress had to decide whether to allow slavery there. Many northerners wanted Congress to ban slavery in all the territories. Many southerners argued that all territories should be open to slavery.

A crisis over how Missouri would enter the Union was settled by the Missouri Compromise of 1820. Congress decided that slavery would be permitted in Missouri. But it banned slavery everywhere else in the Louisiana Purchase north of latitude 36° 30'.

The debate flared once again after the United States conquered new lands after the Mexican-American War. But, once more, members of Congress managed to work out their differences. They approved the Compromise of 1850.

Civil War Begins on April 12, 1861
Confederate troops fired on Fort Sumter. This assault began a war that would last four long years.

The End of Compromise

These agreements began to unravel when Congress organized the territories of Kansas and Nebraska. Senator Stephen A. Douglas proposed "popular sovereignty." Under popular sovereignty, Kansas and Nebraska would be allowed to decide for themselves whether to permit slavery. In 1856, however, bloody fighting broke out in Kansas between proslavery and antislavery settlers.

A year later, the Supreme Court handed down the Dred Scott decision. To the surprise of most northerners, the Court ruled that Congress had no power to outlaw slavery in any territory. It seemed to support the extreme southern position that slavery could be permitted in all territories.

Tensions rose further in 1859 when a northerner named John Brown raided the federal arsenal in Harpers Ferry, Virginia. Brown hoped to lead slaves in an armed uprising. He was captured, tried, and hanged. Many outraged southerners considered Brown's raid a northern plot to destroy the South.

Secession

As these events divided the nation, a new political party, called the Republican Party, formed in the North. Its main goal was to oppose the spread of slavery. The Republican candidate for President, Abraham Lincoln of Illinois, won the election of 1860.

Lincoln's victory convinced southerners that only by seceding, or withdrawing, from the Union could they hope to save their way of life. In December 1860, South Carolina became the first of 11 southern states to secede. Banding together, they formed the Confederate States of America. In April 1861, Confederate forces bombarded federal troops at Fort Sumter in Charleston harbor. War had begun.

War and Emancipation

The Civil War continued for four terrible years. At first it seemed that the Confederacy might prevent a Union victory. White southerners, after all, were defending their homeland. The Confederacy's distinguished military leaders included Robert E. Lee and Thomas "Stonewall" Jackson.

It took the North several years to find a general as skilled as Lee. In the end, the dogged Ulysses S. Grant wore down southern armies. Equally as important to the North were its greater resources: more soldiers, better weapons, many more factories, and a larger railroad network to transport soldiers and supplies.

As the war dragged on, calls for abolition grew stronger. On January 1, 1863, President Lincoln issued the Emancipation Proclamation, freeing all slaves behind Confederate lines. The proclamation changed the character of the war. It became a fight for the freedom of slaves as well as for union.

During the war, over 200,000 African Americans fought for the Union. Furthermore, the war ended sooner because hundreds of thousands of slaves fled southern plantations and crossed Union lines.

On April 9, 1865, Lee surrendered to Grant at Appomattox Court House, Virginia. The "house divided" by slavery had fallen in a ghastly war. The new house—the Union made whole and free—would face new storms.

Events in American History, 1492–1788

1492–1606   **An Age of Exploration**

1492   Columbus reaches America
1513   Balboa sights Pacific Ocean
1517   Protestant Reformation begins in Europe
1587   English colonists settle at Roanoke

1607–1762   **The Early Colonial Period**

1607   Jamestown, first successful colony, founded
1619   First Africans arrive at Jamestown; Virginia House of Burgesses meets
1620   Puritans sign Mayflower Compact and establish Plymouth Colony
1630   Puritans establish Massachusetts Bay Colony
1673   Joliet and Marquette explore Mississippi River
1690s   Spanish missions established in Arizona and California
1754   French and Indian War begins

1763–1788   **The Revolutionary Era**

1763   Treaty of Paris ends French and Indian War
1765   Parliament passes Stamp Act; Stamp Act Congress meets
1773   Parliament passes Tea Act; Boston Tea Party takes place
1774   Parliament passes Intolerable Acts; First Continental Congress meets
1775   Shots fired at Lexington and Concord; Second Continental Congress meets;
                  Battle of Breed's Hill and Bunker Hill fought
1776   Colonists declare independence from Britain
1781   British surrender at Yorktown; Articles of Confederation ratified
1783   Treaty of Paris ends Revolutionary War
1788   Constitution of the United States ratified

Events in American History, 1789–1865

George Washington	1789–1797	1789	Judiciary Act organizes Supreme Court
		1791	Bill of Rights adopted
		1793	Eli Whitney invents cotton gin
John Adams	1797–1801	1798	XYZ affair encourages war fever; Alien and Sedition Acts passed
Thomas Jefferson	1801–1809	1803	Louisiana Territory purchased from France
		1804–1806	Lewis and Clark explore Louisiana Purchase
James Madison	1809–1817	1811	Battle of Tippecanoe fought
		1812	War of 1812 breaks out with Great Britain
		1814	Treaty of Ghent ends war with England
James Monroe	1817–1825	1820	Missouri Compromise adopted
		1823	Monroe Doctrine issued
John Quincy Adams	1825–1829	1825	Erie Canal opens
		1828	Tariff of Abominations passed
Andrew Jackson	1829–1837	1830	Congress passes Indian Removal Act
Martin Van Buren	1837–1841	1837	Panic affects nation
		1838–1839	Indians forced west on Trail of Tears
William Henry Harrison	1841	1841	Harrison is first President to die in office
John Tyler	1841–1845	1842	Massachusetts court allows workers' strikes
James K. Polk	1845–1849	1845	Florida and Texas enter Union
		1846	Mexican War begins
		1847	Mexican War ends; United States receives California and New Mexico territories
Zachary Taylor	1849–1850	1849	California Gold Rush begins
Millard Fillmore	1850–1853	1850	Compromise of 1850 achieved
		1851	Uncle Tom's Cabin published
Franklin Pierce	1853–1856	1854	Congress passes Kansas-Nebraska Act
James Buchanan	1857–1861	1857	Supreme Court issues Dred Scott decision
		1858	John Brown raids Harpers Ferry
		1860	South Carolina secedes from the Union
Abraham Lincoln	1861–1865	1861	Confederate States of America formed
		1862	Homestead Act grants land to farmers
		1863	Lincoln issues Emancipation Proclamation; construction of transcontinental railroad begins
		1865	Civil War ends; Lincoln is assassinated

Unit 5

How was the Civil War a political, economic, and social turning point?

History *Interactive*
Explore Historian's Apprentice Online
Visit: PHSchool.com
Web Code: mvp-5000

Underground Railroad By the middle of the 1830s, opposition to slavery was rising among reformers. Abolitionists aided enslaved people who sought to escape via the Underground Railroad to the North or to Canada.

1830s

Lincoln's Gettysburg Address Lincoln's firm leadership inspired the Union side. In the Gettysburg Address, he vowed that "these dead shall not have died in vain . . . and that government of the people, by the people, for the people, shall not perish from the earth."

1863

Civil War and Reunion

Decision at Gettysburg All attempts at compromise having failed, the United States endured a bloody four-year civil war. After the Battle of Gettysburg, the war turned in favor of the Union army.

1863

A New Voice in Government Before the Civil War, African Americans had no voice in southern government. During Reconstruction, they became a powerful voting force in southern elections. African Americans were elected to public office as sheriffs, mayors, state legislators, and members of Congress.

1868

The Nation Divided

1846–1861

> ## "I then whispered to my wife, 'Come, my dear, let us make a desperate leap for liberty!'"
>
> —*William Craft,*
> **Running a Thousand Miles for Freedom,** *1860*

This painting, *A Ride for Liberty—The Fugitive Slaves*, depicts a black family fleeing toward freedom.

CHAPTER 14

What You Will Learn

Section 1
GROWING TENSIONS OVER SLAVERY
With the addition of new western land, debate over the spread of slavery increased.

Section 2
COMPROMISES FAIL
After all efforts at compromise failed, violent fighting broke out in the Kansas Territory.

Section 3
THE CRISIS DEEPENS
As tensions increased, a new antislavery political party emerged.

Section 4
THE COMING OF THE CIVIL WAR
Abraham Lincoln's election led seven southern states to leave the Union.

↻ Reading Skill
Analyze Cause and Effect In this chapter, you will learn to identify causes and their effects to help connect and understand historical events and issues.

The Nation Divided, 1848–1861

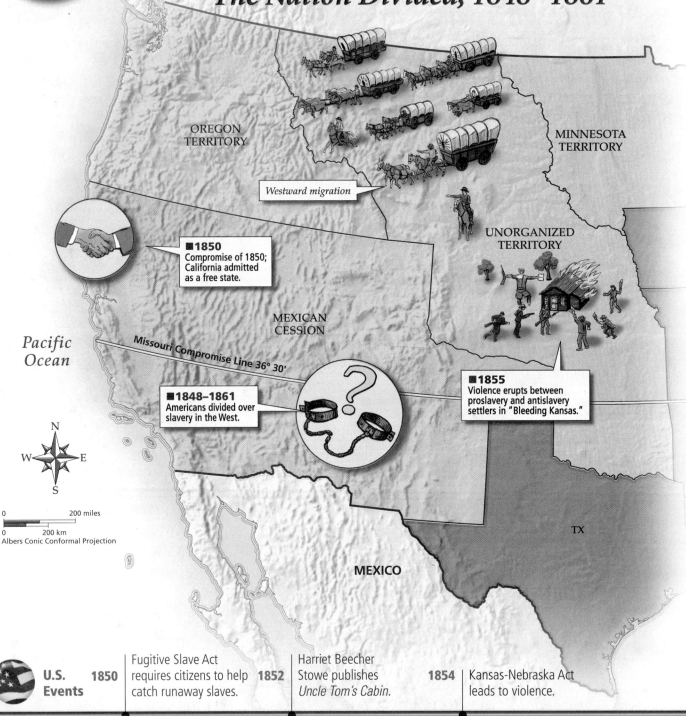

OREGON TERRITORY

MINNESOTA TERRITORY

Westward migration

UNORGANIZED TERRITORY

■1850
Compromise of 1850;
California admitted
as a free state.

MEXICAN CESSION

Missouri Compromise Line 36° 30'

Pacific Ocean

■1848–1861
Americans divided over
slavery in the West.

■1855
Violence erupts between
proslavery and antislavery
settlers in "Bleeding Kansas."

0   200 miles
0   200 km
Albers Conic Conformal Projection

MEXICO

TX

 **U.S. Events** **1850** Fugitive Slave Act requires citizens to help catch runaway slaves.

1852 Harriet Beecher Stowe publishes *Uncle Tom's Cabin.*

1854 Kansas-Nebraska Act leads to violence.

1850   **1853**   **1856**

World Events

1853 Commodore Matthew Perry arrives in Japan to open trade.

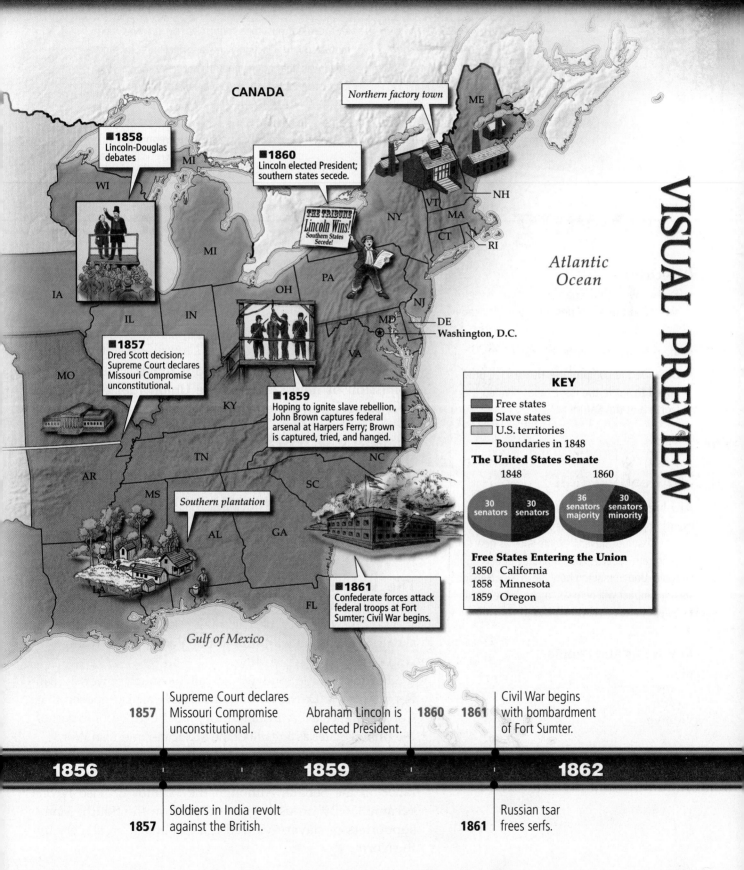

CANADA

Northern factory town

ME

■1858
Lincoln-Douglas debates

MI

■1860
Lincoln elected President; southern states secede.

WI

NH

VT

MA

NY

CT

RI

PA

OH

NJ

Atlantic Ocean

IA

IL

IN

MD

DE
Washington, D.C.

VA

■1857
Dred Scott decision; Supreme Court declares Missouri Compromise unconstitutional.

MO

■1859
Hoping to ignite slave rebellion, John Brown captures federal arsenal at Harpers Ferry; Brown is captured, tried, and hanged.

KY

TN

NC

AR

SC

Southern plantation

MS

AL

GA

LA

FL

■1861
Confederate forces attack federal troops at Fort Sumter; Civil War begins.

Gulf of Mexico

THE TRIBUNE
Lincoln Wins!
Southern States Secede!

VISUAL PREVIEW

KEY

▨	Free states
▧	Slave states
▢	U.S. territories
—	Boundaries in 1848

The United States Senate

1848   1860

| 30 senators | 30 senators | 36 senators majority | 30 senators minority |

Free States Entering the Union
1850 California
1858 Minnesota
1859 Oregon

| 1857 | Supreme Court declares Missouri Compromise unconstitutional. | Abraham Lincoln is elected President. | 1860 | 1861 | Civil War begins with bombardment of Fort Sumter. |

1856 | **1859** | **1862**

| | 1857 | Soldiers in India revolt against the British. | | 1861 | Russian tsar frees serfs. |

The Free-Soil Party

❝Two years ago there existed in this State a party calling itself the "Free Soil" party. . . . opposed, not only to the extension, but to the existence of slavery, and carried out their principles by resolves and mutual political action. One principal item in their creed was, that no member of that party should vote for a slaveholder or a pro-slavery man.❞

—From a letter to the editor, "The Semi-Weekly Eagle," Brattleboro, Vermont, 1850

◀ Free-Soil Party presidential campaign poster, 1848

Growing Tensions Over Slavery

Objectives

- Explain why conflict arose over the issue of slavery in the territories after the Mexican-American War.
- Identify the goal of the Free-Soil Party.
- Describe the compromise Henry Clay proposed to settle the issues that divided the North and the South.

Reading Skill

Analyze Causes Causes are the reasons that events happen. As the United States struggled over the issue of slavery, events such as new laws or important speeches had dramatic effects on the struggle. Understanding how these events made such an impact will help you make sense of this turbulent time in American history.

Key Terms and People

popular
    sovereignty
secede
fugitive

Henry Clay
John C. Calhoun
Daniel Webster

Why It Matters The Missouri Compromise of 1820 seemed to have quieted the differences between North and South. But the American victory in the Mexican-American War added new territory to the United States. As a result, the states renewed their struggle over slavery and states' rights.

❓ **Section Focus Question: How did the question of admission of new states to the Union fuel the debate over slavery and states' rights?**

Slavery and the Mexican-American War

Between 1820 and 1848, four new slaveholding states and four new free states were admitted to the Union. This maintained the balance between free and slaveholding states, with 15 of each. However, territory gained by the Mexican-American War threatened to destroy the balance.

The Wilmot Proviso The Missouri Compromise did not apply to the huge territory gained from Mexico in 1848. Would this territory be organized as states that allowed slavery? The issue was vital to northerners who wanted to stop slavery from spreading.

Fearing that the South would gain too much power, in 1846 Representative David Wilmot of Pennsylvania proposed that Congress ban slavery in all territory that might become part of the United States as a result of the Mexican-American War.

This proposal was called the Wilmot Proviso. The provision was passed in the House of Representatives, but it failed in the Senate. Although the Wilmot Proviso never became law, it aroused great concern in the South. Many supporters of slavery viewed it as an attack on slavery by the North.

An Antislavery Party The <u>controversy</u> over the Wilmot Proviso also led to the rise of a new political party. Neither the Democrats nor the Whigs took a firm stand on slavery. Each hoped to win support in both North and South in the election of 1848.

The Democratic candidate for President in 1848, Senator Lewis Cass of Michigan, proposed a solution that he hoped would appeal to everyone. Cass suggested letting the people in each new territory or state decide for themselves whether to allow slavery. This process, called **popular sovereignty,** meant that people in the territory or state would vote directly on issues, rather than having their elected representatives decide.

Many Whigs and Democrats wanted to take a stronger stand against the spread of slavery. In August 1848, antislavery Whigs and Democrats joined forces to form a new party, which they called the Free-Soil Party. It called for the territory gained in the Mexican-American War to be "free soil," a place where slavery was banned.

The party chose former Democratic President Martin Van Buren as its candidate. Van Buren did poorly in the election. However, he won enough votes from the Democrats to keep Cass from winning. General Zachary Taylor, a Whig and a hero of the Mexican-American War, was elected instead.

☑**Checkpoint** Why was the Free-Soil Party founded?

Vocabulary Builder
<u>controversy</u> (KAHN truh vur see)
n. argument or dispute

The Election of 1848

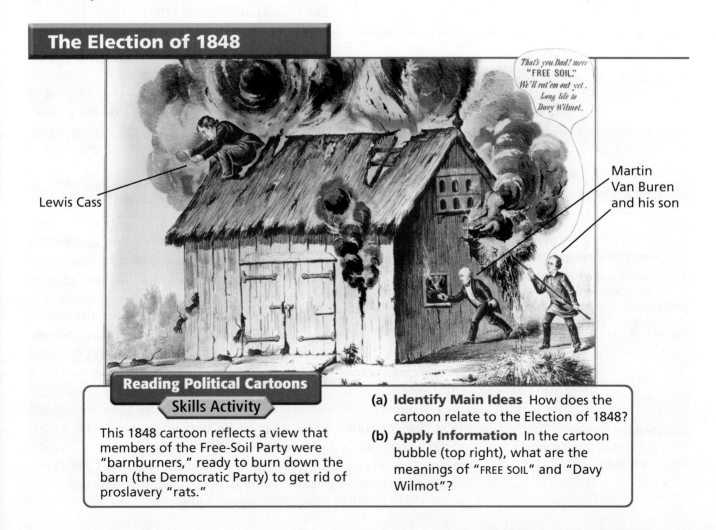

Lewis Cass

Martin Van Buren and his son

That's you Dad! more "FREE SOIL." We'll rat 'em out yet. Long life to Davy Wilmot.

Reading Political Cartoons
Skills Activity

This 1848 cartoon reflects a view that members of the Free-Soil Party were "barnburners," ready to burn down the barn (the Democratic Party) to get rid of proslavery "rats."

(a) **Identify Main Ideas** How does the cartoon relate to the Election of 1848?

(b) **Apply Information** In the cartoon bubble (top right), what are the meanings of "FREE SOIL" and "Davy Wilmot"?

Calhoun Versus Webster

John C. Calhoun

❝[If] something is not done to arrest it, the South will be forced to choose between abolition and secession. . . . If you are unwilling we should part in peace, tell us so; and we shall know what to do when you reduce the question to submission or resistance.❞

—John C. Calhoun, March 4, 1850

Daniel Webster

❝I wish to speak today, not as a Massachusetts man, nor as a Northern man, but as an American. . . . I speak today for the preservation of the Union. . . . I speak today . . . for the restoration to the country of that quiet and that harmony which make the blessings of this Union so rich, and so dear to us all.❞

—Daniel Webster, March 7, 1850

Reading Primary Sources
Skills Activity

During the Senate debate on Clay's Compromise of 1850, John C. Calhoun and Daniel Webster wrote dramatic speeches evaluating the compromise.

(a) Detect Points of View For what region does Daniel Webster claim to be speaking?

(b) Apply Information Calhoun says "[If] something is not done to arrest it, the South will be forced to choose between abolition and secession." To what does "it" refer?

A Bitter Debate

After the discovery of gold in California, thousands of people rushed west. California soon had enough people to become a state. Both sides realized that California's admission to the Union as a free state would upset the balance between free and slave states in the Senate.

Northerners argued that California should be a free state because most of the territory lay north of the Missouri Compromise line. But southerners feared that if free states gained a majority in the Senate, the South would not be able to block antislavery attacks like the Wilmot Proviso. Southern leaders began to threaten to secede, or withdraw, from the nation if California was admitted to the Union as a free state.

There were other issues dividing the North and South. Northerners wanted the slave trade abolished in Washington, D.C. Southerners wanted northerners to catch people who had escaped from slavery. Southerners called for a law that would force the return of fugitives, or runaway enslaved people.

For months it looked as if there was no solution. Then, in January 1850, Senator Henry Clay of Kentucky stepped forward with a plan to calm the crisis. Clay had won the nickname the Great Compromiser for working out the Missouri Compromise. Now, Clay made another series of proposals that he hoped would forever resolve the issues that bitterly divided northerners and southerners.

Analyze Causes
What event did both southerners and northerners worry would destroy the balance of power between them?

Vocabulary Builder
crisis (KRĪ sihs) **n.** turning point or deciding event in history

The Senate's discussion of Clay's proposals produced one of the greatest debates in American political history. South Carolina Senator John C. Calhoun was against compromise. Calhoun was gravely ill and just four weeks from death. He was too weak to give his speech, but he struggled to sit upright while his final speech was read to the Senate.

The admission of California as a free state, Calhoun wrote, would expose the South to continued attacks on slavery. There were only two ways to preserve the South's way of life. One was a constitutional amendment to protect states' rights. The other was secession.

Three days later, Massachusetts Senator Daniel Webster rose to support Clay's proposals and called for an end to the bitter sectionalism that was dividing the nation. Webster argued for Clay's compromise in order to preserve the Union.

Which view would prevail? The very existence of the United States depended on the answer.

✓ **Checkpoint** How did California's proposed admission to the Union affect the debate between the North and the South over slavery?

☆ **Looking Back and Ahead** With the territories acquired by the Mexican-American War, the nation could no longer overlook the slavery issue. Statehood for each of these territories would upset the balance between free states and slaveholding states. For a short while, it seemed to many that Henry Clay's proposed compromise gave concessions to both sides. But, as you will read in the next section, the compromise soon fell apart. When it did, the nation once again plunged down the road to all-out war between the regions.

Section 1 | **Check Your Progress**

Progress Monitoring Online
For: Self-test with instant help
Visit: PHSchool.com
Web Code: mya-5101

Comprehension and Critical Thinking

1. **(a) Recall** What was the Wilmot Proviso?
   (b) Analyze Cause and Effect Did the Wilmot Proviso successfully address the nation's divisions over slavery? What effect *did* it have on the nation?

2. **(a) List** What were the main issues that led to Henry Clay's proposed compromise?
   (b) Detect Points of View Write a sentence describing how you would feel about the need to compromise if you were a member of Congress from the North.

Reading Skill

3. **Analyze Causes** What did southerners want Congress to do about enslaved people who had fled to the North?

Key Terms

Complete these sentences so they clearly show your understanding of the key terms.

4. The status of new western territories would be decided by popular sovereignty, which is _____.

5. If southern states seceded from the Union, then _____.

6. Many northerners would not report fugitives, who were _____.

Writing

7. Consider the broad topic "Conflicts Between Slave States and Free States Before the Civil War." Divide it into four or five narrower topics. Each of these narrower topics should be covered in a research paper of a few pages.

A Harsh Accusation

❝ Sir, the Nebraska Bill was in every respect a swindle. It was a swindle by the South of the North. . . . All efforts were now given to the dismal work of forcing slavery on free soil. ❞

—Senator Charles Sumner of Massachusetts, before being assaulted on the Senate floor, 1856

◄ Newspapers reported Sumner's caning by a southern congressman.

Compromises Fail

Objectives

- Summarize the main points of the Compromise of 1850.
- Describe the impact of the novel *Uncle Tom's Cabin.*
- Explain how the Kansas-Nebraska Act reopened the issue of slavery in the territories.
- Describe the effect of the Kansas-Nebraska Act.

⊙ Reading Skill

Analyze Effects The important events of the 1850s had far-reaching effects around the nation. As you read Section 2, try to identify and understand these effects. Remember that two events do not necessarily have a cause-and-effect link just because they occur in sequence. Use signal words such as *result* to help you identify effects.

Key Terms and People

Harriet Beecher
    Stowe
propaganda

Stephen Douglas
John Brown

Why It Matters Many Americans hoped that Henry Clay's proposed compromise would quiet the controversy over slavery. However, after 1850, the growing divide only worsened.

❓ **Section Focus Question: What was the Compromise of 1850, and why did it fail?**

The Compromise of 1850

In September 1850, Congress finally passed five bills based on Clay's proposals. This series of laws became known as the Compromise of 1850. President Zachary Taylor had opposed the Compromise. However, Taylor died in 1850. The new President, Millard Fillmore, supported the Compromise and signed it into law.

To Please the North The Compromise of 1850 was designed to end the crisis by giving both supporters and opponents of slavery part of what they wanted. To please the North, California was admitted to the Union as a free state. In addition, the Compromise banned the slave trade in the nation's capital. (However, Congress declared that it had no power to regulate the slave trade between slave states.)

To Please the South Under the terms of the Compromise, popular sovereignty would be used to decide the question of slavery in the rest of the Mexican Cession. People in the states created from that territory would vote whether to be a free state or a slave state when they requested admission to the Union. Also, in return for agreeing to outlaw the slave trade in Washington, D.C., southerners got a tough new fugitive slave law.

The Fugitive Slave Act of 1850 allowed special government officials to arrest any person accused of being a runaway slave. Suspects had no right to a trial to prove that they had been falsely accused. All that was required to <u>deprive</u> them of their freedom was for a slaveholder or any white witness to swear that the suspect was the slaveholder's property. In addition, the law required northern citizens to help capture accused runaways if authorities requested assistance.

Outrage in the North The Fugitive Slave Act became the most controversial part of the Compromise of 1850. Many northerners swore that they would resist the hated new law.

Northerners were outraged to see people accused of being fugitive slaves deprived of their freedom. An Indiana man was torn from his wife and children and given to an owner who claimed the man had escaped 19 years earlier. A wealthy African American tailor was carried back to South Carolina after living in New York for years. His friends quickly raised enough money to buy his freedom. But most who were shipped south remained there. Thousands of northern African Americans fled to the safety of Canada, including many who had never been enslaved.

In city after city, residents banded together to resist the Fugitive Slave Law. When two white Georgians arrived in Boston to seize fugitives, Bostonians threatened the slave catchers with harm if they did not leave the city right away. Another group rescued an accused runaway and sent him to safety in Canada. When the mob leaders were arrested, local juries refused to convict them.

John C. Calhoun had hoped that the Fugitive Slave Law would force northerners to admit that slaveholders had rights to their property. Instead, every time the law was enforced, it convinced more northerners that slavery was evil.

☑**Checkpoint** How did the Compromise of 1850 deal with the admission of California to the Union?

Returned to Slavery
Guarded by federal troops, fugitives Anthony Burns and Thomas Sims are captured in Boston and returned to enslavement in South Carolina. Below is a poster distributed by a southern slaveholder. **Critical Thinking: *Draw Conclusions*** *What details show the attitude of Bostonians to the return of Burns and Sims?*

Uncle Tom's Cabin

One northerner deeply affected by the Fugitive Slave Act was Harriet Beecher Stowe. The daughter of an abolitionist minister, Stowe met many people who had escaped from slavery. She decided to write "something that will make this whole nation feel what an accursed thing slavery is."

In 1852, Stowe published *Uncle Tom's Cabin,* a novel about kindly Uncle Tom, an enslaved man who is abused by the cruel Simon Legree. In this passage, Tom dies after a severe beating:

> **"**Tom opened his eyes, and looked upon his master. . . . 'There an't no more ye can do! I forgive ye with all my soul!' and he fainted entirely away.
>
> 'I b'lieve, my soul, he's done for, finally,' said Legree, stepping forward, to look at him. 'Yes, he is! Well, his mouth's shut up, at last,—that's one comfort!'**"**
>
> —Harriet Beecher Stowe, *Uncle Tom's Cabin,* Chapter 38

Analyze Effects
What was one effect of Harriet Beecher Stowe's horror over slavery? What word in this paragraph highlights the cause-effect link?

Stowe's book was a bestseller in the North. It shocked thousands of people who previously had been unconcerned about slavery. As a result, readers began to view slavery as more than just a political conflict. It was a human, moral problem facing every American.

Many white southerners were outraged by Stowe's book. They criticized it as propaganda, false or misleading information that is spread to further a cause. They claimed the novel did not give a fair or accurate picture of the lives of enslaved African Americans.

✓**Checkpoint** What impact did *Uncle Tom's Cabin* have?

Uncle Tom's Cabin
The novel *Uncle Tom's Cabin* had an impact that lasted long after slavery ended. An original illustration from the book and a scene on a decorative plate are shown here. *Critical Thinking: Identify Costs You are a northerner during the 1850s. A fugitive comes to your door seeking help. Will you help her? List the costs and benefits of helping the person.*

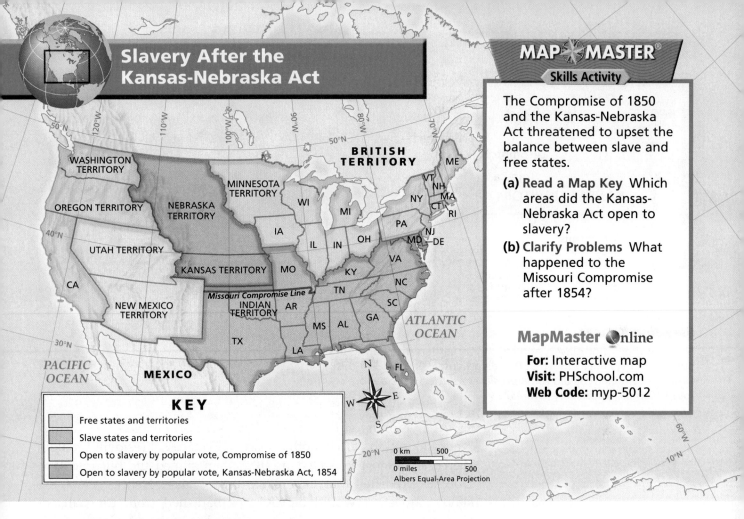

Slavery After the Kansas-Nebraska Act

MAP MASTER®
Skills Activity

The Compromise of 1850 and the Kansas-Nebraska Act threatened to upset the balance between slave and free states.

(a) Read a Map Key Which areas did the Kansas-Nebraska Act open to slavery?

(b) Clarify Problems What happened to the Missouri Compromise after 1854?

MapMaster Online

For: Interactive map
Visit: PHSchool.com
Web Code: myp-5012

KEY
- Free states and territories
- Slave states and territories
- Open to slavery by popular vote, Compromise of 1850
- Open to slavery by popular vote, Kansas-Nebraska Act, 1854

0 km 500
0 miles 500
Albers Equal-Area Projection

The Kansas-Nebraska Act

The nation moved closer to war after Congress passed the Kansas-Nebraska Act in 1854. The act was pushed through by Senator Stephen Douglas. Douglas was eager to develop the lands west of his home state of Illinois. He wanted to see a railroad built from Illinois through the Nebraska Territory to the Pacific Coast.

In 1853, Douglas suggested forming two new territories—the Kansas Territory and the Nebraska Territory. Southerners at once objected. Both territories lay in an area closed to slavery by the Missouri Compromise. This meant that the states eventually created from these territories would enter the Union as free states.

To win southern support, Douglas proposed that slavery in the new territories be decided by popular sovereignty. Thus, in effect, the Kansas-Nebraska Act undid the Missouri Compromise.

As Douglas hoped, southerners supported the Kansas-Nebraska Act. They were sure that slave owners from Missouri would move across the border into Kansas. In time, they hoped that Kansas would enter the union as a slave state.

Northerners, however, were outraged by the Kansas-Nebraska Act. They believed that Douglas had betrayed them by reopening the issue of slavery in the territories. "The more I look at it the more enraged I become," said one northern senator of Douglas's bill. "It needs but little to make me an out-and-out abolitionist."

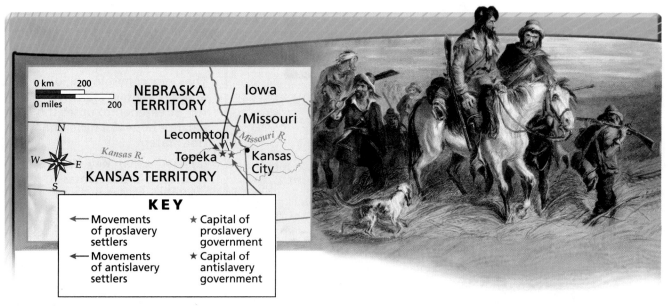

Bleeding Kansas

The migration of proslavery and antislavery settlers into Kansas led to the outbreak of violence known as Bleeding Kansas. **Critical Thinking: Interpret Maps** *Why did some proslavery settlers take a more southerly route than did antislavery settlers?*

After months of debate, southern support enabled the Kansas-Nebraska Act to pass in both houses of Congress. President Franklin Pierce, a Democrat elected in 1852, then signed the bill into law. Douglas predicted that, as a result of the Kansas-Nebraska Act, the slavery question would be "forever banished from the halls of Congress." But events would soon prove how wrong he was.

☑Checkpoint How did Stephen Douglas's plan undo the Missouri Compromise?

Bleeding Kansas

The Kansas-Nebraska Act left it to the white citizens of the territory to decide whether Kansas would be free or slave territory. Both proslavery and antislavery settlers flooded into Kansas within weeks after Douglas's bill became law. Each side was determined to hold the majority in the territory when it came time for the vote.

Thousands of Missourians entered Kansas in March 1855 to illegally vote in the election to select a territorial legislature. Although Kansas had only 3,000 voters, nearly 8,000 votes were cast on election day! Of 39 legislators elected, all but 3 supported slavery. The antislavery settlers refused to accept these results and held a second election.

Vocabulary Builder
impose (ihm POHZ) *v.* to place a burden on someone or something

Growing Violence Kansas now had two governments, each claiming the right to <u>impose</u> their government on the territory. Not surprisingly, violence soon broke out. In April, a proslavery sheriff was shot when he tried to arrest some antislavery settlers in the town of Lawrence. The next month, he returned with 800 men and attacked the town.

Three days later, John Brown, an antislavery settler from Connecticut, led seven men to a proslavery settlement near Pottawatomie (paht uh wah TOH mee) Creek. There, they murdered five proslavery men and boys.

These incidents set off widespread fighting in Kansas. Bands of proslavery and antislavery fighters roamed the countryside, terrorizing those who did not support their views. The violence was so bad that it earned Kansas the name Bleeding Kansas.

Bloodshed in the Senate Even before Brown's raid at Pottawatomie Creek, the violence in Kansas spilled over into the United States Senate. Charles Sumner of Massachusetts was the leading abolitionist senator. In a fiery speech, Sumner denounced the proslavery legislature in Kansas. He then attacked his southern foes, singling out Andrew Butler, an elderly senator from South Carolina.

Butler was not present the day Sumner made his speech. A few days later, however, Butler's nephew, Congressman Preston Brooks, marched into the Senate chamber. Using a heavy cane, Brooks beat Sumner until he fell to the floor, bloody and unconscious. Sumner never completely recovered from his injuries.

Many southerners felt that Sumner got what he deserved. Hundreds of people sent canes to Brooks to show their support. To northerners, however, Brooks's violent act was just more evidence that slavery was brutal and inhuman.

☑**Checkpoint** What was the outcome of the election to select a legislature in the Kansas Territory?

☆ **Looking Back and Ahead** By 1856, all attempts at compromise had failed. The bitterness between the North and the South was about to alter the political landscape of the United States.

Describe the effect of the Kansas-Nebraska Act on Kansas.

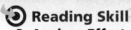

Section 2 | **Check Your Progress**

Progress Monitoring ⬤nline
For: Self-test with instant help
Visit: PHSchool.com
Web Code: mya-5102

Comprehension and Critical Thinking

1. **(a) Recall** What parts of the Compromise of 1850 were included to please the North?
   (b) Draw Conclusions Why do you think northerners were still not satisfied?

2. **(a) Recall** What was the Kansas-Nebraska Act?
   Evaluate Information How did the Kansas-Nebraska Act contribute to tension between the North and the South?

Reading Skill

3. **Analyze Effects** effect of Harriet Beecher Stowe's book *Uncle Tom's Cabin*

Key Terms

Complete the following sentence so that the second part further explains the first part and clearly shows your understanding of the key term.

4. Many white southerners considered propaganda; _____ an unfair picture of slavery.

Writing

5. Imagine that you are researching the effects of Harriet Beecher Stowe's book *Uncle Tom's Cabin*. Write down five questions that would help you focus your research on this topic. The questions should point you to areas where you need to find more information about the influence of Stowe's book.

Literature

Uncle Tom's Cabin
by Harriet Beecher Stowe

Prepare to Read

Introduction

Harriet Beecher Stowe rocked the nation in 1851 when she published *Uncle Tom's Cabin*. The novel won many converts to the antislavery cause. The excerpt below is from the opening chapter. Shelby, a Kentucky slave owner, must sell some of his enslaved servants to Mr. Haley, a slave trader. Haley is especially interested in buying a young woman named Eliza.

Reading Skill

Judging Characters In a work of fiction, characters may say things that the author thinks are wrong. We have to read carefully in order to understand how the author wants us to judge the characters. In the selection below, look for clues as to what Stowe really thinks of Mr. Haley, the slave trader.

Vocabulary *Builder*

As you read this literature selection, look for the following underlined words:

<u>calculation</u> (kal kyoo LAY shuhn) *n.* ability to figure out exactly what something is worth

<u>humane</u> (hyoo MAYN) *adj.* kind; considerate; merciful

<u>candid</u> (KAN dihd) *adj.* frank; honest

<u>virtuous</u> (VIR choo uhs) *adj.* highly moral

Background

Much of *Uncle Tom's Cabin* is written in dialect that reproduces how different types of characters speak. For example, to show the way Haley speaks, Stowe uses "ha'nt" for "haven't," "this yer" for "this here," "uns" for "ones," and "onpleasant" for "unpleasant."

"Come, how will you trade about the gal?—what shall I say for her—what'll you take?"

"Mr. Haley, she is not to be sold," said Shelby. "My wife would not part with her for her weight in gold."

"Ay, ay! women always say such things, cause they ha'nt no sort of <u>calculation</u>. Just show 'em how many watches, feathers, and trinkets, one's weight in gold would buy, and that alters the case, I reckon."

"I tell you, Haley, this must not be spoken of; I say no, and I mean no," said Shelby, decidedly.

"Well, you'll let me have the boy, though," said the trader; "you must own I've come down pretty handsomely for him."

"What on earth can you want with the child?" said Shelby.

"Why, I've got a friend that's going into this yer branch of the business—wants to buy up handsome boys to raise for the market. Fancy articles entirely—sell for waiters, and so on, to rich 'uns, that can pay for handsome 'uns. It sets off one of yer great places—a real handsome boy to open door, wait, and tend. They fetch a good sum; and this little devil is such a comical, musical concern, he's just the article!"

"I would rather not sell him," said Mr. Shelby, thoughtfully; "the fact is, sir, I'm a <u>humane</u> man, and I hate to take the boy from his mother, sir."

"O, you do?—La! yes—something of that ar natur. I understand, perfectly. It is mighty onpleasant getting on with women, sometimes, I al'ays hates these yer screechin', screamin' times. They are *mighty* onpleasant; but, as I manages business, I generally avoids

Slave auction

'em, sir. Now, what if you get the girl off for a day, or a week, or so; then the thing's done quietly,—all over before she comes home. Your wife might get her some ear-rings, or a new gown, or some such truck, to make up with her."

"I'm afraid not."

"Lor bless ye, yes! These critters ain't like white folks, you know; they gets over things, only manage right. Now, they say," said Haley, assuming a <u>candid</u> and confidential air, "that this kind o' trade is hardening to the feelings; but I never found it so. Fact is, I never could do things up the way some fellers manage the business. I've seen 'em as would pull a woman's child out of her arms, and set him up to sell, and she screechin' like mad all the time;—very bad policy—damages the article—makes 'em quite unfit for service sometimes. I knew a real handsome gal once, in Orleans, as was entirely ruined by this sort o' handling. The fellow that was trading for her didn't want her baby; and she was one of your real high sort, when her blood was up. I tell you, she squeezed up her child in her arms, and talked, and went on real awful. It kinder makes my blood run cold to think on 't; and when they carried off the child, and locked her up, she jest went ravin' mad, and died in a week. Clear waste, sir, of a thousand dollars, just for want of management,—there's where 't is. It's always best to do the humane thing, sir; that's been my experience." And the trader leaned back in his chair, and folded his arm, with an air of <u>virtuous</u> decision, apparently considering himself a second Wilberforce.

From *Uncle Tom's Cabin*, by Harriet Beecher Stowe

Analyze LITERATURE

Imagine that you are a northerner in 1851 reading *Uncle Tom's Cabin* for the first time. Write a letter to a friend explaining how this excerpt made you feel about the slave trade.

Judging Characters
Stowe has Haley refer to enslaved Africans as "critters," showing he does not think of them as human beings. Yet, he also claims that slave-trading has not hardened his feelings. What does this indicate about Stowe's view of Haley?

Background
William Wilberforce was a famous English politician who campaigned to end slavery.

If you liked this selection, you might want to read more about the antislavery movement in *Escape From Slavery: Five Journeys to Freedom* by Doreen Rappaport, illustrated by Charles Lilly. Harper Collins Publishers. 1991.

Gross Injustice and Cruelty

❝This rich inheritance of justice, liberty, prosperity, and independence bequeathed by your fathers is shared by you, not by me. . . . What, to the American slave is your Fourth of July? I answer: a day that reveals to him, more than all other days in the year, the gross injustice and cruelty to which he is the constant victim.❞

—Frederick Douglass, Independence Day speech delivered at Rochester, New York, 1852

▲ Slaves laboring on a southern plantation

The Crisis Deepens

Objectives

- Explain why the Republican Party came into being in the 1850s.
- Summarize the issues involved in the Dred Scott decision.
- Identify Abraham Lincoln's and Stephen Douglas's views on slavery.
- Describe the differing reactions in the North and the South to John Brown's raid.

🔵 Reading Skill

Analyze Causes and Effects

Historians often disagree over exactly what caused the Civil War. As you read Section 3, watch carefully for cause-and-effect links. Analyzing these links will help you answer this difficult question for yourself. Remember that sometimes the link is not directly stated. Identify an event, then ask yourself: What caused this event to happen? What were the effects of this event?

Key People

Dred Scott   Abraham Lincoln
Roger B. Taney

Why It Matters Bitterness between northerners and southerners weakened the nation's two major political parties. As a result of the growing struggle over slavery, a new party and new leaders emerged.

❓ **Section Focus Question: Why did the Lincoln-Douglas debates and John Brown's raid increase tensions between the North and South?**

A New Antislavery Party

As the Whig Party split apart in 1854, many northern Whigs joined a new political party. It was called the Republican Party, and its main goal was to stop the spread of slavery into the western territories. The Republicans' antislavery stand also attracted northern Democrats and Free-Soil Party members.

The Republicans quickly became a powerful force in politics. The congressional elections of 1854 were held only months after the party was founded. Of the 245 candidates elected to the U.S. House of Representatives, 105 were Republicans. Republican victories in state races also cost the Democrats control of all but two northern state legislatures.

Two years later, in 1856, the Republican Party ran its first candidate for President. It chose John C. Frémont, the army officer who had helped California win independence during the Mexican-American War. The Republicans waged a strong antislavery campaign. Although the Democrat James Buchanan was elected, Frémont won in 11 of the nation's 16 free states.

☑ **Checkpoint** What was the result of the election of 1856?

The Dred Scott Decision

In March 1857—only three days after Buchanan took office—the U.S. Supreme Court delivered a shattering blow to antislavery forces. It decided the case of *Dred Scott* v. *Sandford*.

Dred Scott was an enslaved person who had once been owned by a U.S. Army doctor. The doctor, and Scott, lived for a time in Illinois and in the Wisconsin Territory. Slavery was illegal in both places. After leaving the army, the doctor settled with Scott in Missouri.

With the help of antislavery lawyers, Scott sued for his freedom. He argued that he was free because he had lived where slavery was illegal. In time, the case reached the Supreme Court. Neither northerners nor southerners were prepared for what the Court decided.

The Court Decides Chief Justice Roger B. Taney wrote the decision for the Court. Scott was not a free man, he said, for two reasons. First, according to Taney, Scott had no right to sue in federal court because African Americans were not citizens. Second, Taney said, merely living in free territory did not make an enslaved person free. Slaves were property, Taney declared, and property rights were protected by the U.S. Constitution.

But the ruling went even further. Taney wrote that Congress did not have the power to prohibit slavery in any territory. Thus, the Missouri Compromise was unconstitutional.

Reaction Supporters of slavery rejoiced at the Dred Scott decision. The decision meant that slavery was legal in all territories—just as white southern leaders had been demanding all along.

Northerners, however, were stunned. African American leaders such as Frederick Douglass condemned the ruling. Still, Douglass declared, "my hopes were never brighter than now." He believed that outrage against the decision would bring more whites to the abolitionist cause.

Indeed, white northerners were also shocked by the ruling. Many had hoped that slavery would eventually die out if it were restricted to the South. Now, however, slavery could spread throughout the West.

One northerner who spoke out against the Dred Scott decision was an Illinois lawyer named Abraham Lincoln. The idea that African Americans could not be citizens, he said, was based on a false view of American history. In a very short time, Lincoln would become a central figure in the fight against the spread of slavery.

☑**Checkpoint** Why did Dred Scott claim he was no longer enslaved?

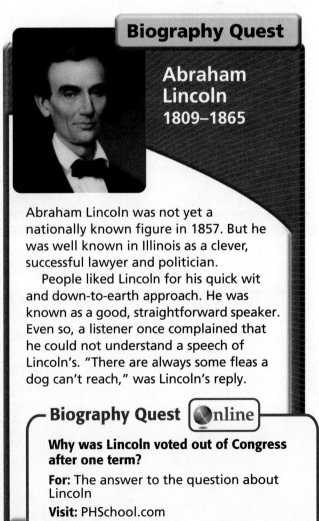

Biography Quest

Abraham Lincoln
1809–1865

Abraham Lincoln was not yet a nationally known figure in 1857. But he was well known in Illinois as a clever, successful lawyer and politician.

People liked Lincoln for his quick wit and down-to-earth approach. He was known as a good, straightforward speaker. Even so, a listener once complained that he could not understand a speech of Lincoln's. "There are always some fleas a dog can't reach," was Lincoln's reply.

Biography Quest ⏺nline

Why was Lincoln voted out of Congress after one term?

For: The answer to the question about Lincoln

Visit: PHSchool.com

Web Code: myd-5013

Links Across Time

Elections and the Media

1858 Americans followed the Lincoln-Douglas debates as telegraph reports circulated around the country.

1960 Americans were for the first time able to watch presidential candidates debate live on television. Richard Nixon and John F. Kennedy debated before an enormous television audience. Many experts believe that the debates played a major role in Kennedy's victory.

Link to Today Online

Elections and the Media Today The digital revolution is again changing American political campaigns. What media do candidates use today?

For: Voting and the media
Visit: PHSchool.com
Web Code: myc-5103

The Lincoln-Douglas Debates

Lincoln had had only a brief career in politics. After serving in the Illinois state legislature, he was elected to Congress as a Whig. There, he voted for the Wilmot Proviso. After a single term, he returned to Illinois to practice law.

Vocabulary Builder
embrace (ehm BRAYS) *v.* to hold tight; to readily accept

Lincoln's opposition to the Kansas-Nebraska Act brought him back into politics, this time <u>embracing</u> the Republican cause. He had long been a rival of Illinois Senator Stephen Douglas, the author of the Kansas-Nebraska Act. Their rivalry was personal as well as political. Both men had courted Mary Todd, who married Lincoln.

A House Divided In 1858, Illinois Republicans chose Lincoln to run for the Senate against Douglas. Accepting the nomination, Lincoln made a stirring speech in favor of the Union:

> **"**A house divided against itself cannot stand. I do not believe this government can endure, permanently, half slave and half free. I do not expect the Union to be dissolved—I do not expect the house to fall—but I do expect it will cease to be divided. It will become all one thing or all the other.**"**
>
> —Abraham Lincoln, Springfield, Illinois, June 16, 1858

Lincoln did not state that he wanted to ban slavery. Still, many southerners became convinced that Lincoln was an abolitionist.

Debating Slavery Lincoln then challenged Douglas to a series of public debates. Thousands of people gathered to hear them speak. Newspapers throughout the nation reported what each man said.

Douglas strongly defended popular sovereignty. "Each state of this Union has a right to do as it pleases on the subject of slavery," he said. "In Illinois we have exercised that sovereign right by prohibiting slavery. . . . It is none of our business whether slavery exists in Missouri." Douglas also painted Lincoln as a dangerous abolitionist who wanted equality for African Americans.

Lincoln took a stand against the spread of slavery. He declared, "If slavery is not wrong, nothing is wrong." Lincoln predicted that slavery would die on its own. In the meantime, he said, it was the obligation of Americans to keep it out of the western territories.

In reply to Douglas, Lincoln stated: "I am not, nor ever have been in favor of bringing about in any way the social and political equality of the white and black races." But he did <u>clarify</u> this view. He insisted that "there is no reason in the world why the Negro is not entitled to all the rights enumerated in the Declaration of Independence, the right to life, liberty and the pursuit of happiness."

In the end, Douglas won the Senate election. However, the debates had made Lincoln known throughout the country. Two years later, the men would be rivals again—this time for the presidency.

Vocabulary Builder
<u>clarify</u> (KLAIR ih fī) **v.** to make the meaning of something clear

☑**Checkpoint** **What position did Douglas take on slavery?**

John Brown's Raid

The nation's attention soon was captured by the actions of John Brown. Driven out of Kansas after the Pottawatomie Massacre, Brown had returned to New England. There he hatched a plot to raise an army and free people in the South who were enslaved.

In 1859, Brown and a small band of supporters attacked the town of Harpers Ferry in Virginia. His goal was to seize guns the U.S. Army had stored there. He thought that enslaved African Americans would support him. He would then give them weapons and lead them in a revolt.

Brown quickly gained control of the arms. But troops commanded by Colonel Robert E. Lee surrounded Brown's force before it could escape. Ten of Brown's followers were killed. Brown was wounded and captured.

Analyze Causes and Effects
Reading Skill How did John Brown's raid affect the national debate over slavery?

John Brown in Kansas

John Steuart Curry began painting this 10-foot-high mural in 1937. It shows John Brown as a fiery abolitionist with a rifle in one hand and a Bible in the other. **Critical Thinking: *Detect Points of View*** *Based on this painting, do you think Curry admired John Brown?*

Death of John Brown

Thomas Hovenden painted this portrait of a saintly John Brown. On his way to his death, Brown stops to kiss a child. Hovenden did not personally witness the events he showed here. **Critical Thinking: Contrast** *Compare this painting to the one on the previous page. How do these two paintings try to stir different emotions?*

At his trial, Brown sat quietly as the court found him guilty of murder and treason. Before hearing his sentence, he gave a moving defense of his actions. The Bible, he said, instructed him to care for the poor and enslaved. "If it is deemed necessary that I should forfeit my life for the furtherance of the ends of justice . . . I say, let it be done." He showed no emotion as he was sentenced to death.

When the state of Virginia hanged Brown for treason on December 2, 1859, church bells across the North tolled to mourn the man who many considered a hero. But southerners were shocked. People in the North were praising a man who had tried to lead a slave revolt! More than ever, many southerners were convinced that the North was out to destroy their way of life.

☑**Checkpoint** **What was John Brown's goal in launching the raid on Harpers Ferry?**

☆ **Looking Back and Ahead** The nation had suffered one dispute after another over the expansion of slavery since the end of the Mexican-American War in 1846. By the election of 1860, talk of the breakup of the United States was everywhere. In the next section, you will read how that breakup came about.

Section 3 | **Check Your Progress**

Progress Monitoring Online
For: Self-test with instant help
Visit: PHSchool.com
Web Code: mya-5103

Comprehension and Critical Thinking

1. **(a) Summarize** Which groups supported the newly formed Republican Party?
   (b) Draw Conclusions How did the outcomes of the elections of 1854 and 1856 affect the Republican Party?

2. **(a) Identify** On what grounds did Dred Scott sue for his freedom in court?
   (b) Draw Conclusions How did Taney's ruling further divide the North and the South?

3. **(a) Recall** What were the Lincoln-Douglas debates?
   (b) Apply Information Why do you think the Lincoln-Douglas debates received national attention?

Reading Skill

4. **Analyze Causes and Effects** Identify one cause and one effect of John Brown's raid. Why did Brown and his followers attack Harpers Ferry? What happened as a result?

Writing

5. Reread the paragraphs in this section that describe the Lincoln-Douglas debates. When you have finished, paraphrase the excerpt from Lincoln's Springfield speech. Remember, when you paraphrase, you restate something said by someone else, using only your own words.

◄ Confederate seal

SECTION 4

The Confederate States

❝In the exercise of a right so ancient, so well-established, and so necessary for self-preservation, the people of the Confederate states . . . passed [laws] resuming all their rights as sovereign and independent States and dissolved their connection with the other States of the Union.❞

—President Jefferson Davis, message to the Confederate Congress, April 29, 1861

◄ Newspaper announcing secession of southern states

The Coming of the Civil War

Objectives
- Describe the results of the election of 1860.
- Explain why southern states seceded from the Union.
- Summarize the events that led to the outbreak of the Civil War.

🎯 Reading Skill

Analyze Multiple Causes or Effects
Many events in history have more than one cause, as the Civil War certainly did. Other events lead to more than one effect, which is also certainly true of the Civil War. As you read about this turning point in American history, look for causes with multiple effects and effects with multiple causes.

Key Term
civil war

Why It Matters John Brown's raid increased tensions between North and South. So did the growing power of the Republican Party. The nation was on the verge of a civil war.

❓ Section Focus Question: Why did the election of Abraham Lincoln spark the secession of southern states?

The Nation Divides

As the election of 1860 drew near, Americans everywhere felt a sense of crisis. The long and bitter debate over slavery had left the nation seriously divided.

Election of 1860 The Republicans chose Abraham Lincoln as their presidential candidate. His criticisms of slavery during his debates with Douglas had made him popular in the North.

Southern Democrats wanted the party to support slavery in the territories. But northerners refused to do so. In the end, the party split in two. Northern Democrats chose Stephen Douglas as their candidate. Southern Democrats picked Vice President John Breckinridge of Kentucky.

Some southerners still hoped to heal the split between North and South. They formed the Constitutional Union Party and nominated John Bell of Tennessee. Bell promised to protect slavery *and* keep the nation together.

Stephen Douglas was sure that Lincoln would win the election. However, he believed that Democrats "must try to save the Union." He pleaded with southern voters to stay with the Union, no matter who was elected. However, when Douglas campaigned in the South, hostile southerners often pelted him with eggs and rotten fruit.

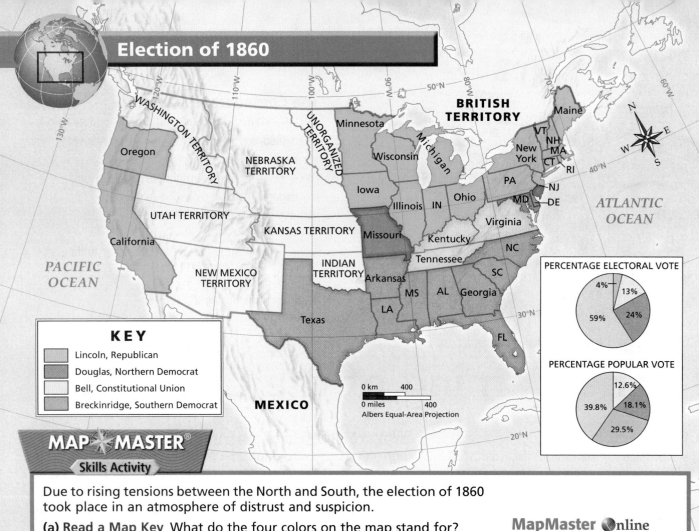

Election of 1860

KEY
- Lincoln, Republican
- Douglas, Northern Democrat
- Bell, Constitutional Union
- Breckinridge, Southern Democrat

PERCENTAGE ELECTORAL VOTE
4% — 13%
59% 24%

PERCENTAGE POPULAR VOTE
12.6%
39.8% 18.1%
29.5%

MAP MASTER
Skills Activity

Due to rising tensions between the North and South, the election of 1860 took place in an atmosphere of distrust and suspicion.

(a) Read a Map Key What do the four colors on the map stand for? Which party won nearly all the northern states? Which party won nearly all the southern states?

(b) Draw Conclusions How does the map show that sectionalism was important in the election?

MapMaster Online

For: Interactive map
Visit: PHSchool.com
Web Code: myp-5104

The election showed just how fragmented the nation had become. Lincoln won in every free state and Breckinridge in all the slave-holding states except four. Bell won Kentucky, Tennessee, and Virginia—all in the upper South. Douglas carried only Missouri. Although Lincoln got only 40 percent of the popular votes, he received enough electoral votes to win the election.

Southern States Secede Lincoln's election sent shock waves through the South. To many southerners, it seemed that the South no longer had a voice in the national government. They believed that the President and Congress were now set against their interests—especially slavery.

One Virginia newspaper expressed the feelings of many southerners. "A party founded on the single sentiment . . . of hatred of African slavery, is now the controlling power," it observed. "The honor, safety, and independence of the Southern people are to be found only in a Southern Confederacy."

South Carolina was the first southern state to secede from the Union. When news of Lincoln's election reached the state, the legislature called for a special convention. On December 20, 1860, the convention passed a declaration that "the union now subsisting between South Carolina and the other states, under the name of the 'United States of America' is hereby dissolved."

The Confederate States of America With the hope of accommodation all but gone, six more states followed South Carolina out of the Union. However, not all southerners favored secession. Tennessee Senator Andrew Johnson and Texas Governor Sam Houston were among those who opposed it. Yet, the voices of the moderates were overwhelmed. "People are wild," said one opponent of secession. "You might as well attempt to control a tornado as attempt to stop them."

In early February, leaders from the seven seceding states met in Montgomery, Alabama, to form a new nation that they called the Confederate States of America. By the time Lincoln took office in March, they had written a constitution and named former Mississippi Senator Jefferson Davis as their president.

✓**Checkpoint** **Why did southern states secede from the Union?**

Vocabulary Builder
accommodation (ak kom moh DAY shuhn) **n.** adjustment; adaptation

The Civil War Begins

On March 4, 1861, Abraham Lincoln became President of a nation facing the greatest crisis in its history. In his inaugural address, he assured the seceded states that he meant them no harm. "I have no purpose, directly or indirectly, to interfere with the institution of slavery where it exists," he promised. But he also warned them about continuing on the course they had chosen:

> **"**In your hands, my dissatisfied fellow countrymen, and not in mine, is the momentous issue of . . . war. The government will not assail [attack] you. . . . We are not enemies, but friends. We must not be enemies. Though passion may have strained, it must not break our bonds of affection.**"**
>
> —Abraham Lincoln, Inaugural Address, March 4, 1861

Lincoln's assurance of friendship was rejected. The seceding states took over post offices, forts, and other federal property within their borders. The new President had to decide how to respond.

Fort Sumter Lincoln's most urgent problem was Fort Sumter, located on an island in the harbor of Charleston, South Carolina. The fort's commander would not surrender it. South Carolina authorities decided to starve the fort's 100 troops into surrender. They had been cut off from supplies since late December and could not hold out much longer.

Abraham Lincoln speaks at his first inauguration

501

ATTACK ON FORT SUMTER

America's most tragic conflict began early on the morning of April 12, 1861, at Fort Sumter. The dark night was suddenly lit up by Confederate shells fired from the mainland. Within a few hours, the fort's wooden barracks had caught fire and portions of the fort had crumbled. At midday, a Confederate shell knocked over the fort's flagpole. The firing went on throughout the day and evening. By the next day, the Union garrison was exhausted and every wooden structure in the fort was ablaze. "The men lay . . . on the ground, with wet handkerchiefs over their mouths and eyes, gasping for breath." **Critical Thinking:** *Analyze Cause and Effect What was the cause of the Confederate attack on Fort Sumter? What were the effects?*

History *Interactive*
Inside Fort Sumter
Visit: **PHSchool.com**
Web Code: **myp-5107**

American flag from
Fort Sumter ▼

▼ **Confederate Troops Fire on the Fort**
Confederate artillery pounded Fort Sumter for 34 hours. Fires raged out of control and threatened to ignite the fort's magazine, where many barrels of gunpowder were stored. Facing shortages of food and ammunition, the Union commander surrendered. The bloodiest of all American wars had begun.

Major Robert ▶
Anderson, Union
commander of
Fort Sumter

Lincoln did not want to give up the fort. But he feared that sending troops might cause other states to secede. Therefore, he announced that he would send food to the fort, but that the supply ships would carry no troops or guns.

Confederate leaders decided to capture the fort while it was isolated. On April 12, Confederate artillery opened fire on the fort. After 34 hours, with the fort on fire, the U.S. troops surrendered.

Vocabulary Builder
isolate (ī sah layt) **v.** to set apart; to separate

Was War Avoidable? The Confederate attack on Fort Sumter marked the beginning of a long civil war. A **civil war** is a war between opposing groups of citizens of the same country.

The Civil War probably attracts more public interest today than any other event in American history. Americans continue to debate why the war took place and whether it could have been avoided.

In 1850, southerners might have been satisfied if they had been left alone. But by 1861, many Americans in both the North and the South had come to accept the idea that war could not be avoided. At stake was the nation's future. Four years later, a weary Lincoln looked back to the beginning of the conflict. He noted:

> **❝**Both parties [condemned] war, but one of them would *make* war rather than let the nation survive, and the other would *accept* war rather than let it perish, and the war came.**❞**
>
> —Abraham Lincoln, Second Inaugural Address, March 4, 1865

Analyze Multiple Causes or Effects According to this section, what were two causes of the Civil War?

✓**Checkpoint** Why was Lincoln reluctant to give up Fort Sumter?

☆ **Looking Back and Ahead** Confederate cannons had nearly destroyed Fort Sumter. To many, it seemed like a huge fireworks display. No one knew that the fireworks marked the beginning of a terrible war that would last four years.

Section 4 | Check Your Progress

Progress Monitoring ⊕nline
For: Self-test with instant help
Visit: PHSchool.com
Web Code: mya-5104

Comprehension and Critical Thinking

1. (a) **Recall** How did divisions among the Democrats help lead to the election of Republican Abraham Lincoln in 1860?
(b) **Explain Problems** What was the South's reaction to Lincoln's election? How did Lincoln try to reassure the South?

2. (a) **Identify** What event marked the start of war between the North and the South?

(b) **Evaluate Information** Explain what Abraham Lincoln meant by the following remark: "Both parties [condemned] war, but one of them would *make* war rather than let the nation survive. . . ."

Reading Skill

3. **Analyze Multiple Causes or Effects** What were three effects of Lincoln's warning to the South?

Key Terms

4. Write two definitions for the key term **civil war**. First, write a formal definition for your teacher. Second, write a definition in everyday English for a classmate.

Writing

5. Based on what you have read in this section, write a thesis statement for an essay explaining why the election of Abraham Lincoln caused the South to secede.

Not everything a writer includes in a selection is equally important. Some information is relevant because it is directly related to the subject of the text. Other information is less relevant because it does not directly relate to the subject. When you read, you must focus your attention on the main topic and the most relevant information. Read the fictional letter below to determine relevance.

The letter below is historical fiction. That means that it is based on history, but is not a primary source. In the letter, William, a farmer who had moved to Kansas Territory, writes to his brother Joseph in Vermont.

November 20, 1854

Dear Joseph,

     I was pleased to receive your last letter. The success of your store is a great achievement. Our new farm continues to prosper and little Sarah has recovered from the fever that had sickened her for a month. Of course, the issue of the Kansas-Nebraska Act continues to trouble me. I do not agree with your support of Senator Stephen Douglas of Illinois; however, I enjoy reading his speeches. Those who oppose slavery, as I do, do not want that cruel system in place in a territory where it had been banned. Under the terms of the Kansas-Nebraska Act, it is up to the people to decide the issue peacefully by voting their hearts. Yet, settlers who are for and against slavery in the territory seem intent on using force, instead of the ballot box. The elections next year will settle the issue once and for all.

Your loving brother,
William

Learn the Skill

Use these steps to determine which information is relevant and which is irrelevant.

1 **Identify the subject or topic.** What is the main topic of the selection?

2 **Identify your purpose for reading the selection.** Ask yourself: What am I trying to find out?

3 **Identify the information that is relevant to the topic.** What information is directly related to the subject? Why is it relevant?

4 **Identify the information that is irrelevant to the topic.** What information is not directly related to the subject? Why is it irrelevant?

Practice the Skill

Answer the following questions about the letter on the page.

1 **Identify the subject or topic.** What is the main topic of the letter?

2 **Identify the purpose for reading the selection.** Why am I reading this letter?

3 **Identify the information that is relevant to the subject.** (a) What are two statements that are directly related to the topic of the letter? (b) Why is each statement relevant?

4 **Identify the information that is irrelevant to the topic.** (a) What are two statements that are not directly related to the subject? (b) Why is each statement irrelevant?

Apply the Skill

See the Review and Assessment at the end of this chapter.

Quick Study Guide

How did the nation try but fail to deal with growing sectional differences?

Section 1
Growing Tensions Over Slavery

- The acquisition of new territories in the West reopened the issue of slavery.
- Lawmakers debated how to keep a balance of power between free and slave-holding states.

Section 2
Compromises Fail

- The Compromise of 1850 attempted to settle the slavery question, but northerners refused to accept the Fugitive Slave Act.
- *Uncle Tom's Cabin* increased northern hatred of slavery and antagonized southern slaveholders.
- Popular sovereignty established by the Kansas-Nebraska Act triggered bloody fighting in Kansas.

Section 3
The Crisis Deepens

- The Republican Party was formed to oppose the spread of slavery.
- In the Dred Scott decision, the Supreme Court ruled that Congress could not ban slavery in any territory.
- Abraham Lincoln became a central political figure when he and Stephen Douglas debated slavery.
- John Brown, an abolitionist, and his followers attacked the federal arsenal at Harpers Ferry, Virginia, to protest slavery.

Section 4
The Coming of the Civil War

- After Lincoln won the presidential election of 1860, some southern states seceded from the Union.
- The Civil War began when Confederate troops fired on Fort Sumter.

? Exploring the Essential Question

Use the online study guide to explore the essential question.

Section 1
How did the question of admission of new states to the Union fuel the debate over slavery and states' rights?

Chapter 14 Essential Question
How did the nation try but fail to deal with growing sectional differences?

Section 2
What was the Compromise of 1850, and why did it fail?

Section 4
Why did the election of Abraham Lincoln spark the secession of southern states?

Section 3
Why did the Lincoln-Douglas debates and John Brown's raid increase tensions between the North and South?

Key Terms
Fill in the blanks with the correct key terms.

1. Many southern states threatened to _____ from the Union if California was admitted as a free state.

2. Southerners claimed that *Uncle Tom's Cabin* was _____ because it did not give a fair picture of the lives of enslaved African Americans.

3. Slavery was the main issue that split the nation apart and led to a violent _____.

Comprehension and Critical Thinking

4. **(a) Recall** Why did Senator Stephen Douglas introduce the Kansas-Nebraska Act?
   (b) Understand Sequence How did the events in Kansas demonstrate the unrest that would eventually take shape throughout the nation?

5. **(a) Summarize** What was the Supreme Court's verdict in the Dred Scott case?
   (b) Detect Points of View How do you think Harriet Beecher Stowe reacted to the verdict?

6. **(a) Identify** What was the main goal of the Republican Party in the election of 1854?
   (b) Distinguish Relevant Information How did Abraham Lincoln represent Republican principles during the Lincoln-Douglas debates?

7. **(a) Identify** What is the subject of the painting below?
   (b) Draw Conclusions Do you agree with the artist's view of this person? Why or why not?

8. **(a) Describe** What happened at Fort Sumter?
   (b) Draw Conclusions Do you think southerners were justified in seceding despite Lincoln's assurances? Explain.

History Reading Skill
9. **Analyze Cause and Effect** Reread the text in Section 4 under the heading "The Nation Divides." How did the election of 1860 affect the unity of the United States?

Writing
10. **Choose one of the following topics for a research report:**
    - the Kansas-Nebraska Act
    - the Dred Scott decision
    - the early career of Abraham Lincoln

    List five questions you would want to pursue if you were going to research that topic. Write a thesis statement for the topic and find supporting evidence for that thesis from the chapter.

11. **Write a Narrative:**
    Imagine you are from a northern farm family and have just heard of the attack on Fort Sumter. Write a narrative describing your hopes and fears about the future.

Skills for Life
Determine Relevance
Use the fictional letter below to answer the questions that follow.

> October 18, 1856
>
> Dear Margaret,
>
> When the Republican Party was formed two years ago, we had no idea it would grow so quickly. I am so pleased with the party's choice of John Frémont as the Republican candidate for President. I know Mother would have agreed with me. I only hope you and I will be able to cast our votes in a presidential election soon.
>
> Your loving sister, Ellen

12. What is the letter about?

13. What is one statement directly related to the subject of the letter? Why is it relevant?

14. What is one statement that is irrelevant to the subject of the letter? Why is it irrelevant?

Test Yourself

1. All of the following were causes of the Civil War EXCEPT

A John Brown's raid on Harpers Ferry.

B the Dred Scott decision.

C the use of child labor in northern factories.

D the publication of Stowe's *Uncle Tom's Cabin.*

Refer to the quotation below to answer Question 2.

> "A house divided against itself cannot stand. . . .
> I do not expect the Union to be dissolved—I do
> not expect the house to fall—but I do expect it
> will cease to be divided. It will become all one
> thing or all the other."

2. What division does this quotation describe?

A church and state

B free states and slaveholding states

C the House of Representatives and the Senate

D Republicans and Democrats

Refer to the pie chart below to answer Question 3.

Percentage of Popular Vote, 1860

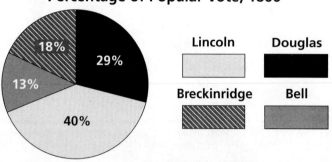

Lincoln   Douglas

Breckinridge   Bell

29% 18% 13% 40%

3. What conclusion can you draw from this pie chart?

A Southerners voted for Douglas.

B Lincoln won most of the popular vote.

C Bell had little support in the North.

D The two Democrats combined won more votes than Lincoln.

Document-Based Questions

Task: Look at Documents 1 and 2, and answer their accompanying questions. Then, use the documents and your knowledge of history to complete this writing assignment:

> Write a two-paragraph essay comparing the goals of the Fugitive Slave Law with its actual effects.

Document 1: In this speech, Senator John Calhoun of South Carolina explained the need for the Fugitive Slave Law. *According to Calhoun, what would happen if Congress did not pass the law?*

> "How can the Union be saved? . . . There is but one way . . . , and that is by adopting such measures as will satisfy . . . the southern section that they can remain in the Union consistently with their honor and their safety. . . .
>
> But can this be done? Yes, easily. . . . The North has only . . . to conced[e] to the South an equal right in [newly] acquired territory, and to caus[e] the stipulations relative to fugitive slaves to be faithfully fulfilled—to cease the agitation of the slave question. . . ."

Document 2: This poster reveals Bostonians' commitment to protect runaways or kidnapped African Americans. *Why were posters like this illegal?*

The Civil War

1861-1865

> *"The wild cries of charging lines,*
> *the rattle of musketry,*
> *the booming of artillery*
> *and the shrieks of wounded were*
> *...like very hell itself...."*

—Lt. Porter Farley,
140th New York Infantry Regiment

In a painting by Don Troiani, a Union soldier and a Confederate soldier fight during the Battle of Gettysburg.

CHAPTER 15

What You Will Learn

Section 1
THE CALL TO ARMS
As the war began and states took sides, the North and the South drew up plans and hoped for an early victory.

Section 2
EARLY YEARS OF THE WAR
The early years of the war were indecisive, as neither side seemed able to defeat the other.

Section 3
THE EMANCIPATION PROCLAMATION
President Lincoln's decision to issue the Emancipation Proclamation opened the way for African Americans to join the Union army.

Section 4
THE CIVIL WAR AND AMERICAN LIFE
The war caused divisions in both North and South while changing the lives of civilians and soldiers alike.

Section 5
DECISIVE BATTLES
Union victories at Gettysburg and Vicksburg in 1863 forced the South's surrender in April 1865.

🔄 Reading Skill
Understand Sequence In this chapter, you will learn to relate the chronological order of events and determine their relationships to one another.

The Civil War

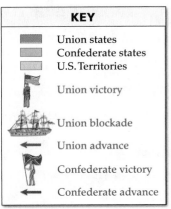

KEY

- Union states
- Confederate states
- U.S. Territories

Union victory

Union blockade

Union advance

Confederate victory

Confederate advance

OR

WASHINGTON TERRITORY

DAKOTA TERRITORY

NEBRASKA TERRITORY

NEVADA TERRITORY

UTAH TERRITORY

COLORADO TERRITORY

CA

NEW MEXICO TERRITORY

Glorieta Pass

• Valverde

MEXICO

Union and Confederate Resources, 1861

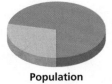

Population
2.5 to 1

Miles of railroad track
2.4 to 1

Wheat production
4.2 to 1

Iron production
15 to 1

Firearms production
32 to 1

Cotton production
1 to 24

 Union resources    Confederate resources

 U.S. Events   1861 | Eleven states secede from the Union.

1862 | President Lincoln announces plan of emancipation.

Vicksburg surrenders to Union forces. | 1863

1861   **1862**   **1863**

 World Events   1861 | Napoleon III sends French troops to invade Mexico.

1862 | Otto von Bismarck becomes prime minister of Prussia.

510

VISUAL PREVIEW

MN

ME

VT

NH

WI

NY

MA

MI

CT

RI

IA

OH

PA

Antietam

Gettysburg

NJ

Bull Run

MD

DE

Fredericksburg

IL

IN

VA

Chancellorsville

Cold Harbor

KY

KS

MO

Seven Days

NC

Petersburg

Chattanooga

Shiloh

TN

Chickamauga

SC

Atlantic Ocean

AR

INDIAN TERRITORY

Atlanta

Fort Sumter

AL

GA

MS

Vicksburg

TX

LA

FL

Port Hudson

New Orleans

Gulf of Mexico

Sabine Pass

Galveston

Mississippi River

N

W E

S

0   300 miles

0   300 km

Albers Conic Equal-Area Projection

| 1863 | Union wins victory at Gettysburg. | Grant invades the South and lays siege to Petersburg. | 1864 | Lee surrenders at Appomattox. | 1865 |

1863   **1864**   **1865**

| 1864 | French-backed Maximilian of Austria becomes emperor of Mexico. |

Miserable Conditions

"Miserable as our condition was, that of the enlisted men was far worse. . . . There was no shelter for them. There was not enough food. They were thinly clad; many had no shoes, few had overcoats, and hundreds had only ragged trousers and shirt to cover their nakedness."

—Maj. Abner B. Small, Sixteenth Maine Volunteers, *Memoirs of a Prisoner of War*

◄ Union troops

The Call to Arms

Objectives

- Identify the states that supported the Union, the states that seceded, and the states whose loyalties were divided.
- Describe the advantages each side had in the war.
- Compare the different strategies used by the North and the South.
- Summarize the results of the First Battle of Bull Run.
- Describe the conditions soldiers in camp faced.

Reading Skill

Understand Sequence of Events The Civil War began as a result of a complex sequence of events. As that war proceeded in its early days, events continued at a furious pace. To form a full understanding of this phase of the war, pause regularly to summarize the sequence of events. Use your own words to recount the important events in the correct order.

Key Terms

border state
neutral

martial law
blockade

Why It Matters As two American nations prepared for war, many Northerners and Southerners were confident that their side would win a quick victory. They were wrong. The Civil War would be a long, bloody, and costly conflict.

⑦ Section Focus Question: Why did each side in the Civil War think the war would be won easily?

Taking Sides in the War

Two days after Fort Sumter's surrender, President Lincoln declared that a rebellion existed in the South. To put it down, he asked the nation's governors to raise 75,000 troops. Across the North, young men eagerly volunteered. Support was so widespread that the governors of Ohio, Indiana, and several other states begged to send more troops than the President had requested.

More States Secede Not all states were so enthusiastic, however. In Tennessee, the governor said that his state "will not furnish a single man" to fight against "our southern brothers." The governors of Kentucky and Missouri made similar replies to Lincoln's request. Maryland and Delaware did not respond at all.

The President's call for troops led more southern states to secede. On April 17, Virginia left the Union. In May, Arkansas, Tennessee, and North Carolina also joined the Confederacy. However, the western counties of Virginia, where there was little support for slavery, refused to secede. In 1863, these 50 counties were admitted to the Union as the state of West Virginia.

The Border States Loyalties remained divided in the border states—slave states that did not secede. Delaware had few enslaved people, and its support of the Union was strong. However, many people in Kentucky, Missouri, and Maryland favored the South. Kentucky and Missouri were important to controlling the Ohio and Mississippi rivers. And unless the Union could hold Maryland, Washington would be surrounded by the Confederacy.

At first, Kentucky declared itself neutral, or not favoring either side. Union generals wanted to occupy Kentucky, but Lincoln refused. He feared that such a move would push the state to secede. His strategy was wise. When Confederate forces invaded it in September 1861, Kentucky decided to support the North.

By contrast, the President acted forcefully to hold Missouri and Maryland. When Missouri's government sided with the South, Union supporters set up their own state government. Fighting broke out within the state. Finally, Lincoln sent troops, and the state stayed in the Union throughout the war.

In Maryland, southern sympathizers destroyed railroad and telegraph lines. So Lincoln placed eastern Maryland under martial law. This is a type of rule in which the military is in charge and citizens' rights are suspended. Maryland officials and others suspected of disloyalty were jailed without trials.

Understand Sequence of Events
Summarize the events as North and South geared up for full-scale conflict. Make sure to recount events in the correct sequence.

☑ **Checkpoint** How did the border states line up in the war?

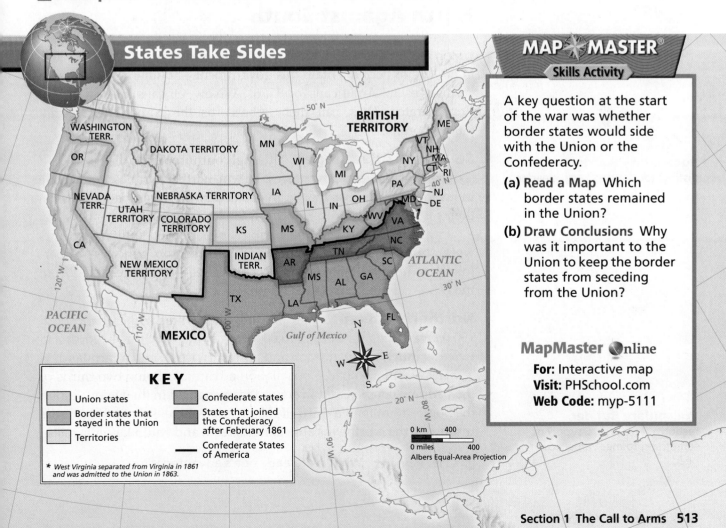

States Take Sides

WASHINGTON TERR.
OR
DAKOTA TERRITORY
MN
BRITISH TERRITORY
ME
VT
NH
MA
CT
RI
NY
WI
MI
PA
NJ
NEVADA TERR.
NEBRASKA TERRITORY
IA
OH
MD
DE
UTAH TERRITORY
COLORADO TERRITORY
KS
IL
IN
WV
VA
CA
MS
KY
NC
NEW MEXICO TERRITORY
INDIAN TERR.
AR
TN
SC
ATLANTIC OCEAN
MS
AL
GA
TX
LA
FL
PACIFIC OCEAN
MEXICO
Gulf of Mexico

KEY
- ☐ Union states
- ☐ Border states that stayed in the Union
- ☐ Territories
- ☐ Confederate states
- ☐ States that joined the Confederacy after February 1861
- — Confederate States of America

West Virginia separated from Virginia in 1861 and was admitted to the Union in 1863.

0 km 400
0 miles 400
Albers Equal-Area Projection

MAP MASTER
Skills Activity

A key question at the start of the war was whether border states would side with the Union or the Confederacy.

(a) Read a Map Which border states remained in the Union?

(b) Draw Conclusions Why was it important to the Union to keep the border states from seceding from the Union?

MapMaster Online
For: Interactive map
Visit: PHSchool.com
Web Code: myp-5111

Comparing Resources, 1861

Percent

100
80
60
40
20
0

Total Population   Factory Production   Railroad Mileage

■ Union states   ■ Confederate states

Source: *The Times Atlas of World History*

Reading Charts

Skills Activity

The Union had an advantage over the Confederacy in a number of resources.

(a) Read a Bar Graph In which of the three comparisons is the Union's advantage the greatest?

(b) Draw Conclusions For each of these three resources, how would you expect the Union to benefit from its advantage?

(c) Make Predictions Based on the information in these graphs, which side would you expect to win the war? Explain.

North Against South

As the armies prepared, people on both sides were confident. A Union soldier declared that he was "willing . . . to lay down all my joys in this life to help maintain this government." Southerners compared themselves to Americans of 1776. A New Orleans poet wrote of Confederates: "Yes, call them rebels! 'tis the name/Their patriot fathers bore."

Southern Advantages Although outnumbered, the South had some <u>distinct</u> military advantages. To win, northern armies would have to invade and conquer the South. Confederates would be fighting on their own territory, with help from the local people.

In addition, most of the nation's experienced military officers were southerners. The Confederacy's three top generals—Albert Johnston, Joseph Johnston, and Robert E. Lee—all had resigned from the U.S. Army to fight for the South.

Northern Advantages In 1861, the United States had about 130,000 factories. Of those, 110,000 were in the North. The North had twice as much railroad track and almost twice as much farmland.

The North also had a population advantage. Some two thirds of the nation's people lived in states that remained in the Union, and in the South more than a third of the people were enslaved. With more <u>resources</u>, the North was able to field, feed, and equip larger armies.

☑**Checkpoint** What were each side's advantages?

Vocabulary Builder
<u>distinct</u> (dihs TIHNKT) **adj.** clear or definite; different in quality

Vocabulary Builder
<u>resource</u> (REE sors) **n.** supply of something to meet a particular need

The Two Sides Plan Strategies

Union leaders hoped to win a quick victory. To isolate the Confederacy, Lincoln had the navy blockade southern seaports. A **blockade** is a military action to prevent traffic from coming into an area or leaving it. Lincoln hoped to cut off the South's supply of manufactured goods and block overseas sales of cotton.

An important part of northern strategy was to gain control of the Mississippi River, the South's major transportation link. This would split the South in two. The Union also planned to invade Virginia and seize Richmond, the Confederate capital. It was just 100 miles from Washington, D.C.

The South's strategy was simpler. The Confederates did not need to invade the North. They had only to defend their land until northerners got tired of fighting. The Confederates sought aid from Britain and other European nations. They hoped that Britain's need of cotton for its textile mills would force the British to support the South.

☑ **Checkpoint**   **How did strategies on the two sides differ?**

Americans Against Americans

On both sides, men rushed to be part of the fight. "I had never dreamed that New England . . . could be fired with so warlike a spirit," wrote Mary Ashton Livermore in Boston. In South Carolina, Mary Chesnut said that men rushed to enlist in the army for "fear the war will be over before they get a sight of the fun."

This war between Americans broke families apart, setting brother against brother, father against son. Kentucky Senator John Crittenden had two sons in the war fighting on different sides. Four brothers of Mary Lincoln, the President's wife, fought for the Confederacy.

Old Enough for War
Soldiers in both the Union and Confederate armies might have been as young as 14. Nearly 4,000 Union troops were 16 or younger. **Critical Thinking: Draw Conclusions** *How do you think the experience of war affected young men?*

Fleeing Bull Run

Before the First Battle of Bull Run, both sides expected an easy victory. But they were wrong. Here, Union soldiers have panicked and are fleeing the Bull Run battlefield. Bull Run was an early sign that the war would be long and costly. **Critical Thinking:** *Draw Conclusions What reasons did each side have to think it would win an early victory? Why were both sides' expectations unreasonable?*

The soldiers came from many backgrounds. Nearly half of the North's troops were farmers. One fourth were immigrants.

Three fourths of the South's 1 million white males between ages 18 and 45 served in the army. Two thirds of the 3.5 million northern males of the same age fought for the Union. Some soldiers were as young as 14.

✔**Checkpoint** **Who were the soldiers in this war?**

First Battle of Bull Run

Union General Irvin McDowell wanted time to turn his soldiers into an effective fighting force. But by July 1861, northern newspapers were demanding the capture of Richmond and a quick end to the war.

McDowell's 30,000 men left Washington and marched southwest into Virginia. About the same number of Confederates waited at Manassas, a railroad center about 25 miles away. Hundreds of people rode out from Washington to see the battle, expecting an easy Union victory.

The armies clashed along Bull Run, a river just north of Manassas, on July 21. At first, the Union army pushed forward. But a southern commander rallied his men to hold firm. "Look, there is Jackson with his Virginians, standing like a stone wall," he shouted. From then on, the general, Thomas Jackson, was known as "Stonewall" Jackson.

Slowly the battle turned in favor of the Confederates. The poorly trained Union troops began to panic. Soldiers and sightseers fled back to Washington. The Confederates were too exhausted to pursue them.

✔**Checkpoint** **What was the result of the First Battle of Bull Run?**

A Soldier's Life

Most soldiers spent three fourths of their time in camp, not fighting. Training took up to 10 hours a day. When not training, soldiers stood guard, wrote home, and gathered firewood. A meal might be simply a dry, cracker-like product called hardtack.

Hardtack

Harsh Conditions Camp conditions were often miserable, especially when wet weather created muddy roads and fields. The lack of clean water was a major health threat. Outbreaks of smallpox, typhoid fever, and other diseases swept through the ranks. It was not unusual for half the men in a regiment to be too sick to fight.

Prisoners of War Both sides built prison camps for captured soldiers. Overcrowded prison camps became deathtraps. Nearly 10 percent of soldiers who died in the war perished in prison camps.

The camps at Elmira, New York, and Andersonville, Georgia, were the worst. Elmira camp, built to hold 5,000 Confederate prisoners, held 10,000. The camp cut rations to bread and water, forcing prisoners to eat rats to survive. Thousands died. At Andersonville, nearly 35,000 Union soldiers lived in a fenced, open field intended to hold 10,000 men. As many as 100 prisoners died each day, usually from starvation or exposure.

✔Checkpoint **What conditions did soldiers have to endure?**

⭐ **Looking Back and Ahead** The North's hopes for an early victory had been dashed. The war would be long and brutal. In the next section, you will read more about the early years of the war.

Section 1 | **Check Your Progress**

Progress Monitoring Online
For: Self-test with instant help
Visit: PHSchool.com
Web Code: mya-5111

Comprehension and Critical Thinking

1. (a) Recall How did President Lincoln respond to the surrender of Fort Sumter?
(b) Apply Information What caused three border states to remain in the Union?

2. (a) List What were three advantages held by the South? What were three advantages held by the North?
(b) Analyze Cause and Effect How did the First Battle of Bull Run shatter the belief that the Civil War would be a quick Union victory?

Reading Skill

3. Understand Sequence of Events Choose a state that wavered about supporting the North or the South. Summarize the sequence of events that led this state to a final decision.

Key Terms

Complete each of the following sentences so that the second part explains the first and shows your understanding of the key term.
4. Union leaders planned a blockade; _____.
5. Lincoln placed Maryland under martial law; _____.

Writing

6. Create an outline that covers the information presented in this section, copying the form below. A few entries have been filled in.

I. Taking sides in the war (first important topic)
  A. More states secede (first issue for that topic)
    1. A number of border states refused to send troops to support the Union (first point)
    2. _____ (second point)
  B.
    1.
    2.
II.

Battlefield Report

❝Our men were vomiting with excessive fatigue, over-exhaustion, and sunstroke; our tongues were parched and cracked for water, and our faces blackened with powder and smoke, and our dead and wounded were piled indiscriminately in the trenches. ❞

—Confederate soldier, describing a battle in Georgia

◄ Confederate troops

Early Years of the War

Objectives

- Explain how new weapons made fighting the war more dangerous.
- Describe the course of the war in the East in 1862.
- Describe the early days of the war in the West and at sea.

🎯 Reading Skill

Distinguish Events in Sequence As you read this section, it is important to keep events in sequence. Ask yourself: Which event happened first? Next? Last? You might number events to help you organize their sequence. This will help you to understand the unfolding drama of the Civil War.

Key Terms and People

ironclad
George McClellan
casualty
Ulysses S. Grant

Why It Matters The Union's crushing defeat at Bull Run made northerners realize that a long and difficult struggle lay ahead. Both the North and South tried to find the strategies and the leaders that would ensure victory and preserve their way of life.

❓ **Section Focus Question: How did each side in the war try to gain an advantage over the other?**

New Technology in the War

New weapons made the Civil War more deadly than any previous war. Traditionally, generals had relied on an all-out charge of troops to overwhelm the enemy. But new rifles and cannons were far more accurate and had a greater range than the old muskets and artillery. They could also be loaded much faster. As a result, the attacking army could be bombarded long before it arrived at the defenders' position.

Unfortunately, Civil War generals were slow to recognize the problem and change tactics. Thousands of soldiers on both sides were slaughtered by following orders to cross open fields against these deadly new weapons.

Both sides also made use of **ironclads.** These were warships covered with protective iron plates. Cannon fire bounced harmlessly off this armor. The most famous naval battle of the war occurred when two ironclads, the Union's *Monitor* and the Confederacy's *Merrimack,* fought to a draw in March 1862. The use of ironclads marked the end of thousands of years of wooden warships. The Confederates used ironclads against the Union's naval blockade. Ironclad Union gunboats played an important role in the North's efforts to gain control of the Mississippi River.

✓**Checkpoint** What new technologies were used in the Civil War?

The War in the East

After the Union's defeat at Bull Run, Lincoln removed McDowell and put General George McClellan in command. The general was a good organizer, but he was very cautious. For seven months, he trained his army but did not attack. "If General McClellan does not want to use the army," a frustrated Lincoln complained, "I would like to borrow it for a time."

In March 1862, McClellan was finally ready. He moved some 100,000 soldiers by boat along Chesapeake Bay to a peninsula southeast of Richmond. As McClellan advanced toward the Confederate capital, he discovered that his force was far <u>superior</u> to the 15,000 enemy soldiers blocking the way. However, McClellan still did not have as many soldiers as he wanted because Lincoln had ordered 37,000 soldiers to stay behind to guard Washington, D.C. The general stopped his advance and asked for more troops.

McClellan waited nearly a month before moving again. This delay gave the Confederates time to <u>reinforce</u> their small army of defenders. On May 31, 1862, the Confederates stopped McClellan's advance near Richmond. In late June, McClellan had to retreat.

With Richmond no longer threatened, Lee decided to invade the North. He hoped that a victory on Union soil would help win support for the South in Europe and turn northern public opinion against the war. In early September, he slipped his army into western Maryland.

Now McClellan had a stroke of luck. A Union officer found a paper showing Lee's battle plan. McClellan thus learned that the Confederate army had divided into two parts.

Vocabulary Builder
<u>superior</u> (sah PIR ee ahr) **adj.** of greater importance or value; above average

Vocabulary Builder
<u>reinforce</u> (ree ihn FORS) **v.** to make stronger; to make more effective

● INFOGRAPHIC
Battle of Two Ironclads

The Civil War introduced ironclad warships. Here, an artist shows the battle between the Confederacy's *Merrimack* (left) and the Union's *Monitor* (right) off Hampton Roads, Virginia, in 1862.
Critical Thinking: *Draw Conclusions* How would you expect an ironclad ship to fare in a battle against an older warship that lacked armor? Explain.

▲ Inset shows the recovery of the *Monitor's* turret, or gun chamber, in 2002.

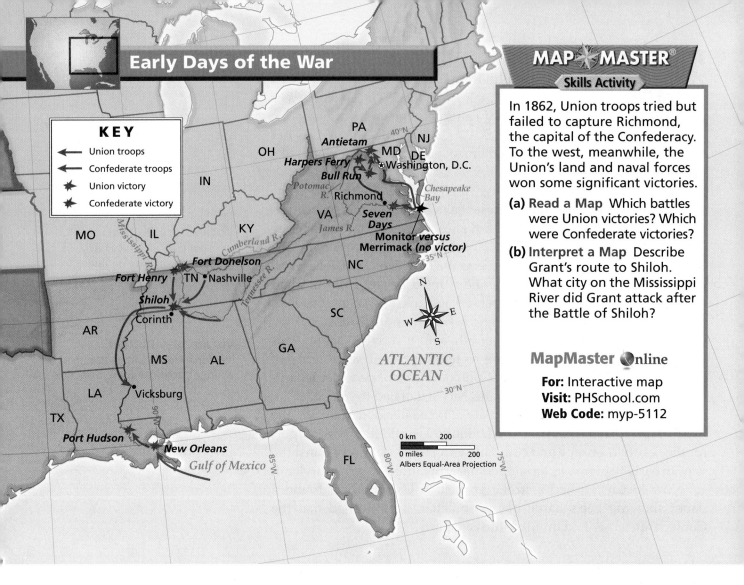

Early Days of the War

KEY
← Union troops
← Confederate troops
✶ Union victory
✶ Confederate victory

MAP MASTER
Skills Activity

In 1862, Union troops tried but failed to capture Richmond, the capital of the Confederacy. To the west, meanwhile, the Union's land and naval forces won some significant victories.

(a) Read a Map Which battles were Union victories? Which were Confederate victories?

(b) Interpret a Map Describe Grant's route to Shiloh. What city on the Mississippi River did Grant attack after the Battle of Shiloh?

MapMaster Online

For: Interactive map
Visit: PHSchool.com
Web Code: myp-5112

McClellan's troops attacked the larger part of Lee's army at Antietam Creek, near Sharpsburg, Maryland, on September 17, 1862. This was the bloodiest day of the Civil War. The Union army attacked again and again. It suffered about 12,000 **casualties**—the military term for persons killed, wounded, or missing in action. Lee lost nearly 14,000 men—almost one third of his army. He was forced to pull his battered army back into Virginia. To Lincoln's dismay, McClellan did not press his advantage by pursuing Lee.

Neither side won a clear victory at the Battle of Antietam. But because Lee had ordered a retreat, the North claimed victory.

✓**Checkpoint** How did McClellan's caution hurt the Union?

The War in the West

As McClellan moved cautiously, Union armies in the West went on the attack. General Ulysses S. Grant led the most successful of these armies. McClellan and Grant were very different. McClellan wore carefully fitted uniforms. Grant, once a poor store clerk, wore rumpled clothes. McClellan was cautious. Grant took chances.

Union forces made major advances in western land and naval battles in 1862, seizing control of most of the Mississippi River. In February 1862, Grant moved his army south from Kentucky. First, he captured Fort Henry on the Tennessee River. Then, he captured Fort Donelson on the Cumberland River.

Two water routes into the western Confederacy were now wide open. Grant's army continued south along the Tennessee River toward Corinth, Mississippi, an important railroad center.

Before Grant could advance on Corinth, Confederate General Albert Sidney Johnston attacked. On April 6, 1862, he surprised Grant's troops at the Battle of Shiloh. (For more on this battle, see the Geography and History feature in this chapter.)

The Battle of Shiloh was costly yet important for both sides. The South suffered nearly 11,000 casualties and the North more than 13,000. However, the Union forced the Confederate army to withdraw from the railroad center. Union forces also gained control of western Tennessee and part of the Mississippi River.

Two weeks after the Battle of Shiloh, a Union fleet commanded by David Farragut entered the Mississippi River from the Gulf of Mexico. On April 26, Farragut captured New Orleans, Louisiana. By summer, nearly the entire river was in Union hands.

Distinguish Events in Sequence
What was the sequence of battles in the West? When did these occur?

☑**Checkpoint** **What was the result of the Battle of Shiloh?**

⭐ **Looking Back and Ahead** Northern and southern generals both tried to carry the war into enemy territory. At first, neither side gained a decisive advantage. In the next section, you will read how the Emancipation Proclamation changed the nature of the war.

Section 2 | **Check Your Progress**

Progress Monitoring ⓞnline
For: Self-test with instant help
Visit: PHSchool.com
Web Code: mya-5112

Comprehension and Critical Thinking
1. **(a) Describe** Explain how new weapons made the Civil War more deadly than previous American wars.
(b) Evaluate Information How did harsh conditions and new technology result in a high number of casualties?

2. **(a) Summarize** Why was General McClellan considered to be an ineffective leader?
(b) Organize Information Make a chart that shows the place, casualties, leaders, outcome, and importance of the battles at Shiloh and Antietam Creek.

Reading Skill
3. **Distinguish Events in Sequence** During the Battle of Shiloh, which came first: Grant captured Fort Henry, Johnston attacked, Grant won a stunning victory? Identify the signal clues that you used.

Key Terms
Read each sentence. If the sentence is true, write YES. If the sentence is not true, write NO and explain why.
4. Both the Union and the Confederacy suffered many casualties.
5. Ironclads were of little importance in the war at sea.

Writing
6. Use library or Internet resources to find more information about one of the topics covered in this section. Suggestions for topics include the ironclad warships, the Battle of Shiloh, or the Battle of Antietam. Then, write a short introduction to a research paper that would present information about the topic.

The Battle of Shiloh

In April 1862, the Confederacy seized an opportunity to attack Union forces in the West. Two Union armies were attempting to join each other in southwestern Tennessee. Confederate troops were camped close by in Corinth, Mississippi. The Confederates attacked near Pittsburgh Landing, Tennessee, on April 6, hoping to crush one Union force before the other could arrive.

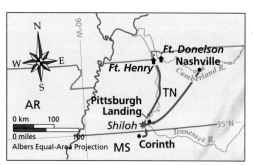

Confederate troops attacked Union forces at the Battle of Shiloh.

KEY
← Union troops
← Confederate troops

1 **A Sunken Road**

The initial Confederate attack caught Union troops by surprise. They retreated a mile before establishing a defensive position along a sunken road. Troops crouched behind the road bank and fought off a dozen Confederate charges.

2 Exposed to Counterattack

Confederate troops marched toward the Union position without the protection of trees or foxholes. Every charge was met with a flurry of bullets from Union soldiers using vegetation and raised mounds of earth as cover.

Understand Effects:
A Bloody Victory

The Battle of Shiloh was one of the bloodiest engagements of the Civil War. Although the Union emerged the victor, both sides suffered heavy losses. Union General Ulysses S. Grant would continue to guide his army as it gradually seized control of the entire Mississippi Valley.

◄ Rifle bullets

Confederate jacket ►

3 The "Hornet's Nest"

As the battle wore on, the Confederates nicknamed the Union position the "Hornet's Nest" because of the intense fire the Confederate soldiers encountered. Union bullets caused many Confederate injuries. One officer's jacket shows the devastating results of the battle.

Analyze **GEOGRAPHY AND HISTORY**

Write a paragraph explaining how northern troops used geography to give themselves an advantage over the Confederates.

Justice Has Awakened

"After two hundred years of bondage and suffering a returning sense of justice has awakened the great body of American people to make amends for the unprovoked wrongs committed against us for over two hundred years."

—African American Tennesseans, letter to the Federal Government, 1865

◄ Artist's representation of Lincoln greeting freed slaves.

The Emancipation Proclamation

Objectives

- Explain why Lincoln issued the Emancipation Proclamation.
- Identify the effects of the proclamation.
- Describe the contributions of African Americans to the Union.

Reading Skill

Explain How Events Are Related in Time President Lincoln and others made many choices in fighting the war. They made these choices in the context of the events at the time. When reading about history, it is important to see how events in a period are related in time. Do events influence the attitudes and decisions of people going forward in time? Do they change people's actions and freedoms?

Key Terms and People

emancipate
Horace Greeley

Why It Matters President Lincoln had been reluctant to abolish slavery. But he changed his mind. His Emancipation Proclamation would dramatically alter the nature of the war, the lives of African Americans, and the future of the United States.

❷ **Section Focus Question: What were the causes and effects of the Emancipation Proclamation?**

Emancipating the Enslaved

Many abolitionists rejoiced when the war began. They urged Lincoln to end slavery and thus punish the South for starting the war.

Lincoln Changes His Mind At first, the President resisted. He knew most northerners did not want to end slavery. "You . . . overestimate the number in the country who hold such views," he told one abolitionist. He feared that any action to emancipate, or free, enslaved African Americans might make the border states secede.

Lincoln said his goal was to restore the Union, even if that meant letting slavery continue. He stated this very clearly in a letter to abolitionist newspaper publisher Horace Greeley.

"If I could save the Union without freeing *any* slave, I would do it, and if I could save it by freeing *all* the slaves, I would do it. . . . What I do about slavery . . . I do because I believe it helps to save the Union."

Gradually, Lincoln began to change his mind. He realized how important slavery was to the South's war effort. He told his Cabinet that he intended to issue an Emancipation Proclamation. But Cabinet members advised him to wait until after a success on the battlefield.

A Famous Proclamation On September 22, 1862, a few days after Lee's retreat from Antietam, Lincoln met again with his Cabinet and issued a <u>preliminary</u> proclamation.

On January 1, 1863, Lincoln issued the final Emancipation Proclamation. This document had little immediate effect, however, because it freed enslaved people only in areas that were fighting the Union. Those were places where the Union had no power. The proclamation did not apply to parts of the South already under Union control. Nor did it free anyone in the border states.

The proclamation was both criticized and praised. Some abolitionists said it should be applied throughout the country. White southerners accused Lincoln of trying to cause a slave revolt. But many Union soldiers were enthusiastic. They welcomed anything that weakened the South. "This army will <u>sustain</u> the Emancipation Proclamation and enforce it with the bayonet," an Indiana soldier said.

Effects of the Proclamation Even though the proclamation freed few slaves at first, it had other important effects. Above all, it changed the Civil War into a struggle for freedom. This was no longer just a fight to save the nation. It was now also a fight to end slavery.

Vocabulary Builder
preliminary (pree LIM uh nehr ee) **adj.** leading up to the main action

Vocabulary Builder
sustain (suh STAYN) **v.** to keep going; to endure; to supply with food; to support as just

The Emancipation Proclamation

❝That on the first day of January, in the year of our Lord [1863], all persons held as slaves within any State or designated part of a State, the people whereof shall then be in rebellion against the United States, shall be then, thenceforward, and forever free. . . .❞

—Emancipation Proclamation, January 1, 1863

A Union general posted the announcement at right, declaring the freedom of enslaved African Americans in the part of Virginia occupied by his troops.

FREEDOM TO SLAVES!

Whereas, the President of the United States did, on the first day of the present month, issue his *Proclamation* declaring "that *all persons held as Slaves in certain designated States, and parts of States, are, and henceforward shall be free,*" and that the Executive Government of the United States, including the Military and Naval authorities thereof, would recognize and maintain the freedom of said persons. *And Whereas,* the county of Frederick is included in the territory designated by the Proclamation of the President, in which the *Slaves should become free,* I therefore hereby notify the citizens of the city of Winchester, and of said County, of said Proclamation, and of my intention to maintain and enforce the same.

I expect all citizens to yield a ready compliance with the Proclamation of the Chief Executive, and I admonish all persons disposed to resist its peaceful enforcement, that upon manifesting such disposition by acts, they will be regarded as rebels in arms against the lawful authority of the Federal Government and dealt with accordingly.

All persons liberated by said Proclamation are admonished to abstain from all violence, and immediately betake themselves to useful occupations.

The officers of this command are admonished and ordered to act in accordance with said proclamation and to yield their ready co-operation in its enforcement.

Winchester Va
Jan. 5th, 1863.

R. H. Milroy,
Brig. Gen'l Commanding.

Reading Primary Sources
Skills Activity

President Lincoln's proclamation specified that it applied only to certain parts of the United States.

(a) Understand Sequence In what order were these two declarations issued?

(b) Compare In what way is the declaration on the right more specific than the one by President Lincoln?

African American Soldiers

These are guards of the 107th Colored Infantry at Fort Corcoran in Washington, D.C. **Critical Thinking: *Apply Information*** *How did conditions for African American soldiers differ from those for white soldiers?*

Also, the Emancipation Proclamation dashed any hopes that Britain would recognize the South's independence. Britain would not help a government that was fighting to keep people enslaved.

In both the North and the South, Lincoln's proclamation united African Americans in support of the war. "We shout for joy that we live to record this righteous decree," wrote Frederick Douglass.

☑**Checkpoint** **How did the proclamation affect the war?**

African Americans Help the Union

Slavery existed in small amounts in the North before the Emancipation Proclamation. Enslaved Africans labored in port towns of New England, and inland they worked in homes or as laborers. But even as African Americans were freed in the North, they received unequal treatment. African American volunteers were not permitted to join the Union army until after the Emancipation Proclamation.

Volunteering for Service Ultimately, 189,000 African Americans served in the Union army or navy. More than half were former slaves who had escaped or been freed by the fighting. All faced extra risks. If captured, they were not treated as prisoners of war. Most were returned to slavery and some were killed.

Black and white sailors served together on warships. In the army, however, African American soldiers served in all-black regiments under white officers. They earned less pay than white soldiers.

Despite these disadvantages, African American regiments fought with pride and courage. "They make better soldiers in every respect than any troops I have ever had under my command," a Union general said of an African American regiment from Kansas.

Explain How Events Are Related in Time
Explain why these two events are related in time: African American soldiers fought for the Union; President Lincoln issued the Emancipation Proclamation.

African American troops took part in about 40 major battles and hundreds of minor ones. The most famous was the attack on Fort Wagner in South Carolina by the 54th Massachusetts Infantry on July 18, 1863. The unit volunteered to lead the assault. As the soldiers charged, Confederate cannon fire rained down. Yet the 54th reached the top of the fort's walls before being turned back in fierce hand-to-hand fighting. The regiment suffered terrible losses. Nearly half of its soldiers were casualties.

Thousands of African Americans supported the Union in noncombat roles. Free northern and emancipated southern African Americans often worked for Union armies as cooks, wagon drivers, and hospital aides.

Resisting Slavery In the South, many enslaved African Americans did what they could to hurt the Confederate war effort. Some provided military and other kinds of information to Union armies. Enslaved people had always quietly resisted slavery by deliberately working slowly or damaging equipment. But with many slaveholders off fighting the war, large numbers of slaves refused to work.

✓**Checkpoint** How did African Americans help the Union cause?

⭐ **Looking Back and Ahead** The Emancipation Proclamation made the Civil War a fight to end slavery. After the war, the Thirteenth Amendment banned slavery throughout the nation. The next section tells how the war affected civilians on both sides.

Section 3 | **Check Your Progress**

Progress Monitoring Online
For: Self-test with instant help
Visit: PHSchool.com
Web Code: mya-5113

Comprehension and Critical Thinking

1. (a) **Identify** Why did Lincoln at first resist identifying slavery as an issue of the Civil War?
   (b) **Analyze Cause and Effect** What effect did the Emancipation Proclamation have on slavery?

2. (a) **Recall** In what ways did African Americans participate in the Civil War?
   (b) **Explain Problems** What were three problems faced by African American soldiers?

Reading Skill

3. **Explain How Events Are Related in Time** Identify events that happened after the Emancipation Proclamation. Explain how these events are connected.

Key Terms

4. Write two definitions for emancipate. First, write a formal definition for your teacher. Second, write a definition in everyday English for a classmate.

Writing

5. Use library or Internet resources to find information about the African American 54th Massachusetts Infantry. Then, list the subtopics to be included in a research paper about the regiment. Write a paragraph about one of those subtopics. Identify some photographs and other nontext items that you would include in a research report on the 54th.

A Nurse's Day

❝[Today] I have covered crutches, ripped up arm slings, washed and made them over, gone to commissary with order from doctor for material for pads for wounded or amputated limbs. . . .❞

—Elvira Powers,
a nurse at a Northern hospital, 1863

▲ A nurse cares for an injured soldier.

The Civil War and American Life

Objectives

- Explain how opposition to the war caused problems for both sides.

- Identify the reasons that both sides passed draft laws.

- Describe the economic hardships the war caused in the North and the South.

- Describe the contributions of women to the war effort.

Reading Skill

Explain How Events Are Related in Time As soldiers were fighting the Civil War on the battlefield, Americans in both the North and the South were facing other wartime challenges. You will have a better understanding of the Civil War Era if you can relate events on the battlefield to events in civilian life.

Key Terms

habeas corpus
draft

income tax
inflation

Why It Matters The Civil War was not just about the winning and losing of battles and the freeing of slaves. The conflict affected men and women from all walks of life. In both the North and the South, civilians had to cope with the pains of war.

❓ Section Focus Question: How did the war affect people and politics in the North and the South?

Divisions Over the War

The Civil War not only divided the nation. It also caused divisions *within* the North and the South. Not all northerners supported a war to end slavery or even to restore the Union. Not all white southerners supported a war to defend slavery or secession.

Division in the South In the South, opposition to the war was strongest in Georgia and North Carolina. Barely half of Georgians supported secession. There were nearly 100 peace protests in North Carolina in 1863 alone. Yet only Virginia provided more troops to Confederate armies than did North Carolina. Generally, regions with large slaveholding plantations supported the war more strongly than poor backcountry regions, where there were fewer enslaved people.

Strong support for states' rights created other divisions. For example, South Carolina's governor objected to officers from other states leading South Carolina troops. And the governors of Georgia and North Carolina did not want the Confederate government to force men from their states to do military service.

Division in the North Northerners were also divided over the war. Many opposed the Emancipation Proclamation. Others believed that the South had a right to secede. Some northern Democrats blamed Lincoln and the Republicans for forcing the South into a war. Northern Democrats who opposed the war were called Copperheads, after the poisonous snake. Copperheads were strongest in Ohio, Indiana, and Illinois. They criticized the war and called for peace with the Confederacy.

Dealing With Disruptions Some people on both sides tried to disrupt the war effort. A common tactic was to encourage soldiers to desert. Some northerners helped Confederate prisoners of war to escape. In the South, peace groups tried to end the war by working against the Confederacy. They tried to prevent men from volunteering for military service and urged Confederate soldiers to desert.

To deal with such problems, both Lincoln and Confederate President Jefferson Davis suspended the right of habeas corpus in some places during the war. Habeas corpus is a constitutional protection against unlawful imprisonment. It empowers judges to order that imprisoned persons be brought into court to determine if they are being legally held. In the North, more than 13,000 people were arrested and jailed without trials.

☑**Checkpoint** How did the Civil War divide both North and South?

Explain How Events Are Related in Time As the Civil War progressed on the battlefield, what was happening at home? Include information about both North and South in your answer.

Copperheads

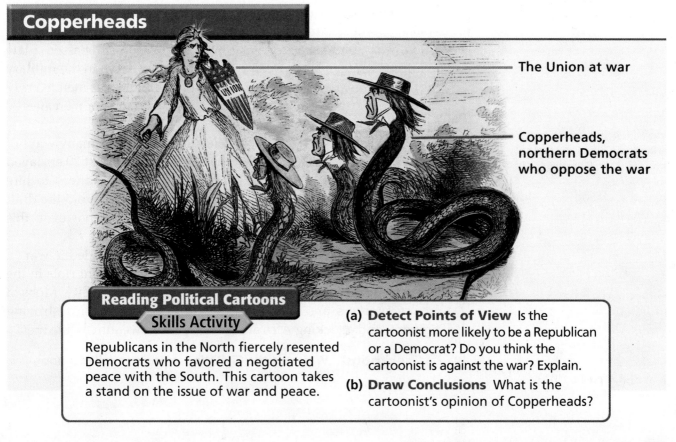

The Union at war

Copperheads, northern Democrats who oppose the war

Reading Political Cartoons

Skills Activity

Republicans in the North fiercely resented Democrats who favored a negotiated peace with the South. This cartoon takes a stand on the issue of war and peace.

(a) Detect Points of View Is the cartoonist more likely to be a Republican or a Democrat? Do you think the cartoonist is against the war? Explain.

(b) Draw Conclusions What is the cartoonist's opinion of Copperheads?

Join or Be Drafted

Volunteers rushed to enlist at first, but antiwar feeling soon grew. During the New York draft riots of 1863, a mob set fire to a home for African American orphans.
Critical Thinking: *Detect Points of View* *What motivated the people who rioted against the draft?*

The Draft Laws

Desertion was a problem for both sides. Between 300,000 and 550,000 Union and Confederate soldiers left their units and went home. About half returned after their crops were planted or harvested. However, at times, from one third to one half of an army's soldiers were away from their units without permission.

To meet the need for troops, each side established a draft, a system of required military service. The South, with its smaller population, was first to act. In April 1862, the Confederacy passed a law requiring white men between ages 18 and 35 to serve in the military for three years. Later, the age range expanded to cover men from 17 to 50. The North adopted a similar draft law in 1863, for men ages 20 to 45.

Exceptions existed, however. Wealthy people had many ways of escaping fighting. In the South, a man who held at least 20 enslaved people did not have to serve. Both sides allowed draftees to hire substitutes to serve in their place. Northerners could avoid the draft by paying the government $300. For many workers, however, this was about a year's pay.

People on both sides complained that the draft made the war "a poor man's fight." Anger against the draft led to violent riots in the North in July 1863. The worst took place in New York City. Mobs of factory workers and laborers rioted for several days, destroying property and attacking African Americans and wealthy white men.

✓**Checkpoint** **Why was the Civil War sometimes called a poor man's fight?**

The War and Economic Strains

Northern industries boomed as they turned out goods the Union needed in the war. Plenty of jobs were available. But the draft drained away workers so there was a constant shortage.

To pay the costs of fighting the war, Congress levied the first income tax in American history in August 1861. An income tax is a tax on the money people receive. The Union also printed $400 million of paper money to help pay its expenses. This was the first federal paper money, or currency. Putting this additional money into circulation led to inflation, or a general rise in prices. In the North, the prices of goods increased an average of 80 percent during the war.

The South was less able than the North to sustain a war. The Union blockade prevented the South from raising money by selling cotton overseas. Shortages made goods more expensive. This led to much greater inflation than in the North. A pair of shoes that had cost $18 dollars in 1862 cost up to $800 in the South in 1864. The price of a pound of beef soared from 12 cents in 1862 to $8 in 1865.

Southern food production fell as invading Union armies destroyed farmland and crops. Shortages of food led to riots in some southern cities. In Richmond, more than 1,000 women looted shops for food, cloth, and shoes in 1863. A woman in North Carolina complained:

> ❝A crowd of we poor women went to Greensboro yesterday for something to eat as we do not have a mouthful of bread nor meat. . . . I have 6 little children and my husband in the army and what am I to do?❞
> —farm woman in North Carolina, April 1863

Enslaved people also suffered from wartime shortages. What little they did have was often seized by Confederate soldiers.

☑Checkpoint   **What strains did the war put on people?**

Women in the Civil War

Women in both the North and the South contributed to the war in many ways. At least 400 women disguised themselves as men and joined the Union or Confederate armies. Others became spies behind enemy lines. Many women took over businesses, farms, and plantations while their fathers, brothers, and husbands served on the battlefields.

In both North and South, women ran farms and plantations. Some southern women worked in the fields to help meet the needs of the Confederacy. They continued to work despite fighting that destroyed their crops and killed their livestock.

Women also ran many northern farms. "I saw more women driving teams [of horses] on the road and saw more at work in the fields than men," a traveler in Iowa reported in 1862.

Vocabulary Builder
levy (LEHV ee) **v.** to impose by law

Vocabulary Builder
currency (KER rehn see) **n.** money used to make purchases

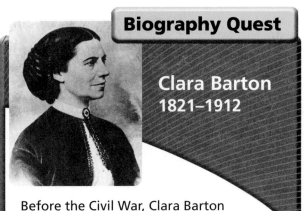

Clara Barton
1821–1912

Before the Civil War, Clara Barton was a clerk in the U.S. Patent Office. When hostilities began, she became a nurse. Her work under dangerous conditions earned her the nickname Angel of the Battlefield from her Union and Confederate patients.

After the war, Barton worked for a time with the International Red Cross. Returning to the United States, Barton helped set up an American branch of the Red Cross.

Biography Quest ◉**nline**

How did Barton become involved in a European war?

For: The answer to the question about Barton
Visit: PHSchool.com
Web Code: myd-5114

Women on both sides did factory work. Some performed dangerous jobs, such as making ammunition. Others took government jobs. For example, the Confederate government employed dozens of women to sign and number Confederate currency.

The war created many new opportunities for women. Some women became teachers. About 10,000 northern women became nurses. Men had dominated these professions before the war.

Barriers to women especially fell in the field of nursing. Elizabeth Blackwell, America's first female physician, trained nurses for the Union army. Social reformer Dorothea Dix became the head of Union army nurses. Harriet Tubman, who continued to lead enslaved people to freedom during the war, also served as a Union nurse. Clara Barton cared for wounded soldiers on the battlefield. Although nursing was not considered a "proper" job for respectable southern women, some volunteered anyway.

✓**Checkpoint** **How did the war affect women?**

☆ **Looking Back and Ahead** Both sides suffered political and economic hardships during the war. Draft laws affected every family, while new jobs opened up for women. In the next section, you will read how the war finally ended in the defeat of the Confederacy.

Section 4 | Check Your Progress

Progress Monitoring ◉**nline**
For: Self-test with instant help
Visit: PHSchool.com
Web Code: mya-5114

Comprehension and Critical Thinking

1. **(a) Identify** What were two reasons some northerners opposed the war? What were two reasons some southerners opposed the war?
(b) Explain Problems Why did the military draft lead some people to describe the war as a poor man's fight?

2. **(a) Describe** Explain the changing role for women during the Civil War.
(b) Identify Costs What effects did the Civil War have on the economies of the North and of the South?

⟳ Reading Skill

3. **Explain How Events Are Related in Time** What was happening to the American economy as the Civil War raged on?

Key Terms

4. Draw a table with four rows and three columns. In the first column, list the key terms from this section: habeas corpus, draft, income tax, inflation. In the next column, write the definition of each term. In the last column, make a small illustration that shows the meaning of the term.

Writing

5. Reread the text under the heading "Women in the Civil War." Then, write a short paragraph about the role that women played in the Civil War. Include material directly quoted from this section. Be sure to copy the quotation exactly, to punctuate it correctly, and to identify the source.

A Valiant Foe

❝I felt . . . sad and depressed at the downfall of a foe who had fought so long and valiantly, and had suffered so much for a cause, though that cause was, I believe, one of the worst for which a people ever fought.❞

—General Grant, expressing his feelings about General Lee

◄ General Grant (left) accepts General Lee's surrender.

Decisive Battles

Objectives

- Describe the significance of the battles at Vicksburg and Gettysburg.
- Explain how Union generals used a new type of war to defeat the Confederacy.
- Explain how the war ended.

⟳ Reading Skill

Relate Events in a Sequence Events in sequence are often connected by a cause-and-effect link. One event causes an event that occurs next. This event in turn can cause another to occur. As you read Section 5, look for sequential events, and then determine if they have a cause-and-effect relationship. Remember, however, that not all events in sequence have this link.

Key Terms and People

siege
William Tecumseh
  Sherman

total war

Why It Matters By 1863, the Civil War had produced hundreds of thousands of dead and wounded. As the fighting raged on, there seemed to be no end in sight. But decisive battles at Gettysburg and Vicksburg would change the war's course and enable the Union to win the Civil War.

❓ **Section Focus Question: How did Lincoln and his generals turn the tide of the war?**

The Tide Turns

After the Union victory at the 1862 Battle of Antietam, the war again began to go badly for the North. As before, the problem was poor leadership. When McClellan failed to pursue Lee's beaten army, Lincoln replaced him with General Ambrose Burnside.

Confederate Victories Burnside knew McClellan had been fired for being too cautious. So Burnside decided on a bold stroke. In December 1862, he marched his army of 120,000 men directly toward Richmond. Lee massed 75,000 men at Fredericksburg, Virginia, to block their path. Using traditional tactics, Burnside ordered charge after charge. The Union suffered nearly 13,000 casualties in the Battle of Fredericksburg and the Confederates nearly 5,000.

Lincoln next turned to General Joseph Hooker, nicknamed "Fighting Joe." "May God have mercy on General Lee, for I will have none," Hooker boasted as he marched the Union army toward Richmond. In May 1863, Hooker's army was smashed at the Battle of Chancellorsville by a force that was half its size. But the victory was a costly one for the South. During the battle, Stonewall Jackson was shot and wounded. A few days later, Jackson died.

The Battle of Gettysburg

The Battle of Gettysburg These Confederate victories made Lee bolder. He was convinced that a major victory on Union soil would force northerners to end the war. In June 1863, Lee's troops crossed Maryland and marched into Pennsylvania. The Union army, which was now commanded by General George Meade, pursued them.

On July 1, some Confederate soldiers approached the quiet town of Gettysburg. They were looking for shoes, which were in short supply in the South because of the Union blockade. Instead of shoes, the Confederates <u>encountered</u> part of Meade's army. Shots were exchanged. More troops joined the fight on both sides. By evening, the southerners had pushed the Union forces back through Gettysburg.

The next day, more than 85,000 Union soldiers faced some 75,000 Confederates. The center of the Union army was on a hill called Cemetery Ridge. The center of the Confederate position was nearly a mile away, on Seminary Ridge. The fighting raged into the next day as Confederate troops attacked each end of the Union line.

On the afternoon of July 3, Lee ordered an all-out attack on the center of the Union line. General George E. Pickett led about 15,000 Confederates across nearly a mile of open field toward Cemetery Ridge. As they advanced, Union artillery shells and rifle fire rained down on them. Only a few hundred men reached the Union lines, and they were quickly driven back. About 7,500 Confederates were killed or wounded in what is known as Pickett's Charge.

Vocabulary Builder
<u>encounter</u> (ehn KOWN ter) **v.** to meet in an unexpected way; to experience

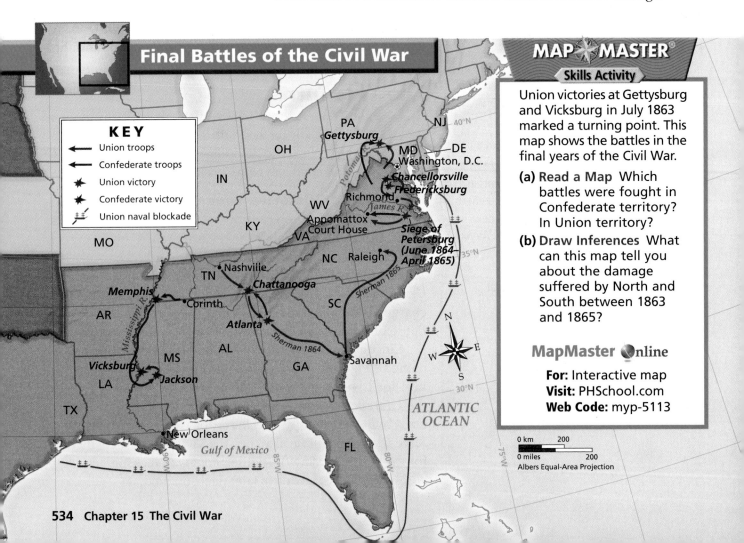

Final Battles of the Civil War

KEY
⟵ Union troops
⟵ Confederate troops
✦ Union victory
✦ Confederate victory
⚓ Union naval blockade

MAP MASTER®
Skills Activity

Union victories at Gettysburg and Vicksburg in July 1863 marked a turning point. This map shows the battles in the final years of the Civil War.

(a) **Read a Map** Which battles were fought in Confederate territory? In Union territory?

(b) **Draw Inferences** What can this map tell you about the damage suffered by North and South between 1863 and 1865?

MapMaster ●nline

For: Interactive map
Visit: PHSchool.com
Web Code: myp-5113

0 km 200
0 miles 200
Albers Equal-Area Projection

In all, the Confederacy suffered more than 28,000 casualties during the three-day Battle of Gettysburg. Union losses <u>exceeded</u> 23,000. For a second time, Lee had lost nearly a third of his troops. "It's all my fault," he said as he rode among his surviving soldiers. "It is I who have lost this fight."

The Fall of Vicksburg On July 4, 1863, as Lee's shattered army began its retreat from Gettysburg, the South suffered another major blow far to the south and west. Vicksburg surrendered to General Grant. It had been one of the last cities on the Mississippi River to remain in Confederate hands. Unable to take Vicksburg by force, Grant had begun a siege of the city in May 1863. A **siege** is an attempt to capture a place by surrounding it with military forces and cutting it off until the people inside surrender.

Day after day, Union guns bombarded Vicksburg. Residents took shelter in cellars and in caves they dug in hillsides. They ate mules and rats to keep from starving. After six weeks, the 30,000 Confederate troops at Vicksburg finally gave up. A few days later, the last Confederate stronghold on the Mississippi River, Port Hudson, Louisiana, also gave up. The entire river was now under Union control.

These events, coupled with Lee's defeat at Gettysburg, make July 1863 the major turning point of the Civil War. Now the Union had the upper hand.

The Gettysburg Address In November 1863, about 15,000 people gathered on the battlefield at Gettysburg to honor the soldiers who had died there. In what is now known as the Gettysburg Address, Lincoln looked ahead to a final Union victory. He said:

Vocabulary Builder
exceed (ehks SEED) **v.** to go beyond what is expected; to be greater than what was planned

Union General Ulysses S. Grant

> **❝**We here highly resolve that these dead shall not have died in vain—that this nation, under God, shall have a new birth of freedom—and that government of the people, by the people, for the people, shall not perish from the earth.**❞**
> —Abraham Lincoln, Gettysburg Address, November 19, 1863

☑ **Checkpoint** **Identify two events that marked turning points in the Civil War.**

Closing In on the Confederacy

In Ulysses S. Grant, President Lincoln found the kind of commander he had long sought. In 1864, the President gave him command of all Union forces. Grant decided that he must attack Richmond, no matter how large the Union losses.

Grant Versus Lee Grant's huge army hammered at the Confederates in a series of battles in northern Virginia in the spring of 1864. Grant was unable to break through Lee's troops. But Grant did not retreat. Instead, he continued the attack.

Cause and Effect

CAUSES
- Issue of slavery in the territories divides the North and South.
- Abolitionists want slavery to end.
- Southern states secede after Lincoln's election.

THE CIVIL WAR

EFFECTS
- Lincoln issues the Emancipation Proclamation.
- Total war destroys the South's economy.
- Hundreds of thousands of Americans killed.

Reading Charts
Skills Activity

The Civil War had multiple causes—and multiple effects.

(a) **Analyze Cause and Effect** Why did the North fear the extension of slavery to the West?

(b) **Draw Conclusions** Which effects were felt mainly in the South? Which effects were felt mainly in the North?

Relate Events in a Sequence

What happened first, the Union's victory in Atlanta or President Lincoln's reelection? Explain how these events are related in sequence.

After seven weeks of fighting, Grant had lost about 55,000 men; the Confederates had lost 35,000. Grant realized that his army could count on a steady stream of men and supplies. Lee, on the other hand, was running out of both.

The two armies clashed at Petersburg, an important railroad center south of Richmond. There, in June 1864, Grant began a siege, the tactic he had used at Vicksburg.

While Grant besieged Lee, another Union army under General William Tecumseh Sherman advanced toward Atlanta. Like Grant, Sherman was a tough soldier. He believed in total war—all-out attacks aimed at destroying an enemy's army, its resources, and its people's will to fight. Sherman later said:

> "We are not only fighting hostile armies, but a hostile people, and must make young and old, rich and poor, feel the hard hand of war."
>
> —William T. Sherman, *Memoirs*, 1886

March to the Sea The Confederates could not stop Sherman's advance. The Union army marched into Atlanta on September 2, 1864. Atlanta's capture gave President Lincoln's reelection campaign a boost. In the months before the capture of Atlanta, many northerners had grown tired of the war. Support for Lincoln had been lagging. But after Atlanta's fall, Lincoln won a huge election victory over General George McClellan, the Democrats' candidate.

In November, Sherman ordered Atlanta burned. He then marched east toward the Atlantic Ocean. Along the way, Union troops set fire to buildings, seized crops and livestock, and pulled up railroad tracks. They left a path of destruction up to 60 miles wide. In February 1865, the army headed north across the Carolinas.

Checkpoint How did Sherman show "the hard hand of war"?

Peace at Last

In March 1865, Grant's army still waited outside Petersburg. For months, Grant had been extending his battle lines east and west of Petersburg. Lee knew it was only a matter of time before Grant would capture the city.

Lincoln, too, saw that the end of the war was near. In his Second Inaugural Address in March 1865, he asked Americans to forgive and forget. "With malice toward none; with charity for all; . . . let us strive together . . . to bind up the nation's wounds," said Lincoln.

Surrender at Appomattox On April 2, Grant's troops finally broke through Confederate lines. By evening, Richmond was in Union hands. Lee's army retreated to the town of Appomattox Court House. There, on April 9, 1865, his escape cut off, Lee surrendered.

Grant offered Lee generous surrender terms. The Confederates had only to give up their weapons and leave in peace. As Lee rode off, some Union troops started to celebrate the surrender. But Grant silenced them. "The war is over," he said. "The rebels are our countrymen again."

The War's Terrible Toll The Civil War was the bloodiest conflict the United States has ever fought. About 260,000 Confederate soldiers gave their lives in the war. The number of Union dead exceeded 360,000, including 37,000 African Americans. Nearly a half million men were wounded. Many returned home disfigured for life.

The war had two key results: It reunited the nation and put an end to slavery. However, a century would pass before African Americans would begin to experience the full meaning of freedom.

☑**Checkpoint** **Why did Lee finally decide to surrender?**

☆ **Looking Back and Ahead** With Lee's surrender, the long and bitter war came to an end. In the next chapter, you will read how U.S. leaders tried to patch the Union together again.

Section 5 | **Check Your Progress**

Progress Monitoring ⊕nline
For: Self-test with instant help
Visit: PHSchool.com
Web Code: mya-5115

Comprehension and Critical Thinking

1. **(a) Identify** Why are the battles at Gettysburg and Vicksburg considered a turning point?
   (b) Understand Sequence How did the advantages of the North at the start of the war continue to be advantages?

2. **(a) Classify** Classify each of the following people as either a Union general or a Confederate general: Ambrose Burnside, Robert E. Lee, Ulysses S. Grant, William Tecumseh Sherman.
   (b) Distinguish Facts From Opinions Write three facts and three opinions Grant might have stated about the Civil War.

⟳ Reading Skill

3. **Relate Events in a Sequence** What events led to the turning point of the Civil War in July 1863? How did those events change the war?

Key Terms

Complete each of the following sentences so that the second part further explains the first part and clearly shows your understanding of the key term.

4. Grant placed Vicksburg under a siege; _____.

5. Sherman pursued a total war; _____.

Writing

6. This section says that the Civil War took more than 620,000 American lives. Research and record the number of American deaths in World War I, World War II, Korea, and Vietnam. Compare the total number of American lives lost in these wars to the number lost in the Civil War. Then, write a paragraph to make a point about your findings. Also, credit the sources of published information you used.

21st Century Learning A primary source is information about people or events presented by someone who lived through what is being described. Speeches are primary sources that can give important information about historical figures and events.

President Lincoln gave this speech at the dedication of the battlefield cemetery at Gettysburg.

Primary Source

"Fourscore and seven years ago our fathers brought forth on this continent a new nation, conceived in Liberty, and dedicated to the proposition that all men are created equal.

Now we are engaged in a great civil war, testing whether that nation, or any nation so conceived and so dedicated, can long endure. We are met on a great battlefield of that war. We have come to dedicate a portion of that field as a final resting place for those who here gave their lives that the nation might live. It is altogether fitting and proper that we should do this.

But in a larger sense, we cannot dedicate, we cannot consecrate, we cannot hallow, this ground. The brave men, living and dead, who struggled here have consecrated it, far above our poor power to add or detract. The world will little note, nor long remember, what we say here, but it can never forget what they did here. It is for us the living, rather, to be dedicated here to the unfinished work which they who fought here have thus far so nobly advanced. It is rather for us to be here dedicated to the great task remaining before us—that from these honored dead we take increased devotion to that cause for which they gave the last full measure of devotion—that we here highly resolve that these dead shall not have died in vain—that this nation, under God, shall have a new birth of freedom—and that government of the people, by the people, for the people, shall not perish from the earth."

—Abraham Lincoln, November 19, 1863

Learn the Skill
Use these steps to analyze a speech.

❶ **Identify the source.** Find out who gave the speech, when it was given, and why it was given.

❷ **Identify the main idea.** Read carefully to discover what the main idea of the speech is. What do you think the speaker wanted to tell his or her audience?

❸ **Identify the point of view.** Often a speechmaker wants to persuade listeners to share his or her feelings. Read carefully to determine the point of view of the speechmaker. Look for language that expresses strong feelings.

Practice the Skill
Answer the questions about the speech above.

❶ **Identify the source.** (a) Who wrote the speech? (b) When was the speech given? (c) Why was it given?

❷ **Identify the main idea.** What is the most important idea in the speech?

❸ **Identify the point of view.** (a) What is the speaker's opinion of the Civil War? (b) What words or phrases express his feelings? (c) Why do you think he feels this way?

Apply the Skill
See the Review and Assessment at the end of this chapter.

Quick Study Guide

How did people, places, and things affect the outcome of the Civil War?

Section 1
The Call to Arms

- The Civil War was a war of Americans against Americans.
- Both the North and the South used their advantages in planning military strategy.

Section 2
Early Years of the War

- New weapons made fighting the war more dangerous.
- Despite many battles early in the war, neither side gained a clear advantage.

Section 3
The Emancipation Proclamation

- The Emancipation Proclamation freed enslaved people in areas of rebellion.
- The Emancipation Proclamation changed the Civil War into a fight to end slavery.
- Approximately 189,000 African Americans served in the Union army and navy.

Section 4
The Civil War and American Life

- The Civil War caused divisions in both the North and the South.
- Draft laws that seemed to favor the wealthy led to protests and riots.
- The Civil War caused economic hardships and also led to changes in women's roles.

Section 5
Decisive Battles

- Major Confederate losses at Gettysburg and Vicksburg marked a turning point.
- Lee surrendered to Grant on April 9, 1865, at Appomattox Court House.
- Some 620,000 soldiers died in the Civil War.

? Exploring the Essential Question

Use the online study guide to explore the essential question.

Section 1
Why did each side in the Civil War think the war would be won easily?

Section 2
How did each side in the war try to gain an advantage over the other?

Chapter 15 Essential Question
How did people, places, and things affect the outcome of the Civil War?

Section 5
How did Lincoln and his generals turn the tide of the war?

Section 3
What were the causes and effects of the Emancipation Proclamation?

Section 4
How did the war affect people and politics in the North and the South?

Key Terms

Answer the following questions in complete sentences that show your understanding of the key terms.

1. Which army, the Union or the Confederate, sustained more casualties?

2. Why did Kentucky cease being neutral?

3. What was both Lincoln's and Davis's purpose in suspending habeas corpus?

4. How did Grant's siege of Vicksburg lead to the surrender of Confederate troops?

Comprehension and Critical Thinking

5. (a) **Recall** Why was it critical to keep Maryland in the Union?
(b) **Analyze Cause and Effect** What was the effect of Lincoln's declaring martial law in Maryland?

6. (a) **Identify** Why did President Lincoln issue the Emancipation Proclamation?
(b) **Explain Problems** What were two limitations of the Emancipation Proclamation?

7. (a) **Describe** What roles did women play in the Civil War?
(b) **Identify Economic Benefits** In what way did the hardships of the Civil War provide new opportunities for women?
(c) **Link Past and Present** Make a list of three opportunities that are open to women today that once were limited to men.

8. (a) **Classify** Create a chart of the battles fought at these places: Bull Run, Antietam Creek, Shiloh, Fredericksburg, Vicksburg, Gettysburg, Petersburg. Classify each battle as either a Union victory or a Confederate victory.
(b) **Detect Bias** Reread the excerpt from Lincoln's Gettysburg Address found in Section 5. Do you think the address gave more comfort to northerners or to southerners? Why?

9. (a) **Summarize** Write three sentences that explain how the Civil War ended.
(b) **Make Predictions** Do you think the surrender of the Confederate army at Appomattox Court House brought an end to the conflict between the northern and southern states? Explain.

History Reading Skill

10. **Understand Sequence** In a paragraph, summarize the events in the Civil War on the battlefield and on the home front. Use signal words to clarify the sequence. Where appropriate, show cause-effect links between events in sequence.

Writing

11. **Write on the following topic:**
Find more information about a Civil War general. Write four paragraphs about him, using the guidelines below.
• The first paragraph should introduce the general and present a thesis.
• The second and third paragraphs should support this thesis by giving some background about the general's life, actions, and character.
• The fourth paragraph should draw a conclusion about the general.

12. **Write a Narrative:**
Choose one of the following roles: soldier, civilian, or nurse. Write two paragraphs of descriptive narrative telling about your experience in the Civil War.

Skills for Life
Analyze a Speech
Use the quotation below to answer the questions.

> ". . . the people of the Confederate States, in their conventions, determined that the wrongs which they had suffered and the evils with which they were menaced required that they should revoke the delegation of powers to the Federal Government which they had ratified in their several conventions. They consequently passed ordinances [laws] resuming all their rights as sovereign and independent States. . . ."
>
> —Jefferson Davis, April 29, 1861

13. (a) Who is the writer?
(b) When was this written?

14. What is the main idea?

15. (a) What words or phrases show the writer's feelings?
(b) Why do you think he feels this way?

Test Yourself

Refer to the quotation below to answer Question 1.

> "I now hold in contemplation of universal law and of the Constitution [that] the Union of these States is perpetual. . . . It follows from these views that no State upon its own mere motion can lawfully get out of the Union. . . ."
>
> —Abraham Lincoln, March 4, 1861

1. This quotation shows that Lincoln wanted to

A allow southern states to secede.

B amend the Constitution.

C abolish slavery.

D preserve the Union.

2. Which of the following granted freedom to all African Americans in areas of rebellion against the Union in 1863?

A Gettysburg Address

B Thirteenth Amendment

C Emancipation Proclamation

D surrender at Appomattox Court House

3. Which of the following was the North's most important advantage in the Civil War?

A Britain and other European nations sent economic aid.

B The nation's most experienced military leaders were northerners.

C The North had a larger population and more resources than the South.

D Northerners were united in their support for the war.

Document-Based Questions

Task: Look at Documents 1 and 2, and answer their accompanying questions. Then, use the documents and your knowledge of history to complete this writing assignment:

> Write an essay describing the disagreement between the Copperheads and northern supporters of the Civil War. Include specific details about each side's position.

Document 1: Clement L. Vallandigham, an Ohio congressman, gave this speech in New York City in March 1863. *What does Vallandigham propose? How does that represent the Copperhead position?*

> "When I see that the experiment of blood has failed, . . . I am not one of those who proclaim . . . that we shall have separation and disunion. I am for going back to the instrumentality through which this Union was first made, and by which alone it can be restored.
>
> I am for peace, because it is the first step toward conciliation and compromise. You cannot move until you have first taken that indispensable preliminary—a cessation of hostilities. . . .
>
> Let men of intelligence judge: let history attest it hereafter. My theory . . . then, is this—stop this war."

Document 2: Copperheads were probably the most outspoken critics of the war in the North. *What opinion of Copperheads does this cartoon present?*

Reconstruction and the New South

New South

1863-1896

"We knowed freedom was on us....
We thought we was going
to get rich like the white folks....
But it didn't turn out that way."

—Felix Haywood,
former slave, on Reconstruction

Students and teachers pose
outside the Freedmen's Bureau
school in Beaufort, South Carolina.

CHAPTER 16

What You Will Learn

Section 1
REBUILDING THE NATION
As the Civil War ended, Americans faced the problem of how to reunite the nation.

Section 2
THE BATTLE OVER RECONSTRUCTION
Disagreements over Reconstruction led to conflict in the government and in the South.

Section 3
THE END OF RECONSTRUCTION
With the end of Reconstruction, African Americans in the South lost many of the rights they had gained.

Reading Skill

Analyze and Evaluate Proposals
In this chapter, you will learn to identify central issues and frame good research questions in order to analyze and evaluate proposals.

543

Reconstruction and the New South

Military Districts, 1867

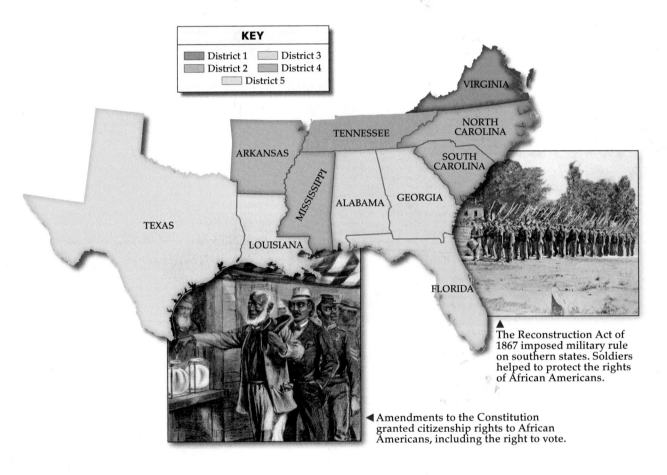

KEY
District 1 District 3
District 2 District 4
District 5

VIRGINIA
NORTH CAROLINA
TENNESSEE
ARKANSAS
SOUTH CAROLINA
MISSISSIPPI
ALABAMA GEORGIA
TEXAS
LOUISIANA
FLORIDA

▲ The Reconstruction Act of 1867 imposed military rule on southern states. Soldiers helped to protect the rights of African Americans.

◀ Amendments to the Constitution granted citizenship rights to African Americans, including the right to vote.

U.S. Events

President Lincoln proposes mild Reconstruction plan. | 1863 | 1865 | Lincoln is assassinated five days after war ends. | 1867 | Radical Reconstruction begins.

1860　　　　**1865**　　　　**1870**

World Events

1867 | Dominion of Canada is formed.

Self-Rule Returns to the South

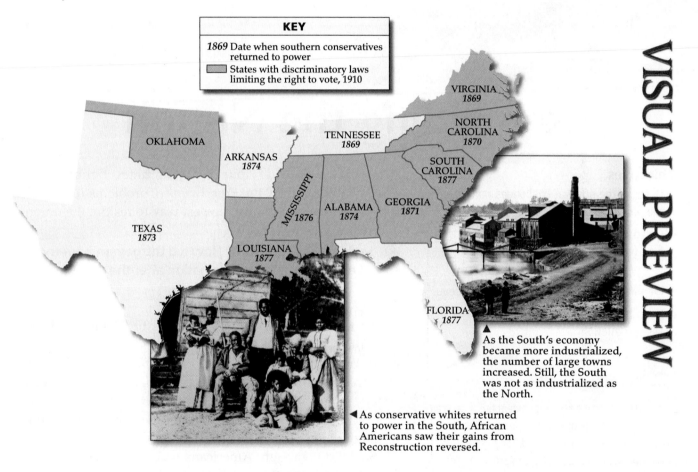

KEY

1869 Date when southern conservatives returned to power

States with discriminatory laws limiting the right to vote, 1910

OKLAHOMA

TEXAS
1873

ARKANSAS
1874

MISSISSIPPI
1876

LOUISIANA
1877

TENNESSEE
1869

ALABAMA
1874

GEORGIA
1871

VIRGINIA
1869

NORTH CAROLINA
1870

SOUTH CAROLINA
1877

FLORIDA
1877

▲ As the South's economy became more industrialized, the number of large towns increased. Still, the South was not as industrialized as the North.

◄ As conservative whites returned to power in the South, African Americans saw their gains from Reconstruction reversed.

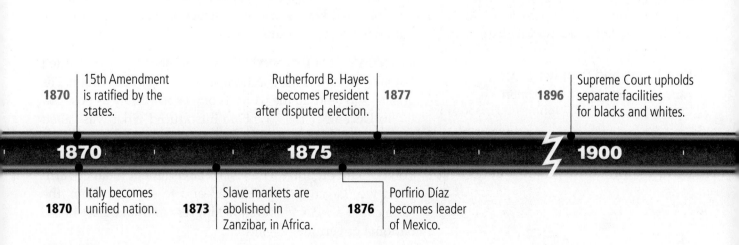

1870 15th Amendment is ratified by the states.

Rutherford B. Hayes becomes President after disputed election. **1877**

1896 Supreme Court upholds separate facilities for blacks and whites.

1870

1875

1900

1870 Italy becomes unified nation.

1873 Slave markets are abolished in Zanzibar, in Africa.

1876 Porfirio Díaz becomes leader of Mexico.

Bind Up the Nation's Wounds

❝ With malice toward none, with charity for all, with firmness in the right as God gives us to see the right, let us strive on to finish the work we are in, to bind up the nation's wounds, to care for him who shall have borne the battle and for his widow and his orphan—to do all which may achieve and cherish a just and lasting peace . . . . ❞

—Abraham Lincoln,
Second Inaugural Address, 1865

◀ As Civil War soldiers returned home, President Lincoln hoped to swiftly heal the nation.

Rebuilding the Nation

Objectives

- Describe the postwar challenges that faced the nation.
- Compare and contrast President Lincoln's plan for Reconstruction with the plan proposed by Congress.
- Identify the goals of the Freedmen's Bureau.
- Describe the immediate impact of Lincoln's assassination.

🎯 Reading Skill

Identify Proposals In turbulent times, such as after the Civil War, people may have many different ideas about how to move forward. They identify goals to achieve and propose solutions to problems. For example, each proposal made by a government leader was intended to achieve a specific goal. As you read Section 1, identify these proposals and goals.

Key Terms and People

Abraham Lincoln   freedman
amnesty   John Wilkes Booth

Why It Matters After four years of bitter fighting, the Union had won the Civil War. Even so, problems remained as Americans tried to find the best way to restore the union and rebuild the nation.

❓ Section Focus Question: How did the government try to solve key problems facing the nation after the Civil War?

Preparing for Reunion

As the Civil War ended, enormous problems faced the nation, especially the South. Vast stretches of the South lay in ruins. What provisions would be made for people who had been freed from slavery? Homeless refugees—both African American and white—needed food, shelter, and work. (For more on conditions in the South after the Civil War, see the Life at the Time feature at the end of this section.)

Somehow, though, Americans had to master their hard feelings and bring the North and the South together again. This process, known as Reconstruction, would occupy the nation for years to come.

Lincoln's Ten Percent Plan Abraham Lincoln wanted to make it easy for the southern states to rejoin the Union. His goal was to bind up the wounds of war as quickly as possible.

In December 1863, Lincoln introduced what was called the Ten Percent Plan. As soon as ten percent of a state's voters swore an oath of loyalty to the United States, the voters could organize a new state government. That government would have to declare an end to slavery. Then, the state could send members to Congress and take part in the national government again.

Lincoln's plan included amnesty for former Confederates who took the loyalty oath. An amnesty is a group pardon. The offer of amnesty did not apply to Confederate government leaders and top military officers.

The Wade-Davis Bill Six months later, Congress passed a much stricter plan for Reconstruction called the Wade-Davis Bill. Under that bill, 50 percent of voters would have to sign a loyalty oath before a state could return to the Union. Moreover, anyone who had <u>voluntarily</u> fought for the Confederacy would be barred from voting for delegates to a convention to write a new state constitution. The bill did not give them a right to vote. Lincoln would not sign the Wade-Davis Bill, so it never became law.

Lincoln and his fellow Republicans hoped to see a strong Republican Party in the new South. Lincoln thought that his "soft," or lenient, Reconstruction policy would win support from influential southerners. Supporters of a strict policy toward the South, known as Radical Republicans, disagreed. They argued that only a strict plan would keep the people who had led the South into secession from regaining power and weakening the control of the Radical Republicans.

✔**Checkpoint** How did Lincoln's plan for Reconstruction differ from that of the Radical Republicans in Congress?

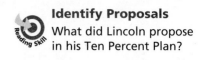

Identify Proposals
What did Lincoln propose in his Ten Percent Plan?

Vocabulary Builder
<u>voluntary</u> (VAHL ahn tair ee) *adj.* not forced; done of one's own free will

Destruction in the South
Parts of Richmond, capital of the Confederacy, lay in ruins at war's end. **Critical Thinking: *Interpret Photographs*** *What do you think would be the most urgent need of the people of Richmond?*

The Freedmen's Bureau

It was urgent to deal with the needs of freedmen, enslaved people who had been freed by the war, as well as other war refugees. Congress created the Freedmen's Bureau in March 1865. The bureau's first duty was to provide emergency relief to people displaced by the war.

Education The Freedmen's Bureau set up schools to teach freedmen to read and write. So great was the hunger for education that many African American communities started schools on their own. To pay a teacher, people pooled their pennies and dollars.

Many teachers were northern white women, but a large number were northern African American women. Edmonia Highgate, the daughter of freed slaves, taught at a Freedmen's Bureau school in Louisiana. "The majority of my pupils come from plantations, three, four and even eight miles distant," she wrote. "So anxious are they to learn that they walk these distances so early in the morning."

Most southern states had lacked systems of public education before the war. Now, public schools began to educate both blacks and whites. The Freedmen's Bureau helped to start schools at which African Americans could extend their education. These schools gave rise to such present-day institutions as Fisk University in Tennessee and Hampton University in Virginia.

Vocabulary Builder
resolve (ree SAHLV) *v.* to decide; to solve

Defending Freedmen The Freedmen's Bureau helped freedmen find jobs and <u>resolved</u> disputes between whites and blacks. Some people tried to cheat the freedmen. The Freedmen's Bureau set up its own courts to deal with such disputes.

✓**Checkpoint** What was the Freedmen's Bureau?

Assassinated! Lincoln's assassination set off an intense hunt for the killer, John Wilkes Booth. *Critical Thinking: Make Predictions* *What effect do you think the assassination of Lincoln would have on the nation?*

Lincoln Is Murdered

As the war drew to a close, President Lincoln hoped for a peaceful Reconstruction. But Lincoln had no chance to put his plans into practice. He was shot dead on April 14, 1865, five days after Lee's surrender.

A Confederate sympathizer, John Wilkes Booth, slipped up behind Lincoln while he and his wife were attending a play at the Ford's Theatre in Washington. Booth fired a single pistol shot into the President's head. Lincoln died a few hours later.

Booth was shot dead two weeks later after pursuers trapped him in a barn and set it on fire. Eight people were convicted and four were hanged for their parts in the plot to kill Lincoln.

News of Lincoln's death shocked the nation. A special funeral train carried Lincoln's body back to Illinois for burial. In town after town, vast crowds paid their last respects.

Lincoln's successor was Vice President Andrew Johnson of Tennessee. Johnson was a southern Democrat who had remained loyal to the Union. Because Johnson had expressed bitterness toward the Confederates, many expected him to take a strict approach to Reconstruction.

✓Checkpoint **Why did many people expect Johnson to take a hard line on Reconstruction?**

⭐ **Looking Back and Ahead** Many people feared the effect of Lincoln's assassination on the process of Reconstruction. In the next section, you will learn how Reconstruction was affected by tensions between Lincoln's successor and members of Congress.

Section 1 | Check Your Progress

Progress Monitoring Online
For: Self-test with instant help
Visit: PHSchool.com
Web Code: mya-5121

Comprehension and Critical Thinking

1. **(a) Recall** What problems faced the South at the end of the Civil War?
   (b) Contrast Why did the South have greater difficulty than the North in recovering from the Civil War?

2. **(a) Recall** How did Lincoln's plan for Reconstruction differ from the Wade-Davis Bill?
   (b) Explain Problems What problems do you see for reuniting the nation in each plan?

Reading Skill

3. **Identify Proposals** Reread the paragraphs under the heading "The Freedmen's Bureau." What did the bureau propose to do to help the freedmen?

Key Terms

Answer the following questions in complete sentences that show your understanding of the key terms.

4. What did former Confederates have to do to get amnesty under Lincoln's plan to rebuild the Union?

5. Who were the freedmen?

Writing

6. Choose the best sentence to end a research paper about Abraham Lincoln. Explain your choice.
   Sentences:
   (a) Abraham Lincoln was humbly born on February 12, 1809, but he went on to be one of our greatest Presidents.
   (b) Because Abraham Lincoln did not win a majority of the votes cast, his presidency turned out to be the nation's most turbulent period.
   (c) His trials as President changed Lincoln into the steady leader who saved the Union in its darkest hour.

The South After the Civil War

The Civil War had a devastating impact on the South. All southerners—rich and poor, black and white—faced a long struggle to rebuild their lives and their land.

Confederate battle flag

Destroyed plantation

▲ Physical Destruction

Most of the fighting during the Civil War took place in the South. After Confederate bombardment at the beginning of the War, the interior of Fort Sumter was destroyed. Cities and plantations lay in charred ruins. Two thirds of the railroads were destroyed.

▶ Wounded Soldiers

A quarter of a million Confederate soldiers died in the war. Thousands more were disabled by their wounds.

Returning Confederate veteran

Freedmen's school

Teaching people to read

▲ Freedmen

For nearly 4 million freedmen, the end of the Civil War was a time of both hope and fear. They were no longer enslaved. But most had no land, no jobs, and no education. The first task was to teach them to read.

Confederate money

◀ Financial Ruin

The economy of the South was ruined. Confederate money was suddenly worthless. Many banks closed, and people lost their life's savings.

Analyze LIFE AT THE TIME

Take one of the following roles: a wounded veteran; a planter whose plantation has been destroyed; a freedman. Write a paragraph explaining how you feel about the end of the war and the possibilities for the future.

Who Shall Rule the South?

" Rebels found themselves in places of trust, while the truehearted Unionists, who had watched for the coming of our flag and ought to have to have enjoyed its protecting power, were driven into hiding places. "

—Senator Charles Sumner, criticizing President Johnson's Reconstruction actions in the South, 1868

◄ President Andrew Johnson

The Battle Over Reconstruction

Objectives

- Explain why conflicts developed over plans for Reconstruction.
- Describe the changes in the South brought about by Radical Reconstruction.
- Explain how Congress tried to remove President Johnson from office.
- Describe how the Ku Klux Klan and other secret societies tried to prevent African Americans from exercising their rights.

🔁 Reading Skill

Analyze Proposals Proposals must be carried out in order to be effective. The proposal must include details on how to put the proposal into action. As you read Section 2, look at the suggested ideas for carrying out proposals.

Key Terms and People

Andrew Johnson
black codes
Hiram Revels
Blanche Bruce
scalawag
carpetbagger
impeachment

Why It Matters The Radical Republicans in Congress wanted a strict form of Reconstruction. However, President Johnson had a more lenient plan. The stage was set for a battle between Congress and the Presidency.

❓ Section Focus Question: How did disagreements over Reconstruction lead to conflict in government and in the South?

A Growing Conflict

Like President Lincoln, Andrew Johnson proposed a relatively lenient plan of Reconstruction. He followed Lincoln's example in putting his plan into effect himself, without consulting legislators.

The Thirteenth Amendment In January 1865, Congress approved a constitutional amendment to abolish slavery throughout the nation. When ratified later that year, the Thirteenth Amendment banned both slavery and forced labor. It gave Congress the power to make laws to enforce its terms.

Johnson's Plan Like Lincoln, Johnson issued a broad amnesty to most former Confederates. Johnson allowed southern states to organize new governments and elect representatives to Congress. Each state, though, was required to abolish slavery and ratify the Thirteenth Amendment. By late fall, most of the states had met Johnson's requirements. When Congress met in December 1865, the representatives and senators elected by white southerners included many former Confederate leaders.

Violence Against Freedmen

Popular magazines carried pictures of violence against freedmen, including the burning of a school (above) and the riots in Memphis (left). **Critical Thinking:** *Make Predictions* *How do you think northerners might have reacted to these pictures?*

Congress quickly rejected Johnson's approach. First, it refused to seat the southern senators and representatives. Next, the two houses appointed a committee to form a new plan for the South.

In a series of public hearings, the committee heard testimony about black codes—new laws used by southern states to control African Americans. <u>Critics</u> claimed that the codes replaced the system of slavery with near-slavery. In Mississippi, for example, African Americans could not vote or serve on juries. If unable to pay a fine as ordered by a court, they might be hired out by the sheriff to any white person who paid the fine.

Anger at these developments led Congress to adopt an increasingly hard line. The hardest line was taken by the Radical Republicans. The Radicals had two key goals. One was to prevent former Confederates from regaining control over southern politics. The other was to protect the freedmen and guarantee them a right to vote.

Vocabulary Builder
<u>critic</u> (KRIHT ihk) ***n.*** someone who makes judgments on the value of objects or actions

☑**Checkpoint** **How did Congress respond to Johnson's plan for Reconstruction?**

The Fourteenth Amendment

The struggle over Reconstruction led to direct clashes between the President and Congress during 1866. At issue were two laws and a constitutional amendment.

Voicing alarm at the treatment of African Americans in the South, Congress passed the Civil Rights Act of 1866. It granted citizenship rights to African Americans and guaranteed the civil rights of all people except Native Americans.

President Johnson vetoed the bill and another one extending the life of the Freedmen's Bureau. Congress voted to overturn both vetoes. Under the Constitution, a vetoed bill becomes law if it wins the votes of two thirds of each house. Both bills received enough votes to become law.

I want a quick reunion.	President Andrew Johnson (1865)	Radical Republicans (1867)	We want real change.
President Andrew Johnson	• Majority of white men must swear oath of loyalty • Must ratify 13th Amendment • Former Confederate officials may vote and hold office	• Must disband state government • Must write new constitution • Must ratify 13th and 14th Amendments • Must allow African American men to vote	Congressman Thaddeus Stevens

Reading Charts
Skills Activity

President Andrew Johnson and Republican members of Congress, led by Thaddeus Stevens, disagreed about the process of Reconstruction.

(a) **Read a Chart** Which plan required states to write new constitutions?

(b) **Detect Points of View** Why did Radical Republicans think Johnson's plan was not strict enough?

Congress also drew up the Fourteenth Amendment to the Constitution, seeking to make sure that the Supreme Court did not strike down the Civil Rights Act. Republicans remembered the Court's Dred Scott decision. In that ruling, the Court declared that no one descended from an enslaved person could be a United States citizen.

The amendment failed at first to win the approval of three fourths of the states. It finally was approved in 1868, after Radicals took control of Reconstruction.

The Fourteenth Amendment says that all people born or naturalized in the United States are citizens. The amendment also declares that states may not pass laws that take away a citizen's rights. Nor can a state "deprive any person of life, liberty, or property, without due process of law; nor deny to any person . . . the equal protection of the laws."

Another provision declares that any state that denies the vote to any male citizen over the age of 21 will have its representation in Congress reduced. That provision was not enforced until the 1970s.

The Fourteenth Amendment became a powerful tool for enforcing civil rights. However, almost a century passed before it was used for that purpose.

Analyze Proposals
Congress proposed the Fourteenth Amendment to give freedmen a way to defend their rights. How would the amendment put that goal into action?

☑Checkpoint **How did the Fourteenth Amendment seek to protect the freedmen?**

Radical Reconstruction

Tempers rose as the elections of 1866 approached. White rioters and police attacked and killed many African Americans in two southern cities, Memphis and New Orleans. Outrage at this violence led Congress to push a stricter form of Reconstruction.

Radicals in Charge By early 1867, the Radical Republicans had won enough support from moderates to begin a "hard" Reconstruction. This period is known as Radical Reconstruction.

The Reconstruction Act of 1867 removed the governments of all southern states that had refused to ratify the Fourteenth Amendment. It then imposed military rule on these states, dividing them into five military districts. Before returning to the Union, each state had to write a new constitution and ratify the Fourteenth Amendment. Each state also had to let African Americans vote.

Under military rule, the South took on a new look. Soldiers helped register southern blacks to vote. In five states, African American voters outnumbered white voters. In the election of 1868, Republicans won all southern states. The states wrote new constitutions and, in June 1868, Congress seated representatives from seven "reconstructed" states.

Vocabulary Builder
register (REJ is tur) **v.** enroll or record officially

Time of Hope and Advancement For the first time, African Americans in the South played an active role in politics. Prominent among them were free-born African Americans—carpenters, barbers, preachers—and former Union soldiers.

African Americans were elected as sheriffs, mayors, judges, and legislators. Sixteen African Americans served in the U.S. House of Representatives between 1872 and 1901. Two others, Hiram Revels and Blanche Bruce, served in the Senate.

Historians once took a critical view of Radical Reconstruction, focusing on the widespread corruption and excessive spending during this period. More recently, however, historians have written about important accomplishments of Reconstruction. They noted that during Reconstruction, southern states opened public schools for the first time. Legislators spread taxes more evenly and made fairer voting rules. They gave property rights to women. In addition, states rebuilt bridges, roads, and buildings destroyed by the war.

Radical Reconstruction brought other sweeping changes to the South. Old leaders lost much of their power. The Republican Party built a strong following based on three key groups. One group, called scalawags by their opponents, were southern whites who had opposed secession. Freedmen voters made up a second group.

The third group were carpetbaggers, a name given by southerners to northern whites who went south to start businesses or pursue political office. Critics claimed that these northerners were in such a rush to head south that they just tossed their clothes into cheap satchels called carpetbags.

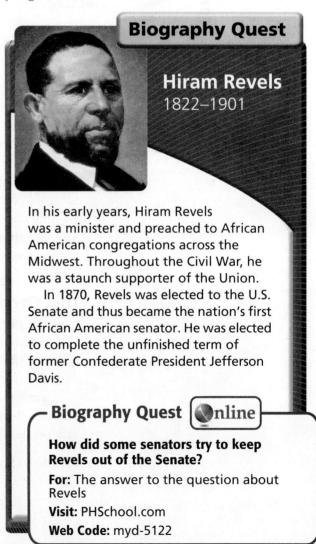

Biography Quest

Hiram Revels
1822–1901

In his early years, Hiram Revels was a minister and preached to African American congregations across the Midwest. Throughout the Civil War, he was a staunch supporter of the Union.

In 1870, Revels was elected to the U.S. Senate and thus became the nation's first African American senator. He was elected to complete the unfinished term of former Confederate President Jefferson Davis.

Biography Quest ⬤nline

How did some senators try to keep Revels out of the Senate?

For: The answer to the question about Revels

Visit: PHSchool.com

Web Code: myd-5122

The terror—"WORSE THAN SLAVERY"

Burning school-house

Targeting President Johnson Meanwhile, the Radicals mounted a major challenge against President Johnson. The Radicals tried to remove Johnson from office by impeachment. Impeachment is the bringing of formal charges against a public official. The Constitution says the House may impeach a President for "treason, bribery, or other high crimes and misdemeanors." After impeachment, there is a trial in the Senate. If convicted, the President is removed from office.

Johnson escaped removal—but barely. The House voted to impeach him in February 1868. The Senate trial took place from March to May. In the end, the votes went 35 for and 19 against Johnson. This was one vote short of the required two-thirds majority.

The Election of 1868 General Ulysses S. Grant, a war hero, won the presidential election for the Republicans in the fall of 1868. With southern states back in the Union under military rule, some 500,000 African Americans voted, mainly for Republicans. Grant won the electoral votes of 26 of the 34 states.

Grant was a moderate who had support from many northern business leaders. With his election, the Radicals began losing their grip on the Republican Party.

Fifteenth Amendment Over opposition from Democrats, Congress approved the Fifteenth Amendment in 1869. It barred all states from denying African American males the right to vote "on account of race, color, or previous condition of servitude."

Some African Americans said the amendment was too weak. It did not prevent states from requiring voters to own property or pay a voting tax. The amendment took effect in 1870, after three fourths of the states gave their approval.

The Ku Klux Klan Angry at being shut out of power, some whites resorted to violence. They created secret societies to terrorize African Americans and their white allies.

The best-known secret society was the Ku Klux Klan. Its members donned white robes with hoods that hid their faces. Klansmen rode by night to the homes of African American voters, shouting threats and burning wooden crosses. If threats failed, the Klan would whip, torture, shoot, or hang African Americans and white Republicans. Klan violence took hundreds of lives during the election of 1868.

The terror went on even after Congress responded with new laws. The Ku Klux Klan Acts of 1870 and 1871 barred the use of force against voters. Although the original Klan dissolved, new groups took its place. In the face of the terrorism, voting by African Americans declined. The stage was set for the end of Reconstruction.

✓**Checkpoint** What were the key elements of Radical Reconstruction?

⭐ **Looking Back and Ahead** Although Reconstruction guaranteed rights to more Americans, huge challenges remained. In the next section, you will learn more about the process of rebuilding the South. You will also learn that as time went on, Americans became less interested in Reconstruction. This set the scene for a return of power to former Confederates.

Terror and Violence

To spread terror, Ku Klux Klan members wore hoods like the one above when they attacked their victims. They also left miniature coffins as warnings. **Critical Thinking: *Draw Conclusions*** *Why do you think the hoods helped spread terror?*

Section 2 | Check Your Progress

Progress Monitoring 🌐nline
For: Self-test with instant help
Visit: PHSchool.com
Web Code: mya-5122

Comprehension and Critical Thinking

1. (a) Recall Which amendment guaranteed African Americans the right to vote: the Thirteenth, Fourteenth, or Fifteenth?
(b) Apply Information How did each of these three amendments help to expand democracy?

2. (a) Recall What was the Ku Klux Klan?
(b) Evaluate Information Why do you think the Klan was not formed before the Civil War?

🔵 **Reading Skill**

3. Analyze Proposals In 1867, the Radical Republicans in Congress proposed the Reconstruction Act. What actions did this proposal involve?

Key Terms

Complete each of the following sentences so that the second part clearly shows your understanding of the key term.
4. Radical Republicans in the House of Representatives tried to remove the President by impeachment, which is _____.

5. Former Confederates wanted to control the lives of freedmen through black codes, which were _____.

Writing

6. Rewrite the following passage to correct the grammar, spelling, and punctuation errors that you find. **Passage:** President Johnson wanting to show mercy to the defeated confederacy. Many of the republicans in Congress, however, opposed him. Because they wanted to protect the freedman. This conflict led congress to held impeechment hearings.

A Southern Viewpoint

❝It would be best for the peace, harmony, and prosperity of the whole country that there should be an immediate restoration, an immediate bringing back of the states into their original practical relations.❞

— Alexander H. Stephens, urging an end to federal control of southern states, 1866

◄ Cartoon criticizing northern carpetbaggers in the South

The End of Reconstruction

Objectives

- Explain why support for Reconstruction declined.
- Describe how African Americans in the South lost many newly gained rights.
- Describe the sharecropping system and how it trapped many in a cycle of poverty.
- Identify the signs that the South began to develop a stronger economy by the 1880s.

Reading Skill

Evaluate Proposals When you read a proposal, ask yourself: Is the proposal likely to work as a way of advancing its goal?

Key Terms and People

poll tax
literacy test
grandfather clause

segregation
Homer Plessy
sharecropper

Why It Matters The South experienced reforms during the Reconstruction era. However, many of the changes were quite temporary. When Reconstruction ended, African Americans were subjected to new hardships and injustices. It would take more than a century to overcome these injustices.

❷ **Section Focus Question: What were the effects of Reconstruction?**

Reconstruction's Conclusion

Support for Radical Republicans declined as Americans began to forget the Civil War and focus on bettering their own lives. Scandals within President Grant's administration played an important role. Grant made poor appointments to public offices, often appointing personal friends. Many of the appointees proved to be corrupt. Although Grant himself had no part in the corruption that took place, his reputation suffered. Grant won reelection in 1872, but many northerners lost faith in the Republicans and their policies.

Self-rule for the South Meanwhile, many people in both North and South were calling for the withdrawal of federal troops and full amnesty for former Confederates. Starting with Virginia in 1869, opponents of Republicans began to take back the South, state by state. Slowly, they chipped away at the rights of African Americans.

In some states, campaigns of terror by secret societies were a major factor in restoring their power. By 1874, Republicans had lost control of all but three southern states. By 1877, Democrats controlled those, too.

The Election of 1876 The end of Reconstruction was a direct result of the presidential election of 1876. Because of disputes over election returns, the choice of the President was decided by Congress. There, a deal between the Republicans and Democrats settled the election—and sealed the fate of Reconstruction.

The candidates in 1876 were Rutherford B. Hayes of Ohio for the Republicans and Samuel J. Tilden of New York for the Democrats. The Republicans said they would continue Reconstruction, and the Democrats said they would end it.

Tilden won the popular vote by 250,000 votes. However, 20 electoral votes were in dispute. Without them, Tilden fell one vote short of the 185 needed to win in the electoral college.

To resolve the issue, Congress appointed a special commission of 15 members. Most of them were Republicans. The commission gave all 20 electoral votes to Hayes. Rather than fight the decision in Congress, Democrats agreed to accept it. Hayes had privately told them that he would end Reconstruction. Once in office, Hayes removed all federal troops from the South.

Evaluate Proposals
What proposal did Hayes make to the Democrats in order to end their opposition? How did this proposal meet the goals of both the Democrats and Republicans?

✓**Checkpoint** **What factors contributed to the end of Reconstruction?**

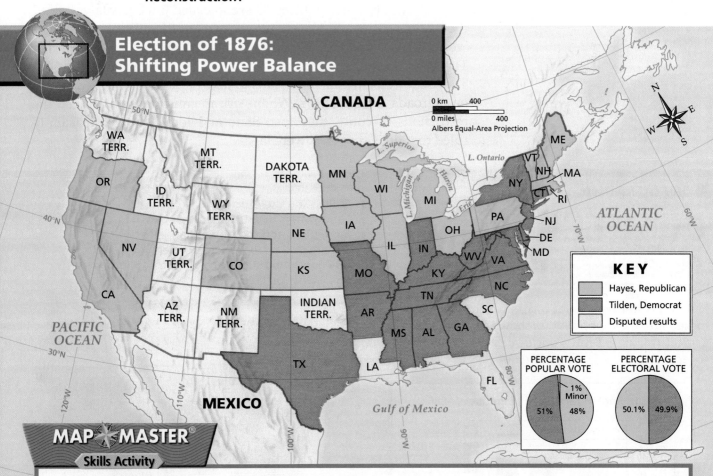

Election of 1876: Shifting Power Balance

KEY
- Hayes, Republican
- Tilden, Democrat
- Disputed results

PERCENTAGE POPULAR VOTE: 51% / 48% / 1% Minor

PERCENTAGE ELECTORAL VOTE: 50.1% / 49.9%

Albers Equal-Area Projection

MAP★MASTER®
Skills Activity

Although Samuel Tilden won the popular vote, Rutherford B. Hayes was declared the winner in the election.

(a) **Read a Map Key** In which region did Tilden have the most support?

(b) **Draw Conclusions** Based on this map, do you think the Civil War ended sectionalism? Explain.

MapMaster ●nline

For: Interactive map
Visit: PHSchool.com
Web Code: myp-5123

African Americans Lose Rights

With the end of Reconstruction, African Americans began to lose their remaining political and civil rights in the South. Southern whites used a variety of techniques to stop African Americans from voting. They passed laws that applied to whites and African Americans but were enforced mainly against African Americans.

One such law imposed a **poll tax**—a personal tax to be paid before voting. This kept a few poor whites and many poor freedmen from voting. Another law required voters to pass a **literacy test,** or a test to see if a person can read and write. In this case, voters were <u>required</u> to read a section of the Constitution and explain it.

However, a grandfather clause allowed illiterate white males to vote. The **grandfather clause** was a provision that allowed a voter to avoid a literacy test if his father or grandfather had been eligible to vote on January 1, 1867. Because no African American in the South could vote before 1868, nearly all were denied the right to vote.

Southern states created a network of laws requiring **segregation,** or enforced separation of races. These so-called Jim Crow laws barred the mixing of races in almost every aspect of life. Blacks and whites were born in separate hospitals and buried in separate cemeteries. The laws decreed separate playgrounds, restaurants, and schools. They required African Americans to take back seats or separate cars on railroads and streetcars. When African Americans challenged the restrictions in court, they lost. State and local courts consistently ruled that Jim Crow laws were legal.

Vocabulary Builder
<u>require</u> (rih KWYR) **v.** to order or command

● **INFOGRAPHIC**

SHARECROPPING
CYCLE OF POVERTY

Farming land they did not own, sharecroppers were locked into a cycle of debt, as shown by the illustration.
Critical Thinking: *Draw Conclusions Why was it hard for sharecroppers to escape the debt cycle?*

1. Planting the Crop
Landowners give the sharecropper land, seed, and tools in exchange for a share in the crop. Sharecroppers buy goods and supplies from the landowner on credit.

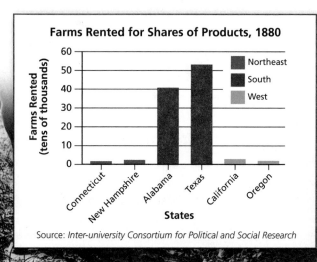

Farms Rented for Shares of Products, 1880

Y-axis: Farms Rented (tens of thousands) — 0, 10, 20, 30, 40, 50, 60
X-axis (States): Connecticut, New Hampshire, Alabama, Texas, California, Oregon
Legend: Northeast, South, West

Source: *Inter-university Consortium for Political and Social Research*

In 1896, the U.S. Supreme Court upheld segregation laws. Homer Plessy had been arrested for sitting in a coach marked "for whites only." In the case of *Plessy* v. *Ferguson,* the Court ruled in favor of a Louisiana law requiring segregated railroad cars. The Court said a law could require "separate" facilities, so long as they were "equal."

This "separate but equal" rule was in effect until the 1950s. In fact, facilities for African Americans were rarely equal. For example, public schools for African Americans were almost always <u>inferior</u> to schools for whites.

Vocabulary Builder
<u>inferior</u> (ihn FIR ee uhr) *adj.* of lower rank or status, or of poorer quality

☑**Checkpoint** **What methods did southern states use to deprive African Americans of their rights?**

A Cycle of Poverty

At emancipation, many freedmen owned little more than the clothes they wore. Poverty forced many African Americans, as well as poor whites, to become sharecroppers. A **sharecropper** is a laborer who works the land for the farmer who owns it, in exchange for a share of the value of the crop.

The landlord supplied living quarters, tools, seed, and food on credit. At harvest time, the landlord sold the crop and tallied up how much went to the sharecroppers. Often, especially in years of low crop prices or bad harvests, the sharecroppers' share was not enough to cover what they owed the landlord for rent and supplies. As a result, most sharecroppers became locked into a cycle of debt.

2. Harvesting the Crop and Settling Accounts
The sharecropper gives the landowner his crop. Landowner sells it and gives the tenant his share, minus the amount owed at the company store.

History *Interactive*
Explore the Sharecropping Cycle
Visit: PHSchool.com
Web Code: myp-5127

3. Cycle of Debt
After a year of hard work, the sharecroppers often owed more than they had earned and had no choice but to offer the landlord a greater percentage of next year's crop.

Links Across Time

1963 Dr. Martin Luther King, Jr., speaks to Americans in Washington, D.C.

Fighting for Civil Rights

1896 In *Plessy* v. *Ferguson*, the Supreme Court upheld segregation laws in the South. These restrictions continued for more than 50 years.

1950s–1960s Some Americans launched a campaign to bring equal rights to African Americans. This civil rights movement used marches, petitions, and other public actions to end discrimination in education, use of public facilities, and voting.

Link to Today Online

Civil Rights Today Did the civil rights movement win equal rights for all Americans? Not everyone agrees. Go online to find out more about recent developments in civil rights.

For: Civil rights in the news
Visit: PHSchool.com
Web Code: myc-5123

Opportunities dwindled for African Americans in southern towns and cities, too. African American artisans who had been able to find skilled jobs during Reconstruction increasingly found such jobs closed to them. Those with some education could become schoolteachers, lawyers, or preachers in the African American community. But most urban African Americans had to take whatever menial job they could find.

✓Checkpoint How did many freedmen and whites become locked in a cycle of poverty?

Industrial Growth

It would be a long process, but during Reconstruction the South's economy began to recover. By the 1880s, new industries appeared. Southerners hailed a "New South," based on industrial growth.

The first element of the South's economy to begin recovery was agriculture. Cotton production, which had lagged during the war, quickly revived. By 1875, it was setting new records. Planters put more land into tobacco production, and output grew.

Southern investors started or expanded industries to turn raw materials into finished products. The textile industry came to play an important role in the southern economy.

The South had natural resources in abundance, but it had done little to develop them in the past. Atlanta newspaper editor Henry Grady described the funeral of a man from Georgia as follows:

> **“**They buried him in the heart of a pine forest, and yet the pine coffin was imported from Cincinnati. They buried him within touch of an iron mine, and yet the nails in his coffin and the iron in the shovel that dug his grave were imported from Pittsburgh.**”**
>
> —Henry Grady to the Bay State Club of Boston, 1889

The South began to develop its own resources. New mills and factories grew up to use the South's iron, timber, and oil. Lumber mills and furniture factories processed yellow pine and hardwoods from southern forests.

Southern leaders took great pride in the region's progress. They spoke of a "New South" that was no longer dependent on "King Cotton." An industrial age was underway, although the North was still far more industrialized.

☑**Checkpoint** **What was the "New South" that was emerging by 1900?**

⭐ **Looking Back and Ahead** When Reconstruction ended in 1877, its record showed many successes and some failures. Most importantly, all African Americans were finally citizens. Laws passed during Reconstruction, such as the Fourteenth Amendment, became the basis of the civil rights movement that took place almost 100 years later.

HISTORIAN'S APPRENTICE ACTIVITY PACK

To further explore the topics in this chapter, complete the activity in the Historian's Apprentice Activity Pack to answer this essential question:

Was Reconstruction a success or a failure?

Factory in the "New South"

Section 3 | Check Your Progress

Comprehension and Critical Thinking

1. (a) Identify Who were share-croppers? How did they differ from landowners?
(b) Draw Conclusions Why did so many sharecroppers live in poverty?

2. (a) Recall What is segregation?
(b) Analyze Cause and Effect How did *Plessy* v. *Ferguson* make the fight against segregation more difficult?

🔵 Reading Skill

3. Evaluate Proposals In *Plessy* v. *Ferguson*, the Supreme Court proposed the idea of "separate but equal" facilities. Do you think this idea meets the goal of ensuring equal rights?

Key Terms

Complete each of the following sentences so that the second part clearly shows your understanding of the key term.
4. African Americans and whites had to pay a poll tax before _____.

5. Because of laws in the South requiring segregation, African Americans and whites _____.

Writing

6. Rewrite the following passage to correct the errors. **Passage:** The 1876 presidential election decided by a special commission. Samuel J. Tilden a democrat won the Popular vote over republican Rutherford B. Hayes. However, their were 20 disputed electoral votes. A special commission made an agreement with the democrats.

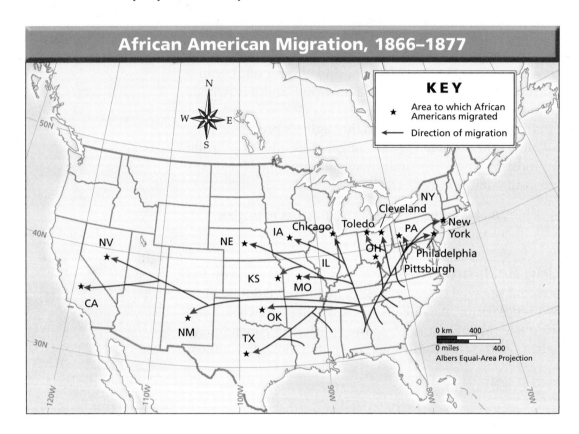

21st Century Learning Thematic maps focus on special topics, such as food products, physical features, or political boundaries. Information presented in a visual way is easier to understand and absorb. One type of thematic map shows the migration or movement of people within a particular area.

African American Migration, 1866–1877

KEY

★ Area to which African Americans migrated

← Direction of migration

0 km 400
0 miles 400
Albers Equal-Area Projection

Learn the Skill

Use these steps to learn how to trace migrations on maps.

1 Identify the subject of the map. Read the title of the map. Look for dates that identify the time period.

2 Look at the map key. The map key explains special symbols and colors used on the map.

3 Determine direction. To trace the route of a migration, use the direction arrows on the compass rose to identify north, south, east, and west. Then, identify the direction or directions of the route.

4 Make a generalization. Use the information on the map to make a general statement about the historic migration.

Practice the Skill

Answer the following questions about the map on this page.

1 Identify the subject of the map. What is the title of the map?

2 Look at the map key. What does the star symbol show?

3 Determine direction. In which direction did African Americans travel to migrate to New York?

4 Make a generalization. In general, to which areas of the country did African Americans migrate during Reconstruction?

Apply the Skill

See the Review and Assessment at the end of this chapter.

Quick Study Guide

What were the short-term and long-term effects of the Civil War?

Section 1
Rebuilding the Nation

- The South faced major economic and social challenges at the end of the Civil War.
- Reconstruction plans and programs like the Freedmen's Bureau were designed to rebuild the South.
- The death of Abraham Lincoln threatened lenient plans for Reconstruction.

Section 2
The Battle Over Reconstruction

- President Andrew Johnson and the Radical Republicans clashed over Reconstruction plans.
- Conflict over Reconstruction led to Andrew Johnson's impeachment.
- During Reconstruction, African American males gained the right to vote. Republicans came to power in each southern state.

Section 3
The End of Reconstruction

- With the end of Reconstruction, African Americans in the South lost many rights they had gained after the Civil War.
- Many African Americans and poor whites were forced to become sharecroppers.
- The South's agriculture revived, and its industries expanded.

? Exploring the Essential Question

Use the online study guide to explore the essential question.

Section 1
How did the government try to solve key problems facing the nation after the Civil War?

Chapter 16 Essential Question
What were the short-term and long-term effects of the Civil War?

Section 2
How did disagreements over Reconstruction lead to conflict in government and in the South?

Section 3
What were the effects of Reconstruction?

Key Terms
Fill in the blanks with the correct key terms.

1. _____ were people who had been enslaved before emancipation.

2. Northerners who moved south after the Civil War were sometimes called _____.

3. Southern states gave _____, which required voters to read and explain part of the Constitution.

4. A _____ farmed land in return for a portion of the value of the crop.

Comprehension and Critical Thinking

5. **(a) Recall** How did the Wade-Davis Bill differ from Lincoln's plan for reuniting the country?
   (b) Make Predictions How do you think southerners would have reacted to Reconstruction if Lincoln's plan had been followed?

6. **(a) Recall** How did Johnson and the Radicals come into conflict?
   (b) Analyze Cause and Effect How effective do you think Johnson was after the failure of the impeachment process?

7. **(a) Recall** What right is guaranteed by the Fifteenth Amendment?
   (b) Interpret Art How does the painting *His First Vote* (below) reflect how the Fifteenth Amendment affected African Americans?

8. **(a) Recall** How did the Freedman's Bureau help African Americans after the Civil War?
   (b) Make Predictions Which of the actions of the Freedmen's Bureau has probably had the longest lasting impact on African Americans? How?

9. **(a) Recall** What were the terms of the compromise that gave Rutherford B. Hayes the presidency in 1876?
   (b) Draw Conclusions How were African Americans in the South affected by this compromise?

History Reading Skill

10. **Analyze and Evaluate Proposals** Review what you have read about the conflict between Johnson and Radical Republicans. What did each side propose? Which proposal makes the most sense to you? Explain.

Writing

11. **Write an essay on the following topic:**
    Explain how events and developments during Reconstruction highlighted differences between North and South, even as the two tried to reunite.
    Your essay should:
    - state a thesis or purpose for writing;
    - explain the subject you are writing about;
    - offer evidence, examples, or details to support your explanation;
    - conclude with a short summary of your main points.

12. **Write a Narrative:**
    Imagine you are Hiram Revels. Write a narrative describing your first days in the Senate.

Skills for Life
Analyze a Migration Map
Use the map in the Skills for Life feature to answer the questions that follow.

13. What time period is covered in this map?

14. What does the arrow symbol show?

15. In which direction did African Americans travel to migrate to Oklahoma and New Mexico?

16. Based on the information in the map, what decision did many African Americans make during Reconstruction?

Test Yourself

Refer to the quotation below to answer Question 1.

> "A system of oppression so rank that nothing could make it seem small except the fact that [African Americans] had already been ground under it for a century and a half."

1. Which system does this quotation refer to?

A amnesty

B Reconstruction

C sharecropping

D segregation

2. How did African Americans benefit from the passage of the Fourteenth Amendment?

A Their right to vote was protected.

B They became citizens.

C They were given land.

D They no longer had to pass literacy tests.

3. A chief goal of the Freedmen's Bureau was to promote

A abolition.

B industrial growth.

C education.

D segregation.

Document-Based Questions

Task: Look at Documents 1 and 2, and answer their accompanying questions. Then, use the documents and your knowledge of history to complete the following writing assignment:

Write a two-paragraph essay about the goals and methods of the Ku Klux Klan. Using specific details, draw a conclusion about whether Document 1 or Document 2 gives a more accurate description of the Klan.

Document 1: The "Organization and Principles" of the Ku Klux Klan, stated below, was written in 1868. It describes the goals of the Klan. *What does the Klan say is its attitude toward violence?*

> "This is an institution of chivalry, humanity, mercy, and patriotism; embodying in its genius and its principles all that is chivalric in conduct, noble in sentiment, generous in manhood, and patriotic in purpose; its peculiar objects being:
>
> First, to protect the weak, the innocent, and the defenseless from the [insults], wrongs, and outrages of the lawless, the violent, and the brutal; to relieve the injured and oppressed. . . .
>
> *Questions to be asked each [Klan] candidate:*
>
> • Are you in favor of a white man's government in this country? . . ."

Document 2: This political cartoon was published in a northern magazine in 1874. *Describe what has happened to the African American family.*

Unit 5

Historian's Apprentice   Workshop

How was the Civil War a political, economic, and social turning point?

DIRECTIONS: Analyze the following documents from the years before, during, and after the Civil War. Answer the questions that accompany each document or set of documents. You will use your answers to build an answer to the unit question.

HISTORIAN'S CHECKLIST

WHO produced the document?

WHERE was it made?

WHEN was it produced?

WHY was it made and for what audience?

WHAT is its viewpoint?

HOW does it connect to what I've learned?

WHY is the document important?

1 Handbill, Boston, 1851

document

CAUTION!!

COLORED PEOPLE

OF BOSTON, ONE & ALL,

You are hereby respectfully **CAUTIONED** and advised, to avoid conversing with the

Watchmen and Police Officers of Boston,

For since the recent **ORDER OF THE MAYOR & ALDERMEN,** they are empowered to act as

KIDNAPPERS

AND

Slave Catchers,

And they have already been actually employed in **KIDNAPPING, CATCHING, AND KEEPING SLAVES.** Therefore, if you value your **LIBERTY,** and the **Welfare of the Fugitives** among you, **Shun** them in every possible manner, as so many **HOUNDS** on the track of the most unfortunate of your race.

Keep a Sharp Look Out for KIDNAPPERS, and have TOP EYE open.

APRIL 24, 1851.

Was this poster antislavery or proslavery? Explain.

2 Battle of Antietam, 1862

document

Why did hostility between the North and the South continue even after the Civil War was over?

568

3 The Emancipation Proclamation

" Coming generations will cele-brate the first of January as the day which brought liberty and man-hood to American slaves.... That paper Proclamation must now be made iron, lead and fire, by the prompt employment of the negro's arm in this contest. "

—*Frederick Douglass, 1863*

What were the effects of the Emancipation Proclamation?

4 Northern Newspaper's Viewpoint

" There is one, and only one, sure and safe policy for the immediate future: namely: the North must remain the absolute Dictator of the Republic until the spirit of the North shall become the spirit of the whole country....

The South is still unpurged of her treason. Prostrate in the dust she is no less a traitor at this hour than when her head was erect.... They cannot be trusted with authority over their former slaves.... The only hope for the South is to give the ballot to the Negro and in denying it to the rebels. "

—The Independent, *May 5, 1865*

Do you think this editorial helped the nation heal after the Civil War? Why or why not?

5 The South's Postwar Economy

" Our losses have been frightful, and we have, now, scarcely a support. My Father had five plan-tations on the coast, and all the buildings were burnt, and the negroes ... are roaming in a starved condition. Our farm near Charleston was aban-doned.... All is now lost, and the negroes, left to themselves ... seek a little food, about the city. Our residence in the city, was sacked ... and the house well riddled by shell & shot. Our handsome Residence in the country was burnt. The Enemy passed over all our property on the coast in their march from Savannah to Charleston, the whole country, down there, is now a howling wilder-ness.... [I]t will be many years, before this once productive country will be able to support itself. "

—*Edward Barnwell Heyward, South Carolina planter, 1866*

How did the Civil War affect the South's economy?

 Go On

6 An African American Senator

"[M]y downtrodden people . . . bear toward their former masters no revengeful thoughts, no hatreds, no animosities. They aim not to elevate themselves by sacrificing one single interest of their white fellow-citizens. They ask but the rights which are theirs by God's universal law . . . [to] enjoy the liberties of citizenship on the same footing with their white neighbors and friends."

—Hiram Revels, speech in the U.S. Senate, March 16, 1870

Do you think Senator Revels' goals could be achieved in the late 1800s? Why or why not?

7 Worse Than Slavery

How did radical white southerners oppose rights for African Americans?

Why did many African American farmers remain trapped in poverty?

Percentage of sharecropped farms (by county)

0%–20%
21%–34%
35%–80%

Conic Projection
0   100   200 mi
0 100 200 km

VIRGINIA
TENNESSEE
NORTH CAROLINA
ARKANSAS
SOUTH CAROLINA
MISS.
ALABAMA
GEORGIA
TEXAS
LOUISIANA
FLORIDA
Atlantic Ocean
Gulf of Mexico
95°W   85°W

N W E S

ACTIVITY

Divide into three groups to prepare a documentary news program on the unit question:

? How was the Civil War a political, economic, and social turning point?

One group should use the Historian's Apprentice Workshop documents to describe the Civil War's political effects. Another group should use the documents to describe the economic effects of the war. The last group should cover the war's social effects. After each group has had time to prepare a presentation, it should report its findings to the rest of the class in the format of a documentary news program.

Unit 6

 **ESSENTIAL QUESTION**

How did the industrialization of the United States change the economy, society, and politics of the nation?

History *Interactive*
Explore Historian's Apprentice Online
Visit: PHSchool.com
Web Code: mvp-6000

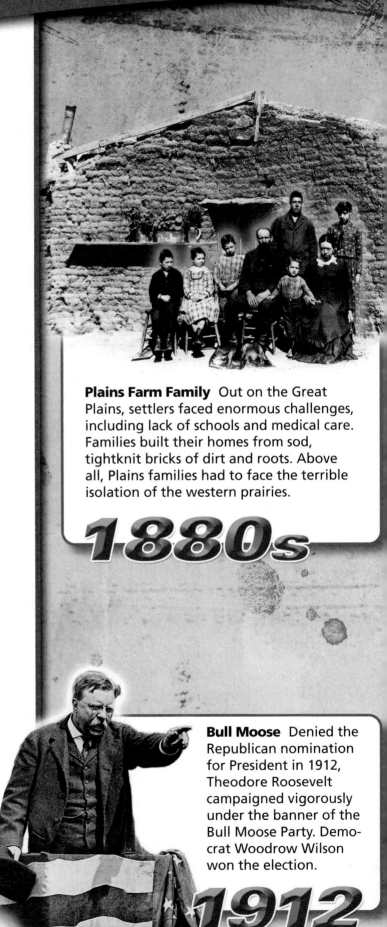

Plains Farm Family Out on the Great Plains, settlers faced enormous challenges, including lack of schools and medical care. Families built their homes from sod, tightknit bricks of dirt and roots. Above all, Plains families had to face the terrible isolation of the western prairies.

1880s

Bull Moose Denied the Republican nomination for President in 1912, Theodore Roosevelt campaigned vigorously under the banner of the Bull Moose Party. Democrat Woodrow Wilson won the election.

1912

An Age of Industry

Geronimo The Apache chief Geronimo led the last important Native American defense against the military might of the United States. In 1886, Geronimo surrendered to a promise of peace. Instead, his people were exiled and imprisoned.

1886

Japanese Immigrants Over 100,000 Japanese immigrated to the United States in the early 1900s. This photo shows a group arriving on the American west coast in the 1920s.

EARLY 1900s

The Fifteen Millionth Ford

The Assembly Line Henry Ford's assembly line greatly reduced the time needed to build a car. Ford could then sell cars at a lower price. Pictured from left are his first Model T from 1908, his first automobile from 1896, and his fifteen millionth Model T.

1920s

The West Transformed

1860-1896

"Ship cattle on the Union Pacific Railroad!... Cattle are now bearing excellent prices east."

—*Union Pacific Railroad advertisement, Wyoming, 1877*

Cowhands drove cattle long distances along dusty trails to reach railroad towns, where the cattle could be shipped east.

Reading Skill

Use Context Clues to Verify Meaning In this chapter, you will learn to use context clues to help you understand the meaning of unfamiliar words or ideas in a text.

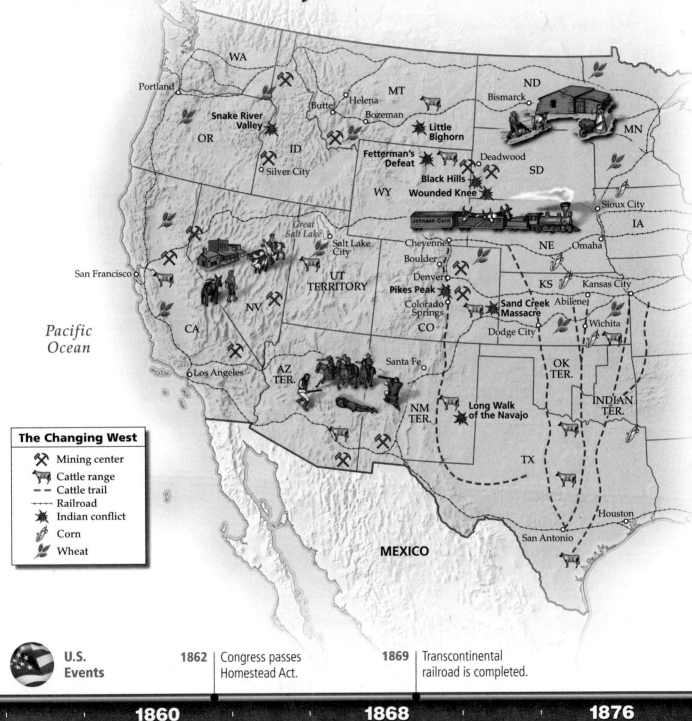

The West Transformed

The Changing West

- ⚒ Mining center
- 🐄 Cattle range
- - - Cattle trail
- ┼┼┼ Railroad
- ✴ Indian conflict
- 🌽 Corn
- 🌾 Wheat

Pacific Ocean

MEXICO

U.S. Events

1862 | Congress passes Homestead Act.

1869 | Transcontinental railroad is completed.

1860   1868   1876

World Events

1864 | Taiping Rebellion in China ends.

1869 | Suez Canal opens.

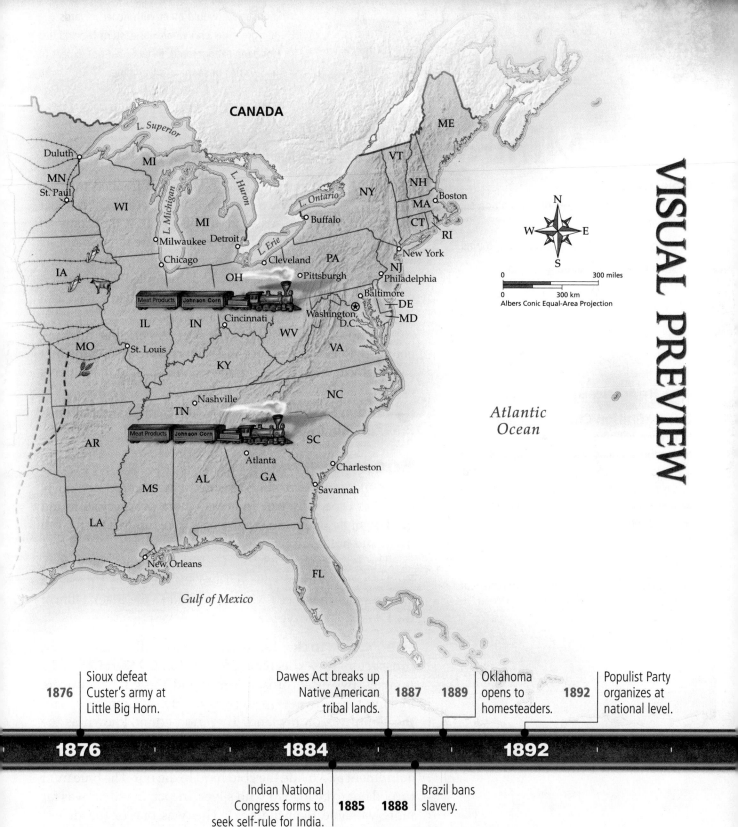

VISUAL PREVIEW

1876 Sioux defeat Custer's army at Little Big Horn.

1887 **1889** Dawes Act breaks up Native American tribal lands.

1889 Oklahoma opens to homesteaders.

1892 Populist Party organizes at national level.

1876

1884

1892

1885 Indian National Congress forms to seek self-rule for India.

1888 Brazil bans slavery.

▼ Western miners

So Many Silver Mines

❝In no country that I have ever seen (not even in California) do I believe that well-directed industry . . . would meet with richer rewards. . . . The great mineral wealth of eastern Nevada has not been exaggerated. In fact I did not expect to find so rich or so many silver mines. **❞**

—Henry Eno, describing mining in Nevada, 1869

Mining and Railroads

Objectives

- Explain how the discovery of gold and silver affected the West.
- Describe life in the western mining towns.
- Summarize how railroads spread and helped the West to develop.

⊙ Reading Skill

Use Definition Clues As you read about history, you will come across unfamiliar words. In this textbook, definitions for many unfamiliar words are included in the text that surrounds the word. When you read a word that you do not know, look at nearby sentences. The unfamiliar word may be repeated and defined.

Key Terms

vigilante
subsidy

transcontinental
railroad

Why It Matters In 1865, America's western frontier stretched from the Mississippi River to the Pacific Ocean. The frontier had prairies, mountains, and forests. It was the home of Native Americans, Mexican settlers, and more recent pioneers who had migrated to California and Oregon. Even so, many Americans thought of the frontier as unsettled. They underestimated the value of the Great Plains, and called it the Great American Desert.

But now, with the Civil War over, Americans' thinking changed. Railroad builders and miners were among the first to transform the West and make it a vital part of the nation's economy.

❓ Section Focus Question: How did mining and railroads draw people to the West?

Boom and Bust

In many parts of the West, settlement came in a rush. This was especially true in areas where prospectors found gold or silver. New mining towns sprang up in a flash—but many did not last long.

The gold rush of 1849 in California excited the nation. Before long, miners spread from California to the Sierra Nevada and the Rocky Mountains and to the Black Hills of the Dakota Territory.

The Comstock Lode Just before the Civil War, prospectors began searching for gold in the Sierra Nevada. In 1859, two Irish prospectors found the gold they were looking for. However, a third man, Henry Comstock, said the claim was on his land. The find became known as the Comstock Lode. A lode is a rich vein of ore.

At the Comstock Lode, a blue-tinted sand stuck to all the equipment and made the gold hard to dig out. The blue mud turned out to be loaded with silver. In fact, the silver was far more valuable than the gold. This was one of the richest silver mines in the world.

In the next 20 years, the Comstock Lode produced $300 million worth of silver and made Nevada a center of mining. A tent city near the mines grew into the boomtown of Virginia City, Nevada.

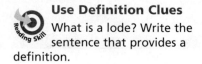

Use Definition Clues
What is a lode? Write the sentence that provides a definition.

The Boom Spreads After the Civil War, prospectors fanned out over the West. They found valuable ores in Montana, Idaho, and Colorado. They made a gold strike in South Dakota's Black Hills. In the 1890s, a gold find drew people from all over the world to Alaska.

Although each strike caused great excitement, few prospectors got rich. The ore was deep underground and expensive to extract. Comstock gave up and sold his mining rights for $11,000 and two mules. Many other prospectors sold their claims to large mining companies. By the 1880s, western mining had become a big business.

Boomtown Life Tent cities like Virginia City often arose around the diggings. Soon hotels, stores, and other wood-frame buildings appeared. Mining camps quickly grew into boomtowns.

Where prospectors went, others followed. Merchants brought mule teams hauling tools, food, and clothing. Nothing was cheap in the boomtown stores. Sometimes, miners paid high prices for bottles of pure drinking water. They did not want to drink from streams that might be polluted with chemicals, like arsenic, used in mining.

Women who joined the mining boom could make a good living. Some opened restaurants. Others washed clothes or took in boarders. One woman just baked pies. In a year, she became quite wealthy.

Nearly half the miners were foreign-born. The streets of the mining towns rang with Irish accents as well as Italian, German, Spanish, Chinese, and other languages. The foreign miners often faced hostility. For example, laws restricted Chinese miners to claims abandoned by others. Mobs often drove the Chinese from towns.

From Boomtown to Ghost Town
In the 1870s, Virginia City, Nevada, had close to 30,000 inhabitants. When the Comstock Lode ran out, Virginia City became a ghost town. Today, it is a thriving tourist attraction. *Critical Thinking: Identify Economic Alternatives* Why did Virginia City become a ghost town? How did it later restore its economy?

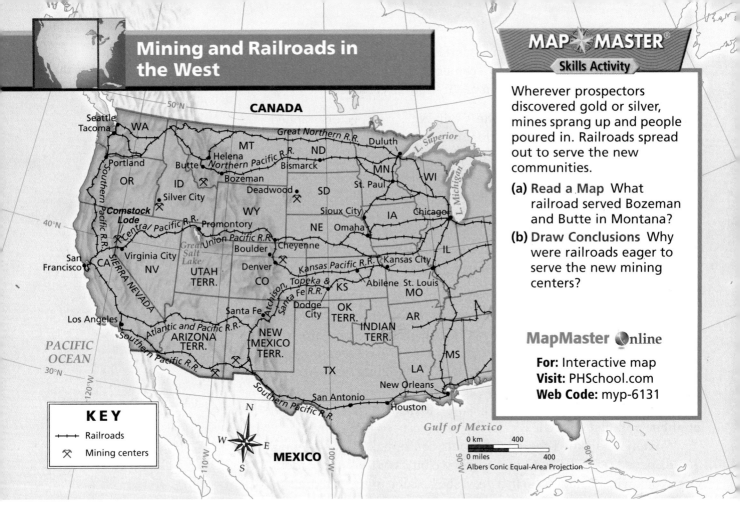

MAP MASTER®

Skills Activity

Wherever prospectors discovered gold or silver, mines sprang up and people poured in. Railroads spread out to serve the new communities.

(a) Read a Map What railroad served Bozeman and Butte in Montana?

(b) Draw Conclusions Why were railroads eager to serve the new mining centers?

MapMaster ●nline

For: Interactive map
Visit: PHSchool.com
Web Code: myp-6131

KEY

+—+—+ Railroads

⚒ Mining centers

Frontier Justice Mining towns sprouted so fast that law and order were hard to find. Miners formed groups of vigilantes, or self-appointed law keepers. Such groups hunted down bandits and imposed their own rough brands of justice.

As boomtowns grew, local residents began to seek more lasting forms of government. Sheriffs, marshals, and judges replaced vigilantes. Colorado, Dakota, and Nevada organized into territories in 1861, followed by Arizona and Idaho in 1863 and Montana in 1864.

In some mining towns, all the ore was soon extracted. Mines shut down and miners moved away. With few customers, businesses failed and merchants left. Boomtowns became ghost towns.

✔**Checkpoint** **Why did boomtowns use vigilante justice?**

The Railroad Boom

Railroads raced to lay track to the mines and boomtowns. They received generous help from the federal government.

Aid to Railroads Before 1860, railroad lines ended at the Mississippi River. Then, the federal government began to offer subsidies. Subsidies are grants of land or money. For every mile of track, the government gave the railroad 10 square miles of land next to the track. Railroads got more than 180 million acres, an area the size of Texas. They also received federal loans.

Spanning the Continent Many westerners dreamed of a transcontinental railroad, a railroad line that spanned the continent. In 1862, Leland Stanford and his partners won the right to build a line eastward from Sacramento. Their railroad was the Central Pacific. Another railroad, the Union Pacific, would build west from Omaha. When the lines met, tracks would stretch from coast to coast.

The railroads hired thousands of workers—native-born whites, Mexican Americans, and African Americans. Workers also <u>immigrated</u> to the United States from Mexico and Ireland. The Central Pacific brought 10,000 Chinese to the United States.

The work was hazardous; the pay low. Cutting through the Sierra Nevada, Chinese <u>manual</u> laborers were lashed by snow and winds. Avalanches buried weeks of work in moments and killed workers by the score. Daily progress sometimes came in inches. (For more on the building of the railroad, see the Geography and History feature.)

At last, on May 10, 1869, the two lines met at Promontory, Utah. Stanford drove the final spike into the last rail with a silver mallet.

Effects of the Railroads New towns sprang up in the West. People and supplies poured in. Gold and silver poured out.

Rapid population growth brought political changes. Nevada became a state in 1864; Colorado in 1876; North Dakota, South Dakota, Montana, and Washington in 1889; Idaho and Wyoming in 1890.

☑Checkpoint **How did the railroads change the West?**

☆ **Looking Back and Ahead** Gold and silver discoveries brought boomtowns to the West. Then came railroads and more settlers. In the next section, you will read how these developments affected the Native Americans who lived in the West.

Vocabulary Builder
immigrate (IHM mah grayt) **v.** to move to a foreign region or country

Vocabulary Builder
manual (MAN yoo ahl) **adj.** involving work done by hand

Section 1 | **Check Your Progress**

Progress Monitoring ●nline
For: Self-test with instant help
Visit: PHSchool.com
Web Code: mya-6131

Comprehension and Critical Thinking

1. **(a) Recall** In 1865, what region of the United States was considered the western frontier?
   (b) Detect Points of View Explain how each of the following groups viewed the western frontier: Americans, Spanish settlers, Native Americans.

2. **(a) Identify** How did the discovery of gold and silver in the West lead to a railroad boom?
   (b) Identify Economic Benefits What incentives did the government offer to railroad builders to extend railroad lines westward?

Reading Skill

3. **Use Definition Clues** Define the term subsidies in the following context, and describe the clue you used: Congress offered generous subsidies to railroads. Subsidies are grants of land or money.

Key Terms

Read each sentence. If the sentence is true, write YES. If the sentence is not true, write NO and explain why.

4. Vigilante groups in the West were replaced by homesteaders.

5. The transcontinental railroad connected the East with the West.

Writing

6. Persuasive writing always centers on an opinion—an idea about which there can be disagreement. Tell whether each of the following statements expresses an opinion or states a fact. **Statements:**
   (a) A valuable gold strike was made in South Dakota's Black Hills.
   (b) The unjust treatment of foreign miners was shameful.
   (c) Creating a coast-to-coast railway was the most important factor in U.S. economic history.
   (d) Some mining camps quickly grew into boomtowns.

Transcontinental Railroad

During the Civil War, Congress passed a bill that provided for the construction of a transcontinental railroad. The new law assigned two companies to build the railroad: the Central Pacific Railroad and the Union Pacific Railroad.

▼ Two Railroads

The Central Pacific headed east from Sacramento. The Union Pacific headed west from Omaha.

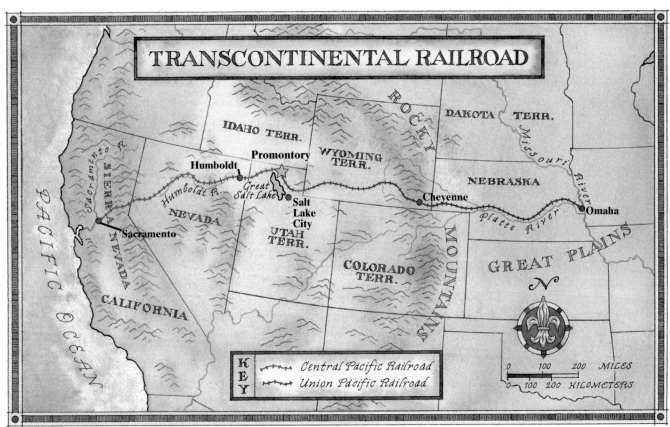

Physical Obstacles ▶

Foul weather and rugged landscapes hampered construction efforts on both lines. The Central Pacific took almost five years to cross the Sierra Nevada.

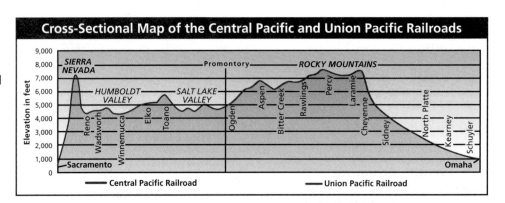

Cross-Sectional Map of the Central Pacific and Union Pacific Railroads

▲ Blasting Through Mountains

The Central Pacific recruited large numbers of Chinese workers to build the railroad. The workers would climb down steep cliffs in the Sierra Nevada and stuff explosives into the rocks to blast tunnels.

Understand Effects:
Moving West

The completion of the transcontinental railroad paved the way for increased settlement of the West. Additional railroads were built in the decades after 1869, and populations of western territories surged. Native Americans were increasingly hemmed in by steady tides of new settlers.

History *Interactive*
Travel the Transcontinental Railroad

Visit: PHSchool.com
Web Code: myp-6137

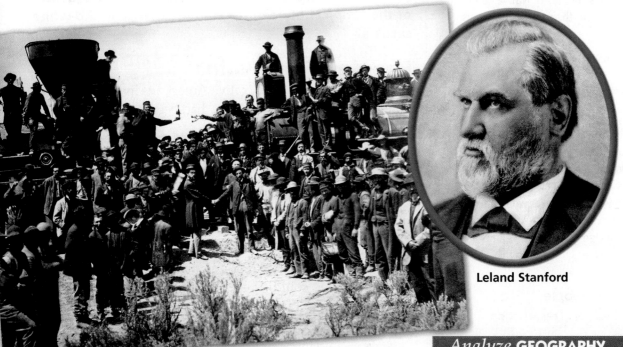

Leland Stanford

▲ A Golden Spike

With the engines No. 119 and Jupiter pulled nose to nose at Promontory, Utah, the railroads were joined by a golden spike on May 10, 1869. Leland Stanford, a railroad executive and later governor of California, supervised construction of the Central Pacific.

Analyze GEOGRAPHY AND HISTORY

Write a paragraph describing how geography affected the construction of the transcontinental railroad. Think about the physical obstacles each railroad company faced along the way.

Leaving the Reservation

❝In the summer of 1883 a rumor was current that the officers were again planning to imprison our leaders. . . . So we held a council ourselves, and fearing treachery, decided to leave the reservation. We thought it more manly to die on the war path than to be killed in prison.❞

—Autobiography of the Apache leader Geronimo

▲ Geronimo (far right)

Native Americans Struggle to Survive

Objectives

- Describe the importance of the buffalo to Native Americans of the Plains.

- Explain how Native Americans and settlers came into conflict.

- Summarize the struggles of Native American groups to maintain their traditional ways of life.

- Explain why Congress passed the Dawes Act in 1887.

🕐 Reading Skill

Use Restatement Clues Like a definition clue, a restatement clue tells you what an unfamiliar word means. It restates in simple language what the word means. Restatement clues often follow the unfamiliar word, linked by a comma and the word *or*. This textbook often uses restatement clues to define key terms and highlights them in blue.

Key Terms and People

travois   reservation
tepee   Sitting Bull

Why It Matters Mining and railroading brought people to the West and turned it into a booming region. However, as people moved to the West, they came into conflict with the Native Americans who lived there. The Indians desperately struggled to preserve their lands and their way of life.

❓ Section Focus Question: What were the consequences of the conflict between the Native Americans and white settlers?

People of the Plains

In 1865, some 360,000 Native Americans lived in the West, mainly on the Great Plains. Many had been there for centuries.

Life in Transition People of the Plains lived by gathering wild foods, hunting, and fishing. Some raised crops. Early Native Americans hunted buffalo and other game on foot. The arrival of the Europeans transformed their lives. Plains nations tamed herds of wild horses, descended from tough breeds brought by the Spanish. They also traded with the French and British for guns.

With guns, Native Americans could kill more game. On horseback, they could travel faster and farther. Even before Europeans arrived though, some groups already traveled far and wide. They carried their belongings on travois (truh VOIZ), or small sleds. They lived in tepees, cone-shaped tents made of buffalo skins.

Many Plains nations followed the buffalo herds. In winter, they trailed the herds into protected valleys and forests. In summer, when grass on the Plains grew tall, hunters tracked the buffalo as they gathered to graze.

People found many uses for the buffalo. Its meat was a protein-rich food. Horns and bones could be made into tools, and tendons could be made into thread. Buffalo hunting thus played a key role in people's survival.

Division of Labors In many Plains nations, women managed village life. They cared for children and prepared food. They carved tools and made clothing and tepees. Sometimes they went to war. In 1876, a Crow woman named The Other Magpie rode against the Sioux for killing her brother. In some groups, a wise woman ruled.

Men were hunters and warriors. Often, they also led religious life. One important ritual was the Sun Dance. The four-day ceremony brought together thousands of Native Americans from many nations. Men would make pledges to the Great Spirit, or ruler of the universe.

☑ **Checkpoint** **Why was the buffalo important to many groups?**

Broken Treaties

U.S. treaties promised to safeguard Native American lands. As miners and railroad crews pushed west, they broke those treaties.

Fort Laramie Treaty In 1851, ten thousand people from many Plains nations gathered near Fort Laramie in Wyoming for a "big talk" with U.S. officials. The officials wanted the nations to stop following the buffalo. If they would settle permanently, the government promised to protect their lands "as long as the grass shall grow."

No sooner had some Native American leaders signed the Fort Laramie Treaty than settlers moved onto their lands. In 1859, a gold strike at Pikes Peak in Colorado sent miners swarming to the region.

Uses of the Buffalo
The buffalo was central to the life of Native Americans living on the Great Plains. It furnished not only food but also many other necessities of life. **Critical Thinking:** *Draw Conclusions Why did the nations of the Plains depend so heavily on the buffalo? How did they cope when the buffalo herds began to disappear?*

Covering Tepees Buffalo hides were used to cover the tepees in which the people of the Plains lived.

Keeping Warm The hairy hides of the buffalo provided clothing and warm coverings, such as this Cheyenne robe. Buffalo tendons made a strong thread for sewing garments together.

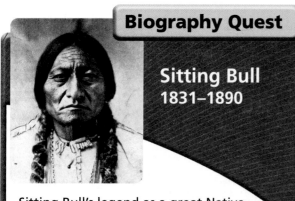

Sitting Bull
1831–1890

Sitting Bull's legend as a great Native American leader began at the age of 10, when he killed his first buffalo. During battle, a warrior would try to get close enough to the enemy to touch him. Sitting Bull excelled at this practice, called "counting coup." He was 14 when he touched his first enemy in battle. He soon became a leader known for his fearlessness in battle.

Biography Quest

What kind of education did Sitting Bull give his children?

For: The answer to the question about Sitting Bull

Visit: PHSchool.com

Web Code: myd-6132

Sand Creek Massacre In the early 1860s, new treaties forced Native Americans to give up land around Pikes Peak. Many warriors resisted. They attacked supply trains and homes.

In response, Colonel John Chivington and 700 volunteers attacked a band of Cheyennes at Sand Creek in eastern Colorado in 1864. These Cheyennes were friendly and under army protection. They raised a white flag to signal peace, but Chivington ordered his men to attack. In the end, more than 100 men, women, and children died.

Buffalo Soldiers The Sand Creek Massacre helped to ignite an era of war. Among the soldiers who fought on the Plains were African American veterans of the Civil War. The Native Americans called them Buffalo Soldiers. The Buffalo Soldiers fought on the Plains for 20 years. They also captured bandits from Texas to the Dakotas.

End of the Buffalo The giant herds of buffalo, so central to Native American life, began to shrink in the 1870s. Railroads had hunters kill the animals to feed their crews. Others also slaughtered buffalo because buffalo robes drew high prices in eastern cities. One hunter might kill 2,000 buffalo in a month.

☑Checkpoint **Why did the buffalo begin to disappear?**

Last Stand for Custer and the Sioux

New treaties in the late 1860s sought to end the wars on the Plains. Federal officials urged Plains nations to settle down and farm.

Reservations Southern Plains nations like the Kiowas, Comanches, and Arapahos moved to reservations in Oklahoma. A reservation is land set aside for Native Americans to live on. Life there was a disaster. Poor soil in Oklahoma made farming difficult.

Many Sioux and Cheyennes gathered on land set aside for them in the Black Hills of the Dakotas. An 1874 gold strike brought a flood of miners. Sitting Bull and Crazy Horse led attacks to keep whites out.

Little Bighorn In June of 1876, under orders to force the Native Americans onto a reservation, Colonel George Armstrong Custer entered the Little Bighorn Valley in Montana Territory. Although outnumbered, he attacked a large band of Sioux and Cheyennes.

Custer and all his men died at the Battle of Little Bighorn. But the victory of Sitting Bull and Crazy Horse was fleeting. One Sioux recalled, "A winter or so later, more soldiers came to round us up on reservations. There were too many of them to fight now."

☑Checkpoint **Why did Custer attack at Little Bighorn?**

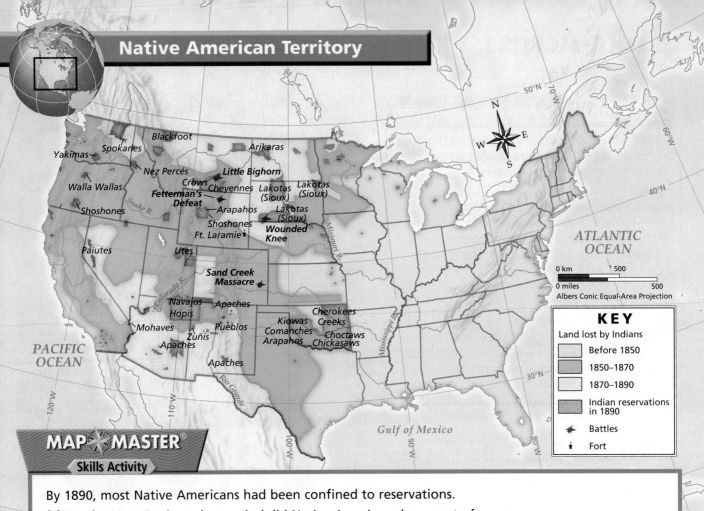

Native American Territory

MAP MASTER
Skills Activity

By 1890, most Native Americans had been confined to reservations.

(a) Read a Map During what period did Native Americans lose most of their land in California?

(b) Draw Conclusions How did being restricted to reservations change the way of life of Native Americans on the Great Plains?

MapMaster Online

For: Interactive map
Visit: PHSchool.com
Web Code: myp-6132

Other Efforts at Resistance

Other Native American nations in the West also came under pressure. Among them were the Nez Percés to the north and the Navajos and Apaches to the south.

The Nez Percés The Nez Percés lived where Idaho, Oregon, and Washington now meet. They bred horses and cattle in the Snake River valley. Under pressure, many agreed to go to a reservation.

Reluctant to see his nation humiliated, Chief Joseph fled toward Canada with a large band of Nez Percés in 1877. The U.S. Army pursued them. In 75 days, the Nez Percés traveled 1,300 miles.

The army caught the Nez Percés near Canada's border. As Chief Joseph surrendered, he said, "I shall fight no more forever."

The Navajos Navajos raised sheep, horses, and cattle in the Southwest. Bands of Navajos also raided settlers' farms for livestock. To stop raids, white settlers called in the army. After a series of wars, the Navajos were defeated in 1864 in Arizona. Soldiers took them on what the Navajos called a "Long Walk" to a spot near the Pecos River. There, they suffered years of disease and hunger.

Vocabulary Builder
reluctant (ree LUHK tehnt) **adj.** not willing to do something

Links Across Time

1968 Native Americans demonstrate in the nation's capital against a bill under consideration by Congress.

Civil Rights for Native Americans

1890 Some 200 Sioux were killed by soldiers at Wounded Knee. This incident brought the period of the Indian Wars to a violent close.

1960s Inspired in part by the civil rights movement, Native Americans organized to demand their rights. Groups such as the American Indian Movement sought to remind Americans of the history of broken treaties between Native Americans and the U.S. government.

Link to Today Online

Native American Rights Today Many Native American rights groups now focus their attention on the Supreme Court. What legal issues affect Native Americans in modern society?

For: Native American rights in the news
Visit: PHSchool.com
Web Code: myc-6132

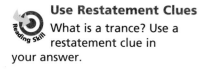

Use Restatement Clues
What is a trance? Use a restatement clue in your answer.

The Apaches Fierce resistance came from Apache warriors like Geronimo, who refused to go to a reservation. From Mexico, Geronimo and his men attacked settlers in Arizona and New Mexico for 10 years. After his capture in 1886, he was sent to a reservation in Oklahoma.

The Ghost Dance Some Native Americans dreamed of returning to old ways. In the late 1880s, Native Americans across the Plains began performing a unique, swaying dance. Dancers fell into a trance, or dreamlike state. They believed they were talking to ghosts of their ancestors, so the dance was called the Ghost Dance. Dancers believed their ancestors and the buffalo would return and white people would leave the Plains. Soldiers guarding reservations saw the dance as the beginning of an uprising. In December 1890, Native American police went to a Sioux village to stop the dances. In a struggle to arrest Sitting Bull, police killed him.

Fearful of further violence, a band of Sioux tried to flee to safety. Army troops surrounded them at Wounded Knee Creek in South Dakota. As the Sioux were giving up their guns, a shot rang out. The troops opened fire with machine guns and rifles. Nearly 200 Sioux men, women, and children were killed. Some 30 soldiers died.

The Battle of Wounded Knee marked the end of the era of Indian Wars. "A people's dream died there," said one chief.

✓**Checkpoint** **What was the purpose of the Ghost Dance?**

The Failure of Reform

Reformers criticized the government for its harsh treatment of Native American nations. Criticism grew as more groups were forced onto reservations in the late 1800s.

Calls for Reform Susette La Flesche knew all about the calamity befalling Native Americans. Her father was an Omaha chief. In lectures and articles, she told of the destruction of native culture.

In 1881, inspired by La Flesche, the poet Helen Hunt Jackson wrote *A Century of Dishonor*. The book recorded the many treaties violated by the government at Native American expense. Alice Fletcher also promoted native rights. She became an agent for the U.S. Bureau of Indian Affairs, which dealt with Native Americans.

Vocabulary Builder
violate (vī ah layt) **v.** to break a rule or law; to disrespect; to disturb

The Dawes Act Hoping to improve Native American life, Congress passed the Dawes Act in 1887. It tried to end Native Americans' wandering and turn them into farmers. Native American males each received 160 acres to farm. The act set up schools to make Native American children more like other Americans.

The Dawes Act failed. Few Native Americans took to farming. Many sold their land cheaply to dishonest whites. Federal agents replaced native leaders, and Native Americans had to give up traditional ways like the buffalo hunt. As a result, they remained poor. Many grew dependent on the government for food and supplies.

✓**Checkpoint** **What was the purpose of the Dawes Act?**

⭐ **Looking Back and Ahead** As settlers poured into the West, buffalo grew scarce. Native Americans were moved onto reservations and forced to change their way of life. In the next section, you will read how some of the settlers made a living in the West.

Section 2 | Check Your Progress

Progress Monitoring ⏺nline
For: Self-test with instant help
Visit: PHSchool.com
Web Code: mya-6132

Comprehension and Critical Thinking

1. (a) Describe How did guns and horses change the lives of Plains Native Americans?
(b) Analyze Cause and Effect What were the short- and long-term effects of hunting buffalo on Native American life?

2. (a) Identify Who was Chief Joseph?
(b) Detect Points of View In 1879, Chief Joseph appeared before Congress. He said, "Treat all men alike. Give them all the same law. Give them all an even chance to live and grow. All men were made by the same Great Spirit Chief." What was Chief Joseph trying to tell Congress? How do you think members of Congress responded to his words?

Reading Skill

3. Use Restatement Clues Use a restatement clue to define the term tepees in the following sentence: They lived in cone-shaped tepees, portable tents made of buffalo skins.

Key Terms

4. Write two definitions for each key term: travois, reservation. First, write a formal definition for your teacher. Second, write a definition in everyday English for a classmate.

Writing

5. Find three pieces of evidence in this section that support or refute the following opinion: In the nineteenth century, the U.S. government treated Native Americans in an unfair way.

CATTLE MEN READ THIS!
Great Inducements to those who wish to
Ship Cattle on the U. P. Railroad!!

Having entered into special arrangements with the U. P. R. R. Company, by which I can ship Cattle East at greatly reduced rates, and having selected a point between Carter and Church Buttes Stations some ten miles East of the former place, near the junction of the Big and Little Muddies, and having Constructed Commodious Lots and Extensive Enclosures, and the Company having put in a Switch capable of holding 40 Cars, I will be Prepared to Commence Shipping on or before the 15th of the Present Month, and will be able to promptly ship any Number of cattle that may be Offered.

We're Almost Froze

❝ When the spring work sets in,
then our troubles will begin
The weather being fierce and cold
We're almost froze, with the water in our clothes
And the cattle we can scarcely hold. ❞

—*Cowboy's Life*, traditional western folk song

◀ Cowboys brought cattle to railroad towns.

The Cattle Kingdom

Objectives

- Explain how the cattle industry began.
- Describe the life of a cowhand on the trail.
- Discuss the myth of the Wild West.
- Identify reasons for the end of the cattle boom.

⟳ Reading Skill

Use Example Clues Writers may offer clues to a word's meaning by giving examples. Consider this sentence: "Canines such as poodles and spaniels make good companions." The examples show that *canines* means "dogs." A writer may describe an example in depth or tell what something does to help you visualize the unfamiliar word. Look for the phrases *such as* and *for example.*

Key Terms

open range
cattle drive
vaquero

cow town
cattle kingdom

Why It Matters As Native Americans were being forced onto reservations, others thrived—at least for a time. For a while, the ranchers who raised cattle on the West's vast open grasslands made great profits. This boom time was relatively short. Even so, the ranchers and the cowboys who worked for them created an American culture that survives to this day.

❷ **Section Focus Question: What factors led to boom and bust in the cattle industry?**

The Rise of the Cattle Industry

For years, wild cattle wandered the open range, or unfenced land, of Texas. Called longhorns for their broad horns, they needed almost no care. They survived on prairie grass and watering holes.

Means and Markets The herds of cattle had grown from strays lost by Spanish ranchers. As American settlers moved in, they set up new ranches. But they did not bother to round up the stray herds because they had no means of getting the cattle to distant markets.

As railroads swept across the Plains in the 1860s, Texans at last saw a way to reach those markets. Protein-rich beef was in demand to feed city dwellers in the East and miners and soldiers in the West.

The Long Drives Ranchers began rounding up the cattle in the 1860s. They hired cowhands—skilled riders who know how to herd cattle—to move the cattle to rail lines in Kansas, Missouri, and Wyoming. Some rail lines were as far away as 1,000 miles.

Spring was an ideal time to begin a cattle drive—the herding and moving of cattle over long distances. Grass grew tall, and rivers flowed full from spring rains. The work was so demanding that cowhands brought a number of horses so that each day a fresh one would be available.

The long drives lasted two to three months. They followed well-worn trails. To the east lay the famous Chisholm Trail from San Antonio, Texas, to Abilene, Kansas. To the west, the Goodnight-Loving Trail led to rail towns in Wyoming. In just one year, as many as 600,000 cattle might be moved north.

☑**Checkpoint** **Why did cattle drives cover long distances?**

Life on the Trail

Life on the trail was hard and dangerous. The long cattle drives tested the nerve and skill of every cowhand.

A Risky Ride Andy Adams had driven many herds north. Never before had he seen cattle going blind with thirst. All he could do was "let them pass." When the crazed cattle finally sniffed out water and drank, their sight returned.

Cowhands such as Andy Adams kept the herds together as the cattle moved along the trails. The cowhands developed nerves of steel, staying calm even in times of extreme stress. Trip after trip, they <u>persisted</u> in performing their exciting but dangerous job.

Herding cattle was certainly risky. A lightning bolt could send a herd stampeding in all directions. Swift river currents sometimes carried the longhorns away, and cowhands would have to struggle to get the panicked animals back on solid ground. Cowhands also fought grass fires, pulled the cattle from swamps, and chased off thieves.

Vocabulary Builder
<u>persist</u> (per SIHST) **v.** to endure; to continue in the face of difficulty

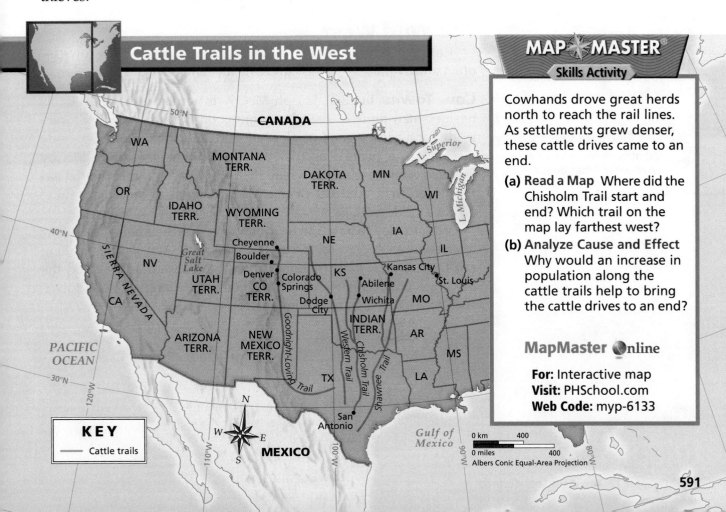

Cattle Trails in the West

KEY

— Cattle trails

MAP★MASTER®

Skills Activity

Cowhands drove great herds north to reach the rail lines. As settlements grew denser, these cattle drives came to an end.

(a) Read a Map Where did the Chisholm Trail start and end? Which trail on the map lay farthest west?

(b) Analyze Cause and Effect Why would an increase in population along the cattle trails help to bring the cattle drives to an end?

MapMaster ●nline

For: Interactive map
Visit: PHSchool.com
Web Code: myp-6133

On the hot, dusty trails, cowhands could spend 18 hours a day in the saddle. Yet, for all their efforts, they earned wages of less than $1 a day. Like mining, cattle ranching relied on a workforce of low-paid laborers.

Spanish Roots The cowhands driving herds north owed much to Spanish and Mexican vaqueros (vah KAYR os). **Vaquero** (from *vaca,* meaning "cow") is the Spanish word for cowhand, or cowboy. Vaqueros tended cattle on ranches in Mexico, California, and the Southwest.

When Americans started to herd cattle, they learned from vaqueros how to ride, rope, and brand. Cowboys wore Mexican spurs and leather chaps that kept their legs safe from thorny shrubs. The broad-brimmed cowboy hat came from the Mexican *sombrero,* or "hat that provides shade." Cowboys used a leather lariat, or lasso (from the Spanish word *lazo*), to catch cattle and horses.

Approximately one third of all western cowhands were Mexican. Many others were African American and white veterans of the Civil War.

☑ **Checkpoint** **What skills did American cowboys learn from Spanish and Mexican vaqueros?**

The Wild West

Cattle drives ended at towns along railroad lines. These towns—often unruly places—helped to create the fantasy of the Wild West.

Cow Towns In 1867, Joseph McCoy hit on an idea. The Illinois businessman figured that after months on the trail, cowboys were ready for a bath, a good meal, a soft bed, and some fun. Also, cattle needed to be penned as they awaited shipment east. So McCoy founded Abilene, Kansas, where the Chisholm Trail met the Kansas Pacific Railroad. Abilene was the first cow town, or settlement at the end of a cattle trail.

With money to be made from cowboys and their herds, rival cow towns such as Wichita and Dodge City, Kansas, soon sprang up along rail lines. Dance halls, saloons, hotels, and restaurants served the cowboys. Gunfights were rare but common enough to lead towns such as Wichita to ban carrying pistols.

Outfitting a Vaquero
Cowhands borrowed much from early Spanish and Mexican vaqueros. **Critical Thinking: Frame Questions** *What question would you want to ask the vaquero pictured here?*

Use Example Clues
What is an example of a cowtown? What does this term mean?

The Myth of the West Rough-and-tumble life in cow towns helped to spread the myth of the West as a place of violence, adventure, and endless opportunity. Easterners called it the Wild West.

No one did more to promote this fantasy than William "Buffalo Bill" Cody. A former buffalo hunter, Cody created a traveling Wild West show in 1883. Gun-slinging cowboys and Native Americans performed daring feats of sharp shooting and horseback riding. They staged performances depicting frontier events, including Custer's Last Stand. Annie Oakley broke the stereotype of the dainty woman with shooting as precise as any man's.

The myth of the Wild West had some basis in fact. But, as you have read, the West was also being transformed. Native Americans were being forced onto reservations. Mining and ranching were big businesses. Independent miners were becoming wage earners, like cowboys. Even wild cow towns were being quieted down by settlers and ministers who wanted peaceful communities for their families and their faiths.

✓**Checkpoint** **How true was the myth of the Wild West?**

Vocabulary Builder
myth (mihth) *n.* story or legend; imaginary object; invented story

Boom and Bust in the Cattle Kingdom

The cattle boom lasted from the 1860s to the 1880s. The region dominated by the cattle industry and its ranches, trails, and cow towns came to be called the **cattle kingdom.** Ranchers made large profits as herds and markets grew. But then the cattle industry collapsed.

The Cattle Boom At the height of the cattle boom, ranchers could buy a young calf for $5 and sell a mature steer for $60. Even after the expense of a cattle drive, profits were extremely high.

Cold Morning on the Range, 1904

by Frederic Remington

Frederic Remington was a Yale-educated easterner who became a famous painter and sculptor of western scenes. His work highlighted such themes as self-reliance and mastery over nature. In *Cold Morning on the Range* (seen here), he portrays a rider in the process of taming a wild horse. **Critical Thinking: *Evaluate Information*** *How do you think Remington's work added to the myth of the Wild West?*

Profits rose still higher with the introduction of new breeds of cattle. These breeds caught fewer diseases and had more meat than longhorns. As a result, backers from the East and Europe invested millions in huge cattle companies. The ranches of one company alone covered almost 800 square miles in three states.

The Boom Ends By the mid-1880s, more than 7 million cattle roamed the open range. That was more than the land could feed. Then, beginning in 1886 and 1887, a cycle of scorching summers and frigid winters killed millions of cattle. Meanwhile, an economic depression threw many city dwellers out of work. Demand for beef dropped.

To make things worse, sheep began competing with cattle for prairie grasses across the Plains. Farmers fenced in the open range to keep cattle away from crops. Without free grazing for their herds, ranchers had to buy expensive feed.

Giant cattle ranches slowly gave way to smaller spreads that grew their own feed. As railroads expanded, their lines moved closer to the ranches. Large roundups and long cattle drives vanished. The cattle boom was over.

☑**Checkpoint** What factors ended the cattle boom?

☆ **Looking Back and Ahead** As railroads pushed across the West, the cattle industry boomed. Cowhands moved herds north on long drives to meet trains that took the cattle east. The cattle boom lasted into the 1880s. In the next section, you will read how farming changed the West.

Texas Longhorn
The horns of longhorn cattle can be six feet wide or more. The cattle use them for both attack and defense.

Section 3 | **Check Your Progress**

Progress Monitoring ⏺nline
For: Self-test with instant help
Visit: PHSchool.com
Web Code: mya-6133

Comprehension and Critical Thinking

1. **(a) Describe** What dangers did cowhands face on cattle drives?
   (b) Draw Conclusions Why do you think cowhands took these risks?

2. **(a) Recall** How did the expansion of railroads help to create a cattle boom?
   (b) Identify Economic Benefits How did the cattle boom lead to economic prosperity for many new towns in the West?

🔁 **Reading Skill**

3. **Use Example Clues** Reread the text following the subheading "Cow Towns." How do example and description help you understand the term cow town? What is a cow town?

Key Terms

Complete each of the following sentences so that the second part further explains the first and clearly shows your understanding of the key term.

4. Cattle drives brought thousands of cattle to rail lines; _____.

5. Vaqueros tended cattle herds; _____.

6. The cattle kingdom supplied meat to a growing nation; _____.

Writing

7. Based on what you have read in this section about the Wild West myth, write an opinion about the effects of this myth on American life. Back up your opinion with reasons and examples from the section and from your own knowledge.

Heavy Burdens

❝ The business of farming has become . . . extremely unprofitable. With the hardest work and the sharpest economy, the average farmer is unable to make both ends meet; every year closes with debt, and the mortgage grows till it devours the land. ❞

— Washington Gladden, a Protestant minister, describing the farmers' plight, 1890

◀ Farmers at work

Farming in the West

Objectives

- Identify what attracted farmers to settle on the Great Plains.
- Describe how people adapted to life on the Plains.
- Summarize the result of the Oklahoma Land Rush.
- Explain how economic issues led farmers to organize to seek reform.

🔍 Reading Skill

Use Comparison or Contrast Clues

Comparison and contrast can also help you define unfamiliar words. Comparison clues show how an unfamiliar word is similar to a familiar word, phrase, or example. Look for signal words such as *similar to* or *like* to highlight these clues. Contrast clues show how an unfamiliar word is different from a familiar word, phrase, or example. Look for signal words such as *unlike* or *instead* to highlight these clues.

Key Terms and People

homesteader
sod
sodbuster
sooner
grange

farm cooperative
inflation
William Jennings
  Bryan

Why It Matters While ranchers and cowhands were building a cattle kingdom, hundreds of thousands of farmers were flooding onto the Great Plains. Again and again, they would face hard times. Some would fail and have to sell their farms. However, others would survive. The crops that they harvested helped to feed the growing nation.

❓ **Section Focus Question: How did farmers on the Plains struggle to make a living?**

Homesteading

By 1900, half a million farmers had settled on the Great Plains. Many were attracted by an offer of free land.

Homestead Act During the Civil War, Congress passed the Homestead Act of 1862. It offered a 160-acre plot to anyone who resided on the land for five years. Congress wanted to give the poor a chance to own farms. Thousands became **homesteaders**—settlers who acquired free land from the government—on the Great Plains.

But few had the money to move west and start a farm. Also, land companies took over large areas illegally. And on the dry Plains, 160 acres was too small a plot to grow enough grain to profit. Only one homesteader in three lasted the required five years.

Railroads Promote Farming In fact, railroads promoted more farming than did the Homestead Act. More farms meant more shipping for western railroads. So the railroads gave away some of the 180 million acres they got from the government. They recruited thousands of people from the eastern United States, Ireland, Germany, and Scandinavia to settle on the Great Plains.

✅ **Checkpoint** How did the Homestead Act help people gain land?

A Hard Life on the Plains

Life on the Great Plains was not easy. Water was scarce, and crops were hard to grow. Farmers struggled to make ends meet.

Busting Sod The first farmers on the eastern Plains staked out sites near water and trees. Later arrivals continued on to the treeless prairie. The farther west one went, the drier the climate became.

The soil of the Plains was fertile. But it was covered with a thick **sod,** or a surface layer of earth in which the roots of grasses tangle with soil. With little rain, sod baked into a hardened mass. Early settlers, lacking wood, cut sod into bricks to build walls. Two rows of sod bricks made walls that kept homes cool in summer and warm in winter.

New Farming Methods Farmers broke through the tough sod with plows. The sod often cracked plows made of wood or iron. In 1837, John Deere of Illinois invented a sodbusting plow made of steel. Steel plows were stronger and lighter than other plows.

Plains farmers, or **sodbusters** as they were known, used machines called drills to plant crops. The drills buried seeds deep in the ground where there was moisture. Farmers used reapers to harvest crops and threshers to beat off the hard coverings of the grains.

Water often lay hundreds of feet below ground. Farmers used windmills to pump the water out. To keep cattle from trampling crops, farmers put up fences. Lacking wood, they used barbed wire. Joseph Glidden, an Illinois farmer, invented this twisted metal wire in 1874.

● **INFOGRAPHIC**

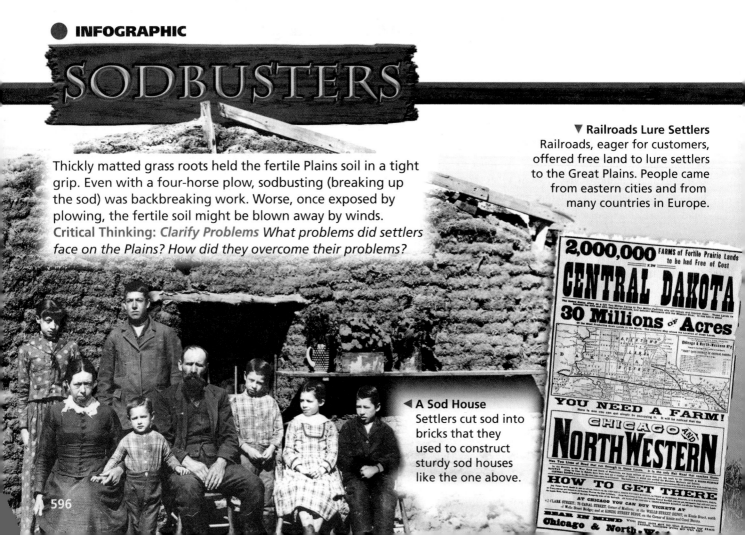

SODBUSTERS

Thickly matted grass roots held the fertile Plains soil in a tight grip. Even with a four-horse plow, sodbusting (breaking up the sod) was backbreaking work. Worse, once exposed by plowing, the fertile soil might be blown away by winds.
Critical Thinking: *Clarify Problems What problems did settlers face on the Plains? How did they overcome their problems?*

▼ **Railroads Lure Settlers**
Railroads, eager for customers, offered free land to lure settlers to the Great Plains. People came from eastern cities and from many countries in Europe.

◄ **A Sod House**
Settlers cut sod into bricks that they used to construct sturdy sod houses like the one above.

2,000,000 FARMS of Fertile Prairie Lands to be had Free of Cost
CENTRAL DAKOTA
30 Millions OF Acres

YOU NEED A FARM!
CHICAGO AND
NorthWestern

HOW TO GET THERE

BEAR IN MIND
Chicago & North.We

Farm Families Whole families worked on the farms. Men labored from dawn to dusk. Children tended animals and helped with other chores. Life was also hard for women. Besides keeping house, they helped plant and harvest. They educated children. They nursed the sick. They sewed clothing, preserved food, and made such basics as candles and soap.

Exodusters Thousands of African Americans, many of them former slaves, streamed onto the Plains. By the early 1880s, perhaps 70,000 African Americans had settled in Kansas. These settlers were known as Exodusters because they believed they were like the Jews fleeing slavery in Egypt, a biblical story told in the book of Exodus.

Some Exodusters took up farming. Others moved to towns. Men often worked as hired hands and women as laundresses.

The Spanish Southwest In the Southwest along the border with Mexico, arriving settlers found Spanish-speaking farmers and sheepherders. Many had <u>resided</u> there since before the Mexican-American War, when the United States had acquired this territory.

The coming of the railroads brought more immigrants from Mexico. Many helped build the new lines. Some of the older Hispanic residents were large landowners, known as *ricos* (REE kos). They fought to keep their lands, deeded under Spanish or Mexican law.

✓**Checkpoint** **Who were the sodbusters and the Exodusters?**

Use Comparison or Contrast Clues
What comparison clue is included in this paragraph to help you define the term *Exodusters*? What are Exodusters?

Vocabulary Builder
<u>reside</u> (ree ZĪD) *v.* to live (in or at); to exist (in)

Scarce Resources ▶
Like the Native Americans, early farm families had few resources to spare. The woman in this picture gathers dried buffalo manure to use as a fuel for heating or cooking, or to use as a fertilizer for crops.

▲ "Grasshopper Plow"
To build their sod houses, early settlers used a spade to dig one brick at a time. But in the late 1800s, a new invention made the job much easier. With the steel "grasshopper plow," a farmer could cut sod into strips 1 foot wide and 4 inches thick. The strips were then cut into about 3-foot lengths.

A Last Rush for Land

By the 1880s, few areas on the Plains remained free to settlers. The federal government agreed to open Oklahoma to homesteaders.

Boomers and Sooners In April 1889, nearly 100,000 people gathered at a line near present-day Oklahoma City. These were the "boomers." They had come to claim some of the 2 million acres of free homesteads in what was once Indian Territory.

At noon, a volley of gunfire signaled the start of the Oklahoma Land Rush. A few people, known as **sooners**, had already sneaked onto the land. They jumped from hiding and grabbed the best land. Other rushes followed until all 2 million acres had been claimed.

The Frontier Closes In 1890, the national census reported that the United States no longer had land available for homesteading. In the West, "there can hardly be said to be a frontier line," the report stated.

✓Checkpoint **Where was the last land rush in the West?**

Farmers Organize

Wheat and grain from Plains farms fed the growing cities of America and Europe. A few big farmers prospered. But small farmers faced an economic crisis and quickly organized to end it.

Crisis on the Farm The more grain that farmers hauled to market, the lower grain prices fell. Farmers were producing a <u>surplus</u> of crops. One Kansas farmer complained that "we are poorer by many dollars than we were years ago."

Small farmers were hit the hardest by low grain prices. Many had borrowed money for land and machinery. As prices fell, Plains farmers could not repay their loans and lost their land. In the South, tenants and sharecroppers fell deeper into debt as cotton prices fell.

Vocabulary Builder
<u>surplus</u> (SER pluhs) **n.** excess; quantity that is left over

Cooperatives and Political Parties Many farmers lived in poverty and isolation. Some communities began to form granges, groups of farmers who met for lectures, sewing bees, and other events. In 1867, local granges joined to form the National Grange.

What began as a social and educational movement evolved into an economic protest. In the 1870s and 1880s, Grangers demanded the same low rates from railroads and warehouses that were given to big farmers. They elected state officials who passed laws limiting rates.

A group called the Farmers' Alliance organized in the late 1870s to help farmers. It set up farm cooperatives—groups of farmers who pool their money to make large purchases of tools, seed, and other supplies at a discount. In the South, both whites and blacks joined the Alliance.

In 1892, unhappy farmers joined with members of labor unions to form the Populist Party. This was a political party that pushed for social reforms. It demanded public ownership of railroads and warehouses to control rates, a tax on income to replace property taxes, an eight-hour workday, and other reforms.

Populists wanted to use silver in addition to gold as a basis for the money supply. With more money circulating, Populists hoped to see inflation, or a general rise in prices. They believed rising grain prices would help farmers pay off their debts. In that way, the farmers could avoid foreclosure—the taking of property to settle a debt. Summing up Populist demands, Kansas activist Mary Elizabeth Lease said:

> ❝We want money, land, and transportation. We . . . want the power to make loans direct from the government. We want the accursed foreclosure system wiped out. . . .❞
>
> —Mary Elizabeth Lease, 1890 speech

The Election of 1896 In the presidential election of 1896, Populists supported Democrat William Jennings Bryan, known as the "Great Commoner." Bryan won the votes of farmers from the South and West for supporting the use of silver to raise prices.

Bankers and business owners claimed rising prices would ruin the economy. They backed Republican William McKinley and his gold-alone standard. McKinley won. Republicans took both the White House and Congress for the first time in decades. The Populists faded. Although the major parties absorbed many of their ideas, most Americans saw no link between farm problems and their own.

These presidential campaign buttons show the two major candidates in 1896. William McKinley (right) won for the Republicans. William Jennings Bryan (left) had the backing of Democrats and Populists but lost.

☑**Checkpoint**   What did the Populists demand?

☆ **Looking Back and Ahead** Farmers found it hard to make a living, so they organized to demand reforms. In the next chapter, you will read about the rise of big business and labor.

Section 4 | **Check Your Progress**

Progress Monitoring ⬤nline
For: Self-test with instant help
Visit: PHSchool.com
Web Code: mya-6134

Comprehension and Critical Thinking

1. (a) Recall What was a homesteader?
(b) Explain Problems What were three problems associated with the Homestead Act?

2. (a) Recall What is a surplus?
(b) Clarify Problems How did a surplus of grain contribute to low grain prices? How did the National Grange, the Farmers' Alliance, and the Populist Party try to address the economic crisis caused by low prices?

🕑 Reading Skill

3. Use Comparison or Contrast Clues Define the term inflation in the following sentence: Like the wind under a child's runaway balloon, inflation pushed prices higher and higher.

Key Terms

Answer the following questions in complete sentences that show your understanding of the key terms.
4. How did tough sod make living on the Great Plains difficult?
5. Why were Great Plains farmers called sodbusters?
6. Who were the sooners?

7. How did forming a farm cooperative help farmers?
8. How did Populists think inflation would help them economically?

Writing

9. Imagine that you will be writing an editorial in support of William Jennings Bryan during the 1896 presidential election. Write a few sentences creating an audience profile describing people who might agree with you. Think about who they are: What kind of work might they do? In what part of the country might they live?

21st Century Learning As you learned in the Skills for Life in the previous chapter, thematic maps focus on topics such as agricultural products, migrations, or physical regions. The map below is a climate map. Climate refers to the average weather of a place over a period of time. The visual information included on a climate map can help you understand the economy of a region.

Climates of the United States

KEY		
	Marine	Abundant rainfall; warm summers and cool winters
	Mediterranean	Hot summers and cool winters
	Highland	Varies, depending on elevation
	Steppe	Limited rainfall; hot summers and cold winters
	Desert	Hot summers and mild-to-cold winters; hot days and cold nights
	Humid continental	Mild summers and cold winters
	Humid subtropical	Hot summers and cool winters
	Tropical	Hot all year
	Tundra	Cold summers and very cold winters
	Subarctic	Cool summers and very cold winters

Learn the Skill

Use these steps to interpret climate maps.

1. **Use the map key to read the map.** The map key explains special symbols and colors used on the map.

2. **Look for patterns on the map.** Study the information on the map to notice trends or patterns.

3. **Make inferences.** Make generalizations. Use the information on the map to make a general statement about the climate.

Practice the Skill

Answer the following questions about the map on this page.

1. **Use the map key to read the map.** What does the key on this map tell you? What do the colors tell you? What other information is on this key?

2. **Look for patterns on the map.** How does the climate change as you move across the Great Plains states from east to west?

3. **Make inferences.** How do you think the climate of the Great Plains affects farming?

Apply the Skill

See the Review and Assessment at the end of this chapter.

How did the growth of big business affect the development of the West?

Section 1
Mining and Railroads

- Gold and silver strikes in the West attracted many newcomers.
- Some mining towns became ghost towns after the metals were mined out.
- Immigrants came to the West from many countries to help build railroads.
- In 1869, a transcontinental railroad linked the East with the West.

Section 2
Native Americans Struggle to Survive

- Native Americans lost their lands, despite treaties aimed at protecting them.
- Native American nations were forced onto reservations.
- Native Americans fought for their way of life.
- The 1887 Dawes Act tried to promote new ways of living among Native Americans.

Section 3
The Cattle Kingdom

- Railroads provided a way for cattle ranchers to get their herds to distant markets.
- Unruly cattle towns helped to give rise to the myth of the Wild West.
- Economic depression, bad weather, and the fencing of crops brought the cattle boom to an end in the late 1800s.

Section 4
Farming in the West

- Free land for homesteaders helped to populate the Great Plains.
- Plains settlers faced a hard and isolated life.
- Disgruntled farmers and workers organized to demand reforms from government.
- The Populist Party shook up American politics in the 1890s.

(?) Exploring the Essential Question

Use the online study guide to explore the essential question.

Section 1
How did mining and railroads draw people to the West?

Section 2
What were the consequences of the conflict between the Native Americans and white settlers?

Chapter 17 Essential Question
How did the growth of big business affect the development of the West?

Section 4
How did farmers on the Plains struggle to make a living?

Section 3
What factors led to boom and bust in the cattle industry?

Key Terms

Complete each of the following sentences so that the second part further explains the first part and clearly shows your understanding of the key term.

1. Plains Indians used travois in their travels; _____.

2. Farmers thought inflation would benefit farm prices; _____.

3. Vaqueros were important in cattle ranching; _____.

4. Railroads benefited from generous government subsidies; _____.

Comprehension and Critical Thinking

5. **(a) Describe** What difficulties did immigrants face in mining towns?
   (b) Evaluate Information How did immigrants help to develop the West?

6. **(a) List** What types of changes did the transcontinental railroad bring to the West?
   (b) Draw Inferences What were the effects of the building of railroads on Native Americans?

7. **(a) List** Describe three ways in which Native Americans made use of buffalo.
   (b) Recall Why did the buffalo begin to disappear from the Great Plains in the 1870s?
   (c) Draw Conclusions How did the disappearance of the buffalo change the lives of Native Americans?

8. **(a) Summarize** How did the U.S. government and settlers treat Native Americans?
   (b) Detect Points of View What do you think the Native American chief meant when he said after the Battle of Wounded Knee, "A people's dream died there"?

9. **(a) Recall** Who was Buffalo Bill Cody?
   (b) Apply Information Why do you think Americans characterize the West as "wild"?

10. **(a) Describe** What was life like for individuals who settled on the Great Plains?
    (b) Draw Conclusions Why do you think families risked moving west?

History Reading Skill

11. **Use Context Clues** Choose four key terms or other unfamiliar words from this chapter. Write sentences that define these words. Include at least one of each clue type: example, comparison or contrast, definition, or restatement.

Writing

12. **Choose one of the following issues discussed in this chapter:**
    • the rise and fall of the cattle kingdom;
    • the settlement of the West and disappearance of the frontier;
    • relations between Native Americans and the U.S. government.

    State an opinion about the issue, and list several facts and reasons from the chapter to support your opinion.

13. **Write a Narrative:**
    Write one or two diary entries from the point of view of a family member who is moving west in the 1870s. Describe why your family is moving west and how you feel about it. Tell what you expect to see in the West and the type of life you think you will have.

Skills for Life

Interpret a Climate Map

Use the map below to answer the questions.

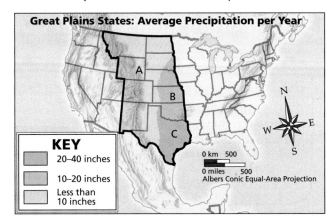

14. Study the key. What does the green color mean?

15. As you move east to west across the Great Plains states, how does the amount of precipitation change?

16. How do you think the amount of rain in the Great Plains states affects farming there?

Test Yourself

1. Which of the following turned Virginia City, Nevada, into a boomtown?

A transcontinental railroad

B Comstock Lode

C Fort Laramie Treaty

D Oklahoma Land Rush

Refer to the quotation below to answer Question 2.

> "Let me be a free man, free to travel, free to stop, free to work, . . . free to choose my own teachers, free to follow the religion of my fathers, free to think and talk and act for myself. . . ."
>
> —Chief Joseph of the Nez Percés, 1879

2. Chief Joseph referred to which situation?

A Battle of Little Bighorn

B passage of the Homestead Act

C building of the Transcontinental Railroad

D confinement of Nez Percés to a reservation

Refer to the photograph below to answer Question 3.

3. The photograph best reflects which of the following?

A gold rush of 1849

B Fort Laramie Treaty

C Populist movement

D Homestead Act

Document-Based Questions

Task: Look at Documents 1 and 2, and answer their accompanying questions. Then, use the documents and your knowledge of history to complete this writing assignment:

> Write an essay about the economic crisis facing farmers in the 1890s.

Document 1: Mary Elizabeth Lease gave this speech in 1890. *What hardship does Lease say farmers are suffering? What does she say is the cause?*

> "After all our years of toil . . . and hardships upon the Western frontier, monopoly is taking our homes from us by an infamous system of mortgage foreclosure. . . . How did it happen? The government, at the bid of Wall Street, repudiated its contracts with the people. . . . As Senator Stewart [of Nevada] puts it, 'For twenty years the market value of the dollar has gone up and the market value of labor has gone down, till today the American laborer . . . asks which is the worst—the black slavery that has gone or the white slavery that has come?'"

Document 2: The more farmers harvested, the less they earned. *How does this graph help to explain the farmers' problem?*

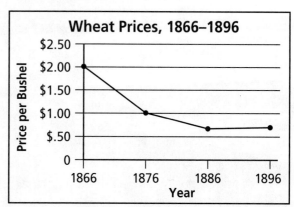

Source: *Historical Statistics of the United States*

Industry and Urban Growth

1865–1915

> "We headed for Fifth Avenue, where we got on a double-decker bus....From our comfortable seats on the upper deck we could soak in the sights—the shiny store windows, then the mansions, and later on the gray panorama of the Hudson River."
>
> —Bernardo Vega, newly arrived immigrant

The Brooklyn Bridge, completed in 1883 to span the East River in New York, linked Manhattan with Brooklyn. Structures like it changed the face of American cities.

CHAPTER 18

What You Will Learn

Section 1
A NEW INDUSTRIAL REVOLUTION
After the Civil War, the United States experienced rapid industrial growth.

Section 2
BIG BUSINESS AND ORGANIZED LABOR
As businesses grew in size and power, workers organized to demand better conditions.

Section 3
CITIES GROW AND CHANGE
Cities grew rapidly, leading to new challenges and a new way of life.

Section 4
THE NEW IMMIGRANTS
Millions of new immigrants came to the United States seeking freedom and opportunities.

Section 5
EDUCATION AND CULTURE
American culture changed as education became more available.

Reading Skill
Use Word Origins In this chapter, you will learn to analyze words by their parts or origins to determine meanings.

605

Industry and Urban Growth, 1865–1915

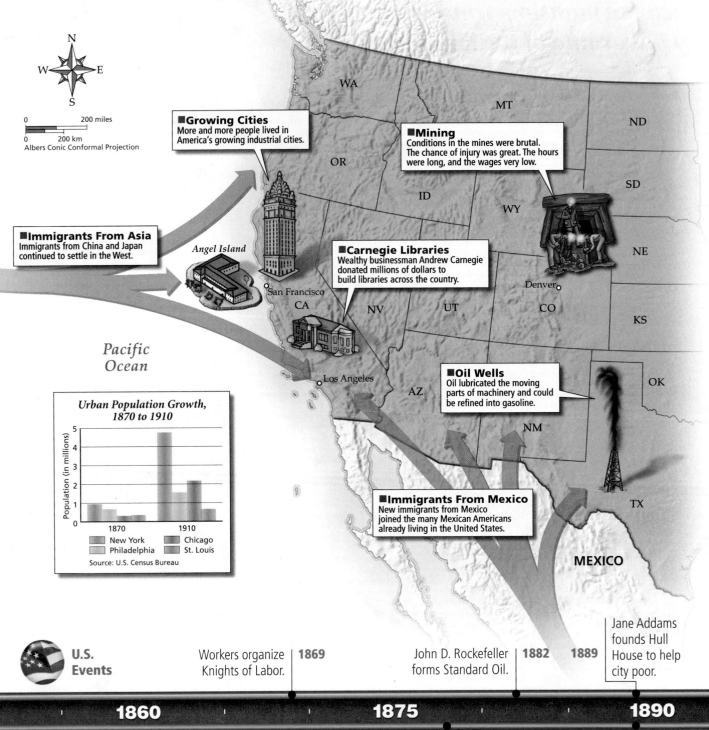

N
W • E
S

0   200 miles
0   200 km
Albers Conic Conformal Projection

■Growing Cities
More and more people lived in America's growing industrial cities.

■Mining
Conditions in the mines were brutal. The chance of injury was great. The hours were long, and the wages very low.

WA

MT

ND

OR

ID

SD

WY

■Immigrants From Asia
Immigrants from China and Japan continued to settle in the West.

Angel Island

■Carnegie Libraries
Wealthy businessman Andrew Carnegie donated millions of dollars to build libraries across the country.

San Francisco
CA

NE

Denver

NV   UT   CO

KS

Pacific
Ocean

Los Angeles

AZ

■Oil Wells
Oil lubricated the moving parts of machinery and could be refined into gasoline.

OK

NM

TX

Urban Population Growth, 1870 to 1910

Population (in millions)

5
4
3
2
1
0
          1870   1910

New York   Chicago
Philadelphia   St. Louis
Source: U.S. Census Bureau

■Immigrants From Mexico
New immigrants from Mexico joined the many Mexican Americans already living in the United States.

MEXICO

Jane Addams founds Hull House to help city poor.

U.S. Events
Workers organize Knights of Labor.   **1869**

John D. Rockefeller forms Standard Oil.   **1882   1889**

1860   **1875**   **1890**

World Events
Salvation Army is formed in London.   **1878**

1889   German engineers build first gas-powered automobile.

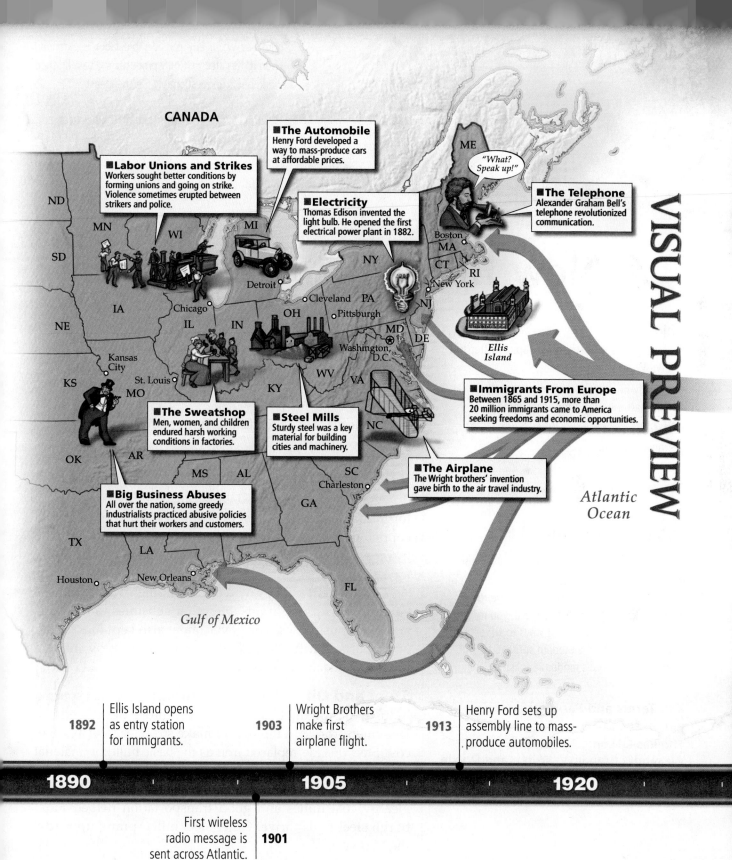

CANADA

■The Automobile
Henry Ford developed a way to mass-produce cars at affordable prices.

■Labor Unions and Strikes
Workers sought better conditions by forming unions and going on strike. Violence sometimes erupted between strikers and police.

■Electricity
Thomas Edison invented the light bulb. He opened the first electrical power plant in 1882.

"What? Speak up!"

ME

■The Telephone
Alexander Graham Bell's telephone revolutionized communication.

ND

MN
WI
MI
Detroit

SD
IA
Chicago
IL
IN
OH
Cleveland
PA
Pittsburgh
NY
Boston
MA
CT
RI
New York
NJ

NE
Kansas City
KY
MD
WV
DE
Washington, D.C.
VA

KS
St. Louis
MO

Ellis Island

■The Sweatshop
Men, women, and children endured harsh working conditions in factories.

■Steel Mills
Sturdy steel was a key material for building cities and machinery.

NC

■Immigrants From Europe
Between 1865 and 1915, more than 20 million immigrants came to America seeking freedoms and economic opportunities.

OK
AR
MS
AL

■Big Business Abuses
All over the nation, some greedy industrialists practiced abusive policies that hurt their workers and customers.

SC
Charleston
GA

■The Airplane
The Wright brothers' invention gave birth to the air travel industry.

Atlantic Ocean

TX
LA
Houston
New Orleans

FL

Gulf of Mexico

VISUAL PREVIEW

1892 | Ellis Island opens as entry station for immigrants.

1903 | Wright Brothers make first airplane flight.

1913 | Henry Ford sets up assembly line to mass-produce automobiles.

1890

1905

1920

First wireless radio message is sent across Atlantic. | **1901**

Steel for Sale

" The price of this Steel is somewhat higher than that of other English brands, but for Tools, Dies, and all purposes when any considerable labor is extended upon it, this steel not only produces the best finished work, but is unquestionably the cheapeast . . . "

—From an 1870 advertisement,
A.J. Wilkinson & Co.

◀ Steel mill

A New Industrial Revolution

Objectives
- List reasons industry grew rapidly after the Civil War.
- Identify inventions and inventors that changed the way Americans lived.
- Describe the advances that revolutionized transportation.

🕐 Reading Skill

Use Greek Word Origins English words may be built on several Greek roots, and each of these may be adapted to modern usage. Thus, once you know the roots of a word, you may need to experiment with different ways to shape an up-to-date word. Use the modern context as your final clue to a word's modern English meaning.

Key Terms and People

patent
Thomas Edison
Alexander Graham
  Bell
Henry Ford
assembly line
Wilbur and Orville
  Wright

Why It Matters You have learned how the Industrial Revolution of the early 1800s changed America. In the late 1800s a new Industrial Revolution transformed life even more. New inventions changed the way Americans worked, traveled, communicated, and played.

❷ Section Focus Question: What conditions spurred the growth of industry?

Why Industry Boomed

As the nation expanded westward, conditions were ripe for industrial growth. Vast deposits of coal, iron, lead, and copper now lay within reach of the miner's pickax. The towering forests of the Pacific Northwest furnished lumber for building.

Government policy favored industrial growth. Congress gave generous land grants and other subsidies to railroads and other businesses. The government also kept high tariffs on imports. Tariffs helped American industry by making foreign goods more expensive.

Steel and Oil Technology was another factor that spurred industrial growth. In the 1850s, inventors developed the Bessemer process, a method to make stronger steel at a low cost. Steel quickly replaced iron as the basic building material of cities and industry.

Pittsburgh became the nation's steel-making capital. Nearby coal mines and good transportation helped Pittsburgh steel mills thrive. Other steel mills sprang up across the Midwest.

Workers near Titusville, Pennsylvania, tapped a new source of energy in 1859. As they drilled into the ground, a stream of dark liquid gushed upward. It was the nation's first oil strike. The oil industry soon devised methods to <u>refine</u> crude oil into lubricants for machines—and, later, into gasoline to power engines and automobiles. Oil was so valuable it became known as "black gold."

A Railroad Boom Railroads fueled industrial growth. Trains carried people and goods to the West and raw materials to eastern factories. Companies improved service by adding sleeping and dining cars and laying down thousands of miles of new tracks.

As more lines were built, railroads sought ways to limit competition and keep prices high. Some big lines consolidated, or combined. They bought up smaller lines or forced them out of business. The Pennsylvania Railroad, for example, consolidated 73 smaller companies. Railroads also gave secret rebates, or discounts, to their best customers. In some places, rival rail lines made agreements to fix rates at a high level.

Such practices helped giant railroads control grain traffic in the West and South. However, high rates angered small farmers, who relied on the railroads to get their goods to market. As a result, many farmers joined the Granger and Populist movements.

☑Checkpoint **How did the government support business?**

Vocabulary Builder
<u>refine</u> (rih FĪN) **v.** purify; make free from impurities

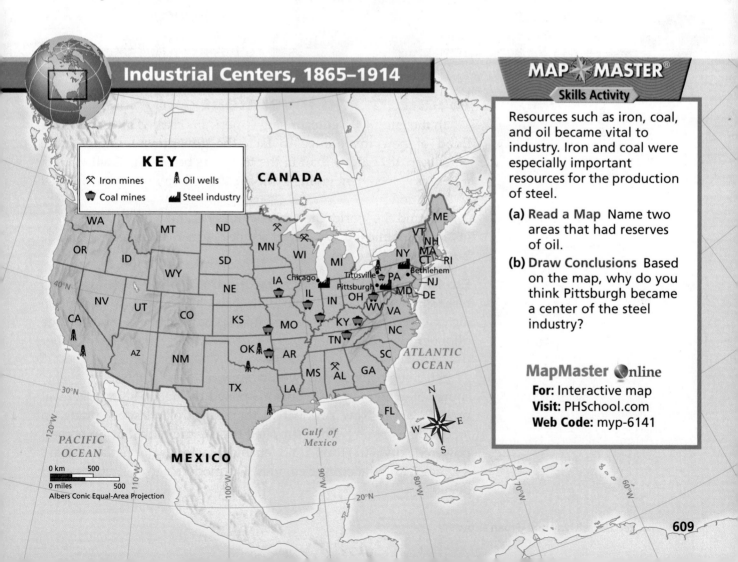

Industrial Centers, 1865–1914

KEY
✗ Iron mines   ⛏ Oil wells
⛫ Coal mines   🏭 Steel industry

MAP MASTER®
Skills Activity

Resources such as iron, coal, and oil became vital to industry. Iron and coal were especially important resources for the production of steel.

(a) Read a Map Name two areas that had reserves of oil.

(b) Draw Conclusions Based on the map, why do you think Pittsburgh became a center of the steel industry?

MapMaster ⬤nline
For: Interactive map
Visit: PHSchool.com
Web Code: myp-6141

609

America: Land of Inventors

Thomas Edison once said, "Genius is one percent inspiration and ninety-nine percent perspiration." This combination of imagination and hard work enabled Americans to produce a flood of new inventions in the late 1800s. **Critical Thinking:** *Evaluate Information Which of the inventions shown here do you think did the most to change daily life? Explain your answer.*

1879
Thomas Edison
Electric light bulb
Extra daylight for work and leisure!

1876
Alexander Graham Bell
Telephone
Instant communication over the miles!

Inventors and Inventions

In the late 1800s, enterprising Americans created an astonishing flood of new inventions. In fact, the government issued more patents in 1897 alone than in the ten years before the Civil War! A **patent** is a document giving someone the sole right to make and sell an invention.

Around the world, the United States became known as a land of invention. Almost every day, it seemed, American inventions made business and life easier.

Edison's Invention Factory In 1876, Thomas Edison set up a research laboratory in Menlo Park, New Jersey. At this "invention factory," Edison and other scientists produced the light bulb, the phonograph, the motion picture camera, and hundreds of other useful devices.

Still, such inventions would be worthless without a reliable source of energy. In 1882, Edison opened the nation's first electrical power plant in New York City. Other power plants soon sprang up all over the country. They supplied the electricity that lit up homes, powered city streetcars, and enabled factories to replace steam engines with safer electric engines. The modern age of electricity had begun.

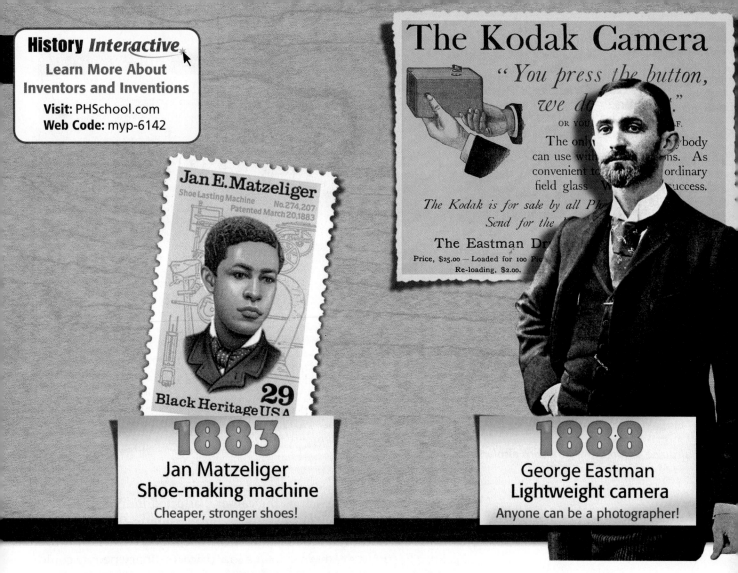

The Kodak Camera

"*You press the button, we d_____*"

OR YOU _____ F.

The onl_____ body can use wit_____ns. As convenient t_____ ordinary field glass _____ uccess.

The Kodak is for sale by all Ph_____
Send for the _____

The Eastman Dr_____

Price, $25.00 — Loaded for 100 Pic_____
Re-loading, $2.00.

Jan E. Matzeliger
Shoe Lasting Machine
No. 274,207
Patented March 20, 1883

29
Black Heritage USA

1883
Jan Matzeliger
Shoe-making machine
Cheaper, stronger shoes!

1888
George Eastman
Lightweight camera
Anyone can be a photographer!

A Communications Revolution Improved communication was vital to growing American businesses. The telegraph, in use since 1844, helped people stay in touch with one another. But Americans still had to wait weeks for news from Europe to arrive by boat. In 1866, Cyrus Field had an underwater telegraph cable laid across the Atlantic Ocean that sped communications from Europe.

The telegraph used a code of dots and dashes. Alexander Graham Bell wanted to build a device that would carry the human voice. Bell worked for years inventing this device, which he called the telephone. Finally, in 1876, he sent the first telephone message to his assistant in another room: "Mr. Watson, come here. I want you."

Bell's patent for the telephone was the most valuable patent ever issued. By 1885, more than 300,000 phones had been sold, most of them to businesses. Instead of going to a telegraph office, people could buy, sell, and get information about prices or supplies simply by picking up the telephone. In time, Bell organized over 100 local companies into the giant American Telephone and Telegraph Company.

Devices for Home and Office Some inventions made office work faster and cheaper. In 1868, Christopher Sholes invented a letter-writing device called the "Type-Writer." Soon, female typists in offices were churning out letters at 60 words per minute.

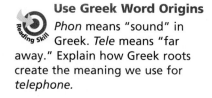

Use Greek Word Origins
Phon means "sound" in Greek. *Tele* means "far away." Explain how Greek roots create the meaning we use for *telephone.*

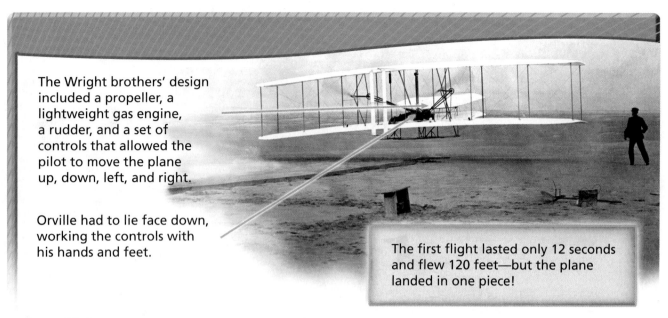

The Wright brothers' design included a propeller, a lightweight gas engine, a rudder, and a set of controls that allowed the pilot to move the plane up, down, left, and right.

Orville had to lie face down, working the controls with his hands and feet.

The first flight lasted only 12 seconds and flew 120 feet—but the plane landed in one piece!

Human Flight

Until the Wright brothers invented the airplane, people had flown only by wind power, in balloons and gliders. The airplane was revolutionary because it powered itself. In addition, the pilot controlled the movement of the plane. This photograph shows the Wright brothers' first flight on December 17, 1903. **Critical Thinking: Contrast** *Identify two ways that the Wright brothers' airplane differed from modern airplanes.*

Some inventions, such as the camera, affected individuals more than businesses. George Eastman introduced a lightweight camera in 1888. It replaced hundreds of pounds of chemicals and equipment. Because Eastman's camera sold at a low price, ordinary people could record their lives on film.

African Americans contributed to the flood of inventions. Jan Matzeliger revolutionized the shoe industry with a machine that sewed the tops to the soles. Granville Woods devised a way to send telegraph messages between moving trains.

☑**Checkpoint** **Why was Edison's power plant important?**

A Transportation Revolution

Technology also revolutionized transportation. For thousands of years, people had traveled by foot or by horse. Railroads went faster and farther but only where tracks ran.

Then, in the late 1800s, European engineers developed the automobile. Suddenly, people were able to travel almost anywhere and at any time. The development of the automobile ushered in an era of freer and faster transportation.

Henry Ford Only 8,000 Americans owned automobiles in 1900. Then, Henry Ford, an American manufacturer, made the automobile available to millions. Ford perfected a system to mass-produce cars and make them available at a lower price.

To speed construction and lower costs, Ford introduced the assembly line in 1913. The **assembly line** is a manufacturing method in which a product is put together as it moves along a belt. As each car frame moved along the belt, one set of workers hooked up the engine, another attached the wheels, and so on. The assembly line sliced production time in half. Lower costs allowed Ford to charge lower prices. By 1917, more than 4.5 million Americans owned cars.

Cars changed the nation's landscape. A web of roads spread across the country. Cities began sprawling into the countryside.

The Wright Brothers Another transportation revolution took place in 1903. Wilbur and Orville Wright tested a gas-powered airplane at Kitty Hawk, North Carolina. On its first flight, the plane stayed in the air for 12 seconds and flew 120 feet. Orville made four flights that day. His longest flight lasted 59 seconds.

Surprisingly, the first flights did not attract much interest. No one could see any practical use for a flying machine. The military uses of the airplane did not become clear until World War I (1914–1918). By the 1920s, the airplane had begun to <u>alter</u> the world by making travel quicker and trade easier.

Vocabulary Builder
<u>alter</u> (AWL ter) **v.** to change; to make different

☑**Checkpoint** **Why did the cost of automobiles decrease?**

⭐ **Looking Back and Ahead** Resources and technology set the stage for growth. In the next section, you will see how business leaders built on this foundation to create giant industries.

Section 1 | Check Your Progress

Progress Monitoring Online
For: Self-test with instant help
Visit: PHSchool.com
Web Code: mya-6141

Comprehension and Critical Thinking

1. **(a) Identify** What factors were in place at the end of the Civil War that helped create a surge in industrial growth?
   (b) Analyze Cause and Effect What effect did the discovery of new energy sources have on the Industrial Revolution?

2. **(a) List** What inventions revolutionized American life in the late 1800s?
   (b) Make Predictions What impact did Ford's assembly line have on changing American lifestyles?

🔎 Reading Skill

3. **Use Greek Word Origins** The Greek root *graph* means "writing," and the Greek root *phon* means "sound." The name of what Edison invention combines these roots?

Key Terms

Answer the following questions in complete sentences that show your understanding of the key terms.
4. How does a patent protect inventors?
5. How did the assembly line revolutionize factories?

Writing

6. Which of the following statements are logical, and which are not logical? Explain why.
   Statements:
   (a) Abundant natural resources aid economic growth because they provide energy and raw materials for manufacturing.
   (b) Secret rebates are unfair because they encourage business but not the arts.
   (c) Secret rebates are unfair because they were given to some customers but not to others.
   (d) Inventions aid industrial growth because they show Americans' special ingenuity.

Out on Strike

❝We, the 20,000 textile workers of Lawrence, are out on strike for the right to live . . . free from overwork and underpay; free from a state of affairs that had become so unbearable and beyond our control, that we were compelled to march . . . in united resistance against the wrongs and injustice of years and years of wage slavery.❞

—Proclamation of the Striking Textile Workers of Lawrence, Massachusetts, 1912

▲ Striking workers in Lawrence

Big Business and Organized Labor

Objectives

- Describe how new business methods helped American industry grow.
- Identify the leaders of "big business" and the practices they used.
- Summarize how working conditions changed as industry grew.
- Describe workers' efforts to organize during the late 1800s.

Reading Skill

Use Latin Word Origins English words may also combine several Latin roots or words to build one word. Knowledge of the several roots can help you make a general guess of the English word's meaning. Context offers confirming information. As you read Section 2, look for words built on Latin word origins. Notice how this ancient language continues to influence English today.

Key Terms and People

entrepreneur
corporation
monopoly
Andrew Carnegie
John D. Rockefeller
trust
free enterprise
Samuel Gompers
collective bargaining

Why It Matters The new Industrial Revolution did not affect all Americans equally. While many business owners earned huge profits, many of their employees endured harsh working conditions and extremely low pay. Today, Americans are still concerned about the gap between rich and poor. We still debate whether or not workers receive a fair share of corporate profits.

❓ Section Focus Question: How did big business change the workplace and give rise to labor unions?

New Ways of Doing Business

Business expansion was led by bold entrepreneurs (ahn treh preh NYOORZ). An **entrepreneur** is someone who sets up new businesses to make a profit. To raise capital, or money, entrepreneurs adopted new ways of organizing business.

The Corporation Many businesses became corporations, or businesses owned by many investors. Corporations raise large amounts of capital by selling stock, or shares. Stockholders receive a share of the profits and pick directors to run the company.

Corporations limited the risk of investors. Owners of other types of businesses could lose their savings, homes, and other property if the business failed. Stockholders risked only the amount of money they had invested.

Banking Banks lent huge amounts of capital to corporations. These loans helped American industry grow faster than ever before. They also made huge profits for the bankers.

One banker, J. Pierpont Morgan, made himself the most powerful force in the American economy. Morgan gained control of key industries, such as railroads and steel. In hard times, Morgan and his friends bought stock in troubled corporations. They then ran the companies in ways that <u>eliminated</u> competition and increased profits.

✓**Checkpoint** How did corporations raise capital?

Vocabulary Builder
<u>eliminate</u> (ee LIHM ih nayt) **v.** to get rid of

Growth of Big Business

As in Jefferson's time, the government took a laissez-faire approach to business in the late 1800s. Congress rarely made laws to regulate business practices. This atmosphere of freedom encouraged the growth of what came to be known as "big business." Entrepreneurs formed giant corporations and monopolies. A **monopoly** is a company that controls most or all business in a particular industry.

Carnegie One of the giants of big business was Andrew Carnegie. A poor Scottish immigrant, he worked his way up in the railroad business. He then entered the growing steel industry. Slowly, Carnegie gained control of every step in making steel. His companies owned iron mines, steel mills, railroads, and shipping lines. In 1892, Carnegie combined his businesses into the giant Carnegie Steel Company. It soon produced more steel than all the mills of England.

As a business leader, Carnegie could be ruthless. Still, he believed that the rich had a duty to improve society. He called his philosophy the Gospel of Wealth. Carnegie donated hundreds of millions of dollars to build libraries and support other charities. "I started life as a poor man," he said, "and I wish to end it that way." Carnegie set up a foundation that continued to fund worthy causes after his death. Many business leaders followed his example.

Rockefeller Another business giant, John D. Rockefeller, also came from humble beginnings. Rockefeller was the son of a peddler in New York. At age 23, he invested in an oil refinery. He used the profits to buy other oil companies. Rockefeller was a brilliant entrepreneur. He also did not hesitate to crush competitors, slashing prices to drive rivals out of business.

In 1882, Rockefeller ended competition in the oil industry by forming the Standard Oil Trust. A **trust** is a group of corporations run by a single board of directors. Other industries followed his lead. By 1900, trusts dominated many of the nation's key industries, from meatpacking to sugar refining to the manufacture of copper wire.

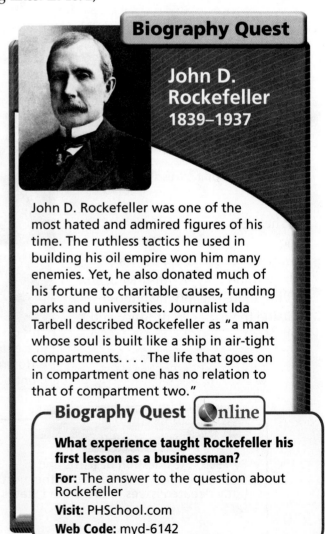

Biography Quest

John D. Rockefeller
1839–1937

John D. Rockefeller was one of the most hated and admired figures of his time. The ruthless tactics he used in building his oil empire won him many enemies. Yet, he also donated much of his fortune to charitable causes, funding parks and universities. Journalist Ida Tarbell described Rockefeller as "a man whose soul is built like a ship in air-tight compartments. . . . The life that goes on in compartment one has no relation to that of compartment two."

Biography Quest ●nline

What experience taught Rockefeller his first lesson as a businessman?

For: The answer to the question about Rockefeller
Visit: PHSchool.com
Web Code: myd-6142

Debate Over Trusts Was big business good or bad for the nation? Americans at the time hotly debated that issue. Today, many historians believe that both views are partly true.

Critics saw trusts as a threat to **free enterprise,** the system in which privately owned businesses compete freely. They saw leaders like Carnegie and Rockefeller as "robber barons" who unfairly eliminated competition. Critics also pointed out that business leaders used their wealth to influence politicians.

Others saw big business leaders as bold "captains of industry" who built up the economy and created jobs. They argued that limiting costly competition allowed companies to lower prices for their products. As a result, American consumers were able to afford more goods and services.

Social Darwinism A new philosophy called Social Darwinism also supported the trend toward trusts. Scientist Charles Darwin had said that, in nature, forms of animal and plant life survived if they could adapt to change better than others. Social Darwinism applied this idea of "survival of the fittest" to human affairs.

Big business leaders used Social Darwinism to justify efforts to limit competition. Businesses that drove out their competitors, they said, were "fittest" and deserved to survive. As you will see, Social Darwinism was also used to justify harsh working conditions.

✔**Checkpoint** How did Rockefeller control the oil industry?

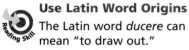
Use Latin Word Origins
The Latin word *ducere* can mean "to draw out." Combine this with *pro-,* meaning "forth." Connect these word origins to the modern usage of the word *products.*

Vocabulary Builder
justify (JUHS tih fī) **v.** to give good reason for an action

Trusts and Monopolies: Good or Bad?

A newspaper editor, quoted below, defends the right of businesses to cooperate in forming trusts and monopolies.

❝The right to cooperate is as unquestionable as the right to compete. . . . The trust denies competition only by producing and selling more cheaply than those outside the trust can produce and sell.❞

—Benjamin R. Tucker, Chicago Conference on Trusts

This cartoon presents a different view of giant business monopolies.

Reading Primary Sources
Skills Activity

By 1900, the question of trusts and monopolies had become one of the most hotly debated issues in the United States.

(a) Interpret Primary Sources According to Tucker, how does the public benefit from trusts?

(b) Detect Points of View How does the view of monopoly expressed in the cartoon differ from Tucker's view?

Changes in the Workplace

Before the Civil War, most factories were small. A boss knew every worker in the shop. As giant industries grew, however, the close relationships between owners and workers ended.

American industry attracted millions of new workers. Most were immigrants or native-born whites. Others were African Americans who left southern farms for northern factories.

Women and Children In some industries, the majority of workers were women. They outnumbered men in the textile mills of New England, the tobacco factories of the South, and the garment sweatshops of New York. A sweatshop is a manufacturing workshop where workers toil long hours under poor conditions for low pay.

Children also worked in industry, often in hazardous jobs. In bottle factories, eight-year-old boys ran with white-hot bottles to cooling racks. Children toiled in textile mills, tobacco factories, coal mines, and garment sweatshops. Most child laborers could not go to school. Therefore, they had little chance of improving their lives.

Dangerous Conditions Factory work could be dangerous. Breathing in fibers or dust all day, textile workers and miners came down with lung diseases. Steelworkers risked burns and death from vats of molten metal. Employers were not required to pay compensation for injuries suffered on the job. Social Darwinists claimed that such harsh conditions were necessary to cut costs, increase production, and ensure survival of the business.

An accident at a New York sweatshop tragically called attention to the dangers many workers faced. On March 25, 1911, fire broke out in the Triangle Shirtwaist Factory. Within minutes, the upper stories were ablaze. Hundreds of workers raced for the exits only to find them locked. The company had locked the doors to keep workers at their jobs. Panicked workers piled up against the exits.

Firetrucks rushed to the scene, but their ladders were too short to reach the fire. One after another, workers trying to escape the flames leaped to their deaths. Nearly 150 people, most of them young women, died in the Triangle Fire. As a result, New York and other states approved safety laws to help protect factory workers.

☑ **Checkpoint** **What dangers did factory workers face?**

Child coal miners

Workers Organize

Since the early days of the Industrial Revolution, factory workers had made attempts to organize. Most early efforts to form unions failed, however. Companies hired private security guards to attack strikers or union organizers. In addition, laws made it illegal for workers to go on strike. Still, workers continued their attempts to form unions, often in secret. Labor unions sought safer working conditions, higher wages, and shorter hours.

A Violent Strike

Strikes often turned violent. This 1877 picture shows a confrontation between Maryland state militia and workers during a railroad strike. At least 10 strikers were killed. **Critical Thinking: Evaluate Information** *How does this picture suggest that there was violence on both sides?*

Knights of Labor In 1869, a group of Philadelphia clothing workers formed a union called the Knights of Labor. At first, the union was small and secret. Then, in 1879, the Knights elected Terence Powderly as president. Powderly rejected the use of strikes as a tool. Instead, he tried to win support by holding public rallies.

Under Powderly, the Knights of Labor admitted women, African Americans, immigrants, and unskilled workers. No earlier labor union had included all workers. For a time, the Knights became the biggest union in the country.

Union successes were undercut by a series of violent labor disputes. One of the worst episodes occurred in Chicago. On May 4, 1886, striking workers rallied in Haymarket Square. Suddenly, a bomb exploded and killed seven policemen. Police sprayed the crowd with bullets. As a result of such violence, public opinion turned against unions. The Knights of Labor, some of whom were at Haymarket Square, lost much of their influence.

Rise of the AFL In 1886, the year of the Haymarket Riot, Jewish immigrant Samuel Gompers formed a new union. It was called the American Federation of Labor, or AFL. The AFL soon replaced the Knights of Labor as the leading union in the country.

Unlike the Knights, the AFL admitted skilled workers only. Gompers argued that skilled workers could create a powerful union because their skills made it costly and difficult to train replacements. He also believed that the most effective way to win improvements was through collective bargaining. In collective bargaining, unions negotiate with management for workers as a group. Gompers believed in using strikes, but only if all else failed.

This practical approach worked well. By 1904, the AFL had grown to more than a million members. But because it barred African Americans, immigrants, and unskilled workers, the AFL still included only a tiny fraction of American workers.

Women in the Labor Movement Women played leading roles in building unions. Mary Harris Jones tirelessly traveled the country, campaigning for unions and giving support to striking miners. She called attention to the hard lives of children in textile mills. Because of her work with children, people began calling her Mother Jones.

Bitter Strikes In 1893, the nation was hit by a severe enconomic depression. Many business owners cut production, fired workers, and slashed wages. A wave of violent strikes swept the country. One of the worst occurred near Chicago. George Pullman, a manufacturer of railroad cars, cut his workers' pay by 25 percent. Still, he refused to lower rents on company-owned housing.

Angry workers struck the Pullman plant. Railroad workers walked off their jobs in support. By July, rail lines were shut down from coast to coast. President Grover Cleveland then sent federal troops to Chicago to end the strike. They were joined by deputies paid by the railroads. Marshals fired on the crowds, killing two protesters.

In such violent labor disputes, the public generally sided with the owners. Most Americans saw striking unions as radical and violent. By 1900, only about 3 percent of American workers belonged to a union.

✓Checkpoint **What methods did the AFL use?**

☆ **Looking Back and Ahead** Big business grew at a rapid pace. Organized labor also grew but faced many obstacles. In the next chapter, you will learn how these trends began to shift.

Mother Jones

Section 2 | **Check Your Progress**

Progress Monitoring Online
For: Self-test with instant help
Visit: PHSchool.com
Web Code: mya-6142

Comprehension and Critical Thinking

1. (a) Recall What big business tactic did Rockefeller use to eliminate competition?
(b) Compare and Contrast How were trusts viewed as both a threat and an advantage to the free enterprise system?

2. (a) List How did changes in the factory system affect workers in the late 1800s?
(b) Draw Conclusions Why was there an effort to organize workers into labor unions?

◎ Reading Skill

3. Use Latin Word Origins Connect the roots *ad-*, meaning "out," and *optare*, meaning "choose or wish," to the modern English word *adopted* as it is used in the following sentence: To raise capital, Americans adopted new ways of organizing business.

Key Terms

4. Draw a table with six rows and two columns. In the first column, list these terms: entrepreneur, corporation, monopoly, trust, free enterprise, collective bargaining. In the next column, write the definition of each word.

Writing

5. Which of the following statements seems the most emotional in its appeal? Which seems the most persuasive? Why?
Statements:
(a) One cause of the Pullman strike was George Pullman's failure to lower rents on company-owned housing.
(b) One cause of the Pullman strike was George Pullman's unfair treatment of workers.
(c) One cause of the Pullman strike was a conflict between George Pullman and his workers over wages and rent.

Big and Busy

❝The things I looked at most was the big buildings and the busy look that everybody had. I thought to myself that in a country where they made things as wonderful as those buildings, anything was possible—even for a farmer boy like me.❞

— Andrew Kokas, Lithuanian immigrant, describing New York City, ca. 1912

◄ New York City's Flatiron Building, under construction in 1902

Cities Grow and Change

Objectives
- Explain why cities grew in the late 1800s.
- Describe the problems city dwellers faced and the efforts to improve city life.
- Identify the attractions and leisure activities cities offered.

🕑 Reading Skill

Use Latin Word Origins Latin roots can be paired with different prefixes or suffixes to create related words. For example, the root *port* means "carry." Paired with the prefix *sub-*, meaning "beneath," it is the root of the English word *support*, meaning "carry from beneath." Paired with the prefix *im-*, meaning "in or toward," it is the root of the English word *import*, meaning "carry into." As you read, look for examples of words that share a Latin root.

Key Terms and People

urbanization
tenement

Jane Addams
settlement house

Why It Matters As the new Industrial Revolution changed the way Americans worked and lived, it also changed where they worked and lived. More and more Americans moved from the rural farmlands to the big cities and the little towns that sprouted all around these cities. This is a trend that still continues today.

❷ Section Focus Question: What were the causes and effects of the rapid growth of cities?

Rapid Growth of Cities

"We cannot all live in cities," wrote journalist Horace Greeley, "yet nearly all seem determined to do so." Greeley was describing the growth of American cities in the late 1800s.

Urbanization The rate of urbanization was astonishing. Urbanization is the rapid growth of city populations. In 1860, only one American in five was a city dweller. By 1890, one in three lived in a city. For the first time, the United States had cities the sizes of London and Paris.

The reason for this rapid urbanization was simple. Cities attracted industry, and industry attracted people. Farmers, immigrants, and African Americans from the South all migrated to cities in search of jobs and excitement.

Many fast-growing cities were located near waterways. New York and San Francisco had excellent ocean harbors. Chicago rose on the shores of Lake Michigan. Cities near waterways drew industry because they provided easy transport for goods.

Growing Out and Up New technology helped cities grow. Elevated trains carried passengers over crowded streets. In 1887, the first electric streetcar system opened in Richmond, Virginia. Ten years later, the nation's first electric subway trains began running beneath the streets of Boston.

Public transportation gave rise to suburbs, living areas on the outskirts of a city. People no longer had to live in cities to work in cities. Steel bridges also <u>accelerated</u> suburban growth. The Brooklyn Bridge, completed in 1883, linked the city center in Manhattan to outlying Brooklyn. As a result, New York City was able to spread out to house its growing population.

Cities began to expand upward as well as outward. In 1885, architects in Chicago constructed the first 10-story building. People called it a "skyscraper" because its top seemed to touch the sky. By 1900, steel-framed skyscrapers up to 30 stories high towered over cities. Electric elevators whisked office workers to the upper floors.

As cities grew outward from their old downtown sections, living patterns changed. Many cities took on a similar shape. Poor families crowded into the oldest sections at the city's center. Middle-class people lived farther out in row houses or new apartment buildings. The rich built fine homes on the outskirts of the city.

☑ **Checkpoint** How did technology change city life?

Problems of Urban Life

Rapid urbanization brought many problems. Fire was a constant threat in tightly packed neighborhoods. In 1871, fire engulfed Chicago. Winds blew flames across the city faster than a person could run. The Chicago Fire leveled 3 square miles of downtown, killed 300 people, and left 18,000 homeless.

Vocabulary Builder
<u>accelerate</u> (ak SEL er ayt) **v.** to increase in speed

Use Latin Word Origins
Use the Latin root *urbanus*, meaning "city," to define the word *urbanization*. Then, name at least one other related word that shows the influence of this root.

A Changing City
Cities underwent great changes in the late 1800s. The photograph shows a Chicago street in 1900. *Critical Thinking: Link Past and Present Describe two ways a picture of this street today might look different.*

Elevated railroad

12-story skyscraper

Rapidly growing population

Electric streetcar

A Tenement Family

This photograph shows a family in their New York tenement apartment. **Critical Thinking: Clarify Problems** *Based on this photograph and your reading, identify one problem this family might face daily.*

Vocabulary Builder

clinic (KLIHN ihk) **n.** place where people receive medical treatment, often for free or for a small fee

Tenement Life In downtown slums, the poor lived in bleak conditions. People crowded into tenements, buildings divided into many tiny apartments. Many apartments had no windows, heat, or indoor plumbing. Often, 10 people might live in a single room. Several families shared a single bathroom.

Slum streets were littered with garbage. Outbreaks of cholera and other diseases were common. Babies ran the greatest risk. In one Chicago slum, half of all babies died before the age of one.

Improving City Life In the 1880s, cities began to improve urban life. They installed streetlights and set up fire, sanitation, and police departments. Public health officials waged war on disease.

Religious groups served the poor. Mother Cabrini, a Catholic nun, set up hospitals and clinics for people who could not afford a doctor. The Salvation Army, founded by a Methodist minister, gave food, clothing, and shelter to the homeless.

Settlement Houses Reformers like Jane Addams worked hard for poor city dwellers. Addams came from a well-to-do family, but she felt strong sympathy for the poor. In 1889, she opened Hull House, a settlement house in the slums of Chicago. A settlement house is a center offering help to the urban poor. Soon, reformers— most of them women—had started settlement houses in other major cities.

At settlement houses, volunteers taught English to immigrants, sponsored music and sports for young people, and provided nurseries for children of working mothers. Addams and other settlement house leaders also pressured state legislatures to outlaw child labor.

☑Checkpoint   **What problems did tenement dwellers face?**

The Excitement of City Life

Despite hardships, cities offered attractions that were not available in the country. Newcomers were awed by electric lights that turned night into day, elevated railroads rumbling overhead, and tall buildings that seemed to pierce the clouds.

Department Stores Downtown shopping areas attracted hordes of people. People came to buy the goods pouring in from American factories. To meet the needs of shoppers, merchants developed a new type of store, the department store.

Earlier, people had bought shirts in one store, boots in another, and lamps in a third. A department store offered all of these goods in separate sections of the same store. Shoppers could wander from floor to floor, bathed in light from crystal chandeliers. Elegant window displays advertised the goods for sale.

Leisure Activities Long hours on the job made people value their free time. This strict division between work and play led to a new interest in leisure. To meet this need, cities provided a wealth of entertainment. Almost every museum, orchestra, art gallery, and theater was located in a city. Circuses drew audiences with elephants, lions, acrobats, and clowns.

In the 1850s, Frederick Law Olmsted planned Central Park in New York. Other cities followed suit. Parks, zoos, and gardens allowed urban dwellers to enjoy green grass and open air.

Cause and Effect

CAUSES

- Growth of industries in cities attracted workers.
- African Americans from the South and immigrants sought a better life.
- Many cities near waterways attracted industries.
- Technological advances led cities to construct subways, trolleys, streetlights, bridges, and skyscrapers.
- Many leisure activities that cities provided drew people to urban areas.

URBANIZATION

EFFECTS

- Urban transportation systems enabled people to live in one part of the city and work in another.
- Flood of people into cities led to teeming neighborhoods that became slums.
- Improvements in transportation gave rise to suburbs.

Reading Charts
Skills Activity

The movement of large numbers of people to cities was one of the biggest social changes of the late 1800s.

(a) Interpret Charts How did technology encourage the growth of cities?

(b) Analyze Cause and Effect Why was the growth of industry a cause of urbanization?

Sports Americans had always enjoyed outdoor games. Not until after the Civil War, however, did professional sports teams begin to spring up in cities. The most popular sport by far was baseball. A guidebook of the time noted:

> "Base ball first taught us Americans the value of physical exercise as an important aid . . . in cultivating the mind up to its highest point. It is to the introduction of base ball as a national pastime, in fact, that the growth of athletic sports in general in popularity is largely due."
> —*Spalding's Official Base Ball Guide,* 1889

The first professional team, the Cincinnati Red Stockings, appeared in 1869. Only seven years later, teams from eight cities formed the National League of Professional Baseball Clubs. A game might draw as many as 5,000 fans, loudly rooting for their city's home team. African American players, banned from the majors in the 1880s, formed their own professional baseball league.

In 1891, James Naismith nailed two peach baskets to the walls of a gym in Springfield, Massachusetts. He handed players a soccer ball and challenged them to throw the ball in the basket. The new game, called basketball, became a favorite winter sport. Football was also popular. At the time, the sport was brutal and dangerous. Players wore no helmets. In one season, 44 college players died of injuries.

✓**Checkpoint** What leisure activities did city dwellers enjoy?

☆ **Looking Back and Ahead** You have already learned that immigration contributed to the growth of cities. In the next section, you will take a closer look at immigrant life.

Early baseball glove and baseball card

Section 3 | Check Your Progress

Progress Monitoring ⬤nline
For: Self-test with instant help
Visit: PHSchool.com
Web Code: mya-6143

Comprehension and Critical Thinking

1. (a) **Describe** Why did cities grow rapidly after the Civil War?
   (b) **Apply Information** What role did technology play in urbanization? Give at least two examples.

2. (a) **Identify** What type of housing did poor city dwellers live in?
   (b) **Identify Benefits** Why do you think many people wanted to live in cities in spite of harsh conditions?

Reading Skill

3. **Use Latin Word Origins** The Latin root *urb* means "city." How does this influence the meaning of the term *suburb*? What other word in Section 3 shows the influence of the root *urb*?

Key Terms

Read each sentence below. If the sentence is true, write YES. If the sentence is not true, write NO and explain why.

4. Urbanization was the result of people moving to western farms.

5. Tenements were apartments used by the wealthy.

6. Settlement houses provided needed services for city dwellers.

Writing

7. "Life in a city is more rewarding than life outside a city." List two or three arguments in favor of this opinion and two or three arguments opposing this opinion.

Three Things Struck Me

❝You see, there were three things that struck me. One was that everyone worked. The factory whistles all over the city blew at seven in the morning, and at six at night. . . . Secondly, everybody had to go to school until they were 16 years old. School, education, was compulsory. And third, military service was voluntary.❞

—Maxwell Lear, immigrant, describing differences between America and Europe, ca. 1900

◀ Doctor examines immigrant children

The New Immigrants

Objectives

- Identify the reasons immigration to the United States increased in the late 1800s.
- Describe the difficulties immigrants faced adjusting to their new lives.
- Discuss how immigrants assimilated and contributed to American life.
- Describe efforts to limit immigration.

Reading Skill

Use Other Word Origins The English language reflects interactions with cultures from around the world. Some words have been adopted in their original form. Others have changed in spelling or pronunciation but still show the influence of the original language.

Key Terms

steerage anarchist
assimilation

Why It Matters The industrial age changed the face of cities with new buildings and bridges. It also changed the population. Millions of new immigrants came to America during the late 1800s and early 1900s. While some Americans welcomed the newcomers, others disliked or even feared them. Today, Americans still wrestle with the issue of how to deal with immigration.

Section Focus Question: How was the experience of immigrants both positive and negative?

A Fresh Start

Between 1865 and 1915, some 25 million immigrants entered the United States—more than the population of the entire country in 1850! They were part of a worldwide surge of migration.

Reasons for Migration There were many reasons for this vast migration. In European nations such as Italy, the amount of farmland was shrinking as populations swelled. Machines were replacing farmhands, forcing more people from the land. They looked to the United States as a "land of opportunity" where they could build a better life.

Other immigrants sought religious freedom. In the 1880s, Jews in Russia became targets of government-sponsored pogroms (POH grohmz), or violent attacks against Jews. Armenian Christians faced similar persecution in Turkey.

Political unrest drove many from their native lands. In 1910, a revolution in Mexico pushed tens of thousands of refugees across the Rio Grande.

Jobs also pulled immigrants to the United States. Steamship companies and railroads, which profited from immigration, sent agents to Asia and Europe to advertise cheap land and plentiful jobs. The promise of freedom also drew people from lands without traditions of democracy and liberty.

Immigration, 1865–1915

Immigration to the United States, 1865–1915

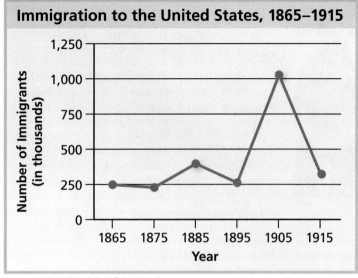

Source: *Historical Statistics of the United States*

Sources of Emigration, 1865–1915

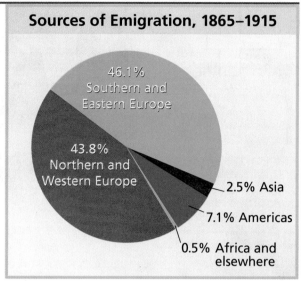

46.1% Southern and Eastern Europe

43.8% Northern and Western Europe

2.5% Asia

7.1% Americas

0.5% Africa and elsewhere

Source: *Historical Statistics of the United States*

Reading Charts
Skills Activity

The line graph shows how the number of immigrants changed in the decades after the Civil War. The pie chart shows where these "new immigrants" in the United States came from.

(a) Read a Graph Approximately how many immigrants entered the United States in 1875? In 1905?

(b) Draw Inferences Based on your reading, how would the pie chart have looked different in the 1830s?

The New Immigrants In the early and mid-1800s, most immigrants were Protestants or Catholics from northern and western Europe. Many spoke English and had experience in democracy.

By contrast, most of the "new immigrants" who began to arrive in the late 1800s came from nations of southern and eastern Europe, such as Italy, Poland, Russia, and Greece. Most were Catholic or Jewish. A smaller number came from Asia and the Pacific. Few understood English or had experience living in a democracy or in a city.

☑Checkpoint Why did many people leave their homelands?

Starting a New Life

The decision to emigrate was difficult. It meant leaving home, family, and friends and starting a strange life. (For more on the immigrants' experiences, see the Life at the Time feature in this chapter.)

Coming to America The passage by boat was miserable. Immigrants were crammed below decks in steerage, large compartments that usually held cattle. The tight, airless berths were breeding grounds for disease. Rough seas sickened the travelers.

Most people coming from Europe landed in New York. After 1892, they went to the receiving center on Ellis Island. Asian immigrants entered through Angel Island in San Francisco Bay after 1910.

New arrivals faced a rigorous physical examination at the receiving centers. Did they limp? Were their eyes free of disease? Those judged to be disabled or seriously ill might be sent home.

Immigrant Neighborhoods Once admitted to the United States, about two thirds of immigrants settled in cities, near other people from the same country. Ethnic neighborhoods helped people feel less <u>isolated</u> in their new homes.

In immigrant neighborhoods, sidewalks rang with the sounds of Italian, Chinese, Yiddish, and other languages. Newcomers celebrated familiar holidays and cooked foods from the old country, such as kielbasa (Polish sausage) and goulash (Hungarian stew). Italians joined social groups such as the Sons of Italy. Greeks read newspapers in Greek. Small storefronts were turned into Jewish synagogues or Buddhist temples.

Vocabulary Builder
<u>isolate</u> (ī sah layt) **v.** to set apart; to separate

☑**Checkpoint** **What hardships did immigrants face?**

Becoming American

Immigrant neighborhoods were springboards to a new life. Organizations called immigrant aid societies helped new arrivals with clothing, housing, and language classes.

Assimilation Newcomers often felt caught between the old world and new. Most clung to traditional modes of worship, family life, and community relations. At the same time, they worked hard to assimilate. Assimilation is the process of becoming part of another culture.

Children of immigrants assimilated more rapidly than their parents. Surrounded by English-speakers in school and on the street, they learned the language quickly. They played baseball and dressed like native-born Americans. Immigrant parents felt both pride and pain as they saw their children change.

Becoming American
Citizenship classes, like the one shown here, were an important step toward assimilation. **Critical Thinking:** *Draw Inferences What subjects do you think students like these might study in citizenship classes?*

This man is labeled *Russian Anarchist.*

This man is labeled *Italian Brigand.* A brigand is a bandit.

A Nativist View of Immigration

In this 1891 cartoon, the man in the suit tells Uncle Sam that he can get rid of anarchy, crime, and other ills by restricting immigration. **Critical Thinking: Detect Bias** *What details create a negative picture of immigrants?*

Still, the fondest dream of many immigrants was to educate their children so that the next generation could be better off. Mary Antin, a Russian Jewish immigrant, called education "the essence of American opportunity, the treasure that no thief could touch . . . surer, safer than bread or shelter."

Contributions of Immigrants The labor of immigrants was essential to the new American economy. Desperate for money, newcomers took whatever jobs they could find. Immigrants worked in steel mills, meatpacking plants, mines, and garment sweatshops. They helped build subways, skyscrapers, and bridges. Chinese, Irish, and Mexican workers laid down hundreds of miles of railroad track in the West.

Through hard work and saving, many immigrants slowly advanced economically. Often, they began by opening small businesses, such as stores or barbershops, to serve their communities. In time, their customers expanded beyond the neighborhood. Outsiders might bring their clothing to Chinese laundries or buy foods they had never tasted before. In this way, ethnic foods such as spaghetti, chow mein, and bagels became part of American life.

Individual immigrants made major contributions. Andrew Carnegie and Alexander Graham Bell were born in Scotland. Samuel Goldwyn and Louis Mayer, Jewish immigrants from Eastern Europe, established the motion picture industry in California. Italian-born Arturo Toscanini became a famous orchestra conductor. Belgian immigrant Leo Baekeland invented the first plastic.

Reading Skill

Use Other Word Origins

Identify the words in this paragraph that came into English from the Yiddish word *beygl,* meaning "ring or bracelet," and the Italian word *spago,* meaning "string or cord."

☑ **Checkpoint** How did immigrants assimilate?

A New Wave of Nativism

As in the 1840s, increased immigration led to a wave of nativism. Nativists sought to preserve the United States for native-born American citizens.

Nativists argued that the new immigrants would not assimilate because their languages, religions, and customs were too different. They also charged that immigrants took jobs away from Americans. Nativists associated immigrants with violence, crime, and anarchy. An **anarchist** is a person who opposes all forms of government.

On the West Coast, nativist feelings against Chinese immigrants ran high. Mobs drove Chinese from mining camps and cities and sometimes killed them. In 1882, Congress passed a law to exclude Chinese laborers from the United States. The Chinese Exclusion Act was the first law limiting immigration based on race. It was finally repealed in 1943.

In 1917, Congress passed a law that denied entry to immigrants who could not read their own languages. Since education at the time was usually restricted to the wealthy, this law barred most of the world's poor people from immigrating to the United States.

Vocabulary Builder
exclude (ehks KLYOOD) **v.** to keep out, expel, or reject

☑ **Checkpoint** **Why did nativists oppose immigration?**

☆ **Looking Back and Ahead** Although immigration slowed after 1917, it never stopped. In the 1960s, Congress finally eased restrictions on immigration.

Section 4 | Check Your Progress

Progress Monitoring Online
For: Self-test with instant help
Visit: PHSchool.com
Web Code: mya-6144

Comprehension and Critical Thinking

1. (a) List Why did people immigrate to the United States in the late 1800s?
(b) Frame Questions What five questions could you ask one of those immigrants?

2. (a) Describe How did immigrants try to assimilate?
(b) Detect Bias How did nativists feel about the ability of immigrants to assimilate?

Reading Skill

3. Use Other Word Origins The text lists *kielbasa* and *goulash*, food items introduced to America by immigrants. The Polish and Hungarian words are used because these foods have no English-word counterparts. On your own or with a partner, name foods from other cultures. Do we use the original name or an English word?

Key Terms

Complete each of the following sentences so that the second part explains the first part and shows your understanding of the term.
4. Many immigrants traveled across the ocean in steerage; _____.
5. Immigrants blended into American life through a process called assimilation; _____.

Writing

6. Imagine that you are writing an editorial in which you object to a bill that excludes immigrants who could not read their own languages. Which of the following arguments is most persuasive? Why? **Arguments:**

(a) Many native-born American citizens do not know how to read, so the bill uses an unfair standard for immigrants.

(b) Immigrants come to this country for a better life, which includes getting an education.

(c) The bill is being used as a trick to restrict all immigration.

An Immigrant's Journey

From all over the world, immigrants poured into the United States. Wherever they came from, these newcomers shared many of the same hopes, fears, and challenges.

 Passage

Immigrants faced a long, difficult ocean crossing crowded into ship holds that were designed to carry cargo or cattle.

"Day after day the weather was bad and the sea stormy. The hatch was tightly closed and there was no circulation of air, so we were all tortured by the bad odor."

—Japanese immigrant describes the voyage

European immigrants arrive in New York

 Arrival

New York's Ellis Island was the point of entry for many European immigrants. Asians were detained on Angel Island outside San Francisco.

"Immigration officials slammed a tag on you with your name, address, country of origin, etc. . . . Then they pushed you and they'd point, because they didn't know whether you spoke English or not."

—Irish immigrant describes arrival at Ellis Island

3 ▸ Ethnic Neighborhoods

Crowded into ethnic neighborhoods, immigrants preserved familiar ways as they adjusted to their new culture.

"When we first arrived we still wore our wooden shoes. . . . We conquered the English language beautifully. My father spoke well. But in the home we spoke Frisian."

–Dutch immigrant describes life in America

A street in a Jewish neighborhood in New York

4 ▸ Citizenship

For many immigrants, becoming a citizen was the proudest moment of their lives.

"I am the youngest of America's children, and into my hands is given all her priceless heritage. . . . Mine is the whole majestic past, and mine is the shining future."

–Russian immigrant expresses pride in becoming U.S. citizen

A new citizen is sworn in

Analyze LIFE AT THE TIME

Suppose that you are an immigrant in 1900. For each stage of the journey from passage to citizenship, write a sentence describing your hopes or your fears.

The Finest High School

"Last Monday the dedication exercises of the finest high school building in the world were held. . . . The building contains eighty classrooms, over a dozen laboratories, [and] three gymnasia . . . What makes the school the greatest in the world, however, is not the outside appearances, but the interior. Every branch of high learning has a place. Botany, biology, chemistry, drawing, cooking—nothing is left out. "

—*The New York Times,* March 1, 1903, describing opening of a new high school

▲ Classroom in Washington, D.C., 1899

Education and Culture

Objectives

- Explain how public education changed after 1870.
- Identify new American writers and the topics they wrote about.
- Describe the growth of the American newspaper industry.

🔄 Reading Skill

Use Popular Word Origins Some words and phrases do not come from formal languages. Instead, they arise from popular use. For example, in the previous section, you saw that *basketball* got its name because it was originally played using peach baskets. The term *basketball* remained even when people stopped using real baskets to play with. Other words and phrases also have origins in popular usage that have since gone out of date.

Key Terms and People

compulsory education
realist
Mark Twain

Joseph Pulitzer
yellow journalism

Why It Matters As industry, urbanization, and immigration all expanded, many Americans felt that the nation's educational system needed to improve. States and local school districts constructed new buildings, hired more teachers, and passed laws requiring more children to attend school. Education expanded, but there was room for more improvement. In fact, we today continue to look for ways to improve the nation's education system.

❓ Section Focus Question: What were the causes and effects of an expanded educational system?

Educating Americans

Before 1870, fewer than half of American children went to school. Many attended one-room schoolhouses, with all age levels and only one teacher. As industry grew, people realized that the nation needed an educated workforce. As a result, states improved public schools at all levels.

Education Expands In 1852, Massachusetts passed the first compulsory education law. **Compulsory education** is the requirement that children attend school up to a certain age. Other states in the North, Midwest, and West followed. Most states required a minimum tenth-grade education.

In the South, which had no tradition of public schools, the Freedmen's Bureau built grade schools for both white and black students. Southern states were more reluctant to pass compulsory education laws than states in the North or West. Still, by 1918, every state required children to attend school.

After the Civil War, many cities and towns built public high schools. By 1900, there were 6,000 high schools in the country. Still, not until 1950 did the majority of Americans of high school age graduate.

Higher education also <u>expanded</u>. New private colleges for both women and men opened. Many states built universities that offered free or low-cost education.

Vocabulary Builder
<u>expand</u> (ek SPAND) **v.** to become bigger

The School Day For elementary school students, the typical school day lasted from 8:00 A.M. to 4:00 P.M. Pupils learned the "three Rs": reading, 'riting, and 'rithmetic.

The most widely used textbooks were *McGuffey's Eclectic Readers.* Students memorized and recited lessons that had titles like "Waste Not, Want Not." Such poems and stories taught not only reading but also moral values and the Christian religion.

Education for Adults Older Americans also got more opportunity to widen their knowledge. Wealthy individuals such as Andrew Carnegie gave money to towns and cities to build public libraries. Libraries offered more than books and magazines. Speakers often gave talks on important topics of the day.

In 1874, a Methodist minister opened a summer school for Bible teachers along Lake Chautauqua (shuh TAWK wuh) in New York. The next year, the camp was opened to the public. Mostly middle-class men and women gathered at Chautauqua to hear lectures on a wide variety of subjects. The Chautauqua Society later began sending out traveling companies on a wide <u>circuit</u>. In time, Chautauquas reached as many as 5 million people in 10,000 towns each year.

Vocabulary Builder
<u>circuit</u> (SIR kuht) **n.** route repeatedly traveled

✓**Checkpoint** **How did states expand public education?**

High School Enrollment, 1880–1910

Number of Students (in thousands) vs. Year (1880, 1890, 1900, 1910)

Source: *Historical Statistics of the United States*

Reading Charts
Skills Activity

The late 1800s saw a dramatic rise in public high school enrollment.

(a) **Read a Chart** How many Americans attended public high schools in 1880? In 1910?

(b) **Distinguish Relevant Information** Which of the following might help you understand the reasons for the trend shown on the graph: a mathematics textbook from 1890; a list showing when states passed compulsory education laws; a population graph? Explain.

New American Writers

As learning became available to more people, Americans began to read more books and magazines. Many bestsellers were dime novels, low-priced paperbacks that often told thrilling tales of the "Wild West." One popular writer, Horatio Alger, wrote "rags-to-riches" stories about poor boys who became successful through hard work, courage, and honesty.

Realism Other American writers were realists, writers who try to show life as it is. They often emphasized the harsh side. Some, such as Stephen Crane, had been newspaper reporters. Crane depicted the hardships of slum life in his novel *Maggie: A Girl of the Streets.*

California-born Jack London wrote of miners and sailors who risked their lives in backbreaking jobs. Kate Chopin shocked readers with *The Awakening,* a novel about an unhappily married woman. The poems of Paul Laurence Dunbar described the joys and sorrows of black life. He was the first African American to earn a living as a writer.

Mark Twain The most popular author of the time was Mark Twain, the pen name of Samuel Clemens. Twain made his stories realistic by capturing the speech patterns of southerners who lived and worked along the Mississippi River.

Twain set his novel *Huckleberry Finn* in the days before the Civil War. Huck, an uneducated boy, and Jim, an escaped slave, raft down the Mississippi River together. Though brought up to believe slavery is right, Huck comes to respect Jim and decides to help him win his freedom.

Some parents complained that Huck was a crude character who would have a bad effect on children. But today, many critics consider *Huckleberry Finn* to be one of the greatest American novels.

☑**Checkpoint** **What kinds of topics did realists write about?**

Use Popular Word Origins
Based on context clues, what do you think the phrase *pen name* means? What do you think was the origin of this term?

Huckleberry Finn
In this passage from Mark Twain's *Huckleberry Finn,* shown below, Huck recounts a conversation with his friend Jim, an escaped slave. **Critical Thinking:** *Evaluate Information How does the language in this passage give a sense of realism?*

Mark Twain

"He was saying how the first thing he would do when he got to a free State he would go to saving up money and never spend a single cent, and when he got enough he would buy his wife, which was owned on a farm close to where Miss Watson lived; and then they would both work to buy the two children, and if their master wouldn't sell them, they'd get an Ab'litionist to go and steal them."

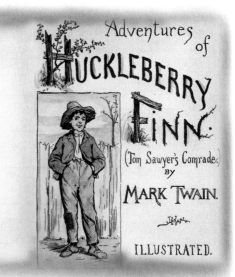

Cover of an early edition of *Huckleberry Finn*

A Newspaper Boom

The number of American newspapers grew dramatically in the late 1800s. By 1900, half the newspapers in the world were printed in the United States.

Causes The spread of education was one reason for the growth of the newspaper industry. As more Americans could read, they bought more newspapers and magazines.

The newspaper boom was also linked to urbanization. In towns and villages, neighbors could share news face to face. In cities, people needed newspapers to stay informed.

A New Kind of Newspaper A Hungarian immigrant, Joseph Pulitzer, created the first modern, mass-circulation newspaper. In 1883, Pulitzer bought the *New York World*. He immediately cut the price so that more people could afford it.

Pulitzer added crowd-pleasing features to his newspaper, including color comics. The Yellow Kid, a tough but sweet slum boy, became the first popular American comic strip character.

The *New York World* became known for sensational headlines that screamed of crime and scandal. Readership skyrocketed, and other papers followed his lead. Because of the Yellow Kid, critics coined the term yellow journalism to describe the sensational reporting style of the *New York World* and other papers.

The Yellow Kid

☑Checkpoint **Why did the newspaper industry grow?**

⭐ **Looking Back and Ahead** In this section, you saw how education increased the popularity and influence of newspapers. In the next chapter, you will see how newspapers and magazines contributed to a growing reform movement.

Section 5 | Check Your Progress

Progress Monitoring Online
For: Self-test with instant help
Visit: PHSchool.com
Web Code: mya-6145

Comprehension and Critical Thinking

1. **(a) Describe** What were schools like before 1870?
   (b) Draw Inferences Why do you think compulsory education laws were important for the industrialized North?

2. **(a) Identify** What were the goals of realists?
   (b) Apply Information How did Mark Twain's use of language make his stories more realistic?

Reading Skill

3. **Use Popular Word Origins** The phrase "yellow journalism" is still used to describe one type of reporting. How has the meaning separated from its origin?

Key Terms

Read each sentence below. If the sentence is true, write YES and explain why. If the sentence is not true, write NO and explain why not.

4. Yellow journalism used sensational headlines to attract readers.

5. Mark Twain was not a realist because he wrote about people.

6. Compulsory education allowed parents to choose whether or not to send children to school.

Writing

7. Do you think memorizing and reciting lessons from books like *McGuffey's Readers* is a useful way for children to learn? Write a paragraph explaining your opinion. Give at least two reasons.

21st Century Learning Economic and social factors often affect political decisions. A cost-benefit analysis is one tool that helps people make these decisions. A cost-benefit analysis compares the costs and benefits, or rewards, that would result if a certain choice were made.

This is an excerpt from the 1902 book *The Battle With the Slum* by Jacob Riis. He was a journalist, photographer, and reformer who focused attention on the conditions in the slums of New York City.

Primary Source

"The East Side, that had been orderly, became a hotbed of child crime. . . . Yesterday, Mayor Low's reform government voted $6 million for new schools. . . . In the most crowded neighborhood in all the world, where the superintendent lately pleaded in vain for three new schools, half a dozen have been built, the finest in this or any other land—great, light, and airy structures, with playgrounds on the roof; and all over the city the like are going up.

The briefest of our laws . . . says that never one shall be built without its playground. And not for the child's use only. The band shall play there yet and neighbor meet neighbor in such social contact as the slum has never known to its undoing . . . Clergymen applaud the opening of the school buildings on Sunday for concerts, lectures, and neighborhood meetings. Common sense is having its day. The streets are cleaned."

—Jacob Riis, *The Battle With the Slum*

Learn the Skill

Use these steps to conduct a cost-benefit analysis.

1. **Identify the issue.** What is the economic, social, or political issue being considered? Look for the main idea and important details.

2. **List the costs and benefits.** Make a two-column chart. List the benefits in the first column and the costs in the second column.

3. **Compare the costs and the benefits.** Are the benefits greater than the costs? Are the costs greater than the benefits?

4. **Make the best decision.** Based on the costs and benefits in the chart, choose the option that makes the best sense. Be able to give reasons for your choice.

Practice the Skill

Answer the following questions about the primary source on this page.

1. **Identify the issue.** (a) What issue is discussed? (b) What are two details relating to the issue?

2. **List the costs and benefits.** Make a chart listing the costs and benefits.

3. **Compare the costs and the benefits.** Are the benefits greater than the costs? Explain.

4. **Make the best decision.** Based on the information in your chart, what decision would you make about the issue? Explain your answer.

Apply the Skill

See the Review and Assessment at the end of this chapter.

Quick Study Guide

How did industrialization increase the speed of change?

Section 1
A New Industrial Revolution

- The discovery of valuable resources fed a major growth in industry.
- Inventions such as the electric light, the telephone, and the automobile changed life.

Section 2
Big Business and Organized Labor

- Industrial growth gave rise to new forms of business, such as corporations and trusts.
- Harsh working conditions led to the formation of labor unions.

Section 3
Cities Grow and Change

- People migrated to cities to find jobs.
- Rapid urbanization created such problems as poor housing and sanitation.

Section 4
The New Immigrants

- Twenty-five million immigrants entered the United States between 1865 and 1915.
- The work of immigrants contributed to the growth of the American economy.
- A new wave of nativists sought to limit immigration.

Section 5
Education and Culture

- Education expanded in response to the needs of industry.
- As more people learned to read, popular books and newspapers boomed.

Immigrant family

? Exploring the Essential Question

Use the online study guide to explore the essential question.

Section 1
What conditions spurred the growth of industry?

Section 2
How did big business change the workplace and give rise to labor unions?

Chapter 18 Essential Question
How did industrialization increase the speed of change?

Section 5
What were the causes and effects of an expanded educational system?

Section 3
What were the causes and effects of the rapid growth of cities?

Section 4
How was the experience of immigrants both positive and negative?

Key Terms

Answer the questions in complete sentences that show your understanding of the key terms.

1. Why did inventors apply for patents?

2. How did forming corporations help entrepreneurs raise capital?

3. Why did Samuel Gompers favor collective bargaining?

4. Why was assimilation a goal of many immigrants?

5. What services did settlement houses provide?

Comprehension and Critical Thinking

6. **(a) Describe** What government policies helped to spark industrial growth?
   (b) Clarify Problems How did the policies of the federal government create problems for small businesses?

7. **(a) Identify** Identify two devices invented by Thomas Edison.
   (b) Draw Conclusions Some people think Edison's creation of a research laboratory was more important than any of his inventions. Give one reason for this opinion.

8. **(a) Recall** What happened at Haymarket Square on May 4, 1886?
   (b) Analyze Cause and Effect How did the events at Haymarket Square and the Pullman plant affect public opinion toward unions?

9. **(a) Summarize** What did Horace Greeley mean when he said, "We cannot all live in cities, yet nearly all seem determined to do so"?
   (b) Identify Costs and Benefits How did the new Industrial Revolution affect the way of life in cities?

10. **(a) Describe** What jobs did immigrants hold after arriving in the United States?
    (b) Identify Economic Benefits Why do you think immigrants were willing to work long hours in dangerous conditions for little pay?

11. **(a) Describe** What was a typical school day like for a child in the 1880s?
    (b) Draw Conclusions What impact did the Industrial Revolution have on education in America?

History Reading Skill

12. **Use Word Origins** Choose an English word from this chapter, and trace its language influences. Use a print or online dictionary. Most entries will show the languages a word has passed through, in order from most recent to most distant. List the languages your chosen word has moved through.

Writing

13. **Write a Persuasive Paragraph:**
    Choose one headline from the list below and write a persuasive paragraph that gives your opinion on the issue. Remember to support your opinion with facts, examples, and reasons.
    - Captains of Industry: Heroes or Tyrants?
    - Immigration: A Benefit or a Danger?
    - The New Industrial Revolution: A Better Life or a Less Human One?

14. **Write a Narrative:**
    Imagine that you are a settlement house worker in a large city in the late 1800s. Write a letter to a friend describing why you have chosen to live among the poor.

Skills for Life

Conduct a Cost-Benefit Analysis

The document below describes piecework, a system in which garment workers are paid a certain amount for each piece of clothing they make. Use the document to answer the questions.

> "The differential rate system of piecework consists briefly in offering two different rates for the same job; a high price per piece, in case the work is finished in the shortest possible time and in perfect condition, and a low price, if it takes a longer time to do the job or if there are any imperfections in the work. . . . The advantages of this [system] are: First, that the manufactures are produced cheaper under it, while at the same time the workmen earn higher wages."
>
> —Frederick Taylor, "A Piece-Rate System," 1895

15. **(a)** What is the cost of the system discussed in the text? **(b)** What is one benefit of the system?

16. Do you think the benefits are greater than the costs? Explain.

Test Yourself

1. **Which of the following most benefited big business?**

   A creation of the Knights of Labor

   B passage of the Chinese Exclusion Act

   C laissez-faire government policies

   D yellow journalism

Refer to the quotation below to answer Question 2.

> "Give me your tired, your poor,
> Your huddled masses yearning to breathe free,
> The wretched refuse of your teeming shore,
> Send these, the homeless, tempest-tossed to me,
> I lift my lamp beside the golden door!"
>
> —poem by Emma Lazarus, inscribed on the Statue of Liberty pedestal

2. **To whom does the poem refer?**

   A inventors   C realists

   B nativists   D immigrants

Refer to the graph below to answer Question 3.

U.S. Rural and Urban Population, 1870–1920

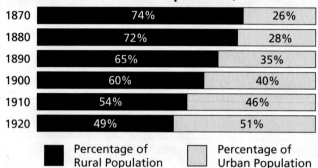

	Percentage of Rural Population	Percentage of Urban Population
1870	74%	26%
1880	72%	28%
1890	65%	35%
1900	60%	40%
1910	54%	46%
1920	49%	51%

Sources: *Historical Statistics of the United States* and *Statistical Abstract of the United States*

3. **In what year was the urban population larger than the rural population?**

   A 1870   C 1910

   B 1890   D 1920

Document-Based Questions

Task: Look at Documents 1 and 2, and answer their accompanying questions. Then, use the documents and your knowledge of history to complete this writing assignment:

Write an essay analyzing the reasons for the success of the AFL.

Document 1: In a speech in 1898, Samuel Gompers described the need for trade unions. *State three purposes of trade unions cited by Gompers.*

> "The trade unions . . . were born of the necessity of workers to protect and defend themselves from encroachment, injustice and wrong. . . . To protect the workers in their inalienable rights to a higher and better life; to protect them, not only as equals before the law, but also in their health, their homes, their firesides, their liberties as men, as workers, and as citizens; to overcome and conquer prejudices and antagonism; to secure to them the right to life; the right to be full sharers in the abundance which is the result of their brain and brawn. . . . The attainment of these is the glorious mission of the trade unions."

Document 2: Unions enjoyed enormous growth in the late 1800s and early 1900s. *What was the increase in union membership between 1897 and 1915?*

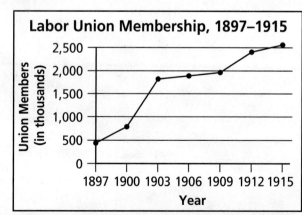

Source: *Historical Statistics of the United States*

Political Reform and the Progressive Era

1870-1920

"*In a crowded city quarter, if the garbage is not properly collected and destroyed, a tenement-house mother may see her children sicken and die.*"

—*Jane Addams,*
Cleaning the Streets of Chicago, *1889*

Photographs like this one by Jacob Riis called public attention to the problems of city slums.

What You Will Learn

Section 1
THE GILDED AGE AND PROGRESSIVE REFORM

Reformers known as Progressives tried to end government corruption and limit the influence of big business.

Section 2
THE PROGRESSIVE PRESIDENTS

Presidents Theodore Roosevelt, William Howard Taft, and Woodrow Wilson backed Progressive reforms.

Section 3
THE RIGHTS OF WOMEN

After decades of effort, women finally won the right to vote.

Section 4
STRUGGLES FOR JUSTICE

African Americans, Mexican Americans, Asian Americans, and religious minorities all faced challenges.

Reading Skill

Identify and Explain Central Issues In this chapter, you will learn to identify central issues and describe them in the context of the times and places in which they occurred.

Political Reform and the Progressive Era

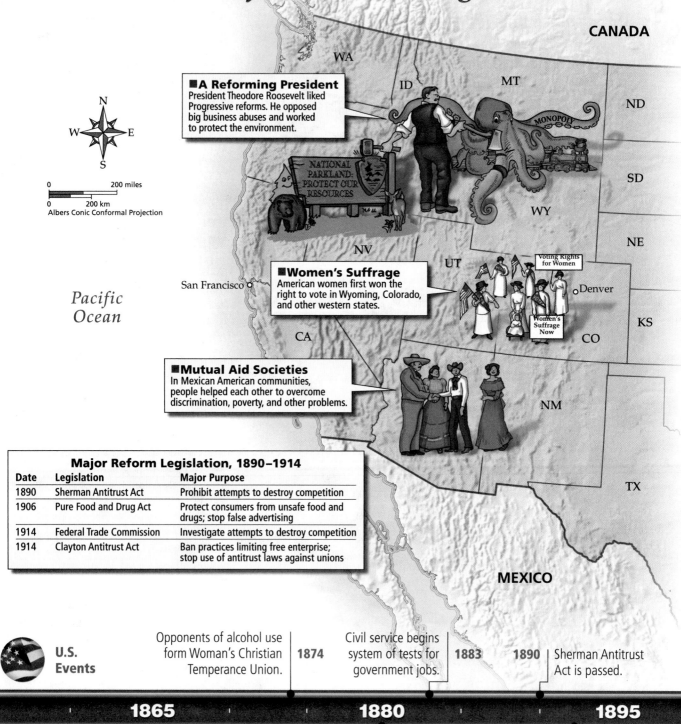

A Reforming President
President Theodore Roosevelt liked Progressive reforms. He opposed big business abuses and worked to protect the environment.

NATIONAL PARKLAND: PROTECT OUR RESOURCES

MONOPOLY

Women's Suffrage
American women first won the right to vote in Wyoming, Colorado, and other western states.

Voting Rights for Women

Women's Suffrage Now

Mutual Aid Societies
In Mexican American communities, people helped each other to overcome discrimination, poverty, and other problems.

CANADA

WA
ID
MT
ND
SD
WY
NE
NV
UT
Denver
KS
CA
CO
San Francisco
Pacific Ocean
NM
TX
MEXICO

N
W E
S

0   200 miles
0   200 km
Albers Conic Conformal Projection

Major Reform Legislation, 1890–1914		
Date	**Legislation**	**Major Purpose**
1890	Sherman Antitrust Act	Prohibit attempts to destroy competition
1906	Pure Food and Drug Act	Protect consumers from unsafe food and drugs; stop false advertising
1914	Federal Trade Commission	Investigate attempts to destroy competition
1914	Clayton Antitrust Act	Ban practices limiting free enterprise; stop use of antitrust laws against unions

U.S. Events

Opponents of alcohol use form Woman's Christian Temperance Union. **1874**

Civil service begins system of tests for government jobs. **1883**

1890 Sherman Antitrust Act is passed.

1865   **1880**   **1895**

World Events

Pogroms against Russian Jews increase. **1880s**

New Zealand is first nation to give women the vote. **1893**

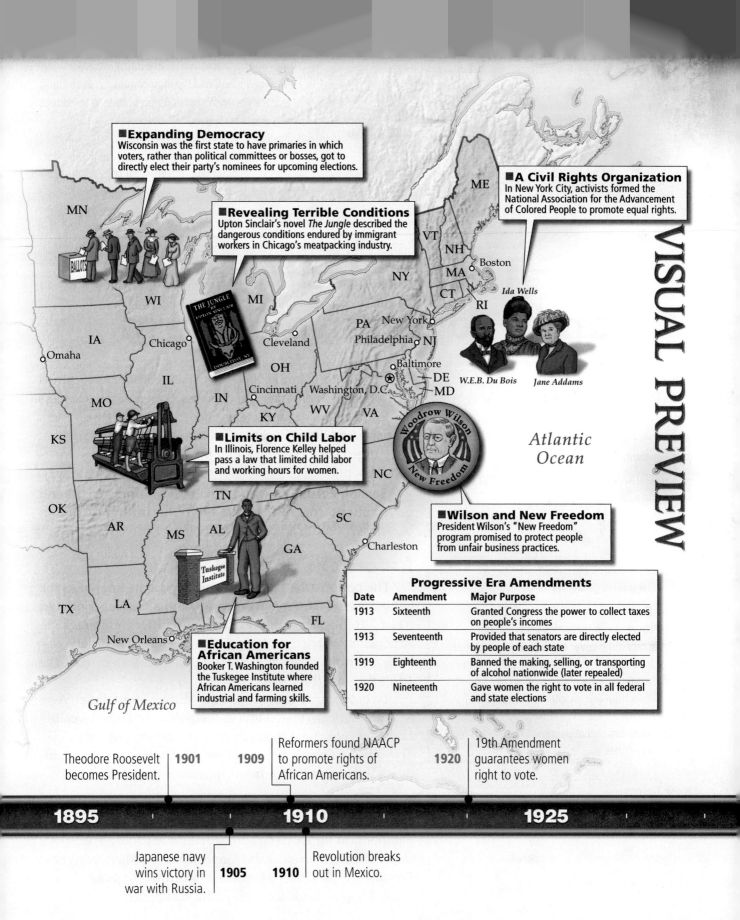

■Expanding Democracy
Wisconsin was the first state to have primaries in which voters, rather than political committees or bosses, got to directly elect their party's nominees for upcoming elections.

■A Civil Rights Organization
In New York City, activists formed the National Association for the Advancement of Colored People to promote equal rights.

■Revealing Terrible Conditions
Upton Sinclair's novel *The Jungle* described the dangerous conditions endured by immigrant workers in Chicago's meatpacking industry.

Ida Wells

W.E.B. Du Bois   *Jane Addams*

■Limits on Child Labor
In Illinois, Florence Kelley helped pass a law that limited child labor and working hours for women.

Atlantic Ocean

Woodrow Wilson
New Freedom

■Wilson and New Freedom
President Wilson's "New Freedom" program promised to protect people from unfair business practices.

■Education for African Americans
Booker T. Washington founded the Tuskegee Institute where African Americans learned industrial and farming skills.

Gulf of Mexico

Progressive Era Amendments

Date	Amendment	Major Purpose
1913	Sixteenth	Granted Congress the power to collect taxes on people's incomes
1913	Seventeenth	Provided that senators are directly elected by people of each state
1919	Eighteenth	Banned the making, selling, or transporting of alcohol nationwide (later repealed)
1920	Nineteenth	Gave women the right to vote in all federal and state elections

Theodore Roosevelt becomes President. **1901**

1909 Reformers found NAACP to promote rights of African Americans.

1920 19th Amendment guarantees women right to vote.

1895   **1910**   **1925**

Japanese navy wins victory in war with Russia. **1905**

1910 Revolution breaks out in Mexico.

Expensive, Inefficient, and Corrupt

❝With very few exceptions, the city governments of the United States are . . . the most expensive, the most inefficient, and the most corrupt. . . . Such cities, like the decaying spots on ripe fruit, tend to corrupt the whole body politic. ❞

—Andrew D. White, educator and diplomat, describing government corruption, 1890

▲ Poor city children

The Gilded Age and Progressive Reform

Objectives
- Identify the problems in American politics during the Gilded Age.
- Describe the political reforms the Progressives supported.
- Explain how journalists contributed to reform efforts.

Reading Skill

Place Events in a Matrix of Time and Place As you read this textbook, notice that chapters often cover overlapping time periods. History is complex and involves many continuing issues. To gain a better understanding of a period, place events from one chapter in the context of other events from the same time period. Think back to other chapters and to your own knowledge for these connections.

Key Terms

civil service
primary
recall
initiative

referendum
graduated income
     tax
muckraker

Why It Matters In the late 1800s, giant corporations gained control of much of American business. Some business leaders abused their power and were aided by corrupt government officials. Americans began to protest against the corruption. They urged government to limit the power of the huge trusts and monopolies.

? Section Focus Question: How did reformers try to end government corruption and limit the influence of big business?

Reform in the Gilded Age

The period after the Civil War came to be known as the Gilded Age. *Gilded* means "coated with a thin layer of gold paint." It suggests falseness beneath surface glitter. Some Americans worried that the glitter of American society was hiding serious problems. The Gilded Age lasted from the 1870s through the 1890s.

Two concerns shaped politics during the Gilded Age. Many Americans feared that industrialists and other wealthy men were enriching themselves at the expense of the public. The other worry was corruption, or dishonesty in government. Bribery and voter fraud appeared to be widespread.

Taming the Spoils System Critics said a key source of corruption was the spoils system, the practice of rewarding political supporters with government jobs. The spoils system had grown since the Age of Jackson. Whenever a new President took office, job seekers swarmed to Washington, demanding rewards for their political support.

In 1881, James Garfield became President. He was soon swamped with people seeking jobs. Four months later, Garfield was shot by a disappointed office seeker. He died two months later. The assassination sparked new efforts to end the spoils system.

Vice President Chester A. Arthur succeeded Garfield. Arthur, a New York politician, owed his own rise to the spoils system. Yet, he worked with Congress to reform how people got government jobs.

In 1883, Arthur signed the Pendleton Act. It created the Civil Service Commission. The **civil service** is a system that includes most government jobs, except elected positions, the judiciary, and the military. The aim of the Civil Service Commission was to fill jobs on the basis of merit. Jobs went to those with the highest scores on civil service examinations. At first, the Commission controlled only a few jobs. Over time, however, the civil service grew to include more jobs.

Controlling Big Business In the late 1800s, big business exerted a strong influence over politics. Railroad owners and industrialists bribed members of Congress in order to secure their votes. Outraged by such actions, many Americans demanded that something be done to limit the power of railroads and monopolies.

Under the Constitution, the federal government has the power to regulate interstate commerce, or trade that crosses state lines. In 1887, President Grover Cleveland signed the Interstate Commerce Act. It forbade practices such as rebates. It also set up the Interstate Commerce Commission to oversee railroads.

Vocabulary Builder
exert (ehks ZERT) **v.** to use; to put into action

The Problem of Corruption

The Capitol building is where Congress meets.

This hand is coming out of a window labeled "Trusts."

Reading Political Cartoons
Skills Activity

In many cities, illegal businesses often paid "protection" to police in order to avoid arrest. This 1894 cartoon compares this practice to corruption in the federal government.

(a) **Interpret Cartoons** Who is the man on the right? What is he getting from the man in the window?

(b) **Draw Inferences** What do you think the giver expects in return?

Thomas Nast cartoon of Boss Tweed

President Benjamin Harrison signed the Sherman Antitrust Act in 1890. It prohibited businesses from trying to limit or destroy competition. The law sounded tough but proved difficult to enforce. Judges sympathetic to business ruled in favor of trusts. Instead of regulating trusts, the Sherman Act was used to limit the power of labor unions. The courts said strikes blocked free trade and thus threatened competition.

Corruption in the Cities Corruption was a particularly serious problem in city governments. As cities grew, they needed to expand services such as sewers, garbage collection, and roads. Often, politicians accepted money to award these jobs to friends. As a result, corruption became a way of life.

In many cities, powerful politicians called bosses controlled work done locally and demanded payoffs from businesses. City bosses were popular with the poor, especially immigrants. The bosses handed out turkeys at Thanksgiving and extra coal in winter. Often, they provided jobs. In return, the poor voted for the boss or his chosen candidate.

William Tweed, commonly known as Boss Tweed, carried corruption to new extremes. During the 1860s and 1870s, he cheated New York City out of more than $100 million. Journalists exposed Tweed's crimes. Cartoonist Thomas Nast pictured Tweed as a greedy giant and as a vulture feeding on the city. Faced with prison, Tweed fled to Spain. There, local police arrested him when they recognized him from Nast's cartoons. Still, when Tweed died in jail in 1878, thousands of poor New Yorkers mourned for him.

☑**Checkpoint** **How did the civil service system limit corruption?**

Progressives and Political Reform

Opposition to corruption led to the rise of the Progressive movement. The Progressives were a <u>diverse</u> group of reformers united by a belief in the public interest, or the good of all the people. The public interest, they said, must not be sacrificed to the greed of a few huge trusts and city bosses.

Vocabulary Builder
<u>diverse</u> (dih VURS) **adj.** different or varied

The Wisconsin Idea Wisconsin was one of the first states to adopt Progressive reforms. Wisconsin governor Robert La Follette, known as Battling Bob, introduced various Progressive reforms that became known as the Wisconsin Idea.

La Follette opposed political bosses. He appointed commissions of experts to solve problems. For example, his railroad commission recommended lowering railroad rates. As rates decreased, rail traffic increased, which helped both railroad owners and customers.

Since the Age of Jackson, party leaders had picked candidates for local and state offices. In 1903, Wisconsin was the first state to adopt a primary run by state government officials. A **primary** is an election in which voters, rather than party leaders, choose their party's candidate. By 1917, all but four states had followed Wisconsin's lead.

Progressive Political Reforms

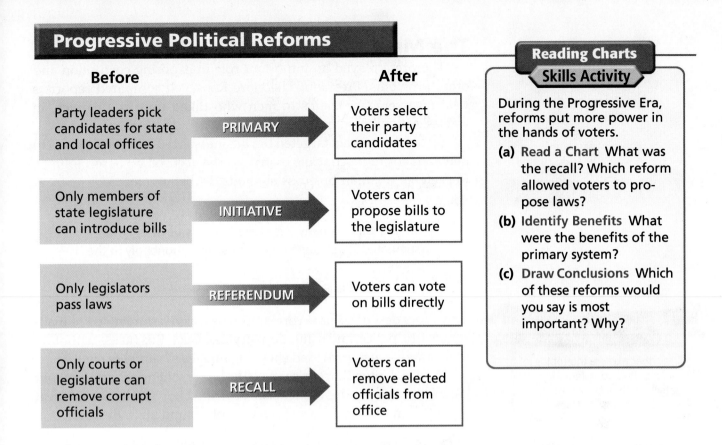

Before		After
Party leaders pick candidates for state and local offices	PRIMARY	Voters select their party candidates
Only members of state legislature can introduce bills	INITIATIVE	Voters can propose bills to the legislature
Only legislators pass laws	REFERENDUM	Voters can vote on bills directly
Only courts or legislature can remove corrupt officials	RECALL	Voters can remove elected officials from office

Reading Charts

Skills Activity

During the Progressive Era, reforms put more power in the hands of voters.

(a) Read a Chart What was the recall? Which reform allowed voters to propose laws?

(b) Identify Benefits What were the benefits of the primary system?

(c) Draw Conclusions Which of these reforms would you say is most important? Why?

More Power to Voters Some states instituted reforms to put more power in the hands of voters. One such reform was the **recall**, a process by which people may vote to remove an elected official from office. The recall made it easier to get rid of corrupt officials.

Other reforms gave voters a direct say in the lawmaking process. The **initiative** is a process that allows voters to put a bill before a state legislature. In order to propose an initiative, voters must collect a certain number of signatures on a petition. The **referendum** is a way for people to vote directly on a proposed new law.

Two Constitutional Amendments Many Progressive reformers backed a **graduated income tax,** a method of taxation that taxes people at different rates depending on income. The wealthy pay taxes at a higher rate than the poor or the middle class. When the Supreme Court ruled that a federal income tax was unconstitutional, Progressives called for a constitutional amendment. The Sixteenth Amendment, which gave Congress the power to pass an income tax, was ratified in 1913.

Since 1789, United States senators had been elected by state legislatures. Powerful interest groups often bribed lawmakers to vote for certain candidates. Progressives wanted to end this abuse by having people vote for senators directly. The Seventeenth Amendment, ratified in 1913, required the direct election of senators.

✔**Checkpoint** What reforms put more power in the hands of voters?

Place Events in a Matrix of Time and Place

In the 1890s, the Populists had also supported an income tax. How did the roots of Populism differ from the roots of Progressivism?

The Muckrakers

The press played an important role in exposing corruption and other problems. President Theodore Roosevelt compared reporters who uncovered problems to men who raked up dirt, or muck, in stables. Muckraker became a term for a crusading journalist.

Some muckrakers targeted big business. Ida Tarbell's work led to demands for more controls on trusts. She accused oil baron John D. Rockefeller of unfair business methods. Tarbell wrote:

> **❝**Every great campaign against rival interests which the Standard Oil Company has carried on has been inaugurated . . . to build up and sustain a monopoly in the oil industry.**❞**
>
> —Ida M. Tarbell, *History of the Standard Oil Company*

Others described how corruption in city government led to inadequate fire, police, and sanitation services. Jacob Riis (REES), a photographer and writer, provided shocking images of slum life.

In 1906, Upton Sinclair's novel *The Jungle* told grisly details about the meatpacking industry. Sinclair described how packers used meat from sick animals and how rats often got ground up in the meat.

✔Checkpoint How did muckrakers stir public opinion?

⭐ **Looking Back and Ahead** The Progressive movement began at local and state levels. In the next section, you will see how three Presidents brought Progressive ideas into the White House.

HISTORIAN'S APPRENTICE ACTIVITY PACK

To further explore the topics in this chapter, complete the activity in the Historian's Apprentice Activity Pack to answer this essential question:

How did industrialization affect the United States?

Section 1 | Check Your Progress

Progress Monitoring Online
For: Self-test with instant help
Visit: PHSchool.com
Web Code: mya-6151

Comprehension and Critical Thinking

1. (a) Recall How was the spoils system reformed during the Gilded Age?
(b) Analyze Cause and Effect What abuses do you think were occurring under the spoils system that made reform necessary?

2. (a) Identify Who were some of the principal muckrakers during the Progressive Era, and what did each try to do?
(b) Link Past and Present What impact do you think their efforts had on life in the United States today?

Reading Skill

3. Place Events in a Matrix of Time and Place Ida Tarbell wrote muckraking articles about the Standard Oil Company. Why did she think this was necessary? How had Standard Oil's business practices changed American industry? Think back to the previous chapter to answer these questions.

Key Terms

Answer the following questions in complete sentences that show your understanding of the key terms.
4. Which jobs are civil service positions?

5. What happens in a primary election?
6. What did muckrakers try to do?
7. What happens in a successful referendum?
8. How are tax rates structured under the graduated income tax?

Writing

9. Write a statement supporting the work of the muckrakers. Then, write a statement opposing their work. For each statement, write one question to ask the muckrakers about their methods and their goals.

Government Over Corporations

❝When I came into office [the Sherman Antitrust Act] was dead; I took it up and for the first time had it enforced. We gained this much by the enforcement: . . . the establishment of the principle that the government was supreme over the great corporations. ❞

—President Theodore Roosevelt, 1912

◀ President Roosevelt was an enthusiastic speaker.

The Progressive Presidents

Objectives

- Describe how Theodore Roosevelt tried to limit the power of business.
- Summarize the main points of Roosevelt's Square Deal.
- Identify the reforms promoted by Presidents Taft and Wilson.

🎯 Reading Skill

Explain Issues From the Past Every era in history has its issues—the ideas or problems that people think about, argue about, and put their energies into. As you read about history, explain these issues to yourself as a way of understanding what mattered to people of that time. Use headings and main ideas to help you identify and explain the issues.

Key Terms and People

Theodore
  Roosevelt
trustbuster
conservation

national park
William Howard
  Taft
Woodrow Wilson

Why It Matters Although Progressives made many gains at the state and local levels, they initially had little success at the national level. That changed, however, in the early 1900s. Several reforming Presidents adopted Progressive ideas, limited the abuses of big business, and tackled other tough national problems.

❓ **Section Focus Question: How did the Progressive Presidents extend reforms?**

The First Progressive President

On September 6, 1901, an unemployed anarchist stood nervously in line at the world's fair in Buffalo, New York. He was waiting to shake the hand of President William McKinley. When McKinley extended his hand, the assassin fired two shots into the President. McKinley died eight days later.

Vice President Theodore Roosevelt then became President. At age 42, he was the youngest President to take office. He was also a strong supporter of Progressive goals.

Teddy Roosevelt Teddy Roosevelt—or TR, as he was called—came from a wealthy New York family. As a child, he suffered from asthma and often was sick. To build his strength, he lifted weights, ran, and boxed. For a time, he worked on a cattle ranch.

TR wanted to serve the public. At the age of 23, he was elected to the New York state legislature. Later, he served on the Civil Service Commission. He then headed New York City's police department and served as assistant secretary of the navy.

In 1898, the United States went to war against Spain. (You will read about this in the next chapter.) Roosevelt led a unit of troops in some daring exploits that received widespread publicity. He returned home to a hero's welcome and was elected governor of New York. Two years later, Roosevelt was elected Vice President under McKinley.

TR and Big Business As President, Roosevelt won a reputation as a trustbuster, a person working to destroy monopolies and trusts. He was not against big business, he said. Indeed, he liked big business. But he saw a difference between "good trusts" and "bad trusts." Good trusts, he said, were efficient and fair and should be left alone. Bad ones took advantage of workers and cheated the public by eliminating competition. The government, he said, must either control bad trusts or break them up.

Roosevelt resolved to do just that. In 1902, he had the government bring a lawsuit against the Northern Securities Company. Northern Securities was a trust that had been formed to control competition among railroads. TR argued that the company used unfair business practices.

In 1904, the Supreme Court ruled that Northern Securities had violated the Sherman Antitrust Act. It ordered the trust to be broken up. The decision was a victory for Progressives. For the first time, the Sherman Antitrust Act had been used to break up trusts, not unions.

Roosevelt later launched suits against other trusts, including Standard Oil and the American Tobacco Company. In time, the courts broke up both trusts because they attempted to limit free trade.

A Boost for Organized Labor Roosevelt also clashed with mine owners. In 1902, Pennsylvania coal miners went on strike for better pay and a shorter workday. Mine owners refused to negotiate with the miners' union.

As winter approached, schools and hospitals ran out of coal. Furious at the owners, Roosevelt threatened to send in troops to run the mines. Finally, the mine owners sat down with the union and reached an agreement. Roosevelt was the first President to side with strikers.

☑ **Checkpoint** What was Theodore Roosevelt's attitude toward big business?

The Square Deal

Roosevelt ran for President in his own right in 1904. During the campaign, he promised Americans a Square Deal. By this, he meant that everyone from farmers and consumers to workers and owners should have the same opportunity to succeed. That promise helped Roosevelt win a huge victory.

Vocabulary Builder
efficient (ee FISH ehnt) *adj.* done in a way that minimizes waste and gets better results

Roosevelt and Conservation

In 1903, President Roosevelt (below left) went camping in California's Yosemite Valley with conservationist John Muir (below right). The trip strengthened Roosevelt's commitment to conservation. Today, you can still enjoy Yosemite National Park.
Critical Thinking: *Link Past and Present* *What do the pictures here suggest about the long-term effects of Roosevelt's conservation policies?*

Conserving Natural Resources Roosevelt took action to protect the nation's wilderness areas. To fuel the nation's surging industrial growth, lumber companies were cutting down entire forests. Miners were removing iron and coal at a frantic pace, leaving gaping holes in the earth.

Roosevelt loved the outdoors and worried about the destruction of the wilderness. He pressed for conservation, or the protection of natural resources. Roosevelt was not against using resources, but he believed they had to be used wisely, with an eye toward the future. For example, he urged lumber companies to plant new trees in the forests they were clearing. Roosevelt declared:

> **"**I recognize the right and duty of this generation to develop and use the natural resources of our land; but I do not recognize the right to waste them, or to rob, by wasteful use, the generations that come after us.**"**
>
> —Theodore Roosevelt, "The New Nationalism"

Under Roosevelt, the U.S. Forest Service was formed in 1905 to conserve the nation's woodlands. Roosevelt also had thousands of acres of land set aside for national parks. A national park is a natural area protected and managed by the federal government.

Reading Skill

Explain Issues From the Past
Explain Roosevelt's reasons for supporting conservation and how they affected his approach to big business.

Protecting Consumers Roosevelt also supported reforms to protect consumers. Upton Sinclair's novel *The Jungle* had shocked Roosevelt. The President made public a report exposing unhealthy conditions in meatpacking plants. The public outcry forced Congress to pass a law in 1906 allowing closer inspections of meatpacking houses.

Muckrakers had also exposed companies for making false claims about medicines and adding harmful chemicals to canned foods. In response, Congress passed the Pure Food and Drug Act, which required food and drug makers to list all the ingredients on their packages.

☑**Checkpoint** **Why did Roosevelt support conservation?**

Taft and Wilson

Roosevelt did not want to run for reelection in 1908. Instead, he backed William Howard Taft, his secretary of war. Taft won easily.

Troubles for Taft Taft's approach to the presidency was far different from Roosevelt's. Unlike the energetic Roosevelt, Taft was quiet and cautious. Roosevelt loved power, Taft was wary of it.

Nevertheless, Taft supported many Progressive causes. He broke up even more trusts than TR. He favored the graduated income tax, approved new safety rules for mines, and signed laws giving government workers the eight-hour workday. He also oversaw the creation of a federal office to make regulations controlling child labor.

Despite such actions, Taft lost Progressive support. In 1909, he signed a bill that raised most tariffs. Progressives opposed the new law, arguing that tariffs raised prices for consumers. Also, Taft modified some conservation policies. Progressives accused the President of blocking conservation efforts.

Election of 1912 By 1912, Roosevelt had broken with Taft. He decided to run against Taft for the Republican nomination. Roosevelt had massive popular support, but Taft controlled the Republican Party leadership. At its convention, the Republican Party nominated Taft.

Roosevelt and his supporters stormed out of the convention. They set up a new party, called the Progressive Party, and chose Roosevelt as their candidate. He accepted, saying, "I feel as strong as a bull moose." Roosevelt's Progressive Party became known as the Bull Moose Party.

Democrats chose Woodrow Wilson, also a Progressive, as their candidate. Wilson had served as president of Princeton University and as governor of New Jersey. Wilson was known as a brilliant

Three-Way Race

TR, the "bull moose" candidate, made the presidential election of 1912 a three-way race. **Critical Thinking: *Draw Inferences*** *Why does the cartoonist show the "moose" nipping at the elephant?*

scholar and a cautious reformer. Though honest and idealistic, he was often criticized for being <u>rigid</u> and unwilling to compromise with others.

Vocabulary Builder
rigid (RIH jihd) *adj.* strict; not easily bent or changed

Together, Taft and Roosevelt won more votes than Wilson. However, they split the Republican vote, and so Wilson won the 1912 presidential election.

Wilson and the New Freedom Wilson hoped to restore free competition among American corporations. He called his program to achieve this goal the New Freedom. To ensure fair competition, Wilson persuaded Congress to create the Federal Trade Commission (FTC) in 1914. The FTC had the power to investigate companies and order them to stop using unfair practices to destroy competitors.

Wilson signed the Clayton Antitrust Act in 1914. The new law banned some business practices that limited competition. In addition, it stopped antitrust laws from being used against unions.

To regulate banking, Congress passed the Federal Reserve Act in 1913. The act set up a system of federal banks and gave the government the power to raise or lower interest rates and control the money supply.

✓**Checkpoint** **How did a split among Republicans enable Woodrow Wilson to become President?**

⭐ **Looking Back and Ahead** Despite Wilson's successes, the Progressive movement slowed after 1914. By then, Progressives had achieved many of their goals. Also, in 1914, war broke out in Europe. Americans worried that the war might soon affect them. You will read about World War I in the next unit.

Woodrow Wilson

Progress Monitoring ⬤nline
For: Self-test with instant help
Visit: PHSchool.com
Web Code: mya-6152

Comprehension and Critical Thinking

1. **(a) Recall** Why did Theodore Roosevelt want to break up Northern Securities and Standard Oil?
   (b) Identify Benefits Which groups of people might have benefited from Roosevelt's actions as a trustbuster?

2. **(a) Recall** Why did the Republican Party split during the 1912 presidential election campaign?
   (b) Draw Conclusions What impact might a powerful third party such as the Bull Moose Party have on a presidential election?

Reading Skill

3. **Explain Issues From the Past** Reread the text following the subheading "A Boost for Organized Labor." Explain the central issues that moved Roosevelt. How did he interact with big business over these issues?

Key Terms

Read each sentence below. If the sentence is true, write YES. If the sentence is not true, write NO and explain why.
4. Theodore Roosevelt was called a trustbuster because he lost the trust of the people.

5. Roosevelt was a strong supporter of conservation, which is the protection of natural resources.

Writing

6. Write the opening paragraph to an editorial evaluating TR's presidency. Complete the following topic sentence, and introduce each point that follows with a transition word: Theodore Roosevelt's Square Deal created a number of reforms that were *(express your opinion here).* For example, he _____. In addition, he _____. Most important *(OR worst of all),* he _____.

The Jungle
by Upton Sinclair

Prepare to Read

Introduction

The main characters in *The Jungle* are a family of immigrants who have recently immigrated to Chicago from Eastern Europe. Several of them find jobs at a meatpacking plant. In this excerpt, Elzbieta, one family member, learns the gruesome details of the sausage-making process.

 Reading Skill

Analyze Symbolism Symbolism is the use of concrete images or objects to represent abstract ideas. Upton Sinclair wrote *The Jungle* in order to make a statement about the excesses of unrestricted free enterprise. As you read this passage, consider what the practices Sinclair describes might represent.

Vocabulary *Builder*

As you read this literature selection, look for the following underlined words:

scheme (skeem) *n.* dishonest plan

hopper (HAH per) *n.* a bin in which material is temporarily stored

nuisance (NOO sehns) *n.* annoyance

enforce (ehn FORS) *v.* bring about by force

⭐ Background

This passage describes, among other things, the working conditions for laborers. Though Sinclair wrote *The Jungle* in order to speak out against working conditions for laborers, the public's reaction was not what Sinclair intended. The public outcry over this book's description of meat-packaging practices helped lead to the passage of the Pure Food and Drug Act of 1906.

The packers were always originating such <u>schemes</u>—they had what they called "boneless hams," which were all the odds and ends of pork stuffed into casings; and "California hams," which were the shoulders, with big knuckle joints, and nearly all the meat cut out; and fancy "skinned hams," which were made of the oldest hogs, whose skins were so heavy and coarse that no one would buy them—that is, until they had been cooked and chopped fine and labeled "head cheese"!

It was only when the whole ham was spoiled that it came into the department of Elzbieta. Cut up by the two-thousand-revolutions-a-minute flyers, and mixed with half a ton of other meat, no odor that ever was in a ham could make any difference. There was never the least attention paid to what was cut up for sausage; there would come all the way back from Europe old sausage that had been rejected, and that was mouldy and white—it would be dosed with borax and glycerine, and dumped into the <u>hoppers</u>, and made over again for home consumption. There would be meat that had tumbled out onto the floor, in the dirt and sawdust, where the workers had tramped and spit uncounted billions of consumption germs. There would be meat stored in great piles in rooms, and the water from leaky roofs would drip over it, and thousands of rats would race about on it. It was too dark in those storage places to see well, but a man could run his hands over these piles of meat and sweep off handfuls of the dried dung of rats. These rats were <u>nuisances</u>, and the packers would put out poisoned bread for them, they would die, and then rats, bread, and meat would go into the hoppers together. This is no fairy story and no joke: the meat would be shoveled into carts, and the man who did the shoveling would not trouble to lift out a rat even when he saw one—there were things that went into the sausage in comparison with which a poisoned rat was a tidbit. There was no place for the men to wash their hands before they ate their dinner, and so they made a practice of washing them in the water that was to be ladled into the sausage. There were the butt-ends of smoked meat, and the scraps of corned beef, and all the odds and ends of the waste of the plants, that would be dumped into old barrels in the cellar and left there. Under the system of rigid economy which the packers <u>enforced</u>, there were some jobs that it only paid to do once in a long time, and among these was the cleaning out of the waste barrels. Every spring they did it; and in the barrels would be dirt and rust and old nails and stale water—and cartload after cartload of it would be taken up and dumped into the hoppers with fresh meat, and sent out to the public's breakfast. Some of it they would make into "smoked" sausage—but as the smoking took time, and was therefore expensive, they would call upon the chemistry department, and preserve it with borax and color it with gelatine to make it brown. All of their sausage came out of the same bowl, but when they came to wrap it they would stamp some of it "special," and for this they would charge two cents more a pound.

From *The Jungle*, by Upton Sinclair. © 1981. Bantam.

Analyze Symbolism

Reading Skill

Upton Sinclair wrote at a time when few laws controlled how people worked and what they produced. Sinclair blamed the capitalist system for these abuses, rather than the lack of laws. Knowing Sinclair's motivation for writing this book, what abstract idea might the "special" and "fancy" packaging of the meat represent?

☑ **Checkpoint** **What was wrong with the way the packers cleaned out the waste barrels?**

Analyze LITERATURE

After reading this passage, what images are the most striking? Are the images powerful? Now imagine that you are a member of the general public reading this passage. Write a short letter to your local newspaper expressing your reaction to this passage.

If you liked this passage from *The Jungle*, you might enjoy reading more about the labor movement in America in *Ashes of Roses* by Mary Jane Auch. Henry Holt and Company, 2002.

The Vote Guarantees Your Liberty

❝The vote is the emblem of your equality, women of America, the guarantee of your liberty. . . . Women have suffered agony of soul which you never can comprehend, that you and your daughters might inherit political freedom. That vote has been costly. Prize it!❞

—Carrie Chapman Catt, 1920

◀ The Nineteenth Amendment became law in 1920.

The Rights of Women

Objectives
- Describe how women won the right to vote.
- Identify the new opportunities that women gained during the Progressive Era.
- Explain how the temperance movement gained strength during the early 1900s.

Reading Skill

Identify Central Issues From the Past
What changes did people of the past work to achieve? As you read Section 3, try to identify the central issues at the core of women's efforts for change. In your own words, answer the questions: What was this struggle about? What change did these people seek?

Key Terms and People

Carrie Chapman Catt
suffragist

Alice Paul
Frances Willard
prohibition

Why It Matters The Progressives' desire for reform did not include a strong interest in women's rights. Women activists struggled for equality without significant help from the Progressives. During this era, however, women finally won the right to vote. They also made other advances. Even so, women knew they had a long way to go before achieving full equality.

❓ **Section Focus Question: How did women gain new rights?**

Women Win the Vote

The Seneca Falls Convention of 1848 marked the start of an organized women's rights movement in the United States. After the Civil War, Elizabeth Cady Stanton and Susan B. Anthony formed the National Woman Suffrage Association. This group pushed for a constitutional amendment to give women the right to vote.

Anthony spoke all over the country for the cause. In 1872, she was arrested for trying to vote. At her trial, she told the judge:

❝My natural rights, my civil rights, my political rights, my judicial rights, are all alike ignored. Robbed of the fundamental privilege of citizenship, I am degraded from the status of a citizen to that of a subject.❞
— *Proceedings of the Trial of Susan B. Anthony*

Women Vote in the West In most states, leading politicians opposed women's suffrage. Still, in the late 1800s, women won voting rights in four western states: Wyoming, Utah, Colorado, and Idaho. Pioneer women had worked alongside men to build farms and cities. By giving women the vote at least in local or state elections, these states recognized the women's contributions.

When Wyoming applied for statehood in 1890, many members of Congress wanted it to bar women from voting. Wyoming lawmakers stood firm. "We may stay out of the Union for 100 years, but we will come in with our women." Wyoming was admitted.

Growing Support In the early 1900s, support for women's suffrage grew. More than 5 million women worked outside the home. Although women were paid less than men, wages gave them some power. Many demanded a say in making the laws.

After Stanton and Anthony died, a new generation of leaders took up the cause. Carrie Chapman Catt devised a detailed strategy to win suffrage, state by state. Across the nation, suffragists, or people who worked for women's right to vote, followed her plan. Their efforts brought steady gains. One by one, states in the West and Midwest gave women the right to vote.

The Nineteenth Amendment Still, in some of these states, women could not vote in federal elections. More women joined the call for a federal amendment to allow them to vote in all elections.

Vocabulary Builder
devise (dee vīz) **v.** to carefully think out; to invent

Identify Central Issues From the Past Identify the central issue, or goal, for suffragists.

Women Get the Vote

KEY

(1918) Full statewide suffrage for women

Partial suffrage for women

No statewide suffrage for women

WY and UT were territories when they extended suffrage to women.

0 km 500
0 miles 500
Albers Equal-Area Projection

MAP MASTER®
Skills Activity

Wyoming was the first state where women could vote in state elections. By 1919, some states (shown in yellow) still did not allow women to vote.

(a) Read a Map In what year did women win suffrage in Colorado? In California?

(b) Apply Information How would this map change after passage of the Nineteenth Amendment?

MapMaster Online

For: Interactive map
Visit: PHSchool.com
Web Code: myp-6153

Vocabulary Builder
<u>commit</u> (kah MIHT) **v.** to make a pledge or promise

As the struggle dragged on, suffragists such as Alice Paul took more forceful steps. Paul met with President Woodrow Wilson in 1913. Paul told Wilson that suffragists had <u>committed</u> themselves to achieving such an amendment. Wilson pledged his support.

By 1919, the tide had turned. Congress passed the Nineteenth Amendment guaranteeing women the right to vote. By August 1920, three fourths of the states had ratified the amendment. The Nineteenth Amendment doubled the number of eligible voters.

☑Checkpoint **Why did suffragists want a constitutional amendment?**

New Opportunities for Women

Besides working for the vote, women struggled to gain access to jobs and education. Most states refused to grant women licenses to practice law or medicine.

Higher Education Despite obstacles, a few women managed to get the higher education needed to enter a profession. In 1877, Boston University granted the first Ph.D., or doctoral degree, to a woman. Slowly, more women earned advanced degrees. By 1900, the nation had 1,000 women lawyers and 7,000 women doctors.

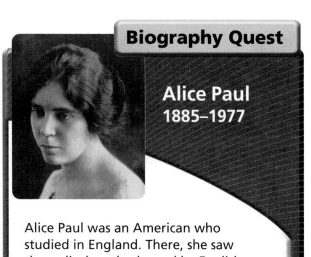

Biography Quest

Alice Paul
1885–1977

Alice Paul was an American who studied in England. There, she saw the radical methods used by English suffragists.

   Returning to the United States, Paul formed a new suffrage group, which merged into the National Woman's Party in 1917. Paul called on President Wilson many times and worked tirelessly for the Nineteenth Amendment.

Biography Quest nline

How did Paul become involved in the struggle for a voting rights amendment?
For: The answer to the question about Paul
Visit: PHSchool.com
Web Code: myd-6153

Women's Clubs During the late 1800s, many middle-class women joined women's clubs. At first, most clubwomen read books and sought other ways to advance their knowledge. In time, many became reformers. They raised money for libraries, schools, and parks. They pressed for laws to protect women and children, to ensure pure food and drugs, and to win the vote.

Faced with racial barriers, African American women formed their own clubs, such as the National Association of Colored Women. They battled to end segregation and violence against African Americans. They also joined the battle for suffrage.

Women Reformers During the Progressive Era, many women committed themselves to reform. Some entered the field of social work, helping the poor in cities.

Florence Kelley investigated conditions in sweatshops. In time, she was made the chief factory inspector for Illinois. Kelley's main concern was child labor. She organized a boycott of goods produced in factories that employed young children.

☑Checkpoint **What gains did women make in education?**

The Crusade Against Alcohol

You have read that reformers began a temperance movement, or campaign against alcohol abuse, in the 1820s. Women took a leading role in the temperance movement. In the late 1800s, the movement gained new strength.

In 1874, a group of women organized the Woman's Christian Temperance Union, or WCTU. Frances Willard became its president in 1879. Willard spoke tirelessly about the evils of alcohol. She called for state laws to ban the sale of liquor. She also worked to close saloons. In time, Willard joined the suffrage movement, bringing many WCTU members along with her.

Carry Nation was a more radical temperance crusader. After her husband died from heavy drinking, Nation often stormed into saloons. Swinging a hatchet, she smashed beer kegs and liquor bottles. Nation won publicity, but her actions embarrassed the WCTU.

After years of effort, temperance leaders persuaded Congress to pass the Eighteenth Amendment in 1917. The amendment enforced prohibition, a ban on the sale and consumption of alcohol. The amendment was ratified in 1919.

✓**Checkpoint** How did supporters of temperance seek to influence public policy?

☆ **Looking Back and Ahead** For many women, the Nineteenth Amendment was a final victory. Others saw it as just one step on the road to full equality. Today, Americans still debate issues involving the roles of women in society, government, the family, and the workplace.

Cartoon of a temperance supporter

Progress Monitoring ⊘nline
For: Self-test with instant help
Visit: PHSchool.com
Web Code: mya-6153

Section 3 | Check Your Progress

Comprehension and Critical Thinking

1. **(a) Recall** What did the Nineteenth Amendment to the Constitution do?
   (b) Link Past and Present How has its passage helped women?

2. **(a) Recall** What did the Eighteenth Amendment to the Constitution do?
   (b) Make Predictions What would be the results of the Eighteenth Amendment? Explain your reasoning.

🔁 Reading Skill

3. **Identify Central Issues From the Past** Reread the text under the heading "New Opportunities for Women." Identify the central issues for the women mentioned in those paragraphs.

Key Terms

Read each sentence below. If the sentence is true, write YES. If the sentence is not true, write NO and explain why.

4. **Suffragists** were people who worked to ban alcohol.

5. During prohibition, the sale and use of tobacco in the United States were outlawed.

Writing

6. Imagine that you are working with a group of people in 1912 promoting women's suffrage. Create four slogans for banners and leaflets supporting the right of women to vote. Then, write a short persuasive paragraph supporting and developing one of those slogans.

Asking for an Equal Chance

❝Through no fault of their own, the condition of the colored people is, in some sections to-day no better than it was at the close of the [Civil War].... Seeking no favors because of our color, nor patronage because of our needs, we knock at the bar of justice, asking an equal chance.❞

—Mary Church Terrell, President, National Association of Colored Women, 1898

◄ African American extended family

Struggles for Justice

Objectives

- Describe the efforts of African American leaders to fight discrimination.
- Describe the life of Mexican Americans and the challenges they faced.
- Explain why some Americans called for limits on Japanese immigration.
- Discuss the problems facing religious minorities.

Reading Skill

Identify Central Problems From the Past Understanding the problems of the past helps you understand the reactions of people from that time. As you read, identify problems and restate them in your own words. Think about how people of that time responded and how people today might respond to similar problems.

Key Terms and People

Booker T. Washington
W.E.B. Du Bois

lynching
parochial school
anti-Semitism

Why It Matters Just as most Progressives were not very interested in women's rights, they also had little interest in minority rights. Jim Crow laws continued to enforce segregation. Violence against African Americans was a growing problem. Meanwhile, Mexican Americans, Asian Americans, and religious minorities faced similar problems. The struggle for social justice and equality would continue well beyond the Progressive Era.

❓ **Section Focus Question: What challenges faced minority groups?**

African Americans

African Americans faced discrimination in the North as well as in the South. Landlords often refused to rent homes in white areas to African Americans. Across the nation, they were restricted to the worst housing and the poorest jobs.

Booker T. Washington During this time, educator Booker T. Washington emerged as the most prominent African American. Born into slavery, Washington taught himself to read. Later, he worked in coal mines, attending school whenever he could. In 1881, Washington helped found the Tuskegee Institute in Alabama. The school offered training in industrial and agricultural skills.

Washington advised African Americans to learn trades and seek to move up gradually in society. Eventually, they would have money and the power to demand equality.

❝No race can prosper till it learns that there is as much dignity in tilling a field as in writing a poem. It is at the bottom of life we must begin, and not at the top. Nor should we permit our grievances to overshadow our opportunities.❞

—Booker T. Washington, speech to Atlanta Exposition, 1895

Washington's practical approach won the support of business leaders such as Andrew Carnegie and John D. Rockefeller. They helped him build trade schools for African Americans. At the same time, Presidents sought his advice on racial issues.

W.E.B. Du Bois W.E.B. Du Bois (doo BOYS) had a different view. A brilliant scholar, Du Bois was the first African American to receive a Ph.D. from Harvard University. He agreed with Booker T. Washington on the need for "thrift, patience and industrial training." However, Du Bois criticized Washington for being willing to accept segregation:

> **❝**So far as Mr. Washington apologizes for injustice, North or South, does not rightly value the privilege and duty of voting . . . and opposes the higher training and ambition of our brighter minds,—so far as he, the South, or the Nation, does this,—we must unceasingly and firmly oppose them.**❞**
>
> —W.E.B. Du Bois, *The Souls of Black Folk*

Du Bois urged blacks to fight discrimination rather than patiently <u>submit</u> to it. In 1909, he joined Jane Addams and other reformers in forming the National Association for the Advancement of Colored People, or NAACP. Blacks and whites in the NAACP worked for equal rights for African Americans.

Campaign Against Lynching In the 1890s, more than 1,000 African Americans in the South and elsewhere were victims of lynching, or murder by a mob. The epidemic of violence worsened after the depression of 1893. Often, jobless whites took out their anger on blacks.

Vocabulary Builder
<u>submit</u> (sahb MIHT) **v.** to yield; to give up power or control

Identify Central Problems From the Past
Reading Skill
Identify the central problems facing African Americans in the late 1800s. How did people of the time respond to those problems?

History *Interactive*
Booker T. Washington and W.E.B. Du Bois
Visit: PHSchool.com
Web Code: myp-6152

Two African American Leaders

Two African American Leaders
Booker T. Washington (left) was the most prominent African American leader of his day. He urged African Americans to work patiently to move up in society. W.E.B. Du Bois (right) admired Washington but criticized many of his ideas. Rather than patiently accepting discrimination, Du Bois urged African Americans to fight it actively.
Critical Thinking: *Contrast* *How did Washington's and Du Bois's ideas about how to fight segregation differ?*

Booker T. Washington

W.E.B. Du Bois

Ida B. Wells Fights Against Lynching

"The real purpose of these savage demonstrations is to teach the Negro that in the South he has no rights that the law will enforce. Samuel Hose [a lynching victim] was burned to teach the Negroes that no matter what a white man does to them, they must not resist. . . . The daily press offered reward for [Hose's] capture and . . . incited the people to burn him as soon as caught."

—Ida B. Wells, "Lynch Law in Georgia," 1899

Antilynching protesters

Reading Primary Sources
Skills Activity

In 1895, journalist Ida B. Wells published an analysis that exposed the truth about the lynching of African Americans.

(a) Interpret a Primary Source According to Wells, why do lynchings occur?

(b) Compare Ida Wells is often classified as a muckraker. How was her work similar to the work of Jacob Riis?

The murders outraged Ida B. Wells, an African American journalist. In her newspaper, *Free Speech,* Wells urged African Americans to protest the lynchings. She called for a boycott of segregated streetcars and white-owned stores. Wells spoke out despite threats to her life.

Setbacks and Successes Few white Progressives gave much thought to the problems faced by African Americans. President Wilson ordered the segregation of workers in the federal civil service. "Segregation is not humiliating, but a benefit," he told protesters who came to talk to him.

Despite obstacles, some African Americans succeeded. Scientist George Washington Carver discovered hundreds of new uses for peanuts and other crops grown in the South. Sarah Walker created a line of hair care products for African American women. She became the first American woman to earn more than $1 million.

Black-owned insurance companies, banks, and other businesses served the needs of African Americans. Black colleges trained young people for the professions. Churches like the African Methodist Episcopal Church became the training ground for generations of African American leaders.

✓**Checkpoint** On what grounds did W.E.B. Du Bois disagree with Booker T. Washington?

Mexican Americans

By 1900, about half a million Mexican Americans lived in the United States. Like African Americans, Mexican Americans often faced legal segregation. In 1910, the town of San Angelo, Texas, built new schools for its Anglo children. Mexican children were forced to go to separate, inferior schools. When Mexican children tried to attend one of the new schools, officials barred their way.

Increased Immigration In 1910, revolution and famine swept Mexico. Thousands of Mexicans fled into the United States. They came from all levels of Mexican society. Many were poor farmers, but some came from middle-class and upper-class families.

At first, 90 percent of Mexican immigrants settled in the Southwest. In time, the migration spread to other parts of the country. People who could not find work in the Southwest began moving to the Midwest and the Rocky Mountain region.

Daily Life Mexican immigrants often worked as field hands, built roads, or dug irrigation ditches. Some lived near the railroads they helped build. Still others worked in city factories under harsh conditions. They were paid less than Anglo workers and were denied skilled jobs.

Like other immigrants, Mexican Americans sought to preserve their language and culture. They created barrios, or ethnic Mexican American neighborhoods. Los Angeles was home to the nation's largest barrio. Its population almost tripled between 1910 and 1920.

Within the barrio, Mexican immigrants and Mexican Americans took many steps to help each other. Some formed mutualistas, or mutual aid groups. These groups worked like other immigrant aid societies. Members of mutualistas pooled money to pay for insurance and legal advice. They also collected money for the sick and needy.

✓**Checkpoint** Why did emigration from Mexico rise after 1910?

Mexican Americans Helping One Another

Like other groups, Mexican Americans formed mutual aid groups. Members of a mutualista in Arizona are shown marching in a parade (bottom left). Below is the symbol of the Cruz Azul Mexicana, or Mexican Blue Cross, which aided poor families.
Critical Thinking: *Draw Conclusions* *Why were mutual aid groups like these important to Mexican American communities?*

Japanese Immigrants Arrive in United States

Japanese immigration to the United States was heavy in the early 1900s. The Gentlemen's Agreement between President Roosevelt and Japan allowed Japanese wives to join their husbands already in the United States. Here, a group of Japanese immigrants arrive on the American west coast in the 1920s.

Asian Americans

As you learned in the previous chapter, the Chinese Exclusion Act of 1882 kept Chinese from settling in the United States. Employers on the West Coast and in Hawaii began hiring workers from other Asian countries, mainly the Philippines and Japan.

Japanese Immigrants More than 100,000 Japanese entered the United States in the early 1900s. Most went first to Hawaii to work on sugar plantations. When the United States annexed Hawaii in 1898, many Japanese decided to seek a better life on the mainland.

Many of the newcomers were farmers. They settled on dry, barren land that Americans thought was useless. Through hard work, the Japanese made their farms profitable. Soon, they were producing a large percentage of southern California's fruits and vegetables.

A Gentlemen's Agreement Prejudice against Asians was high. In 1906, San Francisco forced all Asian students, including Japanese children, to attend separate schools. When Japan protested the insult, the issue threatened to cause an international <u>crisis</u>.

Unions and other groups put pressure on President Theodore Roosevelt to limit immigration from Japan. Because Roosevelt did not want to antagonize a growing naval power, he tried to soothe Japanese feelings. He condemned the segregated schools and proposed that if San Francisco ended segregation, he would restrict Japanese immigration.

In 1907, Roosevelt reached a "Gentlemen's Agreement" with Japan. Japan would stop any more workers from going to the United States. The United States, in exchange, would allow Japanese women to join their husbands who were already in the country.

Anti-Japanese feeling remained high. In 1913, California banned Asians who were not American citizens from owning land.

☑**Checkpoint** What was the Gentlemen's Agreement?

Religious Minorities

Religious minorities also faced prejudice. As you have read, the immigration boom included large numbers of Roman Catholics and Jews. Nativist groups, such as the Anti-Catholic American Protective Association, worked to restrict immigration. Even Jews and Catholics who were not immigrants faced discrimination in jobs and housing.

Anti-Catholic feeling was common in schools. Some teachers lectured against the Pope, and textbooks contained references to "deceitful Catholics." In response, American Catholics set up their own **parochial schools,** or schools sponsored by a church.

The most notorious case of **anti-Semitism,** or prejudice against Jews, in the United States took place in Georgia in 1913. Leo Frank, a Jewish man, was falsely accused of murdering a young girl. Newspapers inflamed public feeling against "the Jew." Despite a lack of evidence, he was sentenced to death. When the governor of Georgia reduced the sentence, a mob took Frank from prison and lynched him.

In response to the lynching and other cases of anti-Semitism, American Jews founded the Anti-Defamation League. (Defamation is the spreading of false, hateful information.) The League worked to promote understanding and fight prejudice against Jews.

Checkpoint **What problems did Jews and Catholics face?**

Looking Back and Ahead Groups such as the NAACP and the Anti-Defamation League were formed to fight discrimination. Today, many Americans continue to work against prejudice.

Section 4 | Check Your Progress

Progress Monitoring Online
For: Self-test with instant help
Visit: PHSchool.com
Web Code: mya-6154

Comprehension and Critical Thinking

1. **(a) Contrast** How did Booker T. Washington and W.E.B. Du Bois propose to improve life for African Americans?
   (b) Draw Conclusions Whose ideas do you think would be more likely to help African Americans in the long run? Explain your reasons.
2. **(a) Identify** What was the Gentlemen's Agreement?
   (b) Analyze Cause and Effect How did the Gentlemen's Agreement affect Japanese immigration?

Reading Skill

3. **Identify Central Problems From the Past** What central problems faced Asian Americans in the late 1800s? How did Japan respond to these problems? Can you connect their problems to the attitudes toward immigrants today?

Key Terms

4. Write two definitions for the key terms lynching and anti-Semitism. First, write a formal definition for your teacher. Second, write a definition in everyday English for a classmate.

Writing

5. Imagine that you are an editorial writer who attended a debate between Booker T. Washington and W.E.B. Du Bois about the best tactics for fighting discrimination. Write a topic sentence that states the central idea of each man's argument. Then, write a paragraph endorsing one of these points of view and explaining your position.

21st Century Learning · Photographs are one type of primary source. By capturing a moment in time, they can provide important details about a historical period or event. The photographs below were taken by Jacob Riis.

Baxter Street, New York
(From *Battle With the Slums,* 1902.)

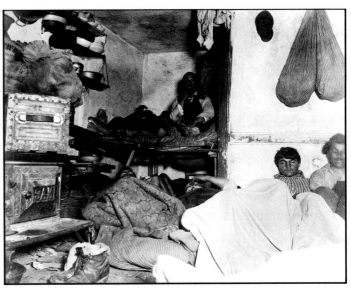

Lodgers in a New York tenement
(From *How the Other Half Lives*, 1890.)

Learn the Skill
Use these steps to analyze photographs.

❶ **Find out information about the photograph.** Read the caption to identify the time and place.

❷ **Identify the subject.** Look carefully at the photograph. What does it show? If there are people in the photograph, what are they doing?

❸ **Decide what the photograph tells about history.** Study the photograph to find out what it illustrates about the past. Try to determine the photographer's point of view or opinion about the scene.

❹ **Decide if the photograph is a reliable source of information.** The photographer may have shot the photograph for a special reason or left out certain details in the scene. You should ask questions to determine the reliability of the photograph.

Practice the Skill
Answer the following questions about the photographs on this page.

❶ **Find out information about the photograph.** (a) Where was the left photograph taken? (b) When was it published?

❷ **Identify the subject.** (a) Who are the people in the right photograph? (b) What are they doing?

❸ **Decide what the photograph tells about history.** (a) What do these photographs show about life in New York City slums at the time? (b) How do you think the photographer felt about these scenes? Explain.

❹ **Decide if the photograph is a reliable source.** Do you think these photographs give a reliable idea of how poor people lived in New York City? Explain.

Apply the Skill
See the Review and Assessment at the end of this chapter.

How did society and politics change during the Progressive Era?

Section 1
The Gilded Age and Progressive Reform

- Corrupt political bosses sometimes gained power over cities during the Gilded Age.
- Progressives supported reforms that gave more power to the voters.
- Muckrakers exposed political, social, and business corruption.

Section 2
The Progressive Presidents

- Theodore Roosevelt tried to break up business trusts that hurt competition.
- Roosevelt's Square Deal called for conservation and consumer protection.
- Roosevelt and Progressive Republicans established the Bull Moose Party.
- Woodrow Wilson continued Progressive reforms in his New Freedom program.

Section 3
The Rights of Women

- The Nineteenth Amendment guaranteed women the right to vote.
- The Eighteenth Amendment banned the sale and consumption of alcoholic beverages.

Section 4
Struggles for Justice

- Booker T. Washington said African Americans should work patiently to move up in society, whereas W.E.B. Du Bois said blacks should actively fight discrimination.
- Mexican immigrants worked in low-paying jobs in the fields and factories and lived in ethnic neighborhoods called barrios.
- Asians faced discrimination, especially on the West Coast.
- Roman Catholics and Jews also faced different forms of discrimination.

? Exploring the Essential Question

Use the online study guide to explore the essential question.

Section 1
How did reformers try to end government corruption and limit the influence of big business?

Section 2
How did the Progressive Presidents extend reforms?

Chapter 19 Essential Question
How did society and politics change during the Progressive Era?

Section 4
What challenges faced minority groups?

Section 3
How did women gain new rights?

Key Terms

Answer the following questions in complete sentences that show your understanding of the key terms.

1. Why would Upton Sinclair be considered a muckraker?

2. Why would William Howard Taft be considered a trustbuster?

3. Why would Alice Paul and Carrie Chapman Catt be considered suffragists?

4. What happened to the more than 1,000 African Americans who were lynched in the South during the 1890s?

Comprehension and Critical Thinking

5. (a) **List** Which legislation did Congress pass to curb big business, and what were the goals of the legislation?
(b) **Make Predictions** How effective do you think the legislation was?

6. (a) **Describe** Which four reforms were instituted during the Progressive Era to give voters more power?
(b) **Apply Information** How would voters in your state use each of these reforms to get what they want done?

7. (a) **Recall** What did Theodore Roosevelt do to protect the nation's natural areas?
(b) **Draw Conclusions** How have Americans benefited from Roosevelt's actions?

8. (a) **Recall** How did the role of President change during the administration of Theodore Roosevelt?
(b) **Evaluate Information** Suggest one reason for the change.

9. (a) **Recall** What was the principal goal of the women's rights movement after the Civil War?
(b) **Draw Inferences** Why was that an important goal?

10. (a) **Summarize** What kind of discrimination did African Americans, Mexican Americans, and Asian Americans face during this period?
(b) **Link Past and Present** How do these groups still face similar discrimination today? Which types of discrimination are no longer legal?

History Reading Skill

11. **Identify and Explain Central Issues** Explain the issues central to corruption in city government, placing them in the context of the nation's growth in the late 1800s. Give an example of a problem that resulted from this corruption. How did people respond to that corruption?

Writing

12. **Write a two-paragraph persuasive composition:**
Choose one particular present-day problem that you feel needs to be corrected. (You do not need to provide a solution.) Express your opinion about this problem, explaining why it needs to be addressed. Include several facts and reasons supporting your opinion. Then, end with a strong statement meant to persuade your readers to take action against the problem.

13. **Write a Narrative:**
Imagine you are a Japanese immigrant in California around 1910. Write a narrative describing your experiences since arriving in the state.

Skills for Life

Analyze Photographs

Use the photograph below by Jacob Riis to answer the questions that follow.

Seventh Avenue night school, New York
(From *Children of the Poor*, 1892.)

14. (a) Who are the people in the photograph?
(b) What are they doing?

15. How do you think the photographer feels about the situation in the photograph? Explain.

16. In general, does the photograph give a reliable idea of how poor people lived in New York City? Explain.

Test Yourself

1. **The principal reason Theodore Roosevelt wanted to break up certain trusts was that he believed they**

   A were unfair to entrepreneurs.

   B hurt workers and the public.

   C made a few Americans rich and kept the majority poor.

   D threatened to slow the growth of foreign trade.

2. **Unlike Booker T. Washington, W.E.B. Du Bois believed that African Americans should**

   A work to achieve equal rights gradually.

   B accept racial segregation laws.

   C actively resist discrimination.

   D focus on gaining industrial and agricultural skills.

Refer to the quotation below to answer Question 3.

> "I recognize the right and duty of this generation to develop and use the natural resources of our land; but I do not recognize the right to waste them, or to rob, by wasteful use, the generations that come after us."

3. **The person who made the above statement would best be described as a**

   A muckraker.

   B suffragist.

   C prohibitionist.

   D conservationist.

Document-Based Questions

Task: Look at Documents 1 and 2, and answer their accompanying questions. Then, use the documents and your knowledge of history to complete this writing assignment:

> Write a short essay about the muckrakers of the late 1800s and early 1900s. Be sure to identify the different muckrakers and to describe their goals and accomplishments. Include information about how they got their name.

Document 1: The excerpt below is from journalist Ida Tarbell's *History of the Standard Oil Company.* *What does Tarbell say is the goal of a trust?*

> "Standard Oil Trust is the most perfectly developed trust in existence; that is, it satisfies most nearly the trust ideal of entire control of the commodity in which it deals. Its vast profits have led its officers into various allied interests, such as railroads, shipping, gas, copper, iron, steel, as well as into banks and trust companies. . . . It has led in the struggle against legislation directed against combinations. Its power in state and Federal government, in the press, in the college, in the pulpit, is generally recognized."

Document 2: In *How the Other Half Lives,* Jacob Riis called attention to the misery of tenement living. *What aspect of tenement living is Riis describing in this excerpt?*

> "It is said that nowhere in the world are so many people crowded together on a square mile as here. . . . In this house . . . there were fifty-eight babies and thirty-eight children that were over five years of age. In Essex Street, two small rooms in a six-story tenement were made to hold a "family" of father and mother, twelve children, and six boarders. These are samples of the packing of the population that has run up the record here to the rate of three hundred and thirty thousand per square mile.
>
> The densest crowding of Old London . . . never got beyond a hundred and seventy-five thousand. Even the alley is crowded out. Through dark hallways and filthy cellars, crowded, as is every foot of the street, with dirty children, the settlements in the rear are reached."

Historian's Apprentice Workshop

How did the industrialization of the United States change the economy, society, and politics of the nation?

DIRECTIONS: Analyze the following documents about the industrialization of the United States. Answer the questions that accompany each document or set of documents. You will use your answers to build an answer to the unit question.

HISTORIAN'S CHECKLIST

WHO produced the document?

WHERE was it made?

WHEN was it produced?

WHY was it made and for what audience?

WHAT is its viewpoint?

HOW does it connect to what I've learned?

WHY is the document important?

document 1 Problems and Reforms

" We need to have, (1.) The minimum age for work fixed at sixteen; (2.) School attendance made compulsory to the same age; (3.) Factory inspectors and truant officers, both men and women, equipped with adequate salaries and traveling expenses, charged with the duty of removing children from mill and workshop, mine and store, and placing them at school. "

—*Florence Kelley, Progressive Reformer, 1889*

What problem was Florence Kelley trying to reform?

document 2 Immigration

IMMIGRATION GROWTH 1895–1905

How was immigration related to industrialization and urbanization?

Ford's Assembly Line

FORD PRICES REDUCED!

EFFECTIVE SEPTEMBER 22, 1920

We are in receipt of a telegram from the Ford Motor Co., announcing a general reduction in the prices of all Ford cars and the Fordson Tractor, as follows:

Runabout	$465.00
Touring	510.00
Coupe	745.00
Sedan	795.00
Truck, pneumatic tires	545.00
Tractor	790.00

All Above Prices f. o. b. factory.

All cars equipped with electric starter. Now booking orders at the new prices. Place your order immediately and avoid disappointment.

Rockingham Motor Co, Inc.
HARRISONBURG, VA.

THE GARRISON PRESS, Harrisonburg, Va.

How did Henry Ford's assembly line affect American life? Explain.

Labor Movement

What methods did workers use to get better working conditions and pay?

Go On

document 5

The Changing West

"A white man was given the position on the reservation of government farmer... he had fenced in a large piece of land, and had that sown and planted with grain and produce of all kinds. The Indians planted it and ... never got any of it."

—*Susette LaFlesche,*
describing life on an Indian reservation, 1870s

How did changes in the West affect Native Americans?

document 6

Struggle for Justice

"The educated colored man must, more and more, go to the farms, into the trades, start brickyards, saw-mills, factories, open coal mines; in short, apply their education to conquering the forces of nature."

—*Booker T. Washington,*
The Story of My Life and Work, 1901

"We claim for ourselves every single right that belongs to a freeborn American ... and until we get these rights we will never cease to protest.... How shall we get them? By voting where we may vote, by persistent, unceasing agitation, by hammering at the truth, by sacrifice and work."

—*W. E. B. DuBois,*
meeting of the Niagara Movement, 1900

How did the views of Washington and Du Bois differ?

7 Government and Big Business

Do you think President Wilson would have agreed or disagreed with this cartoon's message? Explain.

" I am perfectly willing that they should beat any competitor by fair means.... But there must be no squeezing out of the beginner, no crippling his credit; no discrimination against retailers who buy from a rival; no threats against concerns who sell supplies to a rival.... "

—*Woodrow Wilson,*
The New Freedom, 1913

ACTIVITY

Divide into pairs to prepare a debate based on the unit essential question:

 How did the industrialization of the United States change the economy, society, and politics of the nation?

Using the Historian's Apprentice Workshop documents and other information in this unit, one student in each pair should write a couple of paragraphs describing beneficial effects of industrialization in the United States. The other student should write a couple of paragraphs describing harmful effects. Keep in mind the economic, social, and political changes brought by industrialization. Be sure to support your ideas with evidence. Finally, stage a class debate on the question.

Unit 7

How did a more powerful United States expand its role in the world?

History *Interactive*
Explore Historian's Apprentice Online
Visit: PHSchool.com
Web Code: mvp-7000

Americans Look Overseas By 1900, the United States Navy had enlarged and modernized its naval fleet. The nation showed growing interest in overseas trade and in playing a larger role in world affairs.

1900

1917

United States Enters World War I
America joined with France and the other Allies to push back Germany and Austria-Hungary in the First World War. President Wilson hoped this would be the war to make the world "safe for democracy."

A New Role in the World

Panama Canal The United States began building a canal across a narrow strip of land in Central America. The new canal made it possible for oceangoing ships to sail more quickly between the west and east coasts of the United States.

1904

The Roaring Twenties Radios, cars, and motion pictures brought enormous changes to popular culture. New forms of advertising helped popularize products and styles.

1920s

The United States
States
Looks
Overseas

1853-1915

> *"Let us speak courteously, deal fairly, and keep ourselves armed and ready."*
>
> —President Theodore Roosevelt, May 13, 1903

President Theodore Roosevelt followed a "big stick" policy as he sought to block European nations from interfering when Latin American nations could not pay their debts.

Reading Skill

Frame Research Questions In this chapter, you will learn to identify central issues and frame good research questions in order to analyze arguments or proposals.

The United States, East Asia, and the Pacific

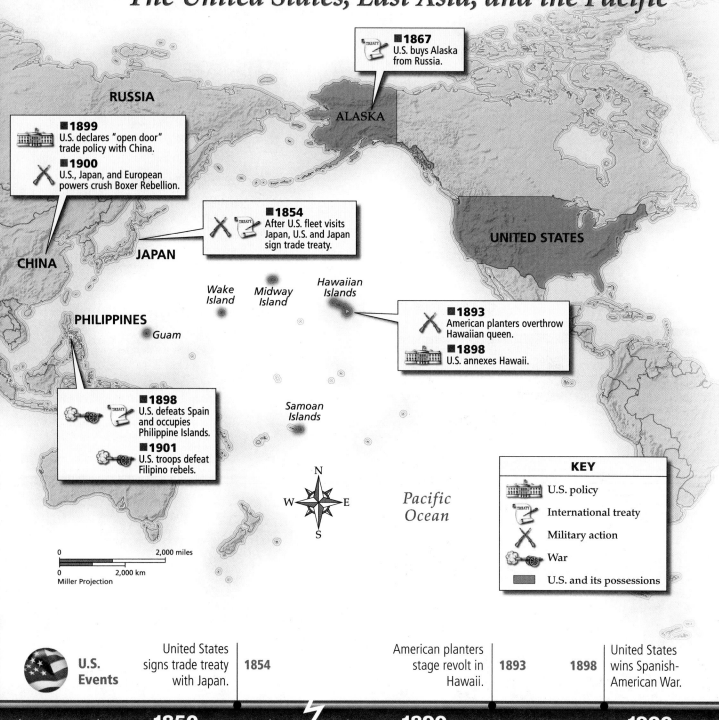

■1867 U.S. buys Alaska from Russia.

■1899 U.S. declares "open door" trade policy with China.

■1900 U.S., Japan, and European powers crush Boxer Rebellion.

■1854 After U.S. fleet visits Japan, U.S. and Japan sign trade treaty.

■1893 American planters overthrow Hawaiian queen.

■1898 U.S. annexes Hawaii.

■1898 U.S. defeats Spain and occupies Philippine Islands.

■1901 U.S. troops defeat Filipino rebels.

RUSSIA

ALASKA

CHINA

JAPAN

Wake Island

Midway Island

Hawaiian Islands

UNITED STATES

PHILIPPINES

Guam

Samoan Islands

Pacific Ocean

N W E S

0   2,000 miles
0   2,000 km
Miller Projection

KEY

U.S. policy

International treaty

Military action

War

U.S. and its possessions

U.S. Events

United States signs trade treaty with Japan. | 1854

American planters stage revolt in Hawaii. | 1893 | 1898 | United States wins Spanish-American War.

1850   1890   1900

World Events

France begins conquest of Indochina. | 1858 | 1880s | European powers carve up Africa.

Boxer Rebellion breaks out in China. | 1900

The United States and Latin America

UNITED STATES

Atlantic Ocean

■1904
President Theodore Roosevelt says that the U.S. will use "police power" to restore order in Latin American countries.

■1909
President Taft urges Americans to pursue profitable business deals in Latin America and Asia.

■1898
U.S. defeats Spain and occupies Cuba and Puerto Rico.

Gulf of Mexico

■1914–1917
U.S. troops get involved in the Mexican Revolution.

■1924–1925
U.S. troops maintain order and protect U.S. interests.

Bahamas

DOMINICAN REPUBLIC

CUBA

MEXICO

HAITI

Puerto Rico
Virgin Is.

Jamaica

GUATEMALA

HONDURAS

Caribbean Sea

EL SALVADOR

NICARAGUA

■1915–1934
U.S. troops maintain order and protect U.S. interests.

■1909–1933
U.S. troops maintain order and protect U.S. interests.

COSTA RICA

PANAMA

VENEZUELA

COLOMBIA

Pacific Ocean

N
W E
S

0   1,000 miles
0   1,000 km
Miller Projection

■1904
After U.S. helps Panama win independence from Colombia, Panama leases land to U.S.

■1914
U.S. completes construction of the Panama Canal.

KEY
🏛 U.S. policy
📜 International treaty
✕ Military action
War
▬ U.S. and its possessions

VISUAL PREVIEW

| United States begins to build Panama Canal. | 1904 | 1914 | United States Navy occupies port of Veracruz, Mexico. |

1900   1910   1920

| | Japan annexes Korea. | **1910** | **1914** | World War I begins in Europe. |

Supremacy in the Pacific
❝For the sake of our commercial supremacy in the Pacific we should control the Hawaiian Islands and maintain our influence in Samoa. ❞

—Senator Henry Cabot Lodge, 1895

◀ U.S. battleships, early 1900s

Eyes on the Pacific

Objectives
- Describe early attempts by the United States to expand in the Pacific.
- List the reasons many Americans came to favor expansion.
- Explain how the United States gained the territories of Samoa and Hawaii.
- Describe how the United States protected its trading rights in China.

🎯 Reading Skill

Ask Extension Questions In discussing one central event, history books will often mention a related event. You may find yourself interested in the related event. Why did it happen? What made it important? How did it affect those involved? Framing questions in specific language will help you research to find the answers.

Key Terms and People

Matthew C. Perry
isolationism
imperialism

Frederick Jackson
  Turner
Liliuokalani
  sphere of influence

Why It Matters Driven by the idea of Manifest Destiny, the United States expanded its borders from the Atlantic Ocean to the Pacific Ocean. However, expansionary dreams did not stop there. In the second half of the 1800s, Americans sought new opportunities overseas.

❓ Section Focus Question: How did the United States acquire new territory and expand trade in the Asia-Pacific region?

The United States Looks Overseas

In the mid-1800s, the United States was ready to take on new challenges. It found new trading partners and acquired more land.

Opening Japan to Trade U.S. merchants longed to engage Japan in a profitable trade. However, for 250 years, Japan had blocked outside trade and barred foreigners from entering or leaving the country.

In 1853, a squadron of heavily armed U.S. warships, commanded by Commodore Matthew C. Perry, sailed into Tokyo Bay. Perry presented the Japanese with a letter from the President calling for Japan to grant trading rights to Americans. The Japanese were awed by Perry's powerful ships and menacing guns. When Perry returned in 1854, they signed a treaty opening Japan for trade.

Perry's visit had another important effect. Faced with the technology and power of the United States, the Japanese recognized their own weakness. They set out to transform their feudal society into an industrial nation that could compete in the modern world.

Purchasing Alaska In 1867, Alaska was a Russian colony. Russia told U.S. Secretary of State William Seward that it wanted to sell Alaska. Seward strongly favored U.S. expansion. He saw Alaska as a stepping stone for trade with Asia and the Pacific.

Alaska is twice the size of Texas. The United States purchased the territory for $7.2 million, about 2 cents an acre. The purchase increased the area of the United States by almost one fifth.

Many Americans opposed the purchase. Some saw Alaska as a frozen wasteland—"Seward's Folly" or "Seward's Icebox." But the <u>critics</u> changed their tune when valuable discoveries of gold led to the Klondike and Alaska gold rushes of 1897–1898. Alaska, it turned out, was rich in an amazing array of resources.

Vocabulary Builder
<u>critic</u> (KRIHT ihk) **n.** someone who makes judgments about objects or actions

☑**Checkpoint** **How did the United States get Japan to open trade?**

The Expansionist Mood

Until the late 1800s, Americans heeded George Washington's advice to "steer clear of permanent alliances." The nation generally pursued a policy of **isolationism**—that is, avoiding involvement in other countries' affairs. Americans stood aside as the nations of Europe undertook a policy of **imperialism**—building empires by imposing political and economic control over peoples around the world.

In the late 1800s, however, a new spirit of expansionism gripped the nation. Americans debated a new sort of Manifest Destiny that would extend overseas. Supporters of expansion offered a variety of arguments for increased involvement in world affairs. These included promoting economic growth and spreading American values. A new view of history also encouraged expansionism.

Seward's Folly

Russia offers Alaska.

Will "Billy" Seward trade?

Reading Political Cartoons

Skills Activity

The cartoonist shows a Russian stranger offering to trade bears, seals, icebergs, and more.

(a) **Recognize Points of View** What is the cartoonist's opinion about the purchase of Alaska? What symbols does the cartoonist use to make the point?

(b) **Apply Information** What did people learn about Alaska after 1898? How would you change the cartoon, based on that information?

Cause and Effect

CAUSES

- Western frontier closes.
- European nations acquire overseas colonies and compete for resources and markets.
- U.S. industry needs to acquire raw materials and to find new markets in which to sell its products.
- Some in the United States want to spread American culture and values to other parts of the world.

U.S. OVERSEAS EXPANSION

EFFECTS

- U.S. Navy grows in size and power.
- United States gains control of territories in the Caribbean and the Pacific.
- The United States issues Open Door Policy, which allows all nations to trade with China.
- U.S. builds Panama Canal.
- United States sends troops to Latin American nations to protect its interests.

Reading a Chart
Skills Activity

American expansionists wanted an overseas empire. By 1900, they had achieved their goal.

(a) Read a Chart Which causes listed on the chart relate to benefits for the U.S. economy?

(b) Apply Information How was a strong navy related to the expansionists' goals?

The Turner Thesis In 1893, historian Frederick Jackson Turner put forth the thesis, or idea, that the western frontier had defined American history. Westward movement, he said, had built individualism and democratic values. Turner concluded:

> ❝And now, four centuries from the discovery of America, at the end of a hundred years of life under the Constitution, the frontier has gone, and with its going has closed the first period of American history.❞
>
> —Frederick Jackson Turner, *The Significance of the Frontier in American History*

Today, few historians accept Turner's thesis. But the idea of a closing frontier influenced expansionists such as Theodore Roosevelt. Overseas expansion, they said, was the new frontier that would help the nation renew its vitality and strength.

Ask Extension Questions

Isolationism and expansionism each had their advantages and disadvantages for the United States. Suggest a possible research question that builds on this topic.

Promoting Economic Growth The United States had a powerful industrial economy. It produced far more than Americans would buy. U.S. leaders watched nervously as European powers seized land in Africa and Asia. If the United States did not act soon, it might be shut out of global markets and denied raw materials.

A top supporter of expansion was Alfred T. Mahan, naval captain and author. Mahan said that future U.S. prosperity depended on building up trade. The key to strong trade, he argued, was a powerful navy that would control the world's sea lanes and thus protect U.S. access to foreign markets.

Spreading American Values In the late 1800s, many Americans believed that Americans of the "Anglo-Saxon race" were superior to "lesser races" in other nations. Therefore, the argument went, Americans had a divine duty to spread Christian values and western civilization around the world.

☑**Checkpoint** **What arguments did expansionists make?**

Gaining Footholds in the Pacific

Supporters of expansion expressed interest in various Pacific islands. They saw them as essential for expanding U.S. influence and trade.

Rivalry for Samoa U.S. steamship companies and missionaries fanned interest in Samoa, a chain of islands in the South Pacific. The steamship companies and the U.S. Navy wanted to set up coaling stations, where ships could stock up on coal.

Britain and Germany also wanted Samoa. Armed conflict loomed in 1889, as Britain, Germany, and the United States all sent warships to Samoa. But fighting was averted when a typhoon struck, disabling or destroying most of the warships. Ten years later, in 1899, the United States and Germany divided the islands of Samoa between them. The people of Samoa, however, had no say in the matter.

Interest in Hawaii Expansionists also eyed Hawaii, a group of islands in the North Pacific. The islands have great natural beauty, sunshine, beaches, and rolling surf. But beauty was secondary. Located between Asia and the United States, Hawaii could serve as a "military and commercial outpost in the Pacific."

The first people to settle Hawaii arrived by canoe from other islands in the Pacific around the 600s. They lived undisturbed until 1778, when Captain James Cook, an English explorer, arrived.

In 1820, the first American missionaries came, hoping to convert Hawaiians to Christianity. Later, other Americans acquired land and set up huge sugar plantations.

As the sugar industry in Hawaii grew, so did the power of American planters. In 1887, planters forced the Hawaiian king, Kalakaua, to accept a new constitution that gave them great influence.

When Kalakaua died in 1891, his sister Liliuokalani (lih lee oo oh kah LAH nee) succeeded him. The new queen was a strong advocate of Hawaiian independence. She refused to recognize the 1887 constitution. She wanted to restore the power of the monarchy and reduce foreign influence in Hawaii.

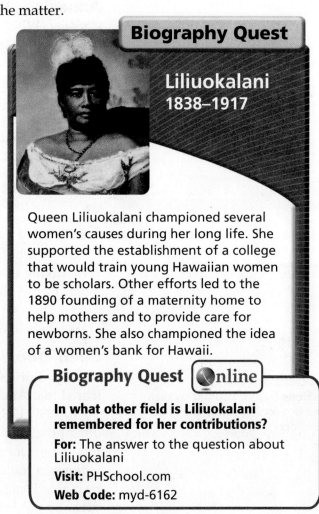

Biography Quest

Liliuokalani
1838–1917

Queen Liliuokalani championed several women's causes during her long life. She supported the establishment of a college that would train young Hawaiian women to be scholars. Other efforts led to the 1890 founding of a maternity home to help mothers and to provide care for newborns. She also championed the idea of a women's bank for Hawaii.

Biography Quest ●nline

In what other field is Liliuokalani remembered for her contributions?

For: The answer to the question about Liliuokalani
Visit: PHSchool.com
Web Code: myd-6162

Annexing Hawaii In 1893, American planters organized an uprising. Without consulting the U.S. government, they persuaded a U.S. official to land 50 U.S. Marines to help overthrow the queen and set up a pro-American government. But President Grover Cleveland rejected a proposal to annex Hawaii. He argued that the revolt had been illegal and was not supported by the people of the islands.

Cleveland's successor, William McKinley, however, favored annexation and supported a treaty to achieve it. On July 7, 1898, Congress voted to make Hawaii a territory of the United States.

☑Checkpoint   How did the United States acquire Hawaii?

Carving Up China

In the late 1800s, China had just emerged from an unsuccessful war. Taking advantage of China's weakness, European powers and Japan forced the Chinese empire to grant them land and trading rights. They set about dividing China into spheres of influence, or areas where another nation has economic and political control.

Open Door Policy At first, Americans were not part of this activity. But as the other powers carved up China, U.S. leaders feared that Americans would be <u>excluded</u> from the China trade.

In 1899, U.S. Secretary of State John Hay issued a message to the other powers. He called on them to keep an "open door" in China. By this, he meant that he wanted them to guarantee the rights of all nations to trade with China on an equal basis. The various nations responded cautiously, most saying neither yes nor no. But Hay declared publicly that the Open Door Policy had been accepted.

Vocabulary Builder
<u>exclude</u> (ehks KLYOOD) **v.** to keep out or expel; to reject or not be considered

Boxer Rebellion Many Chinese resented foreign influences in their country. They organized a secret society to combat the foreigners. The society called itself the Righteous and Harmonious Fists. Europeans called this society and its members Boxers, because they performed ceremonial exercises that resembled shadowboxing.

In the spring of 1900, the Boxers began a rebellion to expel the foreigners. Backed by China's government, they attacked and killed westerners and Chinese Christians. Mobs burned churches and the homes of foreigners. Hundreds of foreigners and some 2,000 Chinese sought safety in a walled section of Beijing, the Chinese capital.

Eventually, the outside powers, including the United States, sent in 18,000 troops armed with modern weapons. The troops freed the trapped foreigners, crushed the rebellion, looted the capital, and killed thousands of Chinese.

The Open Door Again Secretary Hay feared that the other powers would use the Boxer Rebellion as an excuse to seize more Chinese territory. To prevent this, he issued a second Open Door note. In it, he repeated the principle of open trade and made an even stronger statement about American intentions to preserve trade. He also said that China should remain one country and not be broken up into separate pieces.

☑**Checkpoint** What was the goal of the U.S. Open Door Policy?

☆ **Looking Back and Ahead** Under the urging of expansionists, the government promoted U.S. trade and began to acquire territories overseas. In the next section, you will read of how the Spanish-American War gave the United States an empire.

Section 1 | **Check Your Progress**

Progress Monitoring Online
For: Self-test with instant help
Visit: PHSchool.com
Web Code: mya-6161

Comprehension and Critical Thinking

1. **(a) Recall** What benefit did Seward see in acquiring Alaska?
   (b) Detect Points of View Why did people call the purchase of Alaskan lands "Seward's Folly"?

2. **(a) Summarize** In what three ways did U.S. supporters of expansion justify increased involvement in world affairs?
   (b) Identify Economic Benefits How did the division of Samoa and the annexation of the Hawaiian Islands benefit the United States?

Reading Skill

3. **Ask Extension Questions** American acquisition of territory in the Pacific region was controversial. Suggest a possible research question building on this topic.

Key Terms

Complete each of the following sentences so that the second part further explains the first part.

4. During much of the 1800s, the nation followed a policy of isolationism; _____.

5. Competing European nations followed policies of imperialism; _____.

6. China was divided into spheres of influence; _____.

Writing

7. The paragraph that follows contains some vague, incorrect, or illogical arguments. Revise the paragraph to strengthen the passage. **Paragraph:** The United States could no longer be isolated by the rest of the world. The nation had to look overseas to promote economic growth because we were out of raw materials at home. The United States also needed to protect overseas trade, because trade is always useful.

Economic Interests in the Pacific

After the Civil War, the United States became a world leader in industry and agriculture. American leaders believed that expansion was essential in order to compete with European factories. They favored expansion across the Pacific to gain resources, open new markets, and encourage trade.

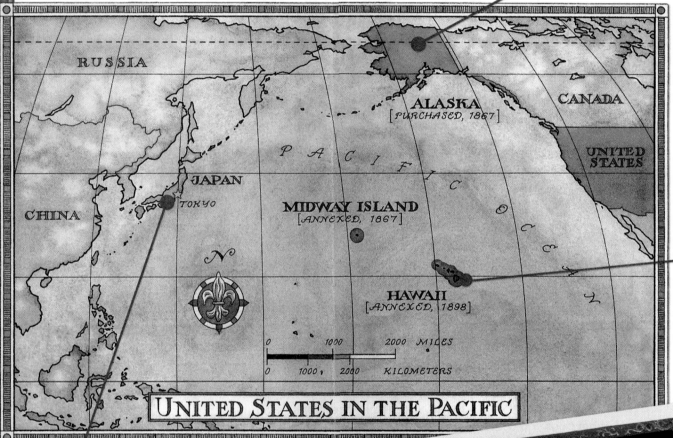

UNITED STATES IN THE PACIFIC

1 **A New Market in Asia**
Seeking to pressure Japan into opening its ports to trade, Commodore Matthew C. Perry led a fleet of warships that entered Tokyo Bay in 1853. Japan realized it could not compete with American naval power. It decided to open trade relations with the United States.

2 "Seward's Folly"

Critics called Alaska "Seward's Folly" because they thought it was an icy wasteland. However, a gold rush in the 1890s proved the critics wrong. These miners pose for a photograph next to their Alaskan claim.

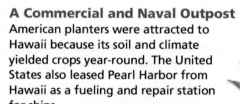

Understand Effects:
America Expands Its Influence

By the start of the Spanish-American War in 1898, the United States had expanded its influence across the entire Pacific Ocean. It acquired valuable raw materials from its new territories and increased its influence on global trade.

Secretary of State William Seward

3 A Commercial and Naval Outpost

American planters were attracted to Hawaii because its soil and climate yielded crops year-round. The United States also leased Pearl Harbor from Hawaii as a fueling and repair station for ships.

Analyze GEOGRAPHY AND HISTORY

What were American goals in the Pacific and Asia? Write a paragraph describing how Hawaii's climate and location made it vital to reaching those goals.

Battle of San Juan Hill

❝ They walked to greet death at every step, many of them, as they advanced, sinking suddenly or pitching forward and disappearing in the high grass, but the others waded on, stubbornly, forming a thin blue line that kept creeping higher and higher. ❞

— Journalist Richard Harding Davis, describing U.S. soldiers at San Juan Hill, 1898

The Spanish-American War

Objectives
- Describe how Americans reacted to the revolt in Cuba.
- Identify the reasons the United States declared war on Spain.
- Explain how the Spanish-American War led to the creation of an American overseas empire.

🕐 Reading Skill

Ask Analytical Questions Reading about history may sometimes leave you puzzled. Ask questions that focus on these puzzles, then research to find answers. Start by looking at what doesn't make sense to you, such as why people acted in a particular way. Use the question starters *who, what, when, why,* and *how* to begin. Then, think about how events changed over time and what caused the changes.

Key Terms and People

reconcentration
José Martí
William Randolph
  Hearst

Emilio Aguinaldo
protectorate

Why It Matters In the previous section, you read how the United States took its first steps on the world stage in the late 1800s. Now, as the century neared its end, the nation was drifting toward war. As a result of this war, America would emerge as a world power with interests around the globe.

❓ Section Focus Question: What were the causes and effects of the Spanish-American War?

War Clouds Loom

Cuba, 90 miles off the coast of Florida, had been under Spanish rule since Columbus came in 1492. Over the centuries, Cubans grew increasingly discontented with Spain's harsh rule. In 1868, the Cubans began an uprising that was finally put down 10 years later.

Rebellion in Cuba Cubans rose up again in 1895. To suppress this new revolt, the Spanish began a policy of reconcentration. **Reconcentration** is the forced movement of large numbers of people into detention camps for military or political reasons. In the Spanish camps, food was scarce and sanitation poor. As a result, an estimated 200,000 Cubans died.

Cuban exiles in the United States, led by José Martí, urged the United States to help the rebels. Martí, Cuba's greatest poet, had long dreamed of an independent Cuba. However, he was killed in a skirmish in Cuba before he could see his dream come true.

Americans React Many Americans were sympathetic to the Cuban rebels. They called on the U.S. government to intervene to oust the Spanish. Other Americans wanted to intervene for economic reasons. They wanted to safeguard American investments in Cuba. At the time, Americans had about $50 million invested in Cuban sugar and rice plantations, railroads, and iron mines.

President Cleveland ignored the calls for intervention. He remarked that "there seems to be an epidemic of insanity in the country." When William McKinley became President in 1897, he also tried to maintain neutrality. Still, the clamor for war continued.

Some of the loudest cries came from the New York press. As you have read, Joseph Pulitzer of the *New York World* had developed a style of reporting that became known as yellow journalism. Pulitzer's rival, William Randolph Hearst of the *New York Journal*, tried to outdo Pulitzer in the use of sensational stories and headlines.

The two publishers focused much of their attention on Cuba. "FEEDING PRISONERS TO THE SHARKS," read one headline in the *Journal*. The *World* called Cuba a land of "blood on the roadsides, blood in the fields, blood on the doorsteps, blood, blood, blood." This daily barrage of horror stories fed American outrage against Spain.

"Remember the *Maine*" Early in 1898, fighting broke out in Havana, Cuba's capital. President McKinley ordered the battleship *Maine* to Havana harbor to protect American lives and property.

On February 15, at 9:40 P.M., a great explosion sank the *Maine* and killed 260 men. To this day, no one knows what caused the explosion. However, the press and the public blamed Spain. With cries of "Remember the *Maine*," Americans demanded revenge.

☑**Checkpoint** Why was the *Maine* in Havana harbor?

Ask Analytical Questions
Reading Skill
The explosion of the *Maine* interested many Americans. Suggest a possible research question on this topic.

The Yellow Press Reports on the *Maine*
Sensational coverage of the explosion of the battleship *Maine* by New York's yellow press helped feed the fever for war. *Critical Thinking: Distinguish Facts From Opinions From these examples and from what you have read, state two facts and two opinions that appeared in coverage of the* Maine.

The United States Goes to War

War fever swept the United States. At first, President McKinley favored a peaceful settlement between Spain and the rebels. He feared that war would disrupt the U.S. economy. In the end, though, McKinley gave in to the public pressure. On April 11, 1898, he asked Congress to declare war on Spain. Nine days later, Congress did so.

Surprise in the Philippines The first great battle of the war was not fought in Cuba. It took place halfway around the world.

Vocabulary Builder
<u>prospect</u> (PRAHS pehkt) *n.* expectation; likely outcome

Assistant Secretary of the Navy Theodore Roosevelt was eager to expand U.S. naval power. After the *Maine* blew up, Roosevelt saw the <u>prospect</u> of war growing. Roosevelt telegraphed Commodore George Dewey, head of the Pacific fleet. He ordered Dewey to move his ships so as to strike the Philippines when war broke out. On May 1, Dewey, with a small fleet of American warships, sank the entire Spanish squadron at Manila Bay, in the Philippines. The Americans did not lose a single ship or life.

Vocabulary Builder
<u>revolt</u> (ree VOHLT) *n.* rebellion

Fall of Manila Like the Cubans, many Filipinos were in <u>revolt</u> against the Spanish. Dewey enlisted Emilio Aguinaldo, a rebel leader, to help him seize Manila from the Spanish. Soon, the United States found itself in control of the Philippine Islands. Aguinaldo was a major help to the Americans. But the Americans overlooked the fact that Aguinaldo was fighting for Philippine independence. Soon he would be fighting against the Americans.

War in the Caribbean The war's focus next shifted to Cuba. The main fighting took place around Santiago and at sea. American ground forces arrived in Santiago in late June. They were poorly trained and poorly equipped—but eager to fight.

One of the best known units was the Rough Riders, led by Theodore Roosevelt. Roosevelt had given up his navy post to join the war. On July 1, Roosevelt helped lead his men in a successful charge up San Juan Hill that became the most celebrated event of the war.

Americans—both black and white—fought in the Santiago campaign. First Lieutenant John J. Pershing wrote:

> **❝**White regiments, black regiments . . . fought shoulder to shoulder, unmindful of race or color . . . and mindful only of their common duty as Americans.**❞**
> —First Lieutenant John J. Pershing, speech, November 27, 1898

Meanwhile, U.S. ships had trapped the Spanish fleet in Santiago harbor. When the fleet tried to escape, U.S. ships destroyed it. The 24,000 Spanish soldiers at Santiago surrendered two weeks later.

After the Spanish surrendered Cuba, American troops invaded Puerto Rico, another Spanish possession in the Caribbean. They quickly brought the island under U.S. control.

Theodore Roosevelt, Rough Rider

✓**Checkpoint** **What lands did Spain lose in the Caribbean?**

Spanish-American War

War in the Caribbean

War in the Pacific

KEY
- - - U.S. Navy
→ U.S. Army
→ Spanish fleet
★ U.S. victories
▬ Spanish colonies

MAP MASTER®
Skills Activity

The two fronts in the Spanish-American War were on opposite sides of the world.

(a) Read a Map Locate these places: Philippine Islands, Manila Bay, Santiago, San Juan. Which are located in the Pacific Ocean? Which are in the Atlantic Ocean or the Caribbean Sea?

(b) Interpret Maps Describe the different routes taken by the U.S. Navy and the U.S. Army to reach Santiago.

MapMaster Online

For: Interactive Map
Visit: PHSchool.com
Web Code: myp-6162

An American Empire

In December 1898, Spain and the United States signed a peace treaty. Spain accepted Cuban independence. It granted Puerto Rico, the Philippines, and the Pacific islands of Guam and Wake to the United States. In return, the United States paid Spain $20 million.

Debating the Treaty The treaty triggered an angry debate in the United States. Many Americans said taking colonies violated the principle of the Declaration of Independence—that all people had a right to self-government. Besides, they said, acquiring colonies brought the risk of future wars.

Expansionists, by contrast, welcomed the treaty. It gave the United States important bases, they said, and provided new business opportunities. Also, they argued, the United States had a duty to spread the ideas of democratic government to other parts of the world.

In a close vote, the Senate ratified the treaty on February 6, 1899. The United States now had an overseas empire.

Governing Cuba and Puerto Rico The United States replaced Spain as the leading Caribbean power. As a result, Cuba did not gain the true independence it sought. In 1902, Congress forced Cuba to include the Platt Amendment in its new constitution. The amendment limited Cuba's power to make treaties or borrow money. It gave the United States a right to intervene in Cuban affairs. It also allowed the United States to keep a naval base at Guantánamo Bay. In effect, it made Cuba a protectorate of the United States. A protectorate is an independent country whose policies are controlled by an outside power. Wrote one Cuban journalist, "The Americans have made our country free. As free as a dog on a leash."

The Foraker Act of 1900 set up a government in Puerto Rico, with a U.S.-appointed governor. The act gave Puerto Ricans limited self-rule. Americans developed Puerto Rico's economy and educational system. In 1917, Puerto Ricans were made citizens of the United States. Still, many Puerto Ricans wanted to be free of outside control.

Revolt in the Philippines When the United States took control of the Philippines, many Filipinos felt betrayed. Led by Emilio Aguinaldo, they renewed their fight for independence. In a three-year war, about 4,000 Americans and 20,000 Filipinos were killed. Finally, in 1901, Aguinaldo was captured and fighting came to an end. Not until 1946 did the Philippines gain independence.

Emilio Aguinaldo

✓Checkpoint How did the treatment of Cuba, Puerto Rico, and the Philippines differ?

☆ **Looking Back and Ahead** The Spanish-American War gave the United States an overseas empire. Next, you will read how the United States extended its influence in Latin America.

Section 2 | **Check Your Progress**

Progress Monitoring ⓦnline
For: Self-test with instant help
Visit: PHSchool.com
Web Code: mya-6162

Comprehension and Critical Thinking

1. **(a) Identify** What role did the press play in rallying American support for a war in Cuba?
   (b) Draw Inferences What motivated the United States to enter into a war with Spain?

2. **(a) List** What were the terms of the peace treaty between the United States and Spain?
   (b) Analyze Cause and Effect How had the United States replaced Spain as a colonial power in the world?

🕐 Reading Skill

3. **Ask Analytical Questions** Reread the text following the subheading "Debating the Treaty." What were the arguments in the debate? Suggest a possible research question on this topic.

Key Terms

Answer the following questions in complete sentences that show your understanding of the key terms.

4. How did reconcentration suppress the people of Cuba?

5. Why did a Cuban describe protectorate status as like being a "dog on a leash"?

Writing

6. Write a persuasive paragraph either for or against the Spanish-American War. Exchange papers with a classmate who took the opposite view. Next, write comments opposing the other person's arguments. Finally, take back your own paper and rewrite it to respond to your classmate's notes.

Profit and Happiness

"... The republics of Central America and the Caribbean possess great natural wealth. They need only a measure of stability ... bringing profit and happiness to themselves and at the same time creating conditions sure to lead to a flourishing interchange of trade with this country."

—President William Howard Taft, 1912

◀ U.S. fruit companies made huge profits in Latin America.

The United States and Latin America

Objectives
- Explain why and how the United States built the Panama Canal.
- Discuss how Presidents expanded the Monroe Doctrine to intervene in the affairs of Caribbean nations.
- Describe how relations between the United States and Mexico became strained under President Wilson.

🔁 Reading Skill

Focus Research Topics Research topics must be specific. Frame questions to a particular time and place. Avoid questions that would require yes or no answers. Connect questions to the context of your history reading. Work toward asking questions that can be answered with evidence from available and reliable research sources.

Key Terms and People

isthmus
William C. Gorgas
corollary

dollar diplomacy
Francisco Villa

Why It Matters By 1902, the United States was a world power with a strong economy and overseas colonies. The nation's leaders were eager to extend American power and influence. They were especially interested in Latin America.

❓ Section Focus Question: How did the United States use the Monroe Doctrine to justify intervention in Latin America?

Linking the Oceans

During the Spanish-American War, the U.S. Navy sent the battleship *Oregon* from San Francisco to Cuba. The trip—14,000 miles around the tip of South America—took more than two months.

Clearly, a shorter route was needed. A canal across Central America would link the Atlantic and Pacific oceans. President Theodore Roosevelt was determined to build that canal. Not only would it improve global shipping, but it would also make it easier for the U.S. Navy to defend the nation's new overseas empire.

Choosing a Site At 50 miles wide, the Isthmus of Panama was the ideal location for a canal. An isthmus is a narrow strip of land joining two larger areas of land. In 1902, Panama was a province of Colombia. Roosevelt offered Colombia $10 million in cash and $250,000 yearly in rent to allow the United States to build a canal through Panama.

Many Colombians opposed the deal because it would give the United States permanent control over a 6-mile-wide stretch of Colombian territory. Other Colombians claimed that the rights were worth far more than the United States had offered. Colombia's government held out for more money. However, Roosevelt was impatient. He did not want to lose time in bargaining.

Revolt in Panama Roosevelt knew that many Panamanians disliked Colombian rule. Secretly, he let them know that the United States would help if they claimed independence. The Panamanians, of course, would then reap the rewards of a canal.

A revolt took place on November 3, 1903. U.S. gunboats waited in the harbor to provide support for the rebels. U.S. Marines landed in Colón to prevent <u>hostile</u> Colombian troops from reaching Panama City. Many Americans were alarmed by Roosevelt's role in the revolt, criticizing his "gunboat diplomacy."

The United States immediately recognized the independent Republic of Panama. Three days later, a Frenchman acting for Panama signed a treaty giving the United States permanent use and control of a 10-mile-wide zone across the Isthmus of Panama. The United States agreed to pay $10 million plus $250,000 a year in rent.

☑ **Checkpoint** **How did the United States help rebels in Panama?**

The Panama Canal

In 1904, the U.S. government began to build a canal across Panama. President Roosevelt urged the engineers to "Make the dirt fly!"

Fighting Disease The first great obstacle to building the canal was not an engineering problem. It was disease. Malaria and yellow fever were widespread in Panama. Real work on the canal could not begin until those diseases were controlled.

William C. Gorgas, an American expert on tropical diseases, took up the problem. Most people at the time believed that the damp night air caused yellow fever and malaria. A major breakthrough came when a Cuban doctor, Carlos Juan Finlay, discovered that yellow fever was transmitted by a certain kind of mosquito. An English doctor, Ronald Ross, found that a different kind of mosquito carried malaria.

At Gorgas's direction, workers cleared brush and drained swamps where mosquitoes lived. The huge effort paid off. By 1906, Gorgas had nearly wiped out yellow fever and reduced malaria in Panama.

The "Big Ditch" Construction of the canal involved three major tasks. Workers had to cut through a mountain, dam a river, and erect the canal's giant locks. By raising or lowering the water level, the locks would allow ships to cross Panama's Cordillera Mountains.

The most challenging job was digging the Gaillard Cut, a 9-mile ditch through the mountains. Thousands of men worked day after day under the tropical sun or in drenching rainstorms. Mudslides were a constant problem. To many workers, it seemed that the digging would never end. One later recalled, "I load cement, I unload cement. I carry lumber until my shoulders peel."

While engineers and supervisors came from the United States, most of the laborers were West Indians of African descent. Some 20,000 were from Barbados. More than 6,000 workers lost their lives during the construction of the canal.

Vocabulary Builder
<u>hostile</u> (HAHS tihl) *adj.* unfriendly; intending to do harm; like an enemy

Focus Research Topics
Suggest a more focused research question that builds on the following topic: How do science and economics work together?

The Panama Canal

The building of the Panama Canal was one of the greatest engineering feats of all time. Construction of the canal began in 1904 and was finished in 1914. When it was completed, the Atlantic and Pacific oceans were linked. **Critical Thinking:** *Synthesize Information* *What were the costs and benefits of building the canal?*

History *Interactive*
Tour the Panama Canal
Visit: PHSchool.com
Web Code: myp-6163

◄ Locks Under Construction
Because of the uneven elevation in the Canal Zone, the canal planners designed a system of locks to raise and lower the water level. This photograph shows construction of a lock in 1913. The huge gates open and close to let water in and out.

UNITED STATES
San Francisco   Jupiter
Atlantic Ocean
4,500 MILES
22 DAYS
12,500 MILES
67 DAYS
PANAMA CANAL
Pacific Ocean

A Shorter Trip ▲
American merchant and naval ships could now travel much more quickly between the Atlantic and Pacific oceans.

Fast Facts

Length: 50 miles

Number of locks: 12 (6 pairs)

Cost to build: $387 million

Time to build: 10 years

Amount of earth removed during construction:
238.9 cubic yards

Source: Panama Canal Authority

◄ Workers and Disease
Tropical diseases killed more than 5,000 workers. Quinine was a drug used to treat malaria.

Quinine Gr...

Despite unexpected delays, work on the canal was finished six months ahead of schedule. The Panama Canal opened on August 15, 1914. After years of work, the Atlantic and the Pacific were joined.

✓Checkpoint **What problems did canal builders overcome?**

Wielding a "Big Stick" in Latin America

Theodore Roosevelt was fond of quoting an old West African proverb: "Speak softly and carry a big stick; you will go far." He wanted the world to know that if diplomacy failed, the United States would not hesitate to use military force to protect its interests.

Roosevelt Corollary Roosevelt applied his "big stick" policy in Latin America. He asserted the claim of the United States to be the leader in the Western Hemisphere. He especially wanted to prevent European nations from becoming too powerful in the region.

In 1904, European nations considered using military force to collect overdue debts from the Dominican Republic. To prevent any such action, Roosevelt announced a new policy. It came to be known as the Roosevelt Corollary to the Monroe Doctrine. A corollary is a logical extension of a doctrine or proposition.

Roosevelt argued that when the neighbors of the United States got into disputes with foreign nations, the United States had the right to "exercise . . . an international police power" to restore order.

Roosevelt sent marines to the Dominican Republic and took over the country's finances. Later Presidents often cited the Roosevelt Corollary when intervening in Latin America.

Dollar Diplomacy William Howard Taft, who followed Roosevelt as President, had a different approach. Taft favored dollar diplomacy, a policy based on the idea that economic ties were the best way to expand American influence. Taft urged U.S. bankers and businesses to invest heavily in Asia and Latin America.

Dollar diplomacy led to as many military interventions as Roosevelt's "big stick." When a revolution broke out in Nicaragua, the United States sent in marines to protect U.S. investments. Later, American troops also occupied Haiti and Honduras. Many Latin Americans bitterly resented interference in their affairs.

✓Checkpoint **How did Roosevelt build on the Monroe Doctrine?**

Vocabulary Builder
invest (ihn VEHST) **v.** to supply money for a project in order to make a profit

The U.S. and Latin America
Fearing European intervention in Latin America, U.S. foreign policy asserted U.S. power in the Western Hemisphere. **Critical Thinking: Identify Effects** *Use information in the text to provide one effect of each policy listed in the chart.*

U.S. Policy in Latin America, 1823–1909		
Monroe Doctrine (1823) Monroe asserts that the United States will not permit European nations to interfere with the free nations of Latin America.	**Roosevelt Corollary** (1904) Theodore Roosevelt reinforces the Monroe Doctrine by claiming the right to use force to prevent intervention in Latin America.	**Dollar Diplomacy** (1909) Taft's policy aims to protect U.S. economic investments in Latin America and in other regions.

Relations With Mexico

Woodrow Wilson, who became President in 1913, had his own ideas about foreign relations. He stated that U.S. foreign policy should aim to support and nurture democracy throughout the world.

Wilson's policy got its first test in relations with Mexico. In 1911, Mexicans had overthrown longtime dictator Porfírio Díaz. Mexico was plunged into a violent revolution that went on until 1917. Wilson at first followed a policy that he called "watchful waiting." He said he hoped Mexico would develop a democratic government.

In 1914, a minor incident led Wilson to intervene in Mexico. U.S. sailors who went ashore in Tampico were briefly arrested. Although they were released promptly with an apology, Wilson sent the navy to occupy the port of Veracruz. More than 100 Mexicans died. The incident brought Mexico and the United States close to war. Tempers cooled after South American nations arranged for peace talks.

Wilson was drawn into Mexican affairs again by the actions of Francisco Villa, a Mexican rebel general nicknamed Pancho. In 1916, Villa's rebels crossed into New Mexico. They raided and burned the town of Columbus, killing 18 Americans.

Mexico's president reluctantly let the United States pursue Villa into Mexico. On Wilson's orders, General John J. Pershing led several thousand soldiers across the border. After 11 months, Wilson ordered Pershing to withdraw without capturing Villa.

✓ **Checkpoint** **What was Wilson's policy toward Mexico?**

⭐ **Looking Back and Ahead** World events provided the backdrop for the withdrawal of troops from Mexico. In 1917, war was raging in Europe and parts of Africa, Asia, and the Pacific. In the next chapter, you will learn about that world war and the U.S. role in it.

Pancho Villa

Progress Monitoring Online
For: Self-test with instant help
Visit: PHSchool.com
Web Code: mya-6163

Section 3 | Check Your Progress

Comprehension and Critical Thinking

1. **(a) Recall** Why was the building of a canal important to the United States?
   (b) Understand Sequence What events led to the eventual building of the Panama Canal?

2. **(a) Describe** According to President Wilson, what was the goal of U.S. foreign policy?
   (b) Compare and Contrast How did the foreign policies of Presidents Roosevelt and Taft differ?

🔄 Reading Skill

3. **Focus Research Topics** Reread the text following the subheading "Roosevelt Corollary." Suggest a more focused research question based on the following: How did Latin Americans respond to U.S. actions under the Roosevelt Corollary?

Key Terms

Read the sentence below. If it is true, write YES. If it is not true, write NO and explain why.

4. Engineers built the canal through an isthmus river bed.

Writing

5. Choose one of the following statements about U.S. support of the Panamanian rebels in 1903. Revise the statement to make its language more restrained and persuasive. **Statements:**

   (a) The greedy Colombian government stood in the way of progress, but Roosevelt found a way around it.

   (b) When Colombia stood up to Roosevelt, he acted like a bully and took what he wanted anyhow.

21st Century Learning You may be asked to give presentations in school or at work. One way to create an effective presentation is by combining text, video, audio, and graphics. Look at the sample storyboard and follow the steps below to learn how to give an effective presentation.

1 (2 mins)	**2** (3 mins)	**3** (3 mins)	**4** (4 mins)	**5** (3 mins)
Why is Hawaii important to the U.S.? Video clip of a Hawaiian beach Introduce topic by explaining historic and modern importance: • Military and commercial outpost in the Pacific • Land of many natural resources and unmatched beauty • Our 50th state (1959)	Photo collage showing pineapple, sugar, shipping, tourism, etc., of Hawaii, with captions	Graphs • Major natural resources in dollars • Largest industries in dollars	Hawaiian music playing in background with pictures • Rich history and interesting culture (show photo of people in traditional Hawaiian dress) • Diverse geography (show photo of volcanoes and landscapes) • Major tourist destination (show people scuba diving)	Summarize by showing how the U.S. might be different if Hawaii had not become a state.

Learn the Skill
Use these steps to learn how to give a multimedia presentation.

1 Define your topic. When choosing a topic, consider the time allotted for the presentation and the complexity of the subject. Multimedia presentations lend themselves to topics that have several subtopics. However, a topic that is too broad is hard to cover adequately in a limited amount of time. Consider how to narrow your topic.

2 Determine what types of media are available for the presentation. Do you have access to a computer and the software to create a podcast, PowerPoint presentation, or slide show? Do you have access to video, film, or audio clips of speeches or historic events?

3 Make a storyboard. Create a storyboard by brainstorming ideas for covering your topic in various media. Then make a detailed outline of the information you will present. Identify the medium that will work best for each part of the presentation. Plan the transitions between the parts of the presentation.

4 Practice your presentation. A trial run gives you a chance to time each segment, identify technical problems, and make sure all participants know their roles.

Practice the Skill
Answer the following questions about the storyboard on this page.

1 Define your topic. How did the presenters narrow or focus the presentation of their topic?

2 Determine what types of media are available for the presentation. What media will be used in the presentation?

3 Make a storyboard. How does the storyboard help the presenters plan their presentation? How will it help the presenters stay within a certain time limit?

4 Practice your presentation. How would you practice the presentation?

Apply the Skill
See the Review and Assessment at the end of this chapter.

How did the United States demonstrate its growing interest in the Pacific and in Latin America?

Section 1
Eyes on the Pacific

- The United States purchased Alaska and acquired Pacific territories.
- The United States recognized the Pacific islands as important military outposts.
- The Open Door Policy was meant to give the United States equal trading opportunities with other nations in China.

Section 2
The Spanish-American War

- The United States went to war against Spain over Cuba and the Philippines.
- Naval and land battles in the Philippines and in Cuba and Puerto Rico resulted in victory for the United States.
- The United States took control of lands from which it had evicted Spain.

Section 3
The United States and Latin America

- The United States built the Panama Canal to improve global shipping and to strengthen American defense.
- Disease and tough terrain made building the Panama Canal very difficult.
- Foreign policy in the early 1900s aimed to build U.S. influence in Latin America.

Teddy Roosevelt

Exploring the Essential Question

Use the online study guide to explore the essential question.

Section 1
How did the United States acquire new territory and expand trade in the Asia-Pacific region?

Chapter 20 Essential Question
How did the United States demonstrate its growing interest in the Pacific and in Latin America?

Section 2
What were the causes and effects of the Spanish-American War?

Section 3
How did the United States use the Monroe Doctrine to justify intervention in Latin America?

Key Terms

Answer the questions in complete sentences that show your understanding of the key terms.

1. How did imperialism conflict with isolationism in U.S. foreign policy?

2. Why did foreign nations want to establish spheres of influence in China?

3. Why was Theodore Roosevelt's foreign policy seen as a corollary to the Monroe Doctrine?

4. What was the goal of Taft's dollar diplomacy?

5. Why was an isthmus a good place to build a canal?

Comprehension and Critical Thinking

6. (a) **Recall** Why was Secretary of State Seward interested in buying Alaska?
   (b) **Detect Points of View** How does the cartoon below reflect what many Americans thought of the purchase at first?
   (c) **Identify Economic Benefits** How did buying Alaska provide economic benefits?

7. (a) **Identify** In which regions of the world did European powers gain control by 1900?
   (b) **Evaluate Information** What impact did the expansion policies of European countries have on the foreign policy of the United States?

8. (a) **Recall** What event was the immediate cause of the Spanish-American War?
   (b) **Draw Conclusions** Do you think this event by itself was enough to start the war? Why or why not?

9. (a) **Explain** How did the United States gain an overseas empire?
   (b) **Detect Points of View** Why do you think some critics felt that having an empire was against American ideals?

10. (a) **Summarize** How did Roosevelt apply his "big stick" policy to Latin America?
    (b) **Compare** How was Taft's dollar diplomacy like the Roosevelt Corollary?

History Reading Skill

11. **Frame Research Questions** Review the sections in this chapter, and frame one research question for each section. Remember to frame questions that go beyond the text and require research to answer.

Writing

12. **Write two persuasive paragraphs about one of the following issues:**
    - American expansionism in the Pacific
    - U.S. relations with Latin America
    - The Spanish-American War

    Your paragraphs should:
    - Include a thesis statement expressing your opinion.
    - Use facts, reasons, and examples from the chapter.

    When you are finished, exchange papers with another student. Correct errors. Try to make the language more persuasive.

13. **Write a Narrative:**
    Imagine you are a Cuban nationalist visiting the United States with José Martí. Write a paragraph describing how you sought U.S. help for Cuba.

Skills for Life

Give a Multimedia Presentation
Use the storyboard on page 698 to answer the following questions.

14. You have only ten minutes for this presentation. How would you change the storyboard?

15. Where would you find the information for this presentation?

16. What are some things you would change in this presentation? Why?

17. What other types of media could be used?

Test Yourself

1. The chief goal of the Open Door Policy was to

A divide China into spheres of influence.

B open Japan for trade.

C put down the Boxer Rebellion.

D protect U.S. trading rights in China.

2. In the late 1800s, expansionists argued that the United States

A should avoid involvement with other nations.

B needed new markets for its products.

C should reject the Turner thesis.

D should accept the Roosevelt Corollary.

Refer to the cartoon below to answer Question 3.

THE BIG STICK IN THE CARIBBEAN SEA

3. What is the subject of this cartoon?

A yellow journalism

B the Spanish-American War

C the Roosevelt Corollary

D the war in the Philippines

Document-Based Questions

Task: Look at Documents 1 and 2, and answer their accompanying questions. Then, use the documents and your knowledge of history to complete this writing assignment:

Write a short essay comparing the viewpoints of supporters and opponents of overseas expansion. Evaluate the validity of the arguments on each side.

Document 1: In January 1899, Senator Orville H. Platt explained why he supported annexing the Philippines. *What arguments does Platt give?*

"I believe the same force was behind . . . our ships in Manila Bay that was behind the landing of Pilgrims on Plymouth Rock. . . . [We] have been chosen to carry forward this great work of uplifting humanity . . . . From the time of the landing on Plymouth Rock in the spirit of the Declaration of Independence, in the spirit of the Constitution, believing that all men are equal and endowed by their Creator with inalienable rights, believing that governments derive their just powers from the consent of the governed, we have spread that civilization . . . until it stood at the Pacific Ocean looking ever westward."

Document 2: Senator George F. Hoar responded to Platt's argument in favor of annexing the Philippines. *Why does Senator Hoar oppose annexing the Philippines?*

"You have no right at the cannon's mouth to impose on an unwilling people your Declaration of Independence and your Constitution and your notions of freedom and notions of what is good. . . . Now the people of the Philippine Islands are clearly a nation— a people three and one-third times as numerous as our fathers were when they set up this nation. . . . The people there have got a government, with courts and judges . . . and it is proposed to turn your guns on them and say, 'We think that our notion of government is better than the notion you have got yourselves.'"

World War I

1914–1919

"Gas cases are terrible. They cannot breathe lying down or sitting up. They just struggle for breath, but nothing can be done... their lungs are gone...."

—Shirley Millard, American nurse, 1918

In this picture, American soldiers fight from trenches in the French countryside in July 1918.

CHAPTER 21

What You Will Learn

Section 1
THE ROAD TO WAR
When World War I broke out in Europe, the United States tried to remain neutral but was drawn into the war.

Section 2
SUPPORTING THE WAR EFFORT
The United States government took strong steps to build the military and to increase support for the war effort.

Section 3
AMERICANS AT WAR
After a long stalemate, the arrival of American troops helped bring the war to an end.

Section 4
SHAPING THE PEACE
Despite President Wilson's efforts, the Allies imposed a harsh peace on Germany.

Reading Skill

Identify and Connect Main Ideas In this chapter, you will learn to improve your reading comprehension by using summaries, outlines, and note taking to identify main ideas.

Imperialism

Alliance Systems

Causes of
World War I

Nationalism

German Submarine Warfare

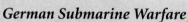

U.S. Events	1912	Woodrow Wilson is elected President.	Wilson declares U.S. neutrality in war in Europe.	1914	1915	128 Americans die when the *Lusitania* is sunk.

1912   **1914**   **1916**

World Events	1914	World War I begins in Europe.

The League of Nations

KEY

- Members of League and territories under their control
- Non-members of League and territories under their control
- Mandates under control of League

Effects of
World War I

American Troops Enter the War

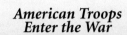

GO OVER THE TOP WITH

U.S. MARINES

Battle Over the Peace

LEAGUE OF NATIONS

AMERICAN PEOPLE

SENATE

Supporting the War Effort

Joan of Arc Saved France

W.S.S. WOMEN OF AMERICA SAVE YOUR COUNTRY *Buy* WAR SAVINGS STAMPS
UNITED STATES TREASURY DEPARTMENT

Little AMERICANS *Do your bit*

Eat Oatmeal-Corn meal mush-Hominy - other corn cereals - and Rice with milk. *Save the wheat for our soldiers.* Leave nothing on your plate

UNITED STATES FOOD ADMINISTRATION

1917 United States declares war on Germany.

1918 Armistice ends World War I.

1919 U.S. Senate rejects Treaty of Versailles.

1916   1918   1920

1917 Revolution in Russia overthrows the tsar.

1918 Treaty of Versailles punishes Germany.

▲ This assassination led to World War I.

Too Much Hatred

❝The situation is extraordinary. It is militarism run stark mad. Unless someone acting for you can bring about a different understanding, there is some day to be an awful cataclysm. No one in Europe can do it. There is too much hatred, too many jealousies.❞

—Colonel E.M. House, advisor to President Woodrow Wilson, 1914

The Road to War

Objectives

- Discover the factors that led to the outbreak of war in Europe.
- Find out why World War I was deadlier than any earlier conflict.
- Learn how the United States moved from neutrality to involvement in the war.

Reading Skill

Identify Main Ideas and Support Look for main ideas within the text paragraphs that begin with subheadings. As you read, use the headings to guide you in identifying main ideas and supporting ideas.

Key Terms

militarism
nationalism
stalemate
trench warfare
propaganda

Why It Matters America was a world power. But when war erupted in Europe, the United States tried to keep out of it. However, the problems that caused the war would soon bring America into the war. Americans were learning the costs and responsibilities of world leadership.

❓ **Section Focus Question: What were the causes of World War I?**

Origins of World War I

In 1914, tensions in Europe erupted into the largest war the world had yet seen. There were many different causes for the conflict that later became known as World War I.

Imperialism European nations competed for trade and territory in Africa, Asia, and the Pacific. France and England looked on distrustfully as Germany expanded its overseas holdings.

Imperialism fed a rise in militarism, or the glorification of the military. For self-protection and for national glory, nations built up their armed forces. Military leaders gained great influence in European governments.

Nationalism A surge of nationalism, or pride in one's nation or ethnic group, boosted tensions. In the Balkan region of southeastern Europe, different national groups sought to break free from Austria-Hungary. Russia encouraged Serbians and other Balkan nationalists to do so. Many people compared the Balkans to a "powder keg," or barrel of gunpowder. A single spark could easily provoke a major war.

Alliance System As tensions mounted, European nations formed alliance systems. Germany formed an alliance with Austria-Hungary. France, Britain, and Russia pledged to come to one another's aid if attacked. The alliance system meant that any conflict between two powers would quickly involve others.

War Begins The spark that set off the war came on June 28, 1914, in the Bosnian city of Sarajevo. A Serbian nationalist assassinated Archduke Franz Ferdinand, heir to the Austro-Hungarian throne. Austria-Hungary accused the government of Serbia of supporting terrorism. On July 29, Austria-Hungary declared war on Serbia.

The alliance system drew one country after another into war. (See the chart below.) In time, more than 20 countries became involved in the fighting. Britain, France, and Russia led the Allies. Opposing them were the Central powers, including Germany, Austria-Hungary, and the Ottoman Empire.

✓Checkpoint **How did nationalism contribute to war?**

The Deadliest War

Both sides hoped for a quick victory. By early September, German forces had advanced to within 30 miles of Paris. At the First Battle of the Marne, however, French and British troops halted the German advance. This area became known as the Western Front. Fighting quickly settled into a long stalemate, or deadlock, in which neither side could score a clear victory. The stalemate dragged on for more than three grueling years.

Along the Western Front, trench warfare fed the stalemate. In trench warfare, soldiers fire on one another from opposing lines of dugout trenches. Between the lines was an unoccupied territory known as "no man's land." After days of shelling, officers would order troops to charge into no man's land and attack the enemy trenches. There, they were mowed down by enemy fire. As death tolls mounted, the two sides fought back and forth over the same patches of land.

The Road to World War I
During the summer of 1914, one European power after another was drawn into the conflict that became known as World War I.
Critical Thinking: *Apply Information* *How does the information on the map help explain the sequence of events listed here?*

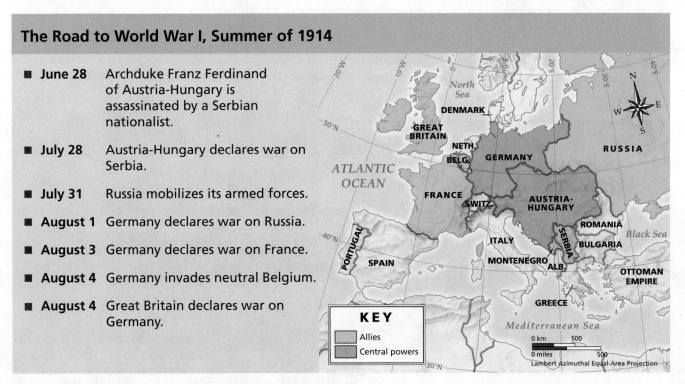

The Road to World War I, Summer of 1914

- **June 28** Archduke Franz Ferdinand of Austria-Hungary is assassinated by a Serbian nationalist.

- **July 28** Austria-Hungary declares war on Serbia.

- **July 31** Russia mobilizes its armed forces.

- **August 1** Germany declares war on Russia.

- **August 3** Germany declares war on France.

- **August 4** Germany invades neutral Belgium.

- **August 4** Great Britain declares war on Germany.

KEY
- Allies
- Central powers

Identify Main Ideas and Support
What is the main idea of the section that begins on the previous page? What are some of the supporting ideas?

Technological advances made the war more lethal. Airplanes, invented a few years before, were used for scouting and support of ground forces. Armored tanks appeared on the battlefield. More than any other weapons, rapid-fire machine guns and heavy artillery raised the death toll.

But the most feared new weapon was poison gas. It was first used by Germany, then by the Allies. Various gases caused choking, blinding, or severe skin blisters. Even some soldiers who survived gas attacks suffered lung problems for years afterward. In 1925, after the war, a group of 140 nations agreed to ban the use of chemical weapons in war.

✓**Checkpoint** **How did technology make the war more deadly?**

American Neutrality

Horrified by the bloodshed, President Woodrow Wilson sought to keep the United States out of the war. Soon after the fighting began, he issued a proclamation of "strict and impartial neutrality."

Ethnic Loyalties Still, many Americans had strong ties to one side or the other. German Americans generally supported the Central powers. Many Irish Americans also favored the Central powers, out of hatred for England's long domination of Ireland.

Vocabulary Builder
dominate (DAHM uh nayt) **v.** to control or rule

● **INFOGRAPHIC**
TRENCH WARFARE

Trenches snaked for miles along the French countryside. Soldiers on both sides endured mud, rats, cold, heat, and—worst of all—the constant threat of death.
Critical Thinking: *Analyze Effects* What impact do you think trench warfare had on the environment?

GAS MASK
A soldier who did not get his gas mask on in time might go blind, suffer agonizing burns and blisters, or choke to death.

HAND GRENADE
The grenade contained powerful explosives. A soldier would pull the safety pin and then throw the grenade by hand at the target.

Other Americans favored the Allies. Britain and the United States shared a common language and history. Americans of Slavic or Italian descent also generally supported the Allied side.

Britain used propaganda to win American support. Propaganda is the spread of information designed to win support for a cause. British propaganda often focused on Germany's brutal treatment of the Belgians at the start of the war. Many of the most horrifying tales were exaggerated or completely made up.

Supplying the Allies Legally, American firms were free to sell to both sides. Still, most American trade was with the Allies. In addition, American banks made large loans to the Allies.

Contributing to this imbalance was a British naval blockade of Germany. British ships stopped supplies from reaching German ports. The British intercepted not only weapons, but also food and cotton. Although Wilson objected, he reached an agreement with Britain. For instance, he required Britain to buy more American cotton to make up for lost sales to Germany.

The *Lusitania* Germany's navy had too few surface vessels to enforce a blockade of Britain and France. But the Germans had a large supply of U-boats, or submarines. In February 1915, Germany announced it would use its U-boats to blockade Britain.

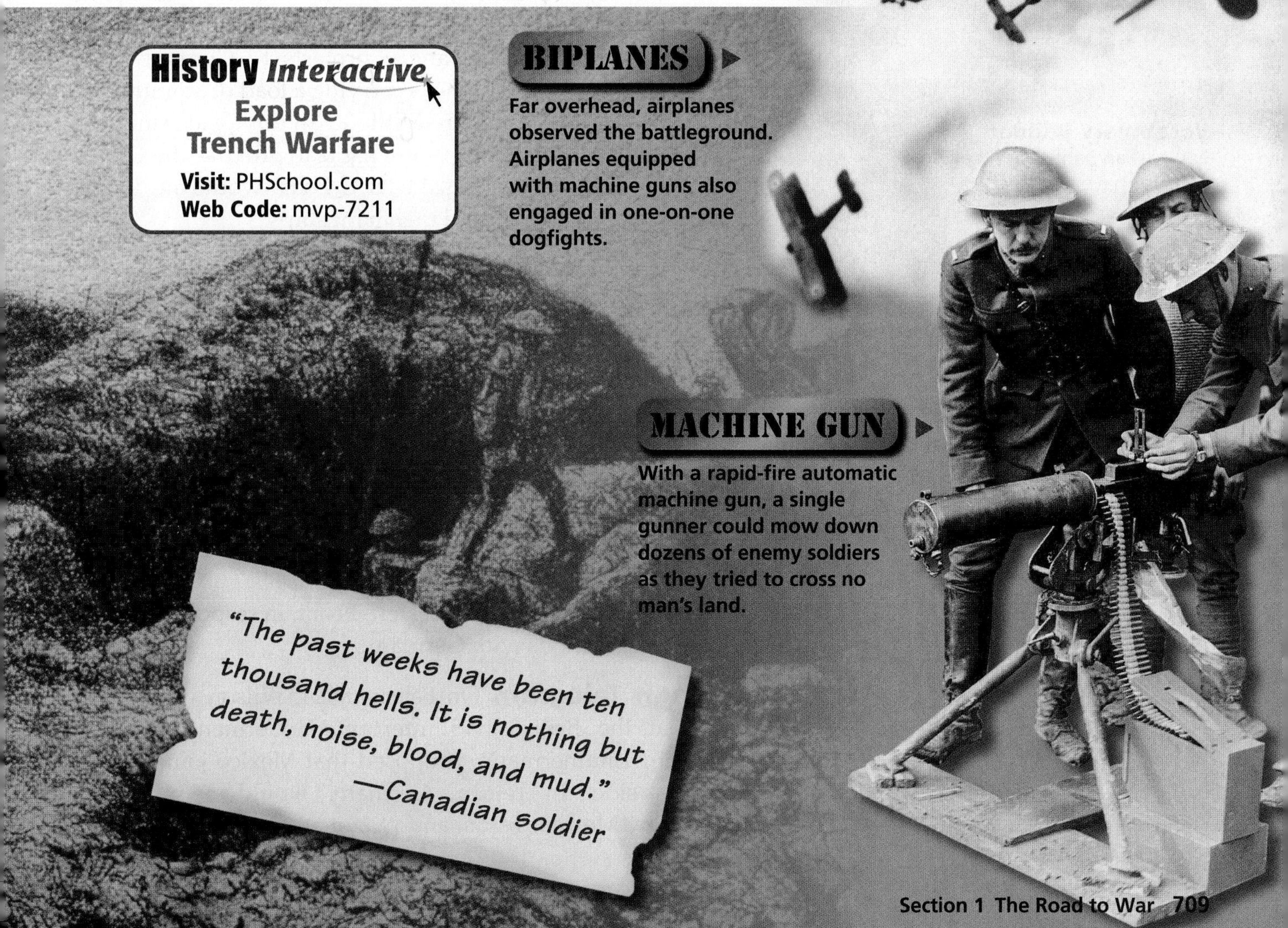

History *Interactive*
Explore Trench Warfare
Visit: PHSchool.com
Web Code: mvp-7211

BIPLANES

Far overhead, airplanes observed the battleground. Airplanes equipped with machine guns also engaged in one-on-one dogfights.

MACHINE GUN

With a rapid-fire automatic machine gun, a single gunner could mow down dozens of enemy soldiers as they tried to cross no man's land.

"The past weeks have been ten thousand hells. It is nothing but death, noise, blood, and mud."
—Canadian soldier

Sinking of the *Lusitania* On May 7, 1915, German U-boats torpedoed the British liner *Lusitania.* One passenger wrote the note shown here, sealed it in a bottle, and tossed it into the sea. ***Critical Thinking: Analyze Cause and Effect*** *What impact did the sinking of the* Lusitania *have?*

Vocabulary Builder
liable (Lī ah bahl) *adj.* likely to cause or have an effect

On May 7, 1915, a U-boat sank a British passenger liner, the *Lusitania,* off the coast of Ireland. Nearly 1,200 people died, 128 of them Americans. Wilson made angry protests to Germany. The Germans responded that the ship was carrying a load of ammunition to England. This argument mattered little to an outraged American public. Fearing that further attacks were <u>liable</u> to provoke the United States to declare war, Germany said its U-boats would no longer target passenger liners and neutral merchant ships.

☑**Checkpoint** **How did the war in Europe divide Americans?**

HISTORIAN'S APPRENTICE ACTIVITY PACK

To further explore the topics in this chapter, complete the activity in the Historian's Apprentice Activity Pack to answer this essential question:

What circumstances can lead to war?

Entering the War

Wilson was reelected in November 1916 on the slogan "He kept us out of war." He then called on the warring powers to accept "peace without victory." Such a peace, he said, should be based on the principles of democracy, freedom of the seas, and the avoidance of "entangling alliances." But Wilson's attempt to make peace failed.

Germany resumed unrestricted submarine warfare in February 1917. Germany hoped that cutting off American supplies to the British would break the stalemate on the Western Front. In response, Wilson cut off diplomatic relations with Germany.

Zimmermann Telegram On February 24, Wilson was shown a telegram that the British had intercepted. Germany's foreign minister, Arthur Zimmermann, proposed that Mexico join the war on Germany's side. In return, Germany would help Mexico "reconquer" New Mexico, Texas, and Arizona.

The Zimmermann Telegram was released to the press on March 1. American anger exploded. Anger soon turned to thoughts of war after U-boats sank three American merchant ships.

Russian Revolution A revolution in Russia removed the final obstacle to America's entry. Russia was one of the three main Allies. Its ruler, Tsar Nicholas II, was an absolute monarch who had long resisted calls for democratic reforms. In March 1917, military defeats and food shortages led to an uprising. The tsar was overthrown. A new government vowed to keep Russia in the war.

The fall of the tsar made it easier for the United States to enter the war. By joining with the Allied powers, the United States would not be siding with a tyrant. Instead, Wilson reasoned, it would be joining with other democracies to fight tyranny.

President Wilson asks Congress to declare war on Germany.

Declaring War On April 2, Wilson asked Congress to declare war against the Central powers. His goal, he declared, was to fight

> **"** . . . for the rights of nations great and small and the privilege of men everywhere to choose their way of life and of obedience. The world must be made safe for democracy. **"**
>
> —Woodrow Wilson, war message, April 2, 1917

Congress overwhelmingly gave its approval. After nearly three years on the sidelines, the United States was at war.

☑**Checkpoint** **How did submarine warfare help lead the United States into World War I?**

⭐ **Looking Back and Ahead** Following its traditional policy of isolationism, the United States tried to stay out of World War I. Now that it had joined the war, American life would be greatly changed.

Section 1 | **Check Your Progress**

Comprehension and Critical Thinking

1. **(a) List** Identify three factors that led to the outbreak of World War I.
   (b) Identify Alternatives What alternatives did European nations face when their Allies entered the war?

2. **(a) Recall** How did Wilson try to maintain neutrality?
   (b) Draw Conclusions Do you think the United States could have avoided entering the war? Why or why not?

🔄 **Reading Skill**

3. **Identify Main Ideas and Support** Reread the text under the heading "American Neutrality." Identify the main idea of this portion of text. Then, list supporting ideas.

Key Terms

Complete each of the following sentences so that the second part further explains the first part and clearly shows your understanding of the key term.

4. Serbs and other ethnic groups favored nationalism, or _____.
5. The British tried to gain support by using propaganda, or _____.
6. Technology contributed to a long stalemate, or _____.
7. War fever was partly the result of militarism, or _____.

Writing

8. Based on what you have read in this section, write a thesis statement for an essay contrasting trench warfare with present-day warfare.

Dearest Myrtle,

❝France certainly is a pretty country. . . . The Americans are doing themselves proud, but the losses are quite a lot. . . . Tell James to be sure to be a good boy. With oceans of love and hugs and kisses for my own sweet little darling, and lots of love for James, I am,

Your loving hubby,
E.J. Williams ❞

—Colonel Ezekiel James Williams, July 1918

▲ American soldiers departing for Europe

Supporting the War Effort

Objectives

- Find out how the United States quickly prepared for entry into World War I.
- Learn what measures the government took to control the wartime economy.
- Discover how the need to build support for the war sometimes clashed with civil liberties.

🔄 Reading Skill

Connect Main Ideas All the ideas in a section relate to one another. Look for several types of connections. For example, these connections may be cause and effect, parts of a category, or comparison-contrast. In addition, some ideas simply provide more information about a larger idea.

Key Terms and People

mobilize
Jeannette Rankin
illiterate

Herbert Hoover
Eugene V. Debs

Why It Matters Now that the United States had declared war on Germany, Americans faced enormous challenges. Like past and future conflicts, this war would dramatically affect both the soldiers on the battlefields and the civilians who remained at home.

❓ **Section Focus Question: What steps did the United States government take to prepare the nation for war?**

Building the Military

The United States entered the war with a large navy. However, it had only the world's sixteenth largest army, numbering just 125,000 men. In order to contribute to an Allied victory, the nation would have to mobilize quickly. To **mobilize** is to prepare for war.

Selective Service Immediately after the United States declared war, eager young men began volunteering for military service. Still, volunteers alone would not be enough to expand the army quickly. Wilson called upon Congress to establish a draft.

After a month of debate, Congress passed the Selective Service Act. The law required all young men between the ages of 21 and 30 to register for the military draft. By war's end, almost four million Americans had served in uniform.

Women in the Military Women were not subject to the draft. Still, American women had a long history of volunteerism, especially during the Progressive Era. More than 30,000 women volunteered for service. Two thirds of these women served in the U.S. Army and U.S. Navy Nurse Corps. The rest performed clerical work, such as filing papers or sending and receiving telegraph messages, as members of the U.S. Navy and U.S. Marine Corps. They became the first women in American history to hold official military rank.

Still, leading American women were divided over the war. Some opposed war under all circumstances. Jane Addams cofounded the Women's Peace Party in 1915 and continued to speak out for peace even after the United States entered the war. Representative Jeannette Rankin of Montana, the first woman elected to Congress, voted against Wilson's war resolution. "As a woman I can't go to war," Rankin said, "and I refuse to send anyone else."

Others, such as suffragist Carrie Chapman Catt, urged women to support the war effort. Catt hoped that women's wartime service would <u>accelerate</u> their drive to win the vote. In fact, this proved to be the case. As you have read, Congress passed the Nineteenth Amendment in 1919, shortly after the end of World War I.

A Diverse Force The military reflected the increasingly diverse makeup of the nation. About one in every five recruits had been born in foreign lands such as the Philippines, Mexico, or Italy. Many others were children of immigrants.

Native Americans were not American citizens at the time. Therefore, they were not subject to the draft. Still, a large number of Native Americans volunteered for service.

African Americans Serve Some 380,000 African Americans also served during the war. Their opportunities were restricted by official segregation and widespread racism. Still, civil rights leader W.E.B. Du Bois encouraged African Americans to support the war effort. "Let us, while the war lasts, forget our special grievances and close ranks . . . with our fellow citizens," Du Bois urged.

Still, African Americans faced discrimination in the military. They were placed in all-black units, of which only 10 percent were sent to combat. Most African American troops were confined to such noncombat duties as unloading ships, working in kitchens, or constructing barracks.

Some African American units fought under French command. Several members of a unit known as the Harlem Hell Fighters received France's highest medal for bravery, the *Croix de Guerre*, or cross of war.

The Military as Educator One in four draftees and recruits were illiterate, or unable to read and write. They could not read newspapers or even write letters home to their families. In addition, some young men from poor rural areas were not used to eating daily meals, taking regular baths, or using indoor plumbing.

For these young men, the military served as a great educator. The army taught millions not only how to fight, but how to read. Recruits learned about nutrition, personal hygiene, and patriotism.

☑**Checkpoint** How did the United States build its military force?

Vocabulary Builder
<u>accelerate</u> (ak SEL er ayt) **v.** to increase in speed; to move faster

An African American Soldier
As in earlier wars, African American soldiers served in separate units. This bugler served in France with the 15th New York Infantry. **Critical Thinking: Evaluate Information** *What image of this soldier does this painting create?*

C. CLARKE BUGLER
15th New York Infantry

Champagne 1918

Raymond Desvarreux

Managing the War Effort

Entry into the war forced a reshaping of the nation's economy. Both agriculture and industry mobilized for war.

Managing Food Supplies President Wilson chose Herbert Hoover to head a new Food Administration. Early in the war, Hoover had directed relief efforts in Belgium. His new job was to assure adequate food supplies for both civilians and troops.

Hoover urged Americans to conserve valuable food resources. To save on food, Americans observed "wheatless Mondays" and "meatless Tuesdays." Many grew their own vegetables in "victory gardens." The President's wife had one on the White House lawn.

Producing for War The war greatly increased demands on American industries. For example, the government placed orders for two million rifles and 130 million pairs of socks. To oversee the shift to war production, Wilson set up a new agency, the War Industries Board (WIB).

At first, the WIB had limited power. The unusually cold winter of 1917 to 1918 caused shortages of fuel and crippling congestion at ports and on railroads. Wilson strengthened the war board and gave it a new head, Jewish financier Bernard Baruch. The board told industries what to produce, how much to charge, and how to use scarce resources. For example, to make sure there was enough tin for military use, the WIB forbade toy makers to use tin for toys.

Finding Workers War brought a labor shortage, as millions of men joined the military. Also, there was a steep drop in immigration, to a tenth of its prewar rate. To meet war demands, American industry needed workers.

To fill the jobs, business owners turned to two main sources. Women took on roles previously denied them, for example, as factory workers or elevator operators. And more than half a million African Americans left the rural South to work in factories of the Midwest and Northeast. They were drawn by the opportunity to earn money and to escape segregation.

☑Checkpoint **What was the role of the War Industries Board?**

Shaping Public Opinion

The government worked to whip up support for the war. At the same time, it took measures to stifle antiwar sentiments.

Calling on Patriotism An effective propaganda tool was the Committee on Public Information, appointed by the President. The committee recruited 75,000 "Four-Minute Men" to deliver brief patriotic speeches at places like movie theaters and ball parks. It also enlisted artists to produce pro-war cartoons and posters. One famous poster had Uncle Sam pointing a finger and sternly saying, "Uncle Sam wants YOU!"

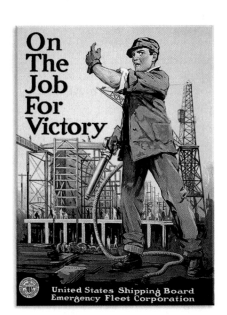

Propaganda posters such as this one encouraged industrial workers to increase production for the war effort.

The government issued Liberty Bonds to help finance the war. Movie stars toured the nation, urging Americans to buy bonds.

Suppressing Dissent The government took stern measures to suppress criticism of the war. Under the Espionage Act of 1917 and the Sedition Act of 1918, authorities closed newspapers and jailed individuals for expressing antiwar views.

Among those jailed was labor leader Eugene V. Debs, a five-time presidential candidate of the Socialist Party. Debs was jailed in 1918 for giving a speech in which he urged workers not to support the war effort. "It is extremely dangerous to exercise the constitutional right of free speech in a country fighting to make democracy safe in the world," Debs commented.

At times, war fever <u>collided</u> with personal freedoms. Private organizations sprang up that encouraged people to spy on their neighbors. The largest of these, the 200,000-strong American Protective League, opened people's mail, tapped phones, and pried into medical records.

Anti-German Hysteria German Americans suffered, too. In towns across the country, citizens shunned, harassed, and even assaulted German Americans who might once have been their friends. Some German Americans were tarred and feathered. Many schools stopped teaching the German language.

Anti-German feeling even affected the language. People referred to sauerkraut as "liberty cabbage." German measles became "liberty measles."

☑Checkpoint **How did the government build public support for the war effort?**

⭐ **Looking Back and Ahead** The war effort deeply affected life at home. In the next section, you will see how America's entry into the war helped to turn the tide in favor of the Allies.

Vocabulary Builder
<u>collide</u> (koh LĪD) **v.** to clash; to come together with great force

Connect Main Ideas
Connect the main ideas following the subheading "Calling on Patriotism" to those following the subheading "Suppressing Dissent."

Section 2 | Check Your Progress

Progress Monitoring ⬤nline
For: Self-test with instant help
Visit: PHSchool.com
Web Code: mva-7212

Comprehension and Critical Thinking

1. **(a) Recall** What steps did the United States take to mobilize for the war?
(b) Identify Alternatives Some Americans opposed the Selective Service Act. Do you think the government had other alternatives? Explain.

2. **(a) Recall** How did the government suppress dissent during World War I?

(b) Support a Point of View Do you think the government is justified in suppressing civil liberties during wartime? Give reasons for your opinion.

🎯 **Reading Skill**

3. **Connect Main Ideas** How are the main ideas of the text under the heading "Managing the War Effort" connected to the main ideas of the text under the heading "Shaping Public Opinion"?

Key Terms

4. Write two definitions of the key term mobilize—one a formal definition for a teacher, the other an informal definition for a younger child.

Writing

5. List supporting information to include in a short essay discussing how the war effort at times conflicted with personal freedom.

On the Home Front

During World War I, all Americans were encouraged to do their part for the war effort. However, some Americans faced the added burden of hatred and mistrust.

Food Will Win the War!

Americans planted "victory gardens" to grow vegetables so that there would be an adequate supply of food. Even children were expected to do their part. ▼

◄ **Mistrust of German Americans**

German Americans faced wartime restrictions and even violence. Here, police in New York fingerprint a German immigrant woman. The passage below describes an attack on a German community in Iowa.

"People acted like savages. They came in mobs from towns all around. . . . One mob got the minister and made him march through town carrying a flag. Then, they made him stand on a coffin which was a rough box and kiss the flag. . . . Then, he was ordered out of town."

Buy a Victory Bond! ▶

To raise money for the war effort, the government issued Victory Bonds and Savings Stamps. Here, Charlie Chaplin—the most popular movie comedian of his day—addresses a huge crowd at a War Bond rally.

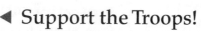

AMERICAN RED CROSS

OUR BOYS NEED
SOX
KNIT YOUR BIT

KEEP HIM FREE

BUY
WAR SAVINGS STAMPS
ISSUED BY THE UNITED STATES TREASURY DEPT.

W.S.S.
WAR SAVINGS STAMPS
ISSUED BY THE
UNITED STATES
GOVERNMENT

◀ Support the Troops!

Volunteer organizations such as the Red Cross worked to keep soldiers healthy and comfortable. You did not have to be somebody's mother to knit a pair of warm socks!

Analyze LIFE AT THE TIME

Choose one of the posters shown on these pages. Restate the message of the poster in your own words and explain how the picture on that poster supports the message.

A Real War

"Machine guns cracking, flares and lights, artillery from both sides. A real war, and we are walking right into the zone, ducking shells all the way."

—Eugene Kennedy,
American soldier, 1918

▲ American soldiers
fighting in Europe

Americans at War

Objectives
- Understand the setbacks that the Allies faced in 1917 and 1918.
- Discover how American forces contributed to the Allied victory.
- Explain the agreement that ended the fighting.

Reading Skill

Connect Main Ideas to Earlier Ideas
Each chapter in this textbook focuses on a different time period or aspect of American history. As you read the chapters, think about how the events of one time period connect to events of other periods. Finding the connections will increase your understanding of history.

Key Terms and People

convoy
John J. Pershing
Vladimir Lenin

communism
armistice

Why It Matters After Congress declared war in April 1917, more than a year passed before U.S. forces engaged in major battles. However, once America's soldiers were in the front lines, they made a difference. World War I would soon end in an overwhelming Allied victory.

? **Section Focus Question: How did the arrival of American troops in Europe affect the course of the war?**

Joining the Fight

While the United States prepared its army, the Allies in Europe were growing increasingly desperate. From February through April 1917, German submarines sank 844 Allied vessels. Britain's top naval official predicted that Germany would win the war unless the flow of supplies from America increased.

Protecting Allied Shipping In order to maintain the flow of products needed to sustain the war effort, Allied naval leaders developed a convoy system. A **convoy** is a large group of merchant vessels sailing together. Light, fast Allied destroyers accompanied the convoys. The first convoys reached Britain in May. Soon, Allied ship losses fell to a fraction of what they had been.

American Expeditionary Force Meanwhile, American forces were preparing to go overseas. The U.S. Army chose John J. Pershing to command the American Expeditionary Force, as American troops in Europe were known. A dashing and dedicated general, Pershing had led the pursuit of Pancho Villa in Mexico.

Pershing insisted that American soldiers fight in separate units under American command. Only rarely were they integrated with British or French units. This was in keeping with Wilson's orders. To influence the postwar settlement, Wilson believed, the United States had to make a victorious showing, on its own, in battle.

The first American troops reached Europe in June 1917. The unit was not ready for combat. Its purpose was to prop up sagging French morale. This First Division symbolized America's commitment to the fight and its intention to send more troops. As the newly arrived Americans paraded through Paris, crowds cheered and threw flowers.

✓**Checkpoint** **How did the convoy system help the Allies?**

Connect Main Ideas to Earlier Events/Ideas
Recall that Pershing already had experience commanding U.S. troops on foreign soil. Connect that main idea to Pershing's role in World War I.

Setbacks and Advances

During 1917, as the Allies waited for more American troops to arrive, their situation grew increasingly desperate. On the Western Front, a three-month British offensive bogged down in the mud in Belgium. To the south, Austria-Hungary and Germany scored a major victory over the Italians at Caporetto.

Russia Makes Peace In Russia, the new government that had replaced the tsar struggled to keep up the war effort. But the Russian army was exhausted. Two million soldiers deserted the front lines. By July, German troops were driving deep into Russia.

Under the leadership of Vladimir Lenin, a radical faction known as the Bolsheviks seized the government on November 7, 1917. Lenin intended to set Russia on the road to communism. **Communism** is an economic and political system based on the idea that social classes and the right to private property should be eliminated. Lenin embraced the ideas of the German thinker Karl Marx, who had predicted that workers around the world would unite to overthrow the ruling class.

Lenin's first order of business was to pull Russia out of the war. In March 1918, Russia and Germany signed a peace agreement, called the Treaty of Brest-Litovsk. It transferred some 30 percent of Russia's territory to Germany.

The peace in the east was a huge setback to the Allies. It allowed the German army to shift 40 divisions to the Western Front. The stage was now set for a crucial showdown. Could Germany knock out the Allies before the bulk of American forces reached Europe?

Germany Attacks On March 21, 1918, the German army unleashed a series of daring attacks. The goal of this "peace offensive," as Germany called it, was to defeat the Allies quickly and bring peace on German terms.

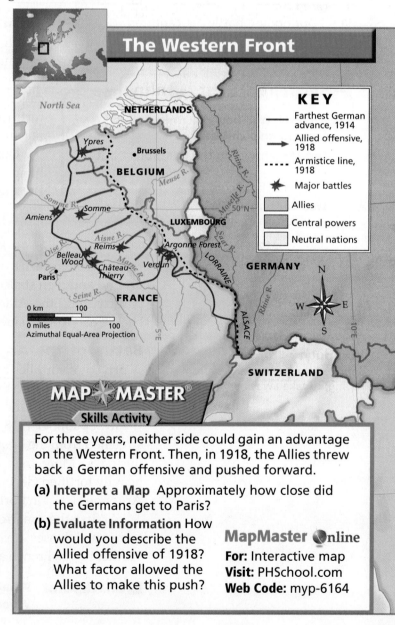

The Western Front

KEY
— Farthest German advance, 1914
→ Allied offensive, 1918
····· Armistice line, 1918
✶ Major battles
▢ Allies
▢ Central powers
▢ Neutral nations

North Sea
NETHERLANDS
Ypres
Brussels
BELGIUM
Meuse R.
Rhine R.
Somme R.
Somme
Amiens
Aisne R.
Oise R.
Reims
LUXEMBOURG
Argonne Forest
Moselle R.
Saar R.
50°N
Belleau Wood
Château-Thierry
Marne R.
Verdun
LORRAINE
GERMANY
Paris
Seine R.
FRANCE
0 km 100
0 miles 100
Azimuthal Equal-Area Projection
5°E
ALSACE
Rhine R.
10°E
SWITZERLAND

MAP◆MASTER®
Skills Activity

For three years, neither side could gain an advantage on the Western Front. Then, in 1918, the Allies threw back a German offensive and pushed forward.

(a) Interpret a Map Approximately how close did the Germans get to Paris?

(b) Evaluate Information How would you describe the Allied offensive of 1918? What factor allowed the Allies to make this push?

MapMaster ⏾nline
For: Interactive map
Visit: PHSchool.com
Web Code: myp-6164

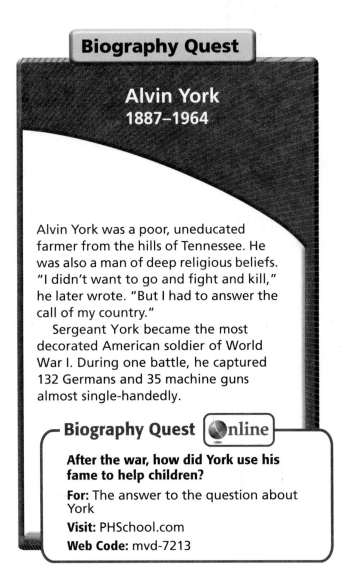

Alvin York
1887–1964

Alvin York was a poor, uneducated farmer from the hills of Tennessee. He was also a man of deep religious beliefs. "I didn't want to go and fight and kill," he later wrote. "But I had to answer the call of my country."

Sergeant York became the most decorated American soldier of World War I. During one battle, he captured 132 Germans and 35 machine guns almost single-handedly.

Biography Quest Online

After the war, how did York use his fame to help children?

For: The answer to the question about York

Visit: PHSchool.com

Web Code: mvd-7213

Vocabulary Builder
<u>deprive</u> (dee PRĪV) **v.** to keep from having; to take away by force

Pershing traveled to the French army's head-quarters to pledge that American troops would now fight under French command. "Infantry, artillery, aviation, all that we have are yours," he declared. "Use them as you wish." The vow, made public, raised French spirits. But two months passed before the Americans could make a significant contribution to the Allied cause.

The advancing Germans broke through Allied lines in Belgium and France. By the beginning of June, Germany had reached the town of Château-Thierry (shah TOE tyeh REE), on the Marne River, less than 50 miles from Paris. As many as a million Parisians fled in panic before the approaching enemy. By this time, however, American troops had arrived to reinforce the Allies.

Turning the Tide American and French troops counterattacked near Château-Thierry. The French commander assigned American units to evict German troops from a narrow, heavily forested area called Belleau (BEH loh) Wood. The Germans had fortified the forest with barbed wire, artillery, and machine guns.

During three weeks of intense, often hand-to-hand combat, U.S. Marines suffered heavy casualties. But, in their first major battle of the war, they succeeded in driving the Germans out.

Germany had lost some 800,000 men since the start of 1918. Yet, the offensive continued. In mid-July, the Germans attempted a new drive toward Paris. The drive gained a bit of ground and then stalled. With more than a quarter million Americans participating, the Allies counterattacked. The Germans had to pull back. Costs to both sides were high in this Second Battle of the Marne.

Battle of the Argonne Forest Weakened by influenza and <u>deprived</u> of supplies by the Allied blockade that had tightened since America's entry into the war, Germany's army was losing the will to fight. Now, it was the Allies' turn to take the offensive.

In September 1918, Allied forces pushed forward along a line that stretched from the North Sea to Verdun. The Americans were toward the right. More than one million American soldiers advanced on heavily fortified German positions between the Meuse River and the Argonne Forest in northeastern France.

At first, the Americans advanced slowly. But as November began, German defenses finally crumbled under the unrelenting assault. Farther north, French and British forces advanced as well.

✓**Checkpoint** **What role did American troops play at Belleau Wood?**

The Armistice

By early autumn, Germany's military and political leaders realized that their cause was lost. Their army had no reserves, whereas the arrival of Americans had assured the Allies of a fresh supply of soldiers. The German leaders decided to seek an armistice. An **armistice** is a halt in fighting that allows peace talks to begin.

Germany knew that France and Britain wanted to impose a harsh settlement. But President Wilson had recently proposed a "Fourteen Points" peace plan, founded on principles for international cooperation. (See Section 4.) On October 6, the head of the German government sent Wilson a note requesting an armistice based on the Fourteen Points. But Wilson ultimately had little say.

A Harsh Armistice France and Britain <u>dictated</u> the terms of the armistice. They required Germany to pull back its troops on the Western Front. Germany also had to cancel the Treaty of Brest-Litovsk and hand over its entire fleet of U-boats.

Meanwhile, the other Central powers—Bulgaria, Austria-Hungary, and the Ottoman Empire—had asked for an armistice, too. None of them was in any position to resist Allied demands.

Wilson's major impact during this period was his insistence that the Kaiser, the absolute monarch of Germany, must step down. On November 9, Kaiser Wilhelm II fled to Holland. There, he soon gave up the throne. Germany became a republic.

Vocabulary Builder
<u>dictate</u> (DIHK tayt) **v.** to direct or order a specific action

Links Across Time

Today An honor guard keeps 24-hour watch at the Tomb of the Unknowns.

Honoring Veterans

1921 The day World War I ended has been remembered ever since. On November 11, 1921, the body of an unidentified American soldier was laid to rest in the Tomb of the Unknowns at Arlington National Cemetery.

1938 November 11 was made a national holiday, Armistice Day. The name of Armistice Day was later changed to Veterans Day.

Link to Today ●nline

Veterans Day Today Each year, on November 11, we continue to honor those who have served in our nation's armed forces.

For: Veterans Day in the news
Visit: PHSchool.com
Web Code: mvc-7213

A wounded soldier returns home

War's Deadly Toll The armistice took effect at 11 A.M. on November 11—the eleventh day of the eleventh month of 1918. The war had finally ended. At the front, soldiers could hardly believe it was true. One American soldier later recalled:

> **"** After the long months of intense strain, of keying themselves up to the daily mortal danger, of thinking always in terms of war and the enemy, the abrupt release from it all was physical and psychological agony. Some suffered a total nervous collapse. **"**
>
> —Thomas Gowenlock, *Soldiers of Darkness*

World War I was the most destructive war history had yet seen. It cost the lives of approximately 10 million military personnel—more than had died in all the wars fought in Europe during the previous 100 years combined.

In Europe, a generation of young men had lost their lives. France suffered approximately 1.3 million military deaths; Britain, 900,000; Germany, 1.6 million; and Russia, 1.7 million. American combat deaths numbered 50,000 in less than a year of fighting. Millions of other soldiers were blinded, lost limbs, suffered permanent lung damage from poison gas, or experienced psychological problems.

No one knows how many civilians died of disease, starvation, or other war-related causes. Some historians believe that as many civilians died as did soldiers. Much of northern France lay in ruins. Millions of children were left orphaned or homeless.

✓Checkpoint How did the war end?

⭐ **Looking Back and Ahead** The war had ended in an overwhelming Allied victory. In Section 4, you will read about the next great challenge: creating the peace.

Section 3 | **Check Your Progress**

Progress Monitoring ⊕nline
For: Self-test with instant help
Visit: PHSchool.com
Web Code: mva-7213

Comprehension and Critical Thinking

1. **(a) Identify** Identify two ways the Americans contributed to the Allied victory.
   (b) Make Predictions How do you think the war might have ended if the United States had not entered? Explain.

2. **(a) Recall** What were the terms of the armistice that ended the war?

(b) Draw Conclusions Why do you think Germany agreed to these terms?

🔁 **Reading Skill**

3. **Connect Main Ideas to Earlier Events** Connect America's role in World War I with its role in the Spanish-American War. What was the United States fighting for in each case?

Key Terms

4. Write a sentence using each of the key terms from this section: convoy, communism, armistice. Include a definition of the key term in each sentence.

Writing

5. Create an outline for an essay tracing the progress of Allied forces during World War I. List the information in the order you would present it in the essay.

Peace and Justice

❝ What we demand in this war . . . is that the world be made fit and safe to live in; and particularly that it be made safe for every peace-loving nation which, like our own, wishes to live its own life, determine its own institutions, be assured of justice. . . .❞

—President Woodrow Wilson, addressing Congress about his Fourteen Points, 1918

◀ Cartoon showing President Wilson's peace efforts

Shaping the Peace

Objectives

- Examine Woodrow Wilson's plan for a lasting and just peace.
- Understand how the Treaty of Versailles punished Germany.
- Explain why many Americans opposed membership in the League of Nations.

🔄 Reading Skill

Connect Main Ideas to Current Events
Events and ideas from history often connect to events and issues of importance today. Finding these connections will bring history to life for you, as well as increase your understanding of current events. Look for these connections as you read this section.

Key Terms and People

self-determination   Henry Cabot Lodge
reparations   deport

Why It Matters After the end of the war, the struggle began to determine the shape of the peace. Wilson's ideas for the postwar sparked a spirited debate. The outcome of this debate would affect America and the world for years to come.

❓ **Section Focus Question: How did the Treaty of Versailles and the League of Nations disappoint President Wilson?**

The Fourteen Points

Even before the war ended, President Wilson had presented his peace plan, known as the Fourteen Points, to Congress. He framed his plan in idealistic terms, saying he hoped to prevent future wars.

The first five points dealt with the factors that had led to the war. Wilson wanted to eliminate secret international agreements. He called for freedom of the seas, free trade among nations, and a sharp reduction in the world's military forces. He also favored settlement of colonial claims, balancing the interests of native populations and colonizing powers.

Points 6 through 13 dealt with specific territorial issues arising from the war. One of these issues involved self-rule for national minority groups in Austria-Hungary and the Ottoman Empire. Later, Wilson turned this point into a call for self-determination. **Self-determination** is the right of a group to decide its own form of government. Wilson knew that one of the causes of World War I was the struggle of Bosnians, Serbs, and other peoples to rule themselves.

For Wilson, Point 14 was the most important. It called for setting up an international organization, or association of nations, to guarantee world peace. Underlying his plan, Wilson said, was "the principle of justice to all peoples and nationalities . . . whether they be strong or weak."

✓ **Checkpoint** **What was the goal of the Fourteen Points?**

Peace Conference in Paris

The victorious powers organized a peace conference in Paris. Although American Presidents had seldom gone abroad, Wilson decided that he himself would lead the American delegation.

The Fourteen Points had thrilled Europe's war-weary population. Two million people turned out to cheer Wilson when he arrived in Paris in January 1919. One newspaper likened him to Moses.

The Big Four At the conference, major decisions were made by the "Big Four." They were Wilson and the prime ministers of the three top European Allies: Georges Clemenceau of France, David Lloyd George of Britain, and Vittorio Orlando of Italy.

The other Allies did not share Wilson's idealistic goal of "peace without victory." They were determined to punish Germany and to ensure that Germany would not threaten its neighbors again. Also, during the war, several Allies had signed secret treaties for dividing up the territories and colonies of the Central powers.

The Treaty of Versailles After difficult negotiations, the Allies came to an agreement. The Treaty of Versailles (ver SĪ) dealt severely with Germany. Various <u>clauses</u> took away territory on Germany's borders and stripped Germany of colonies. The treaty forced Germany to accept full responsibility for the war and to pay the Allies huge **reparations,** or payments to cover war damages. It also placed limits on the size and nature of Germany's military.

Wilson disagreed with these harsh demands. However, he had agreed in order to win his cherished peacekeeping organization. The Treaty of Versailles also called for the creation of an international organization to be called the League of Nations. It would provide a place for countries to meet, settle disputes peacefully, and punish any nation that broke the peace.

On June 28, 1919, German delegates reluctantly signed the treaty. However, German anger at the Treaty of Versailles would later set the stage for another world war.

Other Treaties Negotiators arranged separate treaties with the other Central powers. The treaties applied the principle of self-determination to the peoples of Eastern Europe.

Some changes had already taken place. Austria-Hungary had collapsed. From its ruins arose the separate states of Austria, Hungary, and Czechoslovakia. In addition, the Serbs of Serbia had joined with other Balkan peoples to form Yugoslavia. Poland had declared independence. The peace treaties recognized all these changes, making adjustments to the new borders.

Vocabulary Builder
<u>clause</u> (klawz) **n.** part of a law, treaty, or other written agreement

Lloyd George, Clemenceau, and Wilson (left to right) at the peace talks

Europe After World War I

0 km 500
0 miles 500
Lambert Azimuthal Equal-Area Projection

ATLANTIC OCEAN

FINLAND

NORWAY

SWEDEN

ESTONIA

North Sea

LATVIA

DENMARK

LITHUANIA

Baltic Sea

IRELAND

GER.

RUSSIA

GREAT BRITAIN

NETH.

GERMANY

POLAND

BELG.

LUX.

CZECHOSLOVAKIA

FRANCE

SWITZ.

AUSTRIA

HUNGARY

ITALY

ROMANIA

YUGOSLAVIA

SPAIN

BULGARIA

ALB.

TURKEY

GREECE

Mediterranean Sea

KEY
Territories lost by:
- Austria-Hungary
- Bulgaria
- Germany
- Russia

In 1918, the Treaty of Brest-Litovsk transferred large tracts of Russian territory to Germany. The following year, the peace treaties ending World War I further redrew the map of Europe.

(a) Interpret a Map Which nations lost territory as a result of World War I?

(b) Compare Compare this map to the map in Section 1. Identify one nation that disappeared completely. What country did it become part of?

MapMaster Online

For: Interactive map
Visit: PHSchool.com
Web Code: mvp-7214

However, the peacemakers at Paris did not apply the principle of self-determination to non-Europeans. Britain and France divided up Germany's African colonies, as well as parts of the Ottoman Empire. The Ottoman Empire itself was <u>dissolved</u>, and the new republic of Turkey was created. Many people living in Europe's African and Asian colonies felt betrayed by the peace settlements.

Vocabulary Builder
<u>dissolve</u> (dih ZAHLV) **v.** to break up into smaller parts

☑**Checkpoint** How did the Treaty of Versailles punish Germany?

Battle Over the League

Returning to the United States, Wilson urged the Senate to ratify the Treaty of Versailles. Wilson forcefully backed the treaty's most controversial element, the League of Nations. The United States, he declared, must accept its "destiny" to lead the world on a new path.

Lodge Opposes Many Senators opposed the treaty. Leading the opposition was Henry Cabot Lodge, a powerful Republican from Massachusetts. Lodge's chief objection was to the proposal that the United States join the League of Nations.

U.S. participation is key to building the League of Nations.

The keystone is not in place.

Reading Political Cartoons
Skills Activity

In 1919, the United States Senate voted to reject the Treaty of Versailles and keep the United States out of the League of Nations. This cartoon presents one reaction to the Senate's decision.

(a) **Interpret Cartoons** What does the gap in the bridge represent?

(b) **Detect Points of View** How do you think this cartoonist may have felt about the Senate's decision? What does he convey is likely to happen as a result?

Lodge argued that membership in the League would restrict the right of the United States to act independently in its own interest:

“The United States is the world's best hope, but if you [chain] her in the interests and quarrels of other nations, if you tangle her in the intrigues of Europe, you will destroy her power for good and endanger her very existence. ”

—Henry Cabot Lodge, speech, August 1919

Lodge asked for major changes that would reduce the United States ties to the League. But Wilson refused to compromise.

Wilson's Last Battle In early September, Wilson set out on a nationwide tour to stir public support for his position. Traveling 8,000 miles by train in three weeks, he gave 40 speeches.

On October 2, Wilson suffered a massive stroke that paralyzed his left side. His wife and his physician kept secret the severity of his illness. From his White House sickbed, Wilson continued to reject all compromise on the treaty.

In November 1919, the Senate voted to reject the treaty. The absence of the United States crippled the League's ability to stem the crises that shook the world in the 1930s.

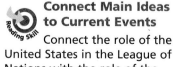

Connect Main Ideas to Current Events
Connect the role of the United States in the League of Nations with the role of the United States in world affairs today.

☑**Checkpoint** Why did Lodge oppose the League of Nations?

Postwar Troubles

The United States did not easily adjust to the return of peace. The postwar years brought a variety of troubles.

Influenza Epidemic Toward the end of the war, troop movements contributed to a worldwide influenza epidemic. In the United States alone, the disease took more than 500,000 lives in 1918 and 1919. Worldwide, the epidemic killed more people than had died in four years of war.

Labor Unrest During the war, unions and businesses had cooperated to meet production goals. But peacetime brought high unemployment, as soldiers came home to seek jobs. With prices rising, unions' demands for higher wages met stiff resistance from management. In 1919, four million laborers—20 percent of the American industrial work force—went on strike.

Red Scare Many Americans feared that Communists, or "Reds," were behind the labor unrest. After all, in Russia, Lenin had called for a worldwide workers' revolution. From 1919 into 1920 a "Red Scare," or fear of Communist revolution, gripped the nation.

Attorney General A. Mitchell Palmer ordered immigrants suspected of radical views to be rounded up and deported, or returned to their home countries. These Palmer Raids reached their height on January 2, 1920, when authorities arrested more than 4,000 people in 33 cities. But public opinion soon turned against Palmer. In time, the panic cooled.

This policeman is wearing a mask to avoid catching influenza.

☑Checkpoint What problems affected the postwar United States?

⭐ **Looking Back and Ahead** After World War I, many Americans longed for a return to peace and prosperity. In the next chapter, you will see how these goals were met in the 1920s.

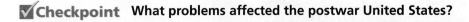

Section 4 | Check Your Progress

Progress Monitoring ⬤nline
For: Self-test with instant help
Visit: PHSchool.com
Web Code: mva-7214

Comprehension and Critical Thinking

1. (a) Describe What were Woodrow Wilson's goals for peace?
(b) Evaluate Information How well did the Treaty of Versailles meet Wilson's goals?

2. (a) Recall Why did Wilson refuse to compromise with critics of the League of Nations?
(b) Support a Point of View Do you think Wilson was right? Why or why not?

Reading Skill

3. Connect Main Ideas to Current Events Reread the text under the heading "Battle Over the League." Connect Wilson's actions to those of current political leaders when seeking support for their policies.

Key Terms

Answer the following questions in complete sentences that show your understanding of the key terms.

4. What was the principle behind the idea of self-determination?
5. What happened to immigrants who were deported?
6. What did the reparations clause require Germany to do?

Writing

7. Write the opening paragraph to an essay taking a stand about whether or not Congress should have ratified the Treaty of Versailles. End the paragraph with a thesis statement expressing your main idea.

People use propaganda to shape public opinion and encourage popular support for or against something, including an idea, political group, or government. During World War I, newspapers and governments on both sides used propaganda to win public support for the war effort. Study the American World War I poster below.

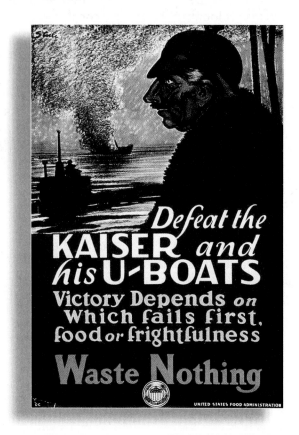

Learn the Skill

Use these steps to recognize propaganda.

① **Identify the point of view.** Study the words and visuals to find the main idea. Identify the person or organization responsible for the propaganda and when it was created.

② **Identify the propaganda technique.** Propaganda can shape public opinion in several ways, such as by (1) using exaggeration, including strong words and images; (2) using symbols and/or offensive names to show the other side in a negative way; and (3) including only some of the facts about the subject or event.

③ **Draw conclusions.** Evaluate the visuals and text. Decide whether or not the propaganda was effective and influenced public opinion.

Practice the Skill

Answer the following questions about the poster.

① **Identify the point of view.** (a) Who created the poster? (b) When was it created? (c) What is the point of view expressed in the poster?

② **Identify the propaganda technique.** What technique or techniques are used in the poster?

③ **Draw conclusions.** How do you think the poster affected public opinion in the United States?

Apply the Skill

See the Review and Assessment at the end of this chapter.

What were the causes and effects of World War I?

Section 1
The Road to War

- The massive war that broke out in Europe in 1914 quickly settled into a long, bloody stalemate.
- At first, President Wilson was determined to maintain American neutrality.
- German submarine warfare and the Zimmermann Telegram contributed to Wilson's decision to declare war on Germany in 1917.

Section 2
Supporting the War Effort

- The United States moved quickly to build up its armed forces.
- To support the war effort, the government took steps to control the economy, build public support for the war, and suppress dissent.

Section 3
Americans at War

- American troops were finally ready for combat in 1918.
- With fresh American troops and supplies, the Allies were able to resist a German advance and push on to victory.
- An armistice ended the war in November 1918.

Section 4
Shaping the Peace

- Wilson's Fourteen Points were an effort to create a just peace and prevent future wars.
- The Treaty of Versailles imposed harsh conditions on Germany.
- Opposition to the League of Nations led the Senate to reject the treaty.

? Exploring the Essential Question

Use the online study guide to explore the essential question.

Section 1
What were the causes of World War I?

Section 2
What steps did the United States government take to prepare the nation for war?

Chapter 21 Essential Question
What were the causes and effects of World War I?

Section 4
How did the Treaty of Versailles and the League of Nations disappoint President Wilson?

Section 3
How did the arrival of American troops in Europe affect the course of the war?

Key Terms

Fill in the blanks with the correct key terms from this chapter.

1. The Treaty of Versailles punished Germany by making it pay _____.

2. In _____, armies fired at each other across a barren patch called no man's land.

3. The principle of _____ meant that nations could choose their own form of government.

4. The use of _____ helped stir support for the war effort.

5. _____ led nations to place great pride and trust in their armies and navies.

Comprehension and Critical Thinking

6. **(a) Describe** Describe the events that led the United States to declare war on Germany.
   (b) Contrast Review what you learned about the Spanish-American War. How were the reasons for declaring war on Spain similar to the reasons for declaring war on Germany? How were they different?

7. **(a) Recall** How did American women support the war effort?
   (b) Analyze Cause and Effect How did the role of women during the war affect their political status?

8. **(a) Recall** What problems did German Americans face during World War I?
   (b) Identify Bias How is the use of an expression such as "liberty cabbage" for "sauerkraut" an example of bias?
   (c) Apply Information Suggest one way that people can avoid such bias during wartime.

9. **(a) Explain** Why did Wilson want American forces to fight separately from French and British armies?
   (b) Evaluate Information Did Wilson's plan succeed?

10. **(a) Recall** How did Wilson and Lodge disagree over the League of Nations?
    (b) Detect Points of View Recall what you learned about George Washington's Farewell Address. Do you think Washington's viewpoint was closer to that of Wilson or to that of Lodge?

History Reading Skill

11. **Identify and Connect Main Ideas** Identify a main idea from each of the four sections in this chapter. Explain how these ideas connect to one another. If possible, find a connection to an earlier event or to a current event.

Writing

12. **Write two paragraphs about one of the following issues involving World War I:**
    - Describe what happened on the "home front" during the war.
    - Evaluate the effectiveness of President Wilson as a leader.
    - Take a stand about America's entry into World War I.

    Your paragraph should:
    - begin with a sentence stating your main idea about your subject;
    - include facts, reasons, and examples from the chapter to develop your ideas.

13. **Write a Letter:**
    Imagine that you are an American soldier in France during World War I. Write a letter home describing your experiences.

Skills for Life

Recognize Propaganda
Use the poster below to answer the questions.

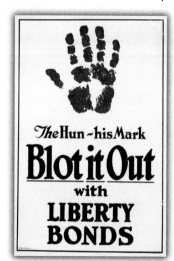

14. **(a)** Who do you think created this poster?
    (b) What did the creator of the poster want people to do?

15. What propaganda techniques are used?

16. Do you think the poster was an effective form of propaganda? Why or why not?

Test Yourself

1. **During World War I, African American soldiers**

   A were banned from joining the army.

   B refused to support the war effort.

   C served in combat with white soldiers.

   D served in segregated units.

Refer to this excerpt from the Treaty of Versailles to answer Question 2.

> "Germany accepts the responsibility of Germany and her allies for causing all the loss and damage to which the Allied and Associated Governments and their nationals have been subjected."

2. **Which of the Big Four would have been most likely to oppose the above clause?**

   A Wilson

   B Lloyd George

   C Clemenceau

   D Orlando

Refer to the graph below to answer Question 3.

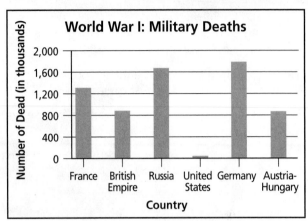

Source: R.E. Dupay and T.N. Dupay, *The Encyclopedia of Military History*

3. **Which Allied power shown on the graph had the most casualties?**

   A Russia

   B Germany

   C France

   D United States

Document-Based Questions

Task: Look at Documents 1 and 2, and answer their accompanying questions. Then, use the documents and your knowledge of history to complete the following writing assignment:

> Write a short essay discussing whether or not the government has the right to limit freedom of speech during wartime.

Document 1: The Espionage Act of 1917 was passed after Congress declared war with Germany. *What is the punishment for someone who violates this portion of the Espionage Act?*

> "SEC. 3 Whoever, when the United States is at war, shall willfully make or convey false reports or false statements with intent to interfere with the operation or success of the military or naval forces of the United States or to promote the success of its enemies . . . or shall willfully obstruct the recruiting or enlistment service of the United States, to the injury of the service or of the United States, shall be punished by a fine of not more than $10,000 or imprisonment for not more than twenty years, or both."

Document 2: Rose Pastor Stokes was a socialist and outspoken critic of the war. In 1918, she was convicted under the Espionage Act and sentenced to 10 years in federal prison for writing to the editor of the *Kansas City Star* the following letter. *Why did Stokes write to the* Kansas City Star?

> "To the Star:
> . . . A headline in the evening's issue of the Star reads: 'Mrs. Stokes for Government and Against War at the Same Time.' I am <u>not</u> for the government. In the interview that follows I am quoted as having said 'I believe the government of the United States should have the unqualified support of every citizen in its war aims.' I made no such statement, and I believe no such thing. No government which is <u>for</u> the profiteers can also be <u>for</u> the people, while the government is for the profiteers.
>
> Rose Pastor Stokes"

The Roaring Twenties

1919~1929

> *"It's the Jazz Age.... Americans were speeding up, moving out, buying more, having fun, dreaming bigger."*
>
> —Donald L. Miller, Professor of History at Lafayette College

The 1920s were years of prosperity for many, as reflected in this scene of Times Square in New York City.

CHAPTER 22

What You Will Learn

Section 1
ADJUSTING TO PEACETIME

After World War I, the United States focused on domestic issues under a series of Republican Presidents.

Section 2
CHANGES IN AMERICAN SOCIETY

The twenties brought many changes to mass culture and to the lives of women and African Americans.

Section 3
THE JAZZ AGE

A burst of creativity energized the worlds of music and literature during what was known as the Jazz Age.

Section 4
THE ECONOMY OF THE 1920s

The twenties were a time of widespread prosperity, but serious economic problems lay just beneath the surface.

Reading Skill

Clarify Understanding In this chapter, you will practice clarifying your understanding of a reading by paraphrasing and summarizing main ideas.

The Roaring Twenties

KEY

- States with a woman governor
- States where women held other statewide offices
- Race riot

N
W E
S

```
0          200 miles
0          200 km
Albers Conic Conformal Projection
```

CANADA

Hundreds of thousands migrate from Canada to the United States.

Seattle
WA
Portland
OR
MT
ID
ND
SD
WY
NE

■The Movies
Millions of Americans go to the movies every week. Most of the films are made in Hollywood.

■Sports Heroes
Born in Manassa, Colorado, Jack Dempsey is one of the era's many sports heroes. He was heavyweight boxing champ.

San Francisco
CA
NV
UT
CO
Denver
KS

KEEP OUT!

■Limits on Immigration
New federal laws limit immigration from Asia.

Pacific Ocean

Los Angeles
AZ
NM
TX

Hundreds of thousands migrate from Mexico to the United States.

MEXICO

Average Price of Selected Stocks, 1921–1929

Average Price Per Share (in dollars)
30
20
10
0
1921 1923 1925 1927 1929
Source: Standard and Poor's

U.S. Events

World War I ends. | **1918**

1920 | The Nineteenth Amendment extends right to vote to women.

1916   **1918**   **1920**   **1922**

World Events

1917 | Bolshevik Revolution gives Communists control of Russia.

The Soviet Union is formed. Mussolini comes to power in Italy. | **1922**

734

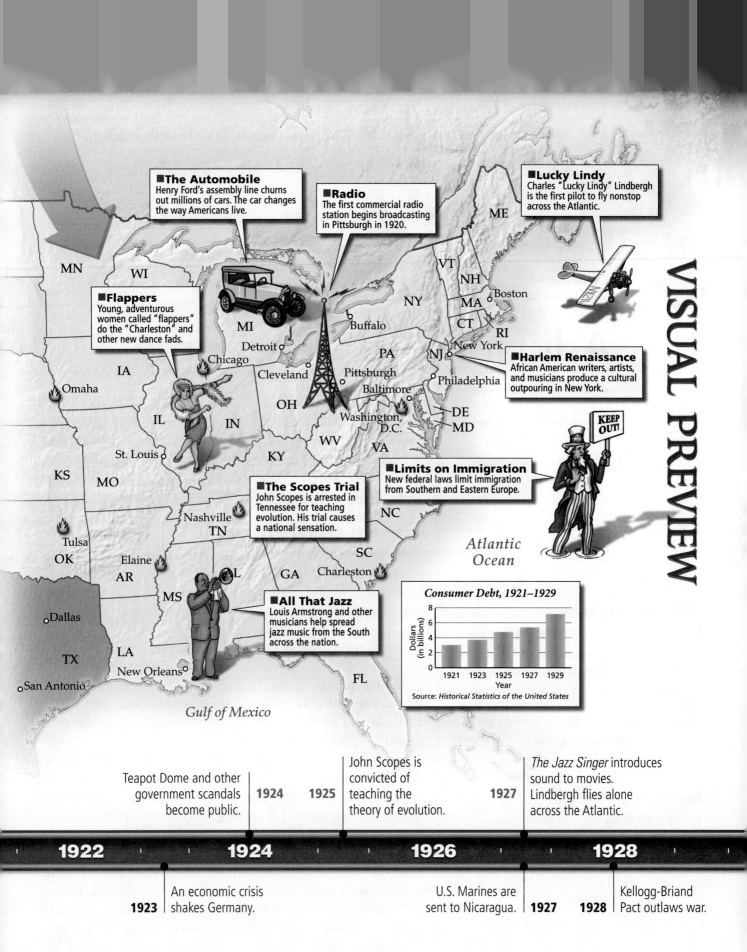

■The Automobile
Henry Ford's assembly line churns out millions of cars. The car changes the way Americans live.

■Radio
The first commercial radio station begins broadcasting in Pittsburgh in 1920.

■Lucky Lindy
Charles "Lucky Lindy" Lindbergh is the first pilot to fly nonstop across the Atlantic.

■Flappers
Young, adventurous women called "flappers" do the "Charleston" and other new dance fads.

■Harlem Renaissance
African American writers, artists, and musicians produce a cultural outpouring in New York.

■Limits on Immigration
New federal laws limit immigration from Southern and Eastern Europe.

KEEP OUT!

■The Scopes Trial
John Scopes is arrested in Tennessee for teaching evolution. His trial causes a national sensation.

■All That Jazz
Louis Armstrong and other musicians help spread jazz music from the South across the nation.

MN, WI, MI, Detroit, Chicago, IA, Omaha, IL, St. Louis, IN, KS, MO, Nashville, TN, Tulsa, OK, Elaine, AR, MS, AL, GA, Dallas, TX, LA, New Orleans, San Antonio, FL

Buffalo, OH, Cleveland, PA, Pittsburgh, Baltimore, Washington, D.C., WV, VA, KY, NC, SC, Charleston

ME, VT, NH, NY, MA, Boston, CT, RI, New York, NJ, Philadelphia, DE, MD

Atlantic Ocean

Gulf of Mexico

Consumer Debt, 1921–1929

Dollars (in billions) — 8, 6, 4, 2, 0

1921, 1923, 1925, 1927, 1929

Year

Source: *Historical Statistics of the United States*

VISUAL PREVIEW

Teapot Dome and other government scandals become public. | **1924** | **1925** | John Scopes is convicted of teaching the theory of evolution. | **1927** | *The Jazz Singer* introduces sound to movies. Lindbergh flies alone across the Atlantic.

1922 | **1924** | **1926** | **1928**

1923 | An economic crisis shakes Germany. | U.S. Marines are sent to Nicaragua. | **1927** | **1928** | Kellogg-Briand Pact outlaws war.

Return to Normalcy
❝America's present need is not heroics...but normalcy; not revolution but restoration; not agitation but adjustment; not submergence in internationality but sustainment in triumphant nationality.❞

— Warren G. Harding, presidential campaign speech, 1920

◄ President Harding and baseball legend Babe Ruth

Adjusting to Peacetime

Objectives
- Explain how economic factors led to the election of Republican Warren Harding.
- Compare and contrast the administrations of Harding and Calvin Coolidge.
- Describe the U.S. policy of isolationism.
- Explain how the threat of communism abroad raised concerns in the United States.

Reading Skill

Paraphrase Text for Understanding
One way to clarify text is to paraphrase. Paraphrasing is simply restating the text in your own words. If you can restate text in your own words, you will be more likely to understand it. As you read Section 1, pause at an indicated side note, read the side note and corresponding text, then paraphrase the idea in your own words.

Key Terms and People

Warren Harding   communism
Calvin Coolidge   anarchist
disarmament

Why It Matters The United States emerged from World War I as a world power. Even so, Americans rejected a major role in world affairs. Instead the nation turned inward, seeking prosperity and a return to "normalcy."

? Section Focus Question: What problems at home and abroad challenged the nation after World War I?

Return to Normalcy

President Woodrow Wilson might have expected to return from the Paris Peace Conference as a popular hero. However, the mishandling of the peace treaty at Versailles and a failing economy at home combined to make Wilson and the Democrats very unpopular.

The end of World War I was followed by an economic recession. During the war, the domestic economy had expanded rapidly to produce all the extra goods needed by the military. With war's end, munitions factories shut down and workers lost their jobs. Soldiers returning from the war found it difficult to find work.

Labor unions had made a no-strike pledge as a patriotic gesture in wartime. But labor disputes led to many strikes after the war. In 1919, four million workers—one fifth of the labor force—took part in strikes. Accounts of strike-related violence filled the newspapers.

Many Americans feared other types of violence as well. Some feared that Communists would overthrow the government, as they had recently done in Russia. Racial violence also frightened some. Many Americans hoped that a change of leadership would restore peace and prosperity.

The Harding Administration In 1920, the Republican nominee for President, Warren Harding of Ohio, promised a return to "normalcy." It was what the public wanted. He won by a landslide.

Harding was a firm supporter of business. He filled his administration with like-minded men. For secretary of the treasury, he chose Andrew Mellon, a banker and industrialist. Mellon was one of the nation's richest men. He got Congress to lower taxes on businesses and the wealthy. He also helped slash the federal budget.

Some of Harding's other appointees were personal friends. Some saw their government jobs as opportunities to make personal fortunes, legally or illegally. Harding's presidency was marred by several major scandals involving these <u>colleagues</u>. In one case, Charles Forbes, the head of the Veterans Bureau, was convicted of taking bribes totaling about $200 million.

The biggest scandal centered on Teapot Dome, Wyoming, a government-owned oil reserve. The secretary of the Department of the Interior, Albert B. Fall, secretly leased the land and its reserves to an oil man. Fall received a bribe of $400,000. After the scandal broke, Fall was tried and convicted. He was the first Cabinet member ever sent to prison.

Harding himself was never linked to any of the crimes and did not live to see the worst of the scandals unfold. In 1923, he suffered a heart attack and died, leaving his Vice President, Calvin Coolidge, to deal with the Teapot Dome and other scandals.

Vocabulary Builder
<u>colleague</u> (KAHL eeg) ***n.*** associate; person who works in the same profession

The Harding Scandals

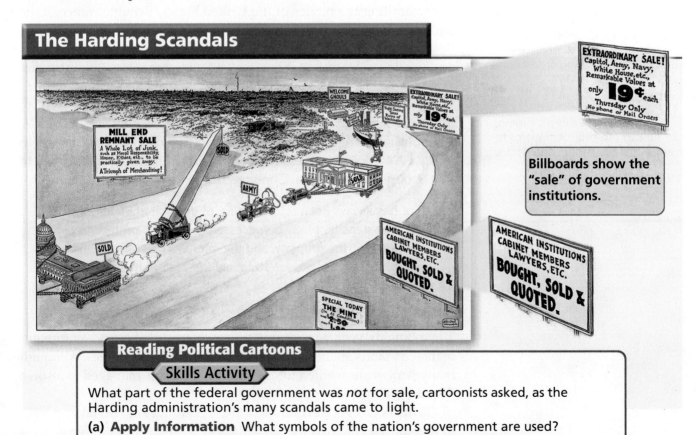

Billboards show the "sale" of government institutions.

Reading Political Cartoons

Skills Activity

What part of the federal government was *not* for sale, cartoonists asked, as the Harding administration's many scandals came to light.

(a) Apply Information What symbols of the nation's government are used?

(b) Detect Points of View Does the cartoonist seem to think the scandals are a serious problem? Explain.

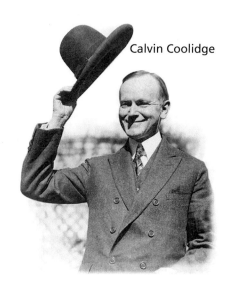
Calvin Coolidge

The Coolidge Administration Coolidge was very different from Harding. He was a soft-spoken, serious New Englander who was known for his honesty and integrity. By cooperating with the investigations into the Harding White House, Coolidge helped to restore the public's trust in government. When Coolidge ran for President in 1924, he won by a large margin.

Coolidge's prospects were helped by the prosperity of the mid-1920s. The postwar recession was over, and the economy had rebounded. The 1920s had begun to "roar," and the voters wanted to keep the Republicans in power.

☑**Checkpoint**   **Why were Wilson and the Democrats unpopular after the war?**

Foreign Policy

World War I had made the United States an international power. Still, most Americans did not want their nation to play a leading role in world affairs. As you have read, this sentiment is known as isolationism.

Isolationism did not mean cutting off contact with the rest of the world. Throughout the 1920s, the United States participated in international conferences intended to promote world peace and to encourage disarmament. Disarmament means the reduction or limitation of military armaments. The United States joined the Washington Naval Arms Conference of 1921. The conference resulted in a treaty limiting the navies of the United States, Britain, France, Italy, and Japan. In 1928, the United States joined France in sponsoring the Kellogg-Briand Pact. The pact condemned military aggression and outlawed war. However, it <u>imposed</u> no punishment on a country that acted aggressively, so it was ineffective at preventing war.

President Coolidge believed that the government had a right to intervene in foreign matters that affected American business. In 1926, a revolution broke out in Nicaragua. Coolidge sent in troops to protect American business interests there. Defending his actions to send troops to Nicaragua, Coolidge stated:

> **❝**It has always been . . . the policy of the United States . . . to take steps that may be necessary for the . . . protection of the lives, the property, and the interests of [U.S.] citizens. In this respect, I propose to follow the path of my predecessors. **❞**
> —Calvin Coolidge, message before Congress, January 10, 1927

The following year, Mexico announced plans to take over all foreign-owned oil lands, including those owned by U.S. companies. Although many Americans wanted to send troops, Coolidge managed to resolve this dispute by diplomacy.

In the Bolshevik Revolution of 1917, Communists had taken power in Russia. They created the Soviet Union, the world's first Communist state. Communism is an economic and political system in which the state owns the means of production and a single party rules. In the Soviet Union, the Communist Party crushed all opposition.

Vocabulary Builder
impose (ihm POHZ) **v.** to place a burden on something or someone

Paraphrase Text for Understanding
Paraphrase this paragraph. Be sure to use your own words to restate the main ideas and details.

In an effort to weaken the Soviet government, the United States refused to grant it diplomatic recognition. In 1918, President Wilson sent troops to aid the opponents of communism. Yet, when a devastating famine hit Russia in 1921, the United States sent aid. That aid may have saved 10 million people from starvation.

☑**Checkpoint** How did President Coolidge solve disputes in Latin America?

The Red Scare

Alarm about communism affected not only American foreign policy but also events at home. The postwar strikes that rocked the United States made some Americans afraid that a revolution was beginning.

The fears reached a fever pitch in the spring and summer of 1919, when a series of bombings occurred. The bombings were the work of **anarchists**, people who oppose all organized government. Many anarchists were foreign-born, and the bombings led to an outcry against all foreigners. During this Red Scare, thousands of anarchists and Communists, or "Reds," were hunted down and arrested. Many were deported, or expelled from the country.

Sacco and Vanzetti In May 1920, at the height of the Red Scare, two Italian immigrants, Nicola Sacco and Bartolomeo Vanzetti, were arrested. They were charged with robbing and murdering two payroll employees in Massachusetts.

At the trial, little evidence was presented that Sacco and Vanzetti, were guilty of the charges. Rather, the prosecution focused on the fact that both defendants were foreigners and anarchists. Sacco and Vanzetti were convicted in 1921 and executed in 1927.

Sacco and Vanzetti
by Ben Shahn

Jewish artist Ben Shahn viewed the execution of Sacco and Vanzetti as an outrage against justice. This portrait of the two men is one in a series of 23 paintings by Shahn about their trial, conviction, and execution. **Critical Thinking: *Apply Information*** *Why did the Sacco-Vanzetti case stir such strong feelings among Americans of the 1920s?*

Mexican workers pick cotton

The case was controversial at the time and remains so today. Were innocent people put to death because of public hysteria? Or did two murderers receive the punishment they deserved?

Limiting Immigration Fears about radicals led to new limits on immigration into the United States. There were other reasons, as well. Many Americans had long worried that the mainstream culture of the United States was being overwhelmed by immigrants from southern and eastern Europe. In addition, American workers were often concerned that newcomers would compete for their jobs.

An emergency immigration law was passed by Congress in 1921. It limited the number of people admitted from eastern and southern Europe. In 1924 and 1929, Congress imposed even more restrictions on immigrants. In addition, the United States completely prohibited immigration from Asia.

The new immigration limits, however, did not apply to people from the Americas. In the 1920s, nearly 500,000 people migrated from Mexico and 950,000 from Canada. Most Mexicans migrated to the Southwest, where their labors played a vital role in the growth of farmlands, railroads, and mines. Canadians, mainly from Quebec, took jobs in factories in New York and New England.

☑ **Checkpoint** What caused the Red Scare after World War I?

⭐ **Looking Back and Ahead** After World War I, Americans elected Republicans, who promised a return to "normalcy" and prosperity. Next we will see how, during the 1920s, the nation experienced an era of social and economic change.

Section 1 | **Check Your Progress**

Progress Monitoring ⓞnline
For: Self-test with instant help
Visit: PHSchool.com
Web Code: mva-7221

Comprehension and Critical Thinking

1. **(a) Recall** How had World War I been good for the economy?
   (b) Analyze Cause and Effect Why might a country face economic problems even after a victorious war?

2. **(a) Recall** Why was secretary of the Interior Albert B. Fall sent to prison?
   (b) Draw Conclusions Why do most historians consider Warren Harding to have been a poor President?

Reading Skill

3. **Paraphrase Text for Understanding** Reread the first paragraph under the heading "The Red Scare." Paraphrase the text, using your own words.

Key Terms

Answer the following questions in complete sentences that show your understanding of the key terms:

4. What is the goal of supporters of disarmament?

5. Who owns the means of production under communism?

6. What are anarchists against?

Writing

7. Based on what you have read in this section, write a thesis statement and one supporting paragraph for an essay about the mood in the country the first few years after World War I.

Something Startling

❝Something startling has happened. . . . In the thick of city traffic—on the streets and boulevards—along the highways and byways—in the mountains—on the plains—their unprecedented performance is changing every notion of what a motor car can be expected to do.❞

—1929 Chrysler advertisement

▲ The automobile changed American life.

Changes in American Society

Objectives

- Identify the causes and effects of the Eighteenth Amendment.
- Explain how the Nineteenth Amendment changed the role of women in society.
- Describe how the automobile, radio, and movies changed American culture.
- Explain why tension and unrest lay beneath the surface during the 1920s.

Reading Skill

Summarize Main Ideas In an earlier chapter, you practiced identifying main ideas. You can build on that skill here, by summarizing main ideas. Clarify your understanding of the text by stating the main ideas. You will find that you must understand the main ideas in order to weave them together into a summary.

Key Terms

prohibition   speakeasy
bootlegger

Why It Matters The political changes of the 1920s were accompanied by far-reaching social changes. A few changes were temporary, but others were enduring. Women assumed an expanded role in society and embraced new attitudes. The automobile, radio, and movies transformed American culture.

② Section Focus Question: How did social change and conflict mark the 1920s?

Prohibition

During the 1800s, many reformers had worked to reduce alcohol use in the United States. Eventually, supporters of temperance began supporting **prohibition,** a total ban on alcoholic drinks. During World War I, support for prohibition grew. Many Americans saw it as a way to conserve grains during the war. In part, due to this reasoning, the states ratified the Eighteenth Amendment in 1919. It prohibited making, selling, or transporting alcohol and began a specific time of federal enforcement known as Prohibition.

The Experiment Fails Saloons shut down, and arrests for drunkenness declined. There was a drop in the amount of alcohol that people consumed, especially working people for whom the high price of illegal liquor was an obstacle.

However, the law proved impossible to enforce. It was easy to smuggle liquor across the border from Canada and the Caribbean. Liquor smugglers, called **bootleggers,** made huge profits importing illegal alcohol. Every large town had its **speakeasies,** or illegal taverns that served liquor.

Dumping Whiskey

Prohibition was intended to solve such social problems as drunkenness and family violence. Yet, the amendment was repealed in 1933. **Critical Thinking: Identify Costs** *What were the unintended consequences of the Prohibition Amendment that led to its repeal?*

The Growth of Organized Crime The money to be made through bootlegging encouraged the growth of organized crime. A series of gang wars broke out in some parts of the country.

By the end of the decade, it was clear that Prohibition had failed. Many people called for the repeal of the Eighteenth Amendment. In February 1933, Congress approved the Twenty-first Amendment, repealing Prohibition. Before the year was out, the states had ratified the amendment and Prohibition was over. The federal government returned the control of alcoholic beverages to the states.

☑**Checkpoint** **Why did many people want to end Prohibition?**

Changing Lives of Women

Due to the Nineteenth Amendment, American women voted in their first presidential election in 1920. They also joined political parties and were elected to offices previously closed to them. In 1924, the first women governors were elected: Nellie Tayloe Ross in Wyoming and Miriam "Ma" Ferguson in Texas.

Vocabulary Builder

<u>restrict</u> (ree STRIHKT) **v.** to confine; to keep within a certain boundary or limit; to place limitations on something or somebody

Other areas of life remained more <u>restricted</u>. Many universities and professional schools still barred women from admission. In some states, women still could not serve on juries or keep their own earnings if they were married. But more women were holding jobs.

Many younger women during the 1920s did not seem interested in women's rights. Called "flappers," these young women shocked the older generation. Flappers rebelled against traditional ways of thinking and acting. They wore bright makeup and short skirts, and also wore their hair in a close-cropped style known as a bob. Even though their numbers were small, the flappers became the symbol of women in the 1920s.

☑**Checkpoint** **How did flappers represent the spirit of the 1920s?**

A New Mass Culture

The automobile also became a symbol of the 1920s—especially the Model T Ford. Henry Ford introduced the assembly line which reduced the time in making cars from about 12 hours to about 1½ hours. Middle-class families could now afford to buy a car since prices dropped.

Impact of the Automobile The automobile changed American life in many ways. In a restless age, it became the symbol of individual freedom and independence. The automobile also created new businesses. Gas stations, roadside restaurants, and cabins sprang up along newly built highways.

Cars affected society in other ways. Cars and new roads made it easier for many families to move to the suburbs. Cars made people in rural areas less <u>isolated</u>. Furthermore, they encouraged tourism.

The Radio Another important part of the new culture was the radio. Introduced in the 1920s, commercial radio was an instant success. Almost any family could afford to buy a radio.

The radio became a leading supplier of entertainment. Families listened together at night after dinner. Radio put Americans in the stands at baseball games and on the floor of political conventions. It turned band leaders, singers, and comedians into household names.

The first commercial radio station, KDKA, began broadcasting in Pittsburgh in 1920. By 1926, there were more than 700 radio stations and a national radio network, NBC. People all over the country could hear the same songs and thrill to the same radio dramas.

Vocabulary Builder
isolate (ī sah layt) **v.** to set apart; to separate

Summarize Main Ideas
Summarize the main ideas under the heading "A New Mass Culture."

Portrait of a Flapper

"She is frankly, heavily made up . . . pallor mortis, poisonously scarlet lips, richly ringed eyes. . . . And there are, finally, her clothes. . . . Her dress . . . is cut low where it might be high, and vice versa. The skirt comes just an inch below her knees, overlapping by a faint fraction her rolled and twisted stockings. The idea is that when she walks in a bit of a breeze, you shall now and then observe the knee. . . . [The flapper's] haircut is also abbreviated. She wears of course the very newest thing in bobs. . . ."

—Bruce Bliven, "Flapper Jane," *The New Republic,* Sept. 9, 1925

Reading Primary Sources
Skills Activity

Some younger Americans shocked their elders by acting with a new freedom during the 1920s. In the quotation above, a magazine writer describes a 19-year-old flapper. **Critical Thinking:** *Evaluate Information* How did changes in American society help to create the flapper generation?

The Movies Movies were another new form of entertainment. They provided an escape from everyday life. Millions of Americans went to the movies at least once a week. The movie industry grew up in Hollywood, where mild weather allowed for filming year-round.

The first films were silent. A pianist or small musical group in each theater provided an accompaniment. In 1927, the first major "talkie," *The Jazz Singer,* created a sensation.

Americans especially loved action films. Comedies were also popular, and actors, such as Charlie Chaplin, became celebrities. Animated movies began in the 1920s, and the Walt Disney company was founded in 1923.

Out of the love of films grew a fascination with movie stars. Fan magazines and gossip columns contributed to the worship of celebrities.

☑**Checkpoint** **What new forms of entertainment became popular in the 1920s?**

Social Conflict

Not everyone shared in the new postwar social values. Some were offended by what they saw. They feared that rapid social and economic changes would destroy a treasured way of life.

The Scopes Trial Some of those conflicts were at the heart of the Scopes trial of 1925. John Scopes was a high school biology teacher in Dayton, Tennessee. He was accused of violating Tennessee law by teaching the theory of evolution to his students.

Evolution is the scientific theory devised by Charles Darwin in the nineteenth century. Darwin claimed that all life evolved, or developed, from simpler forms over a long period of time.

Some religious leaders rejected evolution, saying it denied the word of the Bible. A number of states, including Tennessee, passed laws that banned the teaching of Darwin's theory. Scopes wanted to challenge the law, so he announced that he taught evolution.

The trial became a national sensation. The prosecutor was William Jennings Bryan, who had run for President three times. The defense attorney was Clarence Darrow, a famous Chicago criminal defense lawyer. The trial seemed to pit modern, urban Americans against traditional, rural Americans.

In the end, Scopes was convicted and lost his job. Laws against teaching evolution remained but were rarely enforced.

Racial Conflict African Americans returned from service in World War I with new hope for equality at home. They tried to get better paying jobs and to move to better neighborhoods.

The 1920s saw large numbers of African Americans move north in what was called the Great Migration. Leaving the South, they headed for cities such as Chicago, Detroit, and New York. They crowded into the few neighborhoods that allowed black residents.

Magic of the Silver Screen
Charles Chaplin was among many Hollywood stars who became household names during the 1920s. **Critical Thinking:** *Draw Conclusions How did new forms of mass culture like radio and movies help to bring Americans together?*

This is the great picture upon which the famous comedian has worked a whole year.

6 reels of Joy.

Charles Chaplin IN
"THE KID"
Written and directed by Charles Chaplin
A First National ⊛ Attraction

Racial tensions mounted, and race riots broke out in several cities. Some of the worst violence occurred in Chicago, where 13 days of rioting in 1919 left 38 people dead and some 500 injured.

Under these conditions, the Jamaican immigrant Marcus Garvey gained a wide following. Arriving in America in 1916, Garvey, a spellbinding speaker, created the Universal Negro Improvement Association (UNIA). "Up, you mighty race," Garvey told his followers, "you can accomplish what you will." The UNIA sponsored activities to promote black pride and black unity. It also encouraged African Americans to move permanently to Africa.

The social tensions of the 1920s were also expressed in the growth of the Ku Klux Klan. The whites-only Klan scorned not just blacks but also immigrants, Catholics, and Jews. The organization's power spread from the South to the Midwest and the West. In Oregon and Indiana, Klan-backed candidates were elected as governors.

However, several public scandals at the end of the 1920s cost the Klan much of its support. The general economic prosperity also contributed to the organization's decline.

✓**Checkpoint** **What was one effect of the Great Migration?**

Marcus Garvey

⭐ **Looking Back and Ahead** The economic and social pressures unleashed by World War I greatly changed U.S. society. The changes helped bring a burst of creative energy in the arts.

Section 2 | **Check Your Progress**

Progress Monitoring ⊙nline
For: Self-test with instant help
Visit: PHSchool.com
Web Code: mva-7222

Comprehension and Critical Thinking

1. **(a) List** How did automobiles change the lives of Americans?
   (b) Draw Conclusions How did the production of the automobile change life in small towns?

2. **(a) Recall** What did Marcus Garvey encourage?
   (b) Link Past to Present Which of Garvey's ideas have African Americans embraced and which have they rejected?

🔄 **Reading Skill**

3. **Summarize Main Ideas** Reread the text following the subheading "The Movies." Summarize its main ideas.

Key Terms

Complete the following sentence so that the second part further explains the first part and clearly shows your understanding of the key term.

4. Supporters of the temperance movement favored prohibition, _____.

Writing

5. Which sentence is a better conclusion for a short essay about Prohibition? (a) "The Nineteenth Amendment outlawed the sale of alcohol." (b) "Given its unexpected effects, it is no surprise that Prohibition was repealed."

Breathless and Energetic

❝ Jazz has come to stay because it is an expression of the times, of the breathless, energetic, superactive times in which we are living; it is useless to fight against it. ❞

—Leopold Stokowski, classical music conductor, describing 1920s jazz

◄ Dance contests were popular in the 1920s.

The Jazz Age

Objectives
- Describe the new fads and heroes that emerged during the 1920s and how they affected American culture.
- Identify the origins, importance, and spread of a new musical style—jazz.
- Explain how new literature styles described American society in a new, more critical way.

Reading Skill

Summarize Main Ideas and Essential Details A summary includes more than just main ideas. It must also include essential details. Still, a summary should not repeat everything in the text, but it should include those details necessary for understanding the main ideas. To find these details, ask yourself if the main idea would make sense without a detail. If not, then include the detail.

Key Terms and People

Charles Lindbergh   Sinclair Lewis
jazz   Langston Hughes

Why It Matters The 1920s produced a burst of cultural change and artistic creativity. Americans found new heroes who modeled the fast-paced, fun-loving spirit of the time. A new musical sound earned mass popularity. Writers produced enduring literary works that reflect the complexities of the Jazz Age.

❷ **Section Focus Question: What arts and culture symbolized the Jazz Age?**

Fads and Heroes

The energy and enthusiasm of the 1920s reflected the optimism felt by many Americans of the time. One hit song put it this way: "Ev'ry morning, ev'ry evening, ain't we got fun?"

Dancing and Other Fads As the economy soared and the culture roared, young people expressed their joy for life in dancing. Dance fads became popular quickly and then disappeared. The Charleston swept the nation, followed by the Lindy Hop, the Black Bottom, and then the Breakaway.

Other fads also became part of popular culture in the 1920s. Flagpole sitting was all the rage. Young people competed to see who could sit the longest atop a flagpole. Some did it for hours, others for days. Another fad that tested young people's endurance was the dance marathon. Couples danced for hundreds of hours until only one last bleary-eyed pair remained shuffling wearily about the dance floor.

The Chinese game of mah-jongg became extremely popular. Women went to mah-jongg clubs wearing Chinese-style silk gowns. College students formed their own mah-jongg clubs. Guests brought mah-jongg sets to dinner parties and set up their ivory and bamboo tiles on playing tables.

Heroes of the New Age The growing popularity of sports entertainment produced a new kind of celebrity: the sports hero. Baseball great Babe Ruth became one such celebrity. His record of hitting 60 home runs in one season lasted for more than 30 years.

Other celebrities of the decade included swimmer Johnny Weissmuller, football player Red Grange, golf champion Bobby Jones, tennis stars Bill Tilden and Helen Wills, and boxer Jack Dempsey.

The mass media helped to make these celebrities style setters, too. When Babe Ruth began wearing a camel's-hair coat, so did millions of other Americans.

Charles Lindbergh, nicknamed Lucky Lindy, was the most beloved hero of the era. The handsome young airplane pilot gained his fame by being the first to fly nonstop across the Atlantic in 1927. He became an instant hero. New York City gave him the biggest ticker tape parade ever. Lindbergh seemed to symbolize American energy and optimism.

☑**Checkpoint** **What sports events became popular during the 1920s?**

Biography Quest

Gertrude Ederle
1906–2003

Nobody thought a woman could swim across the English Channel, the 35-mile-wide body of water between England and France. But Gertrude Ederle did it.

On August 6, 1926, Ederle stepped into the water on the French side. And 14 hours and 31 minutes later, she stepped ashore in England. Not only was she the first woman to swim the Channel—she had beaten the existing men's record by nearly 2 hours!

Biography Quest

What problems did Ederle face as a result of her swim?

For: The answer to the question about Ederle

Visit: PHSchool.com

Web Code: mvd-7223

An American Sound

During the 1920s, a new musical sound achieved wide popularity. Jazz was created by black musicians in the nightclubs and dance halls of New Orleans. New Orleans was a major port city, where people and cultures from around the world came together. Jazz combined rhythms from West Africa and the Caribbean, work chants and spirituals from the rural South, and harmonies from Europe into an original new style of music.

Jazz quickly spread to other American cities, following along with the Great Migration. African American musicians also found eager audiences for their music in St. Louis, New York, Chicago, Kansas City, and Detroit. Among the most famous of the new jazz artists were trumpet player and singer Louis Armstrong, singer Bessie Smith, and band leader Duke Ellington. All had roots in the South.

Armstrong, who was known as Satchmo, learned to play the trumpet while growing up in a New Orleans orphanage. Like other jazz players, he developed the ability to take a simple melody and recombine the notes and rhythms in new ways to produce a cascade of rich and exciting sounds. Because of jazz's emphasis on improvisation and experimentation, listeners heard many different versions of the basic tune.

Summarize Main Ideas and Essential Details List three essential details from the text under the heading "An American Sound" that could be used in a summary. Use your own words.

● **INFOGRAPHIC**

THE JAZZ AGE

Jazz spread from the dance halls of New Orleans to Chicago, Harlem, and beyond. Its rollicking beat was soon being heard all over the world.
Critical Thinking: *Apply Information* *How did the Jazz Age open up new opportunities for African Americans?*

Jazz Greats The leading jazz performers were African Americans, such as Louis Armstrong, Duke Ellington, and Bessie Smith. Many became "goodwill ambassadors" abroad, performing in many countries.

Bessie ▶ Smith

The song sheet for ▶ "Tin Roof Blues"

◀ Louis Armstrong

Duke Ellington ▼

Duke Ellington and his band

Radio helped to spread jazz beyond the African American community. During the 1920s, white audiences, white band leaders such as Paul Whiteman, and white composers such as George Gershwin embraced jazz. Jazz became one of the most important American contributions to world culture. It was so popular that the decade of the 1920s became known as the Jazz Age.

However, jazz did not set everyone's feet to tapping. The rhythms of the new music were jarring to many older Americans. And jazz alarmed people who thought it encouraged an overemphasis on frivolity and pleasure and undermined the morals of America's young people.

☑Checkpoint **Why was jazz considered an American art form?**

Literature of the 1920s

American literature flourished during the 1920s. Writers both reflected the exuberance of the era and criticized its excesses. Many writers seemed disillusioned by the postwar generation. They complained that Americans had turned from international idealism to greedy selfishness. Some of these writers found American society so intolerable that they became "expatriates," people who leave their own country to live abroad.

Social Critics F. Scott Fitzgerald's 1925 novel *The Great Gatsby* captured the luxurious society of the wealthy. Fitzgerald was a <u>critic</u> of what he saw as the emptiness of rich people's lives. He seemed both fascinated and disgusted by the people he described.

Fitzgerald's friend Ernest Hemingway was another important writer of the decade. A one-time newspaper reporter, Hemingway was noted for his short, direct sentences using everyday language. Living among American expatriates in France, Hemingway wrote *The Sun Also Rises* (1926) about a group of young Americans who drifted around Spain after the war. Another Hemingway novel, *A Farewell to Arms* (1929), powerfully captured the growing antiwar sentiments of his generation.

Sinclair Lewis reacted against what he saw as the hypocrisies of middle-class culture. In *Babbitt* (1922), Lewis used a fictional real estate agent named George F. Babbitt to criticize American society.

> **❝**Babbitt was virtuous. He advocated, though he did not practice, the prohibition of alcohol; he praised, though he did not obey, the laws against motor-speeding; he paid his debts; he contributed to the church, the Red Cross, and the Y.M.C.A.; he followed the custom of his clan and cheated only as it was sanctified by precedent. . . .**❞**
>
> —Sinclair Lewis, *Babbitt*

Based on this character's moral faults, "babbitry" became a common term for mediocrity combined with an unthinking conformity to middle-class standards and prejudices.

Vocabulary Builder
<u>critic</u> (KRIHT ihk) *n.* someone who makes judgments on the value of objects or actions

F. Scott Fitzgerald's *The Great Gatsby* calls attention to the excesses of the Roaring Twenties.

Zora Neale Hurston

The Harlem Renaissance During the 1920s, a vibrant African American culture grew in Harlem, a part of New York City that attracted thousands of migrants from the South. Writers, musicians, and poets reacted against the prejudice they faced while expressing the hopes of black Americans. Jazz clubs and the music scene were one part of the Harlem Renaissance. Perhaps even more important were the writers.

Poet Langston Hughes won praise not only for the beauty of his poems but also for his moving expressions of racial pride. He wanted his poems to sound like jazz music. He said, "I tried to write poems like the songs they sang on Seventh Street. . . . [These songs] had the pulse beat of the people who keep on going."

James Weldon Johnson was another Harlem Renaissance figure who combined poetry and politics. Johnson wrote editorials for the *New York Age,* one of the most important black-owned newspapers in the country. He also worked as an organizer for the NAACP.

Zora Neale Hurston moved to New York to study anthropology at Barnard College. She, too, became swept up in the cultural excitement of the Harlem Renaissance. Hurston spent much time recording folk songs and folk tales to both preserve and analyze them. She also became an accomplished writer and is most remembered today for her novel *Their Eyes Were Watching God.*

☑**Checkpoint** **What was the Harlem Renaissance?**

⭐ **Looking Back and Ahead** While Americans benefited from the general prosperity of the 1920s, it was easy to overlook a number of disturbing economic trends. In the next section, you will learn why a frenzied stock market boom concealed signs of an economy that was facing serious problems.

Section 3 | **Check Your Progress**

Comprehension and Critical Thinking

1. **(a) Identify** Who was Charles Lindbergh?
   (b) Draw Inferences How did Lindbergh symbolize the American hero of the 1920s?

2. **(a) List** Who were the leading writers of the 1920s and what were their major works?
   (b) Explain Problems Which problems were the writers addressing in their works?

Reading Skill

3. **Summarize Main Ideas and Essential Details** Reread the text following the subheading "The Harlem Renaissance." List three essential details, in your own words, for a summary.

Key Terms
Read the sentence that follows. If the sentence is true, write YES. If the sentence is not true, write NO and explain why.

4. Jazz began in New Orleans when musicians of French heritage combined sounds from Europe with Native American music.

Writing

5. Proofread and correct the following sentences: The Jazz age is similer to currant life in America in a many ways. Four example, the people of both periods warshiped sports heros and other selebrities. Both ages was known for there populous fads. I think I druther live today than in the past.

Prepare to Read

Introduction

Langston Hughes is considered one of the greatest of all African American poets. His short poem "I, Too" expresses two major themes of the Harlem Renaissance. The first is pride in being African American. The second is protest against injustice.

Reading Skill

Analyze Poetic Voices Poets often write in voices other than their own. Sometimes, a poet may take on the voice of a character totally unlike himself or herself. At other times, the "I" of a poem may be symbolic of a group or idea. As you read this poem, look for clues as to who the "I" is supposed to be.

Vocabulary *Builder*

As you read this literature selection, look for the following underlined word:

ashamed (uh SHAYMD) *adj.* feeling sorry and guilty about a wrong action

---

I, too, sing America.

I am the darker brother.
They send me to eat in the kitchen
When company comes,
But I laugh,
And eat well,
And grow strong.

Tomorrow,
I'll be at the table
When company comes.
Nobody'll dare
Say to me,
"Eat in the kitchen,"
Then.

Besides,
They'll see how beautiful I am
And be <u>ashamed</u>—

I, too, am America.

Analyze Poetic Voices The speaker of the poem says, "I am the darker brother." Who do you think the "I" represents? Who are "they" who send the speaker to "eat in the kitchen"? Only by identifying the "I" and "they" can you understand what the poem is saying.

Analyze LITERATURE

Make a two-column chart. In the first column, list the ways in which this poem expresses a sense of injustice. In the second column, list ways in which this poem expresses a sense of optimism and patriotism.

If you want to learn more about the Harlem Renaissance, you might want to read *Harlem Stomp!: A Cultural History of the Harlem Renaissance,* by Laban Carrick Hill. Little, Brown & Co., 2004.

The New **Gainaday**
Electric Washer

Helpful Inventions

66 Shall the men work—or shall you? . . . Back of every great step in woman's progress from a drudge to a free citizen has been some labor-saving invention. 99

—Electric clothes washer advertisement, 1924

◄ Washing machine advertisement

The Economy of the 1920s

Objectives

- Describe the causes and effects of the industrial boom that occurred in the 1920s.

- Explain how rising stock prices encouraged many to borrow money to invest in the stock market.

- Identify groups that did not profit from the prosperity of the 1920s.

- Describe the election of 1928 and Herbert Hoover's victory.

Reading Skill

Summarize a Passage Combine the skills you practiced in Sections 1 through 3 as you read Section 4. Pause after each major portion of text. Summarize the main ideas that fall under the major heading. Remember to paraphrase in your own words and to include all the important ideas.

Key Terms

installment buying   buying on margin
bull market

Why It Matters The cultural changes of the 1920s were accompanied by a period of prosperity. The economic boom produced fortunes for the wealthiest in society. But many others were left out. Some key economic problems lay hidden beneath the surface. By the end of the decade, these problems would lead to a devastating stock market crash and a long-lasting depression.

? **Section Focus Question: What economic problems threatened the economic boom of the 1920s?**

Industrial Growth

The end of World War I was followed by a severe recession in agriculture and industry. For industry, that downturn did not last long. Industrial production recovered, and from 1922 to 1928 it climbed 70 percent. Many companies successfully switched from producing military goods to producing consumer goods. The market was filled with refrigerators, radios, and cars.

As more goods came to market, prices dropped. Meanwhile, rising incomes gave consumers more to spend. To encourage spending, businesses offered installment buying, or buying on credit. In 1925, Americans got 75 percent of their cars on the installment plan.

New forms of advertising surrounded customers with images of things they should consume. Chain stores and mail-order catalogs made it easier for people outside of major cities to buy these goods. A new consumer culture arose.

Middle-class women were especially affected by these changes. Many of the new electric appliances were designed to appeal to the American homemaker. Vacuum cleaners, toasters, washing machines, and refrigerators all lightened the household workload.

Government policies helped boost the economy. High tariffs on imports kept out goods that might compete with domestic products. Taxes on the wealthy were cut to encourage greater spending.

These measures did stimulate the economy. But they also helped Americans develop a recklessness about spending. In 1928, when Ford announced its new Model A, half a million people made a down payment on the car without even having seen it.

☑**Checkpoint** **What factors caused an increase in consumer spending?**

A Booming Stock Market

With a strong economy, more people chose to invest in the stock market. Many people could now afford to purchase stocks, or shares of companies. With money pouring into stocks, stock values kept rising. A period of rising stock prices is called a **bull market.**

Stocks were so profitable that many people began buying on margin—borrowing money in order to buy stocks. The investor put down a portion of a stock's cost and paid the rest later with the profits earned from selling the stock. So long as the market continued to rise, the investor had no problem paying the loan back.

Many Americans grew wealthy buying and selling stocks. Newspapers were filled with stories of investors who <u>accumulated</u> fortunes. However, by 1928, some economists began to worry. High stock prices seemed to have little to do with the actual value of the company that issued them. A few experts warned that the stock market was overvalued. But investors mostly ignored the warnings.

Vocabulary Builder
<u>accumulate</u> (uh KYOOM yoo layt)
v. to slowly collect; to increase in amount over time

History *Interactive*
Buying Stocks on Margin
Visit: PHSchool.com
Web Code: mvl-7224

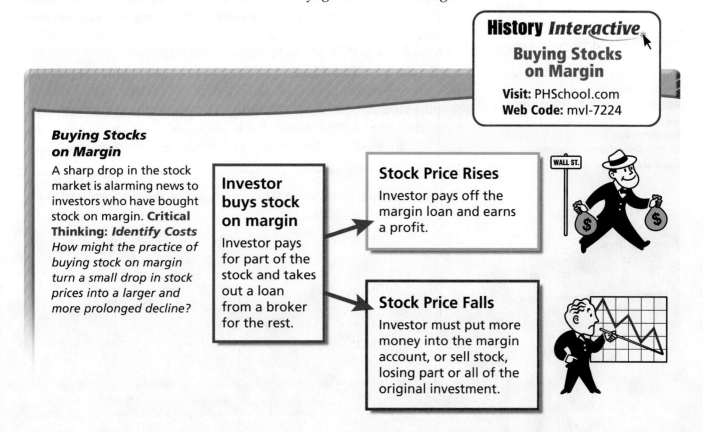

Buying Stocks on Margin
A sharp drop in the stock market is alarming news to investors who have bought stock on margin. **Critical Thinking:** *Identify Costs How might the practice of buying stock on margin turn a small drop in stock prices into a larger and more prolonged decline?*

Investor buys stock on margin
Investor pays for part of the stock and takes out a loan from a broker for the rest.

Stock Price Rises
Investor pays off the margin loan and earns a profit.

Stock Price Falls
Investor must put more money into the margin account, or sell stock, losing part or all of the original investment.

Summarize a Passage
Use what you have learned in this chapter to summarize the text under the heading "A Booming Stock Market."

They preferred to listen to predictions like this one spoken by Irwin Fisher, a professor of economics in 1929: "The nation is marching along a permanently high plateau of prosperity." However, many people at the time were far from prosperous. The wealthiest Americans made up about 5 percent of the population. Most people just worked hard to make ends meet.

✓**Checkpoint** **Why did rising stock prices encourage people to gamble on the stock market?**

Signs of Trouble

There were other signs of potential trouble, too. In fact, for many Americans, the 1920s were years of poverty rather than prosperity.

Farmers Farmers were among the groups that did not participate in the good times. About one fifth of Americans made their living on the land and many of them lived in serious poverty.

There were several reasons for the agricultural depression. American farmers grew far more crops than the American public could consume. Before World War I, farmers had sold their surplus abroad. However, demand for American farm products declined after the war, because many nations were too poor to purchase them.

High debt was another reason for rural poverty. In the good years before the world war, farmers had taken out loans to buy new lands and equipment. After the war, though, sales went down. Many farmers were unable to pay off their debts.

Workers The 1920s were years of mixed results for American workers. On the one hand, wages were rising. Companies also began offering new benefits, such as pensions and paid vacations, in an attempt to keep their workers from joining unions.

On the other hand, unemployment was high. During the 1920s, it was about 5 percent of the workforce each year. Those who had jobs found that their jobs were changing. The assembly line system was squeezing out skilled labor. Each step had been reduced to its simplest methods. Unskilled workers could handle the work—and they received lower pay.

✓**Checkpoint** **Why were farmers left out of the prosperity of the 1920s?**

Vocabulary Builder
participate (pahr TIHS ah payt) **v.** to take part in; to share in an activity

Farmers in Trouble
Drought and erosion contributed to the troubles of farmers, who made up one fifth of the population. **Critical Thinking: Draw Conclusions** *Why might bad times for farmers also be bad for the American economy in general?*

The Election of 1928

The Republicans had held the presidency throughout the 1920s, and they claimed responsibility for the decade's prosperity. For their candidate in the 1928 presidential election, they chose Secretary of Commerce Herbert Hoover. The Democrats nominated New York Governor Alfred E. Smith.

The campaign highlighted some of the continuing divisions in American society. Smith was the first Catholic ever to run for President, and religion became one of the issues. Immigrants, Catholics, and urban residents tended to support Smith. Rural residents and Protestants tended to support Hoover, a Quaker born in Iowa.

The economy was another major issue. Hoover pledged to continue the policies he credited for prosperity. He campaigned on the slogan "a chicken in every pot and a car in every garage." He said the nation was near to "the final triumph over poverty."

Although Alfred Smith won the largest cities, he lost every state but Massachusetts and six Deep South states. Hoover won with special strength in rural areas. Herbert Hoover entered the White House in 1929 with great expectations for a prosperous future.

✓**Checkpoint** Among what groups was Hoover strong?

⭐ **Looking Back and Ahead** A widespread prosperity and sweeping changes in society made the 1920s an exciting time. Within months of Hoover's election, however, a stock market crash plunged the nation into a great depression that spread misery across the land.

Hoover campaign plugs

Progress Monitoring Online
For: Self-test with instant help
Visit: PHSchool.com
Web Code: mva-7224

Section 4 | **Check Your Progress**

Comprehension and Critical Thinking

1. **(a) List** What were the reasons the economy, after a short slump, boomed following World War I?
   (b) Identify Economic Benefits Explain how high tariffs and low taxes boosted the economy during the 1920s.

2. **(a) Recall** Which groups of Americans did not benefit from the prosperity of the 1920s?
   (b) Synthesize Information Why might some farmers have felt government support was necessary at this time?

Reading Skill

3. **Summarize a Passage** Reread and then summarize the text under the heading "Signs of Trouble."

Key Terms

Complete each of the following sentences so that the second part further explains the first part and clearly shows your understanding of the key term.

4. To purchase a car, a person can turn to installment buying, _____.

5. People make money during a bull market, _____.

6. In order to purchase even more stock in the 1920s, people began buying on margin, _____.

Writing

7. Revise the following paragraph by putting the sentences in logical order: In the mid-1920s, however, reduced taxes and extended credit encouraged consumer spending. By 1929, the economy had grown to the point of being overheated. In the early 1920s the economy declined, partly as a result of World War I. The U.S. economy improved a great deal from the beginning to the end of the 1920s. The war had badly weakened European economies, and the overseas market for American goods shrank.

21st Century Learning Facts and figures that measure how an economy is performing are called economic indicators. Examples include wages, income levels, price levels, and interest rates. Sometimes these economic indicators are shown on a graph.

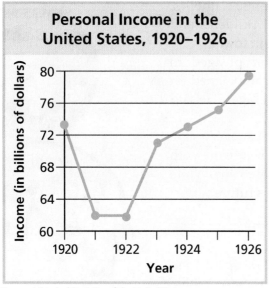

Personal Income in the United States, 1920–1926

Source: *Historical Statistics of the United States*

Average Income per Farm, 1920–1926

Source: *Historical Statistics of the United States*

Learn the Skill

Use these steps to interpret economic data on line graphs.

1 **Identify the topic.** Look for a title, a date, and a source. The title tells you what the subject is; the date tells what time period is covered; the source tells you where the information was found.

2 **Read the labels.** Chart labels identify the given information and how it is measured. Both the horizontal axis and the vertical axis on a graph have labels organizing the information.

3 **Practice interpreting the data.** Find information based on the economic data presented on the graph. The words "in billions" means you must add nine zeroes to the number shown. Sometimes you can compare and contrast information on the graph.

4 **Draw Conclusions.** Use the information on the graph to draw conclusions about the topic. You can also use other information you might know about the subject of the graph.

Practice the Skill

Answer the following questions about the graphs on this page.

1 **Identify the topic.** (a) What is the subject of the first graph (left)? The second graph (right)? (b) What time periods do both graphs show? (c) What is the source for the graphs?

2 **Read the labels.** (a) What do the numbers on the vertical axis of the first graph show? (b) Of the second graph?

3 **Practice interpreting the data.** (a) What was the personal income of all U.S. citizens in 1920? In 1926? (b) What was the average net income per farm in 1920? In 1926? (c) How would you compare the income of farmers to the income of the general population?

4 **Draw conclusions.** (a) What happened to the personal income of Americans in the 1920s? (b) How did the agricultural depression of the 1920s affect the farmer's income during this period?

Apply the Skill

See the Review and Assessment at the end of this chapter.

Quick Study Guide

How did the nation react to change in the 1920s?

Section 1
Adjusting to Peacetime

- A slumping economy and other missteps hurt the Democrats in the election of 1920.
- Scandals marred the Harding administration.
- Calvin Coolidge helped to restore the public trust in government.
- Isolationism and a fear of communism affected U.S. foreign and domestic policy.

Section 2
Changes in American Society

- The United States abandoned Prohibition.
- Flappers became the symbol of 1920s women.
- The automobile, radio, and the movies dramatically changed people's lives.
- Tough living conditions in northern cities led many African Americans to accept the black-pride message of Marcus Garvey.

Section 3
The Jazz Age

- Jazz gains a worldwide audience.
- Americans celebrated heroes, such as aviator Charles Lindbergh who flew nonstop across the Atlantic.
- Writers such as F. Scott Fitzgerald and Ernest Hemingway criticized the excesses of the period.
- The Harlem Renaissance celebrated African American culture.

Section 4
The Economy of the 1920s

- In a time of prosperity, rising stock prices attracted many new investors.
- Farmers and workers did not share in the overall prosperity.
- In 1928, voters elected another Republican President, Herbert Hoover.

? Exploring the Essential Question

Use the online study guide to explore the essential question.

Section 1
What problems at home and abroad challenged the nation after World War I?

Section 2
How did social change and conflict mark the 1920s?

Chapter 22 Essential Question
How did the nation react to change in the 1920s?

Section 4
What economic problems threatened the economic boom of the 1920s?

Section 3
What arts and culture symbolized the Jazz Age?

Key Terms

Answer the following questions in complete sentences that show your understanding of the key terms.

1. Why would anarchists oppose the U.S. government?

2. How did communism abroad affect immigrants in the United States?

3. Why did many in the United States support prohibition?

4. How did bootleggers make a living during the 1920s?

5. When would an investor not want to purchase stocks by buying on margin?

Comprehension and Critical Thinking

6. (a) **Compare** Compare the presidencies of William Harding and Calvin Coolidge.
   (b) **Make Predictions** Had Harding not died in office, would he have made a strong presidential candidate for the Republicans in 1924? Why or why not?

7. (a) **Describe** What is an isolationist foreign policy?
   (b) **Evaluate Information** In your opinion, describe whether the United States did or did not have an isolationist foreign policy during the 1920s.

8. (a) **Recall** What action did the U.S. government take against immigrants and foreigners in the 1920s?
   (b) **Summarize** Why did the government take those actions against immigrants and foreigners?

(c) **Draw Conclusions** What point of view is represented by the artist who painted the picture of Sacco and Vanzetti shown on this page?

9. (a) **Identify** How did businesses make it easy for people to spend more money during the 1920s?
   (b) **Explain Problems** How did that "easy money" threaten the security of the economy?

History Reading Skill

10. **Clarify Understanding** Choose one major portion of text from this chapter. Summarize that text, including its main ideas and essential details. Paraphrase to put the ideas into your own words.

Writing

11. **Write two paragraphs about one of the following topics:**
    - The problems that might arise from an economy built on credit
    - The image of women during the 1920s

    Your paragraphs should:
    - include an introduction and a thesis statement;
    - use facts and examples to develop your ideas;
    - end with a sentence that draws a conclusion about your topic.

    When you are finished, exchange papers with another student. Correct errors. Make sure the ideas flow logically.

12. **Write a Magazine Ad:**
    You are a writer for a magazine. The year is 1920. Your assignment is to write the text for an ad for one of the new consumer products (such as a refrigerator or a mah-jongg set).

Skills for Life
Interpret Economic Data

Use the graphs on the Skills for Life, "Interpret Economic Data," page to answer the following questions.

13. What happened to personal income between the years 1921 and 1922?

14. Did the average income for farmers follow a similar trend during the years 1921–1922?

15. Which group of Americans had more changes in their incomes during the 1920s? Why do you think this happened?

Test Yourself

1. Which term best describes what "Teapot Dome" meant to the Harding administration?

A boon

B success

C scandal

D annoyance

2. How does jazz reflect the spirit of the 1920s?

A Most of the music had a tender, quiet quality.

B The music was based on folk melodies.

C The music was energetic and expressive.

D The music encouraged musicians to play old ballads.

3. How did magazines, radio, and movies help shape new values during the 1920s?

A by reminding consumers to save money

B by encouraging consumers to move to the city

C by popularizing the latest products for living the good life

D by encouraging consumers to borrow money

Document-Based Questions

Task: Look at Documents 1 and 2, and answer their accompanying questions. Then, use the documents and your knowledge of history to complete the following writing assignment:

Use the evidence given here to discuss immigration during the early twentieth century. In your essay, explain whether or not you think that people's views have changed since the early 1900s.

Document 1:
What years showed the greatest increase in immigrants to the United States? The greatest decrease?

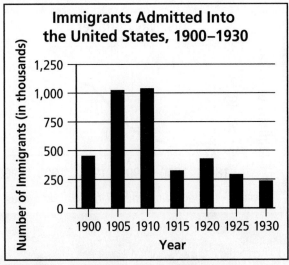

Immigrants Admitted Into the United States, 1900–1930

Number of Immigrants (in thousands)

Year

Source: *Yearbook of Immigration Statistics, 2003*

Document 2: In 1905, Commissioner General of Immigration Francis Sargent made the comments quoted below. In 1921 and again in 1924, Congress enacted laws that limited the number of immigrants allowed to enter from certain nations. These laws remained in effect until 1965. *What do you think Sargent meant by saying the nation would suffer from indigestion?*

"Put me down in the beginning as being fairly and unalterably opposed to what has been called the open door, for the time has come when every American citizen who is ambitious for the national future must regard with grave misgiving the mighty tide of immigration that, unless something is done, will soon poison or at least pollute the very fountainhead of American life and progress. Big as we are and blessed with an iron constitution, we cannot safely swallow such an endless-course dinner, so to say, without getting indigestion and perhaps national appendicitis."

—Francis Sargent, "Are We Facing an Immigration Peril?" *New York Times,* January 29, 1905

How did a more powerful United States expand its role in the world?

DIRECTIONS: Analyze the following documents about America's expanding role in the world in the late 1800s and early 1900s. Answer the questions that accompany each document or set of documents. You will use your answers to build an answer to the unit question.

HISTORIAN'S CHECKLIST

WHO produced the document?

WHERE was it made?

WHEN was it produced?

WHY was it made and for what audience?

WHAT is its viewpoint?

HOW does it connect to what I've learned?

WHY is the document important?

1 U.S. Army Poster, 1898

document

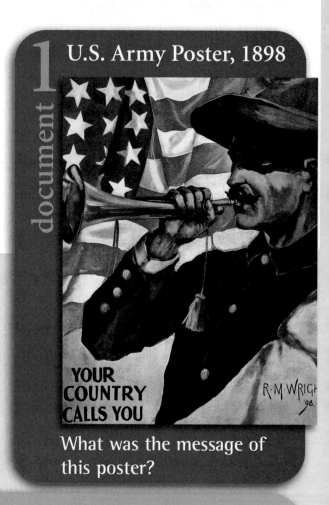

YOUR COUNTRY CALLS YOU

R·M·WRIGH '98.

What was the message of this poster?

2 Small States and Great Nations

document

"Small states are of the past and have no future. . . . The great nations are rapidly absorbing for their future expansion and their present defense all the waste places of the earth. It is a movement which makes for civilization and the advancement of the race. As one of the great nations of the world, the United States must not fall out of line of march."

—*Senator Henry Cabot Lodge, urging American expansion, 1895*

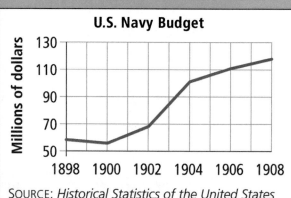

U.S. Navy Budget

SOURCE: *Historical Statistics of the United States*

Do you think Senator Lodge liked the changes in U.S. Navy spending? Explain.

3 An Apology to Hawaii

"Whereas, in pursuance of the conspiracy to overthrow the Government of Hawaii, the United States Minister and the naval representatives of the United States caused armed naval forces of the United States to invade the sovereign Hawaiian nation on January 16, 1893, and to position themselves near the Hawaiian Government buildings and the Iolani Palace to intimidate Queen Liliuokalani.... The Congress ... apologizes to Native Hawaiians on behalf of the people of the United States for the overthrow of the Kingdom of Hawaii on January 17, 1893, with the participation of agents and citizens of the United States, and the deprivation of the rights of Native Hawaiians to self-determination...."

—*"Apology Resolution" adopted by both houses of Congress, November 23, 1993*

Why did the United States Congress apologize to Hawaii in 1993?

4 The Spanish-American War

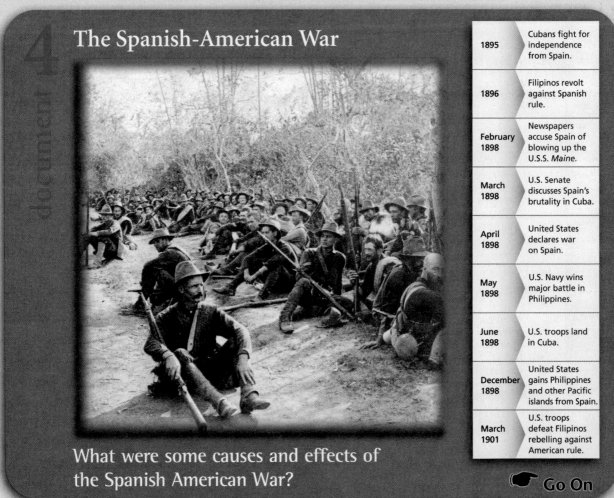

1895	Cubans fight for independence from Spain.
1896	Filipinos revolt against Spanish rule.
February 1898	Newspapers accuse Spain of blowing up the U.S.S. *Maine*.
March 1898	U.S. Senate discusses Spain's brutality in Cuba.
April 1898	United States declares war on Spain.
May 1898	U.S. Navy wins major battle in Philippines.
June 1898	U.S. troops land in Cuba.
December 1898	United States gains Philippines and other Pacific islands from Spain.
March 1901	U.S. troops defeat Filipinos rebelling against American rule.

What were some causes and effects of the Spanish American War?

☞ Go On

5 The Big Stick

What was President Theodore Roosevelt's "big stick" policy?

6 The Panama Canal

How did the Panama Canal benefit the American economy and American military power?

7 Dollar Diplomacy

"The diplomacy . . . has been characterized as substituting dollars for bullets. . . . The republics of Central America and the Caribbean possess great natural wealth. They need only a measure of stability . . . bringing profit and happiness to themselves and at the same time creating conditions sure to lead to a flourishing interchange of trade with this country."

—*President William Howard Taft, 1912*

Why did President Taft think that Latin America was important to the United States?

document

> " What we demand in this war, therefore, is nothing peculiar to ourselves. It is that the world be made fit and safe to live in; and particularly that it be made safe for every peace-loving nation which, like our own, wishes to live its own life, determine its own institutions, be assured of justice and fair dealing by the other peoples of the world as against force and selfish aggression. "
>
> —*Woodrow Wilson,*
> *Fourteen Points speech, 1918*

The United States in International Affairs, 1920–1929 ☑ Quick Study

	Goal	U.S. Action
League of Nations	To prevent war and settle disputes between nations	U.S. membership favored by Wilson; rejected by Senate
World Court	To make judgments in international disputes voluntarily submitted by nations	U.S. participation favored by Harding; rejected by Senate
Washington Naval Conference	To reduce arms race and size of navies of major powers	U.S. agreed with leading naval powers to limit construction of warships.
Kellogg-Briand Pact	To "outlaw war … as an instrument of national policy"	U.S. agreed with many other nations to renounce war as a means of settling international disputes.

How did the United States try to promote peace during and after World War I?

ACTIVITY

Assume the role of a reporter and create a magazine article that addresses the unit question:

 How did a more powerful United States expand its role in the world?

You are a reporter who has traveled around the world covering U.S. foreign policy events. Using the Historian's Apprentice Workshop documents and other information in this unit, identify two different ways in which the United States expanded its role in the world from the 1890s through the 1920s. In your magazine article, be sure to include specific information about events and situations that you witnessed over the years. Your magazine article should include a couple of illustrations, such as a map, drawing, chart, or photograph.

Unit 8

How did the United States deal with crises in domestic and foreign affairs?

History *Interactive*
Explore Historian's Apprentice Online
Visit: PHSchool.com
Web Code: mvp-8000

Dust Bowl and Depression Economic disaster coupled with drought in the prairies caused enormous hardships for Americans all over the country.

1930s

We Can Do It!

United States Joins the Fighting in World War II Americans contributed in many ways to the war effort during World War II. Thousands of soldiers fought in foreign lands, while many who stayed behind—including thousands of women—worked in war industries.

1941

Depression and War

President Roosevelt Launches the New Deal President Franklin D. Roosevelt made frequent radio addresses to the American people. He explained his plans for improving the economy through numerous programs known as the New Deal.

1933

Berlin Airlift When East Germany closed off all access to the city of Berlin, the United States and other nations joined together to supply the city with food and other necessities.

1948

The Great Depression and the New Deal

1929-1941

> "We are still living on the relief.... Will we be evicted? Will our family be broken up, our little girl taken away from us?"
>
> —Ann Rivington, Living on Relief, 1933

The Great Depression threw this little girl and millions of other Americans into poverty.

What You Will Learn

Reading Skill

Analyze Cause and Effect In this chapter, you will learn to identify causes and their effects to help connect and understand historical events and issues.

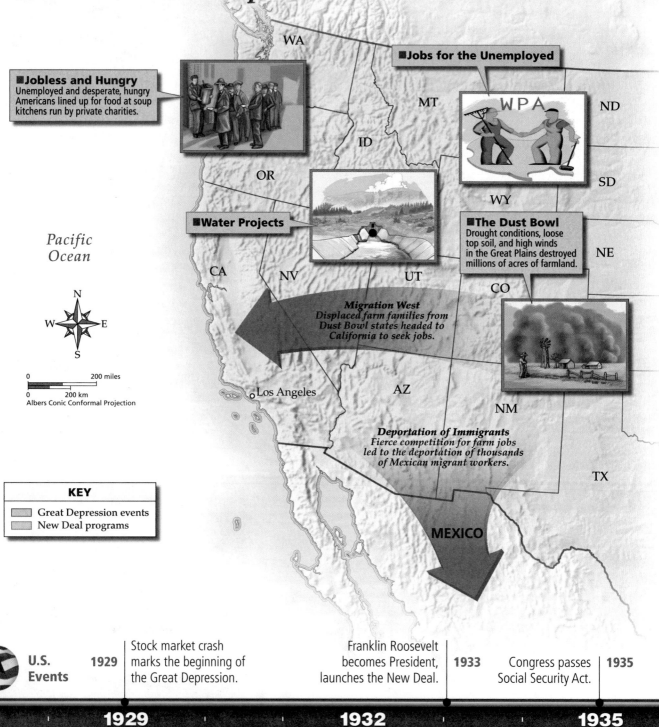

ESSENTIAL QUESTION ?

The Great Depression and the New Deal

WA

■Jobs for the Unemployed

■Jobless and Hungry
Unemployed and desperate, hungry Americans lined up for food at soup kitchens run by private charities.

MT

WPA

ND

ID

OR

SD

WY

■Water Projects

■The Dust Bowl
Drought conditions, loose top soil, and high winds in the Great Plains destroyed millions of acres of farmland.

NE

Pacific Ocean

CA

NV

UT

CO

Migration West
Displaced farm families from Dust Bowl states headed to California to seek jobs.

Los Angeles

AZ

NM

N
W E
S

0   200 miles
0   200 km
Albers Conic Conformal Projection

Deportation of Immigrants
Fierce competition for farm jobs led to the deportation of thousands of Mexican migrant workers.

TX

KEY
Great Depression events
New Deal programs

MEXICO

U.S. Events	**1929** Stock market crash marks the beginning of the Great Depression.	Franklin Roosevelt becomes President, launches the New Deal.	**1933** Congress passes Social Security Act. **1935**

1929   **1932**   **1935**

World Events	**1930** Depression spreads to Europe and Asia.	**1933** Adolf Hitler comes to power in Germany.

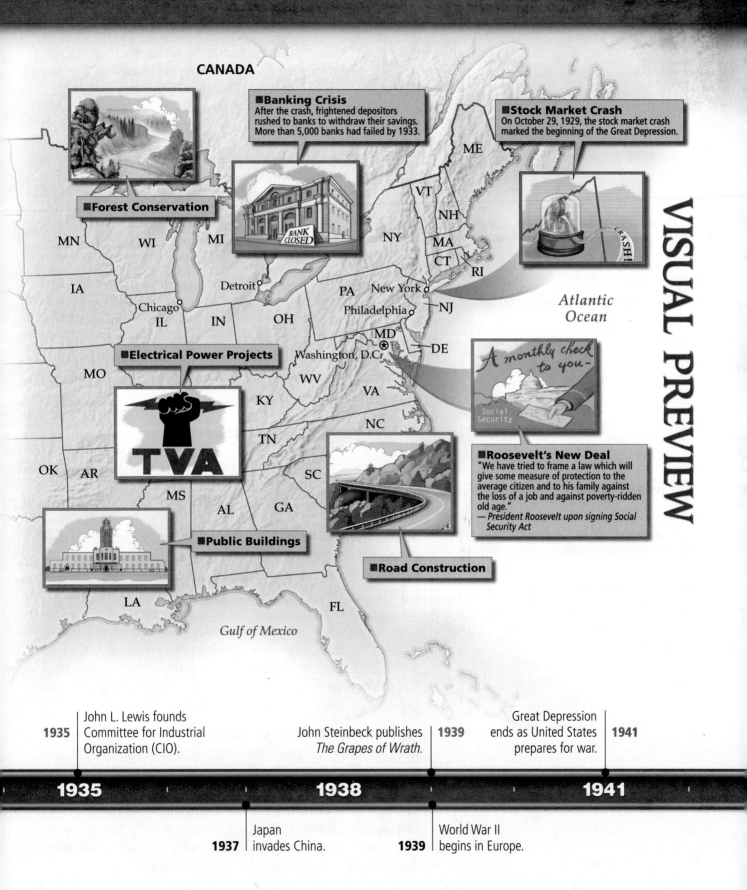

CANADA

■Banking Crisis
After the crash, frightened depositors rushed to banks to withdraw their savings. More than 5,000 banks had failed by 1933.

■Stock Market Crash
On October 29, 1929, the stock market crash marked the beginning of the Great Depression.

■Forest Conservation

MN WI MI
IA
Detroit
Chicago
IL IN OH
MO
■Electrical Power Projects
Washington, D.C.
WV VA
KY
NC
TN
OK AR SC
MS
AL GA
■Public Buildings
LA FL

ME
VT
NH
NY
MA
CT
RI
PA New York
Philadelphia NJ
MD
DE

Atlantic Ocean

A monthly check to you—
Social Security

■Roosevelt's New Deal
"We have tried to frame a law which will give some measure of protection to the average citizen and to his family against the loss of a job and against poverty-ridden old age."
— *President Roosevelt upon signing Social Security Act*

■Road Construction

Gulf of Mexico

VISUAL PREVIEW

1935 John L. Lewis founds Committee for Industrial Organization (CIO).

John Steinbeck publishes *The Grapes of Wrath.* **1939**

Great Depression ends as United States prepares for war. **1941**

1935 **1938** **1941**

1937 Japan invades China.

1939 World War II begins in Europe.

A Family Loses Everything

❝We lost everything.... We tried to struggle along living day by day. Then I couldn't pay the rent. I had a little car, but I couldn't pay no license for it.... I sold it for $15 in order to buy some food for the family. I had three little children.❞

—Ben Isaacs, recalling the Depression, quoted in Studs Terkel's *Hard Times*

◄ A victim of the Great Depression

Hoover and the Crash

Objectives
- Read about America's economic problems during the late 1920s.
- Understand how the Great Depression started.
- Find out how the Depression affected Americans.
- Discover President Hoover's response to the Depression.

Reading Skill

Analyze Causes Analyzing causes will help you to understand the *why* and *how* of history. As you read the following section, try to answer the question: What caused the Great Depression to start? Remember that many causes can combine to yield one effect.

Key Terms
overproduction   default
bankruptcy   bonus

Why It Matters During the 1920s, the stock market boomed and many prospered. However, much of the prosperity was based on borrowed money and buying stock on margin. Then the stock market crashed. The crash was followed by a long, severe economic downturn called the Great Depression.

❓ **Section Focus Question: Why did the economy collapse after the stock market crash?**

A Collapsing Economy

In 1928, Herbert Hoover had predicted that the United States would soon achieve the "final triumph over poverty." In fact, the country was heading for the worst economic crisis in its history.

Signs of Weakness Several signs of economic weakness surfaced during the late 1920s. Older industries, such as coal mining, railroads, and clothing manufacture, were in decline. Agriculture was also experiencing a prolonged downturn.

Yet, as sections of the economy declined, stock prices continued to soar. As you have read, margin buying allowed people to purchase stocks by paying only a fraction of the cost at the outset and owing the balance. Margin buyers gambled that prices would be higher when they were ready to sell. The gamble seemed to pay off—for a while.

The Stock Market Crashes The prices for industrial stocks doubled between May 1928 and September 1929. But soon after, prices began a rapid slide. On Wednesday, October 23, six million shares of stock changed hands. Falling prices caused losses of $4 billion. Brokers who had lent people money to buy on margin now began to recall their loans. Investors who could not pay had to sell their stocks. This caused prices to drop even more.

On October 29, 1929—known as Black Tuesday—the stock market crumbled completely. Panicked traders rushed to sell, but there were no buyers. Prices plummeted. Investors who thought they owned valuable shares of stock were left with worthless pieces of paper. Millionaires lost their fortunes overnight.

Over the next two weeks, stock prices continued to plunge. "Everybody wanted to tell his neighbor how much he had lost," observed a reporter for the *New York Times.* "Nobody wanted to listen. It was too repetitious a tale."

☑**Checkpoint** What happened on Black Tuesday?

The Great Depression Begins

The stock market crash marked the start of a 12-year economic and social disaster known as the Great Depression. The crash, however, was less a cause than a symptom of a deepening crisis.

Troubled Industries One major cause of the Great Depression was **overproduction,** a situation in which the supply of manufactured goods exceeds the demand. Factories were producing more than people could afford to buy. With prices rising faster than salaries, many Americans cut back on their purchases.

At the same time, housing and automobile manufacture were in decline. These industries had supported American prosperity during the 1920s. By the end of the decade, though, most Americans who could afford houses and cars had already bought them. Between 1926 and 1929, spending on construction fell from $11 billion to $9 billion. In the first nine months of 1929, car sales dropped by more than one third.

Vocabulary Builder
<u>decline</u> (dee KLĪN) **v.** to lose strength or power over time

The Stock Market Crash
Screaming newspaper headlines announced the stock market crash of October 1929. Giant fortunes were lost overnight.
Critical Thinking: *Evaluate Information* *What is the young man in this picture trying to do? Do you think he will be successful? Explain.*

Analyze Causes
Identify two sentences on this page or the previous page that give causes of the Depression.

Crisis in Banking A nationwide banking crisis also contributed to the Depression. In the countryside, struggling farmers found it impossible to repay their bank loans. When their farms failed, many banks that had loaned farmers money also went out of business.

City banks failed, too. Some of the largest banks had invested in the stock market or loaned huge amounts to speculators. After the crash, terrified depositors flocked into banks, demanding to withdraw their savings. More than 5,500 banks closed between 1930 and 1933. Many depositors were left penniless.

The Downward Spiral With people unable to buy what factories were producing, many workers lost their jobs. Thus, they had even less money with which to make purchases. In a vicious circle, declining sales led to more factory closings and layoffs. Many companies were forced into bankruptcy. Bankruptcy is financial failure caused by a company's inability to pay its debts. These bankruptcies, of course, caused even more layoffs.

The Great Depression soon spread worldwide. After World War I, many European nations owed America huge sums of money. A slowdown in international trade, however, caused these countries to default, or fail to repay their loans. And as the financial crisis worsened in America, investors cut back on their loans to Europe. The vicious cycle of production cuts, layoffs, and bankruptcies repeated itself as Europe sank into economic depression.

✓Checkpoint How did the Depression spread overseas?

The Human Cost

The Great Depression severely affected more people than any previous downturn. During earlier depressions, most Americans still lived on farms. They could feed their families in times of crisis. By 1930, however, far more Americans lived in cities and worked in factories or offices. When factories or businesses closed, the jobless had no money for food and no land on which to grow food.

The Unemployed Between 1929 and 1933, the unemployment rate skyrocketed from 3 percent to 25 percent. Nationwide, some 13 million people were unemployed. Some cities were harder hit than others. In Toledo, Ohio, four out of five workers had no work.

People lucky enough to have jobs saw their hours cut back and their salaries slashed. Coal miners who had earned $7 a day before the Depression now fought for the chance to work for a dollar.

Growing Poverty Grinding poverty crushed Americans' spirits. In cities, jobless people lined up at soup kitchens, waiting for meals. People tried to sell apples or pencils on the street or to pick up trash for food. Some men hopped freight trains in search of work.

On the outskirts of big cities, homeless people built communities of rundown shacks. They called these makeshift towns Hoovervilles, because they blamed the President for failing to solve the crisis. They slept under "Hoover blankets," or newspapers.

The misery of the Great Depression touched all Americans. Much of the most visible suffering took place in the nation's cities. **Critical Thinking: *Link Past and Present*** *How do you think you would react if another depression like this one struck the United States?*

THE GREAT DEPRESSION: Misery in the Cities

Desperate for food, the jobless lined up at soup kitchens operated by churches and private charities. ▼

◄ Apple sellers were a common sight on street corners.

BUY APPLES 5¢

FREE SOUP COFFEE & DOUGHNUTS FOR THE UNEMPLOYED

FREE SOUP

Unemployment, 1927–1933

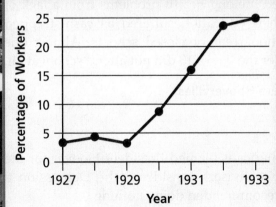

Percentage of Workers

| Year | 1927 | 1929 | 1931 | 1933 |

Source: *Historical Statistics of the United States*

Unemployment reached its highest levels in American history during the 1930s.

The homeless gathered in miserable shantytowns, nicknamed Hoovervilles.

The Bonus Army

In 1932, these World War I veterans headed for Washington, D.C., to demand their bonus. **Critical Thinking: *Evaluate Information*** *What is the meaning of the poster on the right for the years 1918 and 1932?*

Impact on Families The Depression had a harsh effect on American families. Many fathers left their homes in search of work. Others, ashamed of being jobless, quit looking for work or deserted their families. With their futures uncertain, young people put off marriage plans. When couples did marry, they had fewer children.

For children, the Depression brought both hardship and a sense of uncertainty. One woman recalled that, after her father lost his job, her family had to move into a garage heated only by a coal stove:

> **❝**In the morning, we'd get out and get some snow and put it on the stove and melt it and wash around our faces. Never the neck or anything. Put on our two pairs of socks on each hand and two pairs of socks on our feet, and long underwear and lace it up with Goodwill shoes. Off we'd walk, three, four miles to school.**❞**
>
> —Dynamite Garland, quoted in *Hard Times* (Terkel)

Many children suffered lifelong health problems from a lack of food and dental care. Their education suffered as cash-strapped school boards cut the school year or closed schools. Almost one million rural children under the age of 13 did not attend school at all.

✔Checkpoint   What were Hoovervilles?

Hoover Responds

As you saw, many Americans blamed President Hoover for the worsening crisis. Hoover's advisers considered the Depression a temporary setback. They recommended doing nothing.

Government Aid Hoover disagreed. After his brilliant career in mining and foreign aid administration, he believed in taking action. However, he thought business leaders and local governments should take the lead, rather than the federal government.

Hoover met with business executives and encouraged city and state governments to create public works projects to employ jobless people. He also urged private charities to set up soup kitchens.

Eventually, Hoover realized that <u>voluntary</u> action alone would not relieve the crisis. In 1932, he formed the Reconstruction Finance Corporation (RFC) to fund critical businesses, such as banks, insurance companies, and railroads. The RFC also gave money to local governments to fund public-works projects. Despite such measures, the economic situation continued to worsen.

Vocabulary Builder
voluntary (VAHL ahn tair ee) **adj.** not forced; done of one's own free will

The Bonus Army In June 1932, a protest began that would seal the President's fate. Eight years earlier, Congress had approved a bonus, or extra payment, of $1,000 for every veteran of World War I. This bonus was not to be paid until 1945. Made desperate by the Depression, some veterans demanded immediate payment.

When Hoover refused, an angry "Bonus Army" of at least 20,000 veterans marched to Washington, where they camped out. But Congress also rejected their plea. Most marchers left, but about 2,000 stubbornly remained in tents or abandoned buildings. To clear them out, government forces used tear gas, tanks, and machine guns. This lopsided attack killed at least one veteran, injured 100, and left the tent city a smoldering ruin. Many Americans were outraged by the image of government forces firing on unarmed veterans.

☑**Checkpoint** **What was the goal of the Bonus Army?**

⭐ **Looking Back and Ahead** The treatment of the Bonus Army further damaged Hoover's fading popularity. In the next section, you will see how voters turned to a dynamic new leader.

Section 1 | Check Your Progress

Progress Monitoring Online
For: Self-test with instant help
Visit: PHSchool.com
Web Code: mva-8231

Comprehension and Critical Thinking

1. (a) List List the major troubles that industries faced in the Great Depression.
(b) Analyze Cause and Effect How did those troubles cost people their jobs?

2. (a) Describe What actions did President Hoover take to try to ease the economic crisis?
(b) Detect Points of View Why do you think Hoover wanted business leaders and local governments to take the lead?

🔁 Reading Skill

3. Analyze Causes Reread the text following the subheading "The Downward Spiral." Identify the causes in this downward spiral.

Key Terms

Answer the following questions in complete sentences that show your understanding of the key terms.

4. How can overproduction hurt the economy?

5. When would a company declare bankruptcy?

6. What happens when a company or individual defaults on a loan?

Writing

7. Review this section, including photos and other visual elements. List three possible topics for a multimedia presentation that includes non-print media such as photographs, sound recordings, interviews, computer presentations, and film. Choose one of the three topics and write a sentence describing the topic and the kinds of materials you might use in your presentation.

Standing on My Own Two Feet

❝By enrolling in President Roosevelt's peace time army, I managed to retain my self-respect. I did not have to become either a parasite, living off my relatives, or a professional bum. In other words, it gave me a chance to stand on my own two feet.❞

—Robert Miller, worker in California Civilian Conservation Corps, 1933

◀ Franklin Delano Roosevelt campaigning in 1932

Roosevelt and the New Deal

Objectives
- Learn how Franklin Roosevelt won the 1932 presidential election.
- Find out how the New Deal tried to promote economic recovery.
- Understand what new laws regulated America's economic system.
- Identify obstacles and criticisms faced by the New Deal.

Reading Skill

Evaluate Causes and Effects When events have multiple effects, some may be positive and others negative. As you read the following section, look for events that have multiple effects or trigger cause-and-effect chains. Decide if you think the effects are positive or negative.

Key Terms and People

Franklin D. Roosevelt
fireside chat
Huey Long

Francis Townsend
pension
Charles Coughlin

Why It Matters President Hoover's response to the Great Depression did little to revive the economy. So, in 1932, voters elected a new President—Franklin Delano Roosevelt. Some of his new programs helped to improve the economy. Roosevelt dramatically changed the role of the federal government in the U.S. economy.

❓ **Section Focus Question: How did President Roosevelt respond to the Great Depression?**

Franklin D. Roosevelt

The Democrats nominated Franklin D. Roosevelt to run against Hoover in 1932. He became known to Americans as FDR.

Background FDR was a wealthy New Yorker and distant relative of Theodore Roosevelt. He had served as assistant secretary of the navy and was nominated for Vice President in 1920.

A year later, Roosevelt was stricken with polio, a deadly disease. For the rest of his life, he depended on steel leg braces to stand up. Determined to appear strong, Roosevelt never allowed photographers to take his picture in a wheelchair. In fact, most Americans never knew that Roosevelt's legs were paralyzed.

In 1928, he was elected governor of New York. Four years later, the Democrats tapped the popular governor to run for President.

A Voice of Hope During the campaign, Roosevelt pledged "a new deal for the American people." The term *New Deal* would later come to describe his entire political program. The election results were overwhelming. Roosevelt beat Hoover by a margin of 472 electoral votes to 59. Roosevelt received 57.4 percent of the popular vote.

On March 4, 1933, supported on his son's arm, Roosevelt slowly shuffled a few steps to the platform. After taking the oath of office, the new President reassured Americans:

> ❝This great Nation will endure as it has endured, will revive and will prosper. So, first of all, let me assert my firm belief that the only thing we have to fear is fear itself—nameless, unreasoning, unjustified terror which paralyzes needed efforts to convert retreat into advance.❞
>
> —Franklin Roosevelt, First Inaugural Address, 1933

FDR did not <u>specify</u> what actions he would take. Still, the American people were encouraged by the new President's confidence.

Vocabulary Builder
<u>specify</u> (SPEHS ah fī) **v.** to name or describe in exact detail

Bank Holiday An optimistic FDR quickly went into action. The day after he took office, Roosevelt declared a bank holiday, a four-day closing of the nation's banks. Its goal was to halt the nationwide epidemic of bank failures. The bank holiday gave FDR time to propose an Emergency Banking Relief Act, which provided more careful government regulation of banks.

To restore Americans' confidence in their banks, Roosevelt delivered the first of many fireside chats, or radio talks. He told Americans, "It is safer to keep your money in a reopened bank than under the mattress." The next day, most of the nation's banks reopened. A relieved public began to redeposit its savings.

☑Checkpoint **What was the goal of FDR's bank holiday?**

Relief for the Jobless

To decide what legislation to send to Congress, FDR conferred with a group of advisers. FDR's advisers were nicknamed the "brain trust" because several members had been college professors.

History *Interactive*
Explore the Presidency of FDR
Visit: PHSchool.com
Web Code: mvl-8231

Fireside Chat

This coal miner (right) listens intently to a fireside chat by President Franklin Roosevelt (left). A friend of FDR said, "His face would smile and light up as though he were actually sitting on the front porch or in the parlor with them." **Critical Thinking:** *Link Past and Present How do Presidents communicate their ideas to the American people today?*

CCC badge (top) and WPA poster (bottom)

During the whirlwind first hundred days of FDR's administration, Congress passed and the President signed a record 15 new bills. These New Deal measures had three goals: (1) relief for the jobless, (2) economic recovery, and (3) reforms to prevent future depressions.

Unemployment Relief Some measures helped the unemployed by providing financial assistance. The Federal Emergency Relief Administration, or FERA, granted funds to states so they could reopen shuttered relief agencies.

Providing Jobs Other programs employed jobless adults. The Civilian Conservation Corps (CCC) hired city dwellers to work in America's national parks, forests, wilderness areas, and countryside. Millions of young men planted trees, built reservoirs, constructed parks, and dug irrigation canals. In addition to providing jobs, the CCC conserved the nation's natural resources.

Another program, the Works Progress Administration (WPA), put people to work building or repairing public buildings, such as schools, post offices, and government offices. WPA workers paved 650,000 miles of roads, raised more than 75,000 bridges, and built more than 800 airports. The WPA also paid artists to paint murals in post offices and government buildings and hired writers to write stories, state guides, and histories.

✓**Checkpoint** **How did the CCC and WPA help the jobless?**

Promoting Economic Recovery

In 1933, the President faced an enormous challenge. He needed to help two sectors of the economy recover: industry and agriculture.

National Recovery Administration As you saw, one of the causes of the Depression had been overproduction. Some competing businesses lured consumers by slashing prices. As a result, they had to lay off workers or cut wages.

A new federal agency, the National Recovery Administration (NRA) aimed to keep prices stable while boosting employment and buying power. Most of the country's major industries agreed to pay workers a minimum wage, to stop hiring children, and to keep wages and prices from falling too low.

The NRA succeeded in raising prices. However, critics charged that the agency's codes favored large businesses. More important, the NRA failed to improve the economy.

Public Works Administration Another agency, the Public Works Administration (PWA), was granted more than $3 billion to build large public-works projects. The PWA improved the nation's infrastructure and employed many people.

PWA projects included New York's Lincoln Tunnel, Florida's Key West Highway, and the Grand Coulee Dam in Washington. In fact, nearly every county in the nation could boast at least one PWA project. Even so, the Great Depression continued.

Vocabulary Builder
infrastructure (IHN frah struhk chahr) **n.** underlying foundation on which a community or nation depends, such as its roads, bridges, etc.

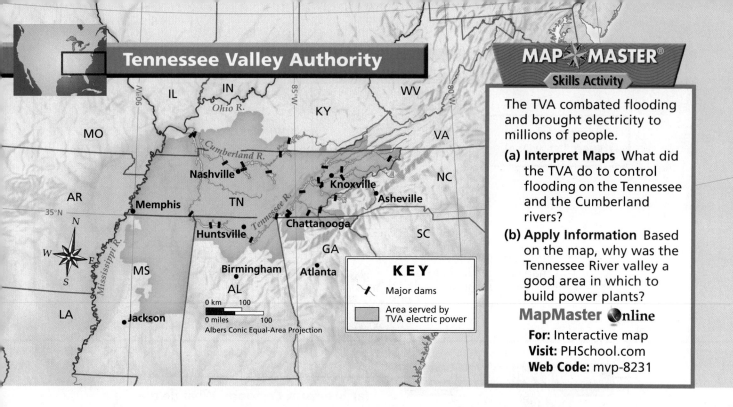

Tennessee Valley Authority

MAP MASTER®
Skills Activity

The TVA combated flooding and brought electricity to millions of people.

(a) Interpret Maps What did the TVA do to control flooding on the Tennessee and the Cumberland rivers?

(b) Apply Information Based on the map, why was the Tennessee River valley a good area in which to build power plants?

MapMaster Online

For: Interactive map
Visit: PHSchool.com
Web Code: mvp-8231

KEY
⤬ Major dams
▢ Area served by TVA electric power

0 km 100
0 miles 100
Albers Conic Equal-Area Projection

Tennessee Valley Authority In 1933, Congress formed the Tennessee Valley Authority (TVA). This agency built giant dams along the Tennessee River. Planners believed that these dams would control flooding, provide cheap electricity, and increase jobs and prosperity in one of the country's poorest rural areas.

The TVA accomplished its major goals. By 1945, power from TVA plants lit thousands of farms that had never before enjoyed electricity. Still, the TVA failed to relieve the region's poverty. Conservatives criticized the TVA for driving some property owners off their land. They also argued that it was unfair for the government to compete with private power companies.

More recently, other critics have claimed that the TVA disrupted the natural environment and that some TVA projects led to increased air pollution. Still, in the 1930s, the popular TVA seemed to symbolize government planning at its best.

✓**Checkpoint** What was the goal of the NRA?

Evaluate Causes and Effects
Evaluate the positive and negative effects of the TVA on the Tennessee Valley region.

Reforming the Economic System

The third part of Roosevelt's plan—reforming the economic system—aimed to prevent future depressions. The Truth-in-Securities Act, for example, required corporations to inform the public fully about their stocks. This act corrected one of the conditions that had contributed to the stock market crash.

The Federal Deposit Insurance Corporation (FDIC), created in 1933, protected bank depositors. It guaranteed individual deposits up to $2,500. By raising public confidence in banks, the FDIC stemmed the tide of bank failures.

FDR beats a drum labeled "New Deal."

This man is Chief Justice Charles Evans Hughes.

Reading Political Cartoons
Skills Activity

Congress passed most New Deal legislation. However, the Supreme Court overturned some key measures. This cartoon is based on a famous painting about the American Revolution.

(a) Interpret Cartoons What do the three figures represent? What seems to be the attitude of FDR and Hughes toward each other?

(b) Draw Conclusions Summarize the main idea of this cartoon.

Other New Deal agencies set fairness and safety standards for various industries. The Federal Power Commission (FPC), for example, helped control the oil and gas industries. The New Deal also strengthened the power of the Food and Drug Administration to ensure product safety.

☑**Checkpoint** How did the FDIC protect bank depositors?

Obstacles to the New Deal

Millions of Americans were enthusiastic about the New Deal. As a result, FDR won reelection in 1936 by a wide margin. Still, the New Deal faced a major challenge in the Supreme Court.

Supreme Court In 1935 and 1936, the Supreme Court declared several New Deal measures, including the NRA, to be unconstitutional. In response, Roosevelt proposed appointing up to six new Supreme Court justices. He claimed that he wanted to relieve the overworked judges. However, conservatives protested. They understood that FDR had designed this "court-packing plan" to gain a majority of justices.

Congress embarrassed the President by defeating his plan. Even so, FDR won a backdoor victory. When a conservative justice resigned in 1937, Roosevelt appointed a liberal in his place. FDR eventually named eight Supreme Court justices.

New Deal Critics Conservatives claimed that the New Deal went too far in regulating businesses and restricting individual freedom. On the other hand, some liberals thought it did not go far enough in helping the poor.

Three New Deal critics attracted widespread attention and some national support. Huey Long, a Democratic senator from Louisiana, argued that the government could end the Depression immediately. Long proposed to tax the wealthy and distribute their wealth to the poor. Long's radio speeches on behalf of what he called the Share Our Wealth plan won many enthusiastic followers.

A California doctor, Francis Townsend, called for a system of government pensions, or retirement payments. Under Townsend's plan, retired Americans over the age of 60 would receive $200 each month as long as they pledged to spend all the money. Congress never approved the Townsend plan, but it later helped set the stage for the government-supported pensions of the Social Security system. You will read about Social Security in Section 4.

Like Huey Long, Father Charles Coughlin used the radio to attract followers. A Catholic priest from Michigan, Coughlin came to distrust Roosevelt's policies on banking and money. Coughlin called on the government to take over the banks.

Supporters of Long, Townsend, and Coughlin eventually joined forces to back a third-party candidate in the 1936 election. However, they were not strong enough to combat FDR's popularity.

Huey Long addresses a rally in Louisiana.

☑Checkpoint **Why did FDR try to increase the size of the Supreme Court?**

⭐ **Looking Back and Ahead** In this section, you have read how Roosevelt tried to tackle the problems of the Great Depression. In the next section, you will see how the Depression affected American life.

Section 2 | **Check Your Progress**

**Comprehension
and Critical Thinking**

1. (a) Recall What were the three goals of the New Deal?
(b) Organize Information Categorize five New Deal measures according to these three goals.

2. (a) Recall How did the Supreme Court threaten the New Deal?
(b) Draw Inferences How might Roosevelt's response have threatened separation of powers in the federal government?

🔊 **Reading Skill**
3. Evaluate Causes and Effects Reread the text under the heading "Relief for the Jobless." Evaluate the effects of FDR's plan to help the poor and unemployed.

Key Terms
Read each sentence below. If the sentence is true, write YES. If the sentence is not true, write NO and explain why.

4. Townsend's pension plan forced retired people to pay higher taxes.
5. In his fireside chats, FDR explained his programs directly to the American people.

Writing
6. List two topics for a multimedia presentation about Franklin Roosevelt's presidency.

From Oklahoma to California

❝ One year the drought killed everything. We made $100—just enough money to pay the rent. . . . We just knew that there was work in California because of what we'd been told and what we'd read in the papers. So we decided to come to California. ❞

—Mildred Ward, recalling why her family migrated during the Great Depression

◀ A family fleeing drought-stricken Oklahoma in the 1930s

Life in the Great Depression

Objectives

- Discover how the Great Depression and the New Deal affected women, African Americans, Mexican Americans, and Native Americans.

- Learn about the causes and effects of the Dust Bowl.

- Understand how art, radio, and movies informed and entertained people during the Depression.

Reading Skill

Analyze Effects Effects are the results of an action, event, or attitude. Often an action, event, or attitude will have several effects. Certainly, the events of the Great Depression had dramatic effects on American business, families, and culture. As you read this section, ask yourself: What happened to businesses and individuals because of these events? How did American culture change because of these events?

Key Terms and People

Eleanor Roosevelt
civil rights
Mary McLeod
 Bethune
Marian Anderson
migrant worker
John Collier
John Steinbeck

Why It Matters Not everyone benefited equally from FDR's New Deal. Poverty and discrimination plagued many. Farmers in the Plains suffered drought and terrible dust storms that destroyed crops. Thousands headed west to California hoping for a better life.

❓ Section Focus Question: How did the Great Depression affect daily life?

Women in the Depression

With so many men out of work, many Americans felt that women should stay at home. Yet, women often had to help support themselves or their families. By the end of the Great Depression, more women were working outside the home than at the start.

Women in the Workplace Women enjoyed two small advantages in the workplace. Female salesclerks and secretaries faced little competition from men. In addition, such jobs were less likely to disappear than the factory jobs many men held.

Still, most women with jobs struggled. For example, women who had trained to become schoolteachers or librarians suddenly found themselves competing for jobs with men who had lost other work. Female factory workers were more likely than men to lose their jobs or to have their wages cut. Many maids, seamstresses, and housekeepers also lost their jobs because fewer people could afford domestic help. African American women were especially hard hit because they held the majority of domestic jobs.

The Great Depression complicated life for most women, whether or not they worked outside the home. To save money, more women found themselves sewing clothes, canning fruits and vegetables, and baking bread instead of buying it.

An Active First Lady The most famous working woman in the country was FDR's wife, Eleanor Roosevelt. After polio had stricken her husband in 1921, Mrs. Roosevelt overcame her shyness to begin speaking and traveling on his behalf.

Eleanor Roosevelt helped transform the role of First Lady. The wives of earlier Presidents had hosted teas and stayed in the background. By contrast, the energetic Mrs. Roosevelt crisscrossed the country, serving as the President's "eyes and ears." Then, she <u>conferred</u> with FDR on what she had seen and what he should do. In 1933 alone, Eleanor Roosevelt logged 40,000 miles, including a trip down into a West Virginia coal mine. She also made frequent radio speeches and wrote a daily newspaper column.

Mrs. Roosevelt used her position to champion women's rights. She held press conferences limited to female reporters. She also urged FDR to appoint more women to government positions.

Vocabulary Builder
<u>confer</u> (kahn FER) **v.** to exchange ideas with someone

☑**Checkpoint** What challenges did women face during the Great Depression?

African Americans in the Depression

African Americans had been hit hard by the Depression. They generally suffered more unemployment, homelessness, illness, and hunger than did whites.

South and North In the South, plunging cotton prices forced many African American sharecroppers off their land. Moving to southern cities, they found that many jobs traditionally done by blacks, such as cleaning streets, were now filled by jobless whites. By 1932, more than half the African Americans in the South were unemployed.

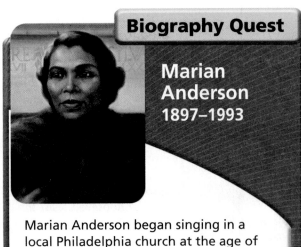

Marian Anderson
1897–1993

Marian Anderson began singing in a local Philadelphia church at the age of six. By 1934, she was singing for the kings of Sweden and Denmark.

Anderson is best remembered for her 1939 concert at the Lincoln Memorial. At first, she shied away from the attention. But she realized, "I had become, whether I liked it or not, a symbol, representing my people."

Biography Quest | Online

What other barriers did Anderson break in her career?

For: The answer to the question about Anderson

Visit: PHSchool.com

Web Code: mvd-8233

The migration of African Americans to the North, which had started after World War I, continued at an even faster pace. Even in northern cities, though, more black than white factory workers lost their jobs. African Americans were usually the last hired and the first fired. In New York, almost 50 percent of blacks were jobless.

FDR's Mixed Record The majority of African American voters had backed Roosevelt. Still, the President had a mixed record on civil rights. Civil rights are the rights guaranteed in the Constitution, especially voting and equal treatment under the law. For example, FDR failed to support a federal antilynching bill, which his wife strongly supported. The President feared that he might lose the support of southern senators for his New Deal programs.

Still, in part due to his wife's prodding, Roosevelt appointed at least 100 African Americans to government posts. Educator Mary McLeod Bethune, a friend of Eleanor Roosevelt's, became the top-ranking African American in the government.

Bethune was a member of FDR's "Black Cabinet," a group of high-ranking appointees who advised the President on African American issues. Other members of the Black Cabinet included William Hastie, who later became the first African American federal judge.

A Symbolic Moment In 1939, the Daughters of the American Revolution (DAR) refused to allow African American singer Marian Anderson to perform at their hall. Eleanor Roosevelt, a DAR member, resigned in protest. She then arranged for Anderson to sing on the steps of the Lincoln Memorial on Easter Sunday.

Anderson's performance drew a crowd of 75,000 listeners. The concert became a key symbol of the struggle for civil rights.

☑ Checkpoint What was the Black Cabinet?

Other Americans in the Depression

All Americans were affected by the Depression. Yet, some faced drastic circumstances. Many Mexicans and Mexican Americans were not only forced out of work but also out of the country. Meanwhile, the New Deal meant a new government policy toward Native Americans.

Vocabulary Builder
 drastic (DRAS tik) **adj.** extreme in effect or action

Mexican Immigrants Are Deported Many Mexican immigrants lived in the Southwest as migrant workers, people who travel from farm to farm picking crops. During good times, farm owners had welcomed the Mexicans, who were willing to toil for low wages under harsh conditions. During the Depression, though, thousands of white migrant workers also flooded the area looking for work.

Many Americans wanted the government to force the Mexicans out of the country. Federal immigration officials rounded up tens of thousands of people and deported them to Mexico. Some of those deported were not immigrants but were citizens who had been born in the United States.

The Indian New Deal A law in 1924 had granted American citizenship to Native Americans. Still, when the Great Depression hit, most of the nation's 170,000 Indians lived in poverty on reservations administered by the government.

Under FDR, John Collier became Commissioner of Indian Affairs. Collier, a white man who had lived among the Pueblo Indians of New Mexico, embarked on an ambitious program that became known as the Indian New Deal. With funding from federal agencies, he hired Native Americans to build needed schools, hospitals, and irrigation systems. Collier also hoped to put reservations under Indian control, stop sales of Native American lands, and encourage Indian schools to teach Native American history and the arts.

Congress approved part of Collier's plan in the Indian Reorganization Act (IRA) of 1934. The IRA did restrict tribal land sales. Yet, it failed to bring self-government to the tribes or to promote education. Native Americans continued to be the poorest Americans.

Native Americans and the New Deal

In addition to the Indian Reorganization Act, Native Americans benefited from other New Deal programs. These farmers display the blue eagle, the symbol of the National Recovery Act. **Critical Thinking: Apply Information** *What was the Indian New Deal?*

☑ **Checkpoint** **Why were many Mexican Americans expelled from the country during the Great Depression?**

The Dust Bowl

In the southwestern Plains, farmers already suffering the effects of the Great Depression faced another disaster. In 1930, very little rain fell. The resulting drought caused widespread crop failure and sent storms of dust swirling across the land. These gigantic dust storms lasted for five years, turning 100 million acres of rich farmland into a wasteland known as the Dust Bowl.

Black Blizzards Modern farming methods contributed to the Dust Bowl. Mechanical farming equipment, which had made farming easier, encouraged farmers to clear huge plots of land. They removed native grasses along with the sod formed by the grass roots. This sod layer, however, had held the dry Plains soil in place. When the rains failed, the rootless soil blew away like powder. (See the Geography and History feature following this section.)

Some dust storms arose so suddenly that people called them "black blizzards." Black blizzards made noon seem like midnight, buried fences, seeped into houses, and killed people and animals. "We went to school with headlights on and with dust masks on," recalled one man.

Analyze Effects Review and analyze the effects of the Great Depression and the Dust Bowl on farmers in the Great Plains.

Okies Head West By the thousands, ruined farm families abandoned their dusty homes to seek work elsewhere. In some of the worst-hit Dust Bowl counties, as many as one family in three left. Many headed west to the rich farmlands of California.

California residents scornfully called the migrants Okies because so many had come from Oklahoma. The migratory agricultural workers found conditions in California almost as miserable as the ones they had left. Unable to buy land, they competed with local workers to pick crops at starvation wages. The police eventually closed some roads entering the state. Still, the migrants kept coming.

☑ **Checkpoint** What were the causes of the Dust Bowl?

Arts and Media of the Depression

In 1939, writer John Steinbeck captured the miseries of the Dust Bowl in *The Grapes of Wrath.* The novel tells the story of the Joads, Okies who seek a better life in California. In one scene, Ma Joad describes how her family has been shattered by hard times:

> ❝They was the time when we was on the lan'. They was a boundary to us then. Ol' folks died off, and little fellas come, an' we was always one thing—we was the fambly—kinda whole and clear. An' now we ain't clear no more. Pa's lost his place. He ain't the head no more. We're cracking up, Tom. There ain't no fambly now.❞
>
> —John Steinbeck, *The Grapes of Wrath*

Steinbeck's novel became the classic example of how American writers and artists tried to cope with the human toll of the Great Depression.

Visual Arts Photographers and painters used the Depression as a theme for their art. Under a New Deal program called the Farm Security Administration, photographer Dorothea Lange recorded the experiences of Dust Bowl migrants. Her classic photograph of a woman migrant farmworker remains the symbol of the Depression.

As you have read, the WPA hired artists to paint murals on public buildings. The realistic, colorful murals of artists such as Thomas Hart Benton paid tribute to the lives of ordinary working people.

Movies and Radio During the Depression, some movies dealt realistically with social problems. These included a 1940 movie version of *The Grapes of Wrath*. Gangster films, such as *The Public Enemy*, depicted the rise of organized crime in American cities.

Most movies of the era, however, were meant to help people forget their problems. Audiences laughed at the antics of Mickey Mouse and thrilled to the adventure fantasy *King Kong*. One of the most popular stars was Shirley Temple, a little girl who symbolized optimism in the face of trouble.

The radio was a vital part of everyday life. Families gathered in their living rooms to listen to FDR's fireside chats. For entertainment, people enjoyed popular bands and comedians. During the day, many listeners tuned in to continuing dramas sponsored by soap companies. Such serials are still known as soap operas.

Poster for the 1933 movie
King Kong

☑Checkpoint **How did movies and radio help Americans during the Great Depression?**

⭐ **Looking Back and Ahead** In this section, you saw how the Great Depression affected Americans of the time. In the next section, you will look at the lasting impact of the New Deal.

Section 3 | **Check Your Progress**

Progress Monitoring ⊙nline
For: Self-test with instant help
Visit: PHSchool.com
Web Code: mva-8233

Comprehension and Critical Thinking

1. **(a) Recall** How did Eleanor and Franklin Roosevelt differ in their position on a proposed antilynching bill?
   (b) Draw Conclusions Why might it have been difficult for FDR to push for civil rights reforms in the 1930s?

2. **(a) Describe** What caused the Dust Bowl in the 1930s?
   (b) Make Predictions What do you think finally ended Dust Bowl conditions?

🔄 Reading Skill

3. **Analyze Effects** Reread the text under the heading "Other Americans in the Depression." Analyze the effects of the Depression on Mexican Americans.

Key Terms

Answer the following questions in complete sentences that show your understanding of the key terms.

4. What is the goal of people who seek civil rights?

5. What did Mexican Americans and Okies do as migrant workers?

Writing

6. Choose one of the general topics from the list that follows. Narrow that topic down to a more specific subtopic that could be covered in a multimedia presentation of 5 minutes. List three elements for that presentation.
   - popular media of the 1930s
   - the Dust Bowl
   - the Depression and women
   - the Depression and African Americans
   - family life in the 1930s

GEOGRAPHY AND HISTORY

The Dust Bowl

As the Depression tightened its grip on the country, a new enemy stalked farmers on the Plains. Drought came in the early 1930s. Farmers had to endure great dust storms, called black blizzards, that blotted out sunlight and swept away farmland. The Great Plains became a Dust Bowl, and thousands of Americans watched as the crops failed.

Windswept soil could bury farmhouses in drifts. ▶

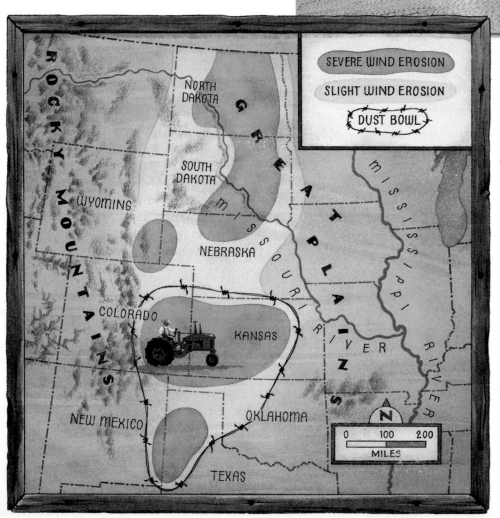

◀ Dust Bowl, 1933–1940

The Dust Bowl spanned parts of six states in the southern plains. Wind erosion wore away soil beds in Nebraska and the Dakotas as well. Dirt from these areas swept east over the Mississippi River— far enough to darken the skies over New York and Washington!

Understand Effects:
A Wave of Migrants

In the face of drought, wind, and low prices for their crops, thousands of Dust Bowl farmers lost their farms. Many headed west to California to look for work. Once they reached California, these displaced laborers often pushed African Americans, Mexican Americans, and Asian Americans out of their jobs.

The painting ▶ at right captures a Dust Bowl landscape after a pounding storm.

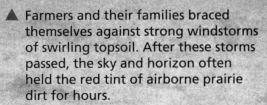

▲ Farmers and their families braced themselves against strong windstorms of swirling topsoil. After these storms passed, the sky and horizon often held the red tint of airborne prairie dirt for hours.

Analyze GEOGRAPHY AND HISTORY

Drought and high winds created terrible dust storms on the Great Plains during the 1930s. Write a journal entry describing the effects of a dust storm on a farm family.

Social Security

❝Social Security has been one of the most successful government programs. Social Security is the foundation of well being for the elderly, the disabled and their families. . . . But today Social Security faces serious long-range financing issues.❞

—James B. Lockhart III, government official testifying before Congress, 2004

◀ Her first Social Security check

Legacy of the New Deal

Objectives

- Discover how the New Deal reformed labor relations.
- Find out how Social Security began.
- Identify the main arguments for and against the New Deal.

Reading Skill

Evaluate Long-Term Effects Important historical events such as the Depression often have far-reaching effects. In fact, the Depression changed America permanently in some areas, such as its culture, political system, and economy. Read this section to identify these long-term effects. Think about how, if at all, they affect your life today.

Key Terms and People

payroll tax
Frances Perkins
collective
  bargaining
John L. Lewis
sit-down strike
deficit spending

Why It Matters FDR's New Deal programs tried to solve the immediate problems of the Great Depression. Yet programs that Roosevelt created in the 1930s had a lasting impact on the American economy and society.

❓ **Section Focus Question: What were the long-term effects of the Great Depression?**

Social Security

"Those suffering hardship from no fault of their own have a right to call upon the government for aid," FDR argued. In 1935, he signed the Social Security Act. It gave the federal government a major and lasting role in providing support for the needy.

A key part of the Social Security Act was Old-Age Insurance. It guaranteed retired people a pension. To fund the pensions, the new law imposed a **payroll tax,** or a tax that removes money directly from workers' paychecks. Employers were required to make matching contributions. Business leaders opposed Old-Age Insurance, arguing that matching payments removed too much money from the economy.

The Social Security Act included Aid to Dependent Children (ADC) to help children whose fathers were dead, unemployed, or not living with the family. The ADC granted federal money to states to help mothers stay home to raise their young children. The Social Security Act also provided financial aid to the disabled and gave the states federal money to make temporary payments to the unemployed.

At first, the Social Security Act excluded some categories of labor. Employers of agricultural and domestic workers were not required to pay into the system. As a result, many African Americans, migrant workers, and poor rural whites did not benefit from Social Security.

✓**Checkpoint** How did the Social Security Act pay for pensions for retired Americans?

Lasting Labor Reforms

The committee that drafted the Social Security Act was chaired by FDR's secretary of labor, Frances Perkins. The first woman to serve in the Cabinet, Perkins backed major labor reforms. She said that "the ideal of government should be, through legislation and through cooperation between employers and workers, to make every job the best that the human mind can devise as to physical conditions, human relations, and wages."

New Laws Favor Workers In 1935, Congress passed the National Labor Relations Act. It became known as the Wagner Act, after the New York senator who sponsored it. The Wagner Act guaranteed workers' rights to organize into unions and prohibited unfair business practices, such as firing union members.

The Wagner Act also upheld collective bargaining, or the right of a union to negotiate wages and benefits for all of its members. A new National Labor Relations Board required employers to participate in collective bargaining with unions. Largely due to the Wagner Act, union membership tripled during the 1930s.

Workers gained additional benefits with the 1938 passage of the Fair Labor Standards Act. The new law set <u>minimum</u> wages at 25 cents per hour and maximum weekly work hours at 44. It also established time-and-a-half payment for overtime work and put an end to child labor in some businesses.

A Powerful New Union In 1935, John L. Lewis, head of the United Mine Workers, formed the Committee for Industrial Organization, later renamed the Congress of Industrial Organizations (CIO). The CIO was an umbrella organization consisting of many other unions. The CIO differed from the older American Federation of Labor (AFL).

The AFL organized member unions by their skills. However, Lewis thought that organizing unions differently would give workers more bargaining power. The CIO combined all the workers in a particular industry, skilled and non-skilled alike. This policy opened up union membership to more women and African Americans, many of whom worked in unskilled positions.

In 1936, the United Auto Workers—a member union of the CIO—launched a sit-down strike at the nation's largest auto factory. In a sit-down strike, workers stay in the factory but stop production. After six weeks, the strikers won their demands for higher wages and shorter hours. The Supreme Court later ruled sit-down strikes illegal.

Vocabulary Builder
minimum (MIHN ah muhm)
adj. smallest or least required or allowed

A Sit-Down Strike
The sit-down strike was a new labor tactic in the 1930s. These auto workers are literally sitting down on the job—on unused car seats. **Critical Thinking: Evaluate Information** *Why do you think sit-down strikes were an effective means of protest?*

☑**Checkpoint** How did the Wagner Act protect workers?

Cause and Effect

CAUSES

- The gap between rich and poor Americans widens.
- Industries decline when people cannot afford new items.
- Margin buying leads to inflated stock prices.
- The stock market crashes in 1929.
- Banks fail because people cannot repay their loans.

THE GREAT DEPRESSION

EFFECTS

- Demand for goods decreases, leading to production cuts in America and Europe. Millions of people lose their jobs.
- The U.S. banking system nears collapse.
- Trade links American economy to Europe. As less U.S. money circulates abroad, businesses fail internationally.
- FDR institutes New Deal legislation to promote economic recovery; the government's role in social welfare increases.
- Totalitarian governments rise in Europe and Asia.

Reading Charts

Skills Activity

The economic collapse known as the Great Depression had multiple causes. Its effects reached every American.

(a) Interpret Charts Identify one economic cause of the Great Depression.

(b) Analyze Cause and Effect In what way are the effects of the Great Depression and the New Deal still felt today?

Scorecard on the New Deal

The Social Security Act and other reforms permanently enlarged the role of the federal government. However, not everyone agreed that the government should take such an active approach to social problems. The debate over the New Deal continues to this day.

Arguments Against the New Deal Since the 1930s, critics have charged that the New Deal gave too much power to the federal government. They argue that government programs threaten both individual freedom and free enterprise. Herbert Hoover warned:

> "Either we shall have a society based upon ordered liberty and the initiative of the individual, or we shall have a planned society that means dictation, no matter what you call it or who does it. There is no halfway ground."
>
> —Herbert Hoover, speech, June 10, 1936

Such critics favor a return to the tradition of laissez faire, which stated that the government should interfere with the economy as little as possible.

Critics of the New Deal also worried about a massive increase in the nation's debt. To pay for his programs, FDR had resorted to a policy of deficit spending. **Deficit spending** is a situation in which the government spends more money than it receives in taxes.

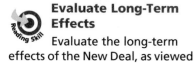

Evaluate Long-Term Effects

Evaluate the long-term effects of the New Deal, as viewed by its critics.

Finally, critics pointed out that the New Deal failed to fulfill its most <u>fundamental</u> goal. FDR's programs did not end the Great Depression. Full economic recovery would not come until 1941, when the United States began producing goods in preparation for entering a new world war.

Arguments for the New Deal Supporters of the New Deal pointed out that FDR's active approach eased many problems. It employed millions of jobless people, ended the banking crisis, reformed the stock market, saved poor families from losing their homes, and improved working conditions. New Deal programs built dams and bridges, preserved 12 million acres of national parkland, brought electricity to rural America, and sponsored the creation of lasting works of art.

For many Americans, the New Deal restored their faith in government. They felt that their government would take care of them. Franklin and Eleanor Roosevelt received millions of letters from admirers. One writer said, "I have always felt like you and your wife and your children were as common as we were." In countless homes, FDR's picture held a place of honor.

☑**Checkpoint** Summarize one argument against the New Deal.

☆ **Looking Back and Ahead** Admirers of the New Deal said that people's faith in FDR helped American democracy survive the Great Depression. By contrast, several nations in Europe and Asia turned from democracy to dictatorship. In the next chapter, you will see how the rise of dictators led to World War II.

Eleanor and Franklin Roosevelt

Section 4 | **Check Your Progress**

Comprehension and Critical Thinking

1. **(a) Identify** What were the main provisions of the Social Security Act?
   (b) Link Past and Present Why is Social Security still important today?

2. **(a) Describe** How was the organization of the CIO different from that of the AFL?
   (b) Identify Benefits How might the organization of the CIO have made it more effective in negotiating with companies on behalf of workers?

🔄 **Reading Skill**

3. **Evaluate Long-Term Effects** Reread "Arguments for the New Deal" on this page. Evaluate the long-term effects of the program, as viewed by its supporters.

Key Terms

Complete each of the following sentences so that the second part further explains the first part and clearly shows your understanding of the key term.

4. Union and company representatives sit down together in collective bargaining, _____.

5. Many people fear a government might hurt the economy through deficit spending, _____.

6. Social Security was funded by a payroll tax, _____.

Writing

7. Create a two-column checklist for a multimedia presentation on a topic from this section. Insert the topic at the top of the checklist. In the left column, list three of these media types: Music; Videos/DVDs; Art; Photographs; Computer Presentations; Interviews. In the right column, describe specific materials you would explore for each type. For example: Interviews (*left column*); Talk to grandmother about Social Security (*right column*).

21st Century Learning Often, paintings and drawings include important evidence about daily life during a particular historical period. Studying works of art helps us draw conclusions about the society that created the art.

Unemployment, by Ben Shahn

Learn the Skill
Use these steps to analyze art.

1 **Identify the subject and artist.** The title or caption often identifies the subject and artist. Details in the painting may also tell you who or what is being shown.

2 **Analyze the details in the work of art.** Look for the most important details to help you identify the focus of the painting.

3 **Draw conclusions based on the work of art.** Use information provided by the work of art and your own knowledge of the period or event. Does the art convey a particular mood or point of view? What can you conclude about the values and culture of the people who lived in that society?

Practice the Skill
Answer the following questions about the mural on this page.

1 **Identify the subject and artist.** (a) What is the title of the mural? (b) Who is the artist? (c) What is the subject matter?

2 **Analyze the details in the work of art.** (a) Who are the people shown in this mural? (b) What are they doing? (c) What details in the mural attract your attention the most?

3 **Draw conclusions based on the work of art.** (a) What mood or feeling is created by this mural? (b) What does this mural show you about American society during this period? (c) What is the artist's point of view about the subject?

Apply the Skill
See the Review and Assessment at the end of this chapter.

How did the Great Depression affect the American people and change the role of government?

Section 1
Hoover and the Crash

- The stock market crash in October 1929 marked the start of the Great Depression.
- Causes of the Depression included overproduction and a banking crisis.
- Unemployment led to widespread misery.
- President Hoover believed business and local government should lead the way out of the Depression.

Section 2
Roosevelt and the New Deal

- In 1933, President Roosevelt launched the New Deal, an ambitious program to bring relief to the jobless, spur economic recovery, and prevent future depressions.
- The Supreme Court overturned several major New Deal measures.
- Some critics felt that the New Deal did not do enough to improve conditions.

Section 3
Life in the Great Depression

- Women, African Americans, and Mexican Americans faced special challenges during the Depression.
- Droughts in the early 1930s turned much of the Plains region into a Dust Bowl.
- Painters, photographers, and writers in the 1930s depicted hard times in their works.

Section 4
Legacy of the New Deal

- The Social Security Act offered assistance to older Americans and others.
- Labor reforms and the founding of the CIO increased the power of unions.
- Critics of the New Deal feared it made the government too powerful, while supporters believed it strengthened faith in the democratic system.

Exploring the Essential Question

Use the online study guide to explore the essential question.

Section 1
Why did the economy collapse after the stock market crash?

Chapter 23 Essential Question
How did the Great Depression affect the American people and change the role of government?

Section 2
How did President Roosevelt respond to the Great Depression?

Section 4
What were the long-term effects of the Great Depression?

Section 3
How did the Great Depression affect daily life?

Key Terms

Read each sentence below. If the sentence is true, write YES. If the sentence is not true, write NO and explain why.

1. The company declared bankruptcy to celebrate profits from selling stock.

2. European countries defaulted on loans, paying off their debts early.

3. His pension provided him with an income after he retired.

4. By spending more money than it took in, the government practiced deficit spending.

5. Migrant workers built permanent homes in the communities where they worked.

Comprehension and Critical Thinking

6. (a) **Summarize** What were the causes of the stock market crash of 1929?
(b) **Analyze Cause and Effect** How did the crash contribute to increased unemployment?
(c) **Apply Information** What measures did Roosevelt take to prevent another crash?

7. (a) **Recall** Why did Americans buy fewer and fewer cars and homes in the late 1920s?
(b) **Analyze Cause and Effect** How did that trend contribute to the Great Depression?

8. (a) **Recall** How did Hoover propose to handle the economic crisis?
(b) **Contrast** How did Roosevelt's approach differ from Hoover's?
(c) **Evaluate Information** Why do you think more Americans responded favorably to Roosevelt's approach than to Hoover's?

9. (a) **Recall** How did the Great Depression affect women? African Americans? Mexican Americans?

(b) **Compare and Contrast** How were Depression experiences similar for all three groups? How were they different?

10. (a) **Describe** How did writers and artists tell the story of Americans during the Depression?
(b) **Contrast** What approaches did the movies take toward the Depression?
(c) **Identify Benefits** Which approach do you think benefited Americans more? Explain.

11. (a) **List** How did Americans benefit from the Social Security Act of 1935?
(b) **Analyze Cause and Effect** Why do you suppose legislators saw a need to pass the act?

Reading Skill

12. **Analyze Cause and Effect** Which effect of the Depression do you think was most devastating? Which effect do you think has caused the greatest change to today's world?

Writing

13. **Plan your research for a short multimedia presentation about one of the following topics:**
   • Contrast Herbert Hoover and Franklin Roosevelt.
   • Show how the New Deal changed daily life.
   • Describe American arts and media in the 1930s.

   Your plan should:
   • narrow the issue into a topic that can be covered in a short multimedia presentation;
   • include a media checklist for that topic;
   • end with a few sentences describing the presentation you would like to create.

14. **Write a Narrative:**
   Write a short narrative describing an argument between two friends in the 1930s who have very different feelings about FDR and the New Deal.

Skills for Life
Analyze Art

Use the painting by William Gropper in Section 3 to answer the questions.

15. (a) What is the title of the painting? (b) Who is the artist? (c) When was the mural painted?

16. (a) What are the people doing? (b) What details attract your attention the most?

17. (a) What mood is created by this painting?
(b) What does it illustrate about American government during this period?

Test Yourself

1. Which New Deal program met the goal of providing jobs for the unemployed?

A Civilian Conservation Corps

B National Recovery Administration

C Social Security Act

D Federal Deposit Insurance Corporation

2. Conservative critics argued that the New Deal

A did too little to help the poor.

B made the federal government too powerful.

C relied too much on private action.

D was unfair to migrant workers.

3. How did margin buying contribute to the stock market crash of October 1929?

A It made it harder to buy stocks.

B It slowed down production of goods.

C It encouraged risky investments.

D It led to deficit spending.

Refer to the graph below to answer Question 4.

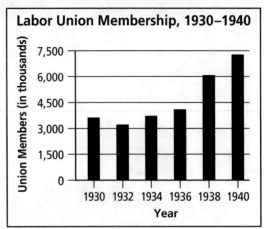

Source: *Historical Statistics of the United States*

4. Which of the following contributed most directly to the trend shown on this graph?

A the Wagner Act

B the Social Security Act

C the National Recovery Act

D the bank holiday

Document-Based Questions

Task: Look at Documents 1 and 2, and answer their accompanying questions. Then, use the documents and your knowledge of history to complete this writing assignment:

Draw a conclusion about whether the New Deal succeeded in meeting Roosevelt's employment goals.

Document 1: In 1933, President Roosevelt asked Congress to take action to ease the crisis. *What three measures did Roosevelt propose?*

"It is essential . . . that measures immediately be enacted aimed at unemployment relief. . . . The first is the enrollment of workers . . . by the Federal Government for . . . public employment. . . . The second is grants to States for relief work. The third extends to a broad public works labor-creating program. . . .

The first of these measures . . . can and should be immediately enacted. I propose to create a civilian conservation corps to be used in . . . forestry, prevention of soil erosion, . . . and similar projects. . . . I estimate that 250,000 men can be given temporary employment by early summer."

—Franklin Roosevelt, March 21, 1933

Document 2: The graph below shows the percentage of American workers who were unemployed between 1933 and 1941. *What trends in unemployment do you see in the graph?*

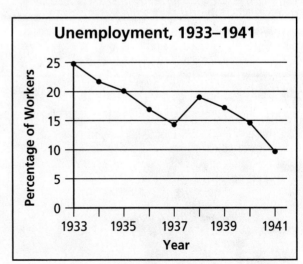

Source: *Historical Statistics of the United States*

Chapter Review and Assessment 797

The World War II Era

1935–1945

CHAPTER 24

> *"I call upon all who love freedom to stand with us now. Together we shall achieve victory."*
>
> —General Dwight D. Eisenhower, radio broadcast on D-Day, June 6, 1944

American soldiers land on the beaches of France on D-Day—June 6, 1944.

CHAPTER 71

What You Will Learn

Section 1
AGGRESSION LEADS TO WAR
In the 1930s, dictators in Germany, Italy, and Japan tried to conquer neighboring nations, sparking a new world war.

Section 2
THE UNITED STATES AT WAR
The United States entered the war after Japanese airplanes bombed the American fleet at Pearl Harbor.

Section 3
THE WAR AT HOME
As the United States organized to win the war, women gained new opportunities, but Japanese Americans faced harsh restrictions.

Section 4
TOWARD VICTORY
The D-Day invasion of France was the first step to final victory in Europe, and the dropping of the atomic bomb brought the war in the Pacific to an end.

Reading Skill
Determine Meanings From Context
In this chapter, you will practice using context and word clues to understand unfamiliar passages in a text.

The World War II Era, 1935–1945

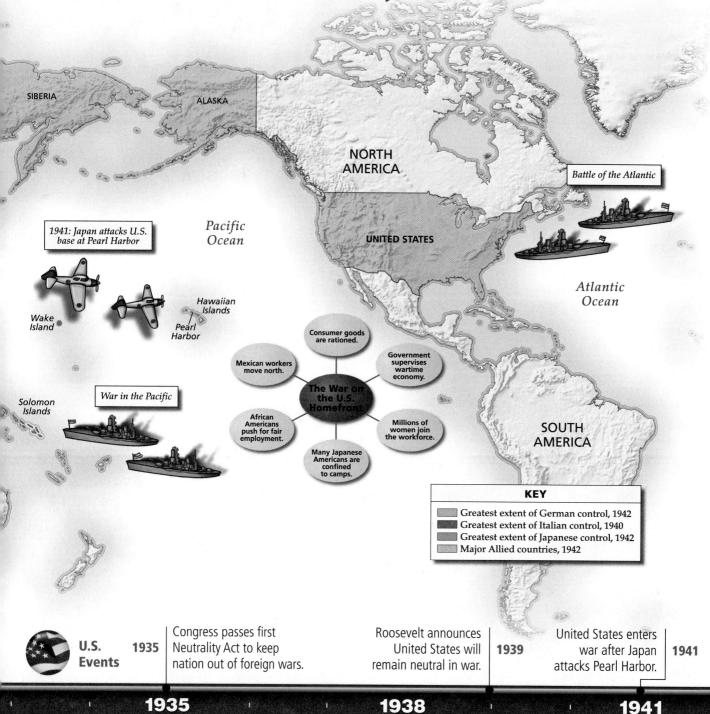

SIBERIA

ALASKA

NORTH AMERICA

UNITED STATES

Pacific Ocean

Battle of the Atlantic

1941: Japan attacks U.S. base at Pearl Harbor

Atlantic Ocean

Wake Island

Hawaiian Islands

Pearl Harbor

War in the Pacific

Solomon Islands

The War on the U.S. Homefront

- Consumer goods are rationed.
- Mexican workers move north.
- Government supervises wartime economy.
- African Americans push for fair employment.
- Many Japanese Americans are confined to camps.
- Millions of women join the workforce.

SOUTH AMERICA

KEY

- Greatest extent of German control, 1942
- Greatest extent of Italian control, 1940
- Greatest extent of Japanese control, 1942
- Major Allied countries, 1942

| U.S. Events | 1935 | Congress passes first Neutrality Act to keep nation out of foreign wars. | Roosevelt announces United States will remain neutral in war. | 1939 | United States enters war after Japan attacks Pearl Harbor. | 1941 |

1935   **1938**   **1941**

| World Events | 1935 | Italy invades Ethiopia. | 1937 | Japan invades China. | 1939 | Germany invades Poland; World War II begins. |

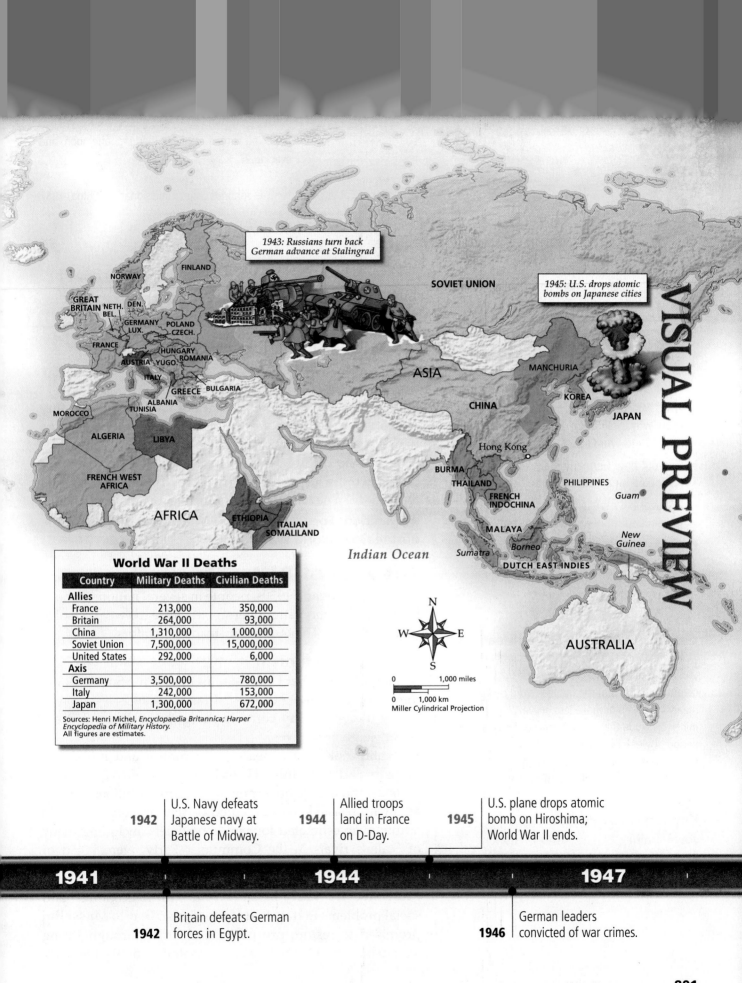

1943: Russians turn back German advance at Stalingrad

1945: U.S. drops atomic bombs on Japanese cities

NORWAY
FINLAND
SOVIET UNION
GREAT BRITAIN
NETH.
DEN.
BEL.
GERMANY
LUX.
POLAND
CZECH.
FRANCE
AUSTRIA
HUNGARY
YUGO.
ROMANIA
ITALY
GREECE
BULGARIA
ALBANIA
TUNISIA
MOROCCO
ALGERIA
LIBYA
ASIA
MANCHURIA
CHINA
KOREA
JAPAN
Hong Kong
BURMA
THAILAND
FRENCH INDOCHINA
PHILIPPINES
Guam
FRENCH WEST AFRICA
AFRICA
ETHIOPIA
ITALIAN SOMALILAND
MALAYA
Sumatra
Borneo
New Guinea
DUTCH EAST INDIES
Indian Ocean
AUSTRALIA

N W E S
0 — 1,000 miles
0 — 1,000 km
Miller Cylindrical Projection

World War II Deaths		
Country	Military Deaths	Civilian Deaths
Allies		
France	213,000	350,000
Britain	264,000	93,000
China	1,310,000	1,000,000
Soviet Union	7,500,000	15,000,000
United States	292,000	6,000
Axis		
Germany	3,500,000	780,000
Italy	242,000	153,000
Japan	1,300,000	672,000

Sources: Henri Michel, *Encyclopaedia Britannica; Harper Encyclopedia of Military History.*
All figures are estimates.

1942 — U.S. Navy defeats Japanese navy at Battle of Midway.

1944 — Allied troops land in France on D-Day.

1945 — U.S. plane drops atomic bomb on Hiroshima; World War II ends.

1941   **1944**   **1947**

1942 — Britain defeats German forces in Egypt.

1946 — German leaders convicted of war crimes.

Japanese Aggression in China
"Those who are suspected of being soldiers, as well as others, have been led outside the city and shot down by the hundreds—yes, thousands. . . . Women are being carried off every morning, afternoon, and evening."

—John McCallum, missionary in China, 1937

▲ Victorious Japanese troops near Nanjing, China, 1937

Aggression Leads to War

Objectives

- Learn why totalitarian dictators gained power after World War I.

- Find out how Germany, Italy, and Japan embarked on a path of military conquest.

- Discover how the United States tried to remain neutral in a new world conflict.

- Understand how World War II began in Europe.

🎯 Reading Skill

Use Word Clues to Analyze Meaning

Start with word clues when you encounter an unfamiliar term such as *economic depression.* It is helpful to know that the familiar word *depress* means "weaken or make less active." Then, you might conclude that an economic depression is a period of weak or less active economy. Finally, learn about a word from its place in a sentence. A verb, for example, will describe an action.

Key Terms and People

Josef Stalin
totalitarian state
Benito Mussolini
fascism

Adolf Hitler
aggression
appeasement
Winston Churchill

Why It Matters The early decades of the twentieth century saw a series of major world crises. World War I and the Russian Revolution destroyed millions of lives and altered the political map of Europe. The Great Depression of the 1930s caused worldwide economic hardship. These conditions set the stage for a new and more destructive world war.

❓ Section Focus Question: What events led to the outbreak of World War II?

The Rise of Dictators

In the 1920s and 1930s, people in several nations came to believe that democratic governments were too weak to solve their problems. They turned instead to dictators.

Soviet Communism By 1929, Josef Stalin was sole dictator of the Soviet Union. Stalin turned the Soviet Union into a totalitarian state. A totalitarian state is a nation in which a single party controls the government and every aspect of people's lives.

Stalin took brutal measures to control and modernize industry and agriculture. He ordered peasants to give crops, animals, and land to government-run farms. Millions of peasants who resisted were executed or sent to labor camps. In addition, an estimated four million Soviets, including many of Stalin's rivals in the Communist Party, were killed or imprisoned on false charges of disloyalty to the state.

Fascism in Italy After World War I, economic and social problems in Italy had led to unrest. Benito Mussolini promised to restore prosperity and order through strong leadership. In October 1922, Mussolini and his followers threatened to overthrow Italy's elected government. In response, the king appointed Mussolini prime minister.

Mussolini turned Italy into the world's first Fascist state. **Fascism is a political system based on militarism, extreme nationalism, and blind loyalty to the state and its leader.** Italy, he said, was a <u>superior</u> nation with a glorious destiny. He spoke of reviving the days when the Roman Empire dominated Europe. He also argued that a superior nation had a right and duty to conquer <u>inferior</u> nations.

Mussolini ended freedom of the press and banned all political parties except his own. Critics were jailed or murdered. In schools, children recited the motto "Mussolini is always right."

Nazi Germany Many Germans were angry over their defeat in World War I and the heavy reparation payments forced on them by the Allies. Among them was an extreme nationalist, Adolf Hitler. By 1921, Hitler had become leader of a small group known as the National Socialist, or Nazi, Party. Nazism was a form of fascism.

Racism lay at the core of Nazi beliefs. Hitler told Germans that they were a "master race," destined to rule over Slavs, Gypsies, and others they considered inferior. The cornerstone of Hitler's racial theories was anti-Semitism, or hatred of Jews. Hitler falsely claimed that Germany had not lost World War I but had been betrayed by Jews and other "traitors." This idea appealed to Germans eager to find a scapegoat, someone on whom to blame their problems.

The Great Depression increased Hitler's popularity. In 1933, he was named chancellor, or leader of the German parliament. Once in power, Hitler quickly created a totalitarian state. All other parties were outlawed. Hitler's secret police enforced strict loyalty.

Germany also passed anti-Semitic laws. Jews were banned from public schools and from professions such as medicine and law. Jewish communities were attacked. In 1938, troops began rounding up Jews and sending them to slave labor camps. But even worse was to come, as you will see.

Vocabulary Builder
<u>superior</u> (soo PIR ee uhr) **adj.** of greater importance or value; of higher quality
<u>inferior</u> (ihn FIR ee uhr) **adj.** of lower rank or status; of poorer quality

Two Fascist Dictators
The Nazi propaganda poster (left) glorifies Adolf Hitler, dictator of Germany. At right, Italian dictator Benito Mussolini strikes a proud pose while standing atop a tank.
Critical Thinking: *Evaluate Information How does the propaganda poster create a heroic image of Hitler?*

CHIESA

Reading Skill

Use Word Clues to Analyze Meaning Use a familiar base word and ending to analyze the meaning of *militarism*.

Militarism in Japan In Japan, too, the Great Depression undermined faith in democratic rule. Military leaders pressured the civilian government to take control of nearby countries. Militarists argued that their island nation needed more space, as well as raw materials for its booming industries.

By 1936, militarists were in complete control of the Japanese government. Like the Nazis in Germany, Japanese militarists preached racism. The Japanese, they said, were superior to other Asians as well as non-Asians.

☑**Checkpoint** **How did the Great Depression aid Hitler?**

Military Aggression

Italy, Germany, and Japan each followed policies of ruthless aggression. **Aggression** is a warlike act by one country against another without cause.

Japan Attacks China In 1931, acting without the approval of Japan's elected government, the Japanese army seized Manchuria in northeastern China. The League of Nations, which had been founded to halt aggression, protested but took no action.

After 1937, Japan stepped up its aggression in China. Japanese armies treated the Chinese brutally. For six weeks, Japanese forces pillaged the Chinese city of Nanjing. In the assault, more than a quarter of a million civilians and prisoners of war were massacred.

Italy Invades Ethiopia In 1935, Mussolini's armies invaded the African country of Ethiopia. Though the Ethiopians fought bravely, their cavalry and outdated rifles were no match for Italy's modern tanks and airplanes.

Ethiopia's emperor, Haile Selassie (Hī lee suh LAS ee), appealed to the League of Nations for aid. However, the League responded weakly. Britain and France were weary of war and caught up in their own economic crises. Without help, Ethiopia fell to the invaders.

German Aggression Hitler vowed to create an empire that united all German-speaking people, including those outside Germany. In defiance of the Treaty of Versailles, he began to rebuild Germany's armed forces. He further defied the treaty by sending troops into the Rhineland region of western Germany in 1936. Two years later, German armies occupied Austria. As Hitler predicted, the European democracies did nothing to stop him.

Still, France and Britain protested when Hitler threatened to invade Czechoslovakia. In September 1938, European leaders met in the German city of Munich to ease the crisis. The leaders of France and Britain hoped to appease Hitler. **Appeasement** is a policy of giving in to aggression in order to avoid war.

In the Munich Pact, Britain and France agreed to let the German leader occupy the Sudetenland (soo DET ehn land), a portion of Czechoslovakia populated largely by people who spoke German. In return, Hitler promised he would seek no further territory.

Haile Selassie addressing the League of Nations

Aggression in Europe to 1939

KEY
- Areas taken over by Germany by September 1939
- Areas taken over by Italy by September 1939
- Areas taken over by the Soviet Union by September 1939

0 km 400
0 miles 400
Azimuthal Equal-Area Projection

NORWAY
SWEDEN
FINLAND
ESTONIA
LATVIA
LITHUANIA
IRELAND
DENMARK
GREAT BRITAIN
North Sea
Baltic Sea
GER.
SOVIET UNION
NETH.
GERMANY
POLAND (Sept. 1939)
BELG.
Rhineland (March 1936)
CZECHOSLOVAKIA (March 1939)
LUX.
Saar Basin
Sudetenland (Sept. 1938)
AUSTRIA (March 1938)
FRANCE
SWITZ.
HUNGARY
ROMANIA
YUGOSLAVIA
ATLANTIC OCEAN
PORTUGAL
SPAIN
Corsica
ITALY
BULGARIA
Sardinia
ALBANIA (April 1939)
GREECE
TURKEY
Sicily
To Ethiopia (1935)
Dodecanese Is. (It.)
Mediterranean Sea
AFRICA

MAP MASTER
Skills Activity

In the late 1930s, aggressive acts by Italy and Germany threatened the peace of Europe and the world.

(a) Interpret a Map What was the earliest act of aggression shown on the map?

(b) Apply Information Based on the map and your reading, describe what happened to Czechoslovakia.

MapMaster Online

For: Interactive map
Visit: PHSchool.com
Web Code: mvp-8241

The British prime minister, Neville Chamberlain, returned from the Munich meeting announcing that he had won "peace for our time." But only a few months later, in March 1939, Hitler occupied the remainder of Czechoslovakia.

☑**Checkpoint** **How did the League of Nations respond to Italian and Japanese aggression?**

American Neutrality

As you have seen, after World War I, the United States returned to a policy of isolationism. As aggression threatened to bring the world to war again, Americans were determined to avoid getting involved.

Neutrality Act In 1935, Congress passed the Neutrality Act. It was the first of several laws designed to keep the United States at peace. The Neutrality Act forbade the President from selling arms, making loans, or giving any other kind of assistance to any nation involved in war.

Good Neighbor Policy At the same time, the United States sought to strengthen ties to Latin America. In 1930, President Herbert Hoover rejected the Roosevelt Corollary to the Monroe Doctrine. The United States, he declared, no longer claimed the right to intervene in Latin American affairs.

Franklin Roosevelt went even further. Under what he called the Good Neighbor Policy, he withdrew American troops from Nicaragua and Haiti. He also cancelled the Platt Amendment, which had limited the independence of Cuba.

☑**Checkpoint** **What was the goal of the Neutrality Act?**

War Begins in Europe

Meanwhile, in Europe, Poland loomed as Hitler's next target. France and Britain now realized that the policy of appeasement had failed. They promised to come to Poland's aid if Germany invaded Poland.

Invasion of Poland In late August 1939, the world was shocked to learn that Hitler and Stalin—two sworn and bitter enemies—had signed a nonaggression agreement. In the Nazi-Soviet Pact, the two dictators promised not to attack one another's countries. Secretly, they agreed to divide up Poland.

On September 1, 1939, Nazi troops invaded Poland. Sixteen days later, the Soviet Union seized eastern Poland. Stalin's forces also invaded Finland and later annexed Estonia, Lithuania, and Latvia.

Two days after Hitler's invasion of Poland, Britain and France declared war on Germany. World War II had begun.

In the early days of the war, Hitler's armies seemed unstoppable. In April 1940, they moved north, seizing Denmark and Norway. In May, they marched west to conquer the Netherlands, Luxembourg, and Belgium. They then moved into France.

Fall of France Britain sent troops to help France resist the assault. The British and French, however, were quickly overpowered. By May, the Germans had forced them to retreat to Dunkirk, a French port on the English Channel. In a bold action, the British sent every available ship and boat across the channel to rescue the trapped soldiers.

Unhindered, German armies entered France and marched on to Paris, the French capital. On June 22, 1940, barely six weeks later, Hitler gleefully accepted the surrender of France.

The Bombing of London
For months, German planes bombed London and other British cities. Here, a group of London women sit outside the rubble of their homes. **Critical Thinking: Draw Conclusions** *Do you think the constant bombing attacks weakened or strengthened the British people? Explain.*

Battle of Britain Now, Britain stood alone against the Nazi war machine. Few thought the island nation stood a chance. Still, Winston Churchill, the British prime minister, expressed confidence:

“We shall defend our island whatever the cost may be, we shall fight on the beaches . . . we shall fight in the fields and in the streets, we shall fight in the hills. We shall never surrender.”

—Winston Churchill, speech, June 4, 1940

Hitler ordered an air assault on Britain. Day after day, German planes attacked British cities. The raids took tens of thousands of lives, yet the British spirit never broke. By night, Londoners slept in subway stations. By day, they cleared the wreckage, buried the dead, and tried to carry on. Overhead, the British air force fought invading planes. The Battle of Britain continued through the summer and into the fall. By then, Hitler had abandoned all plans to invade Britain.

Invasion of the Soviet Union On June 22, 1941, Hitler broke his pact with Stalin. A huge German force crossed into the Soviet Union. The Soviet Union, which had remained out of the early days of the war, now joined Britain in fighting the Germans. Although Churchill and Stalin deeply mistrusted each other, they were now forced to work together to defeat their common enemy.

✓**Checkpoint** **What was the Nazi-Soviet Pact of 1939?**

☆ **Looking Back and Ahead** Only 20 years after the end of World War I, the world was once again plunged into conflict. As you will see, World War II would be even more destructive.

Section 1 | **Check Your Progress**

Progress Monitoring ⦿nline
For: Self-test with instant help
Visit: PHSchool.com
Web Code: mva-8241

Comprehension and Critical Thinking

1. **(a) Describe** What kind of government did Hitler set up in Germany?
(b) Compare How was Nazi Germany similar to the Soviet Union under Stalin?

2. **(a) Recall** How did France and Britain respond to Nazi aggression?
(b) Draw Conclusions Do you think France and Britain could have prevented World War II if they had acted differently? Why or why not?

⊙ **Reading Skill**

3. **Use Word Clues to Analyze Meaning** Explain how the root parts of the word *totalitarian* help you understand the meaning of the word.

Key Terms

Answer the following questions in complete sentences that show your understanding of the key terms.

4. How does a totalitarian state such as Nazi Germany differ from a democratic nation such as the United States?

5. What are the main features of fascism?

6. How did Germany, Italy, and Japan practice aggression?

7. How was the Munich Pact an example of appeasement?

Writing

8. Use library or Internet resources to find more information about one of the topics in this section. Suggestions for topics include Mussolini and fascism, the rise of Hitler, the invasion of Poland, Winston Churchill, and the Battle of Britain. Identify at least three sources of nonprint material on the topic. List the sources you find and describe their contents.

◄ Franklin D. Roosevelt (left) and Winston Churchill (right)

The Struggle for Freedom

❝Freedom means the supremacy of human rights everywhere. Our support goes to those who struggle to gain those rights or keep them. . . . To that high concept there can be no end save victory. ❞

—Franklin Delano Roosevelt, "The Four Freedoms," speech delivered January 6, 1941

The United States at War

Objectives
- Understand how the United States prepared for war and strengthened its ties with the Allies.
- Discover why the United States finally entered World War II.
- Learn how, after many early setbacks, the Allies began to turn the tide of battle in North Africa and the Pacific.

🔁 Reading Skill

Use Sentence Clues to Analyze Meaning After studying a word, look in the sentence for clues to its meaning. For example, you may find descriptions of what a verb does, examples of a noun, or details that explain an adjective.

Key Terms and People

total war
Dwight D.
    Eisenhower

Douglas
    MacArthur

Why It Matters When World War II began, the United States tried to remain neutral. But most Americans opposed dictatorships and aggression. The United States built up its military and sent aid to Great Britain. Finally, in 1941, a Japanese attack on U.S. soil brought America into the war.

❓ Section Focus Question: How did the United States move from neutrality to full involvement in the war?

Moving Toward War

In 1940, President Roosevelt sought reelection to a third term. His decision broke the precedent set by George Washington that Presidents serve only two terms. Roosevelt promised to maintain American neutrality. He told voters, "Your boys are not going to be sent into any foreign wars." FDR won reelection easily.

Lend-Lease Act Roosevelt sympathized with the Allies. Even before Roosevelt had started campaigning, Winston Churchill had appealed to him for military aid. Selling war supplies to Britain would violate the Neutrality Acts. Still, Roosevelt reached a compromise with Congress. The United States could sell supplies to Britain, but Britain would have to pay cash for all goods it received.

However, by the end of 1940, Britain's treasury was empty. Fearing that Britain would fall to the Nazis, Roosevelt persuaded Congress to pass a law he called Lend-Lease. It allowed the United States to lend or lease supplies to Britain and other nations fighting the Nazis. Isolationists objected that the law would draw the United States into war. Most Americans, however, favored the plan.

Lend-Lease convoys soon began moving across the Atlantic. Later, the Lend-Lease arrangement was extended to China and the Soviet Union. Under Lend-Lease, the United States became, in Roosevelt's words, "the great arsenal of democracy."

Military Buildup The United States prepared for possible entry into the war. Congress approved greater spending for the army and navy. In September 1940, it passed a law that set up the first peacetime draft in American history.

Roosevelt took another unprecedented step in 1940. He ordered the Army Air Corps to organize an African American unit under the command of black officers. A flight training program was set up at Tuskegee Army Air Field in Alabama. The Tuskegee Airmen would later compile a superb combat record.

Atlantic Charter In August 1941, Roosevelt and Churchill issued the Atlantic Charter, outlining their goals for the postwar world. They agreed that their nations would seek no territorial gain from the war and <u>emphasized</u> the right of all people to choose their own government. They also called for a new international organization that might succeed where the League of Nations had failed.

Vocabulary Builder
<u>emphasize</u> (EHM fah sīz) **v.** to stress; to give particular importance to

✓**Checkpoint** **What was the Lend-Lease Act of 1941?**

The United States Enters the War

Events in Asia, not Europe, finally drew the United States into war. In July 1941, Japan invaded the French colony of Indochina (present-day Vietnam, Laos, and Cambodia). In response, Roosevelt banned American exports of iron and steel scrap to Japan. He also restricted the sale of oil to Japan.

Facing a shortage of fuel for their navy, Japanese leaders decided on war. Plans for an attack on the United States were soon underway.

The Tuskegee Airmen

"My own opinion was that blacks could best overcome racist attitudes through their achievements, even though those achievements had to take place within the hateful environment of segregation.... The coming war represented a golden opportunity.... We owned a fighter squadron—something that would have been unthinkable only a short time earlier. It was all ours.... Furthermore, we would be required to analyze our own problems and solve them with our own skills."

—Benjamin O. Davis, Jr., *Benjamin O. Davis, Jr., American*

Benjamin Davis at Tuskegee

Reading Primary Sources

〉 **Skills Activity** 〉

Benjamin O. Davis, Jr., commanded the Tuskegee Airmen and later became the first African American general in the Air Force. Here, he describes his feelings about the formation of the flying program.

(a) Detect Points of View How does Davis feel about segregation?

(b) Identify Benefits How does Davis think African Americans might benefit from the United States entering World War II?

Attack on PEARL HARBOR

History *Interactive*

**Learn About
Pearl Harbor**

Visit: PHSchool.com
Web Code: mvl-8242

President Roosevelt called December 7, 1941, "a day that will live in infamy." The attack on Pearl Harbor shocked Americans and propelled the United States into the most extensive war in history. **Critical Thinking: Link Past and Present** *How was the reaction to Pearl Harbor similar to the reaction to terrorist attacks on the United States in our time?*

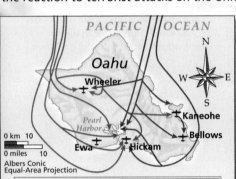

PACIFIC OCEAN

Oahu

Wheeler

Kaneohe

Pearl Harbor

Bellows

Ewa   Hickam

0 km   10
0 miles   10
Albers Conic
Equal-Area Projection

KEY

⟶ Aircraft of the first wave, 7:55 A.M.

⟶ Aircraft of the second wave, 8:54 A.M.

✠ American airfield

EXTRA
RACE RESULTS Los Angeles Times **NIGHT Pictorial**

IT'S WAR!

**Hostilities Declared by Japanese;
350 Reported Killed in Hawaii Raid**

U.S. Battleships Hit;
7 Die in Honolulu

LATE WAR BULLETINS

Air Bombs Rained
on Pacific Bases

▲ Newspaper headlines blared "The nation is now at war!" "Remember Pearl Harbor" became the nation's battle cry.

▲ At Pearl Harbor, the peace of a Sunday morning was shattered by Japanese bombers.

▲ Coming in two waves, the attack destroyed or seriously damaged much of the American fleet and killed thousands of Americans.

Pearl Harbor On December 7, 1941, Japanese bombers launched a surprise attack on American naval, air, and ground forces at Pearl Harbor, on the Hawaiian island of Oahu (oh AH hoo). The attack destroyed nearly half of the island's 400 military aircraft and damaged 8 battleships, two beyond repair. About 2,400 Americans were killed.

The assault on Pearl Harbor caught American military leaders by surprise. Though aware of the possibility of a Japanese attack, they did not expect the attack to come as far east as Hawaii.

The next day, a grave President Roosevelt addressed Congress.

> **"**Yesterday, December 7, 1941, a date which will live in infamy, the United States of America was suddenly and deliberately attacked by naval and air forces of the Empire of Japan.**"**
>
> —Franklin Roosevelt, speech, December 8, 1941

Use Sentence Clues to Analyze Meaning What happened on the "day of infamy"? How did Roosevelt react to the event? What does *infamy* mean?

Later that day, Congress declared war on Japan. Japan's allies, Germany and Italy, then declared war on the United States. Against their wishes, Americans were again involved in a world war.

A Global Conflict Even more than World War I, World War II was truly a global conflict. On one side were the Axis powers, an alliance made up of Germany, Italy, Japan, and six other nations. Opposing the Axis powers were the Allied powers. Before the war was over, the Allied powers would include Britain, France, the Soviet Union, the United States, China, and 45 other countries.

More than any war before it, World War II was a total war. **Total war** is conflict involving not just armies but entire nations. Countries on each side put all their resources into the war effort. Civilian populations often became targets of bombings.

☑**Checkpoint** Why did Japan attack United States forces?

Europe and North Africa

In early 1942, the Allies faced a bleak situation on all fronts. Germany controlled most of Western Europe. Although Britain had not fallen, it was powerless to challenge the Nazi position on the continent. In Eastern Europe, the Nazis had advanced deep into Soviet territory. Soviet losses numbered in the millions. Still, in 1942, the <u>pendulum</u> began to swing in the Allies' favor.

The Soviets Resist Hitler had expected the Soviet Union to collapse swiftly in the face of his ferocious assault. But in December 1941, Soviet troops—assisted by the brutal Russian winter—halted the German advance just miles from Moscow.

The Germans mounted another offensive in mid-1942. A major battle took place in and around the Russian city of Stalingrad. Months of bitter fighting ended in a clear Soviet victory. From then on, the Soviets slowly drove the Germans back westward.

Vocabulary Builder
<u>pendulum</u> (PEHN jah luhm) **n.** hanging weight that swings from side to side in a steady rhythm

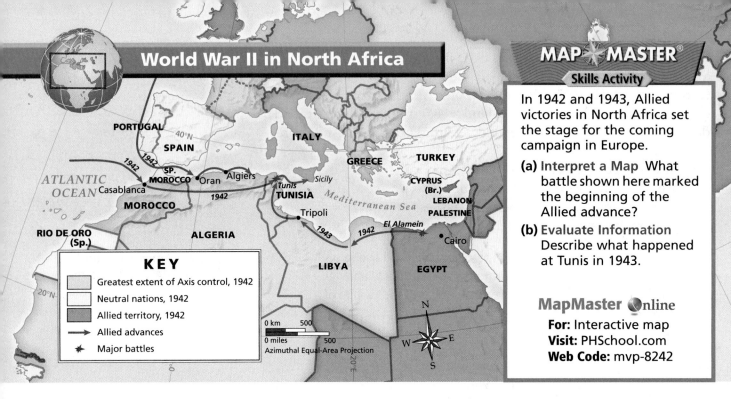

KEY

- Greatest extent of Axis control, 1942
- Neutral nations, 1942
- Allied territory, 1942
- → Allied advances
- ✶ Major battles

0 km 500
0 miles 500
Azimuthal Equal-Area Projection

MAP★MASTER®

Skills Activity

In 1942 and 1943, Allied victories in North Africa set the stage for the coming campaign in Europe.

(a) Interpret a Map What battle shown here marked the beginning of the Allied advance?

(b) Evaluate Information Describe what happened at Tunis in 1943.

MapMaster ⦾nline

For: Interactive map
Visit: PHSchool.com
Web Code: mvp-8242

The Tide Turns in North Africa In North Africa, Erwin Rommel, Germany's most respected general, won a number of quick victories. Then, in October 1942, British troops defeated German forces at El Alamein (el AL uh mayn) in Egypt. Slowly, the British drove Rommel's tank corps westward into Tunisia.

Meanwhile, in November, the first American ground troops in combat landed in North Africa. Under the command of General Dwight D. Eisenhower, they occupied Morocco and Algeria. Hemmed in on both sides, Rommel's army surrendered in May 1943.

✓**Checkpoint** How did Allied fortunes change in North Africa?

Japan Sweeps Through the Pacific

In the days after Pearl Harbor, Japanese armies swiftly took control of Hong Kong, Malaya, Thailand, Burma, Guam, and Wake Island. To the south, they occupied the Dutch East Indies (present-day Indonesia) and the Solomon Islands and threatened Australia.

The Philippines Fall Hours after the attack on Pearl Harbor, Japanese aircraft bombed airfields in the Philippines, the island chain governed by the United States. The Japanese air force destroyed most of the planes that could defend the islands against their invasion.

Two weeks later, a Japanese invasion force landed on Luzon, the key Philippine island. There, General Douglas MacArthur commanded a Filipino–American force. As the enemy closed in on Manila, the capital city, MacArthur withdrew his forces onto the Bataan (bah TAHN) peninsula. He was then ordered by President Roosevelt to go to Australia and take command of all U.S. troops in the region. But as he left the Philippines, MacArthur vowed, "I shall return."

On Bataan and the nearby island of Corregidor, the trapped Americans and Filipinos waged a heroic defense. By early March, they were the only major forces in the Pacific that had not given way to the Japanese. The defenders of Bataan finally surrendered on April 9. Corregidor fell the following month.

Bataan Death March At Bataan, the Japanese captured nearly 70,000 soldiers. Already weak from hunger, the American and Filipino prisoners were then forced to walk 65 miles to a prison camp. Along the way, so many prisoners died of starvation, disease, or violence that their trek soon became known as the Bataan Death March.

Coral Sea and Midway The tide began to turn in the Pacific with two historic naval battles. In May 1942, at the Battle of the Coral Sea, American and Japanese navies waged a new form of warfare. For the first time, opposing ships did not see one another. Instead, planes taking off from the decks of huge aircraft carriers attacked enemy ships many miles away. Both sides suffered heavy losses, but the United States halted the Japanese drive to New Guinea.

A month later, the Japanese sought to take the island of Midway, home of a key American military base. But the Americans sank 4 Japanese aircraft carriers, destroyed 322 Japanese aircraft, and reduced Japan's supply of highly trained pilots. After the Battle of Midway, Japan's navy no longer ruled the Pacific.

✓**Checkpoint** What was the Bataan Death March?

⭐ **Looking Back and Ahead** The attack on Pearl Harbor brought American forces into the biggest war in history. In the next section, you will see how the war affected Americans at home.

Bataan Death March

Section 2 | **Check Your Progress**

Progress Monitoring ⬤nline
For: Self-test with instant help
Visit: PHSchool.com
Web Code: mva-8242

Comprehension and Critical Thinking

1. **(a) Identify** Name two ways that President Roosevelt strengthened ties with Britain in the early years of the war.
   (b) Detect Points of View Why did some Americans view these actions as wrong?

2. **(a) Recall** Why did the situation look bad for the Allies in early 1942?
   (b) Apply Information Explain why each of the following places is considered a turning point in the war: Stalingrad, El Alamein, Midway.

Reading Skill

3. **Use Sentence Clues to Analyze Meaning** Use sentence clues to analyze the meaning of *ferocious* in the following sentence: Hitler had expected the Soviet Union to collapse swiftly in the face of his *ferocious* assault. According to that sentence, what did Hitler think would happen because his assault was ferocious? What does *ferocious* mean?

Key Terms

4. Write two definitions of the term total war—one a formal definition for a teacher, the other an informal definition for a younger child.

Writing

5. Use print or Internet resources to find more information about one of the battles or people discussed in this section. Identify at least three sources of nonprint material on the topic. List the sources you find and describe their contents.

Dauntless: A Novel of Midway and Guadalcanal by Barrett Tillman

Prepare to Read

Introduction

Barrett Tillman is an expert on military aviation and best known for his nonfiction books. Though his 1992 novel *Dauntless* is a work of fiction, it is based on careful research about the war in the Pacific. The novel mixes real and fictional characters. In the excerpt below, Japanese and American fighter pilots prepare for the Battle of Midway in June 1942.

Reading Skill

Analyze Dramatic Irony Often, when we read a novel or see a movie, we know something that the characters do not. This can lead to dramatic irony. Dramatic irony is the contrast between what a character thinks is true and what the audience knows is true. As you read this excerpt, look for two examples of dramatic irony.

Vocabulary *Builder*

As you read this literature selection, look for the following underlined words:

reconnaissance (ree KAHN ah sihns) *n.* act of gathering advance information

disposition (dihs pah SIHSH ahn) *n.* arrangement; placement

cryptanalysis (krihpt ah NAHL uh sihs) *n.* science of breaking codes

latitude (LAH tih tood) *n.* freedom from restrictions

attrition (uh TRIH shuhn) *n.* steady weakening or wearing away

---

Analyze Dramatic Irony

In historical fiction, dramatic irony can occur because the audience knows how events really turned out. Why is the last line of this paragraph an example of dramatic irony?

[Aboard a Japanese ship in the Pacific]

"We are currently here," said Lieutenant Masatake Naito. The ship's air-operations officer pointed to a hash mark along the blue track, indicating a position 700 nautical miles off Japan. His audience, composed of the aircrews who would fly the <u>reconnaissance</u> planes, paid strict attention. After four days at sea, they were about to learn their mysterious destination. . . .

"At dawn four days from now, this force will launch powerful air attacks on the American base at Midway." He tapped the two specks indicating Sand and Eastern Islands, object of the multi-pronged assault. . . .

"We will take the enemy by surprise," Naito continued, "as we have evidence that their remaining fleet units are still in Pearl Harbor." He paused for emphasis, a confident look on his face. "The Americans will be unable to resist coming out to meet us. They must defend Midway or risk leaving Hawaii open to invasion. When they sail to defend Midway, our submarines and fleet units will destroy them in one decisive battle. . . .

"You division commanders—make certain everything is in order. Take nothing for granted." He stood with his hands on his hips, chin jutting forward. "I am counting on each of you. And so is the emperor!" Naito decided against a rousing series of "Banzai" cheers. He would save that emotional moment for later—at the inevitable victory celebration.

[Aboard the American aircraft carrier **Yorktown***]*

The ship's air-operations officer, Commander Murr Arnold, strode to the front of the room. . . . "Gentlemen," Arnold began, I wish to acquaint you with the <u>disposition</u> of our forces as we near Midway." His metallic voice cut through the crowded room, precise and clear. . . .

"Our course is designed to take us well north of the Hawaiian chain and arrive northeast of Midway day after tomorrow. If we remain undetected by the Japanese, we'll be in excellent position to launch surprise air strikes from their flank. We know they're coming, but apparently they don't know that we know."

Arnold then described the Japanese armada steaming toward Midway: the transport group, the main body and supporting force, but he emphasized the striking force of the four veteran carriers. As he did so, Burnett leaned into Rogers and whispered, "I tell you, Buck, that man of ours in Tokyo is worth every dime we pay him."

Rogers stifled a giggle but his mind registered one thought: *cryptanalysis*. . . .

"Admiral Nimitz has given us a great deal of <u>latitude</u> in the conduct of this engagement," Arnold continued. "We will be guided by the principle of calculated risk, employing maximum <u>attrition</u> tactics, but the actual conduct of the battle rests with us." He paused briefly, sweeping the room with his cobra gaze. "There's just one more thing, gentlemen. I have copied a message from Admiral Spruance to Task Force Sixteen, and I want to share it with you. He says, and I quote, 'The successful conclusion of the operations now commencing will be of great value to our country.'" Arnold looked up from the message firmly. "I cannot add anything to that."

From *Dauntless: A Novel of Midway and Guadalcanal* by Barrett Tillman.
Bantam Books, 1992.

United States airplanes attack a Japanese aircraft carrier at the Battle of Midway.

Analyze Dramatic Irony

Sometimes, the reader only recognizes that something is ironic when they read it for the second time, knowing the whole story. Read this paragraph, then reread the scene on the Japanese ship. Identify another example of dramatic irony.

☑Checkpoint **What approach is used, by both the Japanese and the Americans, to prepare pilots for battle?**

Analyze **LITERATURE**

Imagine that you are one of the American pilots on board the *Yorktown* in the excerpt above. Write a letter home expressing your feelings about the coming battle.

If you liked the excerpt from this novel and want to read more about the war in the Pacific, you might read *A Boy at War: A Novel of Pearl Harbor* by Harry Mazer. Simon and Schuster, 2001

Children Contribute to the War Effort

❝Each afternoon after school, everyone rushed for home, not for mitts, bats and balls as in the past but . . . so we could scrounge the garbage cans and alleys for cans, bottles, tires, paper, and anything else required for the war effort.❞

—Donald Brody, describing his childhood during World War II

▲ Garbage could be recycled into war material.

The War at Home

Objectives

- Find out how the United States built its military and converted its economy to meet wartime needs.
- Learn how American women contributed to the war effort.
- Discover how World War II affected Japanese Americans and other groups of people at home.

🔲 Reading Skill

Use Context to Determine Meaning

By examining text around an unfamiliar word, you can often determine its meaning. For example, the unfamiliar word might be referred to or further described in the sentences before or after the sentence in which it is used.

Key Terms and People

rationing
intern

A. Philip Randolph
bracero

Why It Matters World War II involved the people and resources of each nation on a scale that had not been seen before. Americans at home labored in neighborhoods, factories and fields to help their country achieve victory. Some Americans faced discrimination and racism during the war years.

❓ **Section Focus Question: How did the home front respond to American participation in the war?**

Organizing for War

The first challenge the United States faced was to build up its armed forces. Even before Pearl Harbor, Congress had enacted a draft law. Just days after the bombing of Pearl Harbor, Congress revised the law to require people to serve for the entire war.

Building the Military Eventually, more than 15 million volunteers and draftees would wear the American uniform during World War II. The number included Americans from every ethnic and religious group. In newly built military bases around the country, recruits trained to fight in the jungles of the Pacific, the deserts of North Africa, and the farmlands and towns of Europe.

Hundreds of thousands of American women were also in uniform during World War II. They served as nurses or in noncombat roles in special branches such as the Women's Army Corps (WACs). Women pilots ferried bombers from base to base, towed targets, and taught men to fly.

A Wartime Economy Industry quickly converted its output from consumer to military goods. The government established a War Production Board to supervise the changeover and set goals for production. As a result, military output nearly doubled. The war quickly ended the Great Depression. Unemployment fell as millions of jobs opened up in factories. Minority workers found jobs where they had been rejected in the past.

Supporting the War Effort All Americans were expected to play a role in supplying Allied forces with food, clothing, and war equipment. As in World War I, Americans planted victory gardens to <u>supplement</u> food supplies and bought war bonds to help pay military costs.

To conserve needed resources, the government imposed rationing. **Rationing** is the act of setting limits on the amount of scarce goods people can buy. Americans were issued ration coupons to purchase coffee, sugar, meat, shoes, gasoline, tires, and many other goods.

War bond campaigns, rationing, and victory gardens did more than help pay for the war effort. They also gave citizens at home a sense that they were helping to win the war. Thus, they helped maintain public morale during the long struggle.

☑**Checkpoint** **What was the War Production Board?**

Women in Industry

With millions of men in uniform, defense industries needed a new source of labor. The government began a large-scale effort to recruit women for industry.

Millions of women took over jobs in factories and shipyards. Some welded, tended blast furnaces, or ran huge cranes. Others became bus drivers, police officers, or gas station attendants. A fictional character, "Rosie the Riveter," became a popular symbol of all women who worked for the war effort.

Vocabulary Builder
<u>supplement</u> (SUP luh munt) **v.** add to, so as to make up for a lack or deficiency

Use Context to Determine Meaning
Reading Skill To determine the meaning of the word *morale,* use paragraph clues and this question: How do people feel during difficult times?

Rosie the Riveter
This famous poster of Rosie the Riveter (right) assured American women that they were strong enough to handle the challenges of wartime factory work. At left, two real-life "Rosies" work together to build an aircraft. *Critical Thinking: Link Past and Present Why do you think this poster of Rosie the Riveter is still popular with many women today?*

We Can Do It!

Because women were needed in industry, they were able to gain better pay and working conditions. The government agreed that women and men should get the same pay for the same job. Some employers, however, found ways to avoid equal pay.

War work gave many American women a new sense of confidence and independence. "It gave me a good start in life," said welder Nova Lee Holbrook. "I decided that if I could learn to weld like a man, I could do anything it took to make a living."

✔**Checkpoint** **What jobs did women do during the war?**

Ordeal for Japanese Americans

At the start of the war, about 300,000 people of Japanese origin lived in the United States. More than half resided in Hawaii. The rest lived mostly on the West Coast, especially in California.

After the attack on Pearl Harbor, many Americans feared that Japanese Americans would act as spies to help enemy submarines shell military bases or coastal cities. In truth, such suspicions were baseless. There was not a single documented case of disloyalty by a Japanese American.

Internment The intense anti-Japanese fears led President Roosevelt to issue Executive Order 9066 in February 1942. The order was used to intern, or temporarily imprison, some 110,000 Japanese Americans for the duration of the war.

Internees were allowed to bring with them only what they could carry. They had to sell the rest of their possessions quickly, at a fraction of their worth. The U.S. Army then transported them from the West Coast to small, remote internment camps enclosed by barbed wire. Armed soldiers looked down on them from guard towers.

In the 1944 case of *Korematsu* v. *United States,* the Supreme Court ruled that military necessity justified internment. Still, three of the nine justices dissented. One wrote:

❝We must accord great respect and consideration to the judgments of the military authorities who are on the scene and who have full knowledge of the military facts. . . . At the same time, however, it is essential that there be definite limits to military discretion. . . . Individuals must not be left impoverished of their constitutional rights on plea of military necessity that has neither substance nor support.❞

—Frank Murphy, dissenting opinion,
Korematsu v. *United States*

Japanese American Internment

Two frightened boys line up for baggage inspection at an internment camp for Japanese Americans. One internee later recalled, "We didn't know where we were going, how long we'd be gone. We didn't know what to take." **Critical Thinking:** *Apply Information* *Why were these boys forced to leave their homes during World War II?*

As the war ended, the government released the internees. In 1948, it made a small payment to them for the property they had lost. However, a formal apology did not come until 1990. At that time, the government paid $20,000 to each surviving internee.

Japanese Americans in Uniform For Japanese Americans, being imprisoned on such <u>vague</u> charges was a humiliating experience. Still, about 17,000 Japanese Americans showed their loyalty by joining the armed services. All-Japanese units fought in North Africa, Italy, and France, winning thousands of military awards and medals. One group of Japanese American soldiers, the 442nd Nisei Regimental Combat Team, became the most highly decorated military unit in United States history.

Vocabulary Builder
vague (vayg) *adj.* uncertain; not precise or exact

✓**Checkpoint** Why were many Japanese Americans interned?

Tensions at Home

Japanese Americans were not the only group to face wartime restrictions. About 11,000 German Americans and several hundred Italian Americans were also held in government camps as "enemy aliens." Most of these were foreign-born residents who had not yet achieved citizenship. Other German Americans and Italian Americans faced curfews or travel restrictions.

African Americans As in past wars, African Americans served in segregated units during World War II. Groups such as the NAACP and the National Association of Colored Graduate Nurses protested against the racial policy of the armed forces and the military nursing corps.

Discrimination was also widespread in industries doing business with the government. Some African American leaders pointed out that while the nation was fighting for democracy overseas, it still permitted injustice at home.

Union leader A. Philip Randolph, head of the Brotherhood of Sleeping Car Porters, threatened a mass protest unless Roosevelt moved to end discrimination in the armed forces. In response, the President ordered employers doing business with the government to support racial equality in hiring. To enforce the order, he set up the Fair Employment Practices Committee (FEPC) to investigate charges of discrimination.

The FEPC and the growing need for workers opened many jobs that previously had been closed to African Americans. By the end of 1944, about two million African Americans were working in war plants.

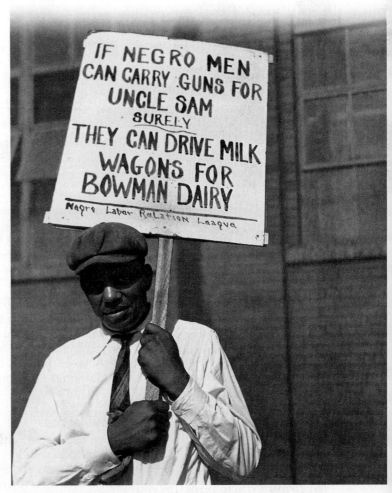

Demanding Fair Employment
This man is picketing at a dairy that hires only white people as drivers. **Critical Thinking: *Analyze Information*** *What is the main idea of the picket sign shown here?*

Young man in a "zoot suit"

However, as employment of African Americans increased, so did racial tension. Thousands of Americans—black people and white people—moved to cities to work in industry. Competition for scarce housing led to angry incidents and even violence. In 1943, race riots broke out in Detroit, New York, and other American cities.

Mexican Americans About half a million Mexican Americans served in the armed forces during World War II. At the same time, the Mexican American population was increasing. Because of the need for workers, the United States signed a treaty with Mexico in 1942. It allowed American companies to hire braceros, or Mexican laborers. As more Mexicans moved north to work on farms and railroads, they often faced prejudice and violent strife.

Young Mexican Americans in Los Angeles often dressed in showy "zoot suits." Their clothing and language set them apart. In June 1943, bands of sailors on shore leave attacked young Mexican Americans, beating them and clubbing them on the streets. The incident sparked several days of rioting.

Newspapers blamed the "Zoot Suit Riots" on the Mexican Americans. But in her newspaper column, Eleanor Roosevelt argued that the riots were the result of "longstanding discrimination against the Mexicans in the Southwest."

✓ **Checkpoint** **How did African Americans seek fairer treatment during the war?**

☆ **Looking Back and Ahead** Despite problems at home, Americans were united in their resolve to push on to victory in Europe and the Pacific. In the next section, you will see how that victory was won.

Section 3 | **Check Your Progress**

Progress Monitoring Online
For: Self-test with instant help
Visit: PHSchool.com
Web Code: mva-8243

Comprehension and Critical Thinking

1. **(a) Recall** What economic restrictions did Americans face during World War II?
(b) Identify Costs and Benefits What were the costs of these restrictions? What were the benefits?

2. **(a) Recall** What happened to Japanese Americans on the West Coast during the war?
(b) Draw Conclusions Do you think restricting people's civil liberties during wartime is ever justified? Why or why not?

Reading Skill

3. **Use Context to Determine Meaning** Reread the text following the subheading "Mexican Americans." Use different clues to determine the meaning of the word *strife*.

Key Terms

4. Write two definitions for each of the following key terms in the section: rationing, intern, bracero. First, write a formal definition for your teacher. Second, write a definition in everyday English for a classmate.

Writing

5. A thesis statement expresses the main idea for a piece of writing. Based on what you have read in this section, write a thesis statement that could be developed using multimedia support on one of the following topics:
• the internment of Japanese Americans
• women's contribution to the war effort
• rationing and other domestic war measures
Follow your thesis statement with a description of the kinds of multimedia materials you would use to support and develop it.

The Tide Has Turned

❝ The tide has turned! The free men of the world are marching together to Victory! I have full confidence in your courage and devotion to duty and skill in battle. We will accept nothing less than full Victory! ❞

—General Dwight D. Eisenhower, speech to troops, June 5, 1944

◄ U.S. troops in Germany, 1945

Toward Victory

Objectives

- Learn how the Allies were finally able to defeat Germany.
- Discover how a powerful new weapon brought the war in the Pacific to a close.
- Explore the horrors of the Holocaust.
- Understand the consequences faced by captured enemy leaders.

🔁 Reading Skill

Use Context to Determine Meaning

Here are additional clues to determine meaning. Draw on your own experience or knowledge. Look for contrast clues, in which a familiar word contrasts with the unfamiliar word. Search for synonym clues, in which a familiar word has a similar meaning.

Key Terms and People

Harry S Truman
island hopping
kamikaze

genocide
war crimes

Why It Matters By mid-1942, the Allies had begun to turn back Axis advances in the Pacific, in North Africa, and in Europe. Ultimately, the Allies were victorious. After the war, the United States assumed the lead in a new global conflict—the Cold War.

❓ Section Focus Question: How did the Allies win World War II and what were the results?

Victory in Europe

In 1943, Russia was bearing the brunt of the Nazi assault. Stalin urged the Americans and British to open up a "second front" in Europe by invading France. However, Roosevelt and Churchill did not think their forces were ready for such a difficult task. Instead, they chose a more realistic goal—removing Italy from the war.

Italy Surrenders In July 1943, American and British troops crossed the Mediterranean from Tunisia. They swiftly took control of the Italian island of Sicily. By fall, they were fighting their way northward along the Italian Peninsula.

The king of Italy dismissed Mussolini from office. On September 8, 1943, the new government surrendered to the Allies. Even so, German troops in Italy continued to fight. The Allies would face a long struggle before they finally controlled Italy.

D-Day In 1944, Allied forces were ready to undertake the invasion of France. Under the command of General Eisenhower, the Allies carefully planned the landing. It would be an operation of massive dimensions, involving thousands of ships and aircraft.

On June 6, 1944—known as D-Day—more than 155,000 American, British, and Canadian troops crossed the English Channel. They landed on five beaches at Normandy, in western France. Troops at four of the beaches quickly overcame German opposition.

On Omaha Beach, however, Americans met an especially fierce German defense. One American survivor of the assault later recalled being wounded by a shell as he tried to come ashore:

> "The shrapnel hit my right shoulder and leg. The explosion and concussion seemed to push me into the ground and knocked the breath out of me. The force of the explosion blew my helmet off and cut the corner of my left eye. . . . The Germans were firing everything they could."
>
> —Roy Arnn, letter, November 10, 1990

By day's end, some 2,500 American soldiers lay dead on Omaha Beach. However, they had succeeded in their mission. Within a month, a million Allied troops had stormed ashore.

On August 25, 1944, the Allies entered Paris. After four years under Nazi rule, French men, women, and children greeted their liberators with joy.

Battle of the Bulge Allied forces pushed eastward. But on December 16, 1944, the Germans counterattacked in Belgium. Hitler poured his remaining reserves into the attack. Bad weather grounded Allied aircraft for the first week of the battle. This allowed German troops to create a "bulge" in the American lines.

The Germans came close to breaking through Allied lines. But, in the end, their attempt to fight off defeat proved futile. German troops were short of critical supplies, especially fuel. Also, though each side lost tens of thousands of men, the Allies had additional troops in reserve. Germany was running out of soldiers.

Fighting in Northern Europe's coldest winter in 40 years, American forces won the Battle of the Bulge. Germany now lay wide open from both east and west.

Germany Invaded In January 1945, a huge Soviet force entered Germany from the east. Soon, the Western Allies also entered in large numbers from the west. While the Allied armies advanced on the ground, their planes bombed German industries and cities.

On April 12, 1945, President Franklin D. Roosevelt died of a stroke. His death shattered Americans. Many could hardly remember anyone else as their leader. At a critical moment, Vice President Harry S Truman was suddenly thrust into the highest office in the country. Truman had little experience dealing with important policy issues. Would he be a decisive leader?

Victory in Europe Meanwhile, Germany was collapsing. On April 16, Soviet troops began an assault on Berlin. Hitler took shelter in a bunker built beneath the city's streets. There, with his Nazi empire in ruins, he committed suicide on April 30, 1945.

A week later, representatives of Germany's armed forces unconditionally surrendered at Eisenhower's headquarters in France. On May 8, the Allies celebrated V-E Day, Victory in Europe.

☑ **Checkpoint** **Why was D-Day important?**

Use Context to Determine Meaning Use clues in these paragraphs to determine the meaning of the word *futile*. Explain all the clues you used.

Anxious American soldiers wait to go into battle.

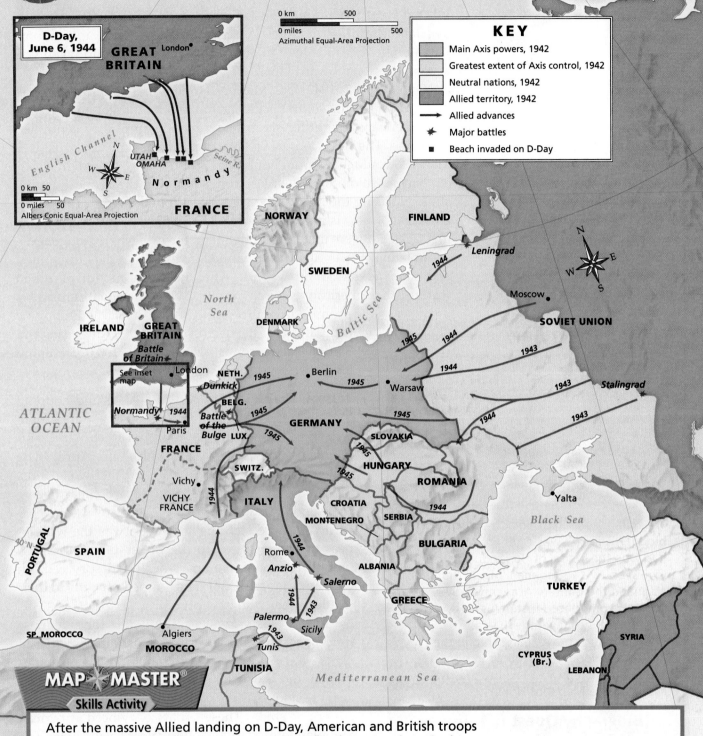

D-Day, June 6, 1944

GREAT BRITAIN

London

English Channel

UTAH
OMAHA

Normandy

FRANCE

Seine R.

0 km 50
0 miles 50
Albers Conic Equal-Area Projection

0 km 500
0 miles 500
Azimuthal Equal-Area Projection

KEY

- Main Axis powers, 1942
- Greatest extent of Axis control, 1942
- Neutral nations, 1942
- Allied territory, 1942
- → Allied advances
- ✳ Major battles
- ■ Beach invaded on D-Day

NORWAY

SWEDEN

FINLAND

Leningrad — 1944

Moscow

SOVIET UNION

North Sea

DENMARK

Baltic Sea

IRELAND

GREAT BRITAIN

Battle of Britain

See inset map

London

NETH.

Berlin — 1945

Warsaw

1945

1944

1943

Stalingrad — 1943

ATLANTIC OCEAN

Dunkirk

BELG.

Battle of the Bulge

LUX.

GERMANY

SLOVAKIA

HUNGARY

ROMANIA

1944

1945

1943

Normandy — 1944

Paris

FRANCE

1944

SWITZ.

Vichy

VICHY FRANCE

ITALY

CROATIA

MONTENEGRO

SERBIA

Yalta

Black Sea

BULGARIA

PORTUGAL

SPAIN

Rome

Anzio

Salerno

1944

1943

ALBANIA

TURKEY

GREECE

SP. MOROCCO

Algiers

MOROCCO

Palermo

Sicily

1943

Tunis

TUNISIA

Mediterranean Sea

CYPRUS (Br.)

SYRIA

LEBANON

40°N

MAP✦MASTER®
Skills Activity

After the massive Allied landing on D-Day, American and British troops pushed steadily eastward toward Germany. At the same time, Soviet troops were already advancing westward.

(a) Interpret a Map Describe the movement of Allied troops on D-Day. Where did they go next?

(b) Evaluate Information Why were there no troop movements or fighting in Spain?

MapMaster Online

For: Interactive map
Visit: PHSchool.com
Web Code: mvp-8244

Victory in the Pacific

The Battle of Midway in 1942 had halted Japan's advance in the Pacific. After that, the Americans went on the offensive.

Island Hopping American commanders adopted a strategy known as island hopping, in which American forces would capture some Japanese-held islands and go around others. Each island taken was a stepping stone toward Japan.

On August 7, 1942, U.S. Marines landed on Guadalcanal (gwah dal cah NAL) in the south Pacific. Hampered by hunger and disease, the Americans fought for six grueling months until they controlled the island. The fierce combat on Guadalcanal was typical of what U.S. Marines would face throughout the island-hopping campaign.

Navajo soldiers made a key contribution to the island-hopping strategy. Using their own language, these code-talkers radioed <u>vital</u> messages from island to island. The Japanese intercepted the messages but were unable to understand the rare Navajo language.

In January 1945, army units landed on Luzon, in the Philippines, and then advanced on Manila. After nearly a month of urban warfare, the Americans secured the city. MacArthur had fulfilled his promise to return to the Philippines. The Philippine campaign cost the lives of over 14,000 Americans and 350,000 Japanese, as well as some 100,000 Filipino civilians.

Japan Holds Firm Meanwhile, island-hopping marines approached Japan. Their last two stops were Iwo Jima (EE woh JEE muh), in February, and Okinawa (oh kuh NAH wuh), in April. The Americans paid a terrible price for the two islands. Six thousand Americans died at Iwo Jima; twelve thousand at Okinawa.

Even more startling, however, was the willingness of the Japanese to die rather than surrender. Only 1 percent of Iwo Jima's defenders survived. On Okinawa, Japanese soldiers jumped off cliffs to their deaths rather than be captured.

In the last days of the war, the Japanese unleashed a deadly new form of combat. It was based on an ancient code, which taught that surrender dishonored a warrior. In kamikaze (kah muh KAH zee) missions, suicide pilots crashed their planes into American ships. These events convinced American war planners that only a full-scale invasion of Japan's home islands would force a surrender.

After Hitler's defeat in Europe, the Allies were able to turn their full attention to the Pacific. By the spring of 1945, American bombers were pounding the Japanese home islands. American ships bombarded the coast and destroyed shipping.

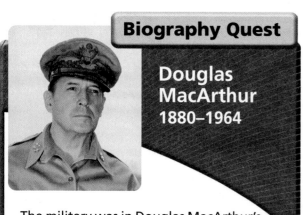

Biography Quest

Douglas MacArthur
1880–1964

The military was in Douglas MacArthur's blood. His father was a general who had won the Medal of Honor during the Civil War. As a young man, MacArthur attended the Military Academy at West Point. He graduated first in his class, with the highest average in years.

MacArthur's brave leadership in the Pacific allowed him to follow in his father's footsteps. In 1942, he, too, was awarded the Medal of Honor.

— **Biography Quest**

How did MacArthur contribute to Japan after World War II ended?

For: The answer to the question about MacArthur

Visit: PHSchool.com

Web Code: mvd-8244

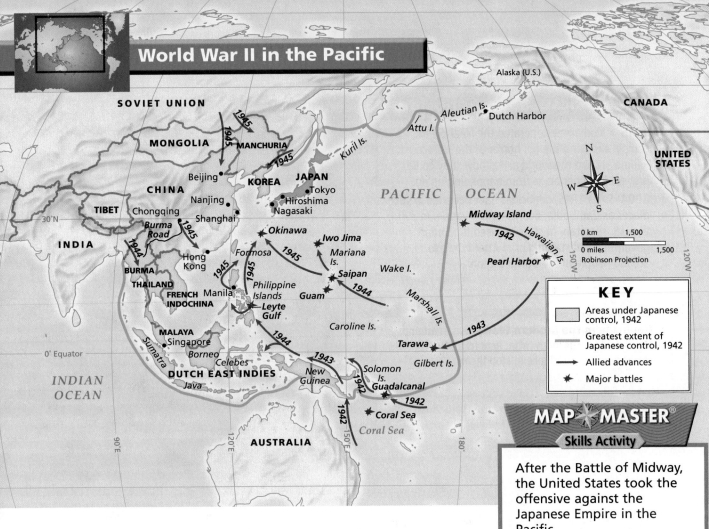

World War II in the Pacific

KEY

- Areas under Japanese control, 1942
- Greatest extent of Japanese control, 1942
- → Allied advances
- ★ Major battles

0 km 1,500
0 miles 1,500
Robinson Projection

MAP MASTER
Skills Activity

After the Battle of Midway, the United States took the offensive against the Japanese Empire in the Pacific.

(a) Interpret a Map How close did the Allied island-hopping campaign get to Japan itself?

(b) Understand Sequence Describe the troop movements and sequence of battles that led to the recapture of the Philippines.

MapMaster Online

For: Interactive map
Visit: PHSchool.com
Web Code: mvp-8244

Millions of Japanese were short of food. Yet, Japanese leaders still talked of winning a glorious victory.

The Atomic Bomb President Truman made plans for invading Japan in the autumn. His military advisers warned him that the invasion might cost half a million American casualties. In July, Truman learned that a secret weapon—the atomic bomb—had been successfully tested in the New Mexico desert. The new weapon could destroy an entire city. Truman decided to use it and save American lives.

On August 6, 1945, an American plane dropped an atomic bomb on the city of Hiroshima. The destruction was like nothing the world had ever seen. Within minutes, the blast and searing heat had killed more than 130,000 people. Still, the Japanese refused to surrender.

On August 9, a second atomic bomb was dropped on the city of Nagasaki. Some 35,000 people died instantly. Many more in both cities would die slower deaths from radiation poisoning.

At last, on August 14, 1945, the emperor of Japan announced that the nation would surrender. That day became known as V-J Day. On September 2, 1945, MacArthur formally accepted Japan's surrender aboard the battleship USS *Missouri*, anchored in Tokyo Bay. World War II was over at last.

☑**Checkpoint** What was kamikaze warfare?

Links Across Time

1945 These survivors of a Nazi death camp can hardly believe they are free.

The Holocaust and Genocide

1945 Allied armies liberated the Nazi death camps, exposing the full horror of the Holocaust. People around the world asked how they could prevent such genocide from happening again.

2004 Since 1945, genocides have occurred in such places as Cambodia, Bosnia, and Rwanda. In 2004, the U.S. secretary of state accused the Sudan government of starving or murdering up to 50,000 people in the Darfur region.

Link to Today

Genocide in the Modern World When attempts at genocide occur today, what actions do the United States and the world take to stop them?

For: The continuing legacy of the Holocaust
Visit: PHSchool.com
Web Code: mvc-8244

The Holocaust

World War II was the bloodiest conflict in human history. It took the lives of up to 60 million people, including about 400,000 Americans. Some two thirds of those killed were civilians. Still, some of the worst horrors were not fully revealed until after Germany's defeat. Only then did the world learn the full extent of Nazi brutality.

Victims of the Nazis As you have read, Nazism was built on racism and extreme anti-Semitism. During the war, Hitler moved beyond restrictions on Jews to what he termed the "final solution to the Jewish problem"—the attempt to annihilate all Jews in Europe.

Some 6 million Jews were murdered under the Nazis. Entire families, from grandparents to infants, were wiped out. This mass slaughter is today known as the Holocaust. As a result of the Holocaust, a new word entered the English language: genocide. Genocide is the deliberate attempt to wipe out an entire nation or group of people.

Other groups also became victims of the Nazis. The Nazis murdered millions of Poles, Slavs, Gypsies, communists, and people with physical or mental disabilities.

Vocabulary Builder
efficient (ee FISH ehnt) **adj.** acting effectively, without wasted cost or effort

Death Camps The Nazis developed an <u>efficient</u> system of mass murder. They built six death camps in Poland. Millions of women, men, and children were transported to these camps in railway cattle cars. Hundreds at a time were killed in gas chambers. Others were subjected to torture or horrifying medical experiments.

As Allied soldiers liberated the death camps, they were shocked by the sight and smell of piles of corpses. The survivors were living skeletons. One American radio reporter told his listeners:

> **❝**In another part of the camp they showed me the children, hundreds of them. Some were only 6 years old. One rolled up his sleeves, showed me his number. It was tattooed on his arm. B-6030, it was. The others showed me their numbers. They will carry them till they die. . . . I could see their ribs through their thin shirts.**❞**
>
> —Edward R. Murrow, *PM*, April 16, 1945

Murrow concluded, "I reported what I saw and heard, but only part of it. For most of it, I have no words."

War Crimes Trials Shocked by the Holocaust and other Nazi actions, the Allies took an unprecedented step. For the first time in history, victors in a war prosecuted leaders of the losing side for war crimes. **War crimes** are wartime acts of cruelty and brutality that are judged to be beyond the accepted rules of war and human behavior.

In the German city of Nuremberg, Allied judges tried prominent Nazis for plunging the world into war and for the horrors of the death camps. In 1946, at the first Nuremberg Trials, 12 defendants were sentenced to death by hanging. Similar trials were held in Manila and Tokyo to try leaders of the Japanese war machine.

A veteran visits the National World War II Memorial.

✔Checkpoint Which people were killed in Nazi death camps?

⭐ **Looking Back and Ahead** After World War I, the United States returned to isolationism. But after World War II, Americans accepted a new role in the world. In the next chapter, you will see how the nation took the lead in a long global conflict—the Cold War.

Section 4 | **Check Your Progress**

Progress Monitoring ⒪nline
For: Self-test with instant help
Visit: PHSchool.com
Web Code: mva-8244

Comprehension and Critical Thinking

1. **(a) Identify** What was D-Day? What did it accomplish?
   (b) Draw Conclusions What do you think might have happened if the D-Day landing had failed?

2. **(a) Recall** Why did the United States decide to drop the atomic bomb on Hiroshima?
   (b) Identify Alternatives What other courses might the Americans have followed? Do you think the decision to drop the bomb was justified?

Reading Skill

3. **Use Context to Determine Meaning** Reread the paragraph with the subheading "Victims of the Nazis." Use different clues to determine the meaning of *annihilate*. Explain *all* the clues you used and where you found them.

Key Terms

Fill in the blanks with the correct key terms from this chapter.

4. The leaders who planned the Nazi death camps were executed for _____.

5. Pilots who carried out _____ missions were certain to die.

6. The _____ campaign allowed Allied forces to inch slowly toward Japan.

7. The Nazi attempt to exterminate Jews was an example of _____.

Writing

8. Create an outline that would develop the following thesis statement for a multimedia report: "The D-Day landing was the single most decisive battle in World War II." Be sure to include ideas for media materials.

21st Century Learning Sometimes the arguments in a primary source are weakened by faulty reasoning, that is, the author makes an error in thinking or argument. Common types of faulty reasoning include incorrectly stating cause-and-effect relationships or misinterpreting a situation, an event, or a character.

Primary Source Read the excerpts below about the political consequences of the 1938 Munich Pact.

"I believe there is sincerity and goodwill on both sides. My main purpose has been to work for the pacification of Europe, for the removal of those suspicions and those [hatreds] which have so long poisoned the air. The path that leads to appeasement is long and bristles with obstacles. This question of Czechoslovakia is the latest and perhaps the most dangerous. Now that we have got past it I feel that it may be possible to make further progress along the road to sanity."

—Neville Chamberlain, address to the House of Commons, October 3, 1938

". . . Many people, no doubt, honestly believe that they are only giving away the interests of Czechoslovakia, whereas I fear we shall find that we have deeply compromised, and perhaps fatally endangered, the safety and even the independence of Great Britain and France. . . . I foresee and foretell that the policy of submission will carry with it restrictions upon the freedom of speech and debate in Parliament, on public platforms, and discussions in the Press."

—Winston Churchill, debate in the House of Commons, October 5, 1938

Learn the Skill

Use these steps to identify faulty reasoning.

1. **Identify the source.** If you know the identity of the speaker or writer, you can place his or her words in historical context.

2. **Find main ideas.** What is the main point of the primary source? Does it support or oppose a particular position?

3. **Compare the primary source with an objective presentation of facts.** What actually happened? Examining the historical events can help you identify mistakes in the writer's or speaker's thinking.

4. **Identify errors in thinking or reasoning.** Frame questions to help you find examples of faulty reasoning. Does the source incorrectly state cause-and-effect relationships? Does the primary source misinterpret facts about a situation, an event, or a person?

Practice the Skill

Answer the following questions about the primary sources on this page.

1. **Identify the source.** When did Churchill deliver his speech?

2. **Find main ideas.** (a) How does Chamberlain defend the Munich Pact? (b) What is the main idea of Churchill's speech?

3. **Compare the primary source with an objective presentation of facts.** (a) How did Chamberlain view events in Czechoslovakia? (b) What actually happened there?

4. **Identify errors in thinking or reasoning.** (a) How does Chamberlain incorrectly state cause-and-effect relationships surrounding the Munich Pact? (b) How does he misinterpret Hitler's character? (c) How does Churchill attack Chamberlain's reasoning?

Apply the Skill

See the Review and Assessment at the end of this chapter.

Quick Study Guide

What were the causes and effects of World War II?

Section 1
Aggression Leads to War

- During the 1920s and 1930s, totalitarian dictators rose in several nations.
- Western democracies took little action to stop Italian, Japanese, and German aggression.
- To avoid involvement in world conflicts, the United States passed the Neutrality Act.
- Germany's invasion of Poland launched World War II.

Section 2
The United States at War

- Though officially neutral, the United States took steps to aid the Allies.
- The United States entered World War II after Japan bombed Pearl Harbor.
- By 1943, the Allies were beginning to turn back Axis advances in Europe, North Africa, and the Pacific.

Section 3
The War at Home

- As the economy switched to wartime production, the government rationed many valuable resources.
- During the war, women took over many jobs usually performed by men.
- On the West Coast, Japanese Americans were shipped to internment camps.

Section 4
Toward Victory

- With Allied troops closing in from the west and east, Germany surrendered in 1945.
- Japan is forced to surrender after two atomic bombs were dropped on Hiroshima and Nagasaki.
- After Germany surrendered, the Allies learned the full extent of the Nazi death camps where millions of people had been murdered.

? Exploring the Essential Question

Use the online study guide to explore the essential question.

Section 1
What events led to the outbreak of World War II?

Section 2
How did the United States move from neutrality to full involvement in the war?

Chapter 24 Essential Question
What were the causes and effects of World War II?

Section 4
How did the Allies win World War II and what were the results?

Section 3
How did the home front respond to American participation in the war?

Key Terms

1. Write one sentence giving the definition of each of these key terms: fascism; aggression; appeasement; total war; rationing; intern; genocide. Then, write a second sentence relating each of the key terms to World War II, its cause or its effects.

Comprehension and Critical Thinking

2. **(a) Describe** Describe the features of a totalitarian state.
(b) Contrast How does a totalitarian government differ from a democratic government, such as that of the United States?

3. **(a) Recall** How did Roosevelt try to improve relations with Latin American countries?
(b) Evaluate Information Why do you think the United States was anxious to strengthen its ties to Latin America in the 1930s?

4. **(a) Recall** Why did the Japanese attack Pearl Harbor?
(b) Apply Information After the attack, a Japanese admiral said, "I'm afraid we have awakened a sleeping tiger." What do you think he meant? Do you think he was correct?

5. **(a) Recall** How did American women contribute to the war effort?
(b) Analyze Cause and Effect How were African Americans able to make some gains toward equality during the war?
(c) Make Predictions What impact do you think these wartime changes might have after the end of the war?

6. **(a) Explain** Why did Stalin want Britain and the United States to open a second front? How was this goal achieved?
(b) Evaluate Information How did the opening of the second front hurt Germany?

7. **(a) Describe** What was the Holocaust?
(b) Apply Information Why were German actions during the Holocaust considered war crimes?
(c) Evaluate Information Explain which of the following actions you would classify as war crimes: the Japanese attack on Nanjing; the German offensive at the Battle of the Bulge; the Bataan Death March.

Reading Skill

8. **Determine Meanings From Context** Find an unfamiliar word in this chapter. Use context clues to analyze its meaning. Explain the clues you used.

Writing

9. **Write a thesis statement and create an outline for a multimedia presentation covering a topic in this chapter. You should**
   - focus on a topic that can be covered in a short multimedia presentation;
   - list the various parts of the presentation order in which they could be organized;
   - include ideas for the photographs, films, recordings, and other multimedia materials.

10. **Create an Interview:**
Create a short radio interview, taking place just after V-J Day, between a journalist covering the war and an American sailor serving on a battleship in the Pacific.

Skills for Life
Identify Faulty Reasoning
Use the excerpt below to answer the questions.

> "Hitler . . . can be stopped and can be compelled to dig in. And that will be the beginning of the end of his downfall. . . . The facts of 1918 are proof that a mighty German Army and a tired German people can crumble rapidly and go to pieces when they are faced with successful resistance."
>
> —Franklin D. Roosevelt, October 27, 1941

11. When was this speech delivered?

12. **(a)** What prediction does Roosevelt make?
(b) On what does he base this prediction?

13. **(a)** How long did the war against Germany actually last after this speech was made?
(b) What may have been the flaw in Roosevelt's reasoning when he made his prediction?

Test Yourself

1. The Supreme Court case of *Korematsu* v. *United States* dealt with the issue of

   A racial segregation in the military.

   B internment of Japanese Americans.

   C equal pay for women who worked in factories.

   D war crimes committed by the Japanese army.

2. **Which of the following was an example of appeasement?**

   A the Munich Pact

   B the Nazi-Soviet nonaggression agreement

   C the Atlantic Charter

   D the Lend-Lease Act

Refer to the table below to answer Question 3.

Item	Amount per Person
Sugar	8–12 ounces per week
Meat	28 ounces per week
Gasoline	3 gallons per week
Shoes	2 pairs per year

Source: *Digital History*

3. **Which wartime economic policy is illustrated by the table above?**

   A conversion to wartime production

   B campaign to sell war bonds

   C rationing of consumer goods

   D hiring of braceros by American industry

Document-Based Questions

Task: Look at Documents 1 and 2, and answer their accompanying questions. Then, use the documents and your knowledge of history to complete this writing assignment:

Use the evidence in the documents to write a newspaper editorial supporting or criticizing President Truman's decision to use the atomic bomb against Japan.

Document 1: In August 1945, the United States dropped two atomic bombs on Japan. The picture shows only a small part of the destruction caused by the bombs. *How was the atomic bomb different from conventional bombs?*

Document 2: In a public statement on August 9, 1945, President Truman gave his reasons for using the atomic bomb against Japan. *Why did Truman decide to use the bomb?*

"Having found the bomb we have used it. We have used it against those who attacked us without warning at Pearl Harbor, against those who have starved and beaten and executed American prisoners of war, against those who have abandoned all pretense of obeying international laws of warfare. We have used it in order to shorten the agony of war, in order to save the lives of thousands and thousands of young Americans.

We shall continue to use it until we completely destroy Japan's power to make war. Only a Japanese surrender will stop us."

The United States in the Cold War

United States

1945–1963

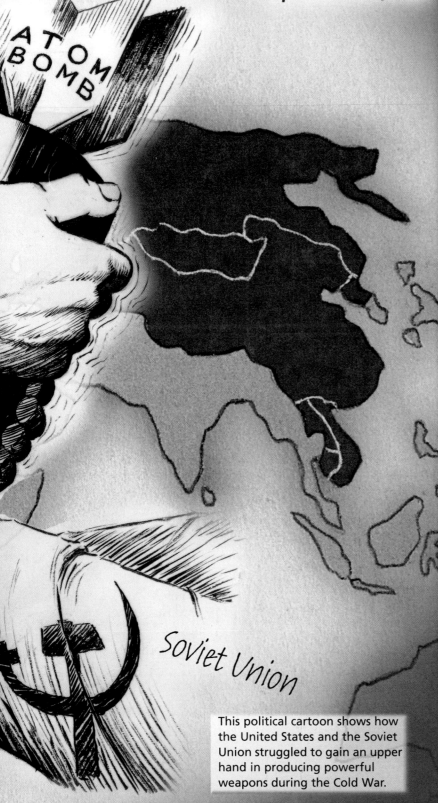

"The only way to win World War III is to prevent it."

—President Dwight D. Eisenhower, September 19, 1956

ATOM BOMB

Soviet Union

This political cartoon shows how the United States and the Soviet Union struggled to gain an upper hand in producing powerful weapons during the Cold War.

CHAPTER 25

What You Will Learn

Section 1
ROOTS OF THE COLD WAR

When Stalin threatened to expand communism, President Truman initiated policies to protect non-Communist nations. It was the beginning of the Cold War.

Section 2
A TIME OF PROSPERITY

After World War II, the economy boomed, the population grew, and many postwar families moved to the suburbs. However, not all Americans shared in the new prosperity.

Section 3
THE KOREAN WAR PERIOD

When North Korea invaded South Korea, the United States and UN forces moved to protect non-Communist South Korea.

Section 4
GLOBAL CONCERNS IN THE COLD WAR

As colonies gained independence, both the United States and the Soviet Union carried their conflict to Africa, Asia, and Latin America.

🔖 Reading Skill

Analyze Cause and Effect In this chapter, you will learn to identify causes and their effects to help connect and understand historical events and issues.

The United States in the Cold War, 1945–1963

■The Korean War
United States and United Nations forces
defended South Korea after it was
invaded by Communist North Korea.

■Arms Race
The United States and the Soviet
Union competed to build more and
more powerful nuclear weapons.

**■Interstate Highway
Act of 1956**
A new system of highways
connected the nation's major cities.

**■Americans Move
to the Suburbs**
The suburbs grew as cars allowed
people to commute to work.

Pacific Ocean

Seattle WA · Portland · OR · ID · MT · WY · CA · NV · UT · Denver CO · Los Angeles · AZ · Albuquerque · NM · MEXICO

N W E S
0 — 250 miles
0 — 250 km
Albers Conic Conformal Projection

The United States and the Cold War	
Truman Doctrine	The United States helped countries threatened by communism.
Marshall Plan	U.S. economic aid helped European nations rebuild after World War II.
Berlin Airlift	The United States airlifted supplies to Berlin after the city was blockaded by the Soviet Union.
NATO	The United States and other democratic nations formed a military alliance to defend against Soviet attack.
Warsaw Pact	The Soviet Union and other Communist nations formed a military alliance in response to NATO.
Korean War	United States and United Nations forces helped South Korea resist an invasion by Communist North Korea.
Cuban Missile Crisis	President Kennedy insisted that the Soviets remove their missiles from Cuba.

**U.S.
Events**

U.S. foreign policy
changes with the
Truman Doctrine and
the Marshall Plan.
1947

United States
joins Allies in
Berlin Airlift.
1948

1952 Dwight D. Eisenhower
is elected President.

1945   **1950**   **1955**

**World
Events**

Soviets successfully
test their first
atomic bomb.
1949

1950 Korean
War begins.

VISUAL PREVIEW

CANADA

United Nations
The United Nations was established after World War II to maintain world peace.

Arms Race
The United States and the Soviet Union competed to build more and more powerful nuclear weapons.

Berlin Airlift
The United States responded to the Soviet blockade of Berlin by airlifting supplies to the city.

Truman Defeats Dewey
Truman's 1948 reelection was one of the biggest upsets in American history.

Dewey Defeats Truman

ND

MN

SD

WI

MI

IA

Detroit

NE

Chicago

Cleveland

VT

NH

Boston

MA

CT

NY

RI

New York

PA

Philadelphia

NJ

Baltimore

OH

DE

Washington, D.C.

MD

WV

IL

IN

KS

St. Louis

KY

VA

MO

Army-McCarthy
Hearings

TN

NC

OK

AR

SC

ELVIS

GA

Rock-and-Roll
Singers like Elvis Presley popularized a new blend of black rhythm-and-blues and country music.

MS

AL

McCarthyism
Senator Joseph McCarthy unjustly accused hundreds of Americans of being Communists.

Marshall Plan
The Marshall Plan provided postwar economic aid to European countries.

MARSHALL PLAN

Berlin Airlift

Dallas

TX

LA

FL

Space Race
Competition between the United States and the Soviet Union extended to outer space.

Gulf of Mexico

Cuban Missile Crisis
The Cuban missile crisis brought the United States and the Soviet Union to the brink of war.

CUBA

Congress creates
the National Aeronautics
and Space Administration.

1958

United States faces
Soviet Union in the
Cuban missile crisis.

1962

1955

1960

1965

Ghana, a former
British colony, gains
independence.

1957

Berlin Wall
is built.

1961

▲ U.S. President Harry Truman (left) and Soviet dictator Josef Stalin (right)

The Threat of Communism

❝The American people desire, and are determined to work for, a world in which all nations and all peoples are free to govern themselves as they see fit. . . . In the pursuit of these aims, the United States and other like-minded nations find themselves directly opposed by a regime with . . . a false philosophy. . . . That false philosophy is communism.❞

—Harry S Truman, inaugural address, January 20, 1949

Roots of the Cold War

Objectives

- Explain how the friendships among the Allies broke down after the war.
- Discover how the United States tried to limit the spread of communism.
- Learn about three new international organizations.
- Understand how the events of 1949 shook America's confidence.

⟳ Reading Skill

Analyze Underlying Causes An event is the effect of a previous cause. However, some causes are not directly stated in the text. To identify these causes, you may need to collect information about how people's emotions affected their actions. For example, think of how the Cold War affected the attitude and actions of the nation.

Key Terms

iron curtain   airlift
satellite   veto
containment

Why It Matters Shortly after the Allies defeated the Axis powers in World War II, the Allies' wartime alliance broke down. The alliance was replaced by a struggle between Communist and non-Communist nations. This struggle, known as the Cold War, would impact American life for nearly half a century.

❓ Section Focus Question: How did the United States respond to the early stages of the Cold War?

Growing Distrust

Differences arose among the wartime Allies even before the war had ended. In the final months of the war, Winston Churchill, Josef Stalin, and Franklin Roosevelt had met at Yalta, a resort in the Soviet Union. There, Stalin promised to hold free elections in the parts of Eastern Europe under his control. At the time, Soviet troops were occupying most of Eastern Europe. Instead, Stalin proceeded to establish Communist governments in these nations. He realized that free elections would result in non-Communist governments. Stalin wanted to construct a ring of friendly countries to protect the western borders of the Soviet Union. After the ring had been built, Stalin hoped to make the Soviet Union the world's dominant power.

Churchill expressed the fears of many in the West. Speaking at a college in Fulton, Missouri, he warned of the Soviet threat:

❝[A]n iron curtain has descended across the continent. Behind that line lie all the capitals of the ancient states of Central and Eastern Europe . . . all these famous cities and populations around them lie in what I must call the Soviet sphere.❞

—Winston Churchill, speech, Westminster College, March 5, 1946

The term **iron curtain** is a way of referring to a barrier to understanding and information. Churchill's use of the term became a popular way of describing the conflict between the democratic nations of the West and the Soviet Union and the Communist-controlled nations of Eastern Europe.

By 1948, most of the nations of Eastern Europe had become satellites of the Soviet Union. A **satellite** is a nation that is dominated politically or economically by a more powerful nation. In addition, <u>hostile</u> Communist threats loomed in Southern and Western Europe. The wartime alliance among the Allies was no more.

☑**Checkpoint**   **Why did nations of the West consider Stalin's actions a threat?**

Analyze Underlying Causes
Why was the West worried about Soviet actions? Use the heading on page 836 to help you infer the underlying cause.

Vocabulary Builder
<u>hostile</u> (HAHS tihl) **adj.** unfriendly; opposing

Containing Soviet Expansion

The Cold War began at a time when many Americans worried about the nation's leadership. Harry S Truman had become President after the sudden death of Franklin Roosevelt in April 1945. Truman was not well known; and, as Vice President, his leadership had not been tested. However, President Truman wasted little time in showing his leadership qualities. The first Cold War challenges he faced were in Greece, Iran, and Turkey. After the war, a Communist-led revolt broke out in Greece. Greek Communists threatened to take over the government. At the same time, the Soviet government began to threaten two nations on its southern border, Turkey and Iran.

The Truman Doctrine and the Marshall Plan In March 1947, President Truman made an urgent request to Congress to aid Greece and Turkey. He declared that the United States would oppose the spread of communism. He stated a principle that became known as the Truman Doctrine:

❝[I]t must be the policy of the United States to support free peoples who are resisting attempted subjugation by armed minorities or by outside pressures.❞
—Harry S Truman, message to Congress, March 12, 1947

Truman's policy of blocking Communist expansion was known as containment. The goal of containment was to contain, or limit, Soviet expansion.

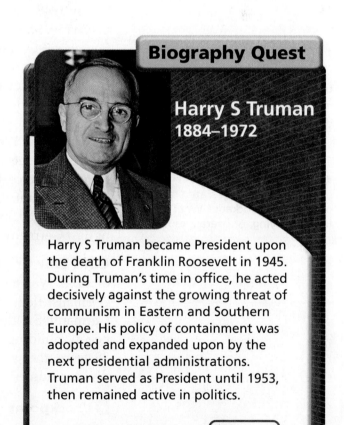

Biography Quest

Harry S Truman
1884–1972

Harry S Truman became President upon the death of Franklin Roosevelt in 1945. During Truman's time in office, he acted decisively against the growing threat of communism in Eastern and Southern Europe. His policy of containment was adopted and expanded upon by the next presidential administrations. Truman served as President until 1953, then remained active in politics.

Biography Quest ⏻**nline**

Why did Truman dismiss MacArthur from his East Asian command in 1951?
For: The answer to the question about Truman and MacArthur
Visit: PHSchool.com
Web Code: mvd-8251

Military aid alone could not contain communism. After World War II, much of Europe lay in ruins. Communists said the capitalist system was powerless to repair the damaged economies. Many desperate Europeans believed them. Communist parties gained strength in both Italy and France.

To meet this crisis, Secretary of State George Marshall proposed a plan in June 1947 that called for the United States to provide economic assistance to European nations. Between 1948 and 1951, the United States loaned 16 Western European countries more than $12 billion.

The Marshall Plan was a huge success. It helped countries such as France, West Germany, and Italy recover from the war. American dollars built new factories, schools, hospitals, railroads, and bridges.

The Berlin Airlift The focus of Cold War hostility now shifted to Germany. At the Yalta Conference, the Allies had agreed to divide Germany into four zones. American, British, French, and Soviet troops would each control one of the zones. Germany's capital city, Berlin, which lay inside Soviet-controlled territory, was also divided into four zones.

By 1948, the Western powers believed that it was time to reunite Germany. Stalin was bitterly opposed to this move. In June 1948, the Soviets set up a blockade around Berlin. They prevented delivery of food supplies to West Berlin's two million residents. Stalin gambled that the Western Allies would accept the Communist takeover of West Berlin. However, the Allies <u>responded</u> with a massive airlift—sending cargo planes to deliver tons of supplies to the people. For almost a year, Western planes delivered supplies to West Berlin.

The Soviets finally called off the blockade in May 1949. In October, France, Britain, and the United States combined their zones into one country, called the Federal Republic of Germany, or West Germany. The Soviet zone became the German Democratic Republic, or East Germany.

Cold War Crisis A divided Germany and Berlin remained a focus of Cold War tensions. Between 1949 and 1961, thousands of East Germans fled to West Berlin. From there, they went to West Germany. Suddenly, in August 1961, the East German government began building a wall between East and West Germany. For 28 years, the wall stood as a symbol of a divided Germany and a divided Europe.

✓**Checkpoint** How did Harry Truman respond to attempts by Greek Communists to seize control of Greece?

International Organizations

After World War II, the United States played a leading role in creating the United Nations (UN). This move signaled a turn away from isolationism.

Vocabulary Builder
<u>respond</u> (rih SPAHND) **v.** to act in return, as if in answer

Analyze Underlying Causes
What was the stated cause of the Berlin blockade? What was the underlying, or overall, cause?

● **INFOGRAPHIC**

THE BERLIN AIRLIFT

During the Berlin Airlift, British and U.S. forces made more than 200,000 flights to deliver goods to the people in West Berlin. **Critical Thinking:** *Draw Conclusions* *Why do you think Stalin chose not to prevent the airlift?*

History *Interactive*

Learn More About the Berlin Airlift

Visit: PHSchool.com
Web Code: mvl-8251

▲ Medal worn by Berlin Airlift workers

Residents of West Berlin watch an approaching cargo plane loaded with food and other goods. At one point, nearly 13,000 tons of goods arrived in West Berlin each day. ▼

▲ A delivery of fresh milk

Division of Berlin, 1949

0   50   100 mi
0   50 100 km

DENMARK

North Sea

NETH.

POL.

Berlin

Elbe R.

Oder R.

WEST GERMANY

Rhine R.

EAST GERMANY

LUX.

CZECH.

FRANCE

Danube R.

West Berlin

East Berlin

Havel R.

Spree R.

Divided City of Berlin

SWITZ.

AUSTRIA

The Cold War in Europe

0 km 400
0 miles 400
Albers Conic Equal-Area Projection

KEY
- NATO nations, 1955
- Warsaw Pact, 1955
- Neutral nations
- Areas added to the Soviet Union after World War II

MAP MASTER®
Skills Activity

By 1955, the Cold War divided Europe into two camps: those nations belonging to NATO and those nations belonging to the Warsaw Pact.

(a) Read a Map Which NATO nations bordered Warsaw Pact nations?

(b) Apply Information Do you think it would be difficult for Yugoslavia to remain neutral? Explain.

MapMaster Online

For: Interactive map
Visit: PHSchool.com
Web Code: mvp-8251

The United Nations The main goals of the UN were to maintain peace and settle international disputes. Under the UN Charter, member nations agreed to bring disputes before the UN.

At the core of the United Nations are the General Assembly and the Security Council. Every nation, large or small, has a single vote in the General Assembly. However, the General Assembly has no way to enforce its decisions. The Security Council has far more power. Its decisions are supposed to be followed by all UN nations. The Security Council has 15 members. Five of them are permanent members—the United States, Russia, China, Britain, and France. Each permanent member has the power to **veto,** or reject, any proposal before the Security Council. If only one permanent member votes no, the Security Council cannot act.

The UN's greatest successes have been in fighting hunger and disease and improving education. Through relief programs, the UN has provided tons of goods, clothing, and medicine to victims of disaster.

NATO and the Warsaw Alliance In April 1949, as Cold War tensions rose, the United States and other Western nations established the North Atlantic Treaty Organization (NATO), a formal military alliance to guard against a Soviet attack. Members of NATO agreed that an attack on one member would be considered an attack against the entire group.

In response, the Soviet Union and the satellite nations of Eastern Europe formed their own alliance, the Warsaw Pact, in 1955.

☑Checkpoint How does the Security Council help the UN meet its goals?

The Shocks of 1949

Until 1949, most Americans were confident that the United States was safe because it alone knew how to build the atomic bomb. However, in September 1949, the Soviet Union exploded its own atomic bomb. Now, the Cold War seemed much more deadly. Each nation had within its reach the power to destroy the other.

Shortly after, Americans received a second shock. Since the 1930s, China had been a battleground between the Chinese Nationalists and the Chinese Communists. In the final months of 1949, the Nationalist government collapsed. China fell under the control of the Communists.

Under their leader, Mao Zedong, the Chinese Communists established the People's Republic of China. The Chinese Nationalists fled to the island of Taiwan. The United States insisted that the Taiwan government was the legal government of China. It refused to recognize the People's Republic and kept the UN from admitting Communist China to China's seat on the Security Council.

☑Checkpoint How did events in the Soviet Union and China in 1949 affect the Cold War?

⭐ **Looking Back and Ahead** The United States faced a world in which the world's largest nation, the Soviet Union, and the world's most populous nation, China, were under Communist rule. While fears stemming from the Cold War haunted Americans, they still held hopes for a better life after 15 years of depression and war.

Dr. Leo Szilard, who participated in the development of the atomic bomb, reads about the Soviet Union's test bomb.

Section 1 | **Check Your Progress**

Progress Monitoring ⊙nline
For: Self-test with instant help
Visit: PHSchool.com
Web Code: mva-8251

Comprehension and Critical Thinking

1. **(a) Recall** What were Stalin's goals for the Soviet Union after World War II?
   (b) Apply Information How did Stalin's goals affect the goals of U.S. foreign policy?

2. **(a) Recall** What is the purpose of the United Nations?
   (b) Evaluate Information Does the organization of the UN make it possible for it to be successful? Explain.

Reading Skill

3. **Analyze Underlying Causes** Reread the text under the heading "International Organizations." Identify the underlying causes for the U.S. decision to join the UN and participate in NATO.

Key Terms

Answer the following questions in complete sentences that show your understanding of the key terms.

4. What was the goal of the American policy of containment of the Soviet Union after World War II?

5. What happens when one country becomes a satellite of another?

Writing

6. Organize the following elements for a multimedia presentation about the UN. Explain the reasons for your choices.
   - Audiotape of opening ceremonies at the UN in 1945
   - Current photograph of the UN
   - Film clip of the Yalta Conference in 1945
   - Audiotape of translators at a General Assembly session

A Nice House on a Lake

❝When we were married, my husband earned $30 a week. We rented a five-room flat, . . . had a baby, etc. Now we have five children and an income of over $25,000 a year. We own our eight-room house—also a nice house on a lake.❞

—Lucille Windam, 1950s housewife

◀ In the 1950s, television became a popular pastime.

A Time of Prosperity

Objectives

- Identify the problems of the postwar economy.
- Explain the effects of a changing society on the lives of Americans during the 1950s.
- Contrast life in the suburbs with life in the cities.

🕒 Reading Skill

Analyze Long-Term Effects Many events in history cause long-term effects. For example, World War II had lasting effects on the American economy and culture. Think about the difficulty of living through these times as you identify long-term effects in this section. Also, note how some of these effects may become the causes for the next effects.

Key Terms and People

closed shop
productivity
standard of living
baby boom

rock-and-roll
Elvis Presley
inner city

Why It Matters As America's leaders waged the Cold War all around the world, important economic, social, and political changes were occurring at home. Many Americans enjoyed a new burst of prosperity. However, not all shared the benefits of the economic boom.

❓ **Section Focus Question: How did the American economy and society change after World War II?**

Adjusting to Peacetime

On the home front, Americans faced important economic challenges after the war. Defense industries had closed or had scaled back employment. Millions of soldiers would have to be absorbed into the postwar economy. The nation faced a serious problem—how to change back to a peacetime economy.

To help meet these needs, Congress had passed an act in 1944 that became known as the GI Bill of Rights. (GI, which stands for "government issue," was the name given to any member of the U.S. armed forces.) The bill gave veterans money to spend on business, homes, and schooling. The GI Bill helped more than two million former soldiers attend college to prepare for new careers.

Inflation During World War II, consumer goods had been in short supply. With the war's end, Americans were ready and eager to buy. Because demand far exceeded the supply of goods, the result was soaring inflation.

As prices rose, workers demanded large pay increases. When employers refused, a wave of strikes swept the nation.

Although President Truman supported labor, he feared that wage increases would lead to even higher prices. In May 1946, he ended a United Mine Workers strike by taking over the mines. When railroad workers struck a month later, Truman threatened to order them back to work. That angered union members. When the President encouraged industries to raise salaries, inflation resulted. That made consumers angry.

During the 1946 elections, Republicans asked voters, "Had enough?" Voters seemed to agree. The election gave Republicans a majority in both the House and the Senate.

Armed with the power to cancel many New Deal programs, Congress passed the Taft-Hartley Act. The act let the government get a court order to delay a strike for 80 days if the strike threatened public safety. The act also forbade unions to contribute to political campaigns. Also, the act banned the closed shop. A **closed shop** is a workplace in which only union members can be hired. Truman vetoed the Taft-Hartley Act, but Congress passed the act over Truman's veto. Eventually, President Truman would try to <u>expand</u> the goal of the New Deal with his Fair Deal reforms.

Analyze Long-Term Effects
What was one long-term effect of the shortage of consumer goods after the war? How do you think Americans felt about it?

Vocabulary Builder
<u>expand</u> (ek SPAND) **v.** to make bigger

The Railroad Strike

Speaking before Congress in 1946, President Truman presented his proposal to end the railroad strike.

"I request . . . legislation [that] after the government has taken over an industry and . . . directed men to remain or return to work, the wage scale should be fixed . . . and . . . it shall be retroactive [effective from a particular date in the past]. This legislation must be . . . fair to capital and labor alike. . . . As part of this legislation, I request Congress to authorize the president to draft into the armed forces . . . all workers who are on strike against their government."

Reading Primary Sources
Skills Activity

(a) Apply Information What role would the government have in Truman's plan?

(b) Draw Conclusions Do you think the workers would be pleased with the plan? Explain.

A Truman Victory

Harry Truman holds an early edition of the *Chicago Tribune* that mistakenly declares Dewey the winner of the 1948 election. **Critical Thinking: *Apply Information*** *What does this headline indicate about the election results?*

The Election of 1948 In early 1948, President Truman's chances for reelection looked slim. Two out of three voters disapproved of the way he was leading the country. Even Truman's own Democrats were split. Angered by Truman's support of civil rights for African Americans, white southern Democrats nominated their own candidate, South Carolina Governor Strom Thurmond. Liberal Democrats, unhappy with Truman's policy of challenging Soviet expansion, formed the Progressive Party. They nominated former Vice President Henry Wallace to run for President.

Confident of victory, the Republicans nominated New York's governor, Thomas Dewey. Dewey did not campaign hard. Truman, on the other hand, campaigned tirelessly. He traveled more than 30,000 miles and made hundreds of speeches. Everywhere Truman went, he attacked what he called the "do-nothing" Republican Congress.

On election night, people still expected a Dewey victory. In fact, the *Chicago Tribune* printed its first edition with the headline "DEWEY DEFEATS TRUMAN."

The election was one of the biggest upsets in American history. Truman squeaked past Dewey to victory. The Democrats also regained control of both the House and the Senate.

President Truman saw his narrow victory as a chance to act on his Fair Deal program, which he had proposed during the campaign. Congress approved a few of the President's Fair Deal proposals. For example, lawmakers increased the minimum wage and provided funds for flood control and low-income housing. However, Congress refused to fund education and national health insurance. It also voted down Truman's proposals to reduce racial discrimination.

Eisenhower's Middle Way In 1952, Truman decided not to run again. In the election of 1952, the Democrats nominated Adlai Stevenson, governor of Illinois. The Republicans chose General Dwight D. Eisenhower, nicknamed Ike. A war hero, Eisenhower won a landslide victory.

In contrast to Roosevelt and Truman, Eisenhower believed that the federal government should play a smaller role in the economy. He called for cutting spending, though not for ending programs that helped people. In fact, he increased the number of people who could receive Social Security benefits.

Generally, Eisenhower followed a middle-of-the-road policy in his two terms as President. Running on a record of "peace, progress, and prosperity" won him another huge victory in 1956.

Perhaps Eisenhower's greatest achievement was the Interstate Highway Act of 1956. It provided funds for a vast system of freeways to link all parts of the United States. Increasingly, Americans used highways instead of railroads for traveling and for transporting goods.

☑**Checkpoint** How did inflation affect the postwar economy?

A Changing Society

The Eisenhower years were prosperous ones for many Americans. Inflation slowed and employment soared. New technologies such as the use of computers helped increase American productivity. **Productivity** is the rate at which workers produce goods. Increasing it meant that workers were able to work more efficiently and produce more goods.

New jobs put money in consumers' pockets. Americans responded by spending money on homes, furniture, and cars. Shoppers also bought new products like televisions and air conditioners.

Throughout the 1950s, the American standard of living rose steadily. The **standard of living** is a measure of how comfortable life is for a person, group, or country. By the end of the decade, 6 out of 10 American families owned homes, and 3 out of 4 had cars. Americans manufactured and bought nearly 1 out of every 2 products produced anywhere in the entire world.

The United States was in the midst of change. After the dangers of war, Americans were looking for security. Many found it in their homes and families.

Baby Boom In the postwar years, Americans married earlier than their parents had. They also raised larger families. The increased birthrate became known as the **baby boom**. The baby boom increased demand for food, housing, and manufactured goods.

Meanwhile, people were living longer thanks to new medicines that became popular in the 1950s. For example, antibiotic medicines could now cure many serious infectious diseases. A new vaccine kept adults and children safe from the crippling disease of polio.

Analyze Long-Term Effects
What caused the economic recovery of the prosperous 1950s? What long-term effects did the recovery cause?

Increase in Car Ownership, 1948–1960

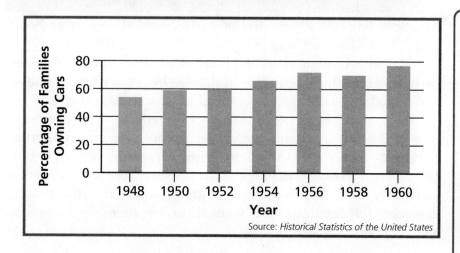

Source: *Historical Statistics of the United States*

Reading Charts
Skills Activity

With the move to the suburbs, people depended more on automobiles. Manufacturers pushed to meet the demands.

(a) **Read a Bar Graph** During which years did automobile ownership remain about the same?

(b) **Identify Causes and Effects** Trace the change in car ownership between 1954 and 1960. List several events (political, social, and economic) that strongly affected the change in ownership at that time.

A New Prosperity

In the decades following World War II, huge numbers of Americans moved to newly developed communities in the suburbs (shown at right). However, not everyone shared this good life. In the cities, housing was often run down (left), and many people were unemployed. **Critical Thinking: Apply Information** *Why do you think a book called* The Other America *was written about American life during this time?*

Vocabulary Builder
negative (NEHG ah tihv) ***adj.*** in opposition to an idea; not positive

Escaping the City Americans bought automobiles as fast as auto plants could make them. Nowhere were these cars more appreciated than in the growing suburbs. During the 1950s, the number of Americans living in the suburbs grew by 50 percent.

Suburbs grew around cities throughout the United States. The growth was most pronounced in the West. As a result, states such as California, Arizona, and Texas gained both people and political power.

Television Of all the new products of the 1950s, the one that had the greatest impact on American life was television. In 1946, only 8,000 homes had a television set. By the mid-1950s, three out of four American homes had one. By the early 1960s, almost every house had one television set, and many homes had more than one.

Television brought news and entertainment into people's homes. Early programs included original dramas by top writers and situation comedies, or sitcoms, about the ideal middle-class family.

There were, however, some <u>negative</u> effects from television. During the 1950s, watching television became the most important activity of family life. In fact, by 1956, Americans were spending almost as much time watching television every week as they spent at work. The first frozen dinners, introduced in the 1950s, were designed for families who wanted to combine mealtime and television viewing.

Rock-and-Roll Television also helped to make popular a new kind of music, rock-and-roll. Rock-and-roll was a blend of black rhythm-and-blues and country music. By far the most popular singer of rock-and-roll was Elvis Presley. With hips shaking and knees bending,

Presley soon became a teen idol and national star. Adults, on the other hand, were shocked at his music and his provocative dance moves. When he appeared on national television, the camera showed only his upper body.

Signs of Trouble Not everyone enjoyed this new prosperity. As jobs and people moved to the suburbs, cities lost important tax money. The **inner cities**, or centers of older cities, became home to poorer, less educated people. Cities could no longer raise enough tax money to repair old apartments, schools, and subways. City schools and other services declined. Crime rose. More and more, the people who stayed in the cities were those who could not afford to move.

Many social critics took note of this division between city and suburb. A small band of critics accused Americans of living in a closed society where differences were not tolerated. One critic, William H. White, wrote *The Organization Man* in 1956. It reported the ways Americans felt pressure to conform to group behavior. Others criticized what they saw as a growing emphasis on material possessions and spending.

Reading Skill — Analyze Long-Term Effects
How did postwar prosperity create long-term changes in American life? Explain how effects became causes that led to more effects.

HISTORIAN'S APPRENTICE ACTIVITY PACK

To further explore the topics in this chapter, complete the activity in the Historian's Apprentice Activity Pack to answer this essential question:

What major influences have helped shape American society and culture?

Checkpoint **How did the changes of the 1950s improve the lives of most Americans?**

Looking Back and Ahead As the United States was poised to enjoy a new burst of prosperity, a conflict was brewing in a faraway corner of the world, the Korean Peninsula. It would draw the United States into a very "hot" and bloody war, and set off a period of self-doubt among Americans.

Section 2 | Check Your Progress

Progress Monitoring Online
For: Self-test with instant help
Visit: PHSchool.com
Web Code: mva-8252

Comprehension and Critical Thinking

1. **(a) Recall** How did Truman attempt to end the strikes by mine workers and railroad workers?
   (b) Evaluate Information Truman claimed to be a friend of labor. Based on his actions, do you think that was true? Explain.
2. **(a) Apply Information** What impact did television have on the American family in the 1950s?
   (b) Link Past and Present How is television different today from television in the 1950s?

Reading Skill

3. **Analyze Long-Term Effects** Reread the text following the subheading "Inflation." Explain that an increased demand for consumer goods led to effects that, in turn, caused other effects. Include the emotions that played a role in the process and identify any long-term effects.

Key Terms

Answer the following questions in complete sentences that show your understanding of the key terms.

4. What would happen to a woman who wanted to work at a closed shop but refused to join a union?
5. What are inner cities? What happened to them in the 1950s?
6. What does a standard of living measure?

Writing

7. Make a list of some materials you would use to prepare a multimedia presentation about American popular culture during the 1950s. (For suggestions, refer to the Life at the Time feature on the pages that follow). Write a few sentences introducing and explaining your choices.

Growing Up in the 1950s

There were a lot of kids growing up in the 1950s. And they enjoyed themselves in ways that had never existed before. The changes that took place in American popular culture back then are still a part of our lives today.

The Baby Boom

During the Great Depression and World War II, couples had fewer children. But after 1946, the birthrate soared.

U.S. Births, 1944–1954

Source: *Historical Statistics of the United States*

The kids at this 1950s soda fountain were part of this postwar baby boom. ▼

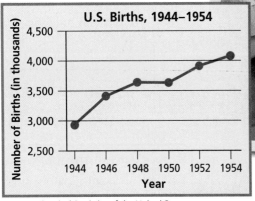

The wild dancing of Elvis Presley outraged many parents. To a generation of teens, Elvis Presley was "The King." ▲

◄ Chuck Berry is often called the Father of Rock-and-Roll. He invented driving guitar riffs that are still being imitated by today's bands.

Rock-and-Roll

The baby boomers were the first generation to grow up with rock-and-roll. The pulsing new music blended elements of rhythm and blues, country and western, and pop music. Concerts by artists such as Chuck Berry and Little Richard brought white and black teenagers together, enjoying the same beat.

Television

Television was invented in the 1920s. Not until the 1950s, however, did the TV set become a familiar feature in most homes. The baby boomers were the first generation to grow up watching "the tube."

The puppet Howdy Doody and his sidekick Buffalo Bob Smith starred in one of the best-loved children's programs of the day.

▼

Analyze LIFE AT THE TIME

Prepare an interview with someone who grew up or went to school during the 1950s. Write 5–7 questions about television, music, or other topics of concern to teenagers.

Communism in Asia

❝ The prestige of the Western world hangs in the balance. . . . It is plainly apparent that here in Asia is where the Communist conspirators have elected to make their play for global conquest. ❞

—General Douglas MacArthur, 1950

◀ American soldiers in Korea

The Korean War Period

Objectives

- Explain how the situation in Korea became the Korean War, the first military conflict of the Cold War.

- Describe how the Korean War ended.

- Explain how the Cold War led to a Red Scare in the United States.

🔁 Reading Skill

Analyze a Cause-and-Effect Chain

Consider how events can snowball out of control when a single cause has multiple effects that, in turn, lead to multiple causes. As the United States entered the Korean War period, this occurred often. Look for the multiple cause-and-effect chains in this section. To find them, read the text following each subheading, and then trace a chain. Watch for events having specific cause-and-effect relationships and not those just occurring in sequence.

Key Terms and People

stalemate
demilitarized zone

Joseph McCarthy
censure

Why It Matters At the outset of the Cold War, the United States used political and economic means to battle against Communism. However, the Cold War suddenly turned hot in the East Asian nation of Korea. As American soldiers fought in the Korean War, other Americans hunted for Communists in America.

❓ Section Focus Question: How did the United States respond to the invasion of Korea and its aftermath?

Conflict in Korea

In 1910, Japan occupied the Korean Peninsula and ruled it harshly. After Japan's defeat in World War II, Korea was divided at the 38th parallel of latitude. The Soviet Union backed a Communist government in North Korea. The United States backed a non-Communist government in South Korea.

Tensions between North and South Korea continued to increase. Then, on June 25, 1950, North Korean troops suddenly invaded South Korea. Armed with Soviet tanks and artillery, the North Koreans shattered the South Korean army and pushed south. Within three days, the invasion had reached South Korea's capital, Seoul (sole). Korea, it appeared, would soon fall to the Communists.

President Truman quickly responded to the attack. At his urging, the UN Security Council voted to send a military force to Korea. Truman appointed World War II hero General Douglas MacArthur to lead the force. Although 16 nations sent troops to fight under the UN flag, 90 percent were American. The Soviet delegate was not present at the UN debate and so failed to veto the proposal.

The first UN forces to arrive at the front were badly outnumbered and poorly supplied. They fought bravely but were pushed back almost to the tip of the Korean Peninsula. As fresh troops and supplies arrived, however, the defensive line held.

Then, in September, General MacArthur launched a bold counterattack. UN forces at Inchon, a port city near Seoul, were able to <u>pursue</u> the North Koreans back across the 38th parallel into North Korea. MacArthur's forces chased the North Koreans almost to the Yalu River, which separates North Korea from China.

China's government responded angrily. As UN soldiers neared the Yalu, masses of Chinese troops crossed the border. The UN forces were overwhelmed. Soon, the battlefront was once again in South Korea. There, the war settled down into a **stalemate,** a situation in which neither side wins.

Truman Versus MacArthur General MacArthur believed that the United States could win in Korea only if it attacked China. MacArthur publicly called for the bombing of supply bases in China. President Truman was more cautious. He believed that an American attack on China might start a new world war. Truman warned MacArthur against making further public statements.

MacArthur disregarded these warnings. He publicly argued that he could not win the war because of politicians in Washington. Truman was furious and fired MacArthur.

Peace Talks Meanwhile, the stalemate in Korea continued. In July 1951, the opposing sides began peace talks. These talks would continue for two long years. All the while, the fighting and the killing continued.

Vocabulary Builder
pursue (per SYOO) **v.** to follow; to attempt to capture or achieve

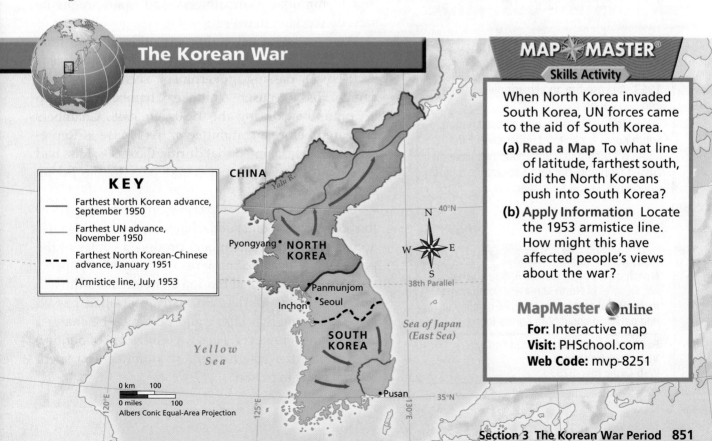

The Korean War

KEY

—— Farthest North Korean advance, September 1950

—— Farthest UN advance, November 1950

- - - Farthest North Korean-Chinese advance, January 1951

—— Armistice line, July 1953

CHINA
Yalu R.
Pyongyang • NORTH KOREA
Panmunjom
Inchon • Seoul
SOUTH KOREA
• Pusan

Yellow Sea

Sea of Japan (East Sea)

N 40°N
W E
S
38th Parallel
35°N
120°E 125°E 130°E

0 km 100
0 miles 100
Albers Conic Equal-Area Projection

MAP MASTER®
Skills Activity

When North Korea invaded South Korea, UN forces came to the aid of South Korea.

(a) Read a Map To what line of latitude, farthest south, did the North Koreans push into South Korea?

(b) Apply Information Locate the 1953 armistice line. How might this have affected people's views about the war?

MapMaster Online

For: Interactive map
Visit: PHSchool.com
Web Code: mvp-8251

A cease-fire finally ended the fighting in July 1953. The border between the warring sides stood almost exactly where it had been before the war. The two sides agreed to establish a demilitarized zone, an area from which military forces are prohibited. It still divides the two countries a half-century later.

The war's toll was horrendous. At least two million Koreans died in the fighting. Most of them were civilians. American losses totaled well over 30,000 dead and more than 100,000 wounded. Thousands of soldiers from other nations also were killed.

With the cease-fire, the fighting ended in Korea. However, tensions between North and South Korea continued well into the next century. Two heavily armed forces continued to face each other across the demilitarized zone.

☑ **Checkpoint** **How did the United States become involved in the Korean War?**

Fears at Home

In Section 1 of this chapter, you learned how American confidence was shaken by the Communist victory in China and Soviet possession of the atomic bomb. The failure to win a decisive victory in the long stalemate in Korea further worried Americans.

Communists in Government? Americans had absorbed a number of blows during the Cold War. Soviet possession of atomic weapons, the fall of China to the Communists, and the stalemate in Korea all led to worries about the ability of the United States to defeat communism. Many Americans worried that Communist sympathizers and spies might be secretly working to overthrow the U.S. government.

Two cases seized public attention. In the first, Alger Hiss, a former State Department official, was accused of passing government secrets to Soviet agents. Hiss's accuser, Whittaker Chambers, had been a Communist during the 1930s. In 1948, Chambers appeared before a committee of the House of Representatives. He claimed that during the 1930s, Hiss had given him top-secret papers to pass to the Soviet Union.

Hiss strongly denied passing any secret papers to the Soviet Union and sued Chambers for making false accusations. Then, Chambers produced copies of the papers. They became known as the "pumpkin papers" because Chambers had hidden them on microfilm in a pumpkin in his garden. So many years had passed since the crime that Hiss could no longer be charged with spying. However, Hiss was convicted of perjury, or lying, to the congressional committee and spent several years in prison.

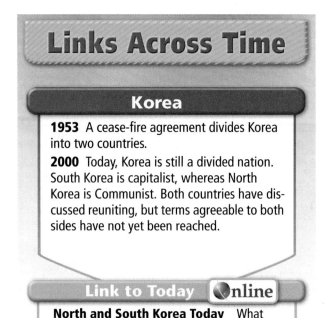

Links Across Time

Korea

1953 A cease-fire agreement divides Korea into two countries.

2000 Today, Korea is still a divided nation. South Korea is capitalist, whereas North Korea is Communist. Both countries have discussed reuniting, but terms agreeable to both sides have not yet been reached.

Link to Today · Online

North and South Korea Today What are the roles of North Korea and South Korea in the global community today? Go online to find out more about both Koreas today.

For: North and South Korea today
Visit: PHSchool.com
Web Code: mvc-8253

The Hunt for Communists

"It's Okay—We're Hunting Communists"

The car is a symbol for the House Un-American Activities Committee.

Tire marks

Reading Political Cartoons
Skills Activity

In 1947, the House Un-American Activities Committee led an investigation to find Communists in the moviemaking industry.

(a) Identify Main Ideas What does the cartoon suggest about the way in which the investigation is being carried out?

(b) Recognize Points of View How does the cartoonist feel about the success of the investigation? Explain.

Fears about America's security rose even higher in 1950 when several Americans were arrested on charges of passing the secret of the atomic bomb to the Soviets. In the most famous trial of the times, a married couple, Julius and Ethel Rosenberg, were found guilty of supplying secret information to the Soviet Union. They were sentenced to death. A worldwide outcry arose, but the Rosenbergs were executed in 1953.

Today, more than half a century after the trials of Alger Hiss and Julius and Ethel Rosenberg, their roles are still debated. However, many questions of their involvement have been <u>resolved</u>. In the 1990s, the U.S. government released copies of secret Soviet messages that had been decoded after years of dedicated work. The messages appeared to show that both Alger Hiss and Julius Rosenberg had spied for the Soviets. Ethel Rosenberg apparently was aware of the spying and may even have assisted her husband.

McCarthyism A climate of fear contributed to the rise of Senator Joseph McCarthy of Wisconsin. McCarthy built his career by threatening to expose Communists. In a speech in Wheeling, West Virginia, in February 1950, McCarthy waved a paper in the air. He claimed it contained the names of 205 Communists who worked in the State Department. McCarthy later reduced this number to 81, then to 57.

Vocabulary Builder
resolve (ree SAHLV) **v.** to settle or decide

McCarthy refused to show the list to anyone. He did not even need to do so because many Americans were eager to believe him. His dramatic charges gained him a large following.

During the next four years, McCarthy's charges became more sensational. He led Senate hearings in which he bullied witnesses and made exaggerated charges. Eventually, the term *McCarthyism* came to mean accusing someone of disloyalty without having any evidence.

Aware of McCarthy's power to destroy careers, few people were brave enough to oppose him and his scare tactics. McCarthy finally lost his following in 1954 when a television audience of millions saw him make false accusations against the United States Army. Many Americans came to realize that McCarthy could not support the charges. Unfortunately, many lives had been ruined by McCarthy's wild charges. Soon after, the U.S. Senate voted to censure, or condemn, him. McCarthy died three years later. By that time, the Communist scare was mostly finished.

✓ **Checkpoint** **What techniques did McCarthy use to accuse people of being Communists?**

⭐ **Looking Back and Ahead** After McCarthy's fall, tensions between the United States and the Soviet Union continued. No one knew that the conflict between the two superpowers would drag on for almost 40 additional years.

Section 3 | Check Your Progress

Progress Monitoring Online
For: Self-test with instant help
Visit: PHSchool.com
Web Code: mva-8253

Comprehension and Critical Thinking

1. **(a) Recall** How did the Korean War start?
(b) Synthesize Information How did the U.S. response to the Korean War reflect the goals of the Truman Doctrine?

2. **(a) Describe** What did Senator McCarthy do in the 1950s?
(b) Analyze Cause and Effect How did McCarthy's actions threaten democratic freedoms in the United States?

Reading Skill

3. **Analyze a Cause-and-Effect Chain** Reread the entire text under the heading "Fears at Home." Analyze the cause-and-effect chain from American worries about global communism to government investigations and spy trials.

Key Terms

Read each sentence below. If the sentence is true, write YES. If the sentence is not true, write NO and explain why.

4. The Korean War ended in a stalemate; boundaries changed little and neither side won the war.

5. The United States censured Senator McCarthy by awarding him the Congressional Medal of Honor for his work fighting communism.

6. The soldiers were preparing to occupy the demilitarized zone.

Writing

7. You are preparing a multimedia presentation about McCarthyism. Write a few sentences to introduce your presentation. Then, write a brief introduction for a film clip of Senator McCarthy speaking. Finally, write a few sentences to conclude your presentation.

If the Bomb Drops . . .

" If you are in the open, drop to the ground instantly, back to the light, and try to shade your bare face, neck, arms, and hands. This will not shield you from gamma rays, but will protect you from burns. "

— "What to Do if Bomb Falls Without Warning," Seattle Civil Defense Manual, 1951

◀ Posters warned Americans about the threat of nuclear war.

Global Concerns in the Cold War

Objectives

- Explain how the Cold War turned into an arms race.
- Describe how the Cold War divided the emerging countries in Asia and Africa.
- Explain how communism gained influence in Latin America.
- Explain why Cuba became a crisis spot during the Cold War.

Reading Skill

Evaluate Short- and Long-Term Effects Some causes lead to both short- and long-term effects. For example, an event might cause an immediate reaction and also change a long-standing pattern in society. The Cold War had many immediate effects on the world. It also had long-term effects.

Key Terms and People

superpower
arms race

stockpile
John F. Kennedy

Why It Matters Tensions between the United States and Communist nations increased during and after the Korean War. As the Cold War intensified, the United States and the Soviet Union competed for power around the world. They engaged in a dangerous competition to build up their supplies of nuclear weapons.

? Section Focus Question: How did the Cold War increase tensions around the world?

The Arms Race

After almost 30 years of totalitarian rule in the Soviet Union, Josef Stalin died in 1953. His death brought no letup in the Cold War tensions. A new Soviet leader, Nikita Khrushchev (KROOSH chawf), predicted that communism would destroy the Western democracies.

By the end of the 1950s, the United States and the Soviet Union had emerged as world superpowers. **Superpowers** are countries whose military, economic, and political strength are so great that they can influence events worldwide.

In the 1950s, the two nations began an expensive and dangerous arms race. An **arms race** is a contest in which nations compete to build more and more powerful weapons. In 1952, Americans exploded the first hydrogen bomb, or H-bomb. Soon, the Soviets had their own H-bomb. China joined the race by exploding its own atomic bomb in 1964. Three years later, China exploded a hydrogen bomb. Britain and France also developed nuclear weapons.

Race to the Moon

The launching of *Sputnik* set a new challenge for the United States. NASA's goal was to send a person into space. The government spent billions of dollars in the effort. John Glenn (shown here), in 1962, became the first American to orbit, or travel around, Earth. His flight lasted nearly five hours. **Critical Thinking: Link Past and Present** *Do you think space exploration is still considered as important today as it was during the 1950s and 1960s? Explain.*

No country wanted to use nuclear weapons and risk a deadly counterattack. Instead, the nuclear nations stockpiled, or collected, their nuclear weapons. By the 1970s, the Soviet Union and the United States had enough weapons stockpiled to destroy each other many times over.

The superpowers also competed in space. In October 1957, the Soviet Union alarmed the West by launching the world's first human-made satellite. *Sputnik* weighed only 184 pounds, but the tiny satellite circling Earth at 18,000 miles an hour gave Americans a huge shock. If the Soviets could send satellites into space, they could also launch nuclear missiles at American cities.

The United States and the Soviets were now also in a race to develop the technology to control outer space. In response to *Sputnik*, Congress created the National Aeronautics and Space Administration (NASA) to launch its own space missions. Congress also passed the National Defense Education Act. Its goal was to produce more scientists and more teachers.

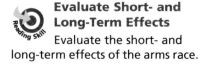

Evaluate Short- and Long-Term Effects
Evaluate the short- and long-term effects of the arms race.

☑ **Checkpoint** How did the launch of *Sputnik* affect Americans?

Emerging Nations

After World War II, many former colonies gained their independence. The United States and the Soviet Union soon were engaged in a competition to win allies among the new nations.

The Peace Corps The Soviet Union made a major effort to win support among the newly independent nations. To counter this appeal, President John F. Kennedy in 1961 proposed that Congress establish a Peace Corps. The new program sought to build friendships between Americans and the people of other nations. It also sought to encourage economic growth in developing countries.

Thousands of Americans, young and old, volunteered to serve in poor villages in Asia, Africa, and Latin America. They shared their skills and knowledge as teachers, doctors, nurses, carpenters, and farmers.

Developments in Africa The Soviet Union quickly extended aid to the new African nations of Ghana and Guinea. To counter Soviet influence, the United States expanded its own aid to other newly independent countries.

The Congo became a flash point for this competition between the United States and the Soviet Union to gain influence in a region. In 1960, the former Belgian Congo gained independence as the nation of Congo. Soon, opposing groups were fighting over control of the new country. The United States backed one side. The Soviet Union aided the other side. Each side supplied airplanes, trucks, and technical advisers to its Congo allies. The war became increasingly violent.

The Philippines With European nations weakened by World War II, many Asians saw an opportunity to seize the independence for which they had long hungered.

The first Asian country to win independence in the postwar period was the Philippine Islands. The United States had promised Filipinos independence in 1934. Twelve years later, in 1946, the United States lived up to its promise.

Unrest soon developed in the Philippines. Many Filipinos wanted reforms, especially land reforms. When the government moved too slowly toward making changes, fighting broke out. Some of the rebels were Communists. By 1954, the government had defeated the rebels. It also made some needed land reforms.

After Ferdinand Marcos became president in 1965, however, the government became less democratic. In the years that followed, many groups continued to push for greater reforms.

Indochina Indochina, which had been under French control, took a different path. After World War II, France struggled to maintain control. In one of the colonies, Vietnam, Ho Chi Minh (HOH CHEE MIHN) led the fight for independence from France. Because Ho was a Communist who had Soviet backing, the United States backed the French. In 1954, Ho's forces defeated the French and won control of the northern part of Vietnam. Fighting in Vietnam would last for almost 30 years. Before it ended, the fighting would draw the United States into a long and bitter war. You will read about the Vietnam War in another chapter.

✓**Checkpoint** How did the Peace Corps help the United States build friendships with other nations?

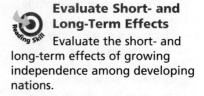

Evaluate Short- and Long-Term Effects Evaluate the short- and long-term effects of growing independence among developing nations.

A Volunteer
This Peace Corps worker strolls with children in Turkey in 1966. She helped start a library, nursery school, and community center in Ankara.

The Cuban Missile Crisis For 13 days in 1962, a standoff between President Kennedy and Soviet leader Nikita Khrushchev over missile bases inside Cuba drew the superpowers dangerously close to a nuclear war. *Critical Thinking: Analyze Cause and Effect How did the Cuban missile crisis affect the arms race?*

Vocabulary Builder
<u>revolt</u> (ree VOHLT) *n.* uprising; rebellion

Latin America and the Cold War

In the 1950s, the Cold War moved close to the United States, in Latin America. The nations of Latin America faced many critical problems, including widespread poverty and poor health care. The United States hoped that moderate Latin American governments would gradually improve these conditions.

Many Latin Americans, however, rejected gradual solutions. Instead, <u>revolts</u> brought anti-American groups to power. Many Americans worried about the threat to American security and American businesses in Latin America. As a result, the United States helped military dictators keep or gain power in several Latin American countries. This policy aroused hostile feelings in Latin America toward the United States.

Fidel Castro Comes to Power In January 1959, Fidel Castro, a Communist, led a successful revolution in Cuba. The Soviet Union promised Castro aid. Castro also began to encourage revolution in other parts of Latin America.

Castro's actions forced thousands of Cubans into exile. An exile is a person who is forced to leave his or her own country. Many came to live in the United States.

In April 1961, a group of Cuban exiles secretly trained by the U.S. Central Intelligence Agency landed at the Bay of Pigs on the southern coast of Cuba. The invasion failed. However, the invasion made Castro more popular in Cuba and embarrassed the United States.

Cuban Missile Crisis The next crisis was even more serious. In 1962, aerial photographs showed American leaders that the Soviets were building nuclear missile bases inside Cuba. The bases could be used to launch missiles against the United States.

Kennedy insisted that Soviet Premier Nikita Khrushchev remove the missiles. Kennedy called them "a threat to world peace." The President imposed a naval blockade on Cuba. He ordered the U.S. Navy to stop any Soviet ship from bringing missiles to Cuba.

For 13 days, the world held its breath, hoping that there would not be an <u>encounter</u> between the two superpowers. Soviet ships packed with more missiles steamed toward Cuba. American armed forces went on alert. Across the country, Americans wondered what would happen if the Soviet ships did not turn back.

At the last moment, the Soviet ships approaching the blockade turned back. Khrushchev agreed to withdraw the missiles. The United States pledged not to invade Cuba. U.S. Secretary of State Dean Rusk described the tense last hours of the crisis: "We were eyeball to eyeball, and I think the other fellow just blinked."

Vocabulary Builder
<u>encounter</u> (ehn KOWN ter) **n.** short, dangerous, or frightening meeting between people, groups, or things

✓Checkpoint **Why were events in Cuba troubling to the American government?**

⭐ **Looking Back and Ahead** Dramatic changes occurred in United States foreign policy after World War II. Isolationism was no longer a valid response to world events. There were also critical changes on the home front, especially in the area of racial relations. You will learn about this historic era in the next chapter.

Section 4 | Check Your Progress

Progress Monitoring Online

For: Self-test with instant help
Visit: PHSchool.com
Web Code: mva-8254

Comprehension and Critical Thinking

1. (a) Recall Why did the United States become involved in the affairs of some Latin American countries?
(b) Detect Points of View How do you think the outcome of the Cuban missile crisis affected Kennedy's reputation in the United States? How do you think it affected Khrushchev's reputation in the Soviet Union?

2. (a) Identify What event in October 1957 shocked the United States?
(b) Draw Conclusions Why was the event seen as a grave threat?

🔵 Reading Skill

3. Evaluate Short- and Long-Term Effects Reread the text following the subheading "Developments in Africa." Evaluate the short- and long-term effects of civil war in the Congo.

Key Terms

Complete each of the following sentences so that the second part further explains the first part and clearly shows your understanding of the key term.
4. In the 1950s, the Soviet Union and the United States engaged in a dangerous arms race, _____.

5. After World War II, the United States and the Soviet Union emerged as the world's two superpowers, _____.

Writing

6. Add to the following list of items to be used in a multimedia presentation about the Cuban missile crisis: photograph of Soviet missiles in Cuba; photograph of Senator Kenneth Keating presenting aerial view of missile sites.

21st Century Learning

Throughout history, nations have made choices about their political futures. Making these choices often involves choosing between alternative, or different, solutions to a serious problem. By studying these alternatives, you can better understand how the actions of political leaders and governments affected history.

The excerpt below is from President Harry S Truman's speech to a joint session of Congress. In it, he discusses what has become known as the Truman Doctrine.

Primary Source

" . . . One aspect of the present situation which I . . . present to you . . . concerns Greece and Turkey. The United States has received from the Greek government an urgent appeal for financial and economic assistance. . . . The very existence of the Greek state is today threatened by the terrorist activities of several thousand armed men, led by Communists, who defy the government's authority at a number of points. . . .

Greece must have assistance if it is to become a self-supporting and self-respecting democracy. The United States must supply that assistance.

. . . I believe that it must be the policy of the United States to support free peoples who are resisting attempted subjugation by armed minorities or by outside pressures. . . . [O]ur help should be primarily through economic and financial aid, which is essential to economic stability and orderly political processes.

. . . I therefore ask the Congress to provide authority for assistance to Greece and Turkey in the amount of $400 million for the period ending June 30, 1948."

—Harry S Truman, March 12, 1947

Learn the Skill

Use these steps to identify alternatives.

1 **Identify the problem.** You must identify the problems before you identify the alternatives. What does the primary source address?

2 **Identify the alternative solutions.** What choices are presented? Look for each main idea.

3 **Evaluate the consequences of each alternative solution.** Alternative solutions will have certain results. Frame questions to help you identify these results, and draw conclusions about the best course of action.

Practice the Skill

Answer the following questions about the primary sources on this page.

1 **Identify the problem.** What political issue is the subject of Truman's speech to Congress?

2 **Identify the alternative solutions.** What solution to the problem does Truman propose?

3 **Evaluate the consequences of each alternative solution.** (a) What do you think may be the result of the solution proposed by Truman? (b) Do you think this is the best plan for dealing with postwar Greece? Explain.

Apply the Skill

See the Review and Assessment at the end of this chapter.

What key foreign and domestic issues affected the United States after World War II?

Section 1
Roots of the Cold War

- Truman established the policy of containment to limit Soviet expansion.
- The United Nations was established to maintain peace and to settle international disputes.
- The Soviet Union exploded its own atomic bomb in 1949, ending the U.S. monopoly on nuclear weapons.

Section 2
A Time of Prosperity

- The Republican Congress passed the Taft-Hartley Act over Truman's veto, limiting the power of unions.
- Truman and the Democrats won the 1948 election.
- The election of Eisenhower in 1952 marked a time of prosperity for most Americans.

Section 3
The Korean War Period

- In the early 1950s, American military forces prevented the Communists from taking over all of Korea.
- Senator Joseph McCarthy begins a career trying to expose Communists.

Section 4
Global Concerns in the Cold War

- The nuclear arms race between the United States and the Soviet Union begins.
- Fidel Castro took over Cuba and made it a Communist nation.
- Castro's attempt to make Cuba a Soviet military base in the Americas was checked by President Kennedy during the Cuban missile crisis.

? Exploring the Essential Question

Use the online study guide to explore the essential question.

Section 1
How did the United States respond to the early stages of the Cold War?

Section 2
How did the American economy and society change after World War II?

Chapter 25 Essential Question
What key foreign and domestic issues affected the United States after World War II?

Section 4
How did the Cold War increase tensions around the world?

Section 3
How did the United States respond to the invasion of Korea and its aftermath?

Key Terms and People

Answer the following questions in complete sentences.

1. How did the airlift in 1948 help people in Berlin?

2. What action did President John F. Kennedy take that brought about an end to the Cuban missile crisis?

3. In the 1950s, why were national television networks fearful of Elvis Presley's guest appearances?

4. What is a demilitarized zone, and what function does it serve?

Comprehension and Critical Thinking

5. **(a) Recall** Why were Americans worried about Truman when he succeeded Roosevelt as President in 1945?
(b) Apply Information Was Truman an effective leader for the United States in the postwar years? Why or why not?

6. **(a) List** Which major international organizations did the United States join in the postwar years to protect its interests?
(b) Identify Benefits How would the United States benefit from being a member of those organizations?

7. **(a) Recall** Which domestic problems did Truman and Eisenhower face during their presidencies?
(b) Apply Information What steps did each take to deal with the problems?
(c) Evaluate Information Whose solutions have had a more lasting impact on the country? Explain your answer.

8. **(a) Describe** How did General MacArthur believe the United States could win the war in Korea?
(b) Make Predictions Describe how history might have played out if MacArthur's proposal had been carried out.

9. **(a) Organize Information** Both the United States and the Soviet Union made gains in the Cold War that they probably considered important "successes." Create a chart of these events.
(b) Evaluate Information How effective do you believe the United States was in containing the spread of communism? Explain.

Reading Skill

10. **Analyze Cause and Effect** Write a paragraph summarizing the major cause-and-effect relationships of two events in this chapter.

Writing

11. **Write an introduction, transitions, and conclusions for a multimedia presentation.**
Review the activity you completed for Section 2 about popular culture during the 1950s. Use the Internet or library to find a few more multimedia sources on this topic. Choose the best order for the presentation.
Your writing should:
- include a thesis statement about popular culture in the 1950s;
- include an introduction and transitions from one multimedia source to the other;
- include an introduction and conclusion for the entire presentation.

12. **Write a Scene:**
Write a short scene in which two children from today open a time capsule from 1952. Include their comments and what they find.

Skills for Life

Identify Alternatives
Use the newspaper excerpt below to answer the questions.

"Moscow, Feb. 19—Western Europe was sternly warned today against the dangers of various economic and political attacks allegedly launched by the United States and Great Britain.
    . . . The countries of western Europe were advised to [keep] their economic independence and to [ignore] proposals for a United States of Europe. As an alternative, they were asked to consider the . . . friendship and postwar cooperation between the Soviet Union, Czechoslovakia, Poland, and Yugoslavia as 'models' of international agreements."

13. What is the political issue discussed?

14. What political alternative is suggested?

15. Based on what you have learned, is this the best alternative to the problem? Explain.

Test Yourself

1. **Which activity took up the most family time in America by the late 1950s?**

   A attending football games

   B watching television

   C listening to rock-and-roll

   D driving around by automobile

2. **What did Winston Churchill mean when he said "an iron curtain has descended across the continent"?**

   A Europe has been divided into two hostile camps.

   B People can now travel anywhere on the continent by railroad.

   C Restricting Western journalists from going to Eastern Europe is breeding ignorance about that region of the world.

   D The whole of Europe has become dangerously oversupplied with weapons.

3. **How did the cases of Alger Hiss and the Rosenbergs contribute to the rise of Joseph McCarthy?**

   A The cases were an alert that laws were needed to protect foreigners.

   B The cases assured Americans that the spread of communism was not a threat.

   C The cases increased Americans' fears about the spread of communism.

   D The cases increased awareness that some investigations were unconstitutional.

Document-Based Questions

Task: Look at Documents 1 and 2, and answer their accompanying questions. Then, use the documents and your knowledge of history to complete this writing assignment:

> Imagine that you live in East Berlin during the Cold War. Write a diary entry describing the building of the wall in 1961 and your reaction to President Kennedy's "Ich bin ein Berliner" speech two years later.

Document 1: The Berlin Wall, which sealed off Communist East Berlin from West Berlin, was a grim symbol of the Cold War. *Why did East Germany build the wall?*

Document 2: In June 1963, U.S. President John F. Kennedy delivered a speech at the Berlin Wall. Berliners loudly cheered his pledge of solidarity with the German people. *Why do you think the United States did not take direct action to remove the wall?*

"Freedom has many difficulties and democracy is not perfect. But we have never had to put a wall up to keep our people in. . . . I know of no town, no city, that has been besieged for 18 years that still lives with the vitality . . . and the determination of the city of West Berlin.

Freedom is indivisible, and when one man is enslaved, all are not free. . . . When all are free, then we can look forward to the day when this city will be joined as one and this country and this great Continent of Europe in a peaceful and hopeful globe.

All free men, wherever they may live, are citizens of Berlin.

And, therefore, as a free man, I take pride in the words 'Ich bin ein Berliner.'"

How did the United States deal with crises in domestic and foreign affairs?

DIRECTIONS: Analyze the following documents on the Great Depression, World War II, and the Cold War. Answer the questions that accompany each document or set of documents. You will use your answers to build an answer to the unit question.

HISTORIAN'S CHECKLIST

WHO produced the document?

WHERE was it made?

WHEN was it produced?

WHY was it made and for what audience?

WHAT is its viewpoint?

HOW does it connect to what I've learned?

WHY is the document important?

1 The Depression

Does the cartoonist think President Hoover reduced the problems of the Great Depression? Explain.

2 The Dust Bowl

"As the naturally occurring grasslands of the southern Great Plains were replaced with cultivated fields, the rich soil lost its ability to retain moisture and nutrients and began to erode. Soil conservation practices were not widely employed by farmers during this era, so when a seven-year drought began in 1931, followed by the coming of dust storms in 1932, many of the farms literally dried up and blew away, creating what became known as the 'Dust Bowl'. Driven by the Great Depression, drought, and dust storms, thousands of farmers packed up their families and made the difficult journey to California where they hoped to find work."

—*Robin A. Fanslow,*
American Folklife Center, Library of Congress, 1998

What were the causes and effects of the Dust Bowl?

document 3 Roosevelt's New Deal

Work Pays America!

PROSPERITY

WORKS PROGRESS ADMINISTRATION

How did government deal with the problems of the Depression and Dust Bowl?

document 4 World War II Home Front

Pitch in and Help!

JOIN THE WOMEN'S LAND ARMY
OF THE U.S. CROP CORPS

How did the sacrifices of citizens on the home front help the United States win World War II?

document 5 World War II

" You are about to embark upon the Great Crusade, toward which we have striven these many months. The eyes of the world are upon you. The hopes and prayers of liberty-loving people everywhere march with you. In company with our brave Allies and brothers-in-arms on other fronts, you will bring about the destruction of the German war machine, the elimination of Nazi tyranny over the oppressed peoples of Europe, and security for ourselves in a free world. "

—*General Dwight D. Eisenhower,
June 6, 1944*

How did Eisenhower's message to American troops help them achieve victory in Europe?

☞ Go On

6 The Nuremberg Trials

"The mere punishment of the defendants, or even of thousands of others equally guilty, can never redress the terrible injuries which the Nazis visited on these unfortunate peoples. For them it is far more important . . . that this Court, as the agent of the United States and as the voice of humanity, stamp these acts, and the ideas which engendered them, as barbarous and criminal."

—*General Telford Taylor, United States Army, 1946*

How did the Allies try to make sure that the Holocaust would never happen again?

7 The Cold War

"The Communist parties, which were very small in all these Eastern States of Europe, have been raised to preeminence and power . . . and are seeking everywhere to obtain totalitarian control."

—*Winston Churchill, "Iron Curtain" speech, 1946*

"United States policy toward the Soviet Union must be that of long-term, patient, but firm and vigilant containment of Russian expansive tendencies. . . . The Soviet pressure against the free institutions of the western world is something that can be contained by adroit and vigilant application of counter-force. . . ."

—*George Kennan, "The Sources of Soviet Conduct," 1947*

Why did the Cold War begin after World War II?

8 The Korean War

"Fifty years ago, on June 25, 1950, armed forces from North Korea . . . crossed the 38th Parallel and launched an invasion of South Korea. The communist forces advanced rapidly. . . . President Truman, recognizing the threat to our South Korean allies and their democracy . . . marshaled international opposition to the invasion and, on June 27, 1950, committed the first U.S. forces to combat in South Korea. . . . Finally . . . on July 27, 1953, North Korea withdrew across the 38th parallel, and the Republic of South Korea regained its status as a free, democratic nation . . . thanks largely to the valor, skill, and perseverance of almost 2,000,000 Americans. . . . NOW, THEREFORE, I, WILLIAM J. CLINTON, President of the United States of America, do hereby urge all Americans to observe the 50th Anniversary of the Korean War."

—*President Bill Clinton, June 23, 2000*

What were the causes and effects of the Korean War?

FAKED LETTER

DOCTORED PHOTO

---from Herblock: A Cartoonist's Life (Times Books, 1998)

Does this cartoon favor or oppose the efforts of Senator McCarthy to expose Communists in America? Explain.

10 The Arms Race

Nuclear Warhead Proliferation					
Year	U.S.	USSR	Britain	France	China
1945	6	0	0	0	0
1950	369	5	0	0	0
1955	3,057	200	10	0	0
1960	20,434	1,605	30	0	0
1965	31,642	6,129	310	4	1

Source: *Bulletin of the Atomic Scientists*

Why did the arms race develop and how did it affect international relations?

ACTIVITY

Divide into small groups that will act as advisory committees to the President of the United States. Using a computer, develop a presentation on the unit question:

 How did the United States deal with crises in domestic and foreign affairs?

Each advisory committee should select one of the crises that affected the United States from the 1930s through the early 1960s. Work together to develop a computer presentation for the President. Your presentation should clearly define the crisis and explain some of its causes and effects. Your presentation should then display and explain several possible solutions to the problem. Finally, the committee should decide which possible solution it thinks is best and why.

Unit 9

How did the United States strive to strengthen democracy at home and to foster democracy abroad?

History *Interactive*
Explore Historian's Apprentice Online
Visit: PHSchool.com
Web Code: mvp-9000

Civil Rights Movement African Americans struggled to gain the rights guaranteed them by the Constitution. Courageous individuals, such as Elizabeth Eckford, braved insults and violence to end segregation in public places and in other areas of American life.

1950s

September 11 Terrorist Attacks Muslim extremists killed thousands in terror attacks in New York, the Washington, D.C., region, and rural Pennsylvania. Americans gathered to mourn the dead and gain strength from one another.

2001

Moving Toward the Future

Vietnam War The United States sent troops to Vietnam to help South Vietnam fight Communists there. By 1968, the number of American forces had reached more than 500,000. Meanwhile, at home, Americans debated whether the nation should be in the war.

1964

The Cold War Ends In 1989, the people in Berlin, Germany, knocked down the wall that had divided their city for nearly 30 years. Within a year, the Communist governments of the Soviet Union and numerous other countries had fallen.

1990

America's Diverse Population The U.S. population continues to grow more diverse, as immigrants come to America from all parts of the world. In recent years, Hispanics have become the largest minority.

21ST Century

The Civil Rights Era

Era

1945-1975

"I am so proud of the people who did something in 1965 that was truly amazing. We were just people, ordinary people, and we did it."

—Sheyann Webb, 9 years old, marching in Selma, Alabama, March 1965

Dr. Martin Luther King, Jr., and his wife, Coretta, lead a peaceful march to protest racial segregation in 1965.

What You Will Learn

Section 1
BEGINNINGS OF THE CIVIL RIGHTS MOVEMENT

The case of *Brown* v. *Board of Education of Topeka* and the Montgomery bus boycott were two early milestones in the civil rights movement.

Section 2
AN EXPANDING ROLE FOR GOVERNMENT

The activism of the Warren Court and the reforms of Presidents Kennedy and Johnson expanded the role of the federal government.

Section 3
THE CIVIL RIGHTS MOVEMENT CONTINUES

During the 1960s, the civil rights movement won major victories but also fragmented into moderate and radical factions.

Section 4
OTHER AMERICANS SEEK RIGHTS

Among the citizens who organized to seek change were women, Latinos, Native Americans, older Americans, and people with disabilities.

Reading Skill

Draw Inferences and Conclusions In this chapter, you will learn how to use details from the text to draw inferences and conclusions.

The Civil Rights Era, 1945–1975

Civil Rights Legislation, 1960s

- Extended voting rights
- Banned segregation in public facilities
- Increased federal authority to enforce school desegregation
- Outlawed discrimination in employment on basis of race, color, and sex
- Eliminated poll tax as voting requirement
- Banned literacy tests as voting requirement
- Empowered the federal government to supervise voter registration and elections
- Banned discrimination in housing

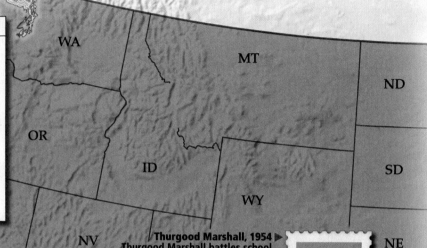

WA

MT

ND

OR

ID

SD

WY

NV

CA

UT

CO

NE

Thurgood Marshall, 1954 ▶
Thurgood Marshall battles school segregation by winning the *Brown* case in the U.S. Supreme Court. Marshall later becomes a Supreme Court justice.

THURGOOD MARSHALL

◀ **César Chávez, 1966**
César Chávez helps to form the United Farm Workers. The UFW seeks higher wages and better working conditions for migrant farm workers, many of whom are Mexican American.

CÉSAR CHÁVEZ

AZ

NM

°Los Angeles

President Lyndon Johnson, 1963 ▶
After President Kennedy is assassinated in Dallas, Lyndon Johnson becomes President. He promotes civil rights, voting rights, education, healthcare, and aid to the poor.

PRESIDENT LYNDON JOHNSON

TX

N
W E
S

0   200 miles
0   200 km
Albers Conic Conformal Projection

*Pacific
Ocean*

MEXICO

**U.S.
Events**

Truman ends segregation in the military. | **1948**

Supreme Court strikes down school segregation in *Brown* v. *Board of Education*. | **1954** | **1955** | African Americans stage bus boycott in Montgomery, Alabama.

1940   **1950**   **1960**

**World
Events**

India wins independence from British rule. | **1947** | **1950** | Korean War begins. | Fidel Castro comes to power in Cuba. | **1959**

872

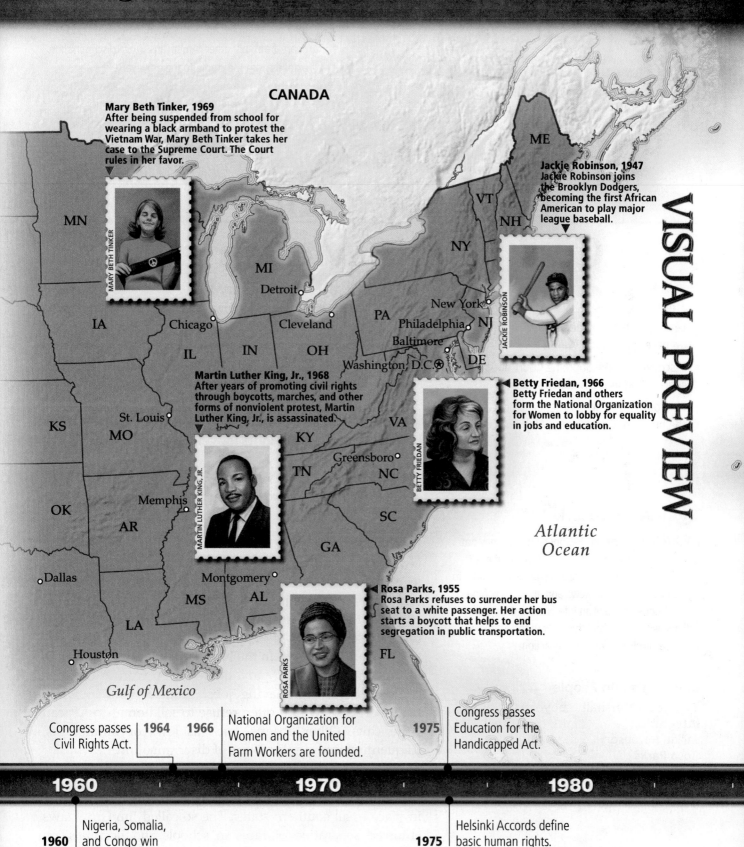

CANADA

Mary Beth Tinker, 1969
After being suspended from school for wearing a black armband to protest the Vietnam War, Mary Beth Tinker takes her case to the Supreme Court. The Court rules in her favor.

MARY BETH TINKER

MN

MI
Detroit

IA
Chicago   Cleveland
IL   IN   OH
PA
Philadelphia   NJ
New York
Baltimore
Washington, D.C.   DE

Jackie Robinson, 1947
Jackie Robinson joins the Brooklyn Dodgers, becoming the first African American to play major league baseball.

ME
VT
NH
NY

JACKIE ROBINSON

Martin Luther King, Jr., 1968
After years of promoting civil rights through boycotts, marches, and other forms of nonviolent protest, Martin Luther King, Jr., is assassinated.

MARTIN LUTHER KING, JR.

KS
St. Louis
MO
KY
Memphis
AR

OK

Dallas
Montgomery
MS   AL
LA

Houston

VA
Greensboro
TN   NC
SC
GA

◄ **Betty Friedan, 1966**
Betty Friedan and others form the National Organization for Women to lobby for equality in jobs and education.

BETTY FRIEDAN

VISUAL PREVIEW

Atlantic Ocean

◄ **Rosa Parks, 1955**
Rosa Parks refuses to surrender her bus seat to a white passenger. Her action starts a boycott that helps to end segregation in public transportation.

ROSA PARKS

FL

Gulf of Mexico

Congress passes Civil Rights Act. | 1964 | 1966 | National Organization for Women and the United Farm Workers are founded. | 1975 | Congress passes Education for the Handicapped Act.

1960   **1970**   **1980**

1960 | Nigeria, Somalia, and Congo win independence.

1975 | Helsinki Accords define basic human rights.

Opposing Segregation

❝We have a society where . . . Negroes, solely because they are Negroes, are segregated, ostracized, and set apart from all other Americans. This discrimination extends from the cradle to the graveyard. ❞

—Thurgood Marshall, civil rights lawyer, in a speech on racial segregation, 1954

◄ Jackie Robinson helped end segregation in baseball.

Beginnings of the Civil Rights Movement

Objectives

- Learn how the campaign for civil rights picked up pace after World War II.
- Discover how the Supreme Court outlawed segregation in the nation's schools.
- Find out why African Americans boycotted the buses in Montgomery, Alabama.

🔁 Reading Skill

Make Inferences History textbooks may not directly state the views of people. Instead, the text may describe people's actions and leave the reader to figure out, or infer, the views and attitudes behind those actions. To make an inference, look at the actions people took and think about the attitudes that most likely produced those actions.

Key Terms and People

Thurgood Marshall
integration
Jackie Robinson
Rosa Parks
boycott
Martin Luther
 King, Jr.

Why It Matters African Americans made important gains after the Civil War. But when Reconstruction ended, most of these gains were lost and many years of inequality and injustice followed. Finally, after decades of little progress, the struggle for equality and civil rights picked up strength after World War II.

❓ **Section Focus Question: What key events marked the beginning of the civil rights movement in the 1950s?**

Separate but Unequal

Racial barriers existed in all parts of the country. However, they took different forms in the North and the South.

In the North Generally, there were no official segregation laws in the North. African Americans could vote and had legal access to jobs and colleges. Still, African Americans and whites rarely mixed. They tended to live in different communities. As a result, their children usually attended different schools.

African Americans in the North often faced prejudice in hiring and housing. Many qualified African Americans could not get high-paying jobs. Homeowners in white neighborhoods would often refuse to sell homes to African Americans. Other groups, such as Jews or immigrants, frequently faced similar forms of discrimination.

In the South In the South, segregation was a way of life supported by law. By the early 1900s, segregation was firmly in place in all southern states. The so-called Jim Crow laws enforced separation of races in schools and hospitals, on public transportation, and in theaters and restaurants. Even drinking fountains were for "whites only" or "colored only."

As you have learned, the 1896 Supreme Court ruling in *Plessy* v. *Ferguson* <u>reinforced</u> segregation. The Court ruled that segregation was legal as long as "separate-but-equal" facilities were provided. In fact, separate schools and other facilities for African Americans were rarely, if ever, equal to those for white southerners.

The NAACP Leads the Fight During the Progressive Era, reformers such as W.E.B. Du Bois and Jane Addams had founded the National Association for the Advancement of Colored People (NAACP). Its goals were to "eradicate . . . race prejudice" and to secure "complete equality before the law."

The NAACP challenged laws that prevented African Americans from exercising their full rights as citizens. It won its first major victory in 1915, when the Supreme Court declared grandfather clauses unconstitutional. As you learned, grandfather clauses had been used in the South to ensure that only whites voted. In the 1920s and 1930s, the NAACP won court victories in the areas of housing, employment, and education.

Thurgood Marshall In 1938, Thurgood Marshall became head of the NAACP's legal section. A brilliant lawyer, Marshall used his knowledge of the Constitution to attack the foundations of segregation. His legal strategy was largely based on the Fourteenth Amendment, which guarantees all citizens "equal protection of the laws."

It also forbids any state from making laws that interfere with the rights of U.S. citizens. Marshall argued that this meant that all rights in the federal Constitution applied to the states as well. Marshall's ultimate goal was integration, or an end to racial segregation. As you will see, his most important victory would come in 1954.

☑**Checkpoint** **Describe one accomplishment of the NAACP.**

Vocabulary Builder
<u>reinforce</u> (ree ihn FORS) *v.* to strengthen; to make more effective

Make Inferences
Why do you think NAACP members went to court to fight against segregation? What do you think was their long-term goal?

Segregation in the South
Legal segregation was a way of life in southern states. The white man and black man at left were forbidden by law from drinking from the same water fountain.
Critical Thinking: *Link Past and Present* *Would you see a road sign like the one shown here today? Why or why not?*

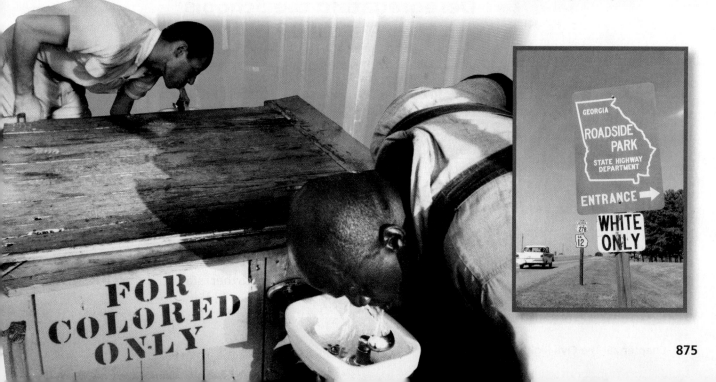

Barriers Begin to Crumble

The campaign for equal rights gained speed after World War II. During the war, African Americans and other minorities had served with distinction in the armed forces. Returning home, they sought an end to discrimination in American society.

Integrating Baseball One of the first barriers to fall was in sports. Professional baseball had long been segregated into the all-white Major Leagues and the Negro League. Branch Rickey, general manager of the Brooklyn Dodgers, wanted to break the "color line" and tap into the vast pool of talent in the Negro League.

In 1947, Rickey signed an African American army veteran named Jackie Robinson. Robinson's first years in the majors were a test of endurance. While some teammates welcomed him, he was ignored by other players and jeered at by fans. Soon, however, his skill and daring on the field won him huge numbers of fans, both white and African American. At the end of his first season, Robinson was named Rookie of the Year. More important, he paved the way for other African American athletes to compete in professional sports.

Integrating the Military President Harry Truman was committed to civil rights. He proposed laws to make lynching a federal crime, to protect the rights of African American voters, and to ban discrimination in hiring. Because of southern opposition, though, not one of these laws was passed.

Still, as commander in chief, Truman did not need congressional approval to end segregation in the military. In 1948, he ordered the integration of all units of the armed forces. As a result, African American and white soldiers fought side by side in the Korean War.

☑**Checkpoint** **What actions did Truman take to further civil rights?**

Postage stamp honoring Jackie Robinson

Desegregating the Schools

Spurred on by small victories, African Americans and their white supporters stepped up the struggle for equal rights. In 1954, the growing civil rights movement achieved a major triumph.

Brown **v.** ***Board of Education*** In 1951, Oliver Brown sued the board of education of Topeka, Kansas. Under Topeka's segregation laws, Brown's daughter Linda had to travel a great distance to a run-down school for African Americans. Brown wanted Linda to attend a school closer to her home, which also had better facilities. But the principal refused, saying that the school was for whites only.

The case of *Brown* v. *Board of Education of Topeka* reached the Supreme Court. Thurgood Marshall represented Brown. Marshall recognized that the moment had come to overthrow the doctrine of "separate but equal." He argued that segregation made equal education impossible. Segregation, he further stated, damaged African American youngsters by making them feel inferior.

The Court agreed. On May 17, 1954, the justices ruled that "in the field of public education, the doctrine of 'separate but equal' has no place." A year later, the Court ordered local school boards to desegregate "with all deliberate speed."

In a few places, schools were integrated smoothly. However, many white southerners were hostile to integration. The biggest battle over school integration took place in Little Rock, Arkansas.

Trouble in Little Rock The Little Rock school board approved a plan for gradual desegregation. According to the plan, nine African American students would attend the city's Central High School. But Arkansas governor Orval Faubus vowed, "No school district will be forced to mix the races as long as I am governor."

On September 4, 1957, Faubus called in the state's National Guard to keep the nine students out of Central High. An angry mob gathered outside the school. A few blocks away, eight of the students met so that they could walk together, protected by a band of black and white ministers. But Elizabeth Eckford did not get the message. Instead, she faced the mob alone. She recalled:

> **❝**Somebody started yelling, 'Lynch her! Lynch her!' . . . I looked into the face of an old woman and it seemed a kind face, but when I looked at her again, she spat on me.**❞**
>
> —Elizabeth Eckford, interview

After several weeks of turmoil, President Eisenhower stepped in. He sent in federal troops to enforce the Supreme Court's ruling. Under their protection, the students finally entered Central High.

☑**Checkpoint** How did the Supreme Court rule in *Brown* v. *Board of Education*?

First Day of School
Elizabeth Eckford is taunted by a mob as she tries to attend school in Little Rock on September 4, 1957. Years later, the woman shown yelling at Eckford apologized to her and they became friends. **Critical Thinking:** *Evaluate Information The day after this photograph was taken, it appeared in newspapers all over the country. How do you think people reacted to it?*

The Montgomery Bus Boycott

Brown v. *Board of Education of Topeka* was a milestone in the civil rights movement. Another milestone took place a year later.

Rosa Parks On December 1, 1955, Rosa Parks, an African American seamstress, boarded a bus in Montgomery, Alabama. Parks was secretary of the local chapter of the NAACP. In accordance with local segregation laws, she sat in the first row for "coloreds." As the bus filled up, the driver ordered her to give up her seat to a white rider. Parks refused. The driver then had her arrested.

News of the arrest spread quickly. Members of the Women's Political Council of Montgomery then took a daring step. At the time, African Americans made up about 70 percent of the city's bus riders. What would happen if they all boycotted, or refused to use, the buses on the day when Parks was brought to trial?

THE Montgomery Bus Boycott

History *Interactive*
Learn About the Montgomery Bus Boycott
Visit: PHSchool.com
Web Code: mvl-9261

The Montgomery bus boycott began when Rosa Parks decided she was no longer going to accept discrimination. It ended with one of the great victories for civil rights.
Critical Thinking: *Draw Conclusions* Why do you think the Montgomery bus boycott succeeded?

Rosa Parks is fingerprinted after ▶ her arrest. A longtime NAACP member, Parks later explained that she was "sick and tired of being sick and tired."

As African ▶ Americans carpool to work, an empty city bus passes in the background.

With the ▶ success of the boycott, these two men no longer have to sit at the back of the bus.

December 1, 1955
Rosa Parks is arrested in Montgomery, Alabama, for refusing to give up her bus seat to a white rider.

December 5, 1955
Led by Dr. Martin Luther King, Jr., African Americans begin boycott of Montgomery bus system.

January 30, 1956
King's house is bombed.

March 14, 1956
Day 100 of bus boycott

June 22, 1956
Day 200 of bus boycott

September 30, 1956
Day 300 of bus boycott

December 13, 1956
U.S. Supreme Court outlaws bus segregation.

December 21, 1956
Boycott ends as King and other African Americans board Montgomery buses.

Members of the Women's Political Council printed and distributed 52,000 fliers. On Monday morning, December 5, there was not a single African American passenger on the city's buses.

The Boycott Grows The protest was originally supposed to last a single day. But that night, some 7,000 people met at a local Baptist church. A young preacher named Martin Luther King, Jr., told the crowd, "There comes a time when people get tired of being trampled over by the iron feet of oppression." At King's urging, the African American community agreed to continue the boycott until the bus segregation laws were taken off the books.

Montgomery's leaders responded to the boycott with outrage. King's home was bombed, and King and others were jailed several times on false charges. But the boycotters <u>persisted</u>. Volunteer drivers transported boycotters between work and home. African Americans walked miles to work or traveled by bicycle. Volunteer chauffeurs drove other protesters between work and home.

The Montgomery bus boycott lasted 381 days. At last, in November 1956, the Supreme Court ruled that segregation on buses was unconstitutional. On December 21, King boarded a bus in Montgomery—and sat in the front seat.

Vocabulary Builder
persist (pehr SIHST) **v.** to continue in the face of opposition or difficulty

✓**Checkpoint** How did the Montgomery bus boycott end?

☆ **Looking Back and Ahead** One important result of the Montgomery bus boycott was the emergence of Martin Luther King, Jr., as a leader of the civil rights movement. Later, you will explore King's ideas and achievements in more detail.

Section 1 | **Check Your Progress**

Progress Monitoring ⊘nline
For: Self-test with instant help
Visit: PHSchool.com
Web Code: mva-9261

Comprehension and Critical Thinking

1. **(a) Recall** How did the Supreme Court ruling in *Plessy* v. *Ferguson* support segregation laws?
   (b) Analyze Cause and Effect What effect did the Supreme Court ruling in *Brown* v. *Board of Education* have on *Plessy* v. *Ferguson*?

2. **(a) Describe** What was the Montgomery bus boycott? How did it begin?
   (b) Evaluate Information Why was a bus boycott an effective tool of protest in Montgomery?

⊘ Reading Skill

3. **Make Inferences** Reread the text following the subheading "Trouble in Little Rock." What can you infer about President Eisenhower's attitude toward Faubus's use of state power to defy a Supreme Court decision?

Key Terms

4. Draw a table with three rows and three columns. In the first column, list the following terms: integration, boycott. In the next column, write the definition of each term. In the last column, make a small illustration that shows the meaning of each term.

Writing

5. Choose one of the photographs in this section. Imagine that you were either one of the people who is shown in the photograph or the photographer who took the picture. Write a few sentences describing the moment when the photograph was taken: what was happening, what you were doing, and how you felt at the time.

Prepare to Read

Introduction

Naomi Long Madgett began writing as a child and published her first book of poetry at age 17. Many of her poems express her pride in her African American heritage. The poem "Midway" was published in 1956, in response to the Supreme Court decision in *Brown* v. *Board of Education of Topeka.*

🎯 Reading Skill

Analyze Titles Some poetry titles describe the subject of the poem. Others are words taken directly from the poem. Still other titles help explain or expand the poem's meaning. As you read this poem, think about what the title "Midway" might mean.

Vocabulary *Builder*

As you read this literature selection, look for the following underlined words:

reap (reep) *v.* to gather a crop

sow (soh) *v.* to plant seeds

abhor (ahb HOHR) *v.* to turn away from in hatred or disgust

deride (dee RĪD) *v.* to ridicule; to make fun of

I've come this far to freedom and I won't turn back.
I'm climbing to the highway from my old dirt track.
  I'm coming and I'm going
  And I'm stretching and I'm growing
And I'll <u>reap</u> what I've been <u>sowing</u> or my skin's not black.

I've prayed and slaved and waited and I've sung my song.
You've bled me and you've starved me but I've still grown strong.
  You've lashed me and you've treed me
  And you've everything but freed me
But in time you'll know you need me and it won't be long.

I've seen the daylight breaking high above the bough.
I've found my destination and I've made my vow,
  So whether you <u>abhor</u> me
  Or <u>deride</u> me or ignore me,
Mighty mountains loom before me and I won't stop now.

From *Star by Star* by Naomi Long Madgett
(Harlo, 1965; Evenill, 1970). Reprinted in *Connected Islands:*
New and Selected Poems (Detroit: Lotus Press, 2004).

🎯 Analyze Titles

What do you think the title "Midway" means? What does it say about events that took place around the time the poem was written? How does the title reflect Madgett's feelings about the future?

If you liked this poem and want to learn more about the early civil rights movement, you might want to read *Rosa Parks: My Story,* by Rosa Parks and James Haskins. Dial Books, 1992.

Analyze LITERATURE

Compare this poem to the poem "I, Too" by Langston Hughes. How are the two poems similar? How can you tell Madgett's poem was written at a later time in history?

The Right to Vote

"Millions of Americans are denied the right to vote because of their color. This law will ensure them the right to vote. . . . The right is one which no American, true to our principles, can deny."

—President Lyndon B. Johnson,
on the Voting Rights Act, 1965

▲ Voter registration drive

An Expanding Role for Government

Objectives

- Describe how the U.S. Supreme Court took on a more activist role under Chief Justice Earl Warren.
- Discover the domestic goals of President Kennedy.
- Find out how President Johnson's Great Society increased the social role of the federal government.

🎯 Reading Skill

Support Inferences With Text Evidence As you know, inferences must be supported by evidence stated in the text. One common focus for inferences is as a tool to learn about people in history. Text evidence can help you infer answers to questions, for example, by describing the person or giving examples of his or her actions. Ask: What were they like?

Key Terms and People

Earl Warren   welfare
Lyndon Johnson

Why It Matters As protest expanded and the call for civil rights and equality grew louder, government responded. After the *Brown* decision on desegregating the schools, new Supreme Court decisions had a powerful impact on American life. Two Presidents of the 1960s supported reforms that transformed the nature of American society.

❷ **Section Focus Question: What was the "Great Society"?**

The Warren Court

In 1953, President Eisenhower appointed former California governor Earl Warren as chief justice of the U.S. Supreme Court. Eisenhower expected the former California governor to keep the Court on its conservative course of respecting past decisions or precedents. Instead, a year later, the Supreme Court broke all precedent with its groundbreaking decision in *Brown* v. *Board of Education of Topeka*.

Extending Individual Rights In the 1960s, the Warren Court continued to make decisions with far-reaching effects. In the 1966 case of *Miranda* v. *Arizona*, the Court overturned the guilty verdict of Ernesto Miranda. Miranda had been convicted on the basis of a confession obtained without access to a lawyer. The Court ruled that this violated the Fifth Amendment. As a result of the *Miranda* ruling, the police must now advise arrested persons of their right to remain silent and to have legal counsel. The Court made other rulings to protect the rights of the accused. Many critics argue that such rulings make it more difficult to combat crime.

Key Decisions of the Warren Court

Case	Decision Based On	Impact
Mapp v. *Ohio* (1961)	**Fourth Amendment:** Protects "against unreasonable searches and seizures."	Evidence from an illegal search cannot be used in a criminal trial.
Gideon v. *Wainwright* (1963)	**Sixth Amendment:** Guarantees accused person "the assistance of counsel for his defense."	If a person accused of a crime cannot afford an attorney, the state must provide one.
Miranda v. *Arizona* (1966)	**Fifth Amendment:** Defendant cannot "be compelled . . . to be a witness against himself."	Before being questioned by police, suspects must be informed of their right to keep silent, as well as to have an attorney.
Tinker v. *Des Moines School District* (1969)	**First Amendment:** Protects "freedom of speech."	A school cannot interfere with a student's right to free speech unless that speech causes major disruption of the school day.

Reading Charts

Skills Activity

Under Chief Justice Earl Warren, the Supreme Court made a number of decisions that continue to have an impact today.

(a) Interpret Charts Which cases shown on the chart involved the rights of accused criminals?

(b) Evaluate Information Which of the decisions shown here do you think had the greatest impact on American life? Explain.

Another case, *Tinker* v. *Des Moines School District* (1969), expanded the concept of freedom of speech guaranteed in the First Amendment. The Court ruled that school administrators had violated the free speech of students by suspending several of them for wearing black arm bands to protest the war in Vietnam.

Judicial Activism Perhaps more important than any individual decision was Warren's approach to the law. Unlike most earlier chief justices, Warren believed that the Constitution must be interpreted flexibly—in light of what the Framers wrote but also in light of what best serves the public interest today. The Warren Court began to strike down laws that the justices regarded as unfair, regardless of past decisions or the exact wording of the Constitution.

This concept of "judicial activism" has stirred controversy. Then and later, critics argue that following their own ideas of fairness gives judges too much power. Only what was written in the Constitution could be written into law, they insist.

☑**Checkpoint** How did the Supreme Court decision in *Miranda* v. *Arizona* affect law enforcement?

Kennedy's Brief Presidency

Election of 1960 In one of the closest presidential elections in history, John F. Kennedy won by about 100,000 of 70 million votes cast. At 43, he became the youngest person ever elected President.

Mixed Success In his inaugural address, the young President sounded an idealistic, optimistic note:

> ❝Let the word go forth from this time and place, to friend and foe alike, that the torch has been passed to a new generation of Americans born in this century, tempered by war, disciplined by a hard and bitter peace, proud of our ancient heritage—and unwilling to witness or permit the slow undoing of those human rights to which this Nation has always been committed, and to which we are committed today at home and around the world.❞
> —John F. Kennedy, First Inaugural Address

Kennedy had been shocked to learn that one fifth of Americans lived below the poverty line. He called on Congress to take action to end poverty, fight disease, and ensure justice for all Americans. Although Kennedy did win some support for his antipoverty measures, Congress rejected most of his <u>domestic</u> proposals. His most lasting accomplishment was the space program. He set a bold goal: to place a man on the moon by the end of the decade.

Kennedy also became convinced of the need for extensive civil rights legislation. But he did not live to achieve this goal.

Assassination On November 22, 1963, Kennedy was in Dallas, Texas, on a political visit. Riding in an open limousine, the President and his wife, Jacqueline, greeted the cheering crowds. Suddenly, shots rang out. Kennedy slumped over. He died shortly afterward.

Within hours, Dallas police arrested Lee Harvey Oswald for the assassination. Two days later, Oswald himself was shot to death while being transferred from one jail to another. Millions of horrified Americans saw the shooting live on television.

Vocabulary Builder
<u>domestic</u> (doh MEHS tihk) *adj.*
relating to matters within one's own country, rather than to foreign affairs

The Kennedy Assassination
Moments after the picture at the left was taken, President Kennedy was shot to death in Dallas. The sign in this New York City store window (right) reflects the nation's shock and grief. **Critical Thinking:** *Make Inferences* Why do you think the store owner referred to the assassination as "a national disgrace"?

The Great Society

"Our society will not be great until every young mind is set free to scan the farthest reaches of thought and imagination. We are still far from that goal. Today, 8 million adult Americans . . . have not finished five years of school. . . . We must give every child a place to sit and a teacher to learn from. Poverty must not be a bar to learning, and learning must offer an escape from poverty."

—Lyndon Johnson, "The Great Society," 1964

Reading Primary Sources
Skills Activity

In May 1964, President Lyndon Johnson outlined his vision of what he called the Great Society. In the excerpt here, Johnson discusses his goals for education.

(a) Interpret Primary Sources What link does Johnson make between education and poverty?

(b) Apply Information How did Head Start relate to Johnson's goals?

The murder of the young, energetic President stunned the nation. A few months later, a commission headed by Earl Warren concluded that Oswald had acted alone. Still, some people continue to question the conclusions of the Warren Commission.

✓**Checkpoint** **What was Kennedy's most lasting success?**

Johnson's Great Society

On the day Kennedy was assassinated, Vice President Lyndon Johnson was sworn in as President. The following year, he was elected President in his own right by a landslide.

Johnson's Background Lyndon Johnson grew up in a poor family in rural Texas. As a young man, he taught at a school for Mexican Americans. Johnson grew deeply attached to his pupils there and became convinced that something needed to be done to help the nation's poor and oppressed.

An ardent supporter of President Franklin Roosevelt, Johnson was elected to Congress in 1937 on a pro–New Deal platform. He won election to the Senate 11 years later, rising to the powerful position of majority leader. He became Vice President in 1961.

Support Inferences With Text Evidence
Give two details from the text to support this inference: Lyndon Johnson was a persuasive politician.

A Flood of Legislation As President, Johnson set out to make his mark with an ambitious program of economic and social reforms. Using his political skills, Johnson persuaded Congress to enact more new laws than at any time since the New Deal. One journalist commented, "Johnson had scarcely settled in office before bills were coming out of Congress like candy bars from a slot machine."

At first, he worked to push through legislation that Kennedy had begun, including a major civil rights law. (See Section 3.) Johnson then turned his attention to his own program, which he called the Great Society. Its goal was to expand opportunity and provide a decent standard of living for all Americans.

Much of this legislation was part of what Johnson called his War on Poverty. The Economic Opportunity Act attacked the causes of poverty, such as illiteracy, unemployment, and inadequate public services. Head Start provided preschool education for needy children. Other Great Society programs provided food stamps and welfare to needy families. Welfare is a system in which government agencies make cash payments to the poor. Johnson also created a Department of Housing and Urban Development (HUD) to oversee the building of middle-income and low-income housing.

Perhaps the most important Great Society legislation was Medicare. This act helped citizens 65 years of age or older to pay their medical bills. A companion act, Medicaid, provided money to assist poor people of all ages who were not covered by Medicare.

Like the New Deal, the Great Society greatly expanded the role of the federal government. Critics said providing for people's needs on such a scale was not the proper <u>function</u> of the federal government. They also charged that, though the Great Society programs cost billions of dollars, many were badly run and did not work.

Johnson displays a newly signed antipoverty law.

Vocabulary Builder
function (FUHNK shuhn) **n.**
purpose; proper use

✓**Checkpoint** **Describe two important laws passed during the administration of Lyndon Johnson.**

⭐ **Looking Back and Ahead** In this section, you saw how Johnson supported social reforms. In the next section, you will see how legislation in the Johnson years advanced civil rights.

Section 2 | **Check Your Progress**

Progress Monitoring ⬤nline
For: Self-test with instant help
Visit: PHSchool.com
Web Code: mva-9262

Comprehension and Critical Thinking

1. **(a) Identify** What were the domestic goals of Kennedy?
   (b) Evaluate Information Was Kennedy's program successful or unsuccessful in the long run? Explain.

2. **(a) Describe** Choose and describe two Great Society programs.
   (b) Draw Conclusions Do you think the federal government should support expensive social programs? Why or why not?

Reading Skill

3. **Support Inferences With Details** Read the text following the subheading "Johnson's Background." Give two details from the text to support this inference: Lyndon Johnson's sympathy for the poor grew from his own experience.

Key Terms

4. Write two definitions of the word welfare—one a formal definition for a teacher, the other an informal definition for a younger child.

Writing

5. Imagine that you are one of the following individuals. Write a few sentences explaining your thoughts and feelings.
   - Police officer reacting to the *Miranda* ruling
   - Resident of Dallas just after Kennedy was shot
   - Poverty-stricken American hearing about Johnson's Great Society program

Make Justice a Reality

❝Now is the time to make real the promises of democracy. Now is the time to rise from the dark and desolate valley of segregation to the sunlit path of racial justice. . . . Now is the time to make justice a reality for all of God's children.❞

—Martin Luther King, Jr., "I have a dream" speech, 1963

◄ Martin Luther King, Jr.

The Civil Rights Movement Continues

Objectives
- Explore Martin Luther King's use of nonviolent protest to gain equal rights.
- Find out how new federal legislation helped protect civil rights.
- Understand why the civil rights movement broke up into several groups.
- Analyze the achievements and failures of the civil rights movement.

🔘 Reading Skill

Draw Logical Conclusions Logic is the cornerstone of drawing conclusions. You must always ask yourself: Does this conclusion make sense? Does it make sense with the evidence in the text? Does it make sense with what I know about these people and their situation? Does it make sense with what I know about the world and how people, in general, act? If the answer to all these questions is yes, you have drawn a logical conclusion.

Key Terms and People

civil disobedience
sit-in
James Meredith
Malcolm X
Stokely Carmichael
ghetto
affirmative action

Why It Matters Emboldened by the gains of the 1950s and the early 1960s, the civil rights movement continued to gain momentum. Dr. Martin Luther King, Jr., led protest actions based on a firm belief in nonviolence. However, other activists felt that stronger methods were needed.

❓ Section Focus Question: How did the civil rights movement gain momentum?

King's Strategy of Nonviolence

The Montgomery bus boycott had brought forth a dynamic civil rights leader in Dr. Martin Luther King, Jr. The boycott also provided the first test of King's belief in civil disobedience, or the peaceful refusal to obey unjust laws. As you have read in Chapter 12, the philosophy of civil disobedience had been developed by the nineteenth-century American writer Henry David Thoreau.

Sources of King's Ideas King's belief in nonviolent protest was rooted in Christian teachings. Like his father and grandfather, King was a Baptist minister. Echoing Jesus, King told his followers that they should always meet hate with love.

King also studied the ideas of India's Mohandas Gandhi. Gandhi had led a campaign of nonviolent resistance to win India's freedom from British colonial rule. Like Gandhi, King taught that one should resist injustice even if it meant going to jail or enduring violence.

In addition, King owed much of his thinking to A. Philip Randolph, the prominent African American labor leader. Randolph championed a strategy of nonviolent mass protest.

SCLC To build on the momentum of the Montgomery bus boycott, King joined with other African American church leaders to found the Southern Christian Leadership Conference (SCLC) in 1957. The goal of the organization was full equality for African Americans. In their first official statement, SCLC leaders declared their commitment to nonviolent civil disobedience:

> “No matter how great the obstacles and suffering, we urge all Negroes to reject segregation. But far beyond this, we call upon them to . . . understand that non-violence is not a symbol of weakness or cowardice, but as Jesus demonstrated, non-violent resistance <u>transforms</u> weakness into strength and breeds courage in face of danger.”
> —Southern Christian Leadership Conference, "A Statement to the South and to the Nation"

Vocabulary Builder
<u>transform</u> (trahns FORM) **v.** to change the form, appearance, or nature of something

The SCLC helped shift the base of the civil rights movement. Most early civil rights activity had been dominated by northerners. Now, African American churches in the South took the lead in organizing resistance to injustice. Under King's leadership, the SCLC would be in the forefront of many civil rights protests in the 1960s.

☑**Checkpoint** **Identify three sources of King's philosophy of nonviolent protest.**

Links Across Time

Gandhi Preaches Nonviolence

1930 Mohandas Gandhi of India led a march to protest British laws which forbade Indians from extracting their own salt from seawater. During the Salt March, tens of thousands of peaceful protesters were arrested or beaten. But they refused to give in.

1955–1968 Inspired by Gandhi's methods, Martin Luther King, Jr., led a series of nonviolent civil rights protests.

Link to Today ⊙nline

Honoring Gandhi and King Today, both Gandhi and King are widely honored for their leadership and courage. A federal holiday in January commemorates King's birthday.

For: The legacy of Martin Luther King, Jr.
Visit: PHSchool.com
Web Code: mvc-9263

1930 Gandhi leads the Salt March

Nonviolent Protest Spreads

Nonviolent protest took many forms. In 1960, four African American college students sat down at a "whites only" lunch counter in Greensboro, North Carolina, and ordered coffee. The students refused to move unless they were served. Word of the incident quickly spread. The **sit-in,** a form of protest in which people sit and refuse to leave, became a common tool to protest segregation.

Civil rights leaders organized the first of many Freedom Rides in 1961. Their goal was to test a recent Supreme Court ruling outlawing segregation in interstate travel. Thirteen Freedom Riders—seven black, six white—set out on two buses for a trip through the Deep South. They successfully integrated several bus stations before being violently attacked in Alabama.

In 1962, a federal court ordered the University of Mississippi to admit James Meredith, an African American student. When Meredith arrived on campus, riots broke out in protest. Two people were killed and hundreds more were injured. President Kennedy sent in federal troops to <u>restore</u> order and allow Meredith to register.

Vocabulary Builder
<u>restore</u> (ree STOR) **v.** to bring back to a normal state

Protests in Birmingham Early in 1963, the SCLC launched massive demonstrations to protest discrimination in Birmingham, Alabama. Thousands of African Americans, including many children, marched peacefully through Birmingham. Police used dogs, fire hoses, and electric cattle prods against the marchers. Horrified Americans watched the violence unfold on television.

Finally, under intense pressure from business interests in the city, Birmingham authorities agreed to desegregate public facilities. They also agreed to hire African American clerks and salespersons.

March on Washington After the events in Birmingham, President Kennedy sent Congress the strongest civil rights bill in the nation's history. To focus attention on the bill, civil rights leaders proposed a march on the nation's capital. The March on Washington took place on August 28, 1963. The sight of nearly 250,000 peacefully assembled citizens stirred more Americans to support civil rights.

Many people, including Christian and Jewish religious leaders, gave speeches that day. But none moved the crowd as did King. His voice rang as he proclaimed, "I have a dream that my four little children will one day live in a nation where they will not be judged by the color of their skins but the content of their character."

☑**Checkpoint** How did Freedom Riders protest segregation?

Civil Rights Legislation

The civil rights movement now progressed to a new stage. Repelled by the violence against peaceful protesters, Americans pressured their representatives in Congress to take action.

Civil Rights Act of 1964 Kennedy was assassinated before he could get his civil rights bill through Congress. The new President, Lyndon Johnson, was determined to move the legislation along.

Pushed hard by Johnson, Congress passed the sweeping Civil Rights Act of 1964. It banned discrimination in public facilities and outlawed discrimination in employment. It also provided for faster school desegregation and further protected voting rights.

Battle for Voting Rights Still, African Americans in the South continued to face barriers to voting. In 1964, civil rights groups mounted an all-out effort to register African American voters in Mississippi. About a thousand volunteers, mostly college students, answered the call. The project had barely begun when three young volunteers disappeared. They were later found murdered. Other violence included beatings, shootings, and church bombings.

In March 1965, King staged a mass protest in Alabama to draw attention to the issue of voting rights. Hundreds of marchers set out from the city of Selma to Montgomery, the state capital. But state troopers set upon marchers with tear gas, clubs, and whips. Again, Americans witnessed the bloodshed on the evening news. Over the next two days, people in more than 80 cities demonstrated against the violence and demanded passage of a voting rights act.

Voting Rights Act In the aftermath of Selma, President Johnson went on national television to support a strong voting rights law. That summer, Congress passed the Voting Rights Act of 1965. It banned literacy tests and other barriers to African American voting.

March on Washington

In one of the largest peaceful demonstrations in American history, a quarter of a million people marched on the nation's capital on August 28, 1963. Here, protesters gather around the reflecting pool in front of the Washington Monument. **Critical Thinking: *Apply Information*** *What was the chief goal of the March on Washington?*

The Voting Rights Act also permitted federal officials to register voters directly in states that practiced discrimination. In the next three years, federal voting examiners registered more than 150,000 African Americans in the South.

✓**Checkpoint** **What were the goals of the Civil Rights Act of 1964?**

The Movement Splinters

Some African Americans grew impatient with the gradual pace of the civil rights movement. They turned to more militant leaders.

Malcolm X One of the best known of these leaders was Malcolm X. Born Malcolm Little, he renounced what he called his "slave name" and adopted "X" as a symbol of his lost African name. He embraced the Nation of Islam, a form of Islam whose members were known as Black Muslims.

Malcolm X rejected the goal of integration altogether. "An integrated cup of coffee isn't sufficient pay for four hundred years of slave labor," he insisted. Instead, he called on African Americans to separate completely from white society.

Later, Malcolm X severed his ties with the Nation of Islam. He rejected separatism and spoke instead of an "honest white-black brotherhood." Before he could fully develop these new ideas, he was shot to death in 1965. Three Black Muslims were convicted of the crime.

Black Power Movement Others also grew frustrated with King's nonviolent approach. Stokely Carmichael argued that African Americans should fight back if attacked. Carmichael and others developed a new approach, called "black power." They urged African Americans to achieve economic independence by starting and supporting their own businesses. They also called on African Americans to take pride in their own heritage.

Militant Voices

Nonviolence dominated the early stages of the civil rights movement. By the mid-1960s, more-militant voices had emerged. **Critical Thinking: Compare** *How did the ideas of Malcolm X and Stokely Carmichael differ from the ideas of Martin Luther King, Jr.?*

Black power movement
Called for economic independence for African Americans

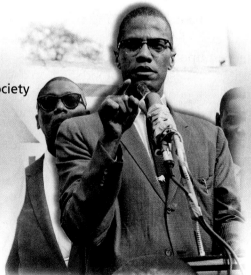

Malcolm X
Called for African Americans to break away from white society

Cause and Effect

CAUSES

- Segregation laws and discrimination lead to the unequal treatment of African Americans.
- The NAACP is formed to fight discrimination.
- African Americans expect equal treatment at home after serving in World War II.

THE CIVIL RIGHTS MOVEMENT

EFFECTS

- *Brown* v. *Board of Education of Topeka* outlaws segregation in schools.
- Martin Luther King, Jr., emerges as a civil rights leader.
- Congress passes Civil Rights Act and Voting Rights Act.
- African Americans make political and economic gains.
- Other groups are inspired to seek equal rights.

Reading Charts
Skills Activity

The long-term causes of the civil rights movement go as far back as the days of slavery. The long-term effects are still being felt today.

(a) Interpret Charts How did World War II help spur the civil rights movement?

(b) Analyze Cause and Effect Which effect of the civil rights movement do you consider the most important? Why?

Protests Turn Violent The civil rights movement had focused mainly on ending segregation in the South. It had done little to ease the hardships of the millions of African Americans who were crowded into ghettos, or poor run-down neighborhoods, in northern cities.

In August 1965, urban discontent exploded into violence. One of the worst incidents occurred in Watts, a primarily African American area of Los Angeles. Angered by what they saw as an act of brutality by police, residents of Watts burned cars and looted stores. More than 1,000 people were killed or injured.

Over the next two years, dozens of other cities exploded with violence and destruction. A presidential commission appointed to study the situation warned, "Our nation is moving toward two societies, one black, one white—separate and unequal."

King Is Killed In 1968, King traveled the country to build support for a Poor People's Campaign to attack economic inequality. On the evening of April 3, King told a gathering in Memphis, Tennessee: "I may not get there with you. But . . . we, as a people, will get to the promised land."

The next day, King was shot to death. A white segregationist was later tried and convicted of the crime. Despite a plea from President Johnson, riots broke out in cities across the nation. With King's death, a major era of the civil rights movement came to an end.

✓Checkpoint What was meant by "black power"?

Draw Logical Conclusions
Reading Skill Draw a conclusion about the reaction of different Americans to the pace of civil rights change.

Summing Up the Civil Rights Era

The civil rights movement of the 1960s achieved many important and lasting results. Although it did not end all inequality, it did end legal segregation and it opened education and voting rights to all.

A Larger Role in Government As more African Americans participated in the political process, the number of African American elected officials increased. For the first time, African American mayors took office in large cities, such as Atlanta, Cleveland, Detroit, Los Angeles, and Newark.

African Americans made gains in the federal government as well. In 1966, Edward Brooke of Massachusetts became the first African American senator since Reconstruction. A year later, President Johnson appointed Thurgood Marshall to the Supreme Court.

Affirmative Action Many gains came as a result of affirmative action programs. Under affirmative action, businesses and schools were encouraged to give preference to members of groups that had been discriminated against in the past.

By the 1970s, thousands of African Americans were attending colleges or entering professions such as medicine or law. Still, a growing number of Americans charged that affirmative action was a form of "reverse discrimination" because it unfairly favored one group of people over another.

Justice Thurgood Marshall

☑ **Checkpoint** **What gains did African Americans make in government?**

☆ **Looking Back and Ahead** African Americans made historic gains during the civil rights era. As you will read in the next section, other groups also sought to win equal rights.

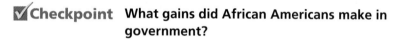

Section 3 | **Check Your Progress**

Progress Monitoring Online
For: Self-test with instant help
Visit: PHSchool.com
Web Code: mva-9263

Comprehension and Critical Thinking

1. (a) Describe What tactics did Martin Luther King, Jr., favor in the fight for civil rights?
(b) Contrast How did the views of Malcolm X differ from those of King?

2. (a) Recall What were the terms of the Voting Rights Act of 1965?
(b) Evaluate Information Why did supporters of the Voting Rights Act favor federal action rather than action on the state level?

Reading Skill
3. Draw Logical Conclusions
What can you conclude about the role of television in the civil rights movement?

Key Terms
Complete each of the following sentences so that the second part further explains the first part and clearly shows your understanding of the key term.
4. In northern cities, poor African Americans often lived in ghettos, _____.

5. Some economic gains came as the result of affirmative action, _____.
6. African Americans who ate at "whites only" lunch counters practiced civil disobedience, _____.

Writing
7. Use the Internet to gather more background information about one of the people or events discussed in this section. Then, list three important details from the information you found.

National Organization for Women

❝There is no civil rights movement to speak for women, as there has been for Negroes and other victims of discrimination. The National Organization for Women must therefore begin to speak.❞

—Betty Friedan, 1966

◄ Women's rights protesters

Other Americans Seek Rights

Objectives

- Discover the gains made by the women's movement.
- Find out how Mexican Americans struggled to win equal treatment.
- Explore how Native Americans, older Americans, and the disabled sought fairer treatment.

🔵 Reading Skill

Support Conclusions With Evidence
Like inferences, conclusions must be supported with evidence. That evidence comes first and foremost from the text but can also come from prior knowledge and personal experience. Identify conclusions that you have made while reading. Then, find the information that led you to that conclusion.

Key Terms and People

Betty Friedan
César Chávez
bilingual

mandatory
retirement
Maggie Kuhn

Why It Matters African Americans were not the only Americans to be denied equal rights, and they were not the only Americans to work for change. Women, Mexican Americans, Native Americans, and others embraced the expanding civil rights movement. Their activities brought dramatic and lasting change.◆

❓ **Section Focus Question: What other groups were swept up in the spirit of reform?**

Women's Rights Movement

By the 1960s, women had won the vote and made other gains. Yet many women believed they still had a long way to go to achieve full equality in jobs and education.

Betty Friedan *The Feminine Mystique,* a 1963 book by Jewish writer Betty Friedan, reignited the women's rights movement. Friedan was a housewife with a degree in psychology. She argued that many women were secretly unhappy with their limited roles in society:

❝The problem lay buried, unspoken, for many years in the minds of American women. It was a strange stirring, a sense of dissatisfaction, a yearning. . . . Each suburban wife struggled with it alone.❞

—Betty Friedan, *The Feminine Mystique*

Friedan's book became an instant bestseller. It challenged traditional ideas about the roles of both men and women. It also inspired thousands of women to seek careers outside the home.

In 1966, Friedan helped found the National Organization for Women (NOW). NOW lobbied Congress for laws that would give women greater equality. It demanded that medical schools and law practices train and hire more women. It also campaigned for day-care facilities for the children of mothers who worked outside the home.

Women in the Workforce, 1950–1975

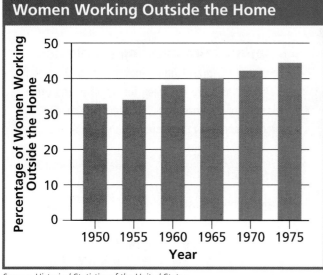

Women Working Outside the Home

Source: *Historical Statistics of the United States*

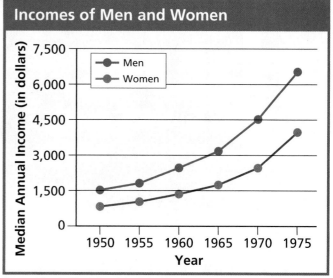

Incomes of Men and Women

Source: *Historical Statistics of the United States*

Reading Charts
Skills Activity

As the women's rights movement continued, more and more women found work outside the home. Still, their incomes continued to lag behind those of men.

(a) Interpret Graphs What percentage of American women worked outside the home in 1950? In 1975?

(b) Make Predictions What do you think will happen to the gap between men's incomes and women's incomes in the future?

Support Conclusions With Evidence

Give evidence to support the conclusion that some American women responded sympathetically to Betty Friedan's point of view and others did not.

The ERA NOW led a campaign to ratify an Equal Rights Amendment (ERA) to the Constitution. The ERA would forbid any form of sex discrimination. Congress passed the amendment in 1972. To become law, it had to be ratified by 38 states.

The ERA touched off a furious debate. Opponents, both men and women, charged that the amendment would undermine traditional values. They warned that women might lose their rights to alimony or be forced to serve in combat. Critics also claimed that the ERA was unnecessary because several laws already protected women's rights. In the end, the ERA did not receive enough votes for ratification.

Notable Gains The women's movement did make notable gains. In 1963, President Kennedy signed the Equal Pay Act, which required equal pay for men and women doing the same jobs. A year later, sex discrimination was included in the Civil Rights Act.

In the workplace, women's salaries continued to lag behind those of men. Still, the number of women working outside the home steadily increased. In addition, more women attended colleges.

Women made gains in the political arena, too. More women were elected to city councils, state legislatures, and the U.S. Congress. In 1969, Shirley Chisholm of New York became the first African American woman elected to Congress. In 1975, Ella Grasso of Connecticut became the first woman elected governor of a state without succeeding her husband.

✓**Checkpoint** **What argument did Betty Friedan make?**

Civil Rights for Mexican Americans

While the African American civil rights movement was taking shape, Mexican Americans were waging their own campaign for equal rights. Mexican Americans were not subject to official segregation laws. However, in the Southwest, all-white schools closed their doors to Mexican American children. Instead, they had to attend poorly equipped "Mexican schools." Custom kept Mexican Americans out of many neighborhoods and jobs.

Organizing for Change In 1948, Mexican American veterans of World War II formed the American GI Forum. Like the NAACP, the Forum supported legal challenges to discrimination.

In 1954—the same year as *Brown* v. *Board of Education of Topeka*—Mexican Americans also won a major Supreme Court victory. A Mexican American man in Texas had been convicted of murder by an all-white jury. His lawyers argued that the conviction was invalid because Mexican Americans were excluded from serving on Texas juries.

In *Hernández* v. *Texas,* the Supreme Court ruled that excluding Mexican Americans from juries was illegal. Other minority groups would later use the *Hernández* decision to help secure their legal rights.

Chávez and the UFW Many Mexican Americans in the Southwest were migrant workers, traveling from farm to farm to pick crops. In 1966, César Chávez helped to form a labor union, the United Farm Workers (UFW). Its goal was to win higher wages and decent working conditions for migrant laborers.

Like King, Chávez favored nonviolent protest. When growers refused to recognize the UFW, he organized a national boycott of California grapes. By 1970, so many Americans had stopped buying grapes that growers agreed to sign a contract with the union.

Protecting Voting Rights During this same period, Mexican Americans organized campaigns to win greater rights. As a result, Congress amended the Voting Rights Act in 1975. It required areas with large numbers of foreign-speaking citizens to hold bilingual elections. Bilingual means "in two languages."

Other laws promoted bilingual education in public schools. Supporters of bilingual education said that it would help students keep up with their work as they learned English.

✔**Checkpoint** What did the Supreme Court decide in *Hernández* v. *Texas*?

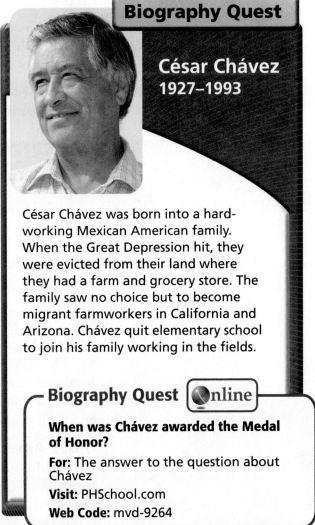

Biography Quest

César Chávez
1927–1993

César Chávez was born into a hard-working Mexican American family. When the Great Depression hit, they were evicted from their land where they had a farm and grocery store. The family saw no choice but to become migrant farmworkers in California and Arizona. Chávez quit elementary school to join his family working in the fields.

Biography Quest ⏺nline

When was Chávez awarded the Medal of Honor?

For: The answer to the question about Chávez

Visit: PHSchool.com

Web Code: mvd-9264

An Era of Protest

The demonstrators in these pictures had different goals. However, all of them believed that they could band together to campaign for change.

Critical Thinking: *Apply Information* How does the Constitution protect the rights of Americans to protest peacefully?

Maggie Kuhn, founder of the Gray Panthers

SPOKESW

Member of the American Indian Movement

A.I.M. DENOUNCES ALL INDIAN EXPLOITATION BOYCOTT BICENTENNIAL

Protesters in wheelchairs, Washington, D.C.

Organizing for Change

The spirit of reform introduced by the civil rights movement spread into every corner of the nation. More groups began to organize in order to achieve greater protection under the law.

Native Americans Indians had long been the poorest segment of the population. They were also subject to shifting federal policy. In the 1960s, activists began to demand change. The National Congress of American Indians sent delegations to Washington to regain land, mineral, and water rights. Increasingly, such efforts succeeded.

The American Indian Movement (AIM) turned to more radical protest. In 1973, armed members of AIM occupied Wounded Knee, South Dakota, for several days. As you have read in Chapter 17, Wounded Knee had been the site of a massacre of Native Americans in 1890. AIM wanted to remind people of the government's long history of unfair dealings with Native Americans.

Not all Native Americans agreed with AIM's militant tactics. But an increasing number showed greater pride in their heritage.

Older Americans The number of Americans over the age of 65 has steadily grown. Often, these older citizens had trouble paying for health care and insurance. Many jobs forced mandatory retirement, a policy that required people to stop working at a certain age. Most companies set 65 as the mandatory retirement age.

Older people organized to <u>exert</u> their political clout. In 1958, the American Association of Retired Persons (AARP) was founded to promote health insurance for retired Americans. The AARP lobbied for passage of programs such as Medicare. Since then, the AARP has taken a stand on a wide range of issues affecting older Americans.

In 1970, Maggie Kuhn was forced to retire because she had reached age 65. She then organized the Gray Panthers to combat age discrimination. The following year, the Gray Panthers gained national attention by staging a protest in Washington during a White House Conference on Aging. Kuhn defined her vision as "young and old working together for a better world for the young to grow old in."

Americans With Disabilities Americans with disabilities also campaigned for equal rights. Disability rights organizations backed laws requiring public buildings to provide access for people with disabilities. As a result, public accommodations were <u>modified</u> to include reserved parking spaces, ramped building entrances, wheelchair lifts on public buses, and Braille buttons on elevators.

Congress also passed laws protecting the educational rights of children with handicaps. The Education for the Handicapped Act of 1975 guaranteed a free education for all children with disabilities. In 1990, Congress passed the Americans With Disabilities Act. It outlawed discrimination in hiring people with physical or mental impairments.

☑ **Checkpoint** **How did older Americans work for change?**

⭐ **Looking Back and Ahead** The civil rights movement was a time of increasing social upheaval. In the next chapter, you will see how the Vietnam War added to this climate of protest.

Vocabulary Builder
<u>exert</u> (ehks ZERT) **v.** to put into action

Vocabulary Builder
<u>modify</u> (MAH dih fī) **v.** to make changes to or in; to alter

Section 4 | Check Your Progress

Progress Monitoring ⦿nline
For: Self-test with instant help
Visit: PHSchool.com
Web Code: mva-9264

Comprehension and Critical Thinking

1. **(a) Identify** What was the Equal Rights Amendment?
   (b) Detect Points of View Identify one argument for and one argument against the ERA.

2. **(a) Recall** Explain one way each of the following groups sought better treatment in the 1960s and 1970s: Mexican Americans, Native Americans, older Americans, people with disabilities.
   (b) Compare How were the efforts of these groups similar?

◉ Reading Skill

3. **Support Conclusions With Evidence** Reread the text following the subheading "Civil Rights for Mexican Americans." Give evidence to support the conclusion that many Mexican Americans faced a language barrier.

Key Terms

Fill in the blank in each question with one of the key terms from this section.

4. _____ ballots were printed in both English and Spanish.

5. Because of _____, many older people had to stop working.

Writing

6. Pick one person below. List three details he or she might observe in the circumstances described:
   • Woman reentering the work force after raising her children
   • Mexican first-grader going to school for the first time in a bilingual class
   • Sixty-five-year-old worker deciding to protest mandatory retirement
   • Physically disabled person entering a building that has no wheelchair ramp

21st Century Learning Decisions involve making choices between alternative courses of action. Understanding the reasons for important historical decisions can help us make decisions in our own lives.

In 1962, Fannie Lou Hamer was arrested in Mississippi after she tried to register to vote. Here she describes what happened next.

Primary Source "After we paid the fine among us, we continued on to Ruleville, and Reverend Jeff Sunny carried me four miles in the rural area where I had worked as a timekeeper and sharecropper for eighteen years. I was met there by my children, who told me the plantation owner was angry because I had gone down to try to register.

After they told me, my husband came, and said that the plantation owner was raising Cain because I had tried to register, and before he quit talking the plantation owner came, and said, 'Fannie Lou, do you know—did Pap tell you what I said?'

And I said, 'Yes, sir.'

He said, 'I mean that,' he said. 'If you don't go down and withdraw your registration, you will have to leave . . . because we are not ready for that in Mississippi.'

And I addressed him and told him and said, 'I didn't try to register for you. I tried to register for myself.'

I had to leave that same night.

On the 10th of September, 1962, sixteen bullets was fired into the home of Mr. and Mrs. Robert Tucker for me. . . ."

— Testimony of Fannie Lou Hamer (August 22, 1964)

Learn the Skill

Use these steps to learn how to make decisions.

❶ **Identify the problem.** What is the issue that must be resolved or the goal that must be achieved?

❷ **Understand the options.** What choices are available?

❸ **Evaluate consequences.** Understand the pros and cons of each alternative.

❹ **Make a decision.** Identify the decision and why it was made.

Practice the Skill

Answer the following questions about the primary source on this page.

❶ **Identify the problem.** (a) What did Hamer want to do? (b) What obstacles did she face?

❷ **Understand the options.** What choices does Hamer have in this situation?

❸ **Evaluate the consequences.** (a) If she does not withdraw her registration, what might happen to Hamer? Why? (b) If she does withdraw her registration, how might she feel?

❹ **Make a decision.** What decision does Hamer make? Why?

Apply the Skill

See the Review and Assessment at the end of this chapter.

Quick Study Guide

How did the civil rights movement change the nation?

Section 1
Beginnings of the Civil Rights Movement

- In the early 1900s, the NAACP challenged segregation laws.
- In *Brown* v. *Board of Education of Topeka*, the Supreme Court ruled that segregation in education was unconstitutional.
- African Americans in Montgomery, Alabama, organized a boycott to protest segregation on city buses.

Section 2
An Expanding Role for Government

- The Warren Court used judicial activism to protect and extend rights.
- John F. Kennedy favored social reforms, but most stalled in Congress.
- Lyndon Johnson's Great Society attempted to attack the causes of poverty.

Section 3
The Civil Rights Movement Continues

- Martin Luther King, Jr., favored nonviolent civil disobedience to achieve civil rights.
- Protests helped persuade Congress to pass civil rights legislation.
- Leaders such as Malcolm X rejected King's approach and supported militant tactics.

Section 4
Other Americans Seek Rights

- The women's movement led more women to work outside the home.
- Mexican American groups sought to end segregation and win better conditions for migrant workers.
- Native Americans organized to protect their rights and call attention to injustice.
- Older Americans and people with disabilities organized to support their interests.

? Exploring the Essential Question

Use the online study guide to explore the essential question.

Section 1
What key events marked the beginning of the civil rights movement in the 1950s?

Section 2
What was the "Great Society"?

Chapter 26 Essential Question
How did the civil rights movement change the nation?

Section 4
What other groups were swept up in the spirit of reform?

Section 3
How did the civil rights movement gain momentum?

Key Terms

Read each sentence below. If the sentence is true, write YES and explain why. If the sentence is not true, write NO and explain why not.

1. As a result of integration, African American and white children attended separate schools.

2. Supporters of civil disobedience were often jailed because they refused to obey laws.

3. César Chávez urged people to boycott grapes in order to increase demand for farm products.

4. Many rural African Americans lived in ghettos.

Comprehension and Critical Thinking

5. **(a) Summarize** What arguments did Thurgood Marshall use in the case of *Brown* v. *Board of Education of Topeka*?
   (b) Apply Information How does the picture below show an effect of the *Brown* case?

6. **(a) Recall** How were the actions of the Warren Court an example of judicial activism?
   (b) Support a Point of View Do you agree or disagree with judicial activism? Explain.

7. **(a) Summarize** What approach to civil rights did Martin Luther King, Jr., favor?
   (b) Apply Information How were sit-ins and freedom rides examples of King's approach?

8. **(a) Recall** What was the goal of affirmative action programs?
   (b) Identify Viewpoints What arguments could be used in favor of affirmative action? What arguments could be used against it?

9. **(a) Recall** What changes in public accommodations did disabled rights groups seek?
   (b) Analyze Cause and Effect How would these changes increase economic opportunities for people with disabilities?

Reading Skill

10. **Make Inferences and Draw Conclusions** Draw a conclusion about Americans' views about discrimination before and after the civil rights movement.

Writing

11. **Write one paragraph on the following topic:** Explain a problem faced by an individual who is a member of one of the groups discussed in this chapter.
    Your paragraph should:
    • describe the individual;
    • identify the time period of the situation you are describing;
    • describe the circumstances of the problem

    When you are finished, exchange papers with another student. Write a brief response to that student's paragraph, looking in particular for details that help create the time period. Revise your own plan in response to your partner's comments.

12. **Write a Narrative:**
    Imagine that you are a young black or white Freedom Rider. Write a letter home explaining why you are going to the South and what problems you face.

Skills for Life
Make Decisions
Use the quotation below to answer the questions.

"The events in Birmingham and elsewhere have so increased the cries for equality that [we cannot] ignore them. . . . We face therefore a moral crisis as a country. . . . It cannot be met by repressive police action. It cannot be left to increased demonstrations in the streets. It cannot be quieted by token moves or talk. . . . I am therefore asking the Congress to enact legislation giving all Americans the right to be served in [public] facilities."

—John F. Kennedy, June 11, 1963

13. **(a)** According to Kennedy, what moral problem faces the United States in 1963? **(b)** What options does he reject?

14. What did Kennedy decide to do? Do you think his decision was correct? Explain.

Test Yourself

Refer to the quotation below to answer Question 1.

> "We shall all be free,
> We shall all be free,
> We shall all be free some day.
> Oh, deep in my heart,
> I do believe
> We shall overcome some day."
>
> —"We Shall Overcome," civil rights anthem

1. Who would have been most likely to disagree with the attitude expressed in this song?

A Malcolm X

B Rosa Parks

C Martin Luther King, Jr.

D Lyndon Johnson

2. The Voting Rights Act of 1965

A gave African Americans the right to vote.

B allowed federal officials to register voters.

C required bilingual elections.

D established literacy tests for voting.

Refer to the symbol below to answer Question 3.

3. The above symbol relates to the activities of

A Maggie Kuhn. C Earl Warren.

B Betty Friedan. D César Chávez.

Document-Based Questions

Task: Look at Documents 1 and 2, and answer their accompanying questions. Then, use the documents and your knowledge of history to complete this writing assignment:

> Summarize the main ideas of Chisholm and Schlafly. Then, explain whose viewpoint you agree with and why.

Document 1: In May 1969, Representative Shirley Chisholm delivered this speech in Congress. *According to Chisholm, why was the ERA needed?*

> "I wish to introduce . . . a proposal that . . . sooner or later must become part of the basic law of the land—the Equal Rights Amendment.
>
> Let me . . . refute two . . . arguments . . . against this amendment. One is that women are already protected under the law. . . . Existing laws are not adequate to secure equal rights for women. . . Women do not have the opportunities that men do.
>
> A second argument . . . is that [ERA] would eliminate legislation . . . giving special protection to women. . . . Women need no protection that men do not need. What we need are laws to protect working people, to guarantee them fair pay, safe working conditions, protection against sickness and layoffs, and provision for dignified, comfortable retirement. Men and women need these things equally."

Document 2: Phyllis Schlafly led the campaign to defeat ERA. In 1986, she summarized her objections. *According to Schlafly, what would have been two negative effects of the ERA?*

> "ERA advocates were unable to show any way that ERA would benefit women or end any discrimination against them. The fact is that women already enjoy every constitutional right that men enjoy. . . .
>
> The opponents of ERA, on the other hand, were able to show many harms that ERA would cause.
> • ERA would take away legal rights that women possessed—*not* confer any new rights on women.
> • ERA would take away women's traditional exemption from military conscription. . . .
> • ERA would make unconstitutional the laws . . . that impose on a husband the obligation to support his wife.
> • ERA would force all schools and colleges, and all the programs and athletics they conduct, to be fully coeducational. . . . ERA would mean the end of single-sex colleges."

The Vietnam Era

1954-1976

"I didn't ask no questions about the war. I thought communism was spreading, and... it was my part to do as much as I could to defeat the Communist from coming here."

—Arthur E. Woodley, Jr.,
Vietnam War veteran

U.S. Marines on patrol in
South Vietnam, 1965

What You Will Learn

Section 1
THE WAR BEGINS
Hoping to block the spread of communism, the United States backed South Vietnam with military aid.

Section 2
AMERICAN INVOLVEMENT GROWS
An expanding war in Vietnam drew a massive commitment of U.S. forces and sharply divided Americans.

Section 3
THE WAR ENDS
After the United States negotiated peace and withdrew its forces, all of Vietnam came under Communist rule.

Section 4
A TIME OF UNCERTAINTY
President Nixon's accomplishments were overshadowed by the Watergate affair, which led to his resignation.

Reading Skill

Ask Questions In this chapter, you will learn what kinds of questions to ask yourself when reading.

What were the causes and effects of

The Vietnam War Era, 1954–1976

The First Indochina War, 1954

KEY
- Communist Vietminh control
- French control

◀ *France wanted to keep its colony in Southeast Asia, but the Communist Vietminh drove the French out.*

Division of Vietnam, 1954–1957

KEY
- Communist government
- Non-Communist government

By international ▶ agreement, Vietnam was divided into two states. War erupted between Vietnamese Communists and non-Communists.

American Involvement Grows, 1960–1968

During the Cold War, the United ▶ States opposed communism. Under President Johnson, more and more U.S. troops were sent to aid South Vietnam's fight against Communist forces.

U.S. Troops in Vietnam

Year	
1964	
1965	
1966	
1967	
1968	

⬤ U.S. Troops (100,000)

Source: U.S. Department of Defense

 U.S. Events

Eisenhower starts U.S. military aid to South Vietnam. **1954**

Kennedy sends military advisers to South Vietnam. **1961**

1964 Congress passes Gulf of Tonkin Resolution.

1952   **1958**   **1964**

 World Events

1954 Vietnam is divided into North Vietnam and South Vietnam.

President Diem of South Vietnam is assassinated. **1963**

Division and Protest at Home, 1965 –1973

▲ More and more Americans became unhappy with events in Vietnam and the rising number of casualties. However, others continued to support the war effort.

Public Support for the Vietnam War

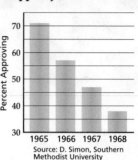

Source: D. Simon, Southern Methodist University

In 1973, President Richard Nixon ▶ ended U.S. involvement in the Vietnam War. In 1975, North Vietnam defeated South Vietnam, and the region's countries fell under communist control.

Southeast Asia, 1975

KEY
- Communist government
- Non-Communist government

Lasting Effects on America

- More than 58,000 Americans died in combat.
- About 300,000 Americans were wounded.
- War's cost (around $200 billion) weakened national economy.
- Trust in American leaders was undermined.
- War Powers Act of 1973 limited President's power.
- Vietnam War Memorial was built in 1982.

Antiwar demonstrations disrupt Democratic National Convention.	**1968**	Last American troops withdraw from Vietnam.	**1973**

Nixon resigns from office as a result of Watergate scandal. **1974**

1964 **1970** **1976**

Student revolts erupt in France. **1968**

Military leaders oust president of Chile. **1973**

South Vietnam falls to Communist North Vietnam. **1975**

Conflict in Vietnam

66 The oppressed the world over are wresting back their independence. We should not lag behind. . . . Under the Vietminh banner, let us valiantly march forward. 99

—Ho Chi Minh, Vietnamese nationalist and Communist leader, 1945

◄ French soldiers in Vietnam

The War Begins

Objectives

- Explain how Vietnam became a focus of conflict after World War II.
- Explain why the United States was concerned about developments in Vietnam.
- Describe how American involvement began to increase under President Kennedy.

Reading Skill

Ask Analytical Questions As you read about history in this textbook, you may find yourself puzzled at times. *Why* did a particular event happen? *Why* did it have the effect that it did? The text may not answer these analytical questions, but raising them will help you in your reading.

Key Terms and People

Ho Chi Minh
domino theory
Ngo Dinh Diem

guerrilla
Lyndon B. Johnson

Why It Matters In the 1950s, the Cold War between the United States and the Soviet Union intensified. America and its allies were determined to stop the spread of Communist dictatorships. After the Korean War, Southeast Asia became a Cold War hot spot. As U.S. involvement slowly grew, few Americans imagined how destructive the war would become.

? Section Focus Question: How did Vietnam become a major battlefield in the war against communism?

Origins of the Conflict

The Vietnam War was the longest war that the United States ever fought. Except for the Civil War, it was the most disruptive. While the war was going on, Americans were bitterly divided about the nation's involvement.

The causes of the war go back into Vietnam's history. Vietnam is a tiny land in Southeast Asia, stretching 1,000 miles along the South China Sea. In the 1800s, France seized Vietnam and ruled it for nearly 100 years as part of the colony of Indochina. During World War II, French rule was interrupted when Japan occupied Vietnam.

Declaring Independence In August 1945, the Japanese surrendered. Some Vietnamese saw the Japanese defeat as an opportunity to free themselves from French colonial rule. Ho Chi Minh (HOH CHEE MINH), a Communist, organized a revolt to end French colonial rule. Earlier, Ho had asked Americans for help. However, the Americans were suspicious because Ho was a Communist. With his followers, who called themselves Vietminh, Ho occupied Hanoi in North Vietnam. He proclaimed an independent Vietnam.

The First Indochina War The French refused to accept Vietnamese independence, and the two sides were soon at war. The United States threw its support, including large sums of money, behind France's struggle to regain control of its former colony. By helping France, U.S. leaders hoped to block any spread of communism.

Fighting between the French and the Vietminh continued for nearly 8 years. Ho's forces steadily gained strength and popular support. The turning point came in 1954, when the Vietminh forced the French to surrender after a 56-day battle at Dienbienphu, in northwestern Vietnam. The defeat was a major blow to the war-weary French, and they agreed to negotiate a settlement. French control over Vietnam was ended.

☑**Checkpoint** **Why did the United States support the French side?**

Ask Analytical Questions

Ask an analytical question about the text in this paragraph. You might focus on comparing America's response to the war in Indochina with its response to Communist movements in Latin America. Recall your reading in a previous chapter.

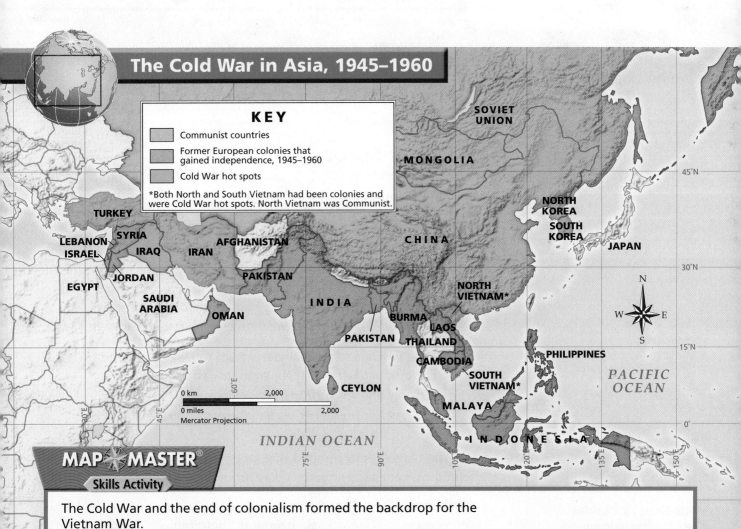

The Cold War in Asia, 1945–1960

KEY

- Communist countries
- Former European colonies that gained independence, 1945–1960
- Cold War hot spots

*Both North and South Vietnam had been colonies and were Cold War hot spots. North Vietnam was Communist.

SOVIET UNION
MONGOLIA
NORTH KOREA
SOUTH KOREA
JAPAN
CHINA
TURKEY
LEBANON
SYRIA
ISRAEL
IRAQ
IRAN
AFGHANISTAN
JORDAN
EGYPT
SAUDI ARABIA
PAKISTAN
OMAN
INDIA
PAKISTAN
BURMA
LAOS
THAILAND
CAMBODIA
NORTH VIETNAM*
SOUTH VIETNAM*
PHILIPPINES
CEYLON
MALAYA
INDONESIA
PACIFIC OCEAN
INDIAN OCEAN

45°N
30°N
15°N
0°

N
W   E
S

0 km   2,000
0 miles   2,000
Mercator Projection

MAP MASTER®
Skills Activity

The Cold War and the end of colonialism formed the backdrop for the Vietnam War.

(a) Interpret Maps Which Asian countries had Communist governments at the time of the Vietnam War?

(b) Explain Problems What problems arose between Communist and non-Communist nations once colonialism ended?

MapMaster ●nline

For: Interactive map
Visit: PHSchool.com
Web Code: mvp-9271

Delicate Balance
Vietnamese villagers often found themselves in a precarious position during the Vietnam War. **Critical Thinking:** *Interpret Photographs* *In what ways would the war have disrupted these people's lives?*

The War Spreads

After World War II, U.S. leaders saw the Soviet Union and its system of communism as a threat to world peace. Adding to their fears, China came under Communist rule in 1949. The Korean War began in 1950, when Communist North Korea attacked South Korea.

When Ho Chi Minh defeated the French in 1954, many U.S. political leaders feared a widespread Communist takeover in Southeast Asia. This idea was called the **domino theory.** If one country fell to the Communists, it was thought that neighboring countries would follow. President Dwight D. Eisenhower explained the idea this way:

> **❝**You have a row of dominoes set up. You knock over the first one, and what will happen to the last one is the certainty that it will go over very quickly.**❞**
> —President Eisenhower, press conference remarks, April 7, 1954

The United States hoped that stopping communism in Vietnam would prevent a Communist takeover in Southeast Asia.

Vocabulary Builder
<u>fate</u> (fayt) *n.* outcome; consequence or final result

Vietnam Divided After the French defeat, an international conference in Geneva, Switzerland, determined Vietnam's <u>fate</u>. Under the resulting Geneva Accords, Vietnam was temporarily divided into two states. North Vietnam, with its capital at Hanoi, was under the Communist rule of Ho Chi Minh. South Vietnam, with its capital at Saigon, was governed by Ngo Dinh Diem (noh din dee EHM). The United States pledged to support the South.

Elections were to <u>unify</u> the country within a few years, but the Diem government blocked them. A South Vietnamese movement organized to oppose Diem. In 1959, the movement launched an armed revolt. Guerrillas, or fighters who carry out hit-and-run attacks, waged a campaign of terror against villages controlled by Diem's officials. Using secret supply lines, the North Vietnamese furnished weapons to the guerrillas, who came to be called the Vietcong.

The American Role Deepens President John F. Kennedy continued Eisenhower's policy of support for South Vietnam. Kennedy sent more aid and many more military advisers.

In the meantime, South Vietnam's government was becoming unpopular. President Diem angered many South Vietnamese by imprisoning people who criticized his policies. Many of his handpicked officials were corrupt. U.S. leaders feared that Diem's actions were increasing support for the Vietcong.

In August 1963, when Diem ordered a crackdown against his opponents, Kennedy withdrew his support for Diem. This was a signal for the South Vietnamese military to act. In November 1963, military leaders seized control of the government and assassinated Diem.

Three weeks later, in an action unrelated to Vietnam, Kennedy himself was assassinated. With his death, Vietnam became the problem of the new President, Lyndon B. Johnson.

Vocabulary Builder
<u>unify</u> (YOO nuh fī) **v.** to unite; to make into one

Missile inspection by President Kennedy

☑ **Checkpoint** What kind of help did the United States give South Vietnam between 1954 and 1963?

⭐ **Looking Back and Ahead** At first, the United States supplied South Vietnam with money, weapons, and military advisers. In the next section, you will read how hundreds of thousands of U.S. troops became involved in a long, difficult war.

Section 1 | Check Your Progress

Progress Monitoring Online
For: Self-test with instant help
Visit: PHSchool.com
Web Code: mva-9271

Comprehension and Critical Thinking

1. (a) Recall After the Japanese surrender in 1945, what happened in Vietnam that led to a new conflict?
(b) Apply Information Why do you think Ho Chi Minh gained a strong following in North Vietnam?

2. (a) Describe How did Ngo Dinh Diem run South Vietnam?
(b) Synthesize Information Why do you think Diem blocked elections during the early years of the government?

🔄 Reading Skill

3. Ask Analytical Questions Reread the text under the heading "The War Spreads." Ask an analytical question about the text. You might focus on the reasons behind the Vietcong fighting style.

Key Terms

Answer the following question in a complete sentence to show your understanding of the key term.
4. How do **guerrilla** soldiers conduct warfare?

Writing

5. Write a paragraph for the place you see in the photograph "Delicate Balance" (on the opposite page). Describe it as if it were a setting for a story in 1958, several years after Vietnam is divided.

Under Fire

❝We were under a lot of fire and we returned a lot of fire, but I think the hardest thing for me was when a lot of our men were wounded—putting them on the helicopters when they were so severely injured and crying for their family and wives and children was devastating.❞

—Tomas Bunting, U.S. Army
4th Infantry Division, in Vietnam

◀ President Johnson meets a soldier in Vietnam.

American Involvement Grows

Objectives

- Describe how President Johnson widened the war in Vietnam.
- Explain how the war in Vietnam was different from any previous war in American history.
- Describe how the Vietnam War divided Americans at home.

🔁 Reading Skill

Ask Inferential Questions Inferential questions help you to infer, or figure out, the reasons behind individual actions or the actions of a nation. For example, asking questions such as "Why did people act in a particular way?" will help you understand how events happened and what motivated people's behavior.

Key Terms

escalate
napalm
hawks

doves
conscientious
    objector

Why It Matters Believing in the domino theory, President Lyndon Johnson feared that if Vietnam fell to communism, so would other countries. In order to prevent this, Johnson was willing to commit more U.S. soldiers to Vietnam. But as the fighting and dying in Vietnam intensified, a growing number of Americans protested against the war.

❓ **Section Focus Question: How did the demands of greater involvement in the Vietnam War divide the nation?**

A Wider War

During his first months as President, Lyndon Johnson tried to continue the policies in Southeast Asia that Eisenhower and Kennedy had set in motion. But before long, he began to expand the U.S. commitment.

Growing American Involvement After the fall of Diem, the government of South Vietnam became increasingly unstable. Military coup followed military coup, with leaders managing to stay in power only a few months. As the ruling generals bickered among themselves, the South Vietnamese military rapidly lost ground to the Vietcong.

Like Eisenhower and Kennedy before him, President Johnson believed in the domino theory. He saw Vietnam as a test of the resolve of the United States to resist the spread of communism. "I am not going to lose Vietnam," Johnson said.

Shortly after taking office, Johnson ordered an increase in economic aid and military advisers to the government and armed forces of South Vietnam. He also authorized a series of secret actions against North Vietnam. Meanwhile, the Soviet Union and China supported the Vietcong with arms and supplies.

The Gulf of Tonkin Incident An event in August of 1964 altered the U.S. role in Vietnam. Reports said North Vietnamese torpedo boats had attacked American destroyers in the Gulf of Tonkin, off the coast of North Vietnam. Details were sketchy. Indeed, the second of two reported attacks may not have taken place at all.

President Johnson, however, was determined to act. He announced that U.S. forces would stage air strikes against North Vietnam. The next day, Johnson asked Congress for the <u>authority</u> to do whatever was needed to resolve, or settle, the conflict. Congress backed the President by passing the Gulf of Tonkin Resolution. It stated:

> **"** . . . Congress approves and supports the determination of the President . . . to take all necessary measures to repel any armed attack against the forces of the United States and to prevent further aggression. **"**
>
> —Gulf of Tonkin Resolution, approved by Congress August 7, 1964

Vocabulary Builder
<u>authority</u> (uh THAWR uh tee)
n. the right to give orders, make decisions, or take action

President Johnson began to **escalate,** or step up, U.S. involvement in the Vietnam War. He cited the resolution as his authority.

☑**Checkpoint** **Why was the Gulf of Tonkin Resolution important?**

An Unconventional War

The Vietnam War was different from many wars the United States had fought before. Under the Constitution, only Congress can declare war. Although the Gulf of Tonkin Resolution gave the President the authority to use military force, it was not a declaration of war. Many Americans would later question the legality of this "undeclared war."

A Massive Buildup Through the fall of 1964, President Johnson was involved in a campaign for reelection, and the United States took limited action in Vietnam. Johnson declared, "We are not about to send American boys . . . to do what Asian boys ought to be doing for themselves." He won the election in a landslide.

Meanwhile, Johnson and his advisers had been working on plans for further actions in Vietnam. Early in 1965, the Vietcong attacked an American base at Pleiku (play KOO), in South Vietnam, killing eight Americans. Johnson responded by ordering a new series of air strikes against North Vietnam. A campaign of sustained U.S. bombing would continue for three years.

U.S. leaders soon realized the need to make plans for an increased commitment of U.S. troops. In March 1965, President Johnson ordered 3,500 marines to protect the American air base in Da Nang—the first American combat troops in Vietnam. Shortly after, he authorized the use of U.S. ground troops for offensive action. Within six weeks, 50,000 American combat troops had arrived in Vietnam; by the end of the year, 184,000 troops were there. In 1968, the figure would reach half a million.

Bombing South Vietnam
U.S. air attacks aimed to kill soldiers and destroy cover.
Critical Thinking: *Evaluate Information* *Why was bombing of only limited value in a war against guerrillas?*

Ask Inferential Questions

Read the text following the subheading "Search and Destroy." Ask an inferential question. You might focus on how American soldiers interacted with Vietnamese civilians.

Search and Destroy American entry into the ground war gave the South Vietnamese government forces a badly needed boost. At the same time, the political situation began to stabilize. A military leader named Nguyen Cao Ky seized power in June 1965 and crushed antigovernment protests by Vietnamese Buddhists. Although Ky's methods were far from democratic, they seemed to be effective in creating a stable government. South Vietnam's government was now able to concentrate on the war against the Vietcong.

The Americans who poured into Vietnam were well trained and equipped with the latest high-tech weapons. They used chemical weapons against the Vietcong. Airplanes dropped bombs containing **napalm,** a jellylike substance that burst into flames when dropped on villages or vegetation. They also sprayed the herbicide Agent Orange across the Vietnamese countryside. It destroyed crops and vegetation where the enemy might hide. Use of Agent Orange was controversial, with critics blaming it for birth defects, cancer, and other long-term health problems among both U.S. soldiers and Vietnamese. (In 1975, the United States declared that it would never again use herbicides in war unless an enemy did so first.)

The Vietcong dug in and kept fighting. They had some advantages of their own. Familiar with the swamps and jungles of Vietnam, the guerrillas employed hit-and-run attacks. Americans did not know what to expect in this jungle warfare, with no clearly defined battle lines. The situation was more confusing because Americans often could not distinguish between enemy and friend.

The Americans in Vietnam also used other new forms of warfare. Heavily armed helicopters carrying hundreds of American troops would locate an enemy stronghold. After heavy machine-gun fire

Soldiers in Vietnam
In 1964, President Johnson promised not to send more troops to Vietnam. However, as U.S. involvement increased, Johnson gave in to the request for more troops. *Critical Thinking: Make Predictions How do you think Johnson's actions would affect him in the 1968 election?*

U.S. Forces in Vietnam, 1963–1969

Military Forces (in thousands) / Year

Source: U.S. Department of Defense, *Military Personnel Historical Reports*

raked the area, U.S. troops landed and fanned out, searching for Vietcong. The goal of these search-and-destroy missions was not to gain territory but to kill as many of the enemy as possible. American military leaders believed that if they could kill enough Vietcong, sooner or later the enemy would give up.

Chinook helicopter picks up supplies

The Tet Offensive On January 31, 1968, the Vietnamese began celebrating Tet, their New Year holiday. Using the celebrations as cover, Vietcong and North Vietnamese soldiers launched attacks on every major city in South Vietnam. In Saigon, they broke through the walls of the American embassy and attacked the presidential palace. Another major assault occurred in the ancient capital of Hue (way). There, the Communists seized the former home of Vietnam's emperors.

Although caught by surprise, American and South Vietnamese forces responded quickly. For weeks, they battled to take back the areas under attack. The Communists fought hard, but in time they yielded to superior U.S. firepower. By February 25, the siege was over. As many as 40,000 North Vietnamese and Vietcong soldiers lost their lives in the fighting.

The Tet offensive set in motion a <u>sequence</u> of events that marked a major turning point of the Vietnam War. On the surface, Tet was a military victory for the United States. But, in fact, Tet dealt a major blow to the U.S. mission in Vietnam. Americans were shocked that enemy forces were capable of such an attack. After Tet, more and more Americans argued that the United States should get out of Vietnam. No matter how many troops the United States sent to Vietnam, they believed, it could never win the war. By now, President Johnson and many of his advisers were also convinced that the United States could not win the war. In addition, the President recognized that support at home for the war was waning.

Vocabulary Builder
<u>sequence</u> (SEE kwehns) **n.** one thing occurring after another; series of events

☑**Checkpoint** **How did fighting the Vietnam War differ from fighting other wars?**

A Nation Divided

As the war dragged on, Americans increasingly became divided. They split into two camps: hawks and doves. Hawks supported the war in Vietnam. However, many challenged President Johnson's policy of gradual escalation. They said the United States was fighting "with one hand tied behind its back." They wanted the government to mount an all-out military effort that would decisively defeat the Vietcong and North Vietnam. Doves believed the Vietnam War could not be won and was morally wrong.

Vietnam Divides the Nation

Critics of the Vietnam War staged massive protest marches. Supporters of the war were no less eager to publicize their views.
Critical Thinking: *Detect Points of View*
Write a paragraph describing why a person might have joined a demonstration for or against the Vietnam War.

Demonstrators oppose the war and support resistance to the draft. ▼

It was a time of deep divisions among Americans. These demonstrators strongly support the war. ▼

VETERANS FOR PEACE IN VIETNAM

DON'T DRAFT OUR SONS TO BOMB AND DESTROY!

END W IN VIE NO

SUPPORT OUR BOYS IN VIETNAM

BOMB HANOI

NO SURRENDER

TEAMSTERS

The doves urged withdrawal of U.S. troops. They organized a wide range of protests against the war, including sit-ins and marches.

The U.S. government had long used the draft to select men to serve in the military. During the Vietnam War, about 1.8 million men were drafted. As opposition to the war rose, so did resistance to the draft. Hundreds of young men burned their draft cards to show opposition to the war. Other young men sought recognition as **conscientious objectors,** people who refuse to participate in war because of a strong belief that war is wrong. Some 100,000 Americans fled to Canada to avoid the war.

In 1965 and after, antiwar protests spread across the nation. The antiwar movement included people from every walk of life. Students, college professors, businesspeople, religious leaders, entertainers, and others spoke out against the U.S. role in the war. At first, most antiwar protests were peaceful, using tactics such as petitions and mass marches. But as the war escalated, protesters adopted more dramatic techniques, such as sit-ins and public draft-card burnings. Violent confrontations with police became common.

Meanwhile, television brought the sights and sounds of battle into American living rooms. The graphic images shocked and sometimes sickened viewers. One theory is that the steady diet of blood and horror on TV helped turn Americans against the Vietnam War.

☑**Checkpoint** **How did doves protest against the war?**

⭐ **Looking Back and Ahead** The commitment of U.S. troops to the Vietnam War in 1965 led to years of warfare. Opposition at home grew as the war dragged on. In the next section, you will read how South Vietnam came under Communist rule.

Section 2 | **Check Your Progress**

Progress Monitoring ⊙nline
For: Self-test with instant help
Visit: PHSchool.com
Web Code: mva-9272

Comprehension and Critical Thinking

1. (a) Recall What event led to the passage of the Gulf of Tonkin Resolution?
(b) Summarize How did President Johnson use the Gulf of Tonkin Resolution?
(c) Analyze Cause and Effect How did the war change after the resolution was passed?

2. (a) Describe What happened in Vietnam in 1968 during Tet, the Vietnamese New Year?
(b) Apply Information How did Americans react to those events?

🔄 Reading Skill

3. Ask Inferential Questions Read the text following the subheading "The Gulf of Tonkin Incident." Ask an inferential question. You might focus on why Johnson sought a congressional resolution even though information was sketchy.

Key Terms

Read each sentence that follows. If the sentence is true, write YES. If the sentence is not true, write NO and explain why.
4. The United States used napalm in South Vietnam to destroy crops and vegetation.

5. Opponents of the Vietnam War adopted the name hawks to show that their cause was wise.
6. A conscientious objector is someone who supports war on religious grounds.

Writing

7. Write a paragraph about a peace march protesting the Vietnam War. Describe one of the following phases of the march: as it begins, as it becomes more active, or as it ends. Include details to make the reader aware of what is happening.

Fighting a Jungle War

American troops faced new challenges in the swamps and jungles of Vietnam. Vietcong guerrillas often used the physical environment to attack—and then flee—American combat patrols. The Vietcong hid in thickets of underbrush to set up a surprise attack. After inflicting damage on unsuspecting American soldiers, the attackers would quickly retreat along hidden paths and tunnels.

American patrols often discovered hidden entrances to Vietcong tunnel systems. Here, soldiers stand guard as an American "tunnel rat" investigates one such entrance. ▶

The Americans had to cut paths through dense jungle foliage in order to fight the Vietcong. Here, American soldiers plunge into a stream while on patrol. ▼

History *Interactive*

Learn About Jungle War in Vietnam

Visit: PHSchool.com
Web Code: mvl-9272

Understand Effects:

Search and Destroy

In previous wars, American soldiers fought along defined battle lines. U.S. military planners in Vietnam quickly realized that a jungle environment erased those lines. In order to combat Vietcong hit-and-run attacks, military planners ordered search-and-destroy missions.

▲ U.S. fighter planes dropped chemical explosives like napalm to destroy Vietcong positions. The fighter above dropped a bomb made of another chemical called phosphorus.

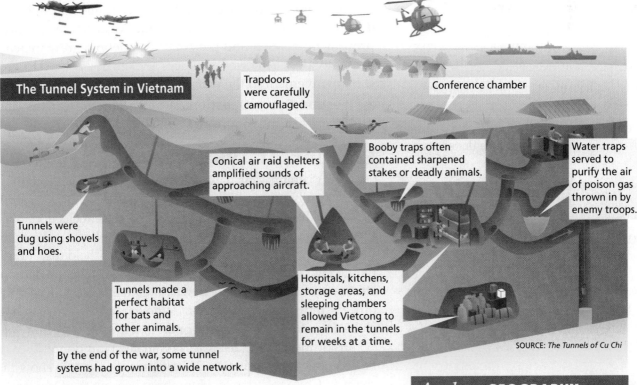

The Tunnel System in Vietnam

Trapdoors were carefully camouflaged.

Conference chamber

Conical air raid shelters amplified sounds of approaching aircraft.

Booby traps often contained sharpened stakes or deadly animals.

Water traps served to purify the air of poison gas thrown in by enemy troops.

Tunnels were dug using shovels and hoes.

Tunnels made a perfect habitat for bats and other animals.

Hospitals, kitchens, storage areas, and sleeping chambers allowed Vietcong to remain in the tunnels for weeks at a time.

By the end of the war, some tunnel systems had grown into a wide network.

SOURCE: *The Tunnels of Cu Chi*

▲ Vietcong guerrillas dug large networks of tunnels throughout the countryside. They used the tunnels to hide their movements and to plan hit-and-run attacks on American soldiers.

Analyze **GEOGRAPHY AND HISTORY**

How did the Vietcong use the physical environment to wage war against American troops? Write a paragraph explaining how the geography of Vietnam affected the war.

We Should Get Out

❝We feel the administration must know that many, many people, those of us who have lost our sons, feel we should get out of this involvement.❞

—Mrs. Ransom, antiwar demonstrator and a soldier's mother, 1969

◀ An American soldier returns home.

The War Ends

Objectives
- Explain how the Vietnam War affected the election of 1968.
- Explain how President Nixon decreased U.S. involvement in Vietnam.
- Describe how the fighting in Vietnam came to an end.
- Describe the long-term impact of the Vietnam War on Southeast Asia and the United States.

🎯 Reading Skill

Ask Questions That Go Beyond the Text There is much more to learn and explore about every topic introduced in this textbook. You can explore topics that interest you through research and discussion. Asking questions will help you. Remember to ask questions that focus on *why* or *how*, rather than questions with yes or no answers.

Key Terms and People

Richard Nixon
Henry Kissinger
boat people

Why It Matters Despite years of fighting and thousands of deaths, the United States and South Vietnam had failed to defeat Communist North Vietnam. Meanwhile, antiwar protests intensified and the American people grew increasingly divided. America's leaders looked for a way to end U.S. involvement in the war.

❷ Section Focus Question: What were the causes and effects of American withdrawal from Vietnam?

Election of 1968

The Vietnam War played a central role in the election of 1968. Heavily criticized by some Democrats for his war policies, President Johnson decided not to seek reelection. Vice President Hubert Humphrey, who backed Johnson's Vietnam policies, then entered the race. The Democrats held their nominating convention in Chicago. Thousands of antiwar demonstrators gathered, too. In what was later deemed a "police riot," officers moved in and struck demonstrators with fists and clubs. Hundreds were injured or arrested.

Inside the hall, the delegates nominated Humphrey. Even as he accepted the nomination, TV cameras cut away to show the chaos in Chicago's streets. Humphrey became the Democratic candidate for President, but the nation was further torn apart.

The Republicans nominated former Vice President Richard Nixon. Nixon promised to restore "law and order" at home and win "peace with honor" in Vietnam. Alabama Governor George Wallace, who had gained national attention by exploiting racial tensions in the South, became a third-party candidate. The election was close, but Nixon won by a small margin.

☑️**Checkpoint** What position did Nixon take on the Vietnam War?

The War Winds Down

Nixon knew that a growing number of Americans believed the war was a mistake. He began looking for a way to get out of Vietnam and still keep his promise of "peace with honor."

Nixon Pursues a New Course To begin scaling down American involvement, in June 1969 Nixon announced a policy known as Vietnamization. Under this plan, American troops gradually withdrew from Vietnam and the South Vietnamese assumed responsibility for fighting the war. The first U.S. combat troops left Vietnam the following month, in July 1969. By August, about 25,000 combat troops returned home. By April 1970, nearly 150,000 soldiers left Vietnam.

At the same time, Nixon expanded the war into Vietnam's neighbor, Cambodia. Cambodia had tried to stay neutral, but North Vietnamese soldiers had been carrying arms and supplies along a mountainous route through Laos and Cambodia into South Vietnam. This route was known as the Ho Chi Minh Trail.

In 1969, the United States began bombing Communist bases in Cambodia. American and South Vietnamese forces also attacked bases on the ground. The bases were being used to mount attacks on American troops in Vietnam. Nixon hoped that the American action

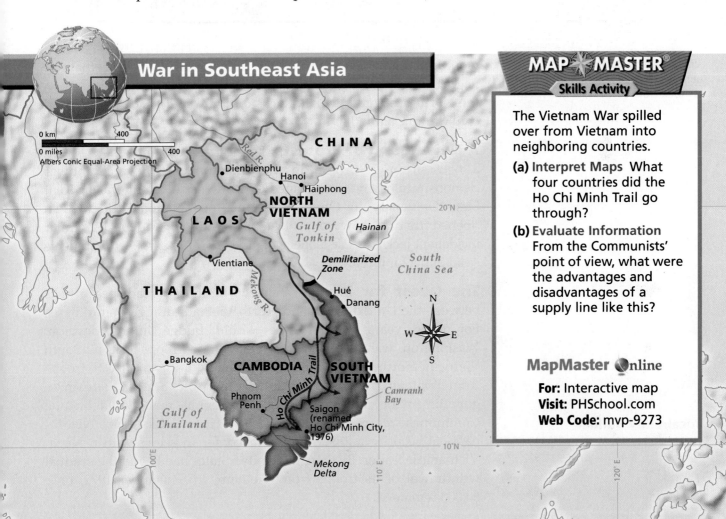

War in Southeast Asia

MAP MASTER
Skills Activity

The Vietnam War spilled over from Vietnam into neighboring countries.

(a) Interpret Maps What four countries did the Ho Chi Minh Trail go through?

(b) Evaluate Information From the Communists' point of view, what were the advantages and disadvantages of a supply line like this?

MapMaster Online

For: Interactive map
Visit: PHSchool.com
Web Code: mvp-9273

A Nurse Reflects

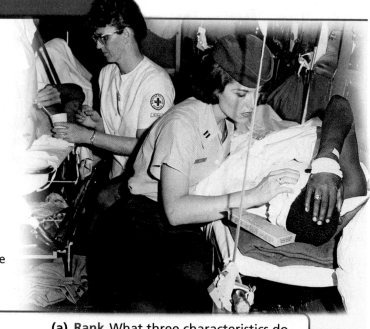

❝Those of us who went to Vietnam practiced a lifetime of nursing in one year—our tour of duty there. We were the young, caring for the young. The average age of the wounded soldier in Vietnam was 19.4 years. The average age of the nurse was 23. We quickly learned that the primary reason we were in Vietnam was to get each other home.❞

—Diane Carlson Evans,
speech, Washington, D.C., 1998

Nurses care for wounded soldiers about to be shipped home.

Reading Primary Sources
Skills Activity

As many as 10,000 women served in uniform with U.S. military forces in the Vietnam War, most as nurses.

(a) Rank What three characteristics do you think were most important for a nurse serving in Vietnam?

(b) Draw Conclusions What does the speaker mean when she says the main goal was "to get each other home"?

Vocabulary Builder
eliminate (ee LIHM ih nayt) **v.** to remove from consideration

would <u>eliminate</u> a military threat and pressure North Vietnam to negotiate peace. In fact, the attacks on Cambodia had little effect on the North Vietnamese. The attacks did, however, lead to chaos and civil war in Cambodia.

A New Round of Protests The attacks on Cambodia triggered a new storm of protest in the United States. Several antiwar demonstrations ended in tragedy. The worst incident was at Kent State University in Ohio, where nervous National Guardsmen opened fire on a crowd of protesters, killing four students. A similar incident at Jackson State College in Jackson, Mississippi, left 2 students dead and 12 injured.

The Quest for Peace While the fighting spread, peace talks between the United States and North Vietnam dragged on in Paris. For three years, neither side would budge in its position. Washington wanted all North Vietnamese troops out of South Vietnam. North Vietnam insisted on the withdrawal of U.S. troops from Vietnam. It also demanded that the South Vietnamese government be replaced with a new regime that would include Communist representatives. In 1970, Henry Kissinger, Nixon's national security adviser, began to <u>confer</u> in secret with a North Vietnamese leader. By then, the United States had begun the gradual withdrawal of its troops from Vietnam. In September 1972, only 60,000 remained.

Vocabulary Builder
confer (kahn FER) **v.** to exchange ideas

In October 1972, just before the U.S. presidential election, Kissinger hinted that an agreement was near. "Peace is at hand," he exclaimed. But his statement proved premature. The South Vietnamese, who had not been consulted, rejected the proposed agreement.

In order to put more pressure on the Communists, President Nixon then ordered new bombings of North Vietnam. After 12 days of concentrated bombing, the North Vietnamese agreed to return to the bargaining table. This time, an accord was reached that all sides accepted. The Paris Peace Accords were signed on January 27, 1973. They closely resembled what had been agreed to in October of the previous year. The last American serviceman to die in combat in Vietnam, Lt. Colonel William B. Nolde, was killed by an artillery shell only 11 hours before a cease-fire went into effect. The last U.S. combat troops were out of Vietnam by March 1973. The longest war in U.S. history was finally over.

Reading Skill **Ask Questions That Go Beyond the Text** Ask a possible research question about Nixon's choice to bomb North Vietnam at this time.

☑**Checkpoint** **What was President Nixon's policy of Vietnamization?**

The Final Years of Conflict

Although direct American involvement in the Vietnam War ended in 1973, the struggle between North and South continued for two more years. The Paris Peace Accords allowed North Vietnam to keep some 150,000 troops in the South. Once the Americans were gone, the Communists set out to seize control of the country.

At the end of 1974, the North Vietnamese launched a series of strikes against the South Vietnamese army. The South Vietnamese army tried without success to stop the Communist advance. In March 1975, the North Vietnamese captured the ancient capital of Hue. At the same time, they forced South Vietnamese troops into a retreat from the Central Highlands, along the Cambodian border. Much of the South Vietnamese army was killed or captured, and other soldiers shed their uniforms and fled into the countryside. Thousands of civilians also perished in what became known as the Convoy of Tears.

By April 29, 1975, North Vietnamese forces were nearing Saigon, the capital of South Vietnam. Fearing a blood bath when the Communists entered the city, the United States carried out a dramatic helicopter evacuation of 1,000 American workers and some 5,500 South Vietnamese supporters. At the same time, American ships rescued thousands of South Vietnamese at sea. The Vietnamese had fled the mainland in any vessel they could find, and many of the vessels proved unseaworthy.

Fleeing Saigon
Vietnamese civilians try to climb aboard a U.S. airplane during the hectic evacuation of Saigon in 1975. **Critical Thinking: Analyze Cause and Effect** *What was the cause of the evacuation, and what were its effects?*

On April 30, North Vietnamese troops entered Saigon. The South Vietnamese government formally surrendered. After decades of fighting, Vietnam was united under a Communist government. And Saigon received a new name: Ho Chi Minh City.

✔**Checkpoint** **What happened in Vietnam after the United States withdrew its combat forces?**

Vietnam Balance Sheet

The Vietnam War was the first foreign war in which American forces suffered defeat. This failure damaged the nation's pride. It also caused Americans to rethink their role in the world.

Effect on the United States The U.S. costs of the war were enormous. More than 58,000 Americans died in combat, and some 300,000 were wounded. On the economic side, the high price tag for the war—around $200 billion—damaged the U.S. economy for years. Unlike veterans of earlier wars, Vietnam vets were not welcomed home with cheering and parades. For many of the survivors, war memories were a nightmare. Many veterans adjusted poorly to civilian life. They suffered high rates of divorce, unemployment, and homelessness.

The Vietnam War undermined the nation's trust in the government and its leaders. In 1971, leading newspapers had published secret government documents known as the Pentagon Papers. They traced the steps by which the United States had committed itself to the Vietnam War and showed that government officials had concealed actions and often misled Americans about their motives.

Two Presidents had sent American troops into battle without a formal declaration of war. Hoping to curb presidential power, Congress passed the War Powers Act in 1973. It declared that a President could not send military forces into action for longer than 60 days without congressional approval.

Another political change resulting from the war was passage in 1971 of the Twenty-sixth Amendment to the Constitution, which lowered the voting age to 18. Supporters of the amendment argued that if 18-year-olds were old enough to fight and die in Vietnam, they were old enough to vote.

Remembering the Vietnam War In 1982, the Vietnam Veterans Memorial was completed in Washington, D.C. Known by many simply as "the Wall," it consists of two slabs of black granite sloping into the ground. Etched into the surface are the names of the more than 58,000 Americans who died

Biography Quest

Maya Lin
born 1959

Maya Lin was a 21-year-old art student when she entered a national contest to design the Vietnam Veterans Memorial. Lin's design for a black granite wall was selected over some 1,400 other entries. Today, the memorial is one of the most visited sites in Washington, D.C.

After that powerful achievement, Lin has gone on to become one of the nation's most respected sculptors and architects.

Biography Quest Online

Why did Lin's design for the Vietnam Veterans Memorial cause controversy?

For: The answer to the question about Lin
Visit: PHSchool.com
Web Code: mvd-9273

in Vietnam. In the words of Jack Wheeler, a Vietnam veteran who played a major role in getting the memorial built, "[the Wall] is probably the single most important step in the process of healing."

Effect on Vietnam Vietnamese losses were huge. South Vietnamese battle deaths exceeded 350,000. Estimates of North Vietnamese battle losses range between 500,000 and one million. Millions of civilians also died. The bombing destroyed much of North Vietnam's industry and transportation, but the greatest damage was in South Vietnam. There, 10 million people were left homeless by the war.

At the end of the war, more than a million people fled the new regime. Those who attempted to escape in small boats were called **boat people.** Perhaps 200,000 boat people died at sea or in refugee camps. Eventually, the United Nations acted to relocate the boat people. The United States took in many refugees, as did other nations. Private groups also worked hard to help the refugees from Vietnam.

✓**Checkpoint** How did the Vietnam War affect the people in North Vietnam and in South Vietnam?

☆ **Looking Back and Ahead** The Nixon administration began withdrawing troops from Vietnam and negotiated a peace pact. After U.S. troops left, fighting resumed and North Vietnam overtook South Vietnam and united the country under communism. In the next section, you will read of other issues that affected the United States in this period.

Section 3 | Check Your Progress

Progress Monitoring ⊙nline
For: Self-test with instant help
Visit: PHSchool.com
Web Code: mva-9273

Comprehension and Critical Thinking

1. **(a) Recall** What campaign promise did Nixon make regarding the war in Vietnam?
   (b) Apply Information Why do you think Nixon broke his campaign promise?

2. **(a) Identify** What is the War Powers Act?
   (b) Explain Problems Why did Congress believe it was necessary to pass the act?

⊙ Reading Skill

3. **Ask Questions That Go Beyond the Text** Ask a possible research question about current Vietnamese views about the war era.

Key Terms

Read the following sentence. If the sentence is true, write YES. If the sentence is not true, write NO and explain why.

4. **Henry Kissinger** did not feel that the United States should withdraw from Vietnam.

Writing

5. Write a paragraph from the viewpoint of one of the following: (a) a Vietnamese refugee settling in the United States in 1975, (b) an American soldier returning home after the war, or (c) a student protesting the invasion of Cambodia. Give the speaker's opinion of the situation in which he or she is involved. Add details to make the experience seem real.

EXTRA
New York Post
NIXON QUITS TONIGHT
Addresses Nation at 9

▲ Vice President Gerald Ford became President after Nixon's resignation.

I Shall Resign the Presidency

" Because of the Watergate matter I might not have the support of the Congress that I would consider necessary to back the very difficult decisions and carry out the duties of this office in the way the interests of the Nation would require. . . . Therefore, I shall resign the Presidency at noon tomorrow. "

—President Richard Nixon, August 1974

A Time of Uncertainty

Objectives

- Explain how President Nixon tried to ease Cold War tensions.
- Describe the impact of the Watergate scandal on the Nixon administration and the nation.
- Identify the challenges faced by President Gerald Ford.

Reading Skill

Ask Questions to Synthesize Information History textbooks contain a great deal of information. Asking questions can help you to reflect on that information and put it into focus. Ask a question that explores the connection between pieces of information, including those from earlier chapters. Answering it will help ensure your understanding of the material.

Key Terms and People

inflation   Jimmy Carter
Gerald Ford

Why It Matters President Nixon dealt with other challenging issues besides the Vietnam War. He eased Cold War tensions and improved relations with Communist China. However, a destructive scandal marred his presidency and changed the way Americans viewed their government.

❷ **Section Focus Question: What successes and failures marked Nixon's presidency?**

Richard Nixon in Office

In running for office, Richard Nixon had criticized the violence and unrest of the Johnson years. The "silent majority," he said, wanted "law and order" and an end to chaos in the streets. Yet, the Nixon years provided their own mix of successes and new troubles.

Moon Landing One success was space exploration. President Kennedy had pledged to land an American on the moon before 1970. That goal was achieved by the *Apollo 11* mission. On July 20, 1969, astronaut Neil A. Armstrong descended from the *Apollo*'s *Eagle* landing craft and set foot on the surface of the moon.

Economic Problems The economy was in trouble when Nixon came into office. High military spending for the Vietnam War had fed inflation, or a steady rise in prices. At the same time, economic growth had stalled, producing an economic recession and high unemployment. Nixon, like most Republicans, asserted that government involvement in the economy should be limited. But when other methods failed to boost the economy, he shocked his fellow conservatives by ordering a temporary freeze on wages, prices, and rents. His policy, however, met little success, and the freeze was soon lifted.

Easing Cold War Tensions Nixon's greatest success was in foreign affairs. Through his policy of détente—or an easing of tensions with Communist powers—he helped to take the edge off the Cold War.

Nixon's most surprising foreign policy move was to open contacts between the United States and Communist China. In 1949, as you have read, Communists led by Mao Zedong won China's civil war by defeating the Nationalists of Chiang Kai-shek. The Nationalists retreated to Taiwan, and the Communists created the People's Republic of China on the mainland. Ever since, the United States had refused to recognize Mao and the Communists as the lawful rulers of China. Instead, the United States treated the Nationalists on Taiwan as China's legitimate rulers. Another reason for hostility between the United States and Communist China was that they had never reached an <u>accommodation</u> after fighting on opposite sides in the Korean War.

Thus, many people were shocked in February 1972 when Nixon announced that he would visit mainland China. Nixon made the trip later that month. He attended banquets with China's Communist leaders. He toured the Great Wall. He met with Chairman Mao Zedong. Nixon said:

> **❝**What we have done is simply opened the door, opened the door for travel, opened the door for trade.**❞**
> —Richard Nixon, July 6, 1972

Nixon also pursued détente with the other great Communist power, the Soviet Union. Several months after visiting China, Nixon went to Moscow. He and Soviet leaders signed the Strategic Arms Limitation Treaty (SALT). SALT restricted the number and type of nuclear warheads and missiles that each nation could build. While it did not end the arms race, SALT showed that the Soviets and Americans were willing to work together to relax tensions.

☑**Checkpoint** Why was Nixon's goal to improve relations with China surprising to many Americans?

Vocabulary Builder
<u>accommodation</u> (ak kom moh DAY shuhn) **n.** agreement or change in what is wanted in order to solve a problem

Breakthrough to China
President Nixon gestures as he stands on the Great Wall of China with Mao Zedong. **Critical Thinking: *Organize Information*** *Describe the issues that divided the United States and Communist China from 1949 to 1972.*

The tapes

Reading Political Cartoons

Skills Activity

Court decisions forced the Nixon administration to turn over evidence of the President's role in the Watergate coverup.

(a) Apply Information What is Richard Nixon caught in?

(b) Make Predictions What might have happened to the President if he had decided not to resign?

Watergate Scandal

Nixon was reelected in 1972. But a political scandal would end in his downfall.

During the 1972 election campaign, police arrested five men who broke into Democratic Party offices in the Watergate complex in Washington, D.C. The men had been hired by Nixon's reelection committee to spy on the Democrats. White House officials paid the burglars "hush money" to keep quiet. But the story soon came out.

In May 1973, a Senate Committee opened nationally televised hearings into the Watergate affair, as the scandal became known. The star witness was John Dean, former White House counsel. He testified that Nixon himself had approved the coverup.

Another witness revealed that Nixon had secretly taped all conversations in his office. At first, Nixon refused to release the tapes. When a Supreme Court order finally forced him to <u>submit</u> the tapes, they largely confirmed Dean's account. The President had conspired to cover up the Watergate burglary and other misdeeds.

In July 1974, the House of Representatives took steps toward impeaching the President. Realizing that enough votes existed to remove him from office, Nixon resigned on August 9, 1974. Vice President Gerald Ford became President.

✓Checkpoint **Why did the Watergate affair bring Nixon down?**

Vocabulary Builder
<u>submit</u> (sahb MIHT) **v.** to give up power or control; to agree to do something

Ask Questions to Synthesize Information
Ask a question connecting the Watergate burglary to the House preparations for impeaching the President.

The Ford Presidency

On taking office, President Ford tried to restore public confidence in the nation's leaders. But trust in him was badly eroded when he granted Richard Nixon a "full, free, and absolute pardon." Ford had acted, he said, to end the "long nightmare" of Watergate.

The nation faced severe economic problems. President Ford began a program of voluntary wage and price controls called Whip Inflation Now (WIN). They had little effect. In fact, the nation slipped into recession, with the highest unemployment rate in years. At Ford's urging, Congress approved a tax cut to stimulate the economy, but recovery was slow and uncertain.

In foreign affairs, Ford generally followed Nixon's policy of easing Cold War tensions with the Soviet Union and China. Though American involvement in the Vietnam War was over, events in Southeast Asia still demanded attention. The President arranged to airlift more than 50,000 South Vietnamese as Communists swept toward Saigon. In neighboring Cambodia, he sent U.S. marines to free the crew of the *Mayaguez,* an American merchant ship that had been seized by Cambodia's Communists.

In 1976, the Republicans nominated Ford to run for President in his own right. The Democrats nominated a little known candidate, Jimmy Carter, former governor of Georgia. Carter promised to restore integrity to Washington. In a close election, Carter won.

Button promoting Ford's voluntary controls

✓**Checkpoint** **What economic problems did President Ford face?**

⭐ **Looking Back and Ahead** In 1977, Jimmy Carter entered office with high hopes. However, he quickly faced a series of perplexing challenges. In the next chapter, you will see how Carter's troubled presidency helped pave the way for a new era in American politics.

Section 4 | **Check Your Progress**

Progress Monitoring Online
For: Self-test with instant help
Visit: PHSchool.com
Web Code: mva-9274

Comprehension and Critical Thinking

1. **(a) List** What were President Nixon's three major actions in foreign affairs?
   (b) Identify Benefits How did each improve U.S. security in the world?

2. **(a) Recall** What was the Watergate break-in?
   (b) Describe What did President Nixon do about it?
   (c) Apply Information How did his actions in the Watergate affair cost him the presidency?

🔁 Reading Skill

3. **Ask Questions to Synthesize Information** Reread the text following the subheading "Easing Cold War Tensions." Ask a question connecting the Vietnam War with Nixon's trips to China and the Soviet Union.

Key Terms

Answer the following question in a complete sentence that shows your understanding of the key term.
4. What happens to prices as a result of inflation?

Writing

5. Write a paragraph describing the viewpoint of one of the following: (a) astronaut Neil Armstrong as his flight to the moon is ready to take off in the summer of 1969 or (b) Richard Nixon during his struggles with the Watergate scandal in 1973.

Synthesize Information

21st Century Learning Synthesizing information enables you to put pieces of evidence together to form conclusions. It often requires analyzing different types of historical information, such as photographs, graphs and charts, and primary sources.

The excerpt below is from a speech Robert Kennedy made two days after he announced his candidacy for the Democratic nomination for President.

Primary Source

"The cost of the war's present course far outweighs anything we can reasonably hope to gain by it, for ourselves or for the people of Vietnam. It must be ended, and it can be ended, in a peace of brave men who have fought each other with a terrible fury, each believing that he alone was in the right. We have prayed to different gods, and the prayers of neither have been answered fully. Now, while there is still time for some of them to be partly answered, now is the time to stop."

—Speech by Senator Robert Kennedy, March 18, 1968

This excerpt is from a speech made by Eugene V. Rostow, who was in the State Department during Lyndon Johnson's presidency.

Primary Source

"This is what is at stake in Vietnam—the credibility of America's support in Southeast Asia, and, indeed, in the many other areas in whose security we have a national interest. Remove this credibility and we will indeed be placed in the position of becoming world policemen, or captives in a fortress America. In theory, there may be better places to fight than Vietnam; in fact, we have no alternative."

—Speech by Eugene V. Rostow, February 20, 1968

Learn the Skill

Use these steps to synthesize information.

1. **Identify key facts and main ideas in each piece of evidence.** Look for the most important idea about the subject. Then, find the key facts that support the main idea. If the evidence is a first-person narrative, identify the speaker's point of view or opinion about the subject.

2. **Compare the pieces of evidence.** Look for similarities and differences in the material to better understand the topic.

3. **Draw conclusions by synthesizing the evidence.** Use the information from various sources to draw conclusions about the topic.

Practice the Skill

Use material on this page and in the chapter to synthesize information.

1. **Identify key facts and main ideas in each piece of evidence.** (a) Who gave the speeches excerpted on this page? (b) Study the map in Section 1. Which nations are considered to be the Cold War hot spots? (c) Look at the full-page feature "Vietnam Divides the Nation," in Section 2. What do some of the signs say?

2. **Compare the pieces of evidence.** (a) What points of view are expressed by Kennedy and Rostow? (b) What do photographs in the feature "Vietnam Divides the Nation" illustrate about public support of the war?

3. **Draw conclusions by synthesizing the evidence.** What can you conclude about the effect of the Vietnam War on U.S. society from the evidence presented?

Apply the Skill

See the Review and Assessment at the end of this chapter.

What were the causes and effects of the Vietnam War?

Section 1
The War Begins

- Ho Chi Minh and the Vietminh fought for Vietnam's independence from France.
- After the Vietminh defeated the French at Dienbienphu in 1954, the Geneva Accords divided Vietnam.
- The United States opposed Ho's Communist government and its attempts to take over South Vietnam.

Section 2
American Involvement Grows

- President Johnson sent half a million U.S. combat soldiers to South Vietnam, citing the Gulf of Tonkin Resolution as his authority.
- The U.S. role in the war caused sharp divisions among Americans.
- The Tet offensive in 1968 shocked Americans and undercut support for the war.

Section 3
The War Ends

- With Democrats divided over the war, Richard Nixon won the presidency in 1968 and began a policy of Vietnamization.
- The Paris Peace Accords of 1973 led to the withdrawal of U.S. troops from Vietnam.
- The war between the Vietnamese continued until South Vietnam was forced under Communist rule in 1975.

Section 4
A Time of Uncertainty

- U.S. astronauts landed on the moon in 1969.
- Nixon's visit to China and a treaty with the Soviet Union eased Cold War tensions.
- Nixon resigned over the Watergate affair, after being forced to reveal evidence that he had conspired to conceal crimes.
- Nixon's successor, Gerald Ford, granted him a pardon.

? Exploring the Essential Question

Use the online study guide to explore the essential question.

Section 1
How did Vietnam become a major battlefield in the war against communism?

Section 2
How did the demands of greater involvement in the Vietnam War divide the nation?

Chapter 27 Essential Question
What were the causes and effects of the Vietnam War?

Section 4
What successes and failures marked Nixon's presidency?

Section 3
What were the causes and effects of American withdrawal from Vietnam?

Key Terms

Read each sentence below. If the sentence is true, write YES. If the sentence is not true, write NO and explain why.

1. Hawks were more likely to take part in antiwar demonstrations than were doves.

2. As part of his Vietnamization program, President Nixon began to escalate U.S. military involvement in Vietnam.

3. Guerrillas are people who oppose a government by holding demonstrations.

4. Conscientious objectors believe it is morally wrong to go to war.

5. According to the domino theory, if the United States sent troops to Vietnam to fight the Communists, other countries would then send troops to help.

Comprehension and Critical Thinking

6. **(a) Describe** What was the South Vietnamese government like under President Diem? What was it like after the fall of Diem?
   (b) Apply Information How did the nature of the South Vietnamese government hamper the fighting of the war?

7. **(a) Summarize** What was the Tet Offensive?
   (b) Apply Information How did the events of the Tet Offensive affect the popularity of President Johnson? Explain.

8. **(a) Identify** What was Nixon's policy of Vietnamization?
   (b) Draw Conclusions How effective was Vietnamization in achieving President Nixon's goal of "peace with honor"?

9. **(a) Classify** Make a table listing the strengths and weaknesses of the American–South Vietnamese side in the Vietnam War.
   (b) Compare Make a similar table showing the strengths and weaknesses of the Communist side.
   (c) Evaluate Information Based on an analysis of the information in your tables, why did the Communists eventually succeed?

10. **(a) Describe** What action did President Gerald Ford take to try to restore confidence in the nation's leaders?
    (b) Clarify Problems How did his action create new problems for his presidency?

Reading Skill

11. **Ask Questions** Ask a useful question about what you have read in this chapter. Remember, when possible, to ask questions that examine the text or require learning beyond the text.

Writing

12. **Write two paragraphs giving an eyewitness view of an event covered in this chapter. Your description should:**
    - identify the eyewitness and the event discussed;
    - indicate why the eyewitness is there;
    - include details appropriate to the time, place, or circumstances of the event;
    - include the eyewitness's description of and response to the event.

13. **Write a Dialogue:**
    A Vietnam veteran meets Maya Lin at the Vietnam Veterans Memorial. Think about the veteran's point of view as a soldier having fought in Vietnam. Then, consider Lin's viewpoint as an artist. Write a conversation the two might have about the memorial.

Skills for Life

Synthesize Information
Study the excerpt and photograph in Section 3, Reading Primary Sources, "A Nurse Reflects." Then, answer the following questions.

14. Who is the author of the primary source?

15. Compare the photograph and the source. What does each reflect about the role of nurses in the Vietnam War?

16. Based on the photograph and the primary source, what can you conclude about women's roles in the Vietnam War?

Test Yourself

1. **The killing of four students by National Guardsmen at Kent State University came after which of these events?**

   A the North Vietnamese attack on American destroyers in the Gulf of Tonkin

   B the Tet offensive

   C the U.S. attack on North Vietnamese bases in Cambodia

   D the fall of Saigon to North Vietnamese forces

2. **One foreign policy change of Richard Nixon's term as President was**

   A important summit meetings with leaders of Eastern European nations.

   B the start of better relations with the People's Republic of China.

   C the start of better relations with Cuba.

   D the signing of nuclear arms agreements with Korea.

Refer to the quotation below to answer Question 3.

"We are pursuing our policy . . . on the grounds that a stable peace . . . is difficult to envisage [view] if 800 million people are excluded from a dialogue with the most powerful nation in the world."

3. **The reasons for which event are explained in the quotation above?**

   A the Geneva Accords after the French defeat at Dienbienphu

   B the Paris Peace Accords that led to the withdrawal of American forces from Vietnam

   C Nixon's meeting in China with Mao Zedong in 1972

   D the signing of the SALT agreement between the United States and the Soviet Union

Document-Based Questions

Task: Look at Documents 1 and 2, and answer their accompanying questions. Then, use the documents and your knowledge of history to complete this writing assignment:

Write an essay describing the effects of the Vietnam War.

Document 1: Thousands of Americans were killed in combat during the Vietnam War. *How does the graph below reflect the pattern of U.S. involvement in Vietnam?*

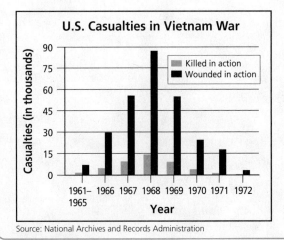

U.S. Casualties in Vietnam War

Source: National Archives and Records Administration

Document 2: In a short essay, Mike Murphy, a Vietnam veteran, describes his experience. *How does Murphy view his Vietnam service? Why?*

"In 1987, I planned a trip to Washington, D.C. I told [my wife] . . . I wanted to see the Museums but the real reason was the Wall. . . . I wanted to see it, . . . but I was also afraid to see it.

On the second day [my wife] asked me where the Vietnam Memorial was; I tell her. . . . As we walk toward the Wall I fall silent, . . . my heart is pounding. . . .

Then I saw the Wall. Black granite half buried in the ground. Half buried like the war, . . . half hidden like the conscience of the country. The tears flowed, I couldn't stop them. . . .

I close my eyes and I am back . . . in Vietnam. I can see it, smell it, touch it and hear it. I quickly open my eyes and I see the Wall. So many names. . . . I close my eyes and let Vietnam flow over me. . . . I cry for the ones that I had known, and for the ones that I did not know. We were all brothers. We went to a land that hated us and came home to a land that hated us. It wasn't supposed to be like that."

New Directions for a Nation

1977–2008

"It is the American story—a story of flawed and fallible people, united across the generations by grand and enduring ideals."

—President George W. Bush,
inaugural address, January 20, 2001

Marines and a marching band parade in front of the U.S. Capitol for the 2001 inauguration of President George W. Bush.

Reading Skill

Compare and Contrast In this chapter, you will learn to look for similarities and differences between events, people, and issues.

United States and the World, 1977–2008

Some American Presidents and Their Domestic Policies

President	Key Domestic Policies
Ronald Reagan	• reduced government spending • reduced federal taxes • increased military spending
Bill Clinton	• reformed welfare system • produced federal budget surpluses
George W. Bush	• reduced federal taxes • reformed nation's schools • organized Homeland Security

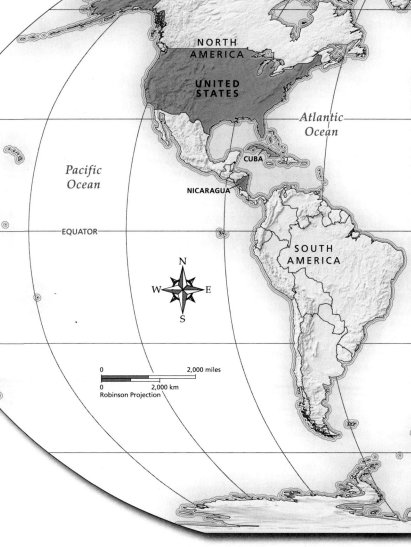

| | 150°W | 120°W | 90°W |
| | | | |

NORTH AMERICA

UNITED STATES

Atlantic Ocean

Pacific Ocean

CUBA

NICARAGUA

EQUATOR

SOUTH AMERICA

N W E S

0   2,000 miles
0   2,000 km
Robinson Projection

U.S. Events

Militants take 53 Americans hostage in Iran. | **1979**

1981 | Ronald Reagan becomes President.

1987 | United States and Soviet Union agree on arms control treaty.

1977   **1983**   **1989**

World Events

1978 | Camp David Accords ease Middle East tensions.

Gorbachev becomes head of Soviet Union. | **1985**

China cracks down on pro-democracy demonstrators. | **1989**

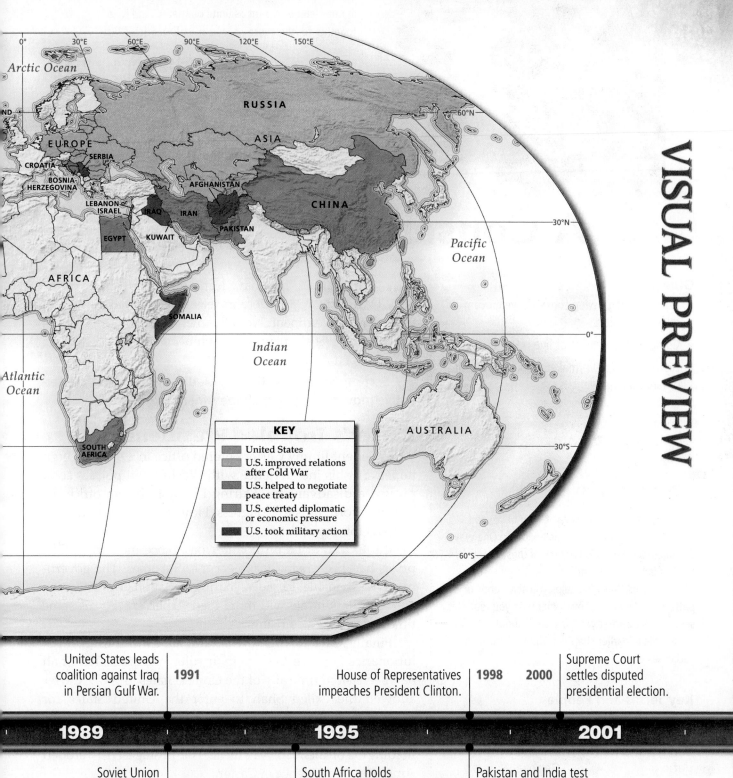

KEY
- United States
- U.S. improved relations after Cold War
- U.S. helped to negotiate peace treaty
- U.S. exerted diplomatic or economic pressure
- U.S. took military action

VISUAL PREVIEW

United States leads coalition against Iraq in Persian Gulf War.	**1991**	House of Representatives impeaches President Clinton.	**1998**	**2000** Supreme Court settles disputed presidential election.

1989	**1995**	**2001**

Soviet Union collapses, ending the Cold War.	**1991**	**1994** South Africa holds multiracial elections.	**1998**	Pakistan and India test nuclear weapons.

The Moral Majority

❝I am convinced that God is calling millions of Americans in the so-often silent majority to join in the moral-majority crusade to turn America around in our lifetime. . . . Let us unite our hearts and lives together for the cause of . . . a moral America.❞

—Reverend Jerry Falwell, 1980

◀ Reverend Jerry Falwell stressed conservative values in politics.

A Conservative Surge

Objectives

- Learn how a growing conservative movement reshaped politics.
- Compare the policies of five U.S. Presidents.
- Discover how policymakers dealt with a series of large budget deficits.

🔄 Reading Skill

Compare and Contrast You have read about many Presidents in this textbook. One way to remember and to keep track of these many leaders is to compare and contrast their achievements. This also helps you see trends or patterns in American government. As you read this section, recall what you have read about Presidents in earlier chapters. Think about their successes and failures.

Key Terms and People

balanced budget
Ronald Reagan
deregulation
deficit
George H.W. Bush

recession
Bill Clinton
surplus
George W. Bush

Why It Matters As you have learned, programs such as the New Deal and Great Society increased the size and power of the federal government. Not all Americans thought this was good. In the 1980s, a new political movement gained strength and reshaped American politics.

❓ Section Focus Question: How did the growing conservative movement help reshape American politics?

Carter's Troubled Presidency

President Jimmy Carter entered office in 1976 with high hopes. But his inexperience with Washington politics soon proved a disadvantage. During his first year in office, he sent 10 reform bills to Congress. However, he could not get support for any of them.

Carter also faced economic woes. Since the early 1970s, prices had been rising far faster than incomes. The government was unable to slow soaring inflation. By 1979, the annual inflation rate was more than 10 percent. At the same time, taxes were also rising.

Finally, Carter faced an international crisis. In Iran, revolutionaries had overthrown their ruler, the Shah. The Shah had been a longtime ally of the United States. In 1979, Carter allowed the exiled Shah to enter the United States for medical treatment. Angry revolutionaries in Iran seized the American embassy in Tehran and took 66 Americans hostage, holding 52 of them for 444 days. The hostage crisis eroded Americans' confidence in Carter.

✅**Checkpoint** What troubles plagued President Carter?

The Conservative Movement

As Carter struggled, a new political movement was gaining strength. This growing conservative movement would reshape American politics.

What Is a Conservative? The terms *liberal* and *conservative* have meant different things at different times. By the late 1970s, liberals were generally those who favored federal government action to regulate the economy and solve social problems. Liberals had supported large-scale federal programs such as Franklin Roosevelt's New Deal and Lyndon Johnson's Great Society.

Conservatives fell into two main categories—political conservatives and social conservatives. Political conservatives wanted to shrink "big government," arguing that it had grown too powerful. They felt that more power should be left with state and local governments because these governments were closer to the people. Conservatives also wanted to lower taxes and curb government regulation of business.

Social conservatives were concerned with "traditional values" such as family, patriotism, and religion. One of their leaders was the Reverend Jerry Falwell. In 1979, he created an organization known as the Moral Majority. Falwell stressed the sacredness of marriage and family and the importance of faith in God. The Moral Majority became active in politics. It organized workshops for people who wanted to enter local politics and endorsed like-minded politicians.

Compare and Contrast Compare and contrast the Moral Majority's goals with those of liberals of the 1960s and 1970s. Recall what you have read in earlier chapters.

The Conservative Movement

"So then Tommy Taxpayer said to the big bully, Godzilla government, 'I am unwilling to pay the bill ...'"

© 1978 by NEA, Inc.   JIM BERRY ©NEA

1978 cartoon ▶

"We [Republicans] see in the sanctity of private property the only durable foundation for constitutional government in a free society. . . . We do not seek to lead anyone's life for him—we seek only to secure his rights and to guarantee him opportunity to strive, with government performing only those needed and constitutionally sanctioned tasks which cannot otherwise be performed. . . . Our towns and cities, then our counties, then our states, then our regional contacts—and only then, the national government. That, let me remind you, is the ladder of liberty."

—Barry Goldwater, speech at the 1964 Republican National Convention

Reading Primary Sources

Skills Activity

The modern conservative movement began with Barry Goldwater, Republican candidate for President in 1964. By the late 1970s, conservatives were gaining strength.

(a) Interpret Primary Sources According to Goldwater, what is the proper role of the federal government?

(b) Detect Points of View Summarize the main point of the cartoon. How does it reflect Goldwater's views?

Election of 1980 By 1980, conservatives were in control of the Republican Party and had a clear strategy to reach their goals. To shrink government, they planned to slash expensive social programs, cut taxes, and balance the federal budget. With a **balanced budget**, government spends only as much money as it collects. Conservatives also wanted to curb regulation of business. They argued that overregulation <u>violated</u> the principles of free enterprise.

The Republicans nominated an outspoken conservative, former California governor Ronald Reagan, to run against Jimmy Carter. Reagan asked voters if they were better off than they had been when Carter took office. Many Americans agreed that they were not. Reagan won a clear victory. Moreover, the Republicans regained control of the Senate for the first time since the election of Eisenhower in 1952.

☑**Checkpoint** **What changes did conservatives want to make?**

Reagan's Presidency

Reagan had a unique background among Presidents. He had been a movie star in the 1940s and 1950s. While president of a screen actors' union, he became interested in politics. In the 1960s, he was elected governor of California.

Reagan entered the White House promising to achieve conservative goals at home. In foreign policy, he vowed to strengthen the military to counter the Soviet Union.

The Great Communicator President Reagan's open manner and infectious optimism added to his popularity. *Critical Thinking: Analyze Cause and Effect* How might a career in movies help to prepare someone to be an effective communicator?

Reagan's skill in presenting ideas in terms that ordinary people could understand gave him great advantages as President. He became known as the Great Communicator. Glowing with optimism, Reagan readily convinced many Americans that he could solve their problems.

Reducing Government "Government is not the solution to our problems," Reagan said. "Government is the problem." Reducing government spending and taxes, he argued, would fire up the economy by giving taxpayers more money to spend and businesses more reasons to manufacture and sell. Reagan's economic program became known as Reaganomics.

Reagan began by slicing more than $40 billion from the federal budget. Most of it came from trimming social programs and cutting federal jobs. In 1981, he persuaded Congress to lower taxes by 25 percent. *Time* magazine concluded that he had done more "to alter the economic direction of the country" than any President in 50 years.

Deregulation, scaling back federal rules for businesses, was another way to limit government. Reagan reduced costly antipollution regulations and opened protected federal lands to oil and lumber companies. Such actions brought praise from business leaders and criticism from environmentalists.

Vocabulary Builder
alter (AWL ter) **v.** to change in some way; to make different

Assessing Reagan Reagan left the White House in 1989, after two terms, as one of the nation's most popular Presidents. His record was mixed. He did not succeed in balancing the budget. In fact, his tax cuts and increases in military spending had led to record federal deficits. A deficit results when the government spends more money than it collects. Meanwhile, critics charged that cuts in social programs and taxes hurt the poor and favored the rich.

Still, Reagan had made good on his promise to limit government by slowing its growth. His policies helped to expand the economy and shrink inflation. Perhaps most important, he restored faith in the presidency. Reagan also made major breakthroughs in ending the Cold War, as you will read in Section 2.

Bush Follows Reagan The victor in the 1988 presidential election was Reagan's Vice President, George H.W. Bush. Bush pledged to continue Reagan's economic policies. "Read my lips," Bush said during the campaign. "No new taxes!"

Facing economic problems, however, Bush broke his promise. As the national debt continued to increase, he concluded that the only way to cut the deficit was to both reduce spending and raise taxes. His call for new taxes outraged many conservatives.

In 1991, the economy fell into a deep recession that lasted more than a year. A recession is a temporary economic slump. Many businesses laid off workers. As unemployment soared, some businesses went bankrupt. Many people blamed the tax hike for causing the recession.

This Bush campaign button compares him to earlier Republican Presidents.

✓**Checkpoint** How well did President Reagan achieve his goals?

The Clinton Years

By the end of Bush's term, voters were upset with deficits, joblessness, and Washington deadlock. Many were angry with Bush for violating his no-tax pledge.

In the presidential election of 1992, Democrats nominated Arkansas Governor Bill Clinton. The election was a three-way contest. Ross Perot, a Texas billionaire, ran on a third-party platform that promised to bring government closer to the needs of Americans. Clinton won the election with 43 percent of the popular vote. Bush received 38 percent and Perot 19 percent.

A New Democrat For the first time in 12 years, a Democrat occupied the White House. Clinton described himself as a "New Democrat" who would steer a middle course between liberalism and conservatism. He vowed to "reinvent" government by slashing its size and its deficits, working with business, and reducing welfare spending. He added that he would not abandon the needy.

President Clinton convinced Congress to raise taxes on higher income groups and reduce some spending. As a result, the deficit was cut in half by 1996. The President also worked with Congress to overhaul welfare. A compromise abolished direct federal spending on welfare and replaced it with grants to states for antipoverty programs. To encourage the jobless to find work, the law limited how long benefits could be paid.

Prosperity and Scandal During the Clinton years, the stock market surged to record highs. Unemployment dropped to a 30-year low. Tax receipts from the growing economy produced federal budget surpluses from 1998 through 2001—the first in 29 years. A **surplus** results when the government collects more money than it spends.

Clinton won reelection in 1996, but scandal dogged his second term. The most serious charge involved an improper relationship with a young White House intern. When he was questioned by investigators, Clinton appeared to have lied under oath.

In December 1998, after a bitter debate, the House voted to impeach Clinton. He was only the second President in history to be impeached, after Andrew Johnson in 1868. The Senate did not convict Clinton, so he remained in office. Despite the scandals, he was still popular with many Americans.

☑**Checkpoint** How was the deficit reduced under Clinton?

Clinton Signs a Bill

Children of minimum-wage earners cluster around President Clinton as he signs a bill to raise the minimum wage. **Critical Thinking:** *Apply Information How might a rise in the minimum wage be related to Clinton's efforts to reduce welfare programs?*

Strengthening America's Families
A New Minimum Wage

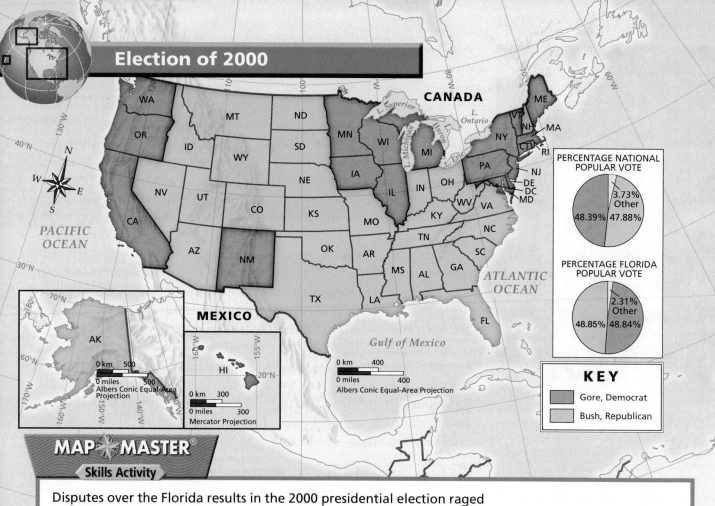

Election of 2000

PERCENTAGE NATIONAL POPULAR VOTE

48.39% — 47.88% — 3.73% Other

PERCENTAGE FLORIDA POPULAR VOTE

48.85% — 48.84% — 2.31% Other

KEY

Gore, Democrat

Bush, Republican

MAP★MASTER®

Skills Activity

Disputes over the Florida results in the 2000 presidential election raged until the U.S. Supreme Court made a ruling.

(a) Interpret Charts What percentage of Florida's votes went to third-party candidates?

(b) Explain Problems Why was the result of the Florida election decisive in determining who would become President?

MapMaster Online

For: Interactive map
Visit: PHSchool.com
Web Code: mvp-9281

President George W. Bush

With Clinton's term nearly over, Republicans hoped to win back the White House. The election of 2000 became one of the most controversial in history.

A Disputed Election Democrats nominated Vice President Al Gore for President. His running mate was Connecticut Senator Joseph Lieberman, the first Jewish candidate nominated for national office by a major party. Republicans nominated Texas Governor George W. Bush, son of former President George H.W. Bush. He and his running mate, Richard Cheney, promised to support conservative goals and restore integrity to the presidency.

Gore won the popular vote by a paper-thin margin, but Bush led in electoral votes. The key was the state of Florida, where Democrats claimed that Bush's small lead was the result of misleading paper ballots and the improper rejection of some votes, many of them in African American precincts. Winning in Florida would have given Gore enough electoral votes to win the presidency. The Democrats took their case to court to force a recount. Finally, the Supreme Court ruled against a recount, and Bush was declared the winner.

No Child Left Behind
President George W. Bush spoke to high school students about a law expanding the use of standardized tests. **Critical Thinking:** *Frame Questions* *Suggest a question that a teacher or school principal might want to ask U.S. leaders about the No Child Left Behind law.*

A Conservative Agenda Despite the controversy, Bush quickly proved to be a strong leader and a powerful conservative voice. Some of his actions sharply divided the country.

In a time of budget surpluses, tax cuts were high on President Bush's agenda. "The budget surplus is the people's money," the President said. Critics claimed Bush's tax cuts favored the wealthy and would lead to more deficits. After an angry debate, Congress enacted the biggest tax cuts since the Reagan years.

Education was another key issue. Bush signed the No Child Left Behind Act. The law made schools more accountable by using standardized testing to measure student progress. Liberals joined in supporting the law. However, some educators worried that it left little room to do anything but "teach for the test." Critics also pointed out that state and local governments would have to pay for most of the program.

In 2004, President Bush won a second term, but his next term brought frustration. Although he succeeded in appointing two conservative justices to the Supreme Court, he failed to reform Social Security and deepen tax cuts. Wars in Iraq and Afghanistan plus an economic collapse at home ate away at budget surpluses and at the President's popularity. By 2008, the federal deficit had ballooned to an all-time high of $455 billion. Bush's public approval ratings sank to 29 percent, among the lowest in history.

☑Checkpoint **What arguments were made for and against President Bush's tax cuts?**

⭐ **Looking Back and Ahead** Riding a surge in conservative voting strength, Republican leaders cut taxes and tried to limit government's role in society. Meanwhile, a buildup of U.S. military strength was putting new pressure on the Soviet Union.

Section 1 | **Check Your Progress**

Progress Monitoring ⊕nline
For: Self-test with instant help
Visit: PHSchool.com
Web Code: mva-9281

Comprehension and Critical Thinking

1. **(a) Describe** How did the conservative movement in 1980 seek to change government?
   (b) Identify Benefits According to Reagan's supporters, how would his conservative policies benefit businesses and average Americans?

2. **(a) Summarize** How did Republican Presidents after Reagan try to continue his policies?
   (b) Evaluate Information In general, do you think the conservative movement succeeded in its goals?

Reading Skill

3. **Compare and Contrast** Reread the text following the subheading "Assessing Reagan." Compare and contrast the public mood during the Reagan presidency and during the Nixon and Carter presidencies.

Key Terms

Answer the following questions in complete sentences that show your understanding of the key terms.

4. How might federal government deregulation affect an industry?

5. What happens to businesses and workers during a recession?

6. How much does a government spend when it wants to keep a balanced budget?

7. What does it mean when a government's budget has a surplus?

Writing

8. Create a plot outline for a narrative about the presidential election of 2000. A plot outline includes the following elements: (1) exposition (background information), (2) central conflict or problem, (3) rising action (develops the conflict), (4) climax (high point), and (5) resolution (how things turn out).

Tear Down This Wall

66 General Secretary Gorbachev, if you seek peace, if you seek prosperity for the Soviet Union and Eastern Europe, if you seek liberalization: Come here to this gate! Mr. Gorbachev, open this gate! Mr. Gorbachev, tear down this wall! 99

—President Ronald Reagan, speech at the Berlin Wall, 1987

◄ The Berlin Wall divided Communist East Berlin from democratic West Berlin.

End of the Cold War

Objectives

- Learn about Cold War struggles in Afghanistan and Central America.
- Discover how the Soviet Union responded to President Reagan's arms buildup.
- Analyze why the Soviet Union dissolved and the Cold War ended.

Reading Skill

Compare and Contrast Effects As different Presidents led America and other nations through the years, their actions led to a range of effects. To compare and contrast those effects, you may have to decide which policies or actions caused which effects. Are later effects the same as earlier ones? Are they different?

Key Terms and People

Mikhail Gorbachev
glasnost

Why It Matters President Nixon had pursued a policy of détente, easing tensions with the Soviet Union and other Communist nations. But the détente soon ended and tensions once again grew. So, as the 1980s began, few imagined that the Soviet Union was about to collapse and the Cold War was about to end.

② Section Focus Question: How did the Cold War end?

The End of Détente

At first, President Carter continued the policy of détente. Then, in 1979, the Soviet Union invaded Afghanistan, its mountainous southern neighbor. President Carter joined world opinion in condemning the invasion. In protest, he withdrew from the Senate a pending arms agreement with the Soviet Union. He also pulled the United States from the 1980 Olympic Games in Moscow and imposed restrictions on trade with the Soviet Union. The invasion of Afghanistan ended the era of détente.

Reagan's Tough Stand Carter's successor, Ronald Reagan, took an even harder line. He denounced the Soviet Union as an "evil empire." He argued that only a well-armed United States could contain the Soviet empire and halt the spread of communism.

Reagan sent millions of dollars in arms to the government of Afghanistan and the Islamic rebels who were fighting the Soviet Union. The rebels were able to inflict heavy casualties on the Soviets.

One of Reagan's first priorities was to strengthen the military posture of the United States. Accordingly, spending on defense projects jumped by more than 50 percent. One of the key projects was the development of a plane that would be almost invisible to enemy radar. The plane was known as the B-2 stealth bomber.

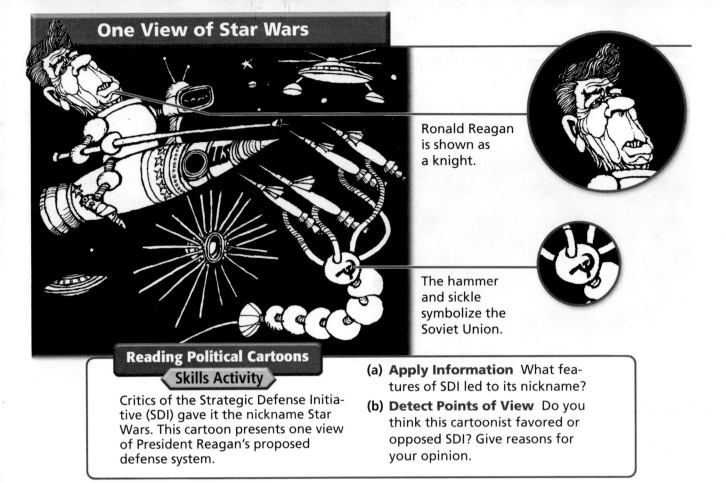

One View of Star Wars

Ronald Reagan is shown as a knight.

The hammer and sickle symbolize the Soviet Union.

Reading Political Cartoons
Skills Activity

Critics of the Strategic Defense Initiative (SDI) gave it the nickname Star Wars. This cartoon presents one view of President Reagan's proposed defense system.

(a) **Apply Information** What features of SDI led to its nickname?

(b) **Detect Points of View** Do you think this cartoonist favored or opposed SDI? Give reasons for your opinion.

Vocabulary Builder
critic (KRIHT ihk) *n.* someone who makes judgments, especially negative judgments

Reagan's boldest arms proposal was a laser-guided defense system to shoot down enemy missiles from space. The system, called the Strategic Defense Initiative (SDI), would cost billions. As research began, critics attacked SDI as an expensive fantasy. They called it Star Wars, after the popular science-fiction movie.

Fighting Leftists in Central America Reagan's determination to halt the spread of communism led to new U.S. involvements in Central America. In Nicaragua, the United States had long supported dictator Anastasio Somoza because of his strong opposition to communism. In 1979, leftist rebels called Sandinistas overthrew Somoza. They set up a government with close ties to Cuba and the Soviet Union.

Reagan supported the Contras, a guerrilla army made up of anti-Communist opponents of the Sandinistas. Some Americans opposed aid to the Contras, charging them with acts of brutality. However, the President secretly ordered the CIA to train and supply the Contras. Involvement in Central America ignited a heated debate in the United States. When Congress learned of the secret aid, angry lawmakers banned all money and military assistance to the Contras.

Frustration with the ban led to a scandal. In 1985, Iranian-backed militants in Lebanon took seven Americans hostage. Administration officials hatched a complicated plot to free the hostages and, at the same time, secretly send aid to the Contras. The officials agreed to sell arms to Iran. In exchange, Iran pressured the militants into releasing some hostages. Meanwhile, U.S. officials used money from the arms sale to buy weapons for the Contras in Nicaragua.

Americans were stunned when word of this "Iran-Contra deal" leaked out. Eventually, seven government officials were convicted of lying to Congress and destroying evidence. President Reagan said he had no knowledge of the deal. Still, the Iran-Contra affair threw a shadow over Reagan's last years as President.

✓**Checkpoint** What was the Iran-Contra scandal?

Compare and Contrast Effects What was the effect of the Iran-Contra affair on the Reagan presidency? Compare and contrast this with the effect of Watergate on President Nixon's presidency.

The Soviet Union in Decline

In the 1980s, the Soviet Union was in decline. Its grip on Eastern Europe grew weaker as new movements for democracy sprang up. Within the Soviet Union, opposition to Communist rule was growing.

Growing Problems The Afghan war had been a major burden on the Soviet economy. It had also sapped the morale of the Soviet people. In 1989, after 10 years, the Soviet Union accepted defeat and withdrew its troops.

The Soviet Union responded to Reagan's military buildup with a buildup of its own. But heavy military spending weakened the Soviet economy and led to severe shortages at home. When Russians went to stores, they waited in long lines and found shelves nearly empty.

A Bold New Leader Mikhail Gorbachev, who became leader of the Soviet Union in 1985, threw his energies into reforming the system. He began to restructure the economy to allow more freedom. He adopted a new policy called **glasnost**, or speaking openly about Soviet problems. However, Gorbachev's reforms only emboldened the Soviet people to demand more changes.

Gorbachev also tried to improve relations with the West. He realized that a continued arms race could overwhelm the Soviet economy. In 1987, he met with Reagan. The two leaders agreed on a new arms control treaty. Both sides promised to destroy short-range and <u>intermediate</u>-range nuclear missiles. For the first time, the two superpowers agreed to give up entire classes of weapons.

Vocabulary Builder
<u>intermediate</u> (ihn ter MEE dee iht) **adj.** happening in between; part way from one extreme to another

Soviet Economic Problems
Consumers in the Soviet Union often found store shelves empty as the economy went through upheaval in the 1980s and 1990s. **Critical Thinking: *Identify Costs*** *How were such shortages related to pressures caused by U.S. policies?*

Eastern Europe Breaks Free The Soviet Union had long controlled most of the Communist governments of Eastern Europe and kept them in power. In 1956, Soviet troops marched into Hungary and smashed a revolt against its Communist leaders. In 1968, Soviet tanks ended democratic reforms in Czechoslovakia.

Under Gorbachev, the Soviet Union lost interest in supporting unpopular leaders in Eastern Europe. One by one, Communist governments there gave in to demands for democratic change. In Poland, the first free elections since World War II produced a non-Communist government in 1989. Communist regimes in Hungary, Romania, and Czechoslovakia soon crumbled. Communism also fell in Yugoslavia, which the Soviet Union had not dominated.

In November 1989, students and workers in East Germany tore down the Berlin Wall, a bitter symbol of Communist oppression. Berliners danced, exchanged hugs, and battered the Berlin Wall with sledgehammers, pickaxes, and bare hands. Within a year, East and West Germany had reunited as a single nation.

The fall of Communist governments unleashed other forces in Eastern Europe. After 1989, national borders shifted. While Germany reunited, Czechoslovakia split into the Czech Republic and Slovakia. Yugoslavia became several loosely joined republics.

☑ **Checkpoint** How did Gorbachev change Soviet policy?

The Cold War Ends

Far-reaching changes affected the Soviet Union, too. It had consisted of 15 republics dominated by a powerful central government in Moscow. As change overtook Eastern Europe, independence movements arose in several Soviet republics.

The Soviet Union Collapses In late 1991, the Soviet Union dissolved. Each republic became an independent state. In the biggest state, Russia, a new president, Boris Yeltsin, vowed to continue the drive for democracy and a strong economy.

"Gorbachev knew how to bring us freedom, but he did not know how to make sausage," complained one Russian. Gorbachev's reforms had failed to solve the problems of shortages and shoddy goods. The new Russia also suffered from unemployment and high prices. Crime and corruption thrived. Many Russians began to question whether democracy could make their lives better.

Unrest in Eastern Europe In Yugoslavia, the fall of communism led to a civil war. Yugoslavia was made up of several republics, including Croatia, Serbia, and Bosnia-Herzegovina. In 1991, Croatia and Bosnia declared independence. However, Serbs in Croatia and Bosnia wanted to remain part of Yugoslavia. With help from Serbia, they fought to prevent the new governments from splitting away. The civil war lasted for four years. More than 250,000 people died, including many children and teenagers.

END OF THE COLD WAR

History *Interactive*
**Explore the
End of the Cold War**
Visit: PHSchool.com
Web Code: mvl-9282

The Cold War had kept international tensions high since the mid-1940s. With the dissolution of the Soviet Union in 1991, the Cold War came to an end. **Critical Thinking:** *Identify Benefits* *What benefits might the Soviet people hope for as a result of the collapse of Communist rule?*

▲ A summit conference between Gorbachev and Reagan in 1988.

● **Soviet Reformer**
Soviet ruler Mikhail Gorbachev sought to reform the Soviet system and ease the arms race to relieve pressure on the Soviet economy.

● **Too Little, Too Late**
Gorbachev's reforms could not save the Communist system in the Soviet Union. In December 1991, the 15 Soviet republics became independent. Russia began experiments with democratic government and a free-market economy.

▲ Demonstrators used sledgehammers to tear down the Berlin Wall in 1989.

● **Eastern Europe Abandons Communism**
A surge of pro-democracy movements helped bring down communism in Eastern Europe from 1989 onward.

Russian schoolchildren sit on a toppled statue of Stalin. ▶

In November 1995, the United States hosted peace talks in Dayton, Ohio. To help enforce the peace, President Clinton sent about 20,000 American troops to Bosnia. Along with Russian and NATO peacekeepers, the troops helped to restore order.

The Dayton Accord did not end trouble in the former Yugoslavia. Ethnic Albanians in Kosovo, a province within Serbia, also sought greater independence. Serbs launched a series of attacks against rebels in Kosovo. Hundreds of thousands of Albanians were killed or forced to flee. In 1999, American and NATO forces bombed Serbia until Serbian troops left Kosovo. After years of negotiations and political infighting, Kosovo declared its independence in 2008.

Cold War Balance Sheet The break-up of the Soviet Union put an end to the 45 years of the Cold War. Americans hailed the emergence of democratic governments in Eastern Europe and the former Soviet Union. U.S. leaders expressed hope that Russia would become a democratic and stable nation.

The United States paid a heavy price during the Cold War. More than 100,000 Americans died fighting "hot" wars in Korea and Vietnam. Taxpayers spent more than $6 trillion on defense.

The Cold War often divided the nation, especially during the Vietnam War. Still, from the perspective of the 1990s, Americans hailed the end of the Cold War as an event worthy of celebration.

☑ **Checkpoint** Why did the Cold War come to an end when it did?

☆ **Looking Back and Ahead** The dissolution of the Soviet Union and the collapse of communism in Eastern Europe brought the Cold War to an end. In the next section, you will read how U.S. policy responded to these changes.

Section 2 | **Check Your Progress**

Progress Monitoring ⊕nline
For: Self-test with instant help
Visit: PHSchool.com
Web Code: mva-9282

Comprehension and Critical Thinking

1. **(a) List** What did President Reagan do to strengthen the American military?
(b) Analyze Cause and Effect How did his actions contribute to the collapse of the Soviet Union?

2. **(a) Describe** What changes did Mikhail Gorbachev make as leader of the Soviet Union?
(b) Analyze Cause and Effect How did his actions help bring about the end of the Soviet Union?

Reading Skill

3. **Compare and Contrast Effects** Compare and contrast the effects that Gorbachev hoped to achieve when he took power in the Soviet Union with the actual effects of his leadership.

Key Terms

Read the sentence below. If the sentence is true, write YES. If the sentence is not true, write NO and explain why.

4. Under the policy of glasnost, critics of the Soviet government were severely punished.

Writing

5. Create a plot outline for an eyewitness narrative of the falling of the Berlin Wall. The plot outline should include the five elements that were listed in the Writing activity in the Section 1 Check Your Progress. Then, write the beginning paragraph of a narrative in which an eyewitness tells about this event.

We Will Not Rest

❝We will not rest until all freedom-loving nations withdraw their support of the apartheid regime. . . . We are committed to the liberation of South Africa because, as Martin Luther King, Jr., said, 'Injustice anywhere is a threat to justice everywhere.'❞

—Coretta Scott King, urging protest against apartheid, 1988

◄ Voters in South Africa

A New Role in the World

Objectives

- See how U.S. foreign policy developed after the Cold War.
- Discover how the United States sought to promote change in South Africa, China, and Cuba.
- Explore efforts to control the spread of nuclear weapons.

🎯 Reading Skill

Analyze Contrasts Reading about different times in history can help you draw conclusions about differences between those times. First, identify contrasts between the policies, attitudes, or actions of different time periods. Then, recall the process of drawing conclusions discussed in a previous chapter. Use details in the text and prior knowledge to link the two time periods.

Key Terms

apartheid
sanction

Why It Matters For nearly 50 years, the struggle with the Soviet Union had guided and limited U.S. foreign policy. That era of U.S. history was now over. The collapse of the Soviet Union and the end of the Cold War enabled the United States to play a new role in the world.

❓ **Section Focus Question: How did the United States use its influence after the Cold War ended?**

Promoting Democracy and Peace

After the Soviet Union dissolved, the United States was the only remaining superpower. President George H.W. Bush said that the United States faced "the rarest opportunities to shape the world and the deepest responsibility to do it wisely." Under Bush and Clinton, the United States stepped up calls for democracy and peace.

South Africa The United States used its influence in many places. In South Africa, a policy of apartheid, or racial separation and inequality, had held democracy in check for decades. The policy barred voting rights for the nonwhite majority.

For years the United States resisted calls for some kind of action against South Africa. Then, in 1986, Congress approved economic sanctions over a veto by President Reagan. Sanctions are penalties applied against a country in order to pressure it to change its policies. U.S. companies were forbidden to invest in South Africa or import South African products. Other countries also applied sanctions.

Along with growing protests inside South Africa, the sanctions took a toll. In 1991, South Africa's white government ended apartheid. Nonwhites were allowed full voting rights, and free elections in 1994 put black leaders in office.

The Philippines In the Philippines, the first free election in 14 years ended the rule of dictator Ferdinand Marcos in 1986. Under the banner of "people power," the new government worked to end the corruption and poverty of the Marcos era. The United States sent economic and military aid, as it had to Marcos.

Northern Ireland In British-ruled Northern Ireland, years of violence between a Protestant majority and a Catholic minority had left thousands dead. In 1998, the United States helped arrange an agreement for sharing power between the two groups. "We can say to the men of violence and those who disdain democracy: Your way is not the way," declared George Mitchell, the U.S. negotiator.

Ferment in China

Pro-democracy demonstrations like this were crushed in Tiananmen Square. **Critical Thinking: *Explain Problems*** *Why did U.S. leaders respond as they did to the Chinese crackdown?*

China In China, workers joined students in a campaign to win democratic reforms. Despite limited reforms that opened its economy to private business, China's Communist government allowed no free elections or free speech.

In May 1989, television news showed hundreds of thousands of people demanding democracy in Tiananmen Square in Beijing, China's capital. A week later, the world watched in horror as the Chinese army routed the demonstrators, killing or wounding many.

The brutal crackdown angered many Americans, including President George H.W. Bush. Still, he said it was important to maintain good relations with China. He pursued a policy of persuasion rather than punishment. President Clinton continued this policy.

Human rights took a back seat to the Summer Olympics in 2008, when China hosted the games for the first time. Chinese authorities cracked down on demonstrators by discouraging applications for protest permits and sometimes arresting those who even applied.

Vocabulary Builder
deprive (dee PRĪV) *v.* to withhold; to take away

Cuba In the 1990s, Cuba fell on hard times. Since 1960, the United States had banned trade with Cuba in an effort to oust Communist dictator Fidel Castro. In 1991, the fall of the Soviet Union <u>deprived</u> Cuba of its chief source of trade and economic aid. The Cuban economy stumbled, and 30,000 Cubans fled to the United States.

For a time, Cuban-American relations improved. In 1994, President Clinton allowed more Cubans to enter the United States. U.S. lawmakers began to debate resuming trade with the island nation. However, President George W. Bush <u>pursued</u> a policy of pressure against Cuba. He refused to relax bans on American trade with and travel to the island nation. In 2006, illness forced Castro to hand over power to his brother Raul, but little changed.

Vocabulary Builder
pursue (per SYOO) *v.* to follow; to chase; to attempt to gain

☑**Checkpoint** **How did the United States seek to promote change in Cuba?**

Easing the Arms Race

In 1972, the United States signed its first arms control treaty with the Soviet Union. The Strategic Arms Limitation Talks (SALT) curbed the number of nuclear warheads and long-range missiles that each side built. Seven years later, the two nations worked out another arms reduction pact (SALT II). But President Carter withdrew the treaty in protest after the Soviet invasion of Afghanistan.

New Approach In 1991, Soviet leader Gorbachev and President George H.W. Bush agreed to a path-breaking arms agreement called the Strategic Arms Reduction Treaty (START). Under START, the powers agreed to destroy about 20 percent of their nuclear weapons.

When the Soviet Union dissolved, Russia inherited most of its nuclear arms. In 1993, the United States and Russia negotiated START II. Revised in 1997, the pact required both countries to cut back long-range nuclear weapons by an astounding two thirds.

Analyze Contrasts

Contrast START with the original Strategic Arms Limitation Treaty. What can you conclude about the factors influencing arms treaties?

Nuclear Weapons Status, 2009

RUSSIA

UNITED KINGDOM

FRANCE

UNITED STATES

ISRAEL

IRAN

CHINA

NORTH KOREA

INDIA

PAKISTAN

ATLANTIC OCEAN

PACIFIC OCEAN

PACIFIC OCEAN

INDIAN OCEAN

KEY

- Nuclear weapon state by 1960
- Nuclear weapon state by 2005
- Suspected of having nuclear weapons programs, 2009

0 km 3,000
0 miles 3,000
Mercator Projection

MAP MASTER®
Skills Activity

U.S. leaders want to halt any further spread of nuclear weapons, especially to nations seen as hostile to American interests.

(a) Interpret Maps What were the first three nations to acquire nuclear weapons?

(b) Draw Conclusions Why was the world so alarmed when both India and Pakistan developed nuclear weapons?

MapMaster Online

For: Interactive map
Visit: PHSchool.com
Web Code: mvp-9283

A Continuing Threat Economic and political instability in the former Soviet Union worried U.S. planners. Russia alone had some 30,000 nuclear weapons; three other republics had some, too. All four pledged to honor existing treaties. In return, Congress sent $400 million per year to help these nations safely store or destroy their nuclear arms.

Another concern was nuclear proliferation—the spread of nuclear arms. Britain, France, and China had long had such weapons, but other nations also sought them. The danger of nuclear war would grow if nuclear weapons spread further.

U.S. intelligence reports said that Israel probably had a nuclear weapon by the late 1960s. Iran and Iraq were also suspected of seeking nuclear arms. South Asia was another problem area. In 1998, feuding neighbors India and Pakistan successfully tested nuclear bombs, sparking fears that many countries might one day possess nuclear arms.

☑ **Checkpoint** **Why would the United States be worried about nuclear proliferation?**

⭐ **Looking Back and Ahead** After the Cold War ended, the United States turned to issues of democratic change and the dangers posed by the spread of nuclear weapons. In the next section, you will read of American efforts to deal with a tangle of dangerous issues in the Middle East.

Section 3 | **Check Your Progress**

Progress Monitoring ⏺nline
For: Self-test with instant help
Visit: PHSchool.com
Web Code: mva-9283

Comprehension and Critical Thinking

1. **(a) Recall** How did U.S. policy encourage political changes in South Africa and Northern Ireland?
   (b) Explain Problems Why do you think the United States was less successful in encouraging change in China?

2. **(a) Describe** How did nuclear weapons spread in the world in the 1990s?
   (b) Explain Problems Why is the spread of nuclear weapons considered one of the greatest dangers facing the world?

🔁 **Reading Skill**

3. **Compare Causes and Reasons** Reread the text following the heading "Promoting Democracy and Peace." Compare the reasons for unrest in Northern Ireland and South Africa. Make a generalization about people's views with regard to freedom and self-determination.

Key Terms

Read each sentence below. If the sentence is true, write YES. If the sentence is not true, write NO and explain why.

4. South Africa's policy of apartheid guaranteed that its black citizens could live and work anywhere they wanted to.

5. The U.S. Congress approved sanctions on South Africa that forbade American companies to invest there.

Writing

6. Create a plot outline for an eyewitness narrative of the military action against the protesters in Tiananmen Square in China in 1991. Then, list several incidents that might be part of the rising action in this narrative. (Rising action builds on the central conflict and increases tension and suspense.)

All Red on the Horizon

❝You could hear the bombs going off. . . . You could see the burning oil well fires. It was all red on the horizon. It's a pretty eerie sight and we're walking towards it.❞

—Mike McCusker, U.S. Marine Corps commander in Kuwait during the 1991 Persian Gulf War

◄U.S. soldiers in Kuwait, 1991

Conflict in the Middle East

Objectives
- Learn why the Middle East has been of vital interest to the United States.
- Examine the causes and effects of Arab-Israeli conflict.
- Explore U.S. involvement in a series of crises in the Middle East.

Reading Skill

Compare Causes and Reasons Why do events in history take place? Examine events from history and compare their causes and reasons. Then, draw conclusions or make generalizations about what motivates people and nations to feel and act as they do. Remember, generalizations are broad statements that fit many situations.

Key Terms and People

Menachem Begin
Yasir Arafat
westernization
Ruholla Khomeini
Saddam Hussein
Norman Schwarzkopf
Colin Powell

Why It Matters After the end of the Cold War, America remained committed to playing a leading role in world affairs. For a time, Americans were optimistic about promoting democracy and peace around the globe. However, tensions and conflict in the Middle East quickly challenged this optimism.

❓ Section Focus Question: How have tensions in the Middle East posed concerns for the United States?

A Vital Region

The Middle East is a term first used by Europeans to describe Southwest Asia. Often, the term has been extended to include Egypt in northeastern Africa, as well as Afghanistan to the east.

Since ancient times, the Middle East has linked the societies of Europe, Asia, and Africa. Three major religions—Judaism, Christianity, and Islam—arose in the region. Today, Islam is the dominant religion of most Middle Eastern nations. Over the centuries, the region has had wars between empires and struggles for political control.

In recent times, the Middle East has gained world attention because of its vast reserves of petroleum, or oil. Nations such as Saudi Arabia and Kuwait became wealthy selling needed oil to the United States and other industrial nations. Arab nations form the backbone of the Organization of Petroleum Exporting Countries (OPEC). OPEC has become a key player in world affairs by setting the level of oil production and raising or lowering the price of oil.

The United States has had to balance conflicting interests in the Middle East. It strongly supports the Jewish nation of Israel. Yet, it also tries to maintain ties with Arab states that oppose Israel.

✓Checkpoint Why is the Middle East of concern to Americans?

Arab-Israeli Conflict

Since the late 1800s, Jews from Europe and elsewhere had been migrating to the land then known as Palestine, which they saw as their ancient homeland. Joining established Jewish communities, they hoped to create a Jewish state there. Arabs there opposed Jewish population growth and attacked Jews. Jews responded with counterattacks. This led to a cycle of violence.

Compare Causes and Reasons
Compare the reasons that Jews went to the region at different times. What can you conclude?

A Series of Wars After the horrors of the Holocaust, many Jews sought refuge in their ancient homeland. Jews formed the independent State of Israel in part of British-controlled Palestine in 1948. The United States and other nations recognized Israel.

However, surrounding Arab countries refused to accept the new state and declared war. An Israeli victory in 1948 left more than half a million Palestinian Arabs homeless. They fled to nearby Arab countries. Similar numbers of Jews fled from Arab countries to Israel.

Further wars followed. In 1956, Israel, Britain, and France attacked Egypt but withdrew under pressure from the United Nations and the United States. War broke out in 1967, and again in 1973, when Arab nations launched a surprise attack. In the 1967 war, Israel seized surrounding territories, including the West Bank and Gaza, home to many Palestinian Arabs. Tensions rose as Israeli settlers moved into the territories.

Camp David Accords In 1977, Egyptian President Sadat tried to break the cycle of war. He became the first Arab leader to visit Israel seeking peace. Still, agreement was not easy to reach.

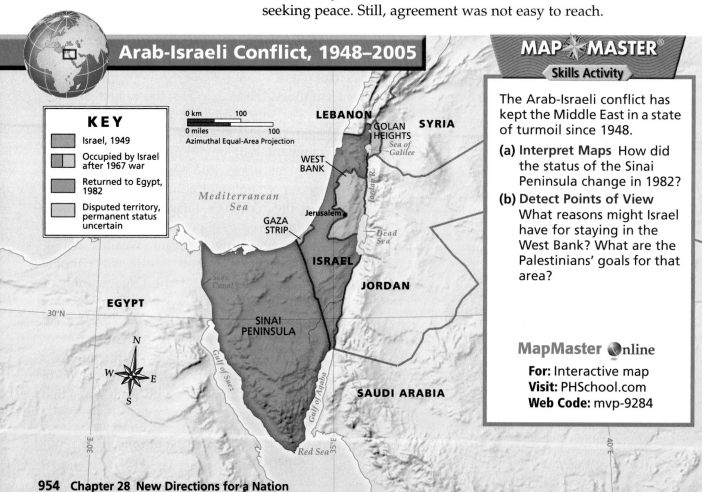

Arab-Israeli Conflict, 1948–2005

MAP MASTER®
Skills Activity

KEY
- Israel, 1949
- Occupied by Israel after 1967 war
- Returned to Egypt, 1982
- Disputed territory, permanent status uncertain

0 km 100
0 miles 100
Azimuthal Equal-Area Projection

LEBANON
GOLAN HEIGHTS
SYRIA
Sea of Galilee
WEST BANK
Jordan R.
Mediterranean Sea
Jerusalem
GAZA STRIP
Dead Sea
ISRAEL
JORDAN
EGYPT
30°N
SINAI PENINSULA
Suez Canal
Gulf of Suez
Gulf of Aqaba
SAUDI ARABIA
Red Sea
30°E
35°E
40°E

The Arab-Israeli conflict has kept the Middle East in a state of turmoil since 1948.

(a) Interpret Maps How did the status of the Sinai Peninsula change in 1982?

(b) Detect Points of View What reasons might Israel have for staying in the West Bank? What are the Palestinians' goals for that area?

MapMaster Online

For: Interactive map
Visit: PHSchool.com
Web Code: mvp-9284

When peace talks faltered, President Jimmy Carter brought Sadat and Israeli Prime Minister Menachem Begin (muh NAKH uhm BAY gihn) to his Maryland retreat, Camp David. There, the leaders signed the Camp David Accords in 1978. Egypt recognized the state of Israel in exchange for return of the Sinai Peninsula.

The Palestinian Issue After 1948, most Palestinians lived in the West Bank or Gaza or in refugee camps in nearby countries. Led by Yasir Arafat, the Palestine Liberation Organization (PLO) did not accept Israel's existence. The PLO launched attacks on Israel, including Israeli civilians. Israel responded with counterattacks.

In 1987, Palestinians in the West Bank and Gaza launched a protest movement or uprising known as the Intifada. The uprising focused world attention on the Palestinian issue.

The United States and other nations tried to broker a peace agreement between the Israelis and Palestinians. In 1993, Israel and the PLO signed a pact setting up limited Palestinian self-rule in the Gaza Strip and part of the West Bank. Arafat agreed to give up violence and accept Israel's existence.

Despite hopes for peace, new disputes developed. Militant groups on both sides refused to accept the peace process. Arab extremists launched a series of suicide bombings in Israeli cities. Israel responded with military force. Accusing Arafat of secretly supporting the bombers, Israeli troops surrounded his headquarters and <u>confined</u> him there.

Still, moderates on both sides continued to seek a solution. On the twenty-fifth anniversary of the Camp David Accords, former President Carter commented that "peace will come to the Mideast only if two things happen." The first was for Israel to give up its settlements in the West Bank and Gaza. The second was recognition of Israel by all Arab nations and their commitment to end Palestinian "acts of terrorism and violence" against Israel.

Contacts picked up after Arafat's death in 2004. The following year, Israel and the new Palestinian leadership announced a cease-fire. In 2005, Israel took a bold step toward peace. Israelis withdrew all Jewish settlements from Gaza and several from the West Bank. President George W. Bush hailed the move as "courageous."

Palestinians welcomed the withdrawal but insisted that Israel withdraw from all of the West Bank. Meanwhile, Hamas, a group considered terrorist by Israel and the United States, took control of Gaza. Israel blockaded Gaza, while Hamas fired rockets into Israel. Israel responded by attacking Gaza in 2009 and maintaining a blockade. Since then, there has been little progress toward peace.

☑ **Checkpoint** Identify the causes of the Israeli-Arab conflict.

Sadat, Carter, and Begin (left to right) celebrate the Camp David Accords.

Vocabulary Builder
<u>confine</u> (kahn FĪN) **v.** to keep within an area; to shut in or imprison

Increasing Tensions

Many Arabs and Muslims have resented American support for Israel. A series of other conflicts increased tensions between the United States and the Muslim world.

Iran and Lebanon As you have read, the United States had long supported the Shah of Iran. The Shah was strongly anti-Communist during the Cold War. However, many Iranians opposed the Shah's harsh, undemocratic rule. Also, devout Muslims opposed his efforts at westernization. Westernization is the adoption of ideas, culture, and technology from Western regions such as the United States and Europe.

In 1979, a revolution forced the Shah to flee. As you have read, the Iranian revolution led to a hostage crisis that contributed to Ronald Reagan's victory over Jimmy Carter.

The United States also became involved in a long, bloody civil war in Lebanon. President Reagan sent American marines as part of a UN peacekeeping force. The forces were later withdrawn after hundreds of American and French troops were killed in suicide bombings in 1983.

An Extreme Form of Islam The force behind the Iranian revolution was a Muslim religious leader, Ayatollah Ruholla Khomeini (roo HOH luh koh MAY nee). Khomeini wanted Iran to return to a very strict form of Islam. The new government banned Western books, movies, and music. New laws limited the rights of women.

Over the next decades, extreme forms of Islam gained influence in parts of the Middle East. The followers of these extreme forms were called Islamists. They saw American culture and Western values as threats to their own beliefs. They resented U.S. economic power and the presence of American troops in nations such as Saudi Arabia. Some Muslim extremists encouraged or committed acts of violence against Americans and other westerners.

Persian Gulf War The nation of Iraq added to tensions in the region. Iraq had long been ruled by a brutal dictator, Saddam Hussein. In 1990, Hussein sent troops to invade neighboring Kuwait. Kuwait is one of the richest oil-producing nations in the Middle East.

President George H.W. Bush feared the invasion of Kuwait was the start of an Iraqi plan to seize Middle Eastern oil. To block such a move, Bush sent troops to Saudi Arabia. He also persuaded the UN to impose economic sanctions on Iraq.

Vocabulary Builder
crisis (KRĪ sihs) *n.* turning point or deciding event in history

Iran Hostage Crisis, 1979
A poster in Tehran depicts U.S. helplessness during the hostage crisis. **Critical Thinking:** *Draw Conclusions* Why were many Iranians angry at the United States?

Bush built a coalition of more than 30 nations, including the Arab nations of Saudi Arabia, Syria, and Egypt. They demanded that Iraq withdraw from Kuwait. When Iraq ignored the demands, the coalition began launching a series of air attacks against the Iraqi capital of Baghdad in January 1991. These were later followed by a ground attack. Military operations were under the command of U.S. General Norman Schwarzkopf and the head of the Joint Chiefs of Staff, Colin Powell.

The Persian Gulf War lasted only six weeks. By February 1991, Hussein was forced to withdraw his troops from Kuwait. The UN then imposed strict economic and military restrictions on Iraq.

Still, Hussein remained in power. Many Americans viewed him as a continuing threat to peace in the Middle East and the world. Of special concern was the suspicion that Hussein was attempting to develop nuclear and biological weapons.

✓**Checkpoint** **What was the outcome of the 1991 Persian Gulf War?**

⭐ **Looking Back and Ahead** Tensions in the Middle East have posed many problems for U.S. foreign policy. After the Persian Gulf War, the United States continued to focus on threats in the region. In the next chapter, you will see how tensions in the Middle East led to a deadly attack within the United States itself.

Biography Quest

Colin Powell
born 1937

In Colin Powell's family, every child was expected to work for a college education. After earning degrees in geology and business administration, he joined the U.S. Army and was awarded the Purple Heart for injury in Vietnam.

Powell became a four-star general and was chairman of the Joint Chiefs of Staff from 1989 to 1993. He was secretary of state from 2001 to 2005—the first African American to hold that office.

Biography Quest

In what year did Powell join the U.S. Army, and what was his rank then?

For: The answer to the question about Powell

Visit: PHSchool.com

Web Code: mvd-9284

Section 4 | **Check Your Progress**

Progress Monitoring Online
For: Self-test with instant help
Visit: PHSchool.com
Web Code: mva-9284

Comprehension and Critical Thinking

1. **(a) Recall** What happened in 1948 that increased tensions between Muslims and Jews in the Middle East?
(b) Draw Inferences Why do you suppose Jews wanted to create the state of Israel?

2. **(a) Identify** Who was Ruholla Khomeini?
(b) Clarify Problems How did his goals clash with those of the United States?

🔴 Reading Skill

3. **Compare Causes and Reasons** Reread the text following the subheadings "Camp David Accords," "The Palestinian Issue," and "Persian Gulf War." Compare U.S. reactions to the Arab-Israeli conflict with the U.S. reaction to Iraq's invasion of Kuwait. Why were the reactions different?

Key Terms

Answer the following question in a complete sentence that shows your understanding of the key term.
4. Why might some people see westernization as a threat to traditional Islamic culture?

Writing

5. Write a paragraph that would be part of the rising action of a narrative about one of the following events:
- Camp David Accords of 1978
- Iranian hostage crisis of 1979–1980
- Persian Gulf War in 1991
- Israeli-PLO agreement in 1993

Indicate your narrator's identity and reason for being there. Include concrete details to make the event come to life.

Global Oil Resources

For millions of years, pools of crude oil collected between rock layers far below the Earth's surface. During the 1850s, people developed technology to drill down to those pools and pump them to the surface for industrial use. Once processed, crude oil becomes petroleum— a resource that has fueled automobiles, energy plants, and everyday products such as bubble gum, crayons, and paint. Although there are oil reserves on nearly every continent, the Middle East rests on a large number of oilfields that make it a vital hub in the global oil network.

Non-OPEC nations also ▶ produce and export their own oil. Russia and Norway are examples of oil exporters outside OPEC ranks. American oil companies drill and pump oil in parts of the United States. However, the United States does not produce enough oil to supply the large U.S. market for gasoline and other products made from oil.

Top World Oil Exporters	Top World Oil Importers
1. Saudi Arabia	1. United States
2. Russia	2. Japan
3. United Arab Emirates	3. China
4. Norway	4. Germany
5. Iran	5. South Korea

Source: *Energy Information Administration*

Venezuela

EQUATOR

MI 0 — 2000

KM 0 — 2000

▲ Venezuelan tanker ships transport oil to bustling ports in South America and across the Pacific Ocean to Asia. Three of the top five oil-importing nations in the world are in East Asia.

OPEC Controls the Flow

Eleven countries make up OPEC (Organization of the Petroleum Exporting Countries). All but three OPEC nations are located in the Middle East or North Africa. This organization guides the flow and price of a sizeable portion of the planet's oil reserves.

◄ Saudi Arabia produces close to ten million barrels of oil every day. Oil derricks like the one shown here support drill bits that grind through desert sand and bedrock.

Understand Effects:
Alternative Energy Sources

Oil is a nonrenewable resource, or a resource that cannot be replaced once it is used. The search for cheap and renewable alternatives to oil is critical to the future of industrialized nations.

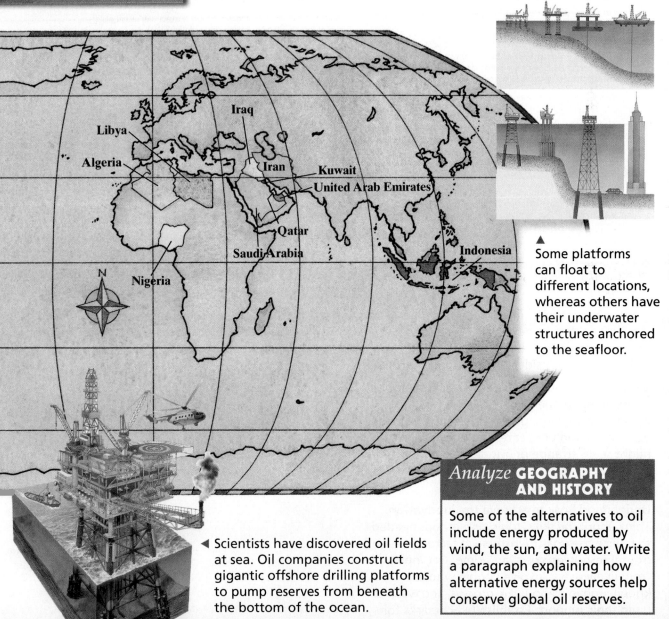

▲ Some platforms can float to different locations, whereas others have their underwater structures anchored to the seafloor.

◄ Scientists have discovered oil fields at sea. Oil companies construct gigantic offshore drilling platforms to pump reserves from beneath the bottom of the ocean.

Analyze GEOGRAPHY AND HISTORY

Some of the alternatives to oil include energy produced by wind, the sun, and water. Write a paragraph explaining how alternative energy sources help conserve global oil reserves.

Innovate and Think Creatively

21st Century Learning

An innovation is a new idea that improves on an existing product or process. The article below is an example of an innovation related to energy, a topic you read about in this chapter. Read the passage below and the innovation steps after the article.

Monday, July 21, 2008

Local Schools Shining Light on Solar Panels

By Jeff Raderstrong, *Seattle Times* staff reporter

Buy a hot dog at an Interlake High School Saints game this fall and save the Earth.

Really?

Well, at least save some electricity.

That's because Interlake's new concession stand will be powered by solar energy. Interlake is one of 12 schools, including Redmond High and Thomas Jefferson High in Auburn, to receive grants from Puget Sound Energy (PSE) for solar panels. The utility plans to give out at least 10 more grants to schools in the next few years.

"There seems to be a lot of demand and excitement in the schools," said PSE spokesman Andy Wappler. . . .

Solar panels act as an additional source of electricity for the main power grid. If the panels can produce more energy than the home or building (or concession stand) needs, the extra energy is sent to the main grid for use by others. The producers then receive energy credits on their next bill. . . .

Redmond High School just received a $150 check, thanks to its 1.1-kilowatt panel, installed in 2006 with a PSE grant. The school, which requires 350 kilowatts to operate, does not consume any of the energy the panel produces. It receives credits on its electricity bill as well as cash from the state's "net-metering" program, which pays solar-energy producers for every watt of solar energy they produce in a year.

In the fall, the Lake Washington School District will install panels at two more schools and expand the Redmond High panel system to include a wind turbine.

Chuck Collins, a consultant contracted by PSE to be resource-conservation manager for Lake Washington district, designed the Redmond High solar program and is looking for other ways to reduce the district's energy bill.

Evergreen Junior High's panels will cost the district $200,000, but, Collins points out, they ultimately will pay for themselves.

"The [junior high] building is supposed to last 40 years," said Collins. "If we can pay off a significant portion of the bill in 15 years, that's a win for the district." . . .

"[There are] a bunch of fallacies of 'solar doesn't work in Washington,'" said Collins. "We're knocking those down, one by one."

Learn the Skill

Use these steps to learn how to think innovatively and creatively.

1 Identify what needs improving. Describe a specific problem to be solved. Are there faster, better, or more efficient ways of getting a job or task done? Consider the intended outcome.

2 Brainstorm solutions. Generate as many ideas as possible. Be open to all ideas. If you are working in a group, don't criticize the ideas of others and don't hesitate to suggest ideas that might seem strange or impractical. Innovation often results from a chain of related ideas leading to an unexpected insight.

3 Understand how to achieve the innovation. Think about the skills, tools, or methods needed to realize the goal. Identify such factors as ease of use, resources, costs, and time. Get input from likely users. Involve people who are knowledgeable about the process, and work to build their support. Establish benchmarks for success and compare the results of the innovation with the original process.

Practice the Skill

Answer the following questions about the article on this page.

1 Identify what needs improving. Based on the information in the article, what was the problem being addressed?

2 Brainstorm solutions. Why was the solution innovative?

3 Understand how to achieve the innovation. How was the innovation achieved?

Apply the Skill

See the Review and Assessment at the end of this chapter.

Quick Study Guide

How did major national and international events affect the nation?

Section 1
A Conservative Surge

- President Carter grappled with many domestic and foreign problems.
- Political and social conservatives helped Ronald Reagan win the presidency in 1980.
- Reagan cut domestic spending and taxes.
- Under Bill Clinton, a growing economy produced budget surpluses.
- The election of George W. Bush in 2000 returned conservatives to power.

Section 2
End of the Cold War

- President Reagan took a strong stand against the Soviet Union and took steps to build defenses.
- Economic problems and political unrest led to the fall of communism in Eastern Europe, the breakup of the Soviet Union, and the end of the Cold War.

Section 3
A New Role in the World

- The United States tried to use its influence to encourage democracy in South Africa, China, and elsewhere.
- The spread of nuclear weapons to other countries became a major concern.

Section 4
Conflict in the Middle East

- The Middle East is the site of vast petroleum reserves and bitter conflicts among nations.
- The United States has tried to balance strong support of Israel with close ties to Arab states.
- An Iranian revolution of 1979 signaled the rise of a new, militant form of Islam.
- In the Persian Gulf War, a U.S.-led coalition turned back an Iraqi invasion of oil-rich Kuwait.

? Exploring the Essential Question

Use the online study guide to explore the essential question.

Section 1
How did the growing conservative movement help reshape American politics?

Section 2
How did the Cold War end?

Chapter 28 Essential Question
How did major national and international events affect the nation?

Section 4
How have tensions in the Middle East posed concerns for the United States?

Section 3
How did the United States use its influence after the Cold War ended?

Key Terms

Fill in the blanks with the correct key terms.

1. Tax cuts and increased spending contributed to a rising budget _____.

2. The introduction of American fashions into the Middle East was an example of _____.

3. To achieve a _____, the government has to spend only as much money as it takes in.

4. By imposing economic _____, the United States tries to influence another nation's policies.

5. Reagan's policy of _____ allowed American businesses to expand more freely.

Comprehension and Critical Thinking

6. (a) **Identify** What were three goals of the conservative movement?
   (b) **Apply Information** Choose two actions of President Reagan, and explain how each fulfilled one of the three goals.
   (c) **Draw Conclusions** Why do you think many people use the term "the Reagan Revolution" to describe Reagan's impact?

7. (a) **Recall** What was the goal of George W. Bush's No Child Left Behind program?
   (b) **Draw Conclusions** Why do you think many recent Presidents have focused on education as an important issue?

8. (a) **List** Why did the Soviet Union collapse?
   (b) **Identify Costs and Benefits** How did the collapse bring both benefits and drawbacks to people of Eastern Europe and Russia?

9. (a) **Summarize** How did the United States promote democracy around the world?
   (b) **Analyze Cause and Effect** How successful was the United States in supporting democratic movements?

10. (a) **Recall** Why is the Middle East considered a vital region for the United States?

(b) **Summarize** How was the United States involved in the conflicts of the region?
(c) **Analyze Cause and Effect** Identify two results of increased American involvement in the Middle East.

Reading Skill

11. **Compare and Contrast** Choose any two Presidents discussed in this chapter. Write a paragraph comparing and contrasting their presidencies. Make a generalization based on your comparison.

Writing

12. **Write an opening and several paragraphs for an eyewitness narrative.**
   Choose one of the narratives that you have been developing in the section activities for this chapter. Use the Internet or library to find more background information about the subject. Then, write two paragraphs describing the rising action for the historical event.
   Your writing should:
   • introduce your eyewitness narrator;
   • focus on a historical event covered in this chapter;
   • make the conflict, or central problem, of the narrative clear;
   • create rising action that builds on the conflict with details and actions.

13. **Write a narrative:**
   Imagine that you are an American negotiator at peace talks in the Middle East. Write a letter home explaining what you hope to accomplish and the challenges you face.

Skills for Life

Innovate and Think Creatively
Use the article on page 960 to answer the following questions.

14. Sometimes one innovative solution can solve multiple problems. How does solar energy address many problems at once?

15. Brainstorm other innovations to solve the problem of the world's dependence on oil and other fossil fuels. What do you think is the best solution?

16. For your "best solution" in question 15, how could this innovation be achieved?

Test Yourself

1. **Which action of President Bill Clinton marked a move away from a conservative policy?**

   A slashing the size of government

   B working with business

   C limiting welfare benefits

   D raising taxes on higher income groups

2. **In the 1990s, the United States sent troops to help enforce peace in**

   A Northern Ireland.

   B Bosnia.

   C Iran.

   D South Africa.

Refer to the map below to answer Question 3.

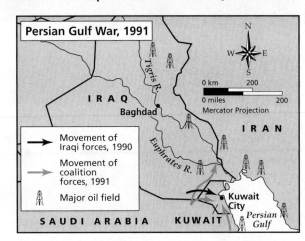

Persian Gulf War, 1991

Movement of Iraqi forces, 1990
Movement of coalition forces, 1991
Major oil field

3. **Based on the map, during the Persian Gulf War, Saudi Arabia**

   A supported Iraq against the U.S.-led coalition.

   B supported the U.S.-led coalition against Iraq.

   C invaded Iraq.

   D was invaded by Iraq.

Document-Based Questions

Task: Look at Documents 1 and 2, and answer their accompanying questions. Then, use the documents and your knowledge of history to complete this writing assignment:

> Write an editorial supporting or criticizing Reaganomics. Be sure to support your arguments with facts.

Document 1: Stephen Moore was an economist and adviser in the Reagan administration. *According to Moore, what were Reagan's main economic ideas?*

> "Ronald Reagan came to the White House with some simple ideas but they weren't simple-minded ideas. These were ideas to cut tax rates. At that time . . . we had a 70 percent top tax rate. That was really discouraging economic growth. The second big problem . . . was raging inflation. . . . And the third thing was Reagan promised to rebuild the military . . . and to try to bring the Cold War to an end victoriously.
>
> What made Ronald Reagan such a great president . . . was that he came in with these three objectives and was able to accomplish them all."

Document 2: Robert Reich was an economist and secretary of labor during the Clinton administration. *According to Reich, what major problem did Reaganomics cause?*

> "Reaganomics had some major problems. For one thing, it created a huge deficit. . . . At the start of the Reagan administration the deficit was about 2.5 percent of the national economy. By the end it was about 5 percent of the national economy. . . .
>
> With that kind of deficit, eventually, you've got to pay the piper. There is a day of reckoning, and the day of reckoning came with a huge recession in 1990 and 1991. . . .
>
> The gap between the rich and the poor began to widen during the Reagan administration and has continued to widen since then."

Challenges for a New Century

1980-Present

"*Our challenges may be new. . . . But those values upon which our success depends-hard work and honesty, courage and fair play, tolerance and curiosity, loyalty and patriotism-these things are old. . . .They have been the quiet force of progress throughout our history.*"

—President Barack Obama,
Inaugural Address,
January 20, 2009

Barack Obama's presidential inauguration was a historic moment, marking the first time an African American had become President.

What You Will Learn

Section 1
THE THREAT OF TERRORISM
The September 11, 2001, terrorist attacks stunned the nation and led to a controversial war in Iraq.

Section 2
ECONOMY AND THE ENVIRONMENT
A global economy and growing concern about environmental problems have linked the world.

Section 3
SCIENCE AND TECHNOLOGY
The computer and other advances in technology and science have transformed modern society.

Section 4
A CHANGING SOCIETY
New immigration and population patterns have led to an increasingly diverse society.

Reading Skill
Make Generalizations In this chapter, you will learn how to use details from the text to make generalizations about a topic.

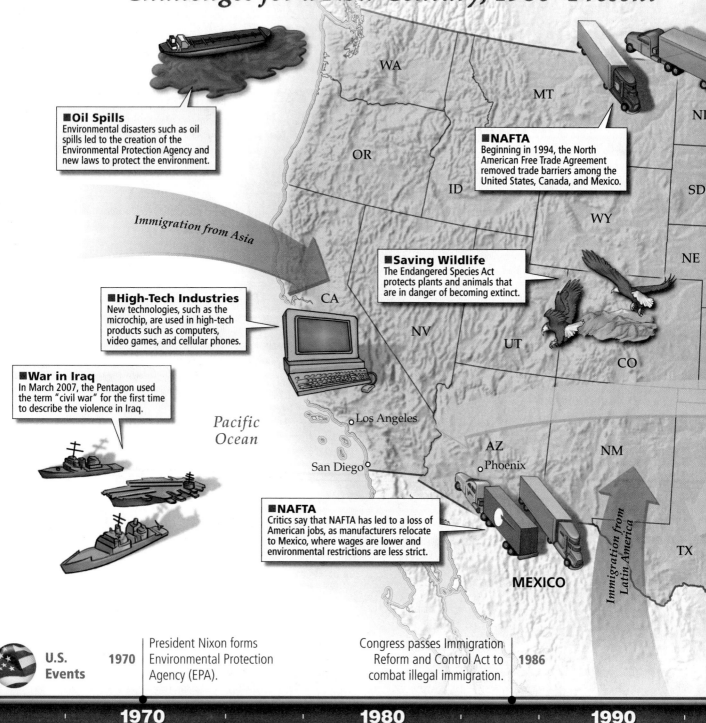

Challenges for a New Century, 1980–Present

■Oil Spills
Environmental disasters such as oil spills led to the creation of the Environmental Protection Agency and new laws to protect the environment.

■NAFTA
Beginning in 1994, the North American Free Trade Agreement removed trade barriers among the United States, Canada, and Mexico.

Immigration from Asia

■Saving Wildlife
The Endangered Species Act protects plants and animals that are in danger of becoming extinct.

■High-Tech Industries
New technologies, such as the microchip, are used in high-tech products such as computers, video games, and cellular phones.

■War in Iraq
In March 2007, the Pentagon used the term "civil war" for the first time to describe the violence in Iraq.

Pacific Ocean

■NAFTA
Critics say that NAFTA has led to a loss of American jobs, as manufacturers relocate to Mexico, where wages are lower and environmental restrictions are less strict.

Immigration from Latin America

WA

MT

NI

OR

ID

SD

WY

NE

CA

NV

UT

CO

Los Angeles

AZ

NM

Phoenix

San Diego

MEXICO

TX

U.S. Events | 1970 | President Nixon forms Environmental Protection Agency (EPA).

Congress passes Immigration Reform and Control Act to combat illegal immigration. | 1986

1970   1980   1990

World Events | 1973 | Arab members of OPEC impose oil embargo.

British scientist proposes World Wide Web. | 1989

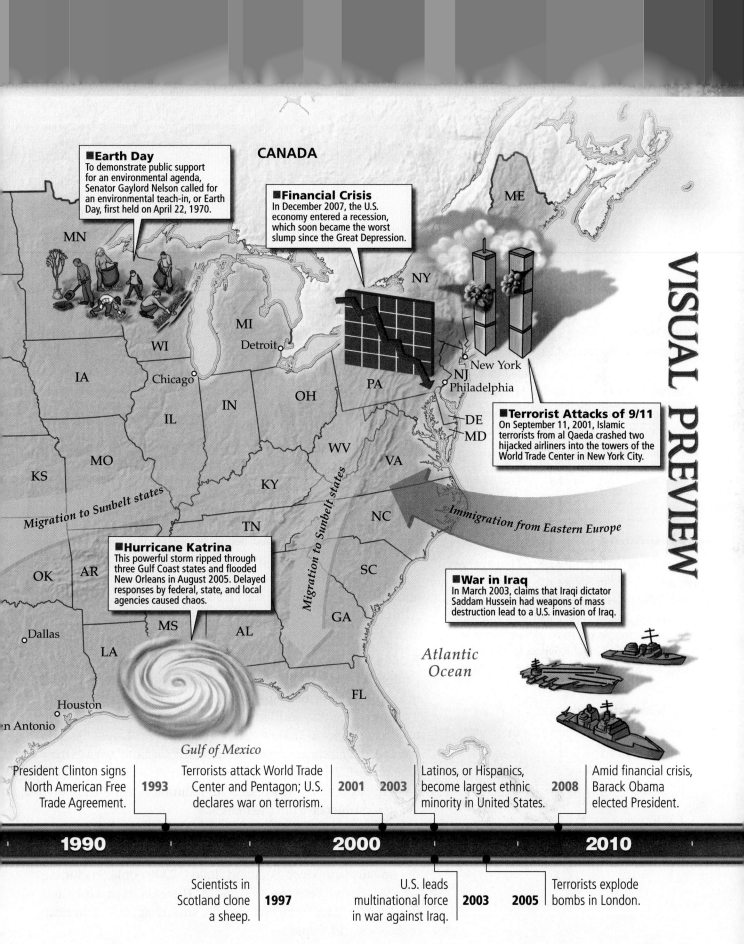

CANADA

■Earth Day
To demonstrate public support for an environmental agenda, Senator Gaylord Nelson called for an environmental teach-in, or Earth Day, first held on April 22, 1970.

■Financial Crisis
In December 2007, the U.S. economy entered a recession, which soon became the worst slump since the Great Depression.

ME

MN

MI

Detroit

WI

NY

IA

Chicago

IN

OH

PA

New York

NJ

Philadelphia

IL

DE

MD

■Terrorist Attacks of 9/11
On September 11, 2001, Islamic terrorists from al Qaeda crashed two hijacked airliners into the towers of the World Trade Center in New York City.

KS

MO

WV

VA

Migration to Sunbelt states

KY

Immigration from Eastern Europe

TN

NC

Migration to Sunbelt states

OK

AR

■Hurricane Katrina
This powerful storm ripped through three Gulf Coast states and flooded New Orleans in August 2005. Delayed responses by federal, state, and local agencies caused chaos.

SC

■War in Iraq
In March 2003, claims that Iraqi dictator Saddam Hussein had weapons of mass destruction lead to a U.S. invasion of Iraq.

Dallas

MS

AL

GA

LA

Atlantic Ocean

FL

Houston

n Antonio

Gulf of Mexico

President Clinton signs North American Free Trade Agreement.

1993

Terrorists attack World Trade Center and Pentagon; U.S. declares war on terrorism.

2001 **2003**

Latinos, or Hispanics, become largest ethnic minority in United States.

2008

Amid financial crisis, Barack Obama elected President.

1990

2000

2010

Scientists in Scotland clone a sheep.

1997

U.S. leads multinational force in war against Iraq.

2003 **2005**

Terrorists explode bombs in London.

▶ New York City
firefighter after
attack of 9/11

The Plane Struck the Towers

❝I arrived just moments after the plane struck the towers. . . . I looked up and saw that the south tower was collapsing. And I don't even know if the word collapse is correct here. It just disappeared. The lines that defined the building dissolved.❞

—Craig Childs, radio reporter, describing the terrorist attack on the World Trade Center, September 11, 2001

The Threat of Terrorism

Objectives

- Learn about the roots of terrorism.
- Explore how Americans responded to the terrorist attacks of September 11, 2001.
- Find out how the United States became involved in wars in Afghanistan and Iraq.
- Examine how the Iraq war led to increasing frustrations in America and abroad.

Reading Skill

Draw Conclusions The story of history often includes many apparently separate and small details. When looked at together, however, these details create a picture of an event, a time, or an important person. As you read the final chapter in this textbook, pay careful attention to the many details. Ask yourself what overall picture they create.

Key Terms and People

terrorism
counterterrorism

Osama Bin Laden

Why It Matters As the United States became more involved in the Middle East, some people in the region grew resentful of America's power and influence. They committed acts of violence against American soldiers and civilians. On September 11, 2001, these terrorists attacked the United States, and a war against terrorism began.

❷ **Section Focus Question: How did the war on terrorism affect American actions at home and abroad?**

Terrorism on the World Stage

In recent decades, terrorism has emerged as a growing threat to world peace and security. Terrorism is the use of violence, often against civilian targets, to force political or social change. Through bombings, hijackings, kidnappings, and other violent acts, terrorists create a climate of fear. Although some attacks are carried out by lone individuals, other terrorists belong to well-organized groups.

Roots of Terrorism Terrorism has a long history. In the United States, for example, the Ku Klux Klan used terror tactics to keep African Americans from voting during Reconstruction.

More recently, individuals and groups have carried out terrorist attacks in nations from Ireland to Sri Lanka. As you have read, Palestinian terrorists used suicide bombings in their war on Israel. Terrorism has also become a tool of Middle Eastern extremists who seek to eliminate American and Western influence from their lands.

Abroad and at Home At first, terrorist attacks against Americans generally occurred abroad. In 1988, an explosion on an airplane over Scotland killed 270 people, including 189 Americans. Between 1996 and 2000, terrorists in Africa and the Middle East launched deadly strikes against American embassies and ships.

In 1993, extremists from the Middle East launched an assault within the United States. A truck bomb exploded beneath one of the twin towers of the World Trade Center, the tallest buildings in New York. Six people died and more than 1,000 were injured. Authorities quickly captured most of the terrorists responsible.

The threat of terrorism was not only <u>external</u>. In 1995, a truck bomb destroyed a federal office building in Oklahoma City. The attack killed 168 people, including children in a day-care center. Investigations found that three young American men who resented the federal government were responsible.

Vocabulary Builder
<u>external</u> (ehks TER nahl) **adj.** on or from the outside

✓**Checkpoint** **Give two early examples of terrorism.**

The Nation Is Attacked

Despite the spread of terrorism, most Americans still felt secure at home. That sense of security vanished in a single day.

A Day of Horror On September 11, 2001, Arab terrorists seized four passenger jets departing from the East Coast. The hijackers crashed two of the planes into the World Trade Center in New York and a third into the Pentagon in Arlington, Virginia, near Washington, D.C. The fourth jet plummeted into a Pennsylvania field after passengers rushed the terrorists. The intended target of the fourth jet was probably the White House or the Capitol Building.

Links Across Time

Acts of Terrorism

1920 On September 16, a wagon filled with explosives shattered Wall Street, the heart of New York's financial district. Some 30 people were killed. The bombing was believed to be the work of anarchists, but no one was ever charged.

1995 On April 19, a truck bomb destroyed a federal office building in Oklahoma City, killing 168 people. A former U.S. soldier was later tried and executed for the crime.

Link to Today   **Online**

Terrorism Today In 2001, the nation was rocked by even deadlier terrorist attacks. How do these devastating acts affect our lives?

For: The impact of terrorism today
Visit: PHSchool.com
Web Code: mvc-9291

1995 The Oklahoma City bombing was the worst terrorist attack on U.S. soil up to that time.

Many people escaped from the main towers of the World Trade Center, but fire and searing heat trapped others on upper floors. Firefighters and police rushed into the buildings to aid in the rescue. Then, as millions of dazed people watched on television or from the streets below, the towers collapsed, one by one.

Nearly 3,000 people were killed at the Pentagon, World Trade Center, and on the airplanes. Victims included citizens of some 80 nations and hundreds of rescuers. The mayor of New York later paid tribute to firefighters killed in the line of duty:

> **"**The New York City firefighters who lost their lives will be remembered among the greatest heroes of American history. Like the brave soldiers who stormed the beaches of Normandy and those who raised the flag over Iwo Jima, our firefighters . . . gave their lives defending our liberty.**"**
>
> —Rudolph W. Giuliani, *Brotherhood*

The Nation Reacts The tragedy of September 11 left Americans stunned, angry, and grief stricken. Yet, they quickly responded to the emergency. Millions lined up to give blood, aid in rescue efforts, or donate money and supplies to help victims and rescuers. Around the nation, Americans flew flags and took part in candlelight vigils. (See the Life at the Time feature in this chapter.) People around the world voiced their sympathy and support.

President George W. Bush expressed the nation's outrage. He vowed to "hunt down and punish those responsible." At the same time, he cautioned Americans not to take out their anger on innocent Arabs and Muslims.

Defending the Homeland To protect the nation, Bush created the Office of Homeland Security to coordinate the country's counterterrorism efforts. Counterterrorism is action taken against terrorism. Counterterrorist goals include identifying and locating terrorists and safeguarding vital transportation, communication, and energy systems.

In December 2001, Bush signed the Patriot Act. It granted authorities sweeping powers to investigate and jail people suspected of having terrorist ties. Under the act, suspects might be held indefinitely without charges being filed and without being allowed to consult a lawyer.

The Patriot Act was controversial. Some people felt such strong measures were necessary for national security. Others believed the law threatened the liberties guaranteed in the Bill of Rights. Even so, in 2006 Congress renewed the Patriot Act, including most of its controversial provisions.

☑**Checkpoint** **How did terrorists destroy the World Trade Center?**

Two Views of the Patriot Act

"The terrorists continue to plot against America and the civilized world. . . . We must continue to give homeland security and law enforcement personnel every tool they need to defend us. And one of those essential tools is the Patriot Act, which allows federal law enforcement to better share information, to track terrorists, to disrupt their cells, and to seize their assets."

—George W. Bush, State of the Union address, January 20, 2004

YES DEAR, I THINK WE WILL BE BETTER OFF UNDER THE NEW DEPARTMENT OF HOMELAND SECURITY...

SCRIBBLE SCRIBBLE

Reading Primary Sources
Skills Activity

In the excerpt above, President Bush explains why he thinks the Patriot Act is necessary. Still, as the cartoon at right shows, many people viewed the new law as a threat to civil liberties.

(a) Interpret Primary Sources According to Bush, how does the Patriot Act make the United States safer?

(b) Detect Points of View Summarize the main point of the cartoon. How do you think Bush would respond?

The War on Terror

A suspect in the September 11 attacks soon emerged. Osama Bin Laden was a wealthy Saudi Arabian who ran a worldwide terrorist network called al Qaeda (al Kī duh).

Invading Afghanistan Bin Laden took refuge in Afghanistan, where the Taliban protected him. The Taliban ruled the country with an iron fist and were bent on creating a fundamentalist Islamic state. Their repressive regime drew worldwide criticism. From a mountain hideout, Bin Laden used cell phones and the Internet to run al Qaeda.

The Taliban refused to surrender Bin Laden. U.S. troops then attacked Afghanistan in October 2001. The United States quickly toppled the Taliban from power and set up a new government to rebuild Afghanistan. In 2004, for the first time, Afghanis elected a president. A year later they voted for their first parliament or legislature. Bin Laden escaped capture and remained a threat.

War in Iraq Bush next targeted Iraq as a threat. Bush accused Iraqi dictator Saddam Hussein of having ties with Bin Laden. He also claimed that Hussein was developing weapons of mass destruction (WMDs), such as nuclear and chemical weapons.

Bush argued that the United States was justified in attacking another country it judged to be a threat, even if that country had not attacked first. This policy caused a rift between the United States and

HISTORIAN'S APPRENTICE ACTIVITY PACK

To further explore the topics in this chapter, complete the activity in the Historian's Apprentice Activity Pack to answer this essential question:

How has the United States tried to remain safe and to defend democracy?

The War in Iraq

An American soldier guards a checkpoint in Baghdad, Iraq, shortly after a deadly car bombing. **Critical Thinking:** *Analyze Cause and Effect Describe a cause-and-effect link of this photograph.*

some of its key European allies, such as France and Germany. Other nations, such as Britain, pledged their support.

In March 2003, the United States led a coalition of about 30 nations in an attack on Iraq. With the United States providing most of the military muscle, coalition forces smashed Iraq's defenses in six weeks. On May 1, Bush announced the end of major combat operations.

Rebuilding Iraq proved difficult. Militants and supporters of Hussein killed American troops and Iraqis. Attacks continued even after Hussein was captured in 2003 and executed in 2006. Meanwhile, no WMDs were found, nor was any link to Bin Laden proved.

Americans Divided Most Americans supported the Iraq War. Bush's strong actions, they said, toppled a brutal dictator and promoted democracy. They hoped that free elections in 2005 would stabilize Iraq and provide a model for other Middle Eastern nations.

An outspoken minority criticized Bush's actions. They felt Iraq had not posed an immediate threat. Some even accused Bush of deceiving Americans about Iraqi WMDs. Other critics charged that the war <u>consumed</u> money, supplies, and troops that were needed to pursue Bin Laden, combat terrorism, and keep the Taliban from regaining control of Afghanistan.

Vocabulary Builder
<u>consume</u> (kahn SYOOM) *v.* to use up

☑**Checkpoint** **Why did President Bush consider Saddam Hussein a threat?**

Frustration at Home and Abroad

The controversy over Iraq gradually weakened Bush's presidency and divided the nation. In 2006, voters vented their frustration with the war in the congressional elections. For the first time since 1994, Democrats won control of both houses of Congress with promises to "bring the troops home."

The situation in Iraq was growing worse every day. Arab terrorists and Iraqi insurgents continued to attack American troops. By 2007, more than 3,000 Americans had died.

Worse still, Iraqis found themselves caught in a web of civil strife. Two sects of Islam, Sunni and Shiite, were fighting for power in Iraq. Most Iraqis are Shiite and suffered under Saddam Hussein. The minority Sunnis supported the dictator. Now, Sunnis and Shiites fought for control of the country. Scores of Iraqis died as a result.

As the killing increased across Iraq, President Bush sent more than 20,000 soldiers to help Iraqis end the violence. Supporters believed that this "surge" helped to stem the bloodshed. However, fighting continued.

American frustrations in Iraq strengthened the hand of Iran, where a fundamentalist Shiite government ruled. As anti-Americanism grew in Iraq, the influence of Iran threatened to expand across the Middle East.

Draw Conclusions
Draw a conclusion about whether Americans generally accepted or opposed the decision to send troops into Iraq.

✓**Checkpoint** **Why was Iraq frustrating for Americans?**

☆ **Looking Back and Ahead** The global war on terrorism showed how events around the world had a powerful impact on Americans. In the next section, you will examine the role of the United States in a growing world economy.

Section 1 | **Check Your Progress**

Progress Monitoring Online
For: Self-test with instant help
Visit: PHSchool.com
Web Code: mva-9291

Comprehension and Critical Thinking

1. **(a) Summarize** How did the United States respond to the terrorist attacks of September 11, 2001?
   (b) Apply Information Agree or disagree with the following statement: The battle between the United States and terrorism did not begin on September 11. Give reasons for your answer.

2. **(a) Describe** Why did President Bush send troops into Afghanistan and Iraq?

(b) Detect Points of View Summarize one argument for the war in Iraq and one argument against it.

Reading Skill

3. **Draw Conclusions** Based on your reading of this section, draw a conclusion to describe how a terrorist differs from a soldier.

Key Terms

4. Write definitions of the key terms terrorism and counterterrorism. Then, based on those definitions, define the prefix *counter-*.

Writing

5. Write a paragraph ending a narrative by someone who was in New York City or in Washington, D.C., on September 11, 2001. The paragraph should sum up the narrator's reactions to the events of that day. It should also explain the long-term effects of September 11 on his or her life.

9/11: Courage and Remembrance

September 11, 2001, has been called "the day that changed America." In the days following the terrorist attacks, Americans responded with sorrow, anger, hard work, and a renewed sense of unity and patriotism.

◄ Rescue and Recovery ▲

The place where the twin towers of the World Trade Center collapsed became known as Ground Zero. For the first few days, rescue teams used specially trained dogs to search for survivors in the rubble. Recovery and clearance efforts went on for many months more.

Coming Together ▲

All over the country, Americans gathered for candlelight vigils.

▶

A rescue worker and a relative of a victim embrace during a memorial service at Yankee Stadium.

◀ ## Remembering the Victims

Americans vowed never to forget the people killed in the attacks. In New York, Washington, and Pennsylvania, people left notes, pictures, flowers, and flags to honor the victims.

Analyze LIFE AT THE TIME

Choose two of the photographs on these pages. For each photograph, write a caption that describes the emotions of the people shown. Then, describe your own feelings as you look at those pictures.

SECTION 2

This New Global Economy

❝ This new global economy will be much different than the industrial economy of the 20th century. . . . It will be fueled by the fusion of different technical and creative fields, and thrive on scholarship, creativity, artistry, and leading edge thinking. ❞

—Deborah Wince-Smith, business leader,
on the global economy, 2007

◀ American shoe factory in Vietnam

Economy and the Environment

Objectives
- Explore the role of the United States in the new global economy.
- Understand the goals of the environmental movement.
- Learn about the problem of energy and possible solutions.

🎯 Reading Skill

Support Conclusions With Evidence
Remember that any conclusions you draw must be supported with evidence. To find this evidence, first read the text carefully. What does it say? What conclusion do you think can be drawn? What details from the text support your conclusion?

Key Terms and People

globalization
trade deficit
outsourcing
free trade
Rachel Carson

environmentalist
renewable
   resource
global warming

Why It Matters As a result of closer economic ties and high-speed technology, the world has become a smaller place. More and more, people around the world are closely connected by business links, energy needs, and environmental concerns.

❓ **Section Focus Question: How do economic and environmental issues link the U.S. and the world?**

A World Linked by Trade and Finance

Since 1970, trade between the United States and other nations has more than doubled. Today, foreign trade accounts for about 25 percent of the American economy. This trend is part of the increasing globalization of the economy. Globalization is the process of creating an international network that also includes a complex web of financial loans and investments.

Trade Deficits American manufacturers face a disadvantage in the global economy. Workers in Latin America, Eastern Europe, and Asia are generally paid less than American workers. As a result, many foreign goods are cheaper to produce and can be sold at lower prices. Competition with low-priced foreign goods has led to trade deficits. A trade deficit occurs when a country buys more from other nations than it sells to them. In 2007, the U.S. trade deficit was more than $711 billion.

In response, more American companies have turned to outsourcing, or having work done in other countries. By building factories in places such as Mexico and Southeast Asia, American manufacturers can take advantage of cheap labor. But critics charge that outsourcing hurts American workers.

Tariffs or Free Trade? Foreign competition has <u>provoked</u> heated debate. Some argue that the United States should protect American profits and jobs by raising tariffs on foreign goods. Others say that tariffs spark expensive "trade wars," leading other nations to raise tariffs on American goods. Instead, opponents of tariffs favor free trade, or the removal of trade barriers. Free trade, they claim, increases business and creates new jobs around the world.

In 1993, President Clinton signed the North American Free Trade Agreement (NAFTA). The treaty removed trade barriers among the United States, Mexico, and Canada. Clinton said:

> **"**We know that it's not just the United States, no wealthy country in the world today can create new jobs without expanding trade. It cannot be done.**"**
>
> —Bill Clinton, Speech, October 20, 1993

Most experts agree that NAFTA, along with global trade regulators such as the World Trade Organization (WTO), has increased trade and generated jobs.

Still, opponents of free trade charge that trade agreements weaken efforts to safeguard workers' rights and the environment. NAFTA, for example, has led American makers of auto parts to move to Mexico, where labor and antipollution laws are less strict.

Vocabulary Builder
<u>provoke</u> (prah VOHK) **v.** to excite; to cause an action

North American Trade

KEY

Imports (in millions of dollars)

Exports (in millions of dollars)

Source: *Statistical Abstracts of the United States, 1995, 1999, 2007*

CANADA

1990	$83,674
1995	$127,226
2000	$178,941
2007	$248,888

UNITED STATES

1990	$30,157
1995	$62,101
2000	$135,926
2007	$210,714

1990	$91,380
1995	$144,370
2000	$230,838
2007	$317,057

1990	$28,279
1995	$46,292
2000	$111,349
2007	$136,092

PACIFIC OCEAN

0 km 500
0 miles 500
Albers Equal-Area Projection

MEXICO

ATLANTIC OCEAN

MAP MASTER®

Skills Activity

The North American Free Trade Agreement of 1993 removed trade barriers among the United States, Canada, and Mexico.

(a) Interpret a Map What was the total value of U.S. exports to Mexico in 1990? In 2000?

(b) Evaluate Information Did the United States have a trade deficit with Canada in 2000? Explain.

MapMaster ●nline

For: Interactive map
Visit: PHSchool.com
Web Code: mvp-9292

Financial Meltdown Late in 2007, the economy of the United States plunged into recession. A recession occurs when the Gross Domestic Product (GDP) shrinks for six months in a row. GDP is the total amount of goods and services produced by an economy. Unemployment rose and consumer spending fell. The stock market dropped by nearly 40 percent, the largest downturn since the Great Depression.

The problem began with mortgages—loans from banks to pay for homes. Over time, borrowers must repay those loans plus additional money (interest) as a charge for borrowing the money. Many banks made risky loans. Some lenders used flexible interest rates that could increase. As the economy slowed, many borrowers found they could not repay what they owed because they lost their jobs or their interest rates increased too much. In 2008, an estimated 1.4 million Americans had to give up their homes because they could not pay their mortgages.

Worse still, big banks repackaged those risky mortgages and sold them to other banks. When borrowers failed to pay their mortgages, banks began to fail because they did not have enough cash to do business. Like an economic virus, the financial crisis spread worldwide, involving many more banks than were originally affected.

Stopping the Slide Nations scrambled to rescue the biggest banks and financial companies. In 2008, Congress agreed to advance up to $750 billion to cash-strapped lenders by creating the Troubled Assets Relief Program, or TARP. Other countries took similar action.

Conservative opponents criticized the government "bailout" of banks. Banks, not taxpayers, should pay for bad business decisions, they said. Other critics wanted the money used to reduce mortgage payments so people could keep their homes. Defenders of TARP countered that without stable banks to lend money, the economy could spiral into a serious depression. As a result, all Americans would suffer.

More federal aid followed. In 2009, Congress enacted a massive aid package to stimulate the economy. Nearly $800 billion was set aside for cities, states, and private industries to help them recover.

☑Checkpoint How did NAFTA encourage free trade?

The Environment

The environment is tied to the global economy. Polluted air or water in one country affects the people and economies of other countries. Natural disasters such as hurricanes, tornadoes, and earthquakes can destroy lives and property and change the landscape.

The Environmental Movement The modern environmental movement began with Rachel Carson. Carson, a marine biologist, published *Silent Spring* in 1962. The book warned that DDT, a chemical used by farmers to destroy insects, remained in the environment, killing birds and fish, and risked contaminating human food supplies. As a result of *Silent Spring*, Congress passed a law restricting the use of the chemical DDT.

Rachel Carson

A series of environmental disasters increased public alarm. In 1969, an oil spill fouled the ocean for hundreds of miles along the California coastline.

Organizations such as the Sierra Club lobbied Congress for laws to protect the environment. In April 1970, environmentalists organized the first Earth Day. An environmentalist is a reformer who seeks to protect the environment.

Taking Action Under public pressure, President Nixon formed the Environmental Protection Agency (EPA). New legislation targeted auto emissions, lakes, and rivers for cleanup.

Local governments also took action. Many communities required residents to recycle glass, paper, and aluminum. Recycling reduces the amount of garbage that must be buried or burned and slows the rate at which resources are consumed.

The environmental movement has spawned controversy. Critics charge that environmental regulations are costly. For example, laws requiring automakers to add pollution control devices raise the price of cars.

In 2001, President George W. Bush called for oil drilling in Alaska's Arctic National Wildlife Refuge to reduce fuel prices and dependency on foreign oil. Environmentalists resisted, but Bush argued that their concerns had to be balanced with economic needs.

The Wrath of Katrina On August 29, 2005, Hurricane Katrina swirled out of the Gulf of Mexico and tore into Louisiana, Mississippi, and Alabama. Winds of up to 175 miles per hour blew down buildings, snapped power lines, and drove people from their homes. New Orleans lay defenseless against surging floodwaters.

For days stranded victims wandered the flooded streets of New Orleans in search of food and clean water. Tens of thousands sought shelter in the Superdome, a large sports arena.

While the federal government began its response, people helped people. Within days, private contributions reached a record $200 million. Families, friends, and strangers opened their doors to survivors. More than 20 countries, including Afghanistan and Honduras, pledged aid.

The economic damage rose to $125 billion. It was the costliest natural disaster in U.S. history. One fourth of U.S. oil output and 10 percent of its refined oil come from the Gulf Coast. When these operations shut down, energy prices spiked upward. In the wake of Katrina, the Gulf Coast states and the nation started on the long road to recovery.

Hurricane Katrina

With winds of up to 175 miles per hour, Hurricane Katrina caused severe damage to coastal communities along the Gulf of Mexico. Here, a helicopter rescues people trapped on the roof of their house. **Critical Thinking: Analyze Cause and Effect** What were some of the social and economic effects of the storm?

☑Checkpoint What steps did the federal government take to protect the environment?

Sources of Energy

Energy Source	Advantages	Disadvantages
Oil	■ Easy to extract and transport ■ Efficient source of energy	■ Produces air pollution ■ A few countries control the supply of oil ■ Nonrenewable source
Coal	■ Inexpensive ■ Large amounts exist in the United States	■ Produces air pollution ■ Nonrenewable source
Wind	■ Free if available ■ Renewable source	■ Varies by place ■ Can affect endangered birds
Solar	■ Produces no waste or pollution ■ Renewable source	■ Requires large equipment ■ Availability depends on the weather
Nuclear	■ Almost limitless energy ■ No air pollution	■ Produces long-lasting radioactive wastes ■ Possible radiation leak

The Energy Supply

The disrupted oil production after Hurricane Katrina underlined the importance of energy conservation. Accounting for less than 5 percent of the world's population, the United States uses over 25 percent of the world's energy supplies. By 2008, the country was importing nearly 60 percent of its oil.

Oil Embargo In 1973, Arab members of OPEC voted to cut off oil supplies to the United States and other nations that supported Israel. The oil embargo deprived the United States of Middle Eastern oil for a year. The price of a barrel of oil quadrupled. Oil shortages became severe. Motorists sometimes waited hours for gasoline.

The need for oil continues to be a problem. As the price of crude oil jumped to over $140 a barrel in 2008, gas prices climbed to more than $4 a gallon. Sales of large, gas-guzzling vehicles dropped. People preferred smaller cars that used less gas. Manufacturers also introduced hybrid cars that ran on gasoline and electric power.

Alternative Energy Sources Dependence on foreign oil, high oil prices, and increasing air pollution have increased pressure to find alternative sources of energy. Each alternative offers drawbacks and advantages.

Fossil fuels, such as petroleum and coal, take thousands of years to form and are not easily replaced. Environmentalists encourage the use of renewable resources, or energy sources that are more easily restored by nature.

Vocabulary Builder
fossil (FAH sihl) *n.* hardened remains of a plant or an animal that lived long ago

Water, solar energy, and wind are renewable resources that can be turned into electricity. However, they also have limitations. These resources are not always available and do not always deliver consistent energy.

Nuclear power plants hold out the hope of near-limitless energy. However, nuclear plants are costly and produce radioactive waste. In 1979, an accident at the Three-Mile Island nuclear power plant in Pennsylvania raised the threat of radiation leaks.

✓**Checkpoint** **What is a major disadvantage of fossil fuels?**

The Question of Global Warming

Environmentalists have become concerned about the possibility of **global warming,** or a worldwide rise in temperatures. Since the late 1800s, scientists have recorded a general rise in world temperatures. Many blamed this trend on "greenhouse gases," such as carbon dioxide, emitted by cars, factories, and homes.

Still, there was disagreement about the possible danger of global warming. Some scientists pointed out that Earth had gone through many cold and warm periods in the past.

In an effort to deal with the possibility of global warming, the United States signed the Kyoto Protocol in 1997. In this agreement, industrialized nations pledged to reduce carbon dioxide emissions. However, President Bush rejected the Kyoto Protocol in 2001.

✓**Checkpoint** **Why does global warming concern many scientists?**

⭐ **Looking Back and Ahead** Although technology is blamed for many environmental problems, it may also hold the key to solving these problems. In the next section, you will explore other ways science and technology have changed the world.

Support Conclusions With Evidence

Find evidence to support the following conclusion: For now, the United States continues to be dependent on foreign oil.

Satellite image of Earth

Section 2 | **Check Your Progress**

Progress Monitoring Online
For: Self-test with instant help
Visit: PHSchool.com
Web Code: mva-9292

Comprehension and Critical Thinking

1. **(a) Explain** Why did the United States experience a trade deficit in the late 1900s?
(b) Identify Alternatives Suggest two ways that the United States might reduce its trade deficit.

2. **(a) Recall** What role did Rachel Carson play in the modern environmental movement?
(b) Compare Recall what you learned about the Progressive Era. How was Carson's role similar to that of muckrakers?

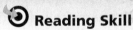 **Reading Skill**

3. **Support Conclusions With Evidence** Give two examples from Section 2 to support the following conclusion: The goal of protecting the environment sometimes conflicts with the goal of expanding the economy.

Key Terms

Complete each of the following sentences so that the second part further explains the first part and clearly shows your understanding of the key term.

4. Solar and water power are renewable resources, _____.

5. Reducing tariffs are one way of encouraging free trade, _____.
6. In 2007, the United States entered a recession, _____.

Writing

7. Rewrite the following sentences to make the time sequence more clear: During the 1950s, gasoline cost about 27 cents per gallon. During the Arab oil embargo, the price more than doubled. In 1925, you could buy a full tank of gas for less than a dollar. Now, more than 30 years later, that 1974 price of 57 cents per gallon looks good!

Higher-Level Skills Are Needed

"In almost every line of work, from high tech to manufacturing, employees need to be able to use computers effectively, communicate clearly, and handle higher-level science and math. . . . But most students are not getting these skills in high school."

—Melinda Gates, of the Bill and Melinda Gates Foundation, on improving high schools, 2005

◄ Students in a computer lab

Science and Technology

Objectives

- Explore the ways in which computers have transformed American life.

- Discover some of the recent achievements of medical science.

Reading Skill

Make Generalizations A generalization is a broad statement that can be applied to a variety of situations. To make a generalization, identify the main points or ideas. Then, develop a general principle or statement that applies to all of the points or ideas. You may need to include main points or ideas from earlier readings or from your own knowledge.

Key Terms

e-commerce   cloning
laser

Why It Matters You have learned how the Industrial Revolution of the 1800s changed the United States and the world. Today, scientific discoveries and technological change continue to transform the world we live in.

❓ **Section Focus Question: How have science and technology transformed modern society?**

The Computer Age

Perhaps no recent technology has revolutionized daily life as much as the computer. With computers, vast amounts of information can be stored, analyzed, and shared in a flash.

Rapid Advances Before the 1970s, machines called mainframes did most of the computing. These costly mainframes weighed tons and filled whole rooms. They were used chiefly by governments, universities, and big businesses.

The invention of transistors, circuits on tiny silicon chips, led to the development of smaller computers. In 1977, a new company, Apple, introduced the first computer for home use. Four years later, International Business Machines (IBM) marketed its own personal computer.

Computer hardware became smaller, and software became easier to use. In the 1970s, Bill Gates, a young Harvard dropout, began developing software that would let ordinary people run computers. Gates cofounded Microsoft, which became one of the world's most successful businesses. By 1990, Americans were buying more than nine million computers every year for their homes, offices, and schools.

An Information Revolution In 1969, the Department of Defense began to link its computers with those in a number of American universities. This electronic network formed the basis of the Internet.

The Internet helped to create an information revolution. In 1989, British scientist Tim Berners-Lee proposed the World Wide Web, a visual presentation of information that was easy to use. By 2008, nearly three-quarters of all Americans used the Internet to find information and communicate.

E-commerce, or buying and selling online, is growing rapidly as companies use the Internet to advertise and conduct business. More people are using the Internet to manage bank accounts, pay bills, and buy airline tickets and other items.

The Internet also enables people to post their own material. By 2006, over 60 million blogs (slang for Web logs) appeared on the Internet. They offer opinions about everything from cooking to politics. Specialized Web sites enable millions of users to post photos, video clips, and other personal information.

Difficult Issues Like all the other technological advances, the information revolution has drawbacks. Today, computers keep records about almost everything we do. As a result, "hackers" who tap into computers can threaten our privacy. Computer hacking has contributed to the spread of a new crime, identity theft. Also, the increased use of e-mails, blogs, chat rooms, and instant messaging, exposes young people to dangerous people on the Web.

Cellular phones, introduced in 1973, have created some social problems. Many Americans favor a ban on the use of cell phones in public places, such as restaurants and airplanes. They argue that no one should be forced to listen to other people's conversations. Cell phone use has also been blamed for many auto accidents. Many states now allow people to use only hands-free cell phones while driving.

✓ Checkpoint How did computers become smaller?

Biography Quest

Bill Gates
born 1955

Computer software made Bill Gates the richest American of his time. He has also given away more money than any American of his time.

In 2004, Gates pledged $1 billion to send minority students to college. Close to 1,000 African American, Latino, Native American, and Asian students will be eligible for these scholarships. Gates has also promised $15 million to help improve educational standards in high schools.

Biography Quest

What did Gates do to promote world health?

For: The answer to the question about Gates

Visit: PHSchool.com

Web Code: mvd-9293

Medical Advances

New technology has aided doctors in the detection and treatment of many medical problems. For example, lasers, or powerful beams of focused light, have become a critical tool for surgeons. Beams of laser light are more <u>flexible</u> than scalpels and can be used to perform delicate eye and skin surgery.

Another new medical tool, magnetic resonance imaging (MRI), provides an accurate view of internal organs and systems. MRIs help doctors identify injuries while reducing the need for surgery.

Vocabulary Builder
flexible (FLEHKS ah bahl) **adj.** easily bent; able to be used in many ways

Technology of
Modern Medicine

Thanks to modern technology, doctors today can diagnose illnesses more accurately than ever before. They can also make repairs to the human body that earlier doctors could only dream of. *Critical Thinking: Apply Information Based on what you have seen or heard, identify one other type of technology used by doctors today.*

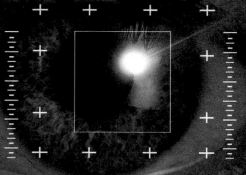

Laser Surgery
Doctors can use a laser to change the shape of a patient's cornea. This type of surgery, known as LASIK, can reduce or eliminate a person's need for eyeglasses. Lasers are also used for many other types of microsurgery.

Magnetic Resonance Imaging
The MRI gives doctors an incredible look inside the human body. Top: The red area indicates a spinal tumor. Bottom: MRI "slices" give a cross section of the brain of a healthy 16-year-old boy.

Bionics
Bionics is the design of mechanized replacement body parts. The woman here demonstrates a bionic arm. Her brain's thought impulses control her artificial limb.

The AIDS Epidemic In recent decades, new diseases have challenged medical science. Perhaps the most deadly is Acquired Immune Deficiency Syndrome (AIDS). Since it began in the 1980s, the AIDS epidemic has killed millions of people in the United States and around the globe. In some African countries, over 20 percent of the population is infected with the virus causing AIDS.

New drugs have extended the lives of many sufferers, but the drugs are too expensive for most people in developing countries. In 2003, President Bush promised a $15 billion program to <u>distribute</u> these medicines in a bold "assault on the global AIDS pandemic."

Vocabulary Builder

<u>distribute</u> (dihs TRIHB yoot) **v.** to spread in an orderly way

Cloning and Stem Cell Research Some medical advances cause heated debate. Cloning, the process of making a genetic double of a plant or an animal, made headlines in 1997 when a Scottish researcher cloned a sheep. Many people worried about the biological and ethical dangers of cloning human beings. In 1997, President Clinton banned federal funding of human cloning.

Similar worries arose regarding stem cell research. Opponents spoke against destroying human embryos to create stem cells that might cure serious illnesses. In 2006, President Bush vetoed a bill allowing federal funding for stem cell research that involved the use of human embryos. Still, many believe that cloning and stem cell research may help find cures for serious medical conditions.

Make Generalizations
Make a generalization about the relationship between science and ethics.

☑**Checkpoint** How has AIDS affected the world?

☆ **Looking Back and Ahead** In this section, you have seen how technology has transformed our lives. In the next section, you will examine other ways that American society has changed.

Section 3 | **Check Your Progress**

Progress Monitoring Online
For: Self-test with instant help
Visit: PHSchool.com
Web Code: mva-9293

Comprehension and Critical Thinking

1. **(a) Summarize** Describe the development of the computer.
   (b) Make Inferences Do you think computers would have had the same impact on society without the development of the transistor?

2. **(a) Recall** What new technologies have aided medical research?
   (b) Detect Points of View How has technology transformed our lives?

Reading Skill

3. **Make Generalizations** Make a generalization about the impact of computers and cellular telephones on American society.

Key Terms

4. Draw a table with three rows and three columns. In the first column, list the following terms: e-commerce, laser, cloning. In the next column, write the definition of each word. In the last column, make a small illustration that shows the meaning of the word.

Writing

5. Revise the following paragraph to improve the style and create a consistent tone: I remember the first time I tried to use a mouse. I was in a computer store in the early 1980s looking at a display for the new computer. I was used to arrow keys. They made the cursor go up and down, back and forth. I was just fine with them. The mouse seemed harder to control. So I gave up and walked away. Who'd've thought I'd be comfortable today?

Citizenship Is Truly a Privilege

"As a citizen, I am more confident to express my thoughts about American history, politics, and society, as well as its remarkable achievements and limitations. American citizenship—with its obligations, responsibilities, and rights—is truly a privilege. "

—Professor Olufemi Vaughan, Nigerian immigrant and American citizen, 2006

▲ New American citizens

A Changing Society

Objectives

- Learn how immigration and population patterns have changed in recent decades.
- Discover how progress toward equal rights has continued for many Americans.
- Explore issues that affect American schools and families.

🕙 Reading Skill

Support Generalizations With Evidence It is important when making generalizations to support them with evidence. Otherwise they can become overstatements or even statements of bias. As you read Section 4, look for evidence to support the generalizations offered.

Key Terms and People

refugee
undocumented worker
guest worker

Condoleezza Rice
Nancy Pelosi

Why It Matters Since colonial times, the United States has drawn immigrants from around the world. Today, new immigration trends and other changing social patterns continue to shape America's diverse society.

❓ **Section Focus Question: How have new immigration and population patterns increased diversity?**

Immigration Affects Society

More immigrants enter the United States every year than at any time since the early 1900s. Back in 1965, a new immigration law ended limits on non-European immigration, dramatically altering immigration patterns. Most immigrants seek economic opportunity or greater political freedom. Some newcomers are **refugees,** people fleeing war or persecution at home.

Latinos: The Largest Minority Today, Latin America rather than Europe is the largest source of immigration. Refugees have fled dictatorships in Cuba and Chile or civil wars in El Salvador and Guatemala. Poverty has driven much immigration from Mexico, Central America, and the Caribbean.

In 2003, Latinos became the largest ethnic minority in the United States, making up 12.5 percent of the population. The term *Latino* refers to people of Latin American birth or descent, as well as to people who speak Spanish as their primary language.

The impact of this shift has been dramatic. The political and economic influence of Latinos has grown. In the 1990s, Miami, Florida, became the first major U.S. city with a Latino majority.

Immigrants From Asia Asian immigration has also grown rapidly. Asian refugees fled war or political oppression in such countries as China and Vietnam. The lure of jobs and education has drawn growing numbers of immigrants from India, Korea, and the Philippines.

By 2007, an estimated 15 million Americans identified themselves as Asian. On average, they enjoyed greater household incomes than any other ethnic group, in part because of high levels of education. Still, in cities with large Asian populations, more Asians than whites work in low-paying jobs.

Debate and Changing Policies Many Americans welcome the new immigrants as hardworking people whose diverse cultures <u>enrich</u> American life. Others claim cheap immigrant labor drives down wages and feel that immigrants drain funds for education, health care, and welfare.

Much of the resentment has focused on undocumented workers, laborers who enter the country without legal permission. The Immigration Reform and Control Act of 1986 imposed stiff penalties on employers who hired such workers. The law also permitted illegal immigrants who came before 1982 to apply for citizenship.

The terrorist attacks of September 11, 2001, raised new concerns about immigration. The attacks were carried out by terrorists from the Middle East. Federal officials feared that other immigrants might be linked to terrorist groups. They monitored foreign-born college students and professors, as well as other immigrants. American authorities also tightened border control. Starting in 2007, they required new passports with "smart chips" to prevent identity fraud.

Vocabulary Builder
<u>enrich</u> (ehn RIHCH) **v.** to make richer or fuller; to improve

 Support Generalizations With Evidence
Find evidence in the text to support this generalization: People become less welcoming when their economic security or sense of safety is threatened.

History *Interactive*
Explore Trends in Immigration
Visit: PHSchool.com
Web Code: mvl-9294

Changing Immigration Patterns

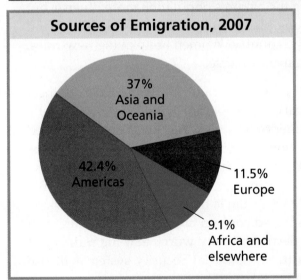

Sources of Emigration, 2007

- 37% Asia and Oceania
- 11.5% Europe
- 9.1% Africa and elsewhere
- 42.4% Americas

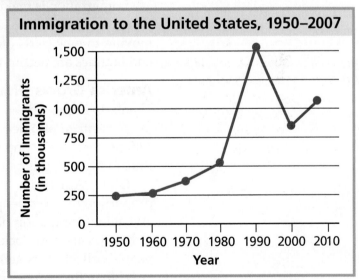

Immigration to the United States, 1950–2007

Number of Immigrants (in thousands) vs. Year

Source: *Yearbook of Immigration Statistics, 2007*

Reading Charts
Skills Activity

In the 1960s, new laws ended many restrictions on immigration. Since then, immigration has increased. The places immigrants come from have also changed.

(a) Interpret Charts How much did yearly immigration rates increase between 1950 and 2000?

(b) Contrast Compare these graphs to the ones in a previous chapter. How have immigration patterns changed since the early 1900s?

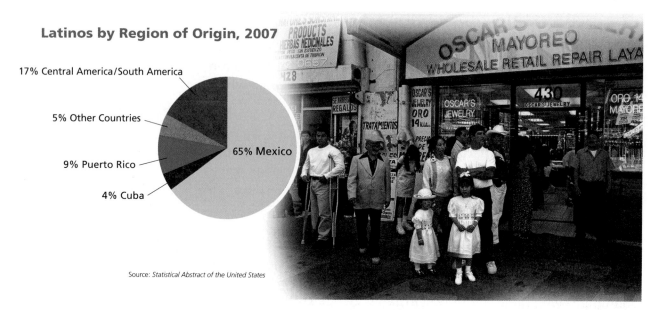

Latinos by Region of Origin, 2007

17% Central America/South America

5% Other Countries

9% Puerto Rico

4% Cuba

65% Mexico

Source: *Statistical Abstract of the United States*

A Growing Population

Latino neighborhoods like this one are now a vital part of most large American cities. The pie graph above shows the varied origins of the nation's growing Latino population. **Critical Thinking: Apply Information** *In which group shown on the pie chart are the people American citizens from birth?*

Even so, in 2004, President Bush proposed a policy allowing more **guest workers,** or temporary immigrant workers, into the country. The goal, he said, was "to match willing foreign workers with willing employers when no Americans can be found to fill the job." Congress refused to act, and the debate continued over how to address illegal immigration.

✓**Checkpoint**   How do Americans view immigration?

A Society Transformed

Immigration is making the nation's population more diverse, but other changes are also taking place. Americans are living longer and moving to new parts of the country. Women are playing new roles, and families are becoming more diverse.

America Grows Older   In recent decades, birthrates have declined. Thanks to improved medical care, people are living longer. As a result, the percentage of older Americans is growing. In 2006, an estimated 12.5 percent of the population was 65 or older. By 2050, the Census Bureau projects this number will nearly double.

Older Americans have gained political strength because the proportion of older people who vote is higher than younger people. The aging population has raised concern about political issues such as health care and Social Security. Many worry that the number of people collecting benefits from the Social Security system will rise faster than the number paying taxes into it.

People on the Move   Centers of population have shifted. More people and industries have moved from the colder states of the Northeast and Midwest to the warmer climates of the South and Southwest, nicknamed the Sunbelt.

The political effects of this population shift have been <u>evident</u>. As their population grew, Sunbelt states won more representation in Congress and more electoral votes in presidential races.

Vocabulary Builder
<u>evident</u> (EHV ih dehnt) *adj.* clear; obvious

Education and the Economy No matter where Americans live, education remains a path to economic opportunity. College graduates earn more than high school graduates, and high school graduates earn more than non-graduates.

However, access to higher education is a major concern. The cost of a college education has skyrocketed. Between 1986 and 2006, the price of a college education almost tripled. In 2006, average costs at private universities topped $30,000 a year for the first time.

The Changing Family In the 1960s, most families consisted of two parents and two to three children. Today, however, families come in many sizes and varieties.

Over the last 50 years, rising rates of divorce and births out of wedlock have led to more families headed by single mothers. In 2007, over 18 million American children, or nearly one in four, lived with a single parent, most of them single mothers. These families tend to be poorer and to have less access to health insurance, medical care, and other social services than two-parent households.

Other kinds of families are growing in number. Some blend two families when divorced or widowed parents remarry. Same-sex unions have sparked controversy.

✓**Checkpoint** **In what ways has American society changed in the 21st century?**

Americans Face Challenges

Americans face many challenges in the twenty-first century. The struggle to provide equal opportunities for all continues. Other challenges include a crisis in health care and a growing drug problem.

Expanding Opportunities The civil rights movement that began in the 1950s and 1960s produced economic and political gains for African Americans. Employment, college enrollment, and entry into the middle class have grown. By 2007, a record number of African Americans occupied national office. Under President George W. Bush, Colin Powell became the first African American secretary of state and Condoleezza Rice was the first African American national security adviser. She later served as secretary of state.

Despite all those gains, problems persist. By 2008, unemployment for African Americans was almost twice that of whites. More than one in three African American children were living in poverty, compared with only one in ten white children.

Latinos, too, have made economic and political strides in the face of ongoing difficulties. By 2007, the U.S. Congress had 26 Latino members. The number of Latino-owned businesses quadrupled in the years between 1980 and 2000. But many Latinos still struggle. Unemployment rates for Latinos are higher than the national average. In 2006, more than one Latino child in four lived in poverty.

Hillary Clinton became Secretary of State in 2009.

Federal health officials have urged Americans to lead active and healthy lives to prevent chronic illness.

Women have also advanced despite obstacles. Many work in jobs once closed to them, such as firefighters and airline pilots. Growing numbers of women are professionals. More women are also becoming leaders in government. Yet, on average, women still earn less than men and often find that top jobs in management go to men.

American Indians have also met with great hardship. According to the 2000 census, 4 million people identified themselves as American Indian or Native American. About one third live on reservations. On reservations, businesses such as banks, factories, and gambling casinos have strengthened tribal economies. But high rates of unemployment, poverty, and juvenile delinquency still plague Indian communities.

Health Care A crisis in health care confronts Americans. While death rates from many forms of cancer have declined, chronic or recurring illnesses continue to afflict Americans. Heart disease remains the nation's number one killer. Diabetes is on the rise. Obesity, or excess body fat, is a growing problem for both children and adults because it contributes to heart disease, diabetes, and other illnesses. To reduce the threat, health professionals urge all Americans to get proper nutrition and regular exercise.

Meanwhile, rising health-care costs have left tens of millions Americans in debt. In 2005, over one in three personal bankruptcies were linked to unpaid medical bills. In 2008, nearly 46 million Americans had no health insurance at all.

The Changing Face of Politics

The election of 2008 produced dramatic changes in Washington. Even before 2008, however, women and minorities were already reshaping politics.

New Faces Growing opposition to the war in Iraq and outrage over the slow federal response to Hurricane Katrina brought new faces to Washington. For the first time in a dozen years, Democrats won control of both houses of Congress. In 2005, African American senator Barack Obama emerged in the national political scene. In 2007, Democrat Nancy Pelosi became the first female speaker of the House of Representatives. By 2009, more women than ever were serving in Congress (17 in the Senate and 74 in the House).

Women and minorities made political gains outside of Washington. In 2006, Alaskans made conservative Republican Sarah Palin their first female governor. Deval Patrick won the governorship of Massachusetts. He was only the second African American ever elected to lead a state. Beating his rivals for governor of Louisiana in 2007, Piyush "Bobby" Jindal became the first Indian-American to hold statewide office.

The Historic Election of 2008 After only two years in the U.S. Senate, Barack Obama won the nomination of Democrats for the presidency by defeating former First Lady and U.S. Senator Hillary Clinton. He was the first African American to be selected by a major party.

Obama promised hope for the future and a less divisive style of politics. His pioneering use of the Internet captured the attention of younger voters and helped him to raise a record $740 million in campaign contributions.

Republicans nominated longtime Arizona senator John McCain. He wooed the party's conservative base by choosing Governor Palin as his running mate. McCain stressed his experience in foreign policy and supported the war in Iraq. Obama, on the other hand, vowed to "bring the troops home."

Many were attracted to Obama's youth, fresh political face, his message of hope and change, and his pledge to meet the growing financial crisis.

Nearly 150 years after the end of slavery, the nation's first African American President headed to the White House. Election Day brought Obama a stunning victory. His win helped Democrats enlarge their majorities in the House and Senate.

Barack Obama took office as President in 2009. He won the election after carrying a majority of votes from African Americans, whites, Latinos, Asians, women, and young people.

☑ **Checkpoint** Why is health care a challenge for many Americans?

☆ **Looking Back and Ahead** How can Americans best meet the challenges of a new century? For many, the answer to that question lies in the enduring ideals on which the country was founded: faith in democracy, respect for individual rights, tolerance for different viewpoints, and the opportunity to build a better future.

Section 4 | **Check Your Progress**

Progress Monitoring ⏻nline
For: Self-test with instant help
Visit: PHSchool.com
Web Code: mva-9294

Comprehension and Critical Thinking

1. (a) Recall How have immigration patterns changed since the 1960s?
(b) Draw Conclusions Why do you think people are still eager to come to the United States?

2. (a) Explain Why has the American population gotten older?
(b) Evaluate Information Agree or disagree with the following statement and give reasons for your answer: Younger Americans should be concerned about issues affecting older Americans.

⏵ Reading Skill

3. Support Generalizations With Evidence Find evidence in the section text to support this generalization: Opportunities for many Americans have improved since the civil rights era.

Key Terms

Read each sentence below. If the sentence is true, write YES. If the sentence is not true, write NO and explain why.

4. Most Americans were eager to let undocumented workers enter the country.

5. Refugees choose to leave their homes in order to find work.

6. President Bush's plan would allow guest workers to enter the country on a temporary basis.

Writing

7. Revise the following paragraph to correct spelling and punctuation errors: I remeber watching the mickey Mouse club show I mean the ariginal one in the 1950s not the one with Britney Spears Sumtimes the announcer woud say to all of we kids in the tV audience You the leaders of the 21th century. That always sent a chill down my back. And now its really the 21th century!

21st Century Learning

To predict consequences, or results, you must analyze what has happened in the past and compare it to the present situation. The data below show demographic, or population, trends. Demographic data help social scientists, as well as town and city planners, form a more complete picture of a certain population and establish trends over a period of time.

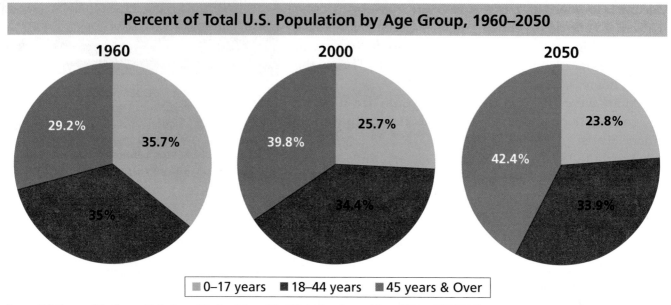

Percent of Total U.S. Population by Age Group, 1960–2050

1960 — 29.2%, 35.7%, 35%

2000 — 39.8%, 25.7%, 34.4%

2050 — 42.4%, 23.8%, 33.9%

■ 0–17 years ■ 18–44 years ■ 45 years & Over

Source: U.S. Bureau of the Census, *Projections of the Population of the U.S., by Age, Sex, and Race: 1995 to 2050* (2002)

Learn the Skill

Use these steps to make predictions.

1 Identify the subject of the data. Read the graph or chart title to understand what is being measured. Always look for the source of the data.

2 Analyze the data. Study the data to see trends or patterns. Remember, information can be presented in different ways: tables, graphs, charts, or as text. Data may appear as percentages or in thousands or millions.

3 Predict possible future developments. Draw conclusions or make generalizations based on the data on the chart.

Practice the Skill

Answer the following questions about the data on this page.

1 Identify the subject of the data. (a) What is the title of the pie graphs? (b) What years are shown on the graphs? (c) What is the source of the data?

2 Analyze the data. (a) What percentage of the population was between 0 and 17 years of age in 1960? (b) Which age group shows the most growth between 1960 and 2050? (c) Which group decreases the most?

3 Predict possible future developments. (a) How do you think changes in the population will affect the construction of schools and houses between 2000 and 2050? (b) What advice would you offer to hospitals and health-care facilities based on this data?

Apply the Skill

See the Review and Assessment at the end of this chapter.

What challenges face the nation in the 21st century?

Section 1
The Threat of Terrorism

- On September 11, 2001, terrorists attacked the World Trade Center and the Pentagon, killing thousands of people.
- In response to the terrorist attacks, the United States took steps to protect the homeland and fight terrorism worldwide.
- Not all Americans agreed when President Bush sent American troops into Iraq.

Section 2
Economy and the Environment

- In response to growing trade deficits, the United States promoted free trade.
- In 2007, the United States plunged into a recession.
- Environmentalists called attention to problems such as air and water pollution.
- In order to reduce dependence on foreign oil, Americans have explored alternative sources of energy.

Section 3
Science and Technology

- The development of computers led to an information revolution.
- Medical science has developed new ways to detect and combat diseases but also faces challenges such as the AIDS epidemic.

Section 4
A Changing Society

- Immigration has increased from regions such as Asia and Latin America.
- The population of the United States has grown more diverse, and the average age of the American people has increased.
- Women and African Americans have made some major economic and political gains. Barack Obama became the first African American President in 2008.

Exploring the Essential Question

Use the online study guide to explore the essential question.

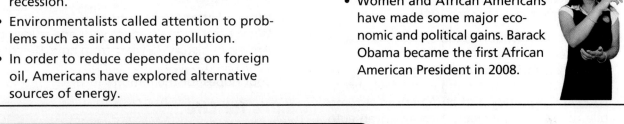

Section 1
How did the war on terrorism affect American actions at home and abroad?

Section 2
How do economic and environmental issues link the U.S. and the world?

Chapter 29 Essential Question
What challenges face the nation in the 21st century?

Section 4
How have new immigration and population patterns increased diversity?

Section 3
How have science and technology transformed modern society?

Key Terms

Fill in the blanks with the correct key terms.

1. A _____ occurs when a nation imports more than it exports.

2. Water, wind, and solar power are _____.

3. Many _____ came to the United States to escape wars in Asia, Africa, or Central America.

4. One goal of _____ is to protect the nation from bombings and other attacks.

5. Immigration laws impose punishments on companies that hire _____.

6. As a result of _____, many American products are manufactured overseas.

Comprehension and Critical Thinking

7. **(a) Summarize** How did Americans respond to the terrorist attacks of September 11, 2001? **(b) Compare** How was this reaction similar to the reaction of Americans to the bombing of Pearl Harbor in December 1941?

8. **(a) Describe** What was the effect of the North American Free Trade Agreement (NAFTA)? **(b) Detect Points of View** Explain how you think each of the following might feel about NAFTA: the president of an American automobile company; a member of an American auto workers union; a Mexican worker.

9. **(a) List** Identify three actions the government took to protect the environment. **(b) Evaluate Information** Why did some business leaders oppose increased environmental regulations? **(c) Make Decisions** Would you be willing to pay higher prices for products in order to protect the environment? Why or why not?

10. **(a) Recall** How did immigration laws change in the 1960s? What were the effects of this change? **(b) Identify Alternatives** What steps has the government taken to control illegal immigration?

11. **(a) Recall** What actions have American schools taken to solve the problems of violence? **(b) Identify Alternatives** Suggest one additional action or approach that might help solve this problem.

Reading Skill

12. **Draw Conclusions and Make Generalizations** Using information from this chapter, draw a conclusion or make a generalization about the challenges that Americans face for the future. Explain the evidence you used to support your conclusion or generalization.

Writing

13. **Write four paragraphs of an eyewitness account of an event or situation described in this chapter.**
    Your account should:
    - identify the eyewitness,
    - include details about the event or situation,
    - describe the eyewitness's thoughts and feelings.

    When you are finished, exchange papers with another student. List one element that you like and one element that you think could be improved. Revise your narrative in response to your partner's list.

14. **Write a Letter to the Future:**
    Write a letter to a student your age studying American history 25 years from now. Describe your feelings about our nation's history and your hopes for the nation's future.

Skills for Life

Make Predictions

Use the graph below to answer the questions.

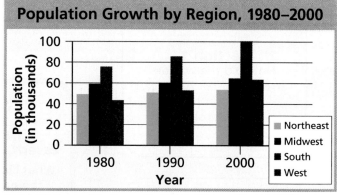

Population Growth by Region, 1980–2000

Source: U.S. Bureau of the Census, *The Statistical History of the U.S.* (1976) and 2000 Census of the U.S. www.census.gov

15. What is being measured by the data?

16. **(a)** In 1980, how many people lived in the Northeast? **(b)** What happened to the population of the South from 1980 to 2000?

17. Make a prediction about how this graph might look in 2020.

Test Yourself

1. **One reason that President George W. Bush gave for sending troops into Iraq in 2003 was that**

   A Iraq had invaded Kuwait.

   B terrorist leader Osama Bin Laden was hiding in Iraq.

   C Iraq was developing weapons of mass destruction.

   D Iraq had imposed an oil embargo against the United States.

2. **Which of the following statements accurately describes one reason the population of the United States has gotten older?**

   A Couples are marrying earlier and having more children.

   B More older people are immigrating to the United States.

   C Science and technology have led to improved medical care.

   D More people have moved to the Sunbelt.

Refer to the quotation below to answer Question 3.

> "It was a spring without voices. On the mornings that had once throbbed with the dawn chorus of robins, catbirds, doves, jays, wrens . . . there was now no sound; only silence lay over the fields and woods and marsh."
>
> —Rachel Carson, *Silent Spring*

3. **The above passage describes a possible effect of**

   A chemical pesticides.

   B solar power.

   C terrorism.

   D cloning.

4. **Companies practice outsourcing in order to**

   A reduce unemployment.

   B increase trade deficits.

   C cut labor costs.

   D create more jobs for women.

Document-Based Questions

Task: Look at Documents 1 and 2, and answer their accompanying questions. Then, use the documents and your knowledge of history to complete this writing assignment:

Write a brief essay comparing the views of technology presented by the two documents. Using specific details, explain which document better represents your view of technology.

Document 1: In testimony before Congress in 1998, journalist Stewart Alsop described great advances that computers have made possible. *What does Alsop mean when he says that computers have "personally empowered" him?*

"I am constantly amazed by what the software industry has delivered to me and to people like me. I am amazed that I can use computers to communicate, produce, calculate, entertain, research, and discover in ways that were not available to people, to my parents and their generation. I have been personally empowered by the technology developed by the software industry and am thankful to have lived in the time when this technology became available."

Document 2: Some people wonder whether computers have really improved our lives. In this cartoon, a "techie" is overwhelmed by his beeping and whirring machines. *How does this cartoon present a negative view of the computer age?*

"ALL THIS TECHNOLOGY... IT'S SO LIBERATING !"

Historian's Apprentice Workshop

How did the United States strive to strengthen democracy at home and to foster democracy abroad?

DIRECTIONS: Analyze the following documents on America from the 1950s to today. Answer the questions that accompany each document or set of documents. You will use your answers to build an answer to the unit question.

HISTORIAN'S CHECKLIST

WHO produced the document?

WHERE was it made?

WHEN was it produced?

WHY was it made and for what audience?

WHAT is its viewpoint?

HOW does it connect to what I've learned?

WHY is the document important?

document 1

Civil Rights Movement

What injustices did Martin Luther King and other activists protest against?

document 2

War on Poverty

"The Economic Opportunity Act of 1964 . . . will give almost half a million underprivileged young Americans the opportunity to develop skills, continue education, and find useful work. . . . It will give dedicated Americans the opportunity to enlist as volunteers in the war against poverty. It will give many workers and farmers the opportunity to break through particular barriers which bar their escape from poverty."

—*President Lyndon B. Johnson, March 16, 1964*

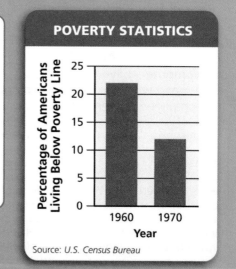

POVERTY STATISTICS

Source: *U.S. Census Bureau*

Does the graph suggest that President Johnson's plan was successful or unsuccessful? Explain.

Women's Rights

"We launched the National Organization for Women in 1966. . . . We have sued, boycotted, picketed, lobbied, demonstrated, marched, and engaged in non-violent civil disobedience. We have won in the courts and in the legislatures; and we have negotiated with the largest corporations in the world, winning unparalleled rights for women. . . . In the past 32 years, women have advanced farther than in any previous generation. Yet still we do not have full equality. . . . We demand an equal share of power in our families and religions, in law, science and technology, the arts and humanities, sports, education, the trades and professions, labor and management, the media, corporations and small businesses as well as government."

—*Declaration of Sentiments of the National Organization for Women, 1998*

What goals does the National Organization of Women seek? What methods have they used?

4

Civil Rights for Mexican Americans

"The United Farm Workers is first and foremost a union. . . . But the UFW has always been something more than a union. . . . The union's survival, its very existence, sent out a signal to all Hispanics that we were fighting for our dignity, that we were challenging and overcoming injustice. . . . The message was clear. If it could happen in the fields, it could happen anywhere: in the cities, in the courts, in the city councils, in the state legislatures. . . . Like the other immigrant groups, the day will come when we win the economic and political rewards, which are in keeping with our numbers in society."

—*Cesar Chavez, 1984*

How did Cesar Chavez's work for the UFW help all Hispanics?

☞ **Go On**

5 No Child Left Behind Act

document

"We're leaving behind the old attitude that it's okay for some students just to be shuffled through the system. That's not okay.... This administration believes, and most people in America believe, that every child can learn. And so we're raising the standards for every public school in America. If you believe every child can learn, then it makes sense to raise the bar, not lower the bar."

—*President George W. Bush, January 2005*

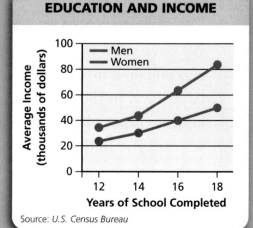

EDUCATION AND INCOME

Average Income (thousands of dollars) vs *Years of School Completed*

— Men
— Women

Source: *U.S. Census Bureau*

Why are educational opportunities important in a democratic society?

---

6 End of the Cold War

document

"In the West today, we see a free world that has achieved a level of prosperity and well-being unprecedented in all human history. In the Communist world, we see failure, technological backwardness, declining standards of health, even want of the most basic kind—too little food. Even today, the Soviet Union still cannot feed itself.... Freedom leads to prosperity. Freedom replaces the ancient hatreds among the nations with comity and peace.... General Secretary Gorbachev, if you seek peace, if you seek prosperity for the Soviet Union and Eastern Europe, if you seek liberalization: Come here to this gate! Mr. Gorbachev, open this gate! Mr. Gorbachev, tear down this wall!"

—*President Ronald Reagan, remarks at Brandenburg Gate, West Berlin, June 12, 1987*

What problems does President Reagan point to as evidence that Soviet Communism failed?

---

7 Humanitarian Aid

document

"The U.S. Agency for International Development (USAID) ... provides economic development and humanitarian assistance around the world.... U.S. foreign assistance has always had the two-fold purpose of furthering America's foreign policy interests in expanding democracy and free markets while improving the lives of the citizens of the developing world."

—*http://www.usaid.gov/about_usaid/*

How and why does the United States distribute aid to people around the world?

Spreading Democracy

" Securing democracy in Iraq is the work of many hands. American and coalition forces are sacrificing for the peace of Iraq and for the security of free nations.... The failure of Iraqi democracy would embolden terrorists around the world, increase dangers to the American people, and extinguish the hopes of millions in the region. "

—*President George W. Bush, November 6, 2003*

How does President Bush's opinion differ from Ambassador Woolcott's? Explain.

" It is unrealistic to expect that, in the Arab world, democracy might start in Iraq, with its history of violence and oppression and with its jarring ethnic and religious components.... Western style democracy in Iraq simply cannot work. "

—*Richard Woolcott, former Australian ambassador to the UN*

ACTIVITY

Work in small groups to develop a graphic advertisement that addresses the unit question:

 How did the United States strive to strengthen democracy at home and to foster democracy abroad?

Review the Historian's Apprentice Workshop documents and other information in this unit. Then create a government publication that focuses on either domestic or foreign policies from the 1960s to today. Start planning by writing a catchy, appealing slogan about how the United States strengthens and expands democracy. Then find photos, cartoons, charts, or other images that illustrate the main idea contained in your slogan. Use a large piece of poster paper to present your slogan and illustrations.

Reference Section

Table of Contents

The Declaration of Independence

The Unanimous Declaration of the Thirteen United States of America

When in the Course of human events, it becomes necessary for one people to dissolve the political bands which have connected them with another, and to assume among the powers of the earth, the separate and equal station to which the Laws of Nature and of Nature's God entitle them, a decent respect to the opinions of mankind requires that they should declare the causes which impel them to the separation.

We hold these truths to be self-evident, that all men are created equal, that they are endowed by their Creator with certain unalienable Rights, that among these are Life, Liberty and the pursuit of Happiness. That to secure these rights, Governments are instituted among Men, deriving their just powers from the consent of the governed. That whenever any Form of Government becomes destructive of these ends, it is the Right of the People to alter or to abolish it, and to institute new Government, laying its foundation on such principles and organizing its powers in such form, as to them shall seem most likely to effect their Safety and Happiness. Prudence, indeed, will dictate that Governments long established should not be changed for light and transient causes; and

The Declaration of Independence has four parts: the Preamble, the Declaration of Natural Rights, the List of Grievances, and the Resolution of Independence. The Preamble states why the Declaration was written. The document will explain to the world the reasons why the colonists feel **impelled**, or forced, to separate from Great Britain.

People set up governments to protect their basic rights. These rights are **unalienable**; they cannot be taken away. The purpose of government is to protect these natural rights. When a government does not protect the rights of the people, the people must change the government or create a new one. The colonists feel that the king's repeated **usurpations**, or unjust uses of power, are a form of **despotism**, or tyranny, that has denied them their basic rights.

The List of Grievances details the colonists' complaints against the British government, and King George III in particular. The colonists have no say in determining the laws that govern them and they feel King George's actions show little or no concern for the well being of the people.

The colonists refuse to **relinquish**, or give up, the right to representation, which they feel is **inestimable**, or priceless.

The king has refused to allow new legislators to be elected. As a result, the colonies have not been able to protect themselves against foreign enemies and **convulsions**, or riots, within the colonies.

The king has tried to stop foreigners from coming to the colonies by refusing to pass naturalization laws. Laws for naturalization of foreigners are laws that set up the process for foreigners to become legal citizens.

The king alone has decided a judge's **tenure**, or term. This grievance later would result in Article 3, Section 1, of the Constitution, which states that federal judges hold office for life.

accordingly all experience hath shown that mankind are more disposed to suffer, while evils are sufferable, than to right themselves by abolishing the forms to which they are accustomed. But when a long train of abuses and usurpations, pursuing invariably the same Object evinces a design to reduce them under absolute Despotism, it is their right, it is their duty, to throw off such Government, and to provide new Guards for their future security. Such has been the patient sufferance of these Colonies; and such is now the necessity which constrains them to alter their former Systems of Government. The history of the present King of Great Britain is a history of repeated injuries and usurpations, all having in direct object the establishment of an absolute Tyranny over these States. To prove this, let Facts be submitted to a candid world.

He has refused his Assent to Laws, the most wholesome and necessary for the public good.

He has forbidden his Governors to pass Laws of immediate and pressing importance, unless suspended in their operation till his Assent should be obtained; and when so suspended, he has utterly neglected to attend to them.

He has refused to pass other Laws for the accommodation of large districts of people, unless those people would relinquish the right of Representation in the Legislature, a right inestimable to them and formidable to tyrants only.

He has called together legislative bodies at places unusual, uncomfortable, and distant from the depository of their public Records, for the sole purpose of fatiguing them into compliance with his measures.

He has dissolved Representative Houses repeatedly, for opposing with manly firmness his invasions on the rights of the people.

He has refused for a long time, after such dissolutions, to cause others to be elected; whereby the Legislative powers, incapable of Annihilation, have returned to the People at large for their exercise; the State remaining in the mean time exposed to all the dangers of invasion from without, and convulsions within.

He has endeavoured to prevent the population of these States; for that purpose obstructing the Laws for Naturalization of Foreigners; refusing to pass others to encourage their migrations hither, and raising the conditions of new Appropriations of Lands.

He has obstructed the Administration of Justice by refusing his Assent to Laws for establishing Judiciary powers.

He has made Judges dependent on his Will alone, for the tenure of their offices, and the amount and payment of their salaries.

He has erected a multitude of New Offices, and sent hither swarms of Officers to harass our people, and eat out their substance.

He has kept among us, in times of peace, Standing Armies without the Consent of our legislatures.

He has affected to render the Military independent of and superior to the Civil power.

He has combined with others to subject us to a jurisdiction foreign to our constitution, and unacknowledged by our laws; giving his Assent to their Acts of pretended Legislation:

For quartering large bodies of armed troops among us:

For protecting them, by a mock Trial, from punishment for any Murders which they should commit on the Inhabitants of these States:

For cutting off our Trade with all parts of the world:

For imposing Taxes on us without our Consent:

For depriving us in many cases, of the benefit of Trial by Jury:

For transporting us beyond Seas to be tried for pretended offences:

For abolishing the free System of English Laws in a neighbouring Province, establishing therein an Arbitrary government, and enlarging its Boundaries so as to render it at once an example and fit instrument for introducing the same absolute rule into these Colonies:

For taking away our Charters, abolishing our most valuable Laws, and altering fundamentally the Forms of our Governments:

For suspending our own Legislatures, and declaring themselves invested with power to legislate for us in all cases whatsoever.

He has abdicated Government here, by declaring us out of his Protection and waging War against us.

He has plundered our seas, ravaged our Coasts, burnt our towns, and destroyed the lives of our people.

He is at this time transporting large Armies of foreign Mercenaries to complete the works of death, desolation, and tyranny, already begun with circumstances of Cruelty and perfidy scarcely paralleled in the most barbarous ages, and totally unworthy the Head of a civilized nation.

He has constrained our fellow Citizens taken Captive on the high Seas to bear Arms against their Country, to become the executioners of their friends and Brethren, or to fall themselves by their Hands.

He has excited domestic insurrections amongst us, and has endeavoured to bring on the inhabitants of our frontiers, the merciless Indian Savages whose known rule of warfare, is an undistinguished destruction of all ages, sexes and conditions.

In every stage of these Oppressions We have Petitioned for Redress in the most humble terms: Our repeated Petitions have been answered only by repeated injury. A Prince, whose character is thus marked by every act which may define a Tyrant, is unfit to be the ruler of a free People.

> Forced by the king, the colonists have been **quartering**, or lodging, troops in their homes. This grievance found its way into the Constitution in the Third Amendment.

> The king has taken away the rights of the people in a nearby province (Canada). The colonists feared he could do the same to the colonies if he so wished.

> The king has hired foreign **mercenaries**, or soldiers, to bring death and destruction to the colonists. The head of a civilized country should never act with the cruelty and **perfidy**, or dishonesty, that the king has.

> The colonists have tried repeatedly to petition the king to **redress**, or correct, these wrongs. Each time, they have been ignored by the king or punished by new laws. Because of the way he treats his subjects, the king is not fit to rule a free people.

The colonists have appealed to the British people. They have asked their fellow British subjects to support them. However, like the king, the British people have ignored the colonists' requests.

The Resolution of Independence boldly asserts that the colonies are now "free and independent states." The colonists have proven the **rectitude**, or justness, of their cause. The Declaration concludes by stating that these new states have the power to wage war, establish alliances, and trade with other countries.

Nor have We been wanting in attentions to our British brethren. We have warned them from time to time of attempts by their legislature to extend an unwarrantable jurisdiction over us. We have reminded them of the circumstances of our emigration and settlement here. We have appealed to their native justice and magnanimity, and we have conjured them by the ties of our common kindred, to disavow these usurpations, which would inevitably interrupt our connections and correspondence. They too have been deaf to the voice of justice and of consanguinity. We must, therefore, acquiesce in the necessity, which denounces our Separation, and hold them, as we hold the rest of mankind, Enemies in War, in Peace Friends.

We, therefore, the Representatives of the United States of America, in General Congress, Assembled, appealing to the Supreme Judge of the world for the rectitude of our intentions, do, in the Name, and by Authority of the good People of these Colonies, solemnly publish and declare, That these United Colonies are, and of Right ought to be Free and Independent States; that they are Absolved from all Allegiance to the British Crown, and that all political connection between them and the State of Great Britain, is and ought to be totally dissolved; and that as Free and Independent States, they have full Power to levy War, conclude Peace, contract Alliances, establish Commerce, and to do all other Acts and Things which Independent States may of right do. And for the support of this Declaration, with a firm reliance on the protection of Divine Providence, we mutually pledge to each other our Lives, our Fortunes and our sacred Honor.

John Hancock, *President*
Charles Thomson, *Secretary*

Georgia
Button Gwinnett
Lyman Hall
George Walton

North Carolina
William Hooper
Joseph Hewes
John Penn

South Carolina
Edward Rutledge
Thomas Heyward, Jr.
Thomas Lynch, Jr.
Arthur Middleton

Maryland
Samuel Chase
William Paca
Thomas Stone
Charles Carroll

Virginia
George Wythe
Richard Henry Lee
Thomas Jefferson
Benjamin Harrison
Thomas Nelson, Jr.
Francis Lightfoot Lee
Carter Braxton

Pennsylvania
Robert Morris
Benjamin Rush
Benjamin Franklin
John Morton
George Clymer
James Smith
George Taylor
James Wilson
George Ross

Delaware
Caesar Rodney
George Read
Thomas McKean

New York
William Floyd
Philip Livingston
Francis Lewis
Lewis Morris

New Jersey
Richard Stockton
John Witherspoon
Francis Hopkinson
John Hart
Abraham Clark

New Hampshire
Josiah Bartlett
William Whipple
Matthew Thornton

Massachusetts
Samuel Adams
John Adams
Robert Treat Paine
Elbridge Gerry

Rhode Island
Stephen Hopkins
William Ellery

Connecticut
Samuel Huntington
William Williams
Oliver Wolcott
Roger Sherman

Signing THE CONSTITUTION

In his *Signing of the Constitution*, painter Howard Chandler Christy captured the moment on September 17, 1787, when delegates signed the historic document that has guided our government for more than 200 years.

1 **Roger Sherman** helped draft the Great Compromise that determined how states would be represented in Congress. After months of bitter debate, the compromise satisfied both large and small states.

2 **George Washington** was voted president of the meeting. His firm leadership held the convention together when it seemed close to breaking up.

3 **Benjamin Franklin,** though frail and ailing, was one of the convention's most respected delegates. At the end, he wrote a masterful speech supporting the Constitution.

4 **James Madison** wrote much of the Constitution and led the fight to get it approved by the states. He is often called the Father of the Constitution.

The Constitution ▶

Critical Thinking: *Interpret Paintings*
How does the artist draw attention to certain Framers?

The Constitution of the United States

A Note on the Text of the Constitution

The complete text of the Constitution, including amendments, appears on the pages that follow. Spelling, capitalization, and punctuation have been modernized, and headings have been added. Portions of the Constitution altered by later amendments or that no longer apply are printed in blue. Commentary appears in the outside column of each page.

> **The Preamble** The Preamble describes the purpose of the government as set up by the Constitution. Americans expect their government to defend justice and liberty and provide peace and safety from foreign enemies.

Preamble

We the people of the United States, in order to form a more perfect union, establish justice, insure domestic tranquillity, provide for the common defense, promote the general welfare, and secure the blessings of liberty to ourselves and our posterity, do ordain and establish this Constitution for the United States of America.

Article I ★ Legislative Branch

Section 1. A Two-House Legislature

> **Section 1** The Constitution gives Congress the power to make laws. Congress is divided into the Senate and the House of Representatives.

All legislative powers herein granted shall be vested in a Congress of the United States, which shall consist of a Senate and House of Representatives.

Section 2. House of Representatives

1. Election of Members The House of Representatives shall be composed of members chosen every second year by the people of the several states, and the electors in each state shall have the qualifications requisite for electors of the most numerous branch of the state legislature.

2. Qualifications No person shall be a representative who shall not have attained to the age of twenty-five years, and been seven years a citizen of the United States, and who shall not, when elected, be an inhabitant of that state in which he shall be chosen.

3. Apportionment Representatives and direct taxes shall be apportioned among the several states which may be included within this Union, according to their respective numbers, which shall be determined by adding to the whole number of free persons, including those bound to service for a term of years and excluding Indians not taxed, three fifths of all other persons. The actual enumeration shall be made within three years after the first meeting of the Congress of the United States, and within every subsequent term of ten years, in such manner as they shall by law direct. The number of representatives shall not exceed one for every thirty thousand, but each state shall have at least one representative; and until such enumeration shall be made, the state of New Hampshire shall be entitled to choose three, Massachusetts eight, Rhode Island and Providence Plantations one, Connecticut five, New York six, New Jersey four, Pennsylvania eight, Delaware one, Maryland six, Virginia ten, North Carolina five, South Carolina five, and Georgia three.

4. Filling Vacancies When vacancies happen in the representation from any state, the executive authority thereof shall issue writs of election to fill such vacancies.

5. Officers; Impeachment The House of Representatives shall choose their Speaker and other officers; and shall have the sole power of impeachment.

Section 3. Senate

1. Composition; Term The Senate of the United States shall be composed of two senators from each state chosen by the legislature thereof, for six years, and each senator shall have one vote.

2. Classification; Filling Vacancies Immediately after they shall be assembled in consequence of the first election, they shall be divided as equally as may be into three classes. The seats of the senators of the first class shall be vacated at the expiration of the second year, of the second class at the expiration of the fourth year, and of the third class at the expiration of the sixth year, so that one third may be chosen every second year; and if vacancies happen by resignation, or otherwise, during the recess of the legislature of any State, the executive thereof may make temporary appointments until the next meeting of the legislature, which shall then fill such vacancies.

Clause 1 Electors refers to voters. Members of the House of Representatives are elected every two years. Any citizen allowed to vote for members of the larger house of the state legislature can also vote for members of the House.

Clause 3 The number of representatives each state elects is based on its population. An enumeration, or census, must be taken every 10 years to determine population. Today, the number of representatives in the House is fixed at 435. Clause 3 contains the Three-Fifths Compromise worked out at the Constitutional Convention. Persons bound to service meant indentured servants. All other persons meant slaves. All free people in a state were counted. However, only three fifths of the slaves were included in the population count. This three-fifths clause became meaningless when slaves were freed by the Thirteenth Amendment.

Clause 4 Executive authority means the governor of a state. If a member of the House leaves office before his or her term ends, the governor must call a special election to fill the seat.

Clause 5 The House elects a Speaker. Only the House has the power to impeach, or accuse, a federal official of wrongdoing.

Clause 2 Every two years, one third of the senators run for reelection. The Seventeenth Amendment changed the way of filling vacancies, or empty seats. Today, the governor of a state must choose a senator to fill a vacancy that occurs between elections.

3. Qualifications No person shall be a senator who shall not have attained to the age of thirty years, and been nine years a citizen of the United States, and who shall not, when elected, be an inhabitant of that state for which he shall be chosen.

4. President of the Senate The Vice President of the United States shall be president of the Senate, but shall have no vote, unless they be equally divided.

5. Other Officers The Senate shall choose their other officers, and also a president pro tempore, in the absence of the Vice President, or when he shall exercise the office of the President of the United States.

6. Impeachment Trials The Senate shall have the sole power to try all impeachments. When sitting for that purpose, they shall be on oath or affirmation. When the President of the United States is tried, the Chief Justice shall preside; and no person shall be convicted without the concurrence of two thirds of the members present.

7. Penalty on Conviction Judgment in cases of impeachment shall not extend further than to removal from office, and disqualification to hold and enjoy any office of honor, trust or profit under the United States: but the party convicted shall nevertheless be liable and subject to indictment, trial, judgment, and punishment, according to law.

Section 4. Elections and Meetings

1. Election of Congress The times, places, and manner of holding elections for senators and representatives, shall be prescribed in each state by the legislature thereof; but the Congress may at any time by law make or alter such regulations, except as to the places of choosing senators.

2. Sessions The Congress shall assemble at least once in every year, and such meeting shall be on the first Monday in December, unless they shall by law appoint a different day.

Section 5. Legislative Proceedings

1. Organization Each house shall be the judge of the elections, returns, and qualifications of its own members, and a majority of each shall constitute a quorum to do business; but a smaller number may adjourn from day to day, and may be authorized to compel the attendance of absent members, in such manner, and under such penalties, as each house may provide.

2. Rules Each house may determine the rules of its proceedings, punish its members for disorderly behavior, and with the concurrence of two thirds, expel a member.

3. Record Each house shall keep a journal of its proceedings, and from time to time publish the same, excepting such parts as may in their judgment require secrecy; and the yeas and nays of the members of either house on any question shall, at the desire of one fifth of those present, be entered on the journal.

Clause 5 Pro tempore means temporary. The Senate chooses one of its members to serve as president pro tempore when the Vice President is absent.

Clause 6 The Senate acts as a jury if the House impeaches a federal official. The Chief Justice of the Supreme Court presides if the President is on trial. Two thirds of all senators present must vote for conviction, or finding the accused guilty. No President has ever been convicted. The House impeached President Andrew Johnson in 1868, but the Senate acquitted him of the charges. In 1998–99, President Bill Clinton became the second President to be impeached and acquitted.

Clause 1 Each state legislature can decide when and how congressional elections take place, but Congress can overrule these decisions. In 1842, Congress required each state to set up congressional districts with one representative elected from each district. In 1872, Congress decided that congressional elections must be held in every state on the same date in even-numbered years.

Clause 1 Each house decides whether a member has the qualifications for office set by the Constitution. A quorum is the smallest number of members who must be present for business to be conducted. Each house can set its own rules about absent members.

Portions of the Constitution altered by later amendments or that no longer apply are printed in blue.

4. Adjournment Neither house, during the session of Congress, shall, without the consent of the other, adjourn for more than three days, nor to any other place than that in which the two houses shall be sitting.

Section 6. Compensation, Immunities, and Disabilities of Members

1. Salaries; Immunities The senators and representatives shall receive a compensation for their services, to be ascertained by law, and paid out of the Treasury of the United States. They shall in all cases, except treason, felony, and breach of the peace, be privileged from arrest during their attendance at the session of their respective houses, and in going to and returning from the same; and for any speech or debate in either house, they shall not be questioned in any other place.

2. Restrictions on Other Employment No senator or representative shall, during the time for which he was elected, be appointed to any civil office under the authority of the United States, which shall have been created, or the emoluments whereof shall have been increased during such time; and no person holding any office under the United States shall be a member of either house during his continuance in office.

Section 7. Law-Making Process

1. Revenue Bills All bills for raising revenue shall originate in the House of Representatives; but the Senate may propose or concur with amendments as on other bills.

2. How a Bill Becomes Law; the Veto Every bill which shall have passed the House of Representatives and the Senate shall, before it become a law, be presented to the President of the United States; if he approve, he shall sign it, but if not, he shall return it, with his objections, to that house in which it shall have originated, who shall enter the objections at large on their journal, and proceed to reconsider it. If after such reconsideration two thirds of that house shall agree to pass the bill, it shall be sent, together with the objections, to the other house, by which it shall likewise be reconsidered, and if approved by two thirds of that house, it shall become a law. But in all such cases the votes of both houses shall be determined by yeas and nays, and the names of the persons voting for and against the bill shall be entered on the journal of each house respectively. If any bill shall not be returned by the President within ten days (Sundays excepted) after it shall have been presented to him, the same shall be a law, in like manner as if he had signed it, unless the Congress by their adjournment prevent its return, in which case it shall not be a law.

3. Resolutions Passed by Congress Every order, resolution, or vote to which the concurrence of the Senate and House of Representatives may be necessary (except on a question of adjournment) shall be presented to the President of the United States; and before the same shall take effect, shall be approved by him, or being disapproved by him, shall be repassed by two thirds of the Senate and House of Representatives, according to the rules and limitations prescribed in the case of a bill.

Clause 4 Neither house can adjourn, or stop meeting, for more than three days unless the other house approves. Both houses must meet in the same city.

Clause 1 Congress decides the salary for its members. While Congress is in session, a member is free from arrest in civil cases and cannot be sued for anything he or she says on the floor of Congress. This allows for freedom of debate. However, a member can be arrested for a criminal offense.

Clause 2 Emolument means salary. A member of Congress cannot hold another federal office during his or her term. A former member of Congress cannot hold an office created while he or she was in Congress. An official in another branch of government cannot serve at the same time in Congress.

Clause 1 Revenue is money raised by the government through taxes. Tax bills must be introduced in the House. The Senate, however, can make changes in tax bills.

Clause 2 A bill, or proposed law, that is passed by a majority of the House and Senate is sent to the President. If the President signs the bill, it becomes law.

A bill can also become law without the President's signature. The President can refuse to act on a bill. If Congress is in session at the time, the bill becomes law 10 days after the President receives it.

The President can veto, or reject, a bill by sending it back to the house where it was introduced. If the President refuses to act on a bill and Congress adjourns within 10 days, then the bill dies. This way of killing a bill without taking action is called the pocket veto.

Congress can override the President's veto if each house of Congress passes the bill again by a two-thirds vote.

Congress's power is expressed directly in the Constitution. Numbered from 1 to 18, these powers are also known as enumerated powers.

Clause 1 Duties are tariffs. Imposts are taxes in general. Excises are taxes on the production or sale of certain goods.

Clause 3 Only Congress has the power to regulate foreign and inter-state commerce. This allows a "common market" with a unified set of laws governing trade. This clause has also been interpreted as giving the federal government authority over Native American nations.

Clause 4 Naturalization is the process whereby a foreigner becomes a citizen. Bankruptcy is the condition in which a person or business cannot pay its debts.

Clause 5 Congressional power to coin money and set its value is one of the keys to creating a stable economy.

Clause 6 Counterfeiting is the making of imitation money. Securities are bonds. Congress can make laws to punish counterfeiters.

Clause 11 Only Congress can declare war. Declarations of war are granted at the request of the President. Letters of marque and reprisal were documents issued by a government allowing merchant ships to arm themselves and attack ships of an enemy nation. They are no longer issued.

Clauses 15, 16 The militia is a body of citizen soldiers. Each state has its own militia, today called the National Guard. Normally, the militia is under the command of a state's governor. However, it can be placed under the command of the President.

Portions of the Constitution altered by later amendments or that no longer apply are printed in blue.

Section 8. Powers of Congress

The Congress shall have power

1. To lay and collect taxes, duties, imposts, and excises, to pay the debts and provide for the common defense and general welfare of the United States; but all duties, imposts and excises shall be uniform throughout the United States;

2. To borrow money on the credit of the United States;

3. To regulate commerce with foreign nations, and among the several states, and with the Indian tribes;

4. To establish an uniform rule of naturalization, and uniform laws on the subject of bankruptcies throughout the United States;

5. To coin money, regulate the value thereof, and of foreign coin, and fix the standard of weights and measures;

6. To provide for the punishment of counterfeiting the securities and current coin of the United States;

7. To establish post offices and post roads;

8. To promote the progress of science and useful arts by securing for limited times to authors and inventors the exclusive right to their respective writings and discoveries;

9. To constitute tribunals inferior to the Supreme Court;

10. To define and punish piracies and felonies committed on the high seas and offenses against the law of nations;

11. To declare war, grant letters of marque and reprisal, and make rules concerning captures on land and water;

12. To raise and support armies, but no appropriation of money to that use shall be for a longer term than two years;

13. To provide and maintain a navy;

14. To make rules for the government and regulation of the land and naval forces;

15. To provide for calling forth the militia to execute the laws of the Union, suppress insurrections, and repel invasions;

16. To provide for organizing, arming, and disciplining the militia, and for governing such part of them as may be employed in the service of the United States, reserving to the states, respectively, the appointment of the officers, and the authority of training the militia according to the discipline prescribed by Congress;

17. To exercise exclusive legislation in all cases whatsoever, over such district (not exceeding ten miles square) as may, by cession of particular states, and the acceptance of Congress, become the seat of the government of the United States, and to exercise like authority over all places purchased by the consent of the legislature of the state in which the same shall be, for the erection of forts, magazines, arsenals, dock-yards, and other needful buildings; —and

18. To make all laws which shall be necessary and proper for carrying into execution the foregoing powers, and all other powers vested by this Constitution in the government of the United States, or in any department or officer thereof.

Section 9. Powers Denied to Congress

1. The Slave Trade The migration or importation of such persons as any of the states now existing shall think proper to admit, shall not be prohibited by the Congress prior to the year one thousand eight hundred and eight, but a tax or duty may be imposed on such importation, not exceeding ten dollars for each person.

2. Writ of Habeas Corpus The privilege of the writ of habeas corpus shall not be suspended, unless when in cases of rebellion or invasion the public safety may require it.

3. Bills of Attainder; Ex Post Facto Laws No bill of attainder or ex post facto law shall be passed.

4. Apportionment of Direct Taxes No capitation, or other direct, tax shall be laid, unless in proportion to the census or enumeration herein before directed to be taken.

5. Taxes on Exports No tax or duty shall be laid on articles exported from any state.

6. Special Preference for Trade No preference shall be given by any regulation of commerce or revenue to the ports of one state over those of another; nor shall vessels bound to, or from, one state, be obliged to enter, clear, or pay duties in another.

7. Spending No money shall be drawn from the Treasury, but in consequence of appropriations made by law; and a regular statement and account of the receipts and expenditures of all public money shall be published from time to time.

8. Titles of Nobility No title of nobility shall be granted by the United States; and no person holding any office of profit or trust under them, shall, without the consent of the Congress, accept of any present, emolument, office, or title, of any kind whatever, from any king, prince or foreign state.

Section 10. Powers Denied to the States

1. Unconditional Prohibitions No state shall enter into any treaty, alliance, or confederation; grant letters of marque and reprisal; coin money; emit bills of credit; make any thing but gold and silver coin a tender in payment of debts; pass any bill of attainder, ex post facto law, or law impairing the obligation of contracts, or grant any title of nobility.

2. Powers Conditionally Denied No state shall, without the consent of the Congress, lay any imposts or duties on imports or exports, except what may be absolutely necessary for executing its inspection laws; and the net produce of all duties and imposts, laid by any state on imports or exports, shall be for the use of the Treasury of the United States; and all such laws shall be subject to the revision and control of the Congress.

Clause 18 Clause 18 gives Congress the power to make laws as needed to carry out the first 17 clauses. It is sometimes called the elastic clause because it lets Congress stretch the meaning of its power.

Clause 1 "Such persons" means slaves. In 1808, as soon as Congress was permitted to abolish the slave trade, it did so.

Clause 2 A writ of habeas corpus is a court order requiring government officials to bring a prisoner to court and explain why he or she is being held. A writ of habeas corpus protects people from unlawful imprisonment. The government cannot suspend this right except in times of rebellion or invasion.

Clause 3 A bill of attainder is a law declaring that a person is guilty of a particular crime. An ex post facto law punishes an act which was not illegal when it was committed. Congress cannot pass a bill of attainder or ex post facto laws.

Clause 7 The federal government cannot spend money unless Congress appropriates it, or passes a law allowing it. The government must publish a statement showing how it spends public funds.

Clause 1 The writers of the Constitution did not want the states to act like separate nations, so they prohibited states from making treaties or coining money. Some powers denied to the federal government are also denied to the states.

Clauses 2, 3 Powers listed here are forbidden to the states, but Congress can pass laws that give these powers to the states.
Clause 2 forbids states from taxing imports and exports without the consent of Congress. States may charge inspection fees on goods entering the states. Any profits go to the United States Treasury.

Clause 3 forbids states from keeping an army or navy without the consent of Congress. States cannot make treaties or declare war unless an enemy invades or is about to invade.

Clauses 2, 3 Some writers of the Constitution were afraid to allow the people to elect the President directly. Therefore, the Constitutional Convention set up the electoral college. Clause 2 directs each state to choose electors, or delegates to the electoral college, to vote for President. A state's electoral vote is equal to the combined number of senators and representatives. Each state may decide how to choose its electors. Members of Congress and federal officeholders may not serve as electors. This much of the original electoral college system is still in effect.

Clause 3 Clause 3 called upon each elector to vote for two candidates. The candidate who received a majority of the electoral votes would become President. The runner-up would become Vice President. If no candidate won a majority, the House would choose the President. The Senate would choose the Vice President.

The election of 1800 showed a problem with the original electoral college system. Thomas Jefferson was the Republican candidate for President, and Aaron Burr was the Republican candidate for Vice President. In the electoral college, the vote ended in a tie. The election was finally decided in the House, where Jefferson was chosen President. The Twelfth Amendment changed the electoral college system so that this could not happen again.

Portions of the Constitution altered by later amendments or that no longer apply are printed in blue.

3. Other Denied Powers No state shall, without the consent of Congress, lay any duty of tonnage, keep troops, or ships of war in time of peace, enter into any agreement or compact with another state, or with a foreign power, or engage in war, unless actually invaded, or in such imminent danger as will not admit of delay.

Article II ★ Executive Branch

Section 1. President and Vice President

1. Chief Executive; Term The executive power shall be vested in a President of the United States of America. He shall hold his office during the term of four years, and, together with the Vice President, chosen for the same term, be elected as follows:

2. Electoral College Each state shall appoint, in such manner as the legislature thereof may direct, a number of electors, equal to the whole number of senators and representatives to which the state may be entitled in the Congress: but no senator or representative, or person holding an office of trust or profit under the United States, shall be appointed an elector.

3. Former Electoral Method The electors shall meet in their respective states, and vote by ballot for two persons, of whom one at least shall not be an inhabitant of the same state with themselves. And they shall make a list of all the persons voted for, and of the number of votes for each; which list they shall sign and certify, and transmit sealed to the seat of the government of the United States, directed to the president of the Senate. The president of the Senate shall, in the presence of the Senate and House of Representatives, open all the certificates, and the votes shall then be counted. The person having the greatest number of votes shall be the President, if such number be a majority of the whole number of Electors appointed; and if there be more than one who have such majority, and have an equal number of votes, then the House of Representatives shall immediately choose by ballot one of them for President; and if no person have a majority, then from the five highest on the list the said House shall in like manner choose the President. But in choosing the President, the votes shall be taken by states, the representation from each state having one vote; a quorum for this purpose shall consist of a member or members from two thirds of the states, and a majority of all the states shall be necessary to a choice. In every case, after the choice of the President, the person having the greatest number of votes of the electors shall be the Vice President. But if there should remain two or more who have equal votes, the Senate shall choose from them by ballot the Vice President.

4. Time of Elections The Congress may determine the time of choosing the electors, and the day on which they shall give their votes; which day shall be the same throughout the United States.

5. Qualifications for President No person except a natural-born citizen, or a citizen of the United States at the time of the adoption of this Constitution, shall be eligible to the office of President; neither shall any person be eligible to that office who shall not have attained to the age of thirty-five years, and been fourteen years a resident within the United States.

6. Presidential Succession In case of the removal of the President from office, or of his death, resignation, or inability to discharge the powers and duties of the said office, the same shall devolve on the Vice President, and the Congress may by law provide for the case of removal, death, resignation or inability, both of the President and Vice President, declaring what officer shall then act as President, and such officer shall act accordingly, until the disability be removed, or a President shall be elected.

Clause 6 The powers of the President pass to the Vice President if the President leaves office or cannot discharge his or her duties. The Twenty-fifth Amendment replaced this clause.

7. Salary The President shall, at stated times, receive for his services, a compensation, which shall neither be increased nor diminished during the period for which he shall have been elected, and he shall not receive within that period any other emolument from the United States, or any of them.

Clause 7 The President is paid a salary. It cannot be raised or lowered during his or her term of office. The President is not allowed to hold any other federal or state position while in office.

8. Oath of Office Before he enter on the execution of his office, he shall take the following oath or affirmation:—"I do solemnly swear (or affirm) that I will faithfully execute the office of the President of the United States, and will to the best of my ability, preserve, protect, and defend the Constitution of the United States."

Section 2. Powers of the President

1. Military Powers The President shall be commander in chief of the army and navy of the United States, and of the militia of the several states, when called into the actual service of the United States; he may require the opinion, in writing, of the principal officer in each of the executive departments, upon any subject relating to the duties of their respective offices, and he shall have power to grant reprieves and pardons for offenses against the United States, except in cases of impeachment.

Clause 1 The President is the head of the armed forces and the state militias when they are called into national service. So the military is under civilian, or nonmilitary, control. The President can get advice from the heads of executive departments. In most cases, the President has the power to grant reprieves and pardons. A reprieve suspends punishment ordered by law. A pardon prevents prosecution for a crime or overrides the judgment of a court.

2. Treaties; Appointments He shall have power, by and with the advice and consent of the Senate, to make treaties, provided two thirds of the senators present concur; and he shall nominate, and by and with the advice and consent of the Senate, shall appoint ambassadors, other public ministers and consuls, judges of the Supreme Court, and all other officers of the United States, whose appointments are not herein otherwise provided for, and which shall be established by law: but the Congress may by law vest the appointment of such inferior officers, as they think proper, in the President alone, in the courts of law, or in the heads of departments.

Clause 2 The President has the power to make treaties with other nations. Under the system of checks and balances, all treaties must be approved by two thirds of the Senate.

The President has the power to appoint ambassadors to foreign countries and to appoint other high officials. The Senate must confirm, or approve, these appointments.

3. Temporary Appointments The President shall have power to fill up all vacancies that may happen during the recess of the Senate, by granting commissions which shall expire at the end of their next session.

Section 3. Duties of the President

He shall from time to time give to the Congress information of the state of the Union, and recommend to their consideration such measures as he shall judge necessary and expedient; he may, on extraordinary occasions, convene both houses, or either of them, and in case of disagreement between them, with respect to the time of adjournment, he may adjourn them to such time as he shall think proper; he shall receive ambassadors and other public ministers; he shall take care that the laws be faithfully executed, and shall commission all the officers of the United States.

Section 4. Impeachment

Section 4
Civil officers include federal judges and members of the Cabinet. High crimes are major crimes. Misdemeanors are lesser crimes. The President, Vice President, and others can be forced out of office if impeached and found guilty of certain crimes.

The President, Vice President and all civil officers of the United States, shall be removed from office on impeachment for, and conviction of, treason, bribery, or other high crimes and misdemeanors.

Article III ★ Judicial Branch

Section 1. Courts, Terms of Office

The judicial power of the United States shall be vested in one Supreme Court, and in such inferior courts as the Congress may from time to time ordain and establish. The judges, both of the Supreme and inferior courts, shall hold their offices during good behavior, and shall, at stated times, receive for their services, a compensation, which shall not be diminished during their continuance in office.

Section 2. Jurisdiction

Clause 1 Jurisdiction refers to the right of a court to hear a case. Federal courts have jurisdiction over cases that involve the Constitution, federal laws, treaties, foreign ambassadors and diplomats, naval and maritime laws, disagreements between states or between citizens from different states, and disputes between a state or citizen and a foreign state or citizen.

1. Scope of Judicial Power The judicial power shall extend to all cases, in law and equity, arising under this Constitution, the laws of the United States, and treaties made, or which shall be made, under their authority;—to all cases affecting ambassadors, other public ministers and consuls;—to all cases of admiralty and maritime jurisdiction;—to controversies to which the United States shall be a party;—to controversies between two or more states; between a state and citizens of another state; —between citizens of different states;—between citizens of the same state claiming lands under grants of different states, and between a state, or the citizens thereof, and foreign states, citizens, or subjects.

Clause 2 Original jurisdiction means the power of a court to hear a case where it first arises. The Supreme Court has original jurisdiction over only a few cases, such as those involving foreign diplomats. More often, the Supreme Court acts as an appellate court. An appellate court does not decide guilt. It decides whether the lower court trial was properly conducted and reviews the lower court's decision.

2. Supreme Court In all cases affecting ambassadors, other public ministers and consuls, and those in which a state shall be a party, the Supreme Court shall have original jurisdiction. In all the other cases before mentioned, the Supreme Court shall have appellate jurisdiction, both as to law and fact, with such exceptions, and under such regulations as the Congress shall make.

Portions of the Constitution altered by later amendments or that no longer apply are printed in blue.

3. Trial by Jury The trial of all crimes, except in cases of impeachment, shall be by jury; and such trial shall be held in the state where the said crimes shall have been committed; but when not committed within any state, the trial shall be at such place or places as the Congress may by law have directed.

Section 3. Treason

1. Definition Treason against the United States shall consist only in levying war against them, or in adhering to their enemies, giving them aid and comfort. No person shall be convicted of treason unless on the testimony of two witnesses to the same overt act, or on confession in open court.

Clause 1 Treason is clearly defined. An <u>overt act</u> is an actual action.

2. Punishment The Congress shall have power to declare the punishment of treason, but no attainder of treason shall work corruption of blood or forfeiture except during the life of the person attained.

Clause 2 Congress has the power to set the punishment for the traitors. Congress may not punish the children of convicted traitors by taking away their civil rights or property.

Article IV ★ Relations Among the States

Section 1. Full Faith and Credit

Full faith and credit shall be given in each state to the public acts, records, and judicial proceedings of every other state. And the Congress may by general laws prescribe the manner in which such acts, records, and proceedings shall be proved, and the effect thereof.

Each state must recognize the official acts and records of any other state. For example, each state must recognize marriage certificates issued by another state. Congress can pass laws to ensure this.

Section 2. Privileges and Immunities of Citizens

1. Privileges The citizens of each state shall be entitled to all privileges and immunities of citizens in the several states.

2. Extradition A person charged in any state with treason, felony, or other crime, who shall flee from justice, and be found in another state, shall on demand of the executive authority of the state from which he fled, be delivered up, to be removed to the state having jurisdiction of the crime.

Clause 2 <u>Extradition</u> means the act of returning a suspected criminal or escaped prisoner to a state where he or she is wanted. State governors must return a suspect to another state. However, the Supreme Court has ruled that a governor cannot be forced to do so if he or she feels that justice will not be done.

3. Fugitive Slaves No person held to service or labor in one state, under the laws thereof, escaping into another, shall in consequence of any law or regulation therein, be discharged from such service or labor, but shall be delivered up on claim of the party to whom such service or labor may be due.

Clause 3 "Persons held to service or labor" refers to slaves or indentured servants. This clause required states to return runaway slaves to their owners. The Thirteenth Amendment replaces this clause.

Section 3. New States and Territories

1. New States New states may be admitted by the Congress into this Union; but no new states shall be formed or erected within the jurisdiction of any other state; nor any state be formed by the junction of two or more states, or parts of states, without the consent of the legislatures of the states concerned as well as of the Congress.

Clause 1 Congress has the power to admit new states to the Union. Existing states cannot be split up or joined together to form new states unless both Congress and the state legislatures approve. New states are equal to all other states.

2. Federal Lands The Congress shall have power to dispose of and make all needful rules and regulations respecting the territory or other property belonging to the United States; and nothing in this Constitution shall be so construed as to prejudice any claims of the United States, or of any particular state.

Section 4. Protection Afforded to States by the Nation

The United States shall guarantee to every state in this Union a republican form of government, and shall protect each of them against invasion; and on application of the legislature, or of the executive (when the legislature cannot be convened) against domestic violence.

Article V ★ Provisions for Amendment

The Congress, whenever two thirds of both houses shall deem it necessary, shall propose amendments to this Constitution, or, on the application of the legislatures of two thirds of the several states, shall call a convention for proposing amendments, which, in either case, shall be valid to all intents and purposes, as part of this Constitution, when ratified by the legislatures of three fourths of the several states, or by conventions in three fourths thereof, as the one or the other mode of ratification may be proposed by the Congress; provided that no amendment which may be made prior to the year one thousand eight hundred and eight shall in any manner affect the first and fourth clauses in the ninth section of the first Article; and that no state, without its consent, shall be deprived of its equal suffrage in the Senate.

Article VI ★ National Debts, Supremacy of National Law, Oath

Section 1. Validity of Debts

All debts contracted and engagements entered into, before the adoption of this Constitution, shall be as valid against the United States under this Constitution, as under the Confederation.

Section 2. Supremacy of National Law

This Constitution, and the laws of the United States which shall be made in pursuance thereof, and all treaties made, or which shall be made, under the authority of the United States, shall be the supreme law of the land; and the judges in every state shall be bound thereby, anything in the constitution or laws of any state to the contrary notwithstanding.

Section 4 In a <u>republic</u>, voters choose representatives to govern them. The federal government must protect the states from foreign invasion and from domestic, or internal, disorder if asked to do so by a state.

The Constitution can be <u>amended</u>, or changed, if necessary. An amendment can be proposed by (1) a two-thirds vote of both houses of Congress or (2) a national convention called by Congress at the request of two thirds of the state legislatures. (This second method has never been used.) An amendment must be <u>ratified</u>, or approved, by (1) three fourths of the state legislatures or (2) special conventions in three fourths of the states. Congress decides which method will be used.

   Congress has proposed each of the 27 amendments to the Constitution by a vote of two-thirds in both houses. The only amendment ratified by constitutional conventions of the states was the Twenty-first Amendment. State legislatures have ratified all other amendments.

Section 2 The "supremacy clause" in this section establishes the Constitution, federal laws, and treaties that the Senate has ratified as the <u>supreme</u>, or highest, law of the land. Thus, they outweigh state laws. A state judge must overturn a state law that conflicts with the Constitution or with a federal law.

Portions of the Constitution altered by later amendments or that no longer apply are printed in blue.

Section 3. Oaths of Office

The senators and representatives before mentioned, and the members of the several state legislatures, and all executive and judicial officers, both of the United States and of the several states, shall be bound by oath or affirmation, to support this Constitution; but no religious test shall ever be required as a qualification to any office or public trust under the United States.

Article VII ★ Ratification of Constitution

The ratification of the conventions of nine states shall be sufficient for the establishment of this Constitution between the states so ratifying the same.

Done in convention by the unanimous consent of the states present the seventeenth day of September, in the year of our Lord one thousand seven hundred and eighty-seven, and of the independence of the United States of America the twelfth. In Witness whereof, we have hereunto subscribed our names.

Article VII During 1787 and 1788, states held special conventions. By October 1788, the required nine states had ratified the United States Constitution.

Attest: William Jackson, SECRETARY
George Washington, PRESIDENT and deputy from Virginia

New Hampshire
John Langdon
Nicholas Gilman

Massachusetts
Nathaniel Gorham
Rufus King

Connecticut
William Samuel Johnson
Roger Sherman

New York
Alexander Hamilton

New Jersey
William Livingston
David Brearley
William Paterson
Jonathan Dayton

Pennsylvania
Benjamin Franklin
Thomas Mifflin
Robert Morris
George Clymer
Thomas Fitzsimons
Jared Ingersoll
James Wilson
Gouverneur Morris

Delaware
George Read
Gunning Bedford, Jr.
John Dickinson
Richard Bassett
Jacob Broom

Maryland
James McHenry
Dan of St. Thomas Jennifer
Daniel Carroll

Virginia
John Blair
James Madison, Jr.

North Carolina
William Blount
Richard Dobbs Spaight
Hugh Williamson

South Carolina
John Rutledge
Charles Cotesworth Pinckney
Charles Pinckney
Pierce Butler

Georgia
William Few
Abraham Baldwin

The Amendments Amendments are changes. The Constitution has been amended 27 times since it was ratified in 1788. The first 10 amendments are referred to as the Bill of Rights. These amendments give rights to the people and states, thus putting limits on the power of government.

First Amendment The First Amendment protects five basic rights: freedom of religion, speech, the press, assembly, and petition. Congress cannot set up an established, or official, church or religion for the nation. It cannot forbid the practice of religion, nor can it force the practice of religion.

Congress may not abridge, or limit, the freedom to speak and write freely. The government may not censor, or review, books and newspapers before they are printed. This amendment also protects the right to assemble, or hold public meetings. Petition means ask. Redress means to correct. Grievances are wrongs. The people have the right to ask the government for wrongs to be corrected.

Second Amendment Americans debate the exact meaning of the Second Amendment. Some believe that it guarantees the right of individuals to own firearms. Others argue that it guarantees the right of each state to maintain a militia. Gun control, or the passage of laws to regulate the ownership and use of firearms, is one of the most controversial issues today.

Third Amendment In colonial times, the British could quarter, or house, soldiers in private homes without permission of the owners. The Third Amendment prevents such abuses.

Portions of the Constitution altered by later amendments or that no longer apply are printed in blue.

Amendments

First Amendment ★

(1791) Freedom of Religion, Speech, Press, Assembly, and Petition

Congress shall make no law respecting an establishment of religion, or prohibiting the free exercise thereof; or abridging the freedom of speech, or of the press; or the right of the people peaceably to assemble, and to petition the government for a redress of grievances.

Second Amendment ★

(1791) Bearing Arms

A well-regulated militia being necessary to the security of a free state, the right of the people to keep and bear arms shall not be infringed.

Third Amendment ★

(1791) Quartering of Troops

No soldier shall, in time of peace, be quartered in any house, without the consent of the owner; nor in time of war, but in a manner to be prescribed by law.

Fourth Amendment ★

(1791) Searches and Seizures

The right of the people to be secure in their persons, houses, papers, and effects, against unreasonable searches and seizures, shall not be violated, and no warrants shall issue, but upon probable cause, supported by oath or affirmation, and particularly describing the place to be searched, and the persons or things to be seized.

Fifth Amendment ★

(1791) Criminal Proceedings; Due Process; Eminent Domain

No person shall be held to answer for a capital, or otherwise infamous, crime, unless on a presentment or indictment of a grand jury, except in cases arising in the land or naval forces, or in the militia, when in actual service in time of war or public danger; nor shall any person be subject for the same offense to be twice put in jeopardy of life and limb; nor shall be compelled, in any criminal case, to be a witness against himself; nor be deprived of life, liberty, or property, without due process of law; nor shall private property be taken for public use, without just compensation.

Sixth Amendment ★

(1791) Criminal Proceedings

In all criminal prosecutions, the accused shall enjoy the right to a speedy and public trial, by an impartial jury of the state and district wherein the crime shall have been committed, which district shall have been previously ascertained by law, and to be informed of the nature and cause of the accusation; to be confronted with the witnesses against him; to have compulsory process for obtaining witnesses in his favor, and to have the assistance of counsel for his defense.

Fourth Amendment This amendment protects Americans from unreasonable searches and seizures. Search and seizure are permitted only if a judge has issued a warrant, or written court order. A warrant is issued only if there is probable cause. This means an officer must show that it is probable, or likely, that the search will produce evidence of a crime.

Fifth Amendment This amendment protects the rights of the accused. Capital crimes are those that can be punished with death. Infamous crimes are those that can be punished with prison or loss of rights. The federal government must obtain an indictment, or formal accusation, from a grand jury to prosecute anyone for such crimes. A grand jury is a panel of between 12 and 23 citizens who decide if the government has enough evidence to justify a trial.

Double jeopardy is forbidden by this amendment. This means that a person cannot be tried twice for the same crime. However, if a court sets aside a conviction because of a legal error, the accused can be tried again. A person on trial cannot be forced to testify, or give evidence, against himself or herself. A person accused of a crime is entitled to due process of law, or a fair hearing or trial.

Finally, the government cannot seize private property for public use without paying the owner a fair price for it.

Sixth Amendment In criminal cases, the jury must be impartial, or not favor either side. The accused is guaranteed the right to a trial by jury. The trial must be speedy. If the government purposely postpones the trial so that it becomes hard for the person to get a fair hearing, the charge may be dismissed. The accused must be told the charges and be allowed to question all witnesses. Witnesses who can help the accused can be ordered to appear in court. The accused must be allowed a lawyer.

Seventh Amendment ★

(1791) Civil Trials

In suits at common law, where the value in controversy shall exceed twenty dollars, the right of trial by jury shall be preserved, and no fact tried by a jury shall be otherwise re-examined in any court of the United States, than according to the rules of the common law.

Eighth Amendment ★

(1791) Punishment for Crimes

Excessive bail shall not be required, nor excessive fines imposed, nor cruel and unusual punishments inflicted.

Ninth Amendment ★

(1791) Unenumerated Rights

The enumeration in the Constitution, of certain rights, shall not be construed to deny or disparage others retained by the people.

Tenth Amendment ★

(1791) Powers Reserved to the States

The powers not delegated to the United States by the Constitution, nor prohibited by it to the states, are reserved to the states respectively, or to the people.

Eleventh Amendment ★

(1795) Suits Against States

The judicial power of the United States shall not be construed to extend to any suit in law or equity, commenced or prosecuted against one of the United States by citizens of another state, or by citizens or subjects of any foreign state.

Seventh Amendment Common law refers to rules of law established by judges in past cases. This amendment guarantees the right to a jury trial in lawsuits where the sum of money at stake is more than $20. An appeals court can set aside a verdict only if legal errors made the trial unfair.

Eighth Amendment Bail is money that the accused leaves with the court as a pledge to appear for trial. If the accused does not appear, the court keeps the money. This amendment prevents the court from imposing bail or fines that are excessive, or too high. The amendment also forbids cruel and unusual punishments, such as physical torture.

Ninth Amendment The rights of the people are not limited to those listed in the Bill of Rights. In the Ninth Amendment, the government is prevented from claiming these are the only rights people have.

Tenth Amendment Powers not given to the federal government belong to the states. Powers reserved to the states are not listed in the Constitution.

Eleventh Amendment A private citizen from one state cannot sue the government of another state in federal court. However, a citizen can sue a state government in a state court.

Portions of the Constitution altered by later amendments or that no longer apply are printed in blue.

Twelfth Amendment ★

(1804) Election of President and Vice President

The electors shall meet in their respective states, and vote by ballot for President and Vice President, one of whom, at least, shall not be an inhabitant of the same state with themselves; they shall name in their ballots the person voted for as President, and in distinct ballots the person voted for as Vice President, and they shall make distinct lists of all persons voted for as President, and of all persons voted for as Vice President, and of the number of votes for each, which lists they shall sign and certify, and transmit sealed to the seat of the government of the United States, directed to the president of the Senate; the president of the Senate shall, in the presence of the Senate and the House of Representatives, open all the certificates and the votes shall then be counted;—the person having the greatest number of votes for President shall be the President, if such number be a majority of the whole number of electors appointed; and if no person have such a majority, then from the persons having the highest numbers not exceeding three on the list of those voted for as President, the House of Representatives shall choose immediately, by ballot, the President.

But in choosing the President, the votes shall be taken by states, the representation from each state having one vote; a quorum for this purpose shall consist of a member or members from two thirds of the states, and a majority of all states shall be necessary to a choice. And if the House of Representatives shall not choose a President whenever the right of choice shall devolve upon them, before the fourth day of March next following, then the Vice President, shall act as President, as in the case of death or other constitutional disability of the President—The person having the greatest number of votes as Vice President, shall be the Vice President, if such a number be a majority of the whole number of electors appointed, and if no person have a majority, then from the two highest numbers on the list, the Senate shall choose the Vice President; a quorum for the purpose shall consist of two thirds of the whole number of senators, and a majority of the whole number shall be necessary to a choice. But no person constitutionally ineligible to the office of President shall be eligible to that of Vice President of the United States.

Thirteenth Amendment ★

(1865) Slavery and Involuntary Servitude

Section 1. Outlawing Slavery Neither slavery nor involuntary servitude, except as a punishment for crime whereof the party shall have been duly convicted, shall exist within the United States, or any place subject to their jurisdiction.

Section 2. Enforcement Congress shall have power to enforce this article by appropriate legislation.

Twelfth Amendment This amendment changed the way the electoral college voted as outlined in Article II, Clause 3.

This amendment provides that each elector choose one candidate for President and one candidate for Vice President. If no candidate for President receives a majority of electoral votes, the House of Representatives chooses the President. If no candidate for Vice President receives a majority, the Senate elects the Vice President. The Vice President must be a person who is eligible to be President.

This system is still in use today. However, it is possible for a candidate to win the popular vote and lose in the electoral college. This happened in 1888 and in 2000.

Thirteenth Amendment The Emancipation Proclamation (1863) freed slaves only in areas controlled by the Confederacy. This amendment freed all slaves. It also forbids involuntary servitude, or labor done against one's will. However, it does not prevent prison wardens from making prisoners work. Congress can pass laws to carry out this amendment.

Fourteenth Amendment ★

(1868) Rights of Citizens

Section 1. Citizenship All persons born or naturalized in the United States, and subject to the jurisdiction thereof, are citizens of the United States and of the state wherein they reside. No state shall make or enforce any law which shall abridge the privileges or immunities of citizens of the United States; nor shall any state deprive any person of life, liberty, or property, without due process of law; nor deny to any person within its jurisdiction the equal protection of the laws.

Section 2. Apportionment of Representatives Representatives shall be apportioned among the several states according to their respective numbers, counting the whole number of persons in each state, excluding Indians not taxed. But when the right to vote at any election for the choice of electors for President and Vice President of the United States, representatives in Congress, the executive and judicial officers of a state, or the members of the legislature thereof, is denied to any of the male inhabitants of such state, being twenty-one years of age, and citizens of the United States, or in any way abridged, except for participation in rebellion, or other crime, the basis of representation therein shall be reduced in the proportion which the number of such male citizens shall bear to the whole number of male citizens twenty-one years of age in such state.

Section 3. Former Confederate Officials No person shall be a senator or representative in Congress, or elector of President and Vice President, or hold any office, civil or military, under the United States, or under any state, who having previously taken an oath, as a member of Congress, or as an officer of the United States, or as a member of any state legislature, or as an executive or judicial officer of any state, to support the Constitution of the United States, shall have engaged in insurrection or rebellion against the same, or given aid or comfort to the enemies thereof. But Congress may, by a vote of two thirds of each house, remove such disability.

Section 4. Public Debt The validity of the public debt of the United States, authorized by law, including debts incurred for payment of pensions and bounties for services in suppressing insurrection or rebellion, shall not be questioned. But neither the United States nor any state shall assume or pay any debt or obligation incurred in aid of insurrection or rebellion against the United States, or any claim for the loss of emancipation of any slave; but all such debts, obligations and claims shall be held illegal and void.

Section 5. Enforcement The Congress shall have power to enforce, by appropriate legislation, the provisions of this article.

Fifteenth Amendment ★

(1870) Right to Vote—Race, Color, Servitude

Section 1. Extending the Right to Vote The right of citizens of the United States to vote shall not be denied or abridged by the United States or by any state on account of race, color, or previous condition of servitude.

Section 2. Enforcement The Congress shall have power to enforce this article by appropriate legislation.

Sixteenth Amendment ★

(1913) Income Tax

The Congress shall have power to lay and collect taxes on incomes, from whatever source derived, without apportionment among the several states, and without regard to any census or enumeration.

Seventeenth Amendment ★

(1913) Popular Election of Senators

Section 1. Method of Election The Senate of the United States shall be composed of two senators from each state, elected by the people thereof, for six years; and each senator shall have one vote. The electors in each state shall have the qualifications requisite for electors of the most numerous branch of the state legislatures.

Section 2. Vacancies When vacancies happen in the representation of any state in the Senate, the executive authority of such state shall issue writs of election to fill such vacancies: provided, that the legislature of any state may empower the executive thereof to make temporary appointments until the people fill the vacancies by election as the legislature may direct.

Section 3. Those Elected Under Previous Procedure This amendment shall not be so construed as to affect the election or term of any senator chosen before it becomes valid as part of the Constitution.

Fifteenth Amendment, Section 1
Previous condition of servitude refers to slavery. This amendment gave African Americans, both former slaves and free African Americans, the right to vote. In the late 1800s, southern states used grandfather clauses, literacy tests, and poll taxes to keep African Americans from voting.

Fifteenth Amendment, Section 2
Congress can pass laws to carry out this amendment. The Twenty-fourth Amendment barred the use of poll taxes in national elections. The Voting Rights Act of 1965 gave federal officials the power to register voters where there was voting discrimination.

Sixteenth Amendment Congress has the power to collect taxes on people's income. An income tax can be collected without regard to a state's population. This amendment changed Article 1, Section 9, Clause 4.

Seventeenth Amendment, Section 1 This amendment replaced Article 1, Section 2, Clause 1. Before it was adopted, state legislatures chose senators. This amendment provides that senators are directly elected by the people of each state.

Eighteenth Amendment ★

(1919) Prohibition of Alcoholic Beverages

Section 1. Ban on Alcohol After one year from the ratification of this article, the manufacture, sale, or transportation of intoxicating liquors within, the importation thereof into, or the exportation thereof from the United States and all territory subject to the jurisdiction thereof for beverage purposes is hereby prohibited.

Section 2. Enforcement The Congress and the several states shall have concurrent power to enforce this article by appropriate legislation.

Section 3. Method of Ratification This article shall be inoperative unless it shall have been ratified as an amendment to the Constitution by the legislatures of the several states, as provided in the Constitution, within seven years from the date of the submission hereof to the states by Congress.

> **Eighteenth Amendment** This amendment, known as Prohibition, banned the making, selling, or transporting of alcoholic beverages in the United States. Later, the Twenty-first Amendment <u>repealed</u>, or canceled, this amendment.

Nineteenth Amendment ★

(1920) Women's Suffrage

Section 1. The Right to Vote The right of citizens of the United States to vote shall not be denied or abridged by the United States or by any state on account of sex.

Section 2. Enforcement Congress shall have power to enforce this article by appropriate legislation.

> **Nineteenth Amendment** Neither the federal government nor state governments can deny the right to vote on account of sex. Thus, women won <u>suffrage</u>, or the right to vote. Before 1920, some states had allowed women to vote in state elections.

Twentieth Amendment ★

(1933) Presidential Terms; Sessions of Congress; Death or Disqualification of President-Elect

Section 1. Beginning of Terms The terms of the President and Vice President shall end at noon on the 20th day of January, and the terms of senators and representatives at noon on the 3rd day of January, of the years in which such terms would have ended if this article had not been ratified; and the terms of their successors shall then begin.

Section 2. Congressional Sessions The Congress shall assemble at least once in every year, and such meeting shall begin at noon on the 3rd day of January, unless they shall by law appoint a different day.

> **Twentieth Amendment, Section 1.** The date for the inauguration of the President was changed to January 20th, and the date for Congress to begin its term changed to January 3rd. Prior to this amendment, the beginning of term date was set in March. The outgoing officials with little or no influence on matters were not effective in office. Being so inactive, they were called "lame ducks."

> Portions of the Constitution altered by later amendments or that no longer apply are printed in blue.

Section 3. Presidential Succession If, at the time fixed for the beginning of the term of the President, the President-elect shall have died, the Vice President-elect shall become President. If a President shall not have been chosen before the time fixed for the beginning of his term, or if the President-elect shall have failed to qualify, the Vice President-elect shall act as President until a President shall have qualified; and the Congress may by law provide for the case wherein neither a President-elect nor a Vice President-elect shall have qualified, declaring who shall then act as President, or the manner in which one who is to act shall be selected, and such person shall act accordingly until a President or Vice President shall have qualified.

Section 4. Elections Decided by Congress The Congress may by law provide for the case of the death of any persons from whom the House of Representatives may choose a President whenever the right of choice shall have devolved upon them, and for the case of the death of any of the persons from whom the Senate may choose a Vice President whenever the right of choice shall have devolved upon them.

Section 5. Date of Implementation Sections 1 and 2 shall take effect on the 15th day of October following the ratification of this article.

Section 6. Ratification Period This article shall be inoperative unless it shall have been ratified as an amendment to the Constitution by the legislatures of three fourths of the several states within seven years from the date of its submission.

> **Twentieth Amendment, Section 3.** If the President-elect dies before taking office, the Vice President-elect becomes President. If no President has been chosen by January 20 or if the elected candidate fails to qualify for office, the Vice President-elect acts as President, but only until a qualified President is chosen.
>
> Finally, Congress has the power to choose a person to act as President if neither the President-elect nor the Vice President-elect is qualified to take office.

Twenty-first Amendment ★

(1933) Repeal of Prohibition

Section 1. Repeal The eighteenth article of amendment to the Constitution of the United States is hereby repealed.

Section 2. State Laws The transportation or importation into any state, territory, or possession of the United States for delivery or use therein of intoxicating liquors, in violation of the laws thereof, is hereby prohibited.

Section 3. Ratification Period This article shall be inoperative unless it shall have been ratified as an amendment to the Constitution by conventions in the several states, as provided in the Constitution, within seven years from the date of the submission hereof to the states by the Congress.

> **Twenty-first Amendment, Section 1** The Eighteenth Amendment is repealed, making it legal to make and sell alcoholic beverages. Prohibition ended December 5, 1933.

Twenty-second Amendment ★

(1951) Presidential Tenure

Section 1. Two-Term Limit No person shall be elected to the office of the President more than twice, and no person who has held the office of President, or acted as President, for more than two years of a term to which some other person was elected President shall be elected to the office of President more than once. But this article shall not apply to any person holding the office of President when this article was proposed by the Congress, and shall not prevent any person who may be holding the office of President, or acting as President, during the term within which this article becomes operative from holding the office of President or acting as President during the remainder of such term.

Section 2. Ratification Period This article shall be inoperative unless it shall have been ratified as an amendment to the Constitution by the legislatures of three fourths of the several states within seven years from the date of its submission to the state by the Congress.

Twenty-third Amendment ★

(1961) Presidential Electors for the District of Columbia

Section 1. Determining the Number of Electors The district constituting the seat of government of the United States shall appoint in such manner as the Congress may direct:

A number of electors of President and Vice President equal to the whole number of senators and representatives in Congress to which the district would be entitled if it were a state, but in no event more than the least populous state; they shall be in addition to those appointed by the states, but they shall be considered, for the purposes of the election of President and Vice President, to be electors appointed by a state; and they shall meet in the district and perform such duties as provided by the twelfth article of amendment.

Section 2. Enforcement The Congress shall have power to enforce this article by appropriate legislation.

Twenty-fourth Amendment ★

(1964) Right to Vote in Federal Elections—Tax Payment

Section 1. Poll Tax Banned The right of citizens of the United States to vote in any primary or other election for President or Vice President, for electors for President or Vice President, or for senator or representative in Congress, shall not be denied or abridged by the United States or any state by reason of failure to pay any poll tax or other tax.

Section 2. Enforcement The Congress shall have the power to enforce this article by appropriate legislation.

Twenty-second Amendment, Section 1
This amendment provides that no President may serve more than two terms. A President who has already served more than half of someone else's term can serve only one more full term. Before Franklin Roosevelt became President, no President served more than two terms in office. Roosevelt broke with this custom and was elected to four terms. The amendment, however, did not apply to Harry Truman, who became President after Franklin Roosevelt's death in 1945.

Twenty-third Amendment, Section 1
This amendment gives the residents of Washington, D.C., the right to vote in presidential elections. Until this amendment was adopted, people living in Washington, D.C., could not vote for President because the Constitution had made no provision for choosing electors from the nation's capital. Washington, D.C., now has three electoral votes.

Twenty-fourth Amendment, Section 1
A poll tax is a tax on voters. This amendment bans poll taxes in national elections. Some states used poll taxes to keep African Americans from voting. In 1966, the Supreme Court struck down poll taxes in state elections, also.

Portions of the Constitution altered by later amendments or that no longer apply are printed in blue.

Twenty-fifth Amendment ★

(1967) Presidential Succession, Vice Presidential Vacancy, Presidential Inability

Section 1. President's Death or Resignation In case of the removal of the President from office or of his death or resignation, the Vice President shall become President.

Section 2. Vacancies in Vice Presidency Whenever there is a vacancy in the office of the Vice President, the President shall nominate a Vice President who shall take office upon confirmation by a majority vote of both houses of Congress.

Section 3. Disability of the President Whenever the President transmits to the President pro tempore of the Senate and the Speaker of the House of Representatives his written declaration that he is unable to discharge the powers and duties of his office, and until he transmits to them a written declaration to the contrary, such powers and duties shall be discharged by the Vice President as acting President.

Section 4. Vice President as Acting President Whenever the Vice President and a majority of either the principal officers of the executive departments or of such other body as Congress may by law provide, transmit to the President pro tempore of the Senate and the Speaker of the House of Representatives their written declaration that the President is unable to discharge the powers and duties of his office, the Vice President shall immediately assume the powers and duties of the office as acting President.

Thereafter, when the President transmits to the President pro tempore of the Senate and the Speaker of the House of Representatives his written declaration that no inability exists, he shall resume the powers and duties of his office unless the Vice President and a majority of either the principal officers of the executive department or of such other body as Congress may by law provide, transmit within four days to the President pro tempore of the Senate and the Speaker of the House of Representatives their written declaration that the President is unable to discharge the powers and duties of his office. Thereupon Congress shall decide the issue, assembling within forty-eight hours for that purpose if not in session. If the Congress, within twenty-one days after receipt of the latter written declaration, or, if Congress is not in session, within twenty-one days after Congress is required to assemble, determines by two-thirds vote of both Houses that the President is unable to discharge the powers and duties of his office, the Vice President shall continue to discharge the same as acting President; otherwise, the President shall resume the powers and duties of his office.

Twenty-fifth Amendment, Section 1
If the President dies or resigns, the Vice President becomes President. This section clarifies Article 2, Section 1, Clause 6.

Twenty-fifth Amendment, Section 3
If the President declares in writing that he or she is unable to perform the duties of office, the Vice President serves as acting President until the President recovers.

Twenty-fifth Amendment, Section 4
Two Presidents, Woodrow Wilson and Dwight Eisenhower, fell gravely ill while in office. The Constitution contained no provision for this kind of emergency. Section 3 provided that the President can inform Congress he or she is too sick to perform the duties of office. However, if the President is unconscious or refuses to admit to a disabling illness, Section 4 provides that the Vice President and Cabinet may declare the President disabled. The Vice President becomes the acting President until the President can return to the duties of office. In case of a disagreement between the President and the Vice President and Cabinet over the President's ability to perform the duties of office, Congress must decide the issue. A two-thirds vote of both houses is needed to find the President is disabled or unable to fulfill the duties of office.

Twenty-sixth Amendment ★

(1971) Right to Vote—Age

Section 1. Lowering the Voting Age The right of citizens of the United States, who are eighteen years of age or older, to vote shall not be denied or abridged by the United States or by any state on account of age.

Section 2. Enforcement The Congress shall have the power to enforce this article by appropriate legislation.

Twenty-seventh Amendment ★

(1992) Congressional Pay

No law, varying the compensation for the services of the senators and representatives, shall take effect until an election of representatives shall have intervened.

Twenty-sixth Amendment, Section 1
In 1970, Congress passed a law allowing 18-year-olds to vote. However, the Supreme Court decided that Congress could not set a minimum age for state elections.

Twenty-seventh Amendment
If members of Congress vote themselves a pay increase, it cannot go into effect until after the next congressional election. This amendment was proposed in 1789. In 1992, Michigan became the thirty-eighth state to ratify it.

Portions of the Constitution altered by later amendments or that no longer apply are printed in blue.

Independence Hall room where the Constitution was signed

Presidents of the United States

1 George Washington (1732–1799)

Years in office:
1789–1797
Party:
none
Elected from:
Virginia
Vice President:
John Adams

2 John Adams (1735–1826)

Years in office:
1797–1801
Party:
Federalist
Elected from:
Massachusetts
Vice President:
Thomas
   Jefferson

3 Thomas Jefferson (1743–1826)

Years in office:
1801–1809
Party:
Democratic
   Republican
Elected from:
Virginia
Vice President:
1) Aaron Burr,
2) George Clinton

4 James Madison (1751–1836)

Years in office:
1809–1817
Party:
Democratic
   Republican
Elected from:
Virginia
Vice President:
1) George Clinton,
2) Elbridge Gerry

5 James Monroe (1758–1831)

Years in office:
1817–1825
Party:
Democratic
   Republican
Elected from:
Virginia
Vice President:
Daniel Tompkins

6 John Quincy Adams (1767–1848)

Years in office:
1825–1829
Party:
National
   Republican
Elected from:
Massachusetts
Vice President:
John Calhoun

7 Andrew Jackson (1767–1845)

Years in office:
1829–1837
Party:
Democratic
Elected from:
Tennessee
Vice President:
1) John Calhoun,
2) Martin Van
   Buren

8 Martin Van Buren (1782–1862)

Years in office:
1837–1841
Party:
Democratic
Elected from:
New York
Vice President:
Richard Johnson

9 William Henry Harrison* (1773–1841)

Years in office:
1841
Party:
Whig
Elected from:
Ohio
Vice President:
John Tyler

10 John Tyler (1790–1862)

Years in office:
1841–1845
Party:
Whig
Elected from:
Virginia
Vice President:
none

11 James K. Polk (1795–1849)

Years in office:
1845–1849
Party:
Democratic
Elected from:
Tennessee
Vice President:
George Dallas

12 Zachary Taylor* (1784–1850)

Years in office:
1849–1850
Party:
Whig
Elected from:
Louisiana
Vice President:
Millard Fillmore

*Died in office

13 **Millard Fillmore** (1800–1874)

Years in office:
1850–1853
Party:
Whig
Elected from:
New York
Vice President:
none

14 **Franklin Pierce** (1804–1869)

Years in office:
1853–1857
Party:
Democratic
Elected from:
New Hampshire
Vice President:
William King

15 **James Buchanan** (1791–1868)

Years in office:
1857–1861
Party:
Democratic
Elected from:
Pennsylvania
Vice President:
John Breckinridge

16 **Abraham Lincoln**** (1809–1865)

Years in office:
1861–1865
Party:
Republican
Elected from:
Illinois
Vice President:
1) Hannibal
   Hamlin,
2) Andrew
   Johnson

17 **Andrew Johnson** (1808–1875)

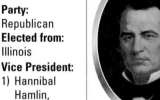

Years in office:
1865–1869
Party:
Republican
Elected from:
Tennessee
Vice President:
none

18 **Ulysses S. Grant** (1822–1885)

Years in office:
1869–1877
Party:
Republican
Elected from:
Illinois
Vice President:
1) Schuyler
   Colfax,
2) Henry Wilson

19 **Rutherford B. Hayes** (1822–1893)

Years in office:
1877–1881
Party:
Republican
Elected from:
Ohio
Vice President:
William Wheeler

20 **James A. Garfield**** (1831–1881)

Years in office:
1881
Party:
Republican
Elected from:
Ohio
Vice President:
Chester A. Arthur

21 **Chester A. Arthur** (1829–1886)

Years in office:
1881–1885
Party:
Republican
Elected from:
New York
Vice President:
none

22 **Grover Cleveland** (1837–1908)

Years in office:
1885–1889
Party:
Democratic
Elected from:
New York
Vice President:
Thomas
   Hendricks

23 **Benjamin Harrison** (1833–1901)

Years in office:
1889–1893
Party:
Republican
Elected from:
Indiana
Vice President:
Levi Morton

24 **Grover Cleveland** (1837–1908)

Years in office:
1893–1897
Party:
Democratic
Elected from:
New York
Vice President:
Adlai Stevenson

**Assassinated

25 **William McKinley**** (1843–1901)

Years in office:
1897–1901
Party:
Republican
Elected from:
Ohio
Vice President:
1) Garret Hobart,
2) Theodore
   Roosevelt

26 **Theodore Roosevelt** (1858–1919)

Years in office:
1901–1909
Party:
Republican
Elected from:
New York
Vice President:
Charles Fairbanks

27 **William Howard Taft** (1857–1930)

Years in office:
1909–1913
Party:
Republican
Elected from:
Ohio
Vice President:
James Sherman

28 **Woodrow Wilson** (1856–1924)

Years in office:
1913–1921
Party:
Democratic
Elected from:
New Jersey
Vice President:
Thomas Marshall

29 **Warren G. Harding*** (1865–1923)

Years in office:
1921–1923
Party:
Republican
Elected from:
Ohio
Vice President:
Calvin Coolidge

30 **Calvin Coolidge** (1872–1933)

Years in office:
1923–1929
Party:
Republican
Elected from:
Massachusetts
Vice President:
Charles Dawes

31 **Herbert C. Hoover** (1874–1964)

Years in office:
1929–1933
Party:
Republican
Elected from:
California
Vice President:
Charles Curtis

32 **Franklin D. Roosevelt*** (1882–1945)

Years in office:
1933–1945
Party:
Democratic
Elected from:
New York
Vice President:
1) John Garner,
2) Henry Wallace,
3) Harry S Truman

33 **Harry S Truman** (1884–1972)

Years in office:
1945–1953
Party:
Democratic
Elected from:
Missouri
Vice President:
Alben Barkley

34 **Dwight D. Eisenhower** (1890–1969)

Years in office:
1953–1961
Party:
Republican
Elected from:
New York
Vice President:
Richard M. Nixon

35 **John F. Kennedy**** (1917–1963)

Years in office:
1961–1963
Party:
Democratic
Elected from:
Massachusetts
Vice President:
Lyndon B.
Johnson

36 **Lyndon B. Johnson** (1908–1973)

Years in office:
1963–1969
Party:
Democratic
Elected from:
Texas
Vice President:
Hubert Humphrey

*Died in office
**Assassinated

37 Richard M. Nixon*** (1913–1994)

Years in office:
1969–1974
Party:
Republican
Elected from:
New York
Vice President:
1) Spiro Agnew,
2) Gerald R. Ford

38 Gerald R. Ford (1913–2006)

Years in office:
1974–1977
Party:
Republican
Appointed from:
Michigan
Vice President:
Nelson
    Rockefeller

39 Jimmy Carter (b. 1924)

Years in office:
1977–1981
Party:
Democratic
Elected from:
Georgia
Vice President:
Walter Mondale

40 Ronald W. Reagan (b. 1911–2004)

Years in office:
1981–1989
Party:
Republican
Elected from:
California
Vice President:
George H.W.
    Bush

41 George H.W. Bush (b. 1924)

Years in office:
1989–1993
Party:
Republican
Elected from:
Texas
Vice President:
J. Danforth
    Quayle

42 William J. Clinton (b. 1946)

Years in office:
1993–2001
Party:
Democratic
Elected from:
Arkansas
Vice President:
Albert Gore, Jr.

43 George W. Bush (b. 1946)

Years in office:
2001–2009
Party:
Republican
Elected from:
Texas
Vice President:
Richard Cheney

44 Barack H. Obama (b. 1961)

Years in office:
2009–
Party:
Democratic
Elected from:
Illinois
Vice President:
Joseph R. Biden

***Resigned

The Fifty States

State	Date of Entry to Union (Order of Entry)	Land Area in Square Miles	Population (In Thousands)	Number of Representatives in House*	Capital	Largest City
Alabama	1819 (22)	50,750	4,447	7	Montgomery	Birmingham
Alaska	1959 (49)	570,374	627	1	Juneau	Anchorage
Arizona	1912 (48)	113,642	5,131	8	Phoenix	Phoenix
Arkansas	1836 (25)	52,075	2,673	4	Little Rock	Little Rock
California	1850 (31)	155,973	33,872	53	Sacramento	Los Angeles
Colorado	1876 (38)	103,730	4,301	7	Denver	Denver
Connecticut	1788 (5)	4,845	3,406	5	Hartford	Bridgeport
Delaware	1787 (1)	1,955	784	1	Dover	Wilmington
Florida	1845 (27)	53,997	15,982	25	Tallahassee	Jacksonville
Georgia	1788 (4)	57,919	8,186	13	Atlanta	Atlanta
Hawaii	1959 (50)	6,423	1,212	2	Honolulu	Honolulu
Idaho	1890 (43)	82,751	1,294	2	Boise	Boise
Illinois	1818 (21)	55,593	12,419	19	Springfield	Chicago
Indiana	1816 (19)	35,870	6,080	9	Indianapolis	Indianapolis
Iowa	1846 (29)	55,875	2,926	5	Des Moines	Des Moines
Kansas	1861 (34)	81,823	2,688	4	Topeka	Wichita
Kentucky	1792 (15)	39,732	4,042	6	Frankfort	Louisville
Louisiana	1812 (18)	43,566	4,469	7	Baton Rouge	New Orleans
Maine	1820 (23)	30,865	1,275	2	Augusta	Portland
Maryland	1788 (7)	9,775	5,296	8	Annapolis	Baltimore
Massachusetts	1788 (6)	7,838	6,349	10	Boston	Boston
Michigan	1837 (26)	56,809	9,938	15	Lansing	Detroit
Minnesota	1858 (32)	79,617	4,919	8	St. Paul	Minneapolis
Mississippi	1817 (20)	46,914	2,845	4	Jackson	Jackson
Missouri	1821 (24)	68,898	5,595	9	Jefferson City	Kansas City
Montana	1889 (41)	145,556	902	1	Helena	Billings
Nebraska	1867 (37)	76,878	1,711	3	Lincoln	Omaha
Nevada	1864 (36)	109,806	1,998	3	Carson City	Las Vegas
New Hampshire	1788 (9)	8,969	1,236	2	Concord	Manchester
New Jersey	1787 (3)	7,419	8,414	13	Trenton	Newark
New Mexico	1912 (47)	121,365	1,819	3	Santa Fe	Albuquerque
New York	1788 (11)	47,224	18,976	29	Albany	New York
North Carolina	1789 (12)	48,718	8,049	13	Raleigh	Charlotte
North Dakota	1889 (39)	68,994	642	1	Bismarck	Fargo
Ohio	1803 (17)	40,953	11,353	18	Columbus	Columbus
Oklahoma	1907 (46)	68,679	3,451	5	Oklahoma City	Oklahoma City
Oregon	1859 (33)	96,003	3,421	5	Salem	Portland
Pennsylvania	1787 (2)	44,820	12,281	19	Harrisburg	Philadelphia
Rhode Island	1790 (13)	1,045	1,048	2	Providence	Providence
South Carolina	1788 (8)	30,111	4,012	6	Columbia	Columbia
South Dakota	1889 (40)	75,898	755	1	Pierre	Sioux Falls
Tennessee	1796 (16)	41,220	5,689	9	Nashville	Memphis
Texas	1845 (28)	261,914	20,852	32	Austin	Houston
Utah	1896 (45)	82,168	2,233	3	Salt Lake City	Salt Lake City
Vermont	1791 (14)	9,249	609	1	Montpelier	Burlington
Virginia	1788 (10)	39,598	7,079	11	Richmond	Virginia Beach
Washington	1889 (42)	66,582	5,894	9	Olympia	Seattle
West Virginia	1863 (35)	24,087	1,808	3	Charleston	Charleston
Wisconsin	1848 (30)	54,314	5,364	8	Madison	Milwaukee
Wyoming	1890 (44)	97,105	494	1	Cheyenne	Cheyenne
District of Columbia		61	572	1 (nonvoting)		

Self-Governing Areas, Possessions, and Dependencies	Land Area in Square Miles	Population (In Thousands)	Capital
Puerto Rico	3,515	809	San Juan
Guam	209	155	Agana
U.S. Virgin Islands	132	121	Charlotte Amalie
American Samoa	77	65	Pago Pago

Sources: Department of Commerce, Bureau of the Census   *As of 108th Congress.

 Alabama
 Alaska
 Arizona
 Arkansas
 California

 Colorado
 Connecticut
 Delaware
 Florida
 Georgia

 Hawaii
 Idaho
 Illinois
 Indiana
 Iowa

 Kansas
 Kentucky
 Louisiana
 Maine
 Maryland

 Massachusetts
 Michigan
 Minnesota
 Mississippi
 Missouri

 Montana
 Nebraska
 Nevada
 New Hampshire
 New Jersey

 New Mexico
 New York
 North Carolina
 North Dakota
 Ohio

 Oklahoma
 Oregon
 Pennsylvania
 Rhode Island
 South Carolina

 South Dakota
 Tennessee
 Texas
 Utah
 Vermont

 Virginia
 Washington
 West Virginia
 Wisconsin
 Wyoming

ILLUSTRATED ATLAS
OF AMERICAN HISTORY

Table of Contents

Introduction

This illustrated atlas contains dramatic maps and vibrant pictures and graphs to bring your study of American history to life. You can use these pages to compare regions or to make connections between past and present. The atlas has been placed at the front of your textbook, so you will have it as a ready reference throughout the year.

Get up-to-date information about any country in the world. Use the World Desk Reference Online to learn about the world today, practice critical thinking skills, and get updated statistics and data.

UNITED STATES
POLITICAL

Golden Gate Bridge, San Francisco, California

115°W 110°W 105°W 100°W

Washington
Seattle
Olympia ★
Spokane ●

Montana
Great Falls ●
Helena ★
Billings ●

Minot ●
North Dakota
Grand Forks ●
Bismarck ★

Portland ●
Salem ★
Eugene ●
Oregon

Boise ★
Idaho
Pocatello ●

Wyoming
Casper ●

South Dakota
Rapid City ●
Pierre ★
Sioux Falls ●

Reno ●
San Francisco ●
Carson City ★
Sacramento ★
Oakland ●
San Jose ●
California
Nevada

Ogden ●
Great Salt Lake
Salt Lake City ★

Cheyenne ★
Nebraska
Lincoln

Utah

Denver ★
Colorado
Colorado Springs ●

Kansas
Wichita ●

Las Vegas ●

Los Angeles ●
Long Beach ●
Salton Sea
San Diego ●

Arizona
Phoenix ★
Tucson ●

Santa Fe ★
Albuquerque ●
New Mexico
Las Cruces ●
El Paso ●

Oklahoma
Oklahoma City ★

Fort Worth ●

Texas
Austin ★

San Antonio ●

125°W

PACIFIC OCEAN

30°N

120°W

115°W

110°W

105°W

100°W

160°W 155°W
Hawaii
Honolulu ★
PACIFIC OCEAN
20°N
0 km 100
0 miles 100
Mercator Projection

160°E 170°E
50°N
PACIFIC OCEAN

180° 70°N 170°W 160°W 150°W
RUSSIA
Arctic Circle
140°W
Alaska
Fairbanks ●
130°W
CANADA
60°N
Anchorage ●
Bering Sea
Gulf of Alaska
Juneau ●
0 km 400
0 miles 400
Albers Conic Equal-Area Projection

MEXICO

100°W
105°W

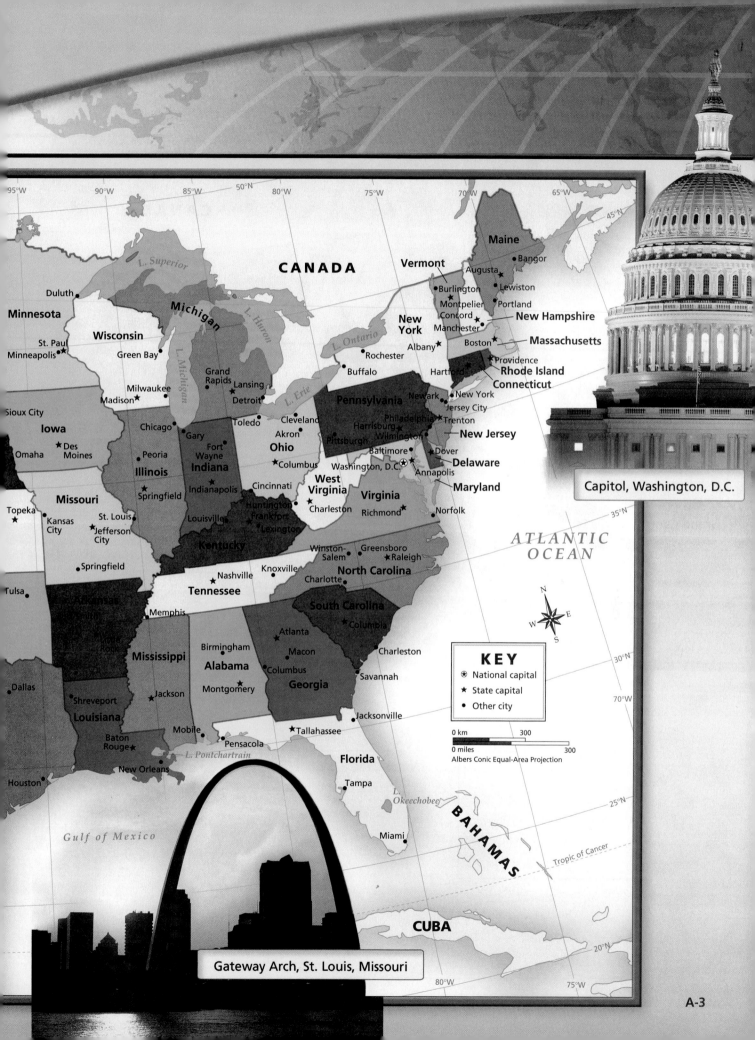

90°W   90°W   85°W   50°N   80°W   75°W   70°W   65°W

45°N

CANADA

L. Superior

Duluth

Minnesota

St. Paul
Minneapolis

Wisconsin

Green Bay

Michigan

L. Huron

Milwaukee
Madison

Sioux City

Iowa

Omaha

Des Moines

Chicago

Gary

Peoria

Grand Rapids

Lansing

Detroit

L. Michigan

L. Erie

Toledo

Cleveland

Akron

Ohio

Columbus

L. Ontario

Rochester

Buffalo

New York

Albany

Maine

Bangor

Augusta

Burlington

Vermont

Montpelier

Concord

Manchester

Lewiston

Portland

New Hampshire

Boston   **Massachusetts**

Hartford

Providence

Rhode Island

Connecticut

Newark

New York

Jersey City

Pennsylvania

Harrisburg

Pittsburgh

Philadelphia

Trenton

New Jersey

Wilmington

Dover

Delaware

Fort Wayne

Indiana

Springfield

Indianapolis

Illinois

Cincinnati

Louisville

West Virginia

Huntington
Frankfort
Lexington

Charleston

Baltimore

Washington, D.C.

Annapolis

Maryland

Virginia

Richmond

Norfolk

35°N

Missouri

Topeka

Kansas City

St. Louis

Jefferson City

Kentucky

Springfield

Nashville

Knoxville

Winston-Salem

Greensboro
Raleigh

North Carolina

Charlotte

ATLANTIC OCEAN

Tulsa

Arkansas

Tennessee

Memphis

South Carolina

Columbia

Atlanta

Birmingham

Macon

Mississippi

Alabama

Columbus

Montgomery

Charleston

Savannah

Georgia

Dallas

Jackson

Shreveport

Louisiana

Mobile

Pensacola

Baton Rouge

New Orleans

L. Pontchartrain

Tallahassee

Jacksonville

KEY
⊛ National capital
★ State capital
• Other city

30°N

70°W

Houston

Florida

Tampa

L. Okeechobee

BAHAMAS

25°N

0 km   300
0 miles   300
Albers Conic Equal-Area Projection

Capitol, Washington, D.C.

Gulf of Mexico

Miami

Tropic of Cancer

CUBA

Gateway Arch, St. Louis, Missouri

20°N

80°W   75°W

A-3

UNITED STATES
PHYSICAL

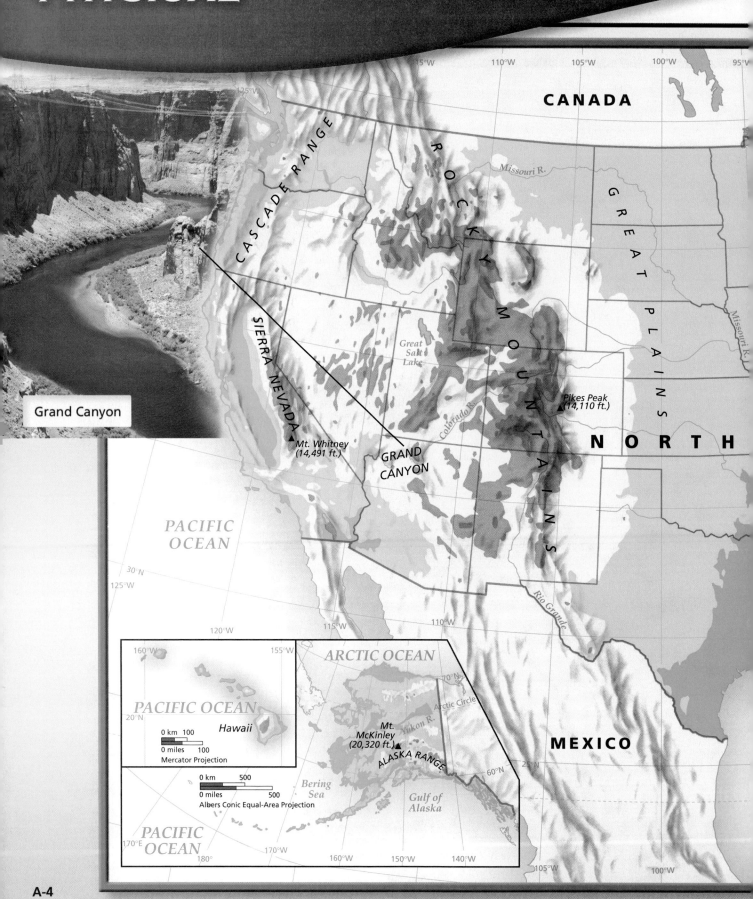

Grand Canyon

CANADA

CASCADE RANGE

R O C K Y

Missouri R.

G R E A T

SIERRA NEVADA

Great Salt Lake

M O U N T A I N S

P L A I N S

Missouri R.

Pikes Peak
(14,110 ft.)

Mt. Whitney
(14,491 ft.)

Colorado R.

GRAND
CANYON

N O R T H

PACIFIC
OCEAN

30°N

125°W

120°W

115°W

110°W

Rio Grande

160°W   155°W
PACIFIC OCEAN
20°N
Hawaii
0 km   100
0 miles   100
Mercator Projection

ARCTIC OCEAN
70°N
Arctic Circle
Mt.
McKinley
(20,320 ft.)
Yukon R.
ALASKA RANGE
60°N

25°N

MEXICO

0 km   500
0 miles   500
Albers Conic Equal-Area Projection

Bering
Sea

Gulf of
Alaska

PACIFIC
OCEAN
170°E
180°   170°W   160°W   150°W   140°W

105°W

100°W

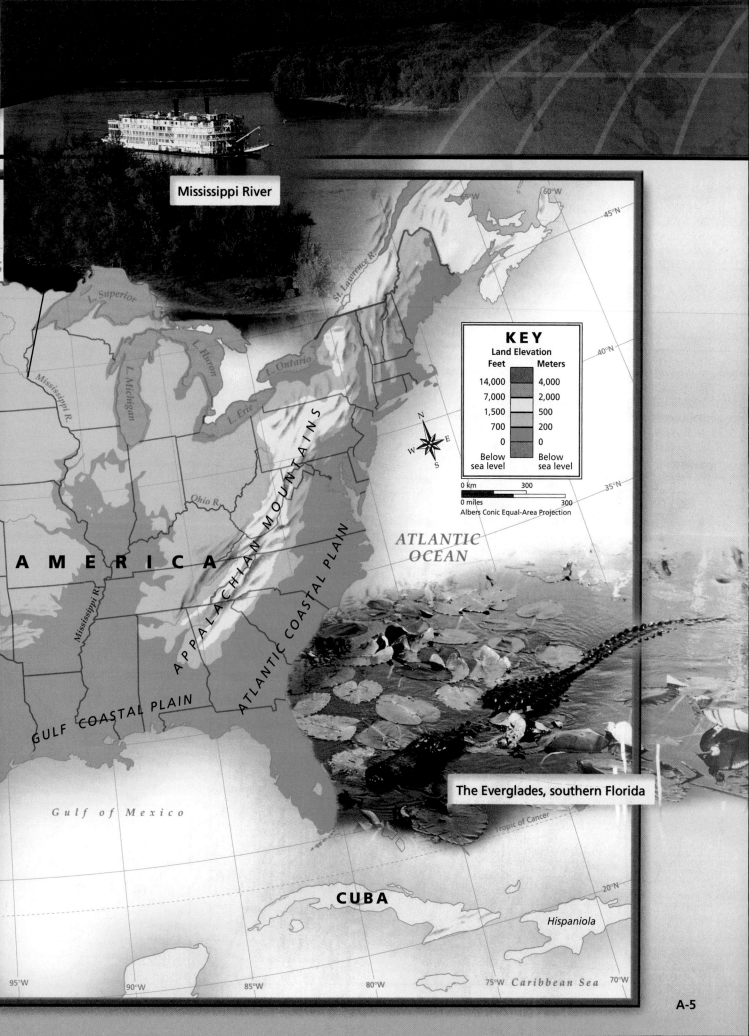

Mississippi River

KEY

Land Elevation

Feet		Meters
14,000		4,000
7,000		2,000
1,500		500
700		200
0		0
Below sea level		Below sea level

0 km   300
0 miles   300
Albers Conic Equal-Area Projection

55°W
60°W
45°N
40°N
35°N

L. Superior

L. Huron

L. Michigan

L. Ontario

L. Erie

St. Lawrence R.

Mississippi R.

Ohio R.

A M E R I C A

A P P A L A C H I A N   M O U N T A I N S

ATLANTIC COASTAL PLAIN

GULF COASTAL PLAIN

ATLANTIC OCEAN

Mississippi R.

Gulf of Mexico

The Everglades, southern Florida

Tropic of Cancer

CUBA

20°N

Hispaniola

95°W   90°W   85°W   80°W   75°W   Caribbean Sea   70°W

UNITED STATES
RESOURCES & THE ECONOMY

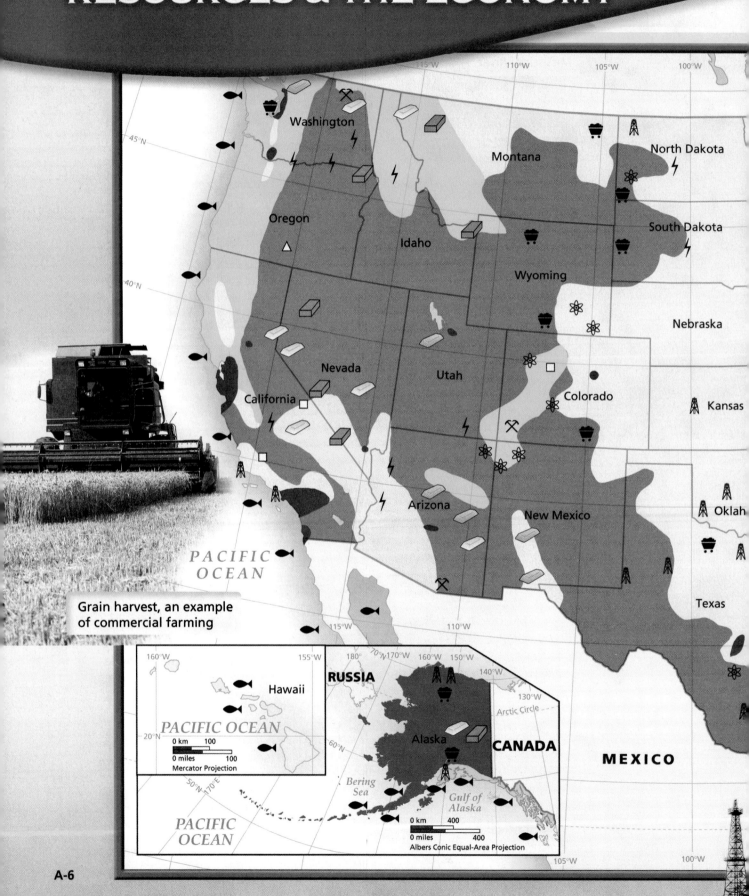

Grain harvest, an example of commercial farming

PACIFIC OCEAN

Washington
Oregon
Idaho
Montana
North Dakota
South Dakota
Wyoming
Nevada
Utah
Colorado
Nebraska
Kansas
California
Arizona
New Mexico
Oklah
Texas

115°W   110°W   105°W   100°W
45°N
40°N

Hawaii
PACIFIC OCEAN
0 km   100
0 miles   100
Mercator Projection

RUSSIA
Bering Sea
Alaska
CANADA
MEXICO
Gulf of Alaska
Arctic Circle

160°W   155°W   180°   170°W   160°W   150°W   140°W   130°W
70°N   20°N   60°N   50°N   170°E

PACIFIC OCEAN

0 km   400
0 miles   400
Albers Conic Equal-Area Projection

115°W   110°W   105°W   100°W

CANADA

L. Superior
Michigan
L. Huron
L. Michigan
L. Ontario
L. Erie

esota
Wisconsin
Iowa
Illinois
Missouri
Arkansas
Louisiana
Mississippi

Minnesota
Indiana
Ohio
Kentucky
Tennessee
Alabama

Pennsylvania
West Virginia
Virginia
North Carolina
South Carolina
Georgia

New York
Vermont
New Hampshire
Massachusetts
Rhode Island
Connecticut
New Jersey
Delaware
Maryland

Maine

Florida

Gulf of Mexico

ATLANTIC OCEAN

Medical research, a key service industry in the U.S. economy

Oil wells pump petroleum, an important natural resource

0 km   300
0 miles   300
Albers Conic Equal-Area Projection

N
W   E
S

KEY

Hunting and gathering	Iron
Forestry	Copper
Livestock raising	Bauxite
Commercial farming	Gold
Manufacturing and trade	Silver
Commercial fishing	Phosphates
Little or no activity	Uranium
Coal	Lead
Petroleum	Nickel
Hydroelectric power	Tungsten

90°W 85°W 80°W 75°W 70°W 65°W
50°N
20°N
75°W

THE WORLD: POLITICAL

100°W 80°W 60°W
Greenland (Den.)

Alaska (U.S.)

60°N

CANADA

NORTH AMERICA

Ottawa

40°N

UNITED STATES

Washington, DC

Bermuda (U.K.)

See inset map

ATLANTIC OCEAN

Tropic of Cancer

Hawaii (U.S.)

20°N

MEXICO

Gulf of Mexico

Mexico City

Caribbean Sea

Caracas

GUYANA

VENEZUELA

Paramaribo

Bogotá

Georgetown

Cayenne

COLOMBIA

French Guiana (Fr.)

SURINAME

Galápagos Is. (Ecuador)

Quito

ECUADOR

SOUTH AMERICA

0° Equator

PACIFIC OCEAN

PERU

BRAZIL

SAMOA

American Samoa (U.S.)

Lima

TONGA

French Polynesia (Fr.)

BOLIVIA

La Paz

Brasília

Sucre

20°S

Cook Is. (N.Z.)

PARAGUAY

Tropic of Capricorn

Pitcairn I. (U.K.)

CHILE

Asunción

International Date Line

Easter Is. (Chile)

Santiago

Buenos Aires

URUGUAY

Montevideo

40°S

ARGENTINA

Falkland Is. (U.K.)

60°S

SOUTHERN OCEAN

Antarctic Circle

ANTARCTICA

Central America and the Caribbean

UNITED STATES

0 km   300

0 miles   300

Azimuthal Projection

Gulf of Mexico

Tropic of Cancer

N

W   E

S

Havana

Nassau

B A H A M A S

CUBA

20°N

MEXICO

DOMINICAN REPUBLIC

Br. Virgin Is. (U.K.)

Belmopan

HAITI

Puerto Rico (U.S.)

ANTIGUA AND BARBUDA

BELIZE

Kingston

Port-au-Prince

Santo Domingo

Guadeloupe (Fr.)

GUATEMALA

JAMAICA

Virgin Islands (U.S.)

ST. KITTS AND NEVIS

Guatemala

Caribbean Sea

DOMINICA

Martinique (Fr.)

HONDURAS

San Salvador

Tegucigalpa

ST. LUCIA

NICARAGUA

Neth. Antilles (Neth.)

ST. VINCENT AND THE GRENADINES

BARBADOS

EL SALVADOR

Managua

Aruba (Neth.)

GRENADA

10°N

COSTA RICA

San José

TRINIDAD AND TOBAGO

PACIFIC OCEAN

Panamá

Caracas

Port of Spain

60°W

ATLANTIC OCEAN

PANAMA

COLOMBIA

VENEZUELA

80°W

GUYANA

A-8

ICELAND
Reykjavik

Svalbard
(Nor.)

See inset map

EUROPE

Moscow

RUSSIA

ASIA

Astana
KAZAKHSTAN
UZBEKISTAN
GEORGIA
TURKEY
ARMENIA
TURK.
AZERBAIJAN
Ankara
T'bilisi
Ashgabat
Tashkent
Bishkek
KYRGYZSTAN
Dushanbe
TAJIKISTAN

Ulaanbaatar
MONGOLIA

Beijing

N. KOREA
P'yongyang
Seoul
S. KOREA

JAPAN
Tokyo

Azores
(Port.)
Madeira Is.
(Port.)
Canary Is.
(Spain)

Tunis
Algiers
CYPRUS
LEBANON
SYRIA
ISRAEL
JORDAN
Jerusalem
Amman
Baghdad
IRAQ
IRAN
Tehran
Kabul
AFGHANISTAN
Islamabad
PAKISTAN

CHINA

TAIPEI
TAIWAN
Hanoi
Hong Kong

PACIFIC OCEAN

MOROCCO
ALGERIA
Tripoli
LIBYA
Cairo
EGYPT
KUWAIT
BAHRAIN
QATAR
Riyadh
Abu Dhabi
U.A.E.
Muscat
SAUDI
ARABIA
OMAN
Sanaa
YEMEN

New
Delhi
Kathmandu
NEPAL
Thimphu
BHUTAN
Dhaka
BANGLADESH

MYANMAR
(BURMA)
Yangon
LAOS
Vientiane
THAILAND
Bangkok

VIETNAM

Manila
PHILIPPINES

Northern
Mariana Is.
(U.S.)
Guam
(U.S.)

Wake I.
(U.S.)

MARSHALL IS.

Western
Sahara
(Mor.)

CAPE
VERDE

See inset
map

AFRICA

NIGER
CHAD
N'Djamena
Khartoum
SUDAN
Addis
Abeba
ERITREA
DJIBOUTI
SOMALIA
ETHIOPIA
CENTRAL
AFRICAN REP.
Bangui
CAMEROON
Yaoundé

INDIA

Colombo
SRI
LANKA

Mogadishu
MALDIVES

Phnom
Penh
CAMBODIA
MALAYSIA
Kuala Lumpur
SINGAPORE

BRUNEI

PALAU

FEDERATED STATES
OF MICRONESIA
NAURU
KIRIBATI

EQ.
GUINEA
SAŌ TOMÉ
& PRĪNCIPE
GABON
Libreville
CONGO
DEM. REP.
OF THE
CONGO
Brazzaville
Kinshasa
UGANDA
Kampala
RWANDA
BURUNDI
Nairobi
KENYA
Dodoma
TANZANIA
Dar es Salaam

SEYCHELLES

INDONESIA
Jakarta

E. TIMOR

PAPUA
NEW GUINEA
Port Moresby

SOLOMON IS.

TUVALU
VANUATU
FIJI IS.

Cabinda
(Angola)
Luanda
ANGOLA
MALAWI
Lilongwe
ZAMBIA
Lusaka
Harare

COMOROS

INDIAN OCEAN

NAMIBIA
Windhoek
ZIMBABWE
BOTSWANA
Gaborone
Pretoria
MOZAMBIQUE
Antananarivo
MADAGASCAR
Maputo
SWAZILAND
MAURITIUS
Réunion
(Fr.)

New Caledonia
(Fr.)

AUSTRALIA

SOUTH
AFRICA
Cape Town
LESOTHO

NEW
ZEALAND
Canberra
Wellington

KEY

⊛ Capital city

N
W   E
S

0 km   2,000
0 miles   2,000
Robinson Projection

SOUTHERN OCEAN

International
Date Line

West Africa inset

Nouakchott
MAURITANIA

0 km   500
0 miles   500
Mercator Projection

N
W   E
S

Dakar
SENEGAL
GAMBIA
Banjul
GUINEA-
BISSAU
Bissau
GUINEA
Conakry
Freetown
SIERRA
LEONE
Monrovia
LIBERIA

MALI
Bamako

Niamey
NIGER
BURKINA
FASO
Ouagadougou

CÔTE
D'IVOIRE
Yamoussoukro
GHANA
Accra
TOGO
Lomé
BENIN
Porto-
Novo

NIGERIA
Abuja

ATLANTIC
OCEAN

Gulf of
Guinea

10°N

10°W

West Africa

Europe inset

Europe

0 km   500
0 miles   500
Azimuthal Projection

0°   10°E   20°E   30°E

60°N
10°W
50°N
40°N

N
W   E
S

FINLAND
Helsinki
NORWAY
Oslo
SWEDEN
Stockholm
ESTONIA
Tallinn
RUSSIA
Riga
LATVIA
LITHUANIA
Vilnius
Minsk
North
Sea
Baltic
Sea

DENMARK
Copenhagen
RUSSIA
BELARUS

Dublin
IRELAND
UNITED
KINGDOM
London
NETHERLANDS
Amsterdam
Berlin
GERMANY
BELGIUM
Brussels
LUX.
Warsaw
POLAND
Kiev
UKRAINE

ATLANTIC
OCEAN

Paris
FRANCE
SWITZ.
LIECH.
Bern
Prague
CZECH
REP.
Vienna
AUSTRIA
SLOVAKIA
Bratislava
Budapest
HUNGARY
SLOVENIA
Ljubljana
Zagreb
CROATIA
Chisinau
MOLDOVA
ROMANIA
Bucharest

PORTUGAL
Lisbon
ANDORRA
Madrid
SPAIN
MONACO
SAN
MARINO
ITALY
Rome
Sarajevo
BOSNIA &
HERZ.
Belgrade
SERBIA
MONT.
Tirana
ALBANIA
MACE.
KOS.
Sofia
BULGARIA
GREECE
Athens
TURKEY

Gibraltar
(U.K.)
Rabat
MOROCCO
Algiers
ALGERIA
Mediterranean
Sea
Tunis
TUNISIA
MALTA

A-9

THE UNITED STATES
A DIVERSE NATION

POLLING PLACE

投票站 CASILLA ELECTORAL
投票所 LUGAR NG BOTOHAN
투표소 PHÒNG PHIẾU

Sign at a California polling place

CANADA

ASIA

UNITED

Asian Migration
According to the 2000 census, 10.2 million Asian Americans make up 3.6 percent of the total U.S. population. Asian immigrants include people from China, Japan, Korea, the Philippines, as well as those from countries in Southeast Asia and South Asia.

N
W E
S

0 km   3,000
0 miles   3,000
Mercator Projection

PACIFIC OCEAN

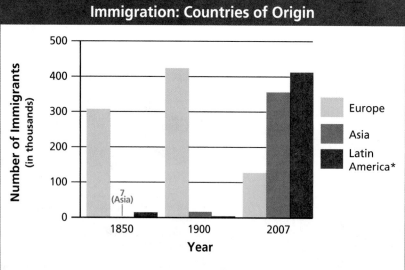

Immigration: Countries of Origin

Number of Immigrants (in thousands)

500
400
300
200
100
7 (Asia)
0

1850   1900   2007
Year

Europe
Asia
Latin America*

*Latin America includes the Caribbean, Mexico, and the countries of Central America and South America.

Sources: *Historical Statistics of the United States* and *Statistical Yearbook of the Immigration and Naturalization Service*

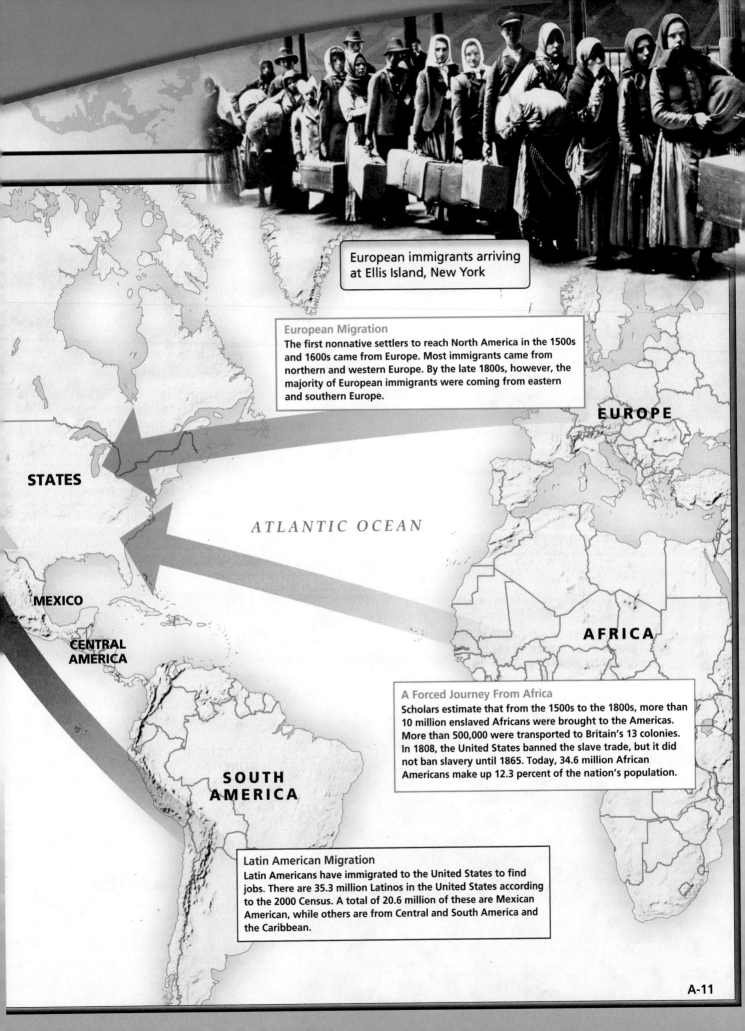

European immigrants arriving at Ellis Island, New York

European Migration

The first nonnative settlers to reach North America in the 1500s and 1600s came from Europe. Most immigrants came from northern and western Europe. By the late 1800s, however, the majority of European immigrants were coming from eastern and southern Europe.

EUROPE

STATES

ATLANTIC OCEAN

MEXICO

CENTRAL AMERICA

AFRICA

SOUTH AMERICA

A Forced Journey From Africa

Scholars estimate that from the 1500s to the 1800s, more than 10 million enslaved Africans were brought to the Americas. More than 500,000 were transported to Britain's 13 colonies. In 1808, the United States banned the slave trade, but it did not ban slavery until 1865. Today, 34.6 million African Americans make up 12.3 percent of the nation's population.

Latin American Migration

Latin Americans have immigrated to the United States to find jobs. There are 35.3 million Latinos in the United States according to the 2000 Census. A total of 20.6 million of these are Mexican American, while others are from Central and South America and the Caribbean.

UNITED STATES
TERRITORIAL EXPANSION
TO 1853

Mandan Village, like the one visited by Lewis and Clark during their exploration of the Louisiana Territory

A covered wagon, the mode of transportation for people moving west in the 1800s

PACIFIC OCEAN

The Alamo, site of a key battle in the war for Texas independence; Texas became part of the Mexican Cession

OREGON COUNTRY
(Agreement with Britain, 1846)

(Ceded by Britain, 1818)

LOUISIANA PURCHASE
(Purchased from France, 1803)

MEXICAN CESSION
(Treaty of Guadalupe-Hidalgo, 1848)

TEXAS ANNEXATION
(Annexed by Congress, 1845)

GADSDEN PURCHASE
(Purchased from Mexico, 1853)

MEXICO

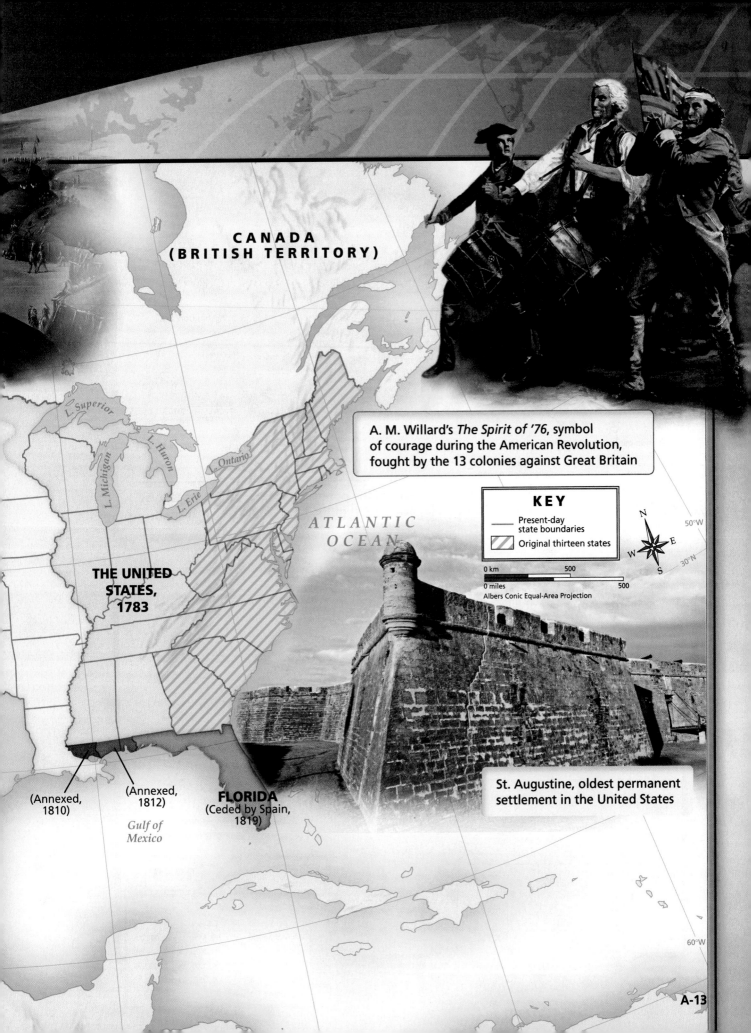

CANADA
(BRITISH TERRITORY)

L. Superior

L. Michigan

L. Huron

L. Ontario

L. Erie

THE UNITED
STATES,
1783

ATLANTIC
OCEAN

A. M. Willard's *The Spirit of '76*, symbol
of courage during the American Revolution,
fought by the 13 colonies against Great Britain

KEY

Present-day
state boundaries

Original thirteen states

N E W S

50°W

30°N

0 km   500

0 miles   500

Albers Conic Equal-Area Projection

(Annexed,
1810)

(Annexed,
1812)

FLORIDA
(Ceded by Spain,
1819)

*Gulf of
Mexico*

St. Augustine, oldest permanent
settlement in the United States

60°W

UNITED STATES
POPULATION DENSITY

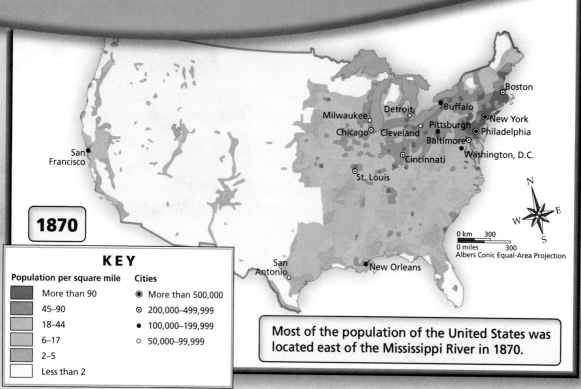

1870

KEY

Population per square mile
- More than 90
- 45–90
- 18–44
- 6–17
- 2–5
- Less than 2

Cities
- More than 500,000
- 200,000–499,999
- 100,000–199,999
- 50,000–99,999

Most of the population of the United States was located east of the Mississippi River in 1870.

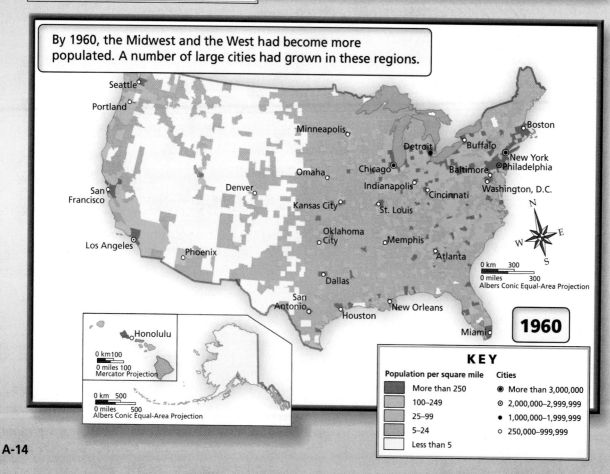

By 1960, the Midwest and the West had become more populated. A number of large cities had grown in these regions.

1960

KEY

Population per square mile
- More than 250
- 100–249
- 25–99
- 5–24
- Less than 5

Cities
- More than 3,000,000
- 2,000,000–2,999,999
- 1,000,000–1,999,999
- 250,000–999,999

In the 1880s, Anaheim, California, outside of Los Angeles was rural. By the twenty-first century Los Angeles, as well as surrounding cities like Anaheim, were modern bustling cities connected by freeways.

Large cities and their suburbs formed huge metropolitan areas by the year 2000. The largest city is New York, followed by Los Angeles and Chicago.

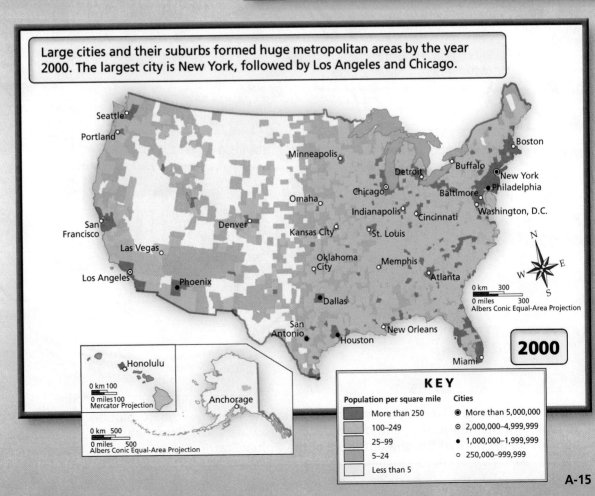

Seattle
Portland
Minneapolis
Detroit
Buffalo
Boston
New York
Philadelphia
Chicago
Baltimore
Omaha
Indianapolis
Cincinnati
Washington, D.C.
San Francisco
Denver
Kansas City
St. Louis
Las Vegas
Oklahoma City
Memphis
Atlanta
Los Angeles
Phoenix
Dallas
San Antonio
New Orleans
Houston
Miami

0 km 300
0 miles 300
Albers Conic Equal-Area Projection

N
W   E
S

2000

Honolulu
0 km 100
0 miles 100
Mercator Projection

Anchorage

0 km 500
0 miles 500
Albers Conic Equal-Area Projection

KEY

Population per square mile

- More than 250
- 100–249
- 25–99
- 5–24
- Less than 5

Cities

- ◉ More than 5,000,000
- ⦿ 2,000,000–4,999,999
- ● 1,000,000–1,999,999
- ○ 250,000–999,999

Symbols OF OUR NATION

Today's American flag has thirteen red and white stripes representing the original thirteen states. Fifty white stars stand for the current number of states. The first official flag had thirteen stars and was approved in 1777.

Thirteen white stars

American bald eagle

Scroll reading *E Pluribus Unum* ("Out of Many, One")

Olive branch (symbol of peace)

Thirteen arrows (symbol of war)

The Great Seal of the United States was designed after the American Revolution to represent the new nation, and the values of its founders. The Great Seal appears on the back of the one-dollar bill of the United States.

Contents

The Economics Handbook will provide you with key economic concepts and terms, so you may understand economic issues and decision making throughout history.

As you study history, you will learn certain rights and responsibilities of being an American citizen. The Civics Handbook will show you how to conduct important civics activities.

What is Economics?

Making Choices About Resources

Which sweater to buy? How many hours to study? Which restaurant to go to? If you are like most people, you constantly face decisions because you don't have enough time and money to do everything. Economics is the study of how people make choices when they face a limited supply of resources.

The study of economics begins with the idea that people cannot have everything they need and want. A need is something like air, food, or shelter. A want is an item that we would like to have but that is not necessary for survival. Because people cannot have everything they need or want, they must consider their choices and decide how best to fill their needs.

As an individual, you have to decide what to do with your time and money. Businesses have to decide how many people to employ and how much to produce. A city government may have to decide whether to spend its budget to build a park or a library.

Trade-offs and Opportunity Costs

When people make decisions, they face trade-offs because they choose one course of action over another. A person who chooses one item gives up other opportunities. The thing a person gives up is called the opportunity cost. Suppose you have to choose between sleeping late or getting up early to study for a test. The opportunity cost of extra study time is less sleep.

Review Questions

1. What is economics?
2. Define trade-off and opportunity cost.

Scarcity

Why Must People Make Choices?

People have to make choices because of scarcity. Scarcity is the term used to explain that there are not enough resources to meet everyone's wants or needs. One person may be able to buy hundreds of bicycles or guitars, but no one can have an unlimited supply of everything. At some point, a limit is reached. Scarcity always exists because our needs and wants are always greater than our resource supply.

Meeting Basic Needs
Agriculture allowed early Native Americans to grow and store food for survival.

Meeting Needs and Wants

Until modern times, people mostly focused on resources related to agriculture to meet their needs and wants. They farmed the land to produce food, mainly for their own use. This traditional way of meeting basic needs still exists in some countries today. However, modern societies have also developed other economic systems to deal with increased trade and industry. An economic system is the method used by a society to produce and distribute goods and services.

Review Questions

1. What is scarcity?

2. How does scarcity cause people to make choices?

Basic Economic Questions

Through its economic system, society answers three key questions. **1)** What goods and services should be produced? **2)** How should goods and services be produced? **3)** Who consumes the goods and services? Goods are objects, such as cars and clothes. Services are actions that people do for others, such as teaching. Producers make and sell goods and services. Consumers buy and use goods and services.

How a society answers these three questions shows what economic goals it values and shapes its economic system.

Three Key Economic Questions		
What goods and services should be produced?	**How should goods and services be produced?**	**Who consumes the goods and services?**
How much of our resources should we devote to national defense, education, public health, or consumer goods? Which consumer goods should we produce?	Should we produce food on large corporate farms or on small family farms? Should we produce electricity with oil, nuclear power, coal, or solar power?	How do goods and services get distributed? The question of who gets to consume which goods and services lies at the very heart of the differences between economic systems. Each society answers the question of distribution based on its combination of social values and goals.

Economic Goals	
Economic efficiency	Making the most of resources
Economic freedom	Freedom from government intervention in the production and distribution of goods and services
Economic security and predictability	Assurance that goods and services will be available, payments will be made on time, and a safety net will protect individuals in times of economic disaster
Economic equity	Fair distribution of wealth
Economic growth and innovation	Innovation leads to economic growth, and economic growth leads to a higher standard of living.
Other goals	Societies pursue additional goals, such as environmental protection.

Review Questions

1. List examples of both goods and services.

2. Which economic goals are most valued in the U.S.?

Modern Economic Systems

As you read on page 1037, an economic system is the method a society uses to produce and distribute goods and services. Four different economic systems have developed as societies attempt to answer the three economic questions according to their goals. This table provides information about the main economic systems in the world today.

Modern Economic Systems			
	Description	**Origin**	**Location Today**
Traditional	People make economic decisions based on custom or habit. They produce what they have always produced and just as much as they need, using long-established methods.	Accompanied the rise of agriculture and home crafts	Mainly in rural areas within developing nations
Market (Capitalist, Free-Enterprise)	Economic decisions are made in the marketplace through interactions between buyers and sellers according to the laws of supply and demand. Individuals own the means of production. Government regulates some economic activities and provides such "public goods" as education.	Capitalism has existed since the earliest buying and selling of goods in a market. The market economic system developed in response to Adam Smith's ideas and the shift from agriculture to industry in the 1800s.	Australia, Canada, Japan, United States, and a handful of other nations
Centrally Planned (Command, Socialist, Communist)	Central government planners make most economic decisions for the people. In theory, the workers own the means of production. In practice, the government does. Some private businesses, but government is in control.	In the 1800s, criticism of capitalism by Karl Marx and others led to calls for distributing wealth according to need. After the 1917 Russian Revolution, the Soviet Union developed the first command economy.	Communist countries, including Cuba, North Korea, Venezuela and Vietnam
Mixed (Social Democratic, Liberal Socialist)	A system with markets in which the government plays an important role in making economic decisions.	The Great Depression of the 1930s ended laissez-faire capitalism in most countries. People insisted that government take a stronger role in fixing economic problems. The fall of communism in Eastern Europe in the 1990s ended central planning in most countries. People insisted on freer markets.	Most nations, including Brazil, France, India, Italy, Poland, Russia, and Sweden

The Market Economy

Individuals Buy and Sell

What do a crafts fair, a music store, and the New York Stock Exchange all have in common? All are examples of markets. A market is an arrangement that allows buyers and sellers to exchange things.

Markets exist because none of us can make, or produce, all we require to satisfy our needs and wants. You probably didn't grow the wheat used to make the cereal you had for breakfast. Instead, you purchased your cereal at a store, which is an example of a market. Markets allow us to exchange the things we have for the things we want.

In a market system, people and businesses have the freedom to make, to sell, and to buy what they want. Producers choose what to make and sell. Consumers decide what goods and services to buy. In other words, individuals answer the three key economic questions that you learned about on page 1038. It is an efficient system because producers make only what buyers want, when they want it, and generally at prices they are willing to pay.

New York Stock Exchange

Review Questions

1. Why do markets exist?

2. In a free market, who decides what to make, to sell, and to buy?

Centrally Planned Economies

The Government Decides

In a centrally planned economy, the central government alone answers the key economic questions. Centrally planned economies are sometimes called command economies because a central authority is in command of the economy. It owns all resources and decides what is produced and at what price things will be sold.

The government in centrally planned economies tries to encourage faster economic growth and more equal distribution of goods and services. Economic growth means there is an increase in production and people are spending more money.

Often, the government has a hard time making a plan that will meet these goals. There is no competition among sellers and producers do not keep the profit if they make better products. As a result, producers do not try to improve their products, and consumers must accept poorly made merchandise.

Centrally planned economies mostly exist in countries with a communist form of government, such as North Korea and the former Soviet Union. In communist countries, the government controls both economic and political decisions. Individual freedoms are limited.

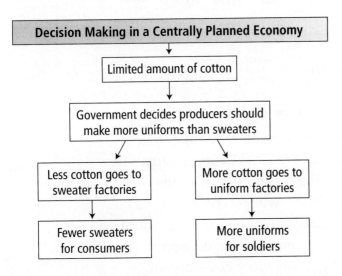

Decision Making in a Centrally Planned Economy

Limited amount of cotton

Government decides producers should make more uniforms than sweaters

Less cotton goes to sweater factories

More cotton goes to uniform factories

Fewer sweaters for consumers

More uniforms for soldiers

Review Questions

1. In a centrally planned economy who makes the important economic decisions?

2. **Diagram Skills** How does the government's decision affect consumers and soldiers?

Mixed Economies

Government Helps the Economy

No country has an economy that is strictly a free market or a command economy. Most economies are actually market economies, with some level of government involvement. This is called a mixed economy. While most areas of the economy may be free, the government may step in to provide certain goods and services. In a mixed economy, the government generally provides defense, education, and public roads.

Review Questions

1. Describe a mixed economy.

2. In a mixed economy, the government enforces safety standards. If a product is found to be unsafe, the government requires that the product be recalled, or removed from stores. Do research on the Internet to identify two products that have been recalled in the last year. Explain the reasons for the recalls.

A Continuum of Economic Systems

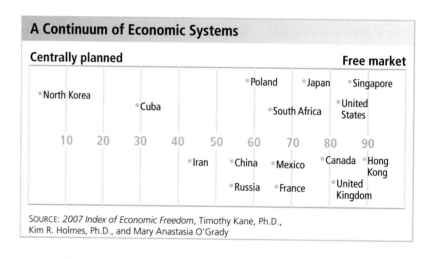

SOURCE: *2007 Index of Economic Freedom*, Timothy Kane, Ph.D., Kim R. Holmes, Ph.D., and Mary Anastasia O'Grady

How Involved Is the Government?

As you read on page 1039, the economic systems of the nations around the world vary greatly. The chart above shows the continuum or range of economic systems in the world. The countries on the left side of the diagram have a large amount of government involvement in the economy. The countries on the right have less government involvement in the economy. Compared to most other countries, the United States has an economy with little government involvement and a great deal of economic freedom. Its system is called a free enterprise system.

Economics at Work

Factors of Production

Now that you are familiar with the different economic systems that exist, it is important to understand how producers make decisions about resources and how the marketplace works.

All the resources that are used to make all goods and services are called factors of production. As the diagram below shows, there are three types: land, labor, and capital. Because resources are scarce, societies try to make the most of the resources they have to work with. When societies use resources efficiently, the economy grows. Efficiency means an economy is using resources in such a way as to maximize the production of goods and services.

The Marketplace

In a local market, goods and services are exchanged among people who live within a smaller community such as a town or city. Over the years, however, technology and improved transportation systems have allowed producers to exchange goods with people who live across the world. As you will read on the next page, the relationship between sellers and buyers help decide how much to produce and at what price.

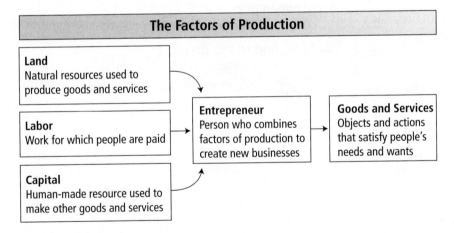

The Factors of Production

Land
Natural resources used to produce goods and services

Labor
Work for which people are paid

Capital
Human-made resource used to make other goods and services

Entrepreneur
Person who combines factors of production to create new businesses

Goods and Services
Objects and actions that satisfy people's needs and wants

Entrepreneurs are individuals who take risks to develop new ideas and start businesses. Their efforts help the economy grow.

Consumer Demands

Producers make decisions about how to use resources, but consumers decide which goods to buy and use. Economists use the term demand to describe the ability and desire of consumers to buy a good.

In a market system, buyers demand goods and sellers supply those goods. Both buyers and sellers help to set prices through their interactions. For example, more people will buy a slice of pizza if it costs $1 than if it costs $10. As the price of an item increases, people will buy less of it. As the price goes down, people will buy more of the same item. Buying more when prices are low, and buying less when prices are high is called the law of demand.

When fewer people buy pizza because the price is too high, economists say that the quantity demanded of pizza has dropped. When prices drop and people buy more, they say the quantity demanded of pizza has increased.

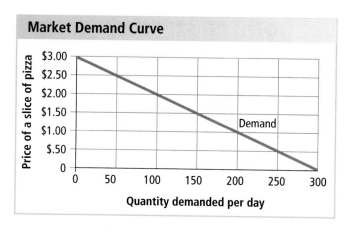

Market Demand Curve

Economists use a line graph to show how price and the demand for a good relate to each other. Because quantity demanded increases as prices decrease, the line on the graph above slopes down to the right.

Review Questions

1. What is the relationship between price and consumer demand?

2. According to the graph, at $.50 per slice, what is the demand for pizza per day?

The Supply of Goods and Services

When demand for a good increases, the price rises. In order to make more money, companies will supply more of the good or service as prices increase. Supply is the amount of goods available in the marketplace. When prices rise, other companies might begin producing the good because they also want to make money. As a result, there is a greater supply of the good available to consumers. If the price of a good decreases, companies will produce less and some companies may stop selling the good completely. The law of supply states that producers will offer more of a good if prices rise, and less of a good if prices fall.

Market Supply Curve

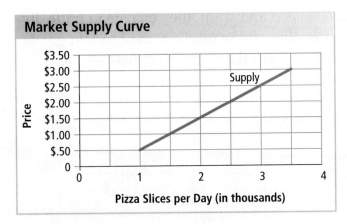

The line on a supply graph will always rise from left to right. The line shows that higher prices lead to higher production. If the price of a slice of pizza is $2.00, all the pizzerias in a city will produce 2,500 slices.

Review Questions

1. According to the law of supply, what happens to the quantity of goods produced if prices fall?

2. **Graph Skills** According to the graph, how many slices of pizza will be produced if the cost per slice is $1.00?

Why Nations Trade

Making the Best Use of Resources

As you have read, markets exist because people cannot produce all we require to satisfy our needs and wants. This is true of nations, as well.

Countries produce different goods and services because they have different resources. They focus on certain products that they can make easily and cheaply. For example, coffee can be grown easily in warm areas like Central America, so it is inexpensive to produce there. If Canadians wanted to produce coffee, however, they would have to grow it in greenhouses, which would be more difficult and costly. Because countries cannot efficiently produce everything their citizens need and want, they engage in trade. By specializing or focusing on the production of certain goods and services, nations make the best use of their resources.

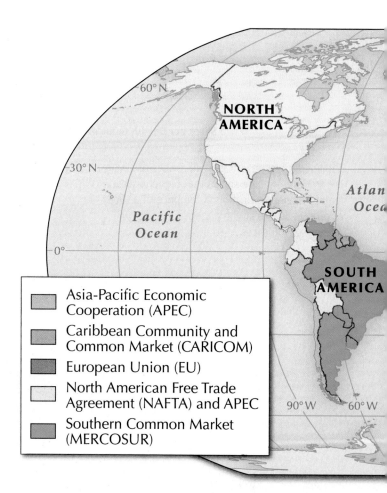

Asia-Pacific Economic Cooperation (APEC)

Caribbean Community and Common Market (CARICOM)

European Union (EU)

North American Free Trade Agreement (NAFTA) and APEC

Southern Common Market (MERCOSUR)

Nations Work Together

Trading among nations is an exchange of goods and services in an international market. It has played an important role in the U.S. economy. Free-trade zones help encourage trade among nations. A free-trade zone is a region where a group of countries agree to reduce or eliminate tariffs, or taxes on imported goods. These agreements make trading less expensive.

The North American Free Trade Agreement (NAFTA) was developed to eliminate all fees and other trade barriers between Canada, Mexico, and the United States. Supporters of NAFTA say the agreement increases trade between the countries. Approximately 100 trading organizations like NAFTA operate throughout the world today.

Major Trade Organization Members

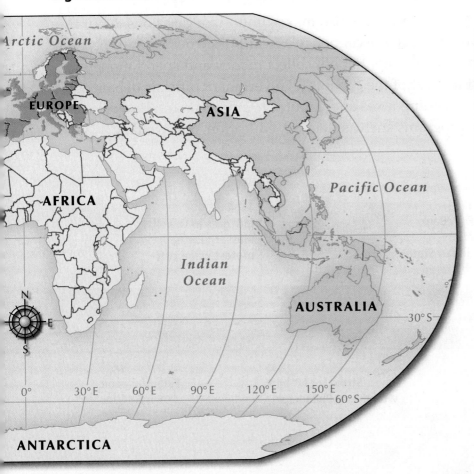

Review Questions

1. How does trade help societies meet their needs and wants?

2. How do countries join together to encourage economic growth for all?

The American Economy

A Tradition of Free Enterprise

The United States economy encourages free enterprise, which means people are allowed to try out their business ideas and compete in the free market. Its vast land, resources, and many people who are willing to work have all contributed to economic growth in the United States.

The free market has helped the economy in the United States, but the government set up the foundation for economic success. Government laws, such as those protecting the right to private property and enforcing contracts, help Americans profit from free enterprise. The Constitution also specifies limits on how government can tax, and it prohibits government from interfering in business contracts. Federal and state agencies regulate industries whose goods and services affect the well-being of the public.

The Government's Role in the Economy

The federal government also makes important decisions about the economy by setting fiscal policy. Fiscal policy means that the government decides how to both collect money and spend money in the best interest of the economy. Government officials debate about raising or cutting taxes and about how much should be spent on specific programs such as defense, education, and welfare.

Key Events in American Economic History

1791 First Bank of the United States chartered

1834 Mill girls in Lowell, Massachusetts, protest wage cuts

1867 Knights of Labor formed

1750   1800   1850

1835 Strike for 10-hour workday in Philadelphia

1869 Financial panic sweeps nation

Americans often argue about the proper balance of government involvement in the economy. Some people want more government services, while others say that the government already intervenes too much in the economy.

Sometimes government fiscal policy decisions bring gradual shifts or changes to an established system. For example, in the United States during the Great Depression many new federal programs changed the role of the government in the American economy. With the New Deal, the federal government moved away from laissez faire, or leaving the economy alone. Instead, the federal government took specific actions to improve the economy.

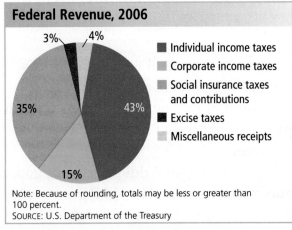

Federal Revenue, 2006

- 3%
- 4%
- 43%
- 35%
- 15%

- ■ Individual income taxes
- □ Corporate income taxes
- ■ Social insurance taxes and contributions
- ■ Excise taxes
- □ Miscellaneous receipts

Note: Because of rounding, totals may be less or greater than 100 percent.
SOURCE: U.S. Department of the Treasury

This graph shows the revenue sources or sources of money in the government's budget.

Review Questions

1. Describe the economic system of the United States.

2. Graph Skills What are the largest sources of the U.S. Government's income?

3. What are two ways the government encourages economic growth in the U.S. economy?

| 1886 American Federation of Labor formed | 1913 Federal Reserve System created | 1929 Stock market crash | 1947 Taft-Hartley Act | 1955 AFL and CIO merge | 1980 Savings and Loan crisis begins | 2007 United States plunges into recession |

1900

1950

2000

| 1892 Homestead Strike in Pennsylvania | 1930 Great Depression begins | 1933 Federal Deposit Insurance Corporation (FDIC) created | 1963 Equal Pay Act | 1997 More than 160,000 ATMs operate in United States |

Measuring the Economy

The Federal Reserve or Fed is the central banking system of the United States. It functions as a bank for other banks and for the federal government. The Fed is responsible for monetary policy, which means it makes decisions that help to manage the growth of the economy. The Fed attempts to encourage economic growth by controlling the money supply, availability of credit, and interest rates.

Monetary policy is based on careful study of economic indicators including the rate of inflation and the Gross Domestic Product (GDP). These factors help economists predict changes in the economy.

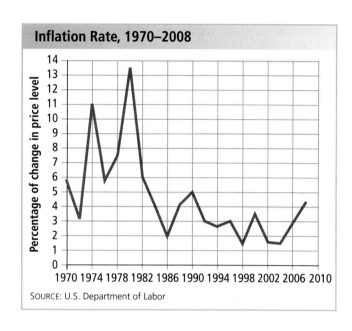

Inflation Rate, 1970–2008

SOURCE: U.S. Department of Labor

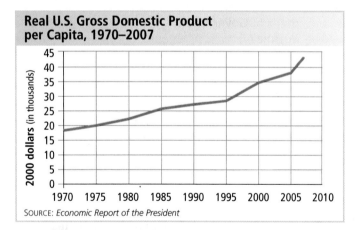

Real U.S. Gross Domestic Product per Capita, 1970–2007

SOURCE: Economic Report of the President

Review Questions

1. What is monetary policy?

2. What factors do economists study to measure the economy?

Inflation is a general increase in prices. In a period of inflation, as prices rise, the same amount of money buys less. As a result, people cannot afford to buy as many goods and services.

The GDP is the total dollar value of goods produced in a country. The GDP grows when more goods and services are being produced. If consumers spend less, fewer goods and services will be produced and the GDP decreases.

The strength of the economy can also be measured by how much people are saving and investing. When you save money, it doesn't just stay in the bank. Banks use your saved money to make loans to businesses. This investment helps the economy grow.

How to Volunteer

Americans are known for their strong tradition of community involvement. You too can become involved by contributing your time and talents to make a difference in your school and community.

Below, Carlos Lopez describes his experience looking for a volunteer job. As you read, think about the steps he took to become a volunteer for a program that teaches inline skating to inner city children.

Carlos Lopez comes from a family of volunteers. His mother, a teacher, volunteers her time after school to help recent immigrants learn English. His father helps out once a month in a local soup kitchen.

Carlos too wanted to help his community, so he looked into possibilities for community service. He talked to friends in the Service Learning Club at school. He also looked online to learn more about national organizations such as Habitat for Humanity and Meals on Wheels. He looked at volunteer opportunities listed in his local newspaper. Soon Carlos had a list of ten possibilities to consider.

Carlos then had to decide how much time he could spend volunteering. Between homework, chores, and sports, Carlos figured he could volunteer about three hours a week, as long as his volunteer job was close by.

Carlos also considered his strengths and interests in choosing where to volunteer. He liked teaching younger children, and he wanted to be outdoors.

Carlos saw a notice at school asking for volunteers to teach inline skating to inner city children, using donated skates and gear. He talked to classmates who volunteered for the program and visited it the next week.

Today the children are learning a new skill and getting fresh air and exercise. Carlos has the satisfaction of helping others who would not otherwise have this opportunity.

Learn the Skill

To find a volunteer job, follow these steps:

❶ **Research your options.** Find out about possible volunteer jobs in your community.

❷ **Determine your strengths, interests, and availability.**

Practice the Skill

❶ Make a list of at least five volunteer opportunities you have heard or read about.

❷ List your own strengths, interests, and availability.

❸ Decide which volunteer opportunities on your list would be best for you.

Apply the Skill

Find out about volunteer opportunities in your community. Research one and report your findings to the class.

How to Cast Your Vote

One of the most important ways to voice your opinion is through your vote. By voting for those representatives who reflect your own opinions, you can exercise some influence over the choices the government makes. The process of casting a vote is quite simple. See the box below for some of the most frequently asked questions and answers about voting.

Who can vote?

- American citizens
- at least 18 years of age
- who live in the state in which they wish to vote

How do you register to vote?

- Go to city hall or the county courthouse, or register when you apply for or renew your driver's license.
- Take proof of your age along, such as a birth certificate.
- Check to see if you can register on the Internet.

Who should you vote for?

- Read newspaper and magazine articles that tell you the candidates' views on important issues.

- Check online to see if the candidates have Web sites that tell you more about them.
- Listen to candidates' speeches.

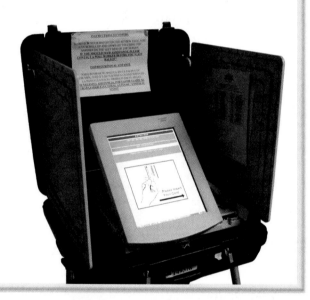

Learn the Skill

To cast your vote, follow these steps:

1. **Find the location of your polling place.** Your voter registration card should identify your polling place.

2. **Go to your polling place on Election Day.** Your name will be checked against a list of registered voters.

3. **Cast your vote.** You will mark your ballot or make your choices on a touch screen or another type of voting device.

Practice the Skill

Call your local courthouse or city hall to find out where you should register to vote. Then find out where people in your area go to cast their votes.

Apply the Skill

Choose a recent presidential election. Decide for whom you would have voted in that election.

How to Evaluate Leadership

What sort of person should you choose to represent you? Part of the answer depends on the position being filled. You may find certain qualities important for town supervisor and others important for U.S. Senator.

No matter what the position, you must evaluate the candidate before you cast your ballot. Consider the scenario below, which describes one citizen's evaluation of a candidate for state representative.

Hannah is planning to vote in an upcoming election for state representative. Three people are running for the office—a Democrat, a Republican, and a third-party candidate.

Hannah decides that a few qualities top her list as the most important for a public servant to possess. They are honesty, experience, and creative approaches to solving problems. Hannah also knows that her state is suffering from high unemployment and a substandard educational system.

Hannah watches the candidates on television, reads newspaper articles, and visits their Web sites. She learns that the third-party candidate is mainly concerned with a narrow list of issues and decides to eliminate him.

Hannah learns that the Republican candidate has served in public office before, while the Democratic candidate is new to politics.

Since she believes that an experienced candidate can accomplish more, she is considering eliminating the Democrat. She continues her research and finds that the Republican was a high school teacher for 15 years before entering politics and that during his time as mayor of a small city, he boosted the local economy. Based on these factors, Hannah decides to vote for the Republican candidate.

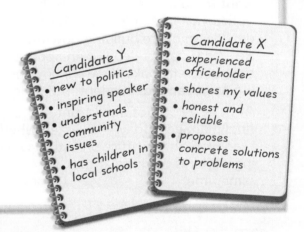

Candidate Y
- new to politics
- inspiring speaker
- understands community issues
- has children in local schools

Candidate X
- experienced officeholder
- shares my values
- honest and reliable
- proposes concrete solutions to problems

Learn the Skill

To learn how to evaluate leadership, follow these steps.

1 **Choose the qualities that make a good leader.** Make a list of your criteria.

2 **Rate your subject.** Using your criteria, rate the person you are evaluating on the basis of their actions, speeches, and other's experiences with them.

Practice the Skill

1 What resources does Hannah use to find out about the candidates?

2 What state issues does Hannah believe her representative will have to address?

Apply the Skill

Choose someone in a leadership position, such as a member of Congress or the President. Evaluate that person based on your leadership criteria.

How to Work on a Political Campaign

If you are interested in politics, consider volunteering to work on a political campaign. It takes the support of hundreds of volunteers to run for national office. State and local campaigns also depend on volunteer help. The diary entries below describe how one volunteer found work on a political campaign.

July 20th Talked to Tyler today about the upcoming election. We both support the Independent Party. I like their position on the environment, and Tyler supports their government reform efforts.

August 12th Tyler and I have both decided to volunteer to work on Adam Santini's campaign for governor! I was on Adam's Web site and noticed that they had a form to fill out for people who want to help in the campaign. Tyler noticed a "Santini for Governor" sign outside an office building downtown. He went in and filled out an application to volunteer. Looks like we'll both be trying to get an Independent into office!

August 27th Got a call from the Santini field manager today, who asked whether I can work in the office on Saturday mornings. Tyler is working at the same time.

September 3rd I sure had my eyes opened at the Santini headquarters today! It takes a lot of work, and a lot of workers, to get someone elected! There are field workers, communications workers, a policy team, a fundraising department, and a scheduling department.

October 15th Things are really heating up now that the election is so close. We've been handing out fliers and making phone calls. Other people are making posters and entering data into the computer. We need all the help we can get!

November 10th Well, the election is officially over and—WE WON!! It was a lot of hard work, but we did it together and now we can watch things change with Santini in office!

Learn the Skill

To work on a political campaign, follow these steps:

① Choose a candidate. Why did the volunteers above decide to work for Santini?

② Find out how to contact the candidate's organization. How did the volunteers get in touch with the Santini campaign?

③ Find out about volunteer opportunities. What tasks did the volunteers do?

Practice the Skill

① Choose a candidate you wish to support in the next national, state, or local election.

② Think about your availability and what kind of transportation you will need.

Apply the Skill

Contact the candidate's campaign headquarters to learn about volunteer opportunities.

How to Write a Letter to the Editor

The Constitution of the United States guarantees all citizens the right to express their views on political issues. One way to do this is to write a letter to the editor of your local newspaper. If your letter is printed, other citizens will be able to read your opinion.

Below is a letter to the editor from a concerned citizen. Read the letter, and think about the citizen's opinion. Has he expressed it clearly? Has he given good reasons for feeling the way he does? Does the letter influence you?

Editor:

Thank you for the articles in your paper identifying the importance of recycling. It is the responsibility of every citizen to care for our environment, and recycling is a simple and effective way of caring. Before our family began recycling, we were not aware of how much newspaper, glass, aluminum, paper, and plastic we used. We have been amazed at the amounts we accumulate each week.

The new city program offering curbside pickup service makes recycling easy and convenient. We urge everyone to participate in the new program. To learn more, contact the city manager's office.

Sincerely,

Matt Reilly

Learn the Skill

To write an effective letter to the editor, follow these steps:

1. **Find out about volunteer opportunities.** What tasks did the volunteers do?

2. **State your opinion.** Give two reasons why you feel the way you do. Support your reasons with evidence or examples.

3. **Reaffirm your point of view.** You may also share your suggestions for overcoming the problem or working out the issue.

Practice the Skill

1. Brainstorm a list of three issues. For each one, write one statement that expresses your opinion. Write at least two reasons or examples to support your opinion.

2. Take turns sharing your ideas with a classmate. You should be able to understand each other's views on the issues each of you has chosen.

Apply the Skill

1. Select one of your three issues and write a letter to the editor.

2. Send your letter to the editor of your local newspaper.

How to Conduct a Poll

The United States is a representative democracy. This means that public officials act on behalf of the citizens who elected them. To do this effectively, they must know how citizens feel about different issues.

Polls are a good way of determining public opinion. A poll is a list of questions like those below. Many people answer these questions. The results of a poll give a good idea of how people may feel about different issues.

Forced-Choice Questions

A forced-choice question makes the person give a definite answer. For example, the person may have to choose either "yes" or "no."

Example: The minimum voting age should be raised to 21.

_____ yes _____ no

Scaled Questions

Scaled questions ask a person to gauge how strongly they feel about an issue.

Example: Circle your reaction to the following statement: The Constitution continues to meet the needs of Americans today.

Disagree   Uncertain   Agree

Ranked Questions

A ranked question gives a list of items. The person must put them in order of importance to him or her.

Example: Rank the following in order of importance. Use a 1 for the freedom you think is most important and a 3 for the freedom you think is least important.

_____ freedom of the press

_____ freedom of speech

_____ freedom of assembly

Learn the Skill

To conduct a poll, follow these steps:

1 Choose an issue and write poll questions that ask about people's opinions of it. Think of an issue that is of importance to many people. Include each type of question in your poll.

2 Ask people to take the poll. Ask at least ten people.

3 Compile the results. How many people answered each question the same way?

Practice the Skill

1 Write two examples of each type of question.

2 Have a partner read your questions to make sure they are clear and worded fairly.

Apply the Skill

1 Choose an issue and write six poll questions about it.

2 Ask 20 people to complete your poll.

3 Compile the results and report them to the class.

How to Use the Internet as a News Source

If you have a particular news topic you'd like to research, you can use a combination of magazines, newspapers, and Internet sources. The major television networks, newspapers, and magazines all have Web sites.

Reggie wanted to learn about the President's recent visit to Latin America. Read the material below to find out how he went about his search for information.

8:30 a.m.

"Let's see. The President went to Latin America on Monday. The press should have been covering his visit all week. First, I'll look in the local newspaper for information, starting on Tuesday. . . .

9:00 a.m.

"Our paper had one story about the visit. I think I'll stop at the library and see what some of the bigger newspapers and news magazines reported. . . .

11:00 a.m.

"That was interesting. Those sources included some photographs, and the main newspapers discussed the President's visit each day. I wonder what I can find on the Internet? . . .

1:00 p.m.

"Wow! A search online turned up lots of news articles on the subject. Each article had links to related articles on the same subject. The search also turned up some editorials on the President's trip and official news releases from the White House. It will be easy to compare their different points of view."

Learn the Skill

To learn how to use the Internet as a news source, follow these steps.

❶ Use a search engine to find Internet news sources.

❷ Be sure that your sources have a reputation for accurate news coverage. If you are unsure of a source's reliability, compare it to sources you know to be trustworthy.

Practice the Skill

❶ What information was Reggie able to locate online?

❷ How did the online information differ from the print information?

Apply the Skill

❶ Choose a topic in the news. Type a keyword or phrase about the topic into a search engine.

❷ Follow those results that appear to be good news sources.

❸ Explain how each site helped broaden your understanding of the topic.

How to Write a Letter to a Public Official

Public officials are elected in order to carry out the political goals of citizens. One way to participate in government is to let your elected representatives know how you feel about certain issues.

You can write a letter to convey your opinion about an issue. Your letter should state your views clearly and give reasons why you feel the way you do. Below, a concerned citizen asks her representative to take action on an issue.

> 2213 Essex Road
> Castle City, CA 94320
> August 28, 1994
>
> The Honorable Carmen Mendoza
> House of Representatives
> Washington, D.C. 20515
>
> Dear Representative Mendoza:
>
> Last evening, I saw your interview on the news. You said you were concerned about the lack of recreational facilities for teenagers in many areas. I share your concern. Unlike me, you can do much to solve this problem. You could propose a bill that provides federal funds to build such facilities.
>
> Opponents of this bill might say that building such facilities would be very expensive. But what would be more expensive in the long run—abandoning many teens to a life of crime or providing an alternative to life on the streets? Many older people have testified that they were saved from the evils of street life by an opportunity to channel their energies into sports and other programs provided at recreational centers.
>
> I have seen you express your concern on television. Now I would like to know what you plan to do about this problem.
>
> Respectfully yours,
> Cleotis Larkin

Learn the Skill

To write a letter to a public official, follow these steps:

1 **Find out to whom you should write.** Do some research or call a few offices to find the best person to hear your comments.

2 **Address the letter.** Follow the correct format for a letter.

3 **Clearly state your purpose.** Provide reasons to back it up.

Practice the Skill

1 Read the letter above. Find the writer's address, the receiver's address, the greeting, and the signature.

2 Analyze the body of the letter. Did the writer convey her purpose clearly?

Apply the Skill

1 Choose an issue that concerns you. Find out which public official handles that issue.

2 Write a letter. Have a teacher or classmate read it over. Send it to the public official.

How to Analyze Television News Programs

Most Americans get information about local, national, and world events by watching the news on television. This means that television has a great influence on public opinion. When you watch the news, you should think critically about how information is presented to you.

A news program can make people think a certain way about issues. It could leave out important information without which you might think differently. Also, television news networks choose which stories to report and how much time to spend on them.

For a school project, Darius Heely is tracking the news. Every evening for the past two weeks, he has watched the same news program. He sits by the television with his notebook in hand.

When the program starts, he gets his pencil and his stopwatch ready. For each story, Darius jots down the subject and records the time. He makes notes, such as whether a story was national or international, if it covered violent content, or if it seemed more like entertainment than news.

At the end of the program, Darius reads over the notes that he has taken. Sometimes he disagrees with how the news was presented by this program.

For the last part of his project, Darius will compare his notes about all of the news content aired during the two weeks. He will see which stories were reported several days in a row and which got the most attention. By doing this, Darius will get a good idea of how the news networks shape public issues.

Learn the Skill

To analyze the news, follow these steps:

1. **Make a chart.** The columns should show the subject, length of time, location, and other notes.

2. **Watch the news.** Fill in the chart.

3. **Think about it.** What did you think was the most important story? Which was given the most emphasis? Were some less important than others? How long were most stories?

Practice the Skill

1. Watch the news with a friend or family member. Each of you should fill out a chart.

2. Decide which story you thought was the most important. Choose one thing you liked and one thing you didn't like about the program.

3. Compare your reactions with others.

Apply the Skill

1. With a group of classmates, read through a newspaper.

2. Plan a television news program with the stories from the newspaper.

3. Explain your group's decisions to the class.

How to Serve on a Jury

The Constitution of the United States guarantees all persons the right to trial by jury. Ordinary citizens serve on a jury. They are the ones to hear and judge the facts in a case.

As major participants, jurors are vitally important in the American system of justice. If you are called to serve on a jury, keep in mind that you will help to ensure that the defendant will be treated fairly by the courts.

A Juror's Responsibilities

When the Court . . .	the Juror must . . .
sends the potential juror a summons to appear in court on a specific date and time, . . .	. . . appear in court as requested.
requests the juror to swear that he or she will tell the truth, . . .	. . . swear an oath.
questions the juror to determine whether he or she is qualified and suitable to serve on the jury, . . .	. . . answer truthfully.
presents the case against the defendant . . .	. . . give careful attention to the testimony and evidence.
excuses the jury to deliberate and decide the case, . . .	. . . weigh the evidence and decide the case, being careful to follow the steps below.

Learn the Skill

To learn how to serve on a jury, follow these steps.

❶ **Avoid bias.** Do not allow likes or dislikes for either side to influence you.

❷ **Remember that the defendant is presumed innocent.** The government must prove guilt "beyond a reasonable doubt."

Practice the Skill

❶ As a juror, how might you avoid bias?

❷ Consider the phrase "beyond a reasonable doubt." What does this phrase mean?

Apply the Skill

❶ Consider the following: A woman named Linda Wright has been accused of stealing from the cash drawer at the store where she works. She claims to be innocent.

❷ Conduct a mock jury trial as a class based on the scenario above.

How to Identify Your Political Roots and Attitudes

A person's political roots can be traced back to early childhood and the influence of family, friends, and teachers.

The excerpt below is from the Web site of a fictional presidential candidate. As you read, look for hints about his political roots and attitudes.

"My name is Joshua Heckman, and I am running for President. Since I wouldn't vote for someone whom I know nothing about, I wouldn't expect you to, either. I've set up this Web site to help you get to know me.

"I was born into a working class neighborhood in Detroit, Michigan. I went to public school and played baseball and basketball. When I was 12 years old, my dad got sick. He couldn't work anymore, and we didn't have any health insurance, so things got pretty tight financially. My mom went to work, but we still had to sell our house. A few years later, my dad recovered and things improved enough that I was able to attend college by taking out several student loans.

"I studied public administration in college, and got a job as business manager of a large Michigan hospital. My years there taught me a lot about people and the challenges they face. Later I ran for the state legislature and have served there for 10 years. I believe these experiences will motivate and enable me to make a real difference for the people of the United States."

Learn the Skill

To learn how to identify your political roots and attitudes, follow these steps.

1. **Identify any early political experiences you have had.** Recall, for example, family conversations about politics.

2. **Identify the influences of the place where you live, your ethnic and religious ties, and your personal interests.**

3. **Consider the effects of personal experiences.** Describe an experience with a specific person or event that influenced your political attitudes.

Practice the Skill

In what ways would you expect Heckman's background to influence his later political attitudes?

Apply the Skill

Interview a friend or family member. Use the steps above to help this person identify the influences on his or her political attitudes.

How to Participate in Public Debate

Government institutions and policies affect citizens' lives every day. You may sometimes disagree with the way the government has handled an issue, or you may have a suggestion for solving a public problem. There are many ways you can share your views with government officials.

Mia Renatti was upset by her city's plan to tear down her school and build a new one. As you read about Mia, think about what issues you might want to speak out about.

Mia Renatti lives in one of the oldest neighborhoods in her city. She attends the same school that her older sisters, her father, and her grandmother attended. She lives just down the street from the school and grew up playing on its playground.

Mia was very upset when the city announced that it was considering tearing down the school and completely rebuilding it. Mia didn't think a whole new building was necessary. She thought about the different ways she could convince her neighborhood to fight the new school.

Mia decided she could reach out to other concerned citizens by speaking at a public school board meeting. She thought about all the reasons why her school was important to her and about how expensive the long-term construction project would be.

The day of the meeting came, and Mia was very nervous. But she knew that many people in the audience felt the way she did. She delivered her speech, and everyone applauded. At the end of the meeting, the school board decided that it would be best to preserve the old school.

Learn the Skill

To express your views publicly, follow these steps:

❶ Identify a local issue.

❷ Find out which government bodies are involved. Do some research on the issue to find out which offices handle it and what impact they have on the issue.

❸ Decide the best way to express your opinion. Write a letter to one of the government offices, attend a city council meeting, or speak with your neighbors.

Practice the Skill

❶ With a partner, research a community issue.

❷ Contact relevant local organizations to receive information.

❸ Send a letter to one organization expressing your views on the issue.

Apply the Skill

❶ Prepare a short speech about the issue you have researched.

❷ Hold a "city council meeting" in class and deliver your speech.

The glossary defines all high-use words and many key historical words and terms. The high-use words appear underlined the first time that they are used in the text. The key words and terms appear in blue type the first time that they are used. Each word in the glossary is defined in both English and Spanish. The page number(s) after the English definition refers to the page(s) on which the word or phrase is defined in the text. For other references, see the index.

Pronunciation Key

When difficult names or terms first appear in the text, they are respelled to help you with pronunciation. A syllable printed in small capital letters receives the greatest stress. The pronunciation key below lists the letters and symbols that will help you pronounce the word. It also includes examples of words using each of the sounds and shows how each word would be pronounced.

Symbol	Example	Respelling
a	hat	(hat)
ay	pay, late	(pay), (layt)
ah	star, hot	(stahr), (haht)
ai	air, dare	(air), (dair)
aw	law, all	(law), (awl)
eh	met	(meht)
ee	bee, eat	(bee), (eet)
er	learn, sir, fur	(lern), (ser), (fer)
ih	fit	(fiht)
ī	mile	(mīl)
ir	ear	(ir)
oh	no	(noh)
oi	soil, boy	(soil), (boi)
oo	root, rule	(root), (rool)
or	born, door	(born), (dor)
ow	plow, out	(plow), (owt)

Symbol	Example	Respelling
u	put, book	(put), (buk)
uh	fun	(fuhn)
yoo	few, use	(fyoo), (yooz)
ch	chill, reach	(chihl), (reech)
g	go, dig	(goh), (dihg)
j	jet, gently bridge	(jeht), (JEHNT lee), (brihj)
k	kite, cup	(kīt), (kuhp)
ks	mix	(mihks)
kw	quick	(kwihk)
ng	bring	(brihng)
s	say, cent	(say), (sehnt)
sh	she, crash	(shee), (krash)
th	three	(three)
y	yet, onion	(yeht), (UHN yuhn)
z	zip, always	(zihp), (AWL wayz)
zh	treasure	(TREH zher)

A

abolitionist (a boh LIH shuhn ihst) person who wanted to end slavery (p. R 1)
abolicionista persona que quería abolir la esclavitud

accelerate (ak SEL er ayt) to increase in speed (pp. 621, 713)
acelerar aumentar la velocidad

accommodation (ak kom moh DAY shuhn) adjustment; adaptation (pp. 501, 925)
acomodo ajuste; adaptación

accumulate (uh KYOOM yoo layt) to collect slowly; to increase in amount over time (p. 753)
acumular reunir lentamente; aumentar una cantidad con el tiempo

affirmative action (uh FERM uh tihv AK shuhn) program to provide more job and education opportunities for people who faced discrimination in the past (p. 892)
acción afirmativa programa diseñado para proporcionar más oportunidades de trabajo y educación a la gente que sufrió discriminación en el pasado

aggression (uh GREHSH uhn) warlike act by one country against another without cause (p. 804)
agresión acto de guerra de un país en contra de otro sin causa alguna

airlift (AIR lihft) emergency shipment of supplies sent via airplane (p. 838)
puente aéreo envío de mercancía de emergencia por avión

alter (AWL ter) to change; to make different (pp. 613, 911, 939)
alterar cambiar; hacer algo diferente

amendment (ah MEHND mehnt) revision or addition to a bill, law, or constitution (p. R 4)
enmienda revisión o adición a un proyecto de ley, ley o constitución

amnesty (AM nehs tee) government pardon (p. 547)
amnistía indulto que otorga el gobierno

analyze (AN ah līz) to examine something in detail in order to determine its nature (p. 750)
analizar examinar algo en detalle para establecer su naturaleza

anarchist (AN ahr kehst) person who opposes all forms of government (pp. 629, 739)
anarquista persona que se opone a todas las formas de gobierno

annex (an NEHKS) to add on or take over (p. R 7)
anexar agregar o apoderarse de algo

anti-Semitism (an tee SEH mih tihz uhm) prejudice against Jews (p. 665)
antisemitismo prejuicio contra los judíos

apartheid (uh PAHR tayt) in South Africa, policy of strict racial segregation (p. 949)
apartheid en Sudáfrica, política de estricta segregación racial

appeasement (uh PEEZ mehnt) policy of giving into aggression in order to avoid war (p. 804)
apaciguamiento política de consentir la agresión para evitar la guerra

armistice (AHR muh stis) halt in fighting that allows peace talks to begin (p. 720)
armisticio suspensión en la lucha de guerra que permite que comiencen las charlas de paz

arms race (ahrmz rays) contest in which nations compete to build more and more powerful weapons (p. 855)
carrera armamentista lucha en la cual las naciones compiten por construir armas cada vez más potentes

assembly line (ah SEHM blee līn) manufacturing method in which a product is put together as it moves along a conveyor belt (p. 613)
línea de montaje método de manufactura por el cual se arma un producto a medida que se desplaza en una banda transportadora

assimilation (ah sih mih LAY shuhn) process of becoming part of another culture (p. 627)

asimilación proceso de convertirse en parte de otra cultura

authority (uh THAWR uh tee) the right to give orders, make decisions, or take action (p. 911)
autoridad el derecho a dar ordenes, tomar decisiones o actuar

B

baby boom (BAY bee boom) large increase in the birthrate from the late 1940s through the early 1960s (p. 845)
baby boom gran aumento de la tasa de natalidad entre la segunda mitad de la década de 1940 y la primera mitad de la década de 1960

balanced budget (BAL ehnst BUHJ iht) condition that exists when a government spends only as much as it collects (p. 938)
presupuesto equilibrado condición que existe cuando un gobierno gasta sólo tanto como lo que recibe

bankruptcy (BANK ruhpt see) financial failure caused by an inability to pay one's debts (p. 772)
quiebra fracaso financiero causado por la incapacidad para pagar las deudas

bilingual (bī LIHNG gwuhl) in two languages; describing a person that has the ability to speak two languages fluently (p. 895)
bilingüe en dos idiomas; descripción de una persona que tiene la habilidad para hablar dos idiomas con fluidez

black codes (blak kohds) southern laws that severely limited the rights of African Americans after the Civil War (p. 553)
códigos negros leyes sureñas que limitaron severamente los derechos de los afroamericanos después de la Guerra Civil

blockade (BLAHK ayd) shutting a port or roadway to prevent people or supplies from coming into or leaving an area (p. 515)
bloqueo cierre de un puerto o camino para impedir que entren o salgan personas o provisiones en cierta zona

boat people (boht PEE puhl) after the Vietnam War, refugees who escaped from Vietnam in small boats (p. 923) *balseros* después de la Guerra de Vietnam, refugiados que huyeron de Vietnam a bordo de botes pequeños

bonus (BOH nuhs) additional sum of money (p. 775)
bono suma de dinero adicional

bootlegger (BOOT lehg uhr) person who smuggled liquor into the United States during Prohibition (p. 741)
contrabandista de alcohol persona que contrabandeaba alcohol a Estados Unidos durante el período de la Prohibición

border state (BOR der stayt) slave state that remained in the Union during the Civil War (p. 513)
estado fronterizo estado esclavista que permaneció en la Unión durante la Guerra Civil

boycott (BOI kaht) organized campaign to refuse to buy or use certain goods and services (p. 877)
boicot campaña organizada para rehusar comprar o usar ciertos bienes y servicios

bracero (bruh SER oh) Mexican laborer (p. 820)
bracero trabajador mexicano

bull market (bool MAHR kiht) period of increased stock trading and rising stock prices (p. 753)
mercado alcista período de aumento en la transacción de acciones y aumento de sus precios

buying on margin (BĪ ihng ahn MAHR jihn) borrowing money in order to buy stocks (p. 753)
comprar sobre la base de margen pedir prestado dinero para poder comprar acciones

C

carpetbagger (KAHR peht BAG er) uncomplimentary nickname for a northern white who went to the South after the Civil War to start a business or pursue a political career (p. 555)
carpetbagger sobrenombre despreciativo dado a los norteños blancos que se mudaron al Sur después de la Guerra Civil para emprender un negocio o seguir una carrera política

casualty (KA su ahl tee) military term for a person killed, wounded, or missing in action (p. 520)
baja término militar que describe a una persona muerta, herida o desaparecida en combate

cattle drive (KAT tl drīv) herding and moving of cattle over long distances, usually to railroads (p. 590)
arreo de ganado conducción y traslado de ganado a grandes distancias, por lo regular hacia los ferrocarriles

cattle kingdom (KAT tl KING duhm) region dominated by the cattle industry and its ranches, trails, and cow towns (p. 593)
región ganadera región donde predomina la industria ganadera y sus ranchos, sendas y pueblos vaqueros

censure (SEHN sher) to officially condemn (p. 854)
censura condenar oficialmente

charter (CHAHR ter) official document that gives certain rights to an individual or a group (p. R 2)
carta de privilegio documento oficial que confiere ciertos derechos a un individuo o grupo

checks and balances (chehks and BAL an sez) a principle of the U.S. Constitution that gives each branch of government the power to check, or limit, the actions of the other branches (p. R 4)
control y equilibrio principio de la Constitución de Estados Unidos que otorga a cada rama del gobierno el poder de controlar o limitar las acciones de las otras ramas

circuit (SIR kuht) route repeatedly traveled; circular trip around an area (p. 633)
circuito trayecto que se recorre una y otra vez; un recorrido circular en torno a un área

civil disobedience (SIHV ihl dih soh BEE dee ehns) idea based on nonviolence that people have a right to disobey a law they consider unjust, if their consciences demand it (p. 886)
desobediencia civil idea de que las personas tienen derecho, sin usar la violencia, a desobedecer una ley que consideren injusta, si su conciencia así lo exige

civil rights (SIHV uhl rīts) rights guaranteed in the Constitution, especially voting and equal treatment under the law (p. 784)
derechos civiles derechos garantizados en la Constitución, especialmente el derecho a voto y el trato igualitario ante la ley

civil service (SIHV ihl SER vihs) system that includes most government jobs, except elected positions, the judiciary, and the military (p. 645)

administración pública sistema que incluye a la mayoría de los trabajos del gobierno, excepto a los cargos elegidos, a los judiciales y a los militares

civil war (SIHV ihl wor) war between people of the same country (p. 503)
guerra civil guerra entre habitantes de un mismo país

clarify (KLAIR ih fī) to make the meaning of something clear (p. 497)
aclarar explicar el significado de algo

clause (klawz) part of a law, treaty, or other written agreement (p. 724)
cláusula parte de una ley, tratado u otro acuerdo escrito

clinic (KLIHN ihk) place where people receive medical treatment, often for free or for a small fee (p. 622)
clínica lugar donde las personas reciben asistencia médica, en muchos casos gratuitamente o a cambio de un pago reducido

cloning (KLOHN ihng) process of making a genetic double of a plant or an animal (p. 985)
clonar proceso de hacer una duplicación genética de una planta o animal

closed shop (klohzd shahp) workplace in which only union members can be hired (p. 843)
plantilla de sindicación obligatoria lugar de trabajo en el cual sólo se puede contratar a trabajadores sindicalizados

colleague (KAHL eeg) person who works in the same profession (p. 737)
colega persona que trabaja en la misma profesión

collective bargaining (koh LEHK tihv BAHR gehn ing) negotiation between company management and a union representing a group of workers about wages, benefits, and working conditions (pp. 618, 791)
negociación colectiva negociación entre un sindicato que representa a un grupo de trabajadores y la dirección de una compañía acerca de los salarios, prestaciones y condiciones de trabajo

collide (koh LĪD) to come together with great force or violence; to crash (p. 715)
colisionar encontrarse con gran fuerza o violencia; chocar

communism (KAHM yoo nihz uhm) economic and political system in which the state owns the means of production and a single party rules (pp. 719, 738)
comunismo sistema económico y político en el que el estado es dueño de los medios de producción y gobierna un partido único

compulsory education (kuhm PUHL sor ee ehd jyoo KAY shuhn) requirement that children attend school up to a certain age (p. 632)
educación obligatoria exigencia de que los niños asistan a la escuela hasta una edad determinada

confer (kuhn FER) to exchange ideas with someone (pp. 783, 920)
conferir intercambiar ideas con alguien

confine (kuhn FĪN) to keep within certain limits; to shut or imprison (p. 955)
confinar mantener dentro de ciertos límites; encerrar o encarcelar

conscientious objector (kahn shee EHN shuhs ahb JEHK tehr) person who refuses to take part in war because of a strong belief that war is wrong (p. 915)
objetor de conciencia persona que rehúsa participar en la guerra debido a su fuerte creencia de que la guerra es algo erróneo

conservation (kahn ser VAY shuhn) protection of natural resources (p. 651)
conservación protección de los recursos

consume (kuhn SYOOM) to use up (p. 972)
consumir usar

containment (kuhn TAYN muhnt) policy of limiting the expansion or influence of a hostile power; America's method to limit Soviet expansion during the Cold War (p. 837)
contención política de limitar la expansión o influencia de una potencia hostil; método de EE.UU. de limitar la expansión soviética durante la Guerra Fría

controversy (KAHN truh vur see) argument or dispute (p. 483)
controversia discusión o disputa

convoy (KAHN voy) a large group of merchant vessels sailing together (p. 718)
convoy grupo de barcos mercantiles que navegan en conjunto

Copperhead (KAHP er hehd) northerner who opposed using force to keep the southern states in the Union (p. 531)
Copperhead norteño que se oponía al uso de la fuerza para mantener a los estados sureños dentro de la Unión

corollary (KOR oh lair ee) a logical extension of a doctrine or proposition (p. 696)
corolario una extensión lógica de una doctrina o proposición

corporation (kor por AY shuhn) business owned by many investors (p. 614)
compañía empresa que es propiedad de muchos inversionistas

counterterrorism (kownt er TEHR ehr ihz uhm) action taken against terrorism (p. 970)
contraterrorismo acción tomada en contra del terrorismo

crisis (KRĪ sihs) turning point or deciding event; situation involving great risk (pp. 484, 664, 956)
crisis momento crucial o acontecimiento decisivo; una situación que implica un gran riesgo

critic (KRIHT ihk) someone who makes judgments about objects or actions (pp. 553, 681, 749, 944)
crítico persona que hace juicios sobre objetos o acciones

currency (KER rehn see) money used to make purchases (p. 531)
moneda dinero que se usa para realizar compras

D

decline (dee KLĪN) to lose strength or power over a period of time (p. 770)
decaer perder fuerza o poder a lo largo de cierto tiempo

default (dee FAWLT) failure to repay loans (p. 772)
no pago incumplimiento del pago de los préstamos

deficit (DEHF uh siht) debt that results when more money is spent than earned (p. 939)
déficit deuda que resulta de gastar más dinero del que se gana

deficit spending (DEHF uh siht SPEHND ihng) government practice of spending more money than is taken in from taxes (p. 792)

déficit presupuestario práctica gubernamental de gastar más dinero del que se recauda con los impuestos

demilitarized zone (DMZ) (dee MIHL uh tuh rīzd zohn) area from which military forces are prohibited (p. 852)
zona desmilitarizada área en la que se prohibe la entrada a fuerzas militares

deport (dee PORT) to expel from a country (p. 727)
deportar expulsar de un país

deprive (dee PRĪV) to keep from happening; to take away something needed by force or intent (pp. 487, 950)
privar impedir que suceda; tomar por la fuerza o con intención algo que se necesita

deregulation (dee rehg yuh LAY shuhn) reduction of federal or state restrictions on businesses (p. 939)
desregulación reducción de las restricciones federales o estatales sobre los negocios

devise (dee VĪZ) to carefully think out; to invent (p. 657)
idear hacer planes cuidadosamente; inventar

dictate (DIHK tayt) to direct or order a specific action (p. 721)
dictar dirigir u ordenar una acción específica

dimension (duh MEHN shuhn) size or extent; length, width, or height (p. 821)
dimensión tamaño o alcance; longitud, anchura o altura

disarmament (dihs AHR muh mehnt) reduction or limitation of armed forces and military weapons (p. 738)
desarme reducción o limitación de las fuerzas armadas o armas militares

dissolve (dih ZAHLV) break up into smaller parts (p. 725)
disolver separar en partes más pequeñas

distinct (dihs TIHNKT) clear or definite; clearly different in its quality (p. 514)
distinto claro o definido; que difiere claramente en cuanto a su calidad

distribute (dihs TRIHB yoot) to spread in an orderly way (p. 985)
distribuir diseminar de manera ordenada

diverse (dih VURS) different or varied (p. 646)
variado que tiene diversidad

dollar diplomacy (DAHL er dih PLOH mah see) idea that economic ties were the best way to expand American influence (p. 696)
diplomacia del dólar idea de que los lazos económicos eran el mejor recurso para expandir la influencia estadounidense

domestic (doh MEHS tihk) having to do with the home or household; pertaining to a country's internal affairs (pp. 736, 782, 883)
doméstico relacionado con la casa o el hogar; relativo a los asuntos internos de un país

dominate (DAHM uh nayt) to rule or control (p. 708)
dominar regir o controlar

domino theory (DAHM uh noh THEER ee) idea that if one country fell to communism, neighboring countries would follow (p. 908)
teoría del efecto domino idea de que si un país caía bajo control comunista, los países vecinos lo seguirían

doves (duhvz) those who oppose war (p. 913)
palomas quienes se oponen a la guerra

draft (draft) system of required military service (p. 530)
leva sistema del servicio militar obligatorio

drastic (DRAS tik) extreme in effect or action (p. 784)
drástico que es extremo en su efecto o en acción

E

e-commerce (ee KAHM ers) business and trade over the Internet (p. 983)
comercio electrónico negocio y comercio a través de Internet

efficient (ee FISH ehnt) acting effectively, without wasted cost or effort (pp. 650, 826)
eficiente que actúa con eficacia, sin desperdiciar costos ni esfuerzos

eliminate (ee LIHM ih nayt) to get rid of (pp. 615, 723, 920)
eliminar deshacerse de algo

emancipate (ee MAN sih payt) to set free (p. 524)
emancipar liberar

embrace (ehm BRAYS) to accept; to hold tight to; to readily accept (p. 496)
abrazar aceptar; aferrarse a; aceptar sin dificultad

emphasize (EHM fah sīz) to stress; to make more important (p. 809)
recalcar destacar; dar más importancia

encounter (ehn KOWN ter) battle or fight (p. 859)
encuentro batalla o lucha

enrich (ehn RIHCH) to make wealthy; to improve or increase in quality or wealth (pp. 644, 987)
enriquecer hacer rico; mejorar o aumentar en cuanto a calidad o riqueza

entrepreneur (ahn treh preh NEWR) someone who sets up new businesses to make a profit (p. 614)
empresario persona que establece negocios nuevos para obtener ganancias

environmentalist (ehn vī ruhn MEHNT uhl ihst) person who works to protect the environment (p. 978)
ambientalista persona que trabaja para proteger el medio ambiente

escalate (EHS kuh layt) to increase or expand (p. 911)
escalar aumentar o ampliar

established church (ee STAB lihsht church) a religion that is officially supported by a nation's government (p. R)
iglesia official religión elegida por un Estado

evident (EHV ih dehnt) clear; easy to understand; obvious (p. 988)
evidente claro; fácil de entender; obvio

exceed (ehks SEED) to go beyond what is expected; to outdo or be greater than what was planned (p. 535)
exceder ir más allá de lo esperado; superar lo proyectado

exclude (ehks KLOOD) to keep out or expel; to reject or not be considered (pp. 629, 684)
excluir mantener fuera o expulsar; rechazar o no considerar

executive branch (ehks ZEHK you tihv branch) branch of government that carries out the laws (p. R 3)
rama ejecutiva rama del gobierno que hace cumplir las leyes

exert (ehks ZERT) to use; to put into action (pp. 645, 897)
ejercer utilizar; poner en acción

expand (ek SPAND) to become or make bigger (pp. 633, 843)
expandir volverse o hacerse más grande

external (ehk STER nuhl) from the outside; having to do with foreign countries (p. 969)
externo de afuera; relacionado con países extranjeros

F

factory system (FAK tor ee SIHS tehm) methods of production that bring workers and machinery together in one place (p. R 6)
sistema de fábricas métodos de producción que reúnen trabajadores y maquinaria en un mismo lugar

farm cooperative (fahrm koh AH per at ihv) group of farmers who pool their money to make large purchases of tools, seeds, and other supplies at a discount (p. 598)
cooperativa agrícola grupo de agricultores que forman un fondo común con su dinero para hacer compras grandes de herramientas, semillas y otras provisiones a precio con descuento

fascism (FASH ihz uhm) political system based on militarism, extreme nationalism, and blind loyalty to the state and its leader (p. 803)
fascismo sistema político basado en el militarismo, en el nacionalismo extremo y en la lealtad ciega al estado y su líder

fate (fayt) outcome; consequence or final result (p. 908)
destino resultado; consecuencia o resultado final

federalism (FEHD er uhl ihz uhm) principle of the U.S. Constitution that establishes the division of power between the federal government and the states (p. R 3)
federalismo principio de la Constitución de Estados Unidos que establece la división de poderes entre el gobierno federal y los estados

fireside chat (FIR sīd chat) informal radio speech first given by President Franklin D. Roosevelt while in office (p. 777)
charla informal discurso radial informal dado inicialmente por el presidente Franklin D. Roosevelt mientras estaba en el cargo

flexible (FLEHKS ah bahl) capable of change; easily bent (p. 983)

flexible capaz de cambiar; que se dobla facilmente

fossil (FAHS uhl) hardened remains of a plant or animal that lived long ago (p. 980)
fósil restos endurecidos de una planta o animal que vivió hace mucho tiempo

fragment (FRAG mehnt) broken part or piece; small section of something (p. 501)
fragmento parte rota o pieza de algo; sección pequeña de algo

free enterprise (free EHN ter prīz) economic system in which each privately owned business decides what to produce, how much to produce, and what prices to charge (p. 616)
libre empresa sistema económico en el que cada empresa de propiedad privada decide qué producir, cuánto producir y qué precios cobrar

free trade (free trayd) agreement between countries to buy and sell without quotas or tariffs on imports or exports (p. 977)
libre comercio acuerdo entre países para vender y comprar sin cupos o aranceles sobre las importaciones o exportaciones

freedmen (FREED mehn) men and women who were legally freed from slavery after the Civil War (p. 548)
libertos hombres y mujeres liberados jurídicamente de la esclavitud después de la Guerra Civil

fugitive (FYOO jih tihv) runaway (p. 484)
fugitivo persona que huye

function (FUHNK shuhn) purpose; proper use; official duty (p. 885)
función propósito; uso adecuado; responsabilidades que conlleva un cargo

fundamental (fuhn duh MEHN tahl) most important part; foundation of an idea or action; the essential quality (p. 793)
fundamental lo más importante; la base de una idea o acción; la cualidad esencial

G

genocide (JEHN uh sīd) deliberate attempt to kill or destroy an entire nation or group of people (p. 826)

genocidio intento deliberado de matar o destruir a toda una nación o grupo de personas

ghetto (GEHT oh) poor run-down neighborhood where one group of people live due to poverty or prejudice (p. 891)
gueto vecindario pobre y decadente donde vive un grupo de gente por motivos de pobreza o prejuicios

glasnost (GLAHS nawst) policy in the Soviet Union of speaking openly about society's problems (p. 945)
glasnost (apertura) política de la Unión Soviética de hablar abiertamente sobre los problemas de la sociedad

global warming (GLOH buhl WAWRM ihng) slow but steady worldwide rise in temperatures (p. 981)
calentamiento global aumento lento, pero constante, de las temperaturas en el mundo

globalization (gloh buhl ī ZAY shuhn) process of creating an international network of trade, communication, and culture (p. 976)
globalización proceso de crear una red internacional de comercio, comunicación y cultura

graduated income tax (GRAD yoo ay tehd IHN kuhm taks) tax on earning that charges different rates for different income levels (p. 647)
impuesto sobre la renta escalonado impuesto sobre las ganancias que aplica tasas diferentes a los distintos niveles de ingreso

grandfather clause (GRAND fah ther klawz) law that excused a voter from a literacy test if his father or grandfather had been eligible to vote on January 1, 1867 (p. 560)
cláusula del abuelo ley que eximía a un votante de la prueba de alfabetización si su padre o abuelo había tenido derecho a votar el 1 de enero de 1867

grange (graynj) group of farmers who met for lectures, sewing bees, and other events (p. 598)
grange grupo de agricultores que se reunían para participar en conferencias, círculos de costura y otras actividades

guerrilla (guh RIHL uh) fighter who works as part of a small band to make hit-and-run attacks (p. 909)
guerrillero combatiente dentro de un pequeño grupo que realiza ataques relámpago

guest worker (gehst WER ker) temporary immigrant worker (p. 987)
trabajador visitante trabajador inmigrante temporero

H

habeas corpus (HAY bee ihs KOR puhs) the right not to be held in prison without first being charged with a specific crime; constitutional protection against unlawful imprisonment (p. 529)
habeas corpus derecho a no ser encarcelado sin antes haber sido acusado de un delito específico; protección constitucional contra el encarcelamiento ilegal

hawks (hawks) those who support, or are in favor of, a particular war (p. 913)
halcones personas que apoyan o están a favor de una guerra específica

homesteader (HOHM steh der) settler who acquired free land offered by the government (p. 595)
finquero colono que adquirió tierras gratis ofrecidas por el gobierno

hostile (HAHS tihl) unfriendly; intending to do harm (pp. 694, 837)
hostil poco amistoso; que se propone hacer daño

I

illiterate (ih LIT ur ut) unable to read and write (p. 713)
analfabeto que no sabe leer ni escribir

immigrate (IHM mah grayt) to move into a foreign region or country (p. 581)
inmigrar mudarse a una región o país extranjero

impeachment (ihm PEECH mehnt) process of bringing formal charges against a public official (p. 556)
juicio político proceso que consiste en presentar una acusación formal contra un funcionario público

imperialism (ihm PIR ee uhl ihz uhm) building empires by imposing outside rule on peoples around the world (p. 681) *imperialismo* construcción de imperios imponiendo un gobierno extranjero a pueblos de otras partes del mundo

impose (ihm POHZ) to place a burden on something or someone (pp. 490, 555, 738)
imponer colocar una carga sobre algo o alguien

income tax (IHN kuhm taks) tax on the money people earn or receive (p. 531)
impuesto a los ingresos impuesto sobre el dinero que la gente gana o recibe

inferior (ihn FIR ee uhr) less worthy; less valuable; of lower rank; of poorer quality (pp. 561, 803)
inferior menos digno; menos valioso; de categoría más baja; de menor calidado

inflation (ihn FLAY shuhn) general rise in prices (pp. 531, 599, 924)
inflación aumento generalizado de los precios

infrastructure (IHN frah struhk cher) basic public works needed for a society to function, including the systems of roads, bridges, and tunnels (p. 778)
infraestructura obras públicas básicas necesarias para el funcionamiento de una sociedad, como los sistemas de carreteras, puentes y túneles

initiative (ihn IH shee ah tihv) process that allows voters to put a bill before a state legislature (p. 647)
iniciativa procedimiento que permite a los votantes presentar un proyecto de ley ante una legislatura estatal

inner city (IHN er SIHT ee) center of an older city (p. 847)
centro urbano la zona centro de una ciudad con bastantes años

installment buying (ihn STAWL mehnt BĪ ihng) buying on credit (p. 752)
compra a plazos compra por medio de crédito

integration (ihn tuh GRAY shuhn) mixing of different racial groups (p. 875)
integración mezcla de diferentes grupos raciales

intermediate (ihn ter MEE dee iht) happening in between; in the middle (p. 945)
intermedio que ocurre entre determinadas cosas; en medio

intern (IHN tern) to temporarily imprison so as to keep from leaving a country (p. 818)

recluir encarcelar temporalmente con el fin de evitar la huida del país

invest (ihn VEHST) to purchase something with money with the hope that its value will grow; to supply money for a project in order to make a profit (p. 696)
invertir adquirir algo a cambio de dinero con la esperanza de que su valor aumente; facilitar dinero para un proyecto para que dé ganacias

iron curtain (Ī ern KERT uhn) barrier of secrecy and censorship that keeps a country isolated from the rest of the world (p. 837)
telón de acero barrera de secretismo y censura que mantiene a un país aislado del resto del mundo

ironclad (Ī ern klad) warship covered with protective iron plates (p. 518)
acorazado barco de guerra cubierto con placas protectoras de hierro

island hopping (Ī luhnd HAHP ihng) Allied strategy used during World War II to gain control of the Pacific Islands (p. 824)
salto de isla a isla estrategia aliada usada durante la Segunda Guerra Mundial para obtener el control de las islas del Pacífico

isolate (Ī soh layt) to set apart; to separate (pp. 503, 627, 743)
aislar apartar; separar

isolationism (Ī soh LAY shuhn ihz uhm) avoiding involvement in other countries' affairs (p. 681)
aislacionismo práctica de evitar la participación en los asuntos de otros países

isthmus (IHS muhs) narrow strip of land having water on each side and joining two larger areas of land (p. 693)
istmo franja estrecha de tierra con agua a ambos lados y que une dos extensiones de tierra más grandes

J

jazz (jaz) original style of music that combined rhythms from West Africa and the Caribbean, work chants and spirituals from the rural South, and harmonies from Europe (p. 747)
jazz estilo original de música que combina ritmos de África occidental y el Caribe, cantos laborales y religiosos del sur rural estadounidense y harmonías de Europa

judicial branch (jyoo DIH shuhl branch) system of courts to settle disputes involving national issues (p. R 3)
poder judicial sistema de tribunales para dirimir pleitos referentes a cuestiones nacionales

justify (JUHS tih fī) to give good reason for an action (p. 616)
justificar dar buenas razones para una acción

K

kamikaze (kah muh KAH zee) World War II Japanese pilot trained to make a suicidal crash attack, usually upon a ship (p. 824)
kamikaze piloto japonés de la Segunda Guerra Mundial entrenado para realizar ataques suicidas, estrellándose generalmente sobre un barco

L

laser (LAY zer) device that sends out a powerful beam of focused light (p. 983)
láser dispositivo que emite un potente haz de luz concentrada

legislative branch (LEHJ ihs lay tihv branch) branch of government that passes laws (p. R 3)
rama legislativa rama del gobierno que aprueba las leyes

levy (LEHV ee) to impose a tax by law; to force to be paid (p. 531)
gravar imponer una contribución por ley; obligar a que se pague

liable (LĪ ah bahl) likely to cause or have an effect (p. 710)
responsable probable que cause o tenga un efecto

literacy test (LIH ter ah see tehst) examination to see if a person can read and write; used in the past to restrict voting rights (p. 560)
prueba de alfabetización examen para establecer si una persona sabe leer y escribir, se usaba en el pasado para restringir el derecho al voto

lynching (LIHNCH ihng) when a mob illegally seizes and executes someone (p. 661)
linchamiento cuando una multitud captura y ejecuta ilegalmente a una persona

M

mandatory retirement (MAN duh tawr ee ree TĪR mehnt) policy that requires people to stop working at a certain age (p. 896)
jubilación obligatoria política que obliga a la gente a dejar de trabajar a cierta edad

Manifest Destiny (MAN uh fest DEHS tuh nee) in the 1800s a belief Americans had the right to spread across the continent (p. R 7)
destino manifiesto creencia que se dieminó en el siglo XIX de que los estadounidenses tenían el derecho y la obligación de ocupar todo el continente, hasta el Pacífico

manual (MAN yoo ahl) involving work done by hand (p. 581)
manual referente al trabajo que se hace con las manos

martial law (MAHR shuhl law) type of rule in which the military is in charge and citizens' rights are suspended (p. 513)
ley marcial tipo de gobierno en el que los militares están al mando y se suspenden los derechos de los ciudadanos

mercantilism (MER kan tihl ihz uhm) economic policy that held that a nation prospered by exporting more goods to foreign nations than it imported from them (p. R 5)
mercantilismo principio económico según el cual una nación prospera exportando más bienes a países extranjeros que los que importa de ellos

migrant worker (MĪ grehnt WER ker) person who moves from one region to another in search of work (p. 784)
trabajador migrante persona que se muda de una región a otra en busca de trabajo

militarism (MIHL uh tuh rihz uhm) glorification of the military (p. 706)
militarismo glorificación de los militares

minimum (MIHN ah muhm) smallest amount possible or allowed (p. 791)
mínimo cantidad más pequeña posible o permitida

mobilize (MOH buh lyz) to prepare for war (p. 712)
mobilizar preparar para la guerra

modify (MAHD ih fī) to change to or in (p. 897)
modificar cambiar a algo o en algo

monopoly (muhn AH poh lee) company that controls all or nearly all business in a particular industry (p. 615)
monopolio compañía que controla toda o casi toda la actividad de una industria en particular

muckraker (MUHK rak er) crusading journalist (p. 648)
muckraker periodista que busca poner en evidencia las ruindades de las personas

myth (mihth) story or legend; imaginary object; invented story (p. 593)
mito cuento o leyenda; objeto imaginario; relato inventado

N

napalm (NAY pahm) explosive, jelly like substance that would burst into flames when dropped on villages and vegetation (p. 912)
napalm sustancia explosiva de tipo gelatinosa que estalla en llamas al dejarse caer sobre aldeas y campos de vegetación

national park (NA shuhn uhl pahrk) natural area protected and managed by the federal government (p. 651)
parque nacional extensión natural protegida y administrada por el gobierno federal

nationalism (NA shuhn uhl ihz uhm) devotion to the interests of one's own country; pride in one's own nation or ethnic group (p. 706)
nacionalismo lealtad a los intereses del propio país; orgullo respecto a la propia nación o grupo étnico

negative (NEHG ah tihv) in opposition to an idea; not positive (p. 846)
negativo opuesto a una idea; no positivo

neutral (NEW truhl) not favoring either side in a dispute (p. 513)
neutral que no favorece a ninguna de las partes en un pleito

O

open range (OH pehn raynj) unfenced land (p. 590)
campo abierto terreno no cercado

outsourcing (OWT sors ihng) having work done in other countries; sending out work to an outside provider or manufacturer in order to cut costs (p. 976)
subcontratación realizar el trabajo en otros países; enviar el trabajo a un proveedor o manufacturero exterior con el fin de recortar costes

overproduction (oh ver proh DUHK shuhn) situation in which the supply of manufactured goods exceeds the demand (p. 771)
superproducción situación en la cual la oferta de bienes manufacturados excede la demanda

P

parochial school (pah ROH kee uhl skool) school sponsored by a church (p. 665)
escuela parroquial escuela auspiciada por una iglesia

participate (pahr TIHS ah payt) to take part in; to share in an activity (p. 754)
participar tomar parte en algo; compartir una actividad

patent (PAT ehnt) document that gives someone the sole right to make and to sell an invention (p. 610)
patente documento que otorga a una persona el derecho exclusivo a fabricar y vender un invento

payroll tax (PAY rohl tax) money the government is authorized to remove from a worker's salary and used to help support the government (p. 790)
impuestos sobre sueldos cantidad de dinero que el gobierno está autorizado a retirar del salario de los trabajadores y que se usa para el mantenimiento del gobierno

pendulum (PEHN jah luhm) hanging weight that swings from side to side in a steady rhythm (p. 811)
péndulo peso que cuelga y que oscila de lado a lado a ritmo constante

pension (PEHN shuhn) sum of money paid regularly as a retirement benefit (p. 781)
pensión cantidad de dinero pagada regularmente como beneficio o prestación de jubilación

persist (per SIHST) to endure; to continue in the face of difficulty (pp. 591, 879)
resistir soportar; continuar a pesar de la dificultad

poll tax (pohl taks) personal tax to be paid before voting (p. 560)
impuesto al voto impuesto personal que debía pagarse para poder votar

popular sovereignty (PAH pyoo lahr SAH ver ehn tee) principle that asserts that people are the primary source of the government's authority; right of people to vote directly on issues (p. 483)
soberanía popular principio que afirma que la gente es la fuente primaria de la autoridad de los gobiernos; derecho de la gente a votar directamente sobre cietas cuestiones

preliminary (pree LIM uh nehr ee) leading up to the main action (p. 525)
preliminar preámbulo a la acción principal

primary (PRĪ mair ee) election in which voters, rather than party leaders, choose their party's candidate for an election (p. 646)
primaria elección donde los votantes, y no los dirigentes de un partido, eligen el candidato de su partido para una elección

productivity (proh duhk TIHV uh tee) rate at which workers produce goods (p. 845)
productividad índice de producción de bienes de los trabajadores

prohibition (proh ih BIH shuhn) total ban on the sale and consumption of alcohol (pp. 659, 741)
ley seca prohibición total de la venta y consumo de alcohol

propaganda (prah peh GAN dah) false or misleading information that is spread to further a cause; information used to sway public opinion (pp. 488, 709)
propaganda información falsa o engañosa que se difunde para apoyar una causa; información usada para influir en la opinión pública

prospect (PRAHS pehkt) expectation; something to look forward to happening (p. 690)
prospecto expectativa; algo que se desea que ocurra

protectorate (proh TEHK tor ayt) independent country whose policies are controlled by an outside power (p. 692)

protectorado país independiente cuya dirección está bajo el control de una potencia extranjera

provoke (prah VOHK) to cause to anger; to excite; to cause an action (p. 977)
provocar incitar al enojo; excitar; dar lugar a una acción

pursue (per SYOO) to chase after; to try to capture (pp. 851, 950)
perseguir ir tras de algo; tratar de capturar

R

rationing (RASH uhn ihng) limits set on the amount of certain goods people can buy (p. 817)
racionar establecer límites sobre la cantidad de ciertos bienes que la gente puede comprar

realist (REE uhl ihst) writer or artist who tries to show life as it is (p. 634)
realista escritor o artista que intenta mostrar la vida tal como es

recall (REE kawl) process by which voters can remove an elected official from office (p. 647)
destitución proceso por el cual los votantes pueden retirar de su cargo a un funcionario electo

recession (rih SEHSH uhn) temporary economic slump that is milder than a depression (p. 938)
recesión descenso económico temporal menos grave que una depresión

reconcentration (ree kahn sehn TRAY shuhn) forced movement of large numbers of people into detention camps for military or political reason (p. 688)
reconcentración traslado de un gran número de personas a campos de confinamiento por motivos militares o políticos

referendum (reh fer EHN duhm) process by which citizens vote directly on a bill (p. 647)
referéndum procedimiento por el cual los ciudadanos votan directamente respecto a un proyecto de ley

refine (ree FĪN) to purify; to make free from impurities (p. 609)
refinar purificar; quitar impurezas

refugee (REHF yoo jee) person who flees his or her homeland to seek safety elsewhere (p. 986)
refugiado persona que escapa de su país de origen en busca de seguridad en otro lugar

register (REJ is tur) enroll or record officially (p. 555)
registrar inscribir o anotar oficialmente

reinforce (ree ihn FORS) to make stronger; to strengthen; to make more effective (pp. 519, 875)
reforzar hacer más fuerte; fortalecer; hacer más eficaz

reluctant (ri LUK tuhnt) not willing to do something (p. 587)
reacio que no tiene la voluntad de hacer algo

renewable resource (rih NOO uh buhl REE sors) energy source that can be quickly restored by nature (p. 980)
recurso renovable fuente energética que puede ser restablecida rápidamente por la naturaleza

reparations (rep uh RAY shunz) payments to cover war damages (p. 724)
indemnizaciones pagos para cubrir daños o perjuicios causados por la guerra

require (rih KWYR) to order or command (p. 560)
requerir ordenar o mandar

reservation (reh zer VAY shuhn) area set aside by the government for Native Americans to live on (p. 586)
reservación territorio que el gobierno destina a ser habitado por indígenas americanos

reside (ree ZĪD) to live in; to dwell for a while; to exist in (p. 597)
residir vivir en algún lugar; habitar por un tiempo; existir

resolve (ree SAHLV) to decide; to solve (pp. 548, 853)
resolver decidir; dar solución

resource (REE sors) supply of something to meet a particular need (p. 514)
recurso abasto de algo que satisface una necesidad en particular

respond (rih SPAHND) to react (p. 838)
responder reaccionar

restore (ree STOR) to bring back to a normal state; to put back; to reestablish (pp. 524, 888)

restaurar devolver a una condición normal; reponer; restablecer

restrict (ree STRIHKT) to confine; to keep within a certain boundary or limit; to place limitations on something or somebody (p. 742)
restringir confinar; mantener dentro de ciertas fronteras o límites; poner limitaciones a algo o alguien

revival (ree VĪ vuhl) huge outdoor religious meeting (p. R 1)
reunión evangelista encuentro religioso de grandes proporciones al aire libre

revolt (ree VOHLT) uprising; rebellion; to rebel (pp. 690, 858)
revuelta sublevación; rebelión

rigid (RIH jihd) strict; not easily bent or changed (p. 653)
rígido estricto; que no se dobla o cambia con facilidad

rock-and-roll (RAHK and rohl) style of music derived from rhythm and blues and country music (p. 846)
rocanrol estilo de música derivada del rhythm-and-blues y country

S

sanction (SANK shuhn) penalty applied against a country in order to pressure it to change its policies (p. 949)
sanción castigo aplicado a un país con el fin de presionarlo para que cambie su política

satellite (SAT uhl īt) nation that is dominated politically and economically by a more powerful nation (p. 837)
satélite nación dominada política y económicamente por otra más poderosa

scalawag (SKAL eh wag) southern white who had opposed secession (p. 555)
scalawag blanco sureño que se oponía a la secesión

secede (seh SEED) to withdraw from membership in a group (pp. R 9, 484)
separarse retirarse como miembro de un grupo

segregation (sehg reh GAY shuhn) enforced separation of races (p. 560)
segregación separación obligada de dos razas

self-determination (self di tur muh NAY shun) right of a group to decide its own form of government (p. 723)
autodeterminación derecho de un grupo de decidir su propio régimen político

separation of powers (seh pahr AY shuhn uhv POW ers) principle by which the powers of government are divided among separate branches (p. R 4)
separación de poderes principio por el cual los poderes del gobierno se dividen entre sus distintas ramas

sequence (SEE kwehns) one thing occurring after another; series of events (p. 913)
secuencia cuando una cosa ocurre después de otra; serie de acontecimientos

settlement house (SEHT ehl mehnt hows) center offering help to the urban poor (p. 622)
centro comunitario centro que ofrece ayuda a los habitantes pobres de una ciudad

sharecropper (SHAIR krah per) person who rents a plot of land and farms it in exchange for a share of the crop (p. 561)
aparcero persona que alquila un terreno y lo cultiva a cambio de una parte de la cosecha

siege (seej) military blockade or bombardment of an enemy town or position in order to force it to surrender (p. 535)
sitio cerco militar o bombardeo de una población o posición enemiga a fin de obligarla a rendirse

sit-down strike (SIHT down strīk) form of protest in which workers remain in the workplace, but refuse to work until a settlement is reached (p. 791)
huelga de brazos caídos forma de protesta en la que los trabajadores permanecen en el lugar de trabajo, pero en la que rechazan trabajar hasta que se consiga un acuerdo

sit-in (SIHT ihn) form of protest in which people sit and refuse to leave (p. 888)
sentada forma de protesta en la cual la gente se sienta y se niega a irse

sod (sahd) soil held together by the tangled roots of grasses (p. 596)
tepe pedazo de tierra sujetado por las raíces enmarañadas del pasto

sodbuster (SAHD buhs ter) farmer on the Great Plains in the late 1800s (p. 596)
sodbuster granjero de las Grandes Llanuras de la segunda mitad del siglo XIX

sooner (SOO ner) person who sneaked onto the land before the start of the Oklahoma land rush (p. 598)
sooner persona que se introdujo a escondidas en las tierras antes de que comenzara la carrera por las tierras de Oklahoma

speakeasy (SPEEK ee zee) illegal tavern that served liquor during Prohibition (p. 741)
taberna clandestina taberna ilegal donde se servían bebidas alcohólicas durante la Prohibición

specify (SPEHS uh fī) to describe or to point out in detail (p. 777)
especificar describir o señalar en detalle

sphere (sfeer) rounded shape; area of interest or influence (p. 836)
esfera figura redondeada; zona de interés o influencia

sphere of influence (sfir uhv IHN floo ehns) area of one nation where another nation had special economic and political control (p. 684)
esfera de influencia zona de una nación donde otra ejercía un control económico y político

stalemate (STAYL mayt) deadlock; situation in which neither side wins (pp. 707, 851)
estancamiento situación en la que ningún contendiente gana

standard of living (STAN derd uhv LIHV ihng) index based on the amount of goods, services, and leisure time people have (p. 845)
nivel de vida índice basado en la cantidad de bienes, servicios y tiempo de ocio que posee la gente

steerage (STIR ihj) large compartments of ships that usually held cattle (p. 626)
tercera clase grandes compartimientos de los barcos en los que normalmente se transportaba ganado

stockpile (STAHK pīl) to collect (p. 856)
almacenar hacer acopio o acumular

submit (suhb MIHT) to give up power and control (pp. 661, 926)
someterse ceder el poder y el control

subsidy (SUHB sih dee) grant of land or money (p. 580)
subsidio concesión de tierras o dinero

suffragist (SUH frihj ihst) person who worked for women's right to vote (p. 657)
sufragista persona que luchaba por el derecho al voto de las mujeres

superior (suh PIR ee er) of greater importance or value; above average in quality; higher in position or rank (pp. 519, 803)
superior de mayor importancia o valor; por encima del promedio en cuanto a calidad; que ocupa una posición o categoría más alta

superpower (SOO per pow er) country with the military, political, and economic strength to influence events worldwide (p. 855)
superpotencia país con la fuerza militar, política y económica para influir en los acontecimientos a nivel mundial

supplement (SUP luh munt) add to, so as to make up for a lack or deficiency (p. 817)
suplementar adicionar para compensar por alguna deficiencia

surplus (SER pluhs) excess; quantity that is left over (pp. 598, 940)
superávit excedente; cantidad sobrante

sustain (suh STAYN) to keep going; to support as just (pp. 525, 718)
sostener mantener en marcha; apoyar como justo

T

tenement (TEHN eh mehnt) building divided into many tiny apartments (p. 622)
conventillo un edificio dividido en muchos apartamentos pequeños

tepee (TEE pee) portable tent made of buffalo skins (p. 584)
tipi tienda portátil construida con pieles de búfalo

terrorism (TEHR er ihz uhm) deliberate use of violence, often against civilian targets, to achieve political or social goals (p. 968)
terrorismo uso deliberado de la violencia, a menudo en contra de objetivos civiles, con el fin de alcanzar objetivos políticos o sociales

total war (TOH tuhl wor) all-out attacks aimed at destroying not only an enemy's army but also its resources and its people's will to fight (pp. 536, 811)
guerra total ataques masivos encaminados a destruir no sólo al ejército enemigo, sino también sus recursos y la voluntad de luchar de la población

totalitarian state (toh tal uh TER ee uhn stayt) nation in which a single party controls the government and every aspect of people's lives (p. 802)
estado totalitario país en el que un sólo partido político controla el gobierno y todos los aspectos de la vida de las personas

trade deficit (trayd DEHF uh siht) occurs when a country buys more from other nations than it sells to them; an excess of imports over exports (p. 976)
déficit comercial hecho que ocurre cuando un país compra a otras naciones más de lo que les vende; exceso de importaciones sobre las exportaciones

transcontinental railroad (trans kahn tihn EHN tuhl RAYL rohd) rail line that spans the continent (p. 581)
ferrocarril transcontinental sistema ferroviario que cruza un continente de costa a costa

transform (trans FORM) to change in appearance or form; to change the condition of something (pp. 584, 887)
transformar cambiar la apariencia o la forma; cambiar la condición de algo

travois (trav OI) small sled (p. 584)
travois trineo pequeño

trench warfare (trench WOR fayr) type of fighting in which soldiers fire on one another from opposing lines of dugout trenches (p. 707)
guerra de trincheras lucha en la cual soldados combaten desde líneas estáticas de trincheras cavadas en el suelo, ambas enfrentadas

trust (truhst) group of corporations run by a single board of directors (p. 615)
trust grupo de compañías dirigidas por un solo consejo directivo

trustbuster (TRUHST buhs ter) person who worked to destroy monopolies and trusts (p. 650)
trustbuster persona que lucha para destruir los monopolios y trusts

U

undocumented worker (uhn DAHK yuh mehnt īhd WER ker) laborers who enter the country without legal permission (p. 987)
trabajador indocumentado obreros o jornaleros que entran en el país sin permiso legal

unify (YOO nuh fī) to unite; to make into one (p. 909)
unificar unir; juntar

urbanization (er ban ihz AY shuhn) movement of large numbers of people from rural areas to cities; rapid growth of city populations (p. 620)
urbanización desplazamiento de un gran número de personas de las zonas rurales a las ciudades; crecimiento rápido de la población de las ciudades

V

vague (vayg) uncertain; not precise or exact (p. 819)
vago incierto; no preciso o exacto

vaquero (vah KAIR oh) Spanish word for cowboy (p. 592)
vaquero término que se aplica a los ganaderos mexicanos o hispanos

veto (VEE toh) to reject, as when the President rejects a law passed by Congress (p. 840)
vetar rechazar, como cuando el Presidente rechaza una ley aprobada por el Congreso

vigilante (vihj ihl AN tee) self-appointed law enforcer (p. 580)
vigilante persona que se designa a sí misma para hacer cumplir la ley

violate (VĪ ah layt) to break a rule or law; to disrespect; to disturb (pp. 589, 938)
violar no cumplir una regla o ley; ofender; molestar

vital (VĪ tuhl) necessary for life; of great importance; spirited; lively (pp. 482, 824)

vital necesario para la vida; de gran importancia; lleno de vida; animado

voluntary (VAHL ahn tair ee) not forced; done of one's free will (pp. 547, 775)
voluntario no forzado; hecho por voluntad propia

W

war crime (wor crīm) wartime act of cruelty and brutality that is judged to be beyond the accepted rules of war and human behavior (p. 827)
crimen de guerra acto cruel y brutal realizado en tiempo de guerra que sobrepasa las reglas establecidas para la guerra y el comportamiento humano

welfare (WEHL fair) system in which government agencies make cash payments to the poor (p. 885)
asistencia social sistema en el cual las agencias gubernamentales efectúan pagos en efectivo a las personas pobres

westernization (wehs tern ih ZAY shuhn) adoption of ideas, culture, and technology from Western regions such as the United States and Europe (p. 956)
occidentalización adopción de ideas, cultura y tecnología de las regiones occidentales como de los Estados Unidos y Europa

Y

yellow journalism (YEHL oh JER nahl ihz uhm) style of reporting and displaying news in a sensational way that distorts the truth (p. 635)
periodismo amarillista estilo de reseñar y presentar noticias de un modo sensacionalista que deforma la verdad

Identify: central issues from the past, 656, 657, 659; central problems from the past, 660, 665; and connect main ideas, *704q*, 730; evidence, HT 5; and explain central issues, 668; main ideas and support, 706, 708, 711; proposals, 546, 547, 549

Judging characters, *492–493q*

Make: generalizations, *966q*, 982, 985; inferences, 874, 879; inferences and draw conclusions, 900

Paraphrase text for understanding, 736, 738, 740

Place events in a matrix of time and place, 644, 647, 648

Relate events in a sequence, 533, 536, 537

Summarize: main ideas, 741, 743, 745; main ideas and essential details, 746, 747, 750; passage, 752, 754, 755

Support: conclusions with evidence, 893, 894, 897, 976, 980, 981; generalizations with evidence, 986, 987, 991; inferences with text evidence, 881, 884, 885

Understand: sequence, 540; sequence of events, HT 7, 512, 513, 517

Use: comparison or contrast clues, 595, 597, 599; context clues, HT 7, 602; context clues to verify meaning, *576q*; context to determine meaning, 816, 817, 820, 821, 822, 827; definition clues, 578, 581; example clues, 590, 594; Greek word origins, 608, 611, 613; Latin word origins, 614, 616, 619, 620, 624; other word origins, 625, 628, 629; popular word origins, 632, 634, 635; restatement clues, 584, 588, 589; sentence clues to analyze meaning, 808, *811q*, 813; word clues to analyze meaning, 802, 804, 807; word origins, *606q*, 638

Reagan, Ronald W., *938p*, *1033p*
and Cold War, *934–935m*, *947p*, *998q*
as President, 938–939, 949, 990
on role of religion, *934q*
strengthening defense, 943–944, *944i*

Reaganomics, 939, *963q*

real estate speculation (1920s), *734q*

recall, voter, 647

recession, 939

reconcentration, 688

Reconstruction, *544–545m*
conclusion of, 558–563, *569q*
conflicts over, 552–557
early, *477i*, 546–549, *550–551i*
successes/failures of, *565c*, *569q*

Reconstruction Act of 1867, 555

Reconstruction Finance Corporation (RFC), 775

recycling, 978

Red Cross, *717p*

Red Ribbon Week, *990p*

Red Scare, 727, 739–740

referendum, voter, 647

reform movements
for civil rights. *See* civil rights movement
against corruption, 644–648
against discrimination, 660–665
to extend New Deal reforms, 843, 844
to improve 1930's economy, 779–780
to improve environment, 978–981
to improve health/welfare, 622, 659
to improve labor, 618–619, 791
to improve Social Security, 973
for Native Americans, 589, 896
for older Americans, 896–897
for voters rights. *See* voting rights
for women's rights. *See* women's rights movement

refugees, 923, 986

Reich, Robert, *963q*

religion. *See specific religion or tradition*

religion, freedom of, *1019q*

religious toleration, 665, 745, 948

religious values, *934q*

Remington, Frederic, *593i*

renewable resources, 980

reparations, 724

representative government, 989, *1017q*, *1023q*

republic, *1017q*

Republicans (1850s–present)
in 1920s, 755
in 1940s to 1950s, 844
in 1960s to 1970s, 918, 924
in 1980s, 938–939, *939p*
in 2000s, 941–942, 973
after Civil War, 547, 556, *559m*
vs. Populists, 599, 652
roots/formation of, 494
on slavery/Union, 499
after World Wars I and II, 737–738, 843

Republicans (1863), Radical, 547, 553–558, *554c*

research paper/report, HT 24

reservation, Indian, 586

resources
in late 1800s, 562–563, 608–609, 681
conserving (1900s), 651, *651p*
during World War I, 714, 817
in 2005, *958–959m*, 979–980, *980c*

retail industry, 623, 628, 847

retirement, mandatory, 896–897

Revels, Hiram, *545p*, 555, *555p*, *570q*

Rice, Condoleezza, 989, *989p*

Richmond (VA), 537, *547p*

Rickey, Branch, 876

Ride for Liberty–The Fugitive Slaves (Johnson), *479i*

Righteous and Harmonious Fists, 685

rights. *See specific kind*

Riis, Jacob, *641p*, 648, *666p*, *668p*, *669q*

riots. *See* protests; racial conflict/violence

roads, 845

"Roaring Twenties," *675i*. *See also* culture

Robinson, Jackie, 876, *876p*

Robinson Projection, HT 11

Rock and Roll music, 846–847

Rockefeller, John D., 615, *615p*, *648q*, 661

Roman Catholics, 626, 665, 745, 755, 950

Romania, 946

Roosevelt, Eleanor, 783, *783p*, *793p*

Roosevelt, Franklin D., *1032p*
on Good Neighbor Policy, 806
and New Deal, *765p*, 776–781, 793
on Pearl Harbor attack, *811q*
as President, 776, *777q*, 780, *780i*, *793p*, 808–809, *808p*, 822
on unemployment, *797q*
at Yalta conference, 836

Roosevelt, Theodore "Teddy"
"big stick" policy of, *677i*, 696
on conservation, *651q*
on journalists, 648
national parks, *642–643m*
as President, *572p*, 649–652, 693, *1032p*
on segregation, 664
in Spanish-American War, 690, *690i*

Roosevelt Corollary, 696, *696c*, 806

Rosenberg, Ethel, 853

Rosenberg, Julius, 853

Rosie the Riveter, *817i*

Ross, Nellie Tayloe, 742

Ross, Ronald, 694

Rostow, Eugene V., *928q*

Acknowledgments

Staff Credits

The people who made up the **America: History of Our Nation**—team—representing design services, editorial, editorial services, education technology, manufacturing and inventory planning, market research, marketing services, planning and budgeting, project planning, production services, publishing processes, and rights and permissions—are listed below. Boldface type denotes the core team members.

Scott Andrews, Rosalyn Arcilla, **Jane Breen, Laura Chadwick, Eugennie Chang,** Bob Craton, **Brett Creane,** Harold DelMonte, **Glenn Diedrich, Jim Doris, Kerry Dunn,** Patricia Fromkin, **Elizabeth Good, Shelby Gragg,** Michael Hornbostel, Judie Jozokos, **Patrick Keithahn,** John Kingston, **Doreen Kruk, Ann-Michelle Levangie, Marian Manners, Grace Massey, Anne McLaughlin,** Michael McLaughlin, **Xavier Niz, Jennifer Paley, Paul Ramos, Ryan Richards, Melissa Shustyk,** Kristen VanEtten, **Al Velasquez, Roberta Warshaw**

Map and Art Credits

Maps Mapping Specialist Limited, except where noted with additional type set by Justin Contursi **Visual Preview Maps** XNR Productions 480–481, 510–511, 544–545, 576–577, 606–607, 642–643, 678–679, 704–705, 734–735, 768–769, 800–801, 834–835, 872–873, 904–905, 934–935, 966–967 and TLAH Maps 131, 373, 472, 475, 571, 762 **Illustrated Maps** Tim Barker 480–481 Anthony Morse 582, 686, 788 with additional type set by Artur Mkrtchyan

Art Keithley and Associates, all charts/graphs/instructional art and photo composites except where noted **Timelines** Humberto Ugarte **Illustrations** XNR 480–481, 510–511, 544–545, 576–577, 606–607, 642–643, 678–679, 704–705, 734–735, 768–769, 800–801, 834–835, 872–873, 904–905, 934–935, 966–967 **Instructional Art/Photo Composites** Kerry Cashman 502, 560–561, 596–597 John Kingston 610–611, 695, 914, 984 Lisa Smith-Ruvalcaba 810, 839, 878, 947 Humberto Ugarte 708–709, 748, 773 Justin Contursi **Atlas design and Skills Activity photo treatments** GDPS **Skills for Life art** Brainworx 522–523, 550–551, 582–583, 630–631, 686–687

Every effort has been made to credit all vendors. Any omissions brought to our attention will be corrected in subsequent printings.

Photo Credits

Cover and Title Page: © Bob Gelberg/Masterfile **A-1** Getty Images; **A-2 T** Chee-Onn Leong/Shutterstock; **A-3 B** Dallas and John Heaton/CORBIS; **A-3 T** AP/Wide World Photos; **A-4 T** akva/Shutterstock; **A-5 T** Julie Habel/CORBIS; **A-5 B** Marvin Newman; **A-6 T** © DK Images; **A-7 T** Darren Baker/Shutterstock; **A-7 B** Bill Ross/CORBIS; **A-10** Larry Downing/Reuters/CORBIS; **A-11** © CORBIS; **A-12 TL** Connie Ricca/CORBIS; **A-12 TR** Smithsonian American Art Museum, Washington, DC/Art Resource, NY; **A-12 B** Bettmann/CORBIS; **A-13 T** Bettmann/CORBIS; **A-13 B** Henryk Sadura/Shutterstock; **A-15 T** Anaheim Public Library; **A-15 B** D. Boone/CORBIS; **A-16 TL** © Royalty-Free/Corbis; **A-16 B** © CORBIS; **ii** Jamestown-Yorktown Educational Trust, VA, USA/The Bridgeman Art Library, London/New York; **v** John Guthrie, Guthrie Studios; **vii** AP/Wide World Photos; **viii** The Granger Collection; **ix** CORBIS; **x** Bettmann-CORBIS; **xi** AP/Wide World; **xii** © Royalty-Free/Corbis; **xv** Courtesy of the Library of Congress; **xvii** Kim Mould/Omni-Photo Communications, Inc.; **xviii** The Granger Collection, New York; **xx** © CORBIS/Bettmann; **HT 01** Armstrong Roberts/ClassicStock/The Image Works; **HT 02 L** Courtesy National Archives; **HT 02 R** Picture History/Newscom; **HT 03** Lawrence Migdale/Pix; **HT 04** © CORBIS/Bettmann; **HT 05** © Picture Partners/Alamy; **HT 08 L** David Stoecklein/CORBIS; **HT 08 R** Sime s.a.s./eStock/PictureQuest; **HT 10** Silver Burdett Ginn; **HT 14** Copyright © North Wind/North Wind Picture Archives—All rights reserved.; **HT 15** akva/Shutterstock; **HT 16** Mary Evans Picture Library; **HT 17** The Granger Collection, New York; **HT 21** KAL/The Baltimore Sun/CartoonArts International/CWS; **HT 24** Brand X Pictures/PictureQuest; **HT 23** © Jeff Greenberg/PhotoEdit Inc. **R 1** The Granger Collection, New York; **R 2** © Bettmann/CORBIS; **R 5** The Granger Collection, New York; **R 6** O.C. Seltzer, Lewis and Clark with Sacagawea, at the Great Falls of the Missouri River, #0137.871. From the Collection of Gilcrease Museum, **R 8** The Granger

Collection, New York; **R 10** © CORBIS; **476 B** © CORBIS; **477 T** Mary Evans Picture Library; **477 B** His First Vote, 1868 (oil on canvas), Wood, Thomas Waterman (1823–1903)/Private Collection, Christie's Images/www.bridgeman.co.uk/The Bridgeman Art Library, London/New York; **478–479** The Granger Collection, New York; **482** © David J. & Janice L. Frent Collection/CORBIS; **483** Courtesy of the Library of Congress; **484 L** Clemson University; **484 R** The Granger Collection, New York; **486 L** The Granger Collection; **486 R** TK; **487 L** Copyright © North Wind/North Wind Picture Archives—All rights reserved.; **487 R** Illinois State University; **488** © Bettmann/CORBIS; **488 Inset** Rèunion des Musèes Nationaux/Art Resource, NY; **493 T** The Granger Collection, New York; **493 B** Pearson Education/PH School Division; **494** © Bettmann/CORBIS; **494** Courtesy of the Library of Congress; **495** John Henry Brown, "Abraham Lincoln" (1809–1865), Sixteenth US President. Watercolor on ivory, c. 1860. National Portrait Gallery, Smithsonian Institution/Art Resource, NY. (detail); **496** © CORBIS/Bettmann; **497** Kansas State Historical Society; **498** The Granger Collection, New York; **499** National Portrait Gallery, Smithsonian Institution/Art Resource, NY (NPG.71.29); **499** © Bettmann/CORBIS; **499** © CORBIS; **501** Hulton-Deutsch Collection/CORBIS; **502 B** The Granger Collection, New York; **502 T** United States Department of the Interior; **502 M** Adoc-photos/Art Resource, NY; **506** Kansas State Historical Society; **507** The Granger Collection, New York; **508–509** Painting by Don Troiani/historicalartprints.com; **512** © Medford Historical Society Collection/CORBIS; **515 L** Armstrong Roberts/ClassicStock/The Image Works; **515 R** Picture History/Newscom; **516** Courtesy Beverley R. Robinson Collection, US Naval Academy Museum; **517** Dave King/Dorling Kindersley (c) Confederate Memorial Hall, New Orleans; **518** The Granger Collection, New York; **519 L** © Bettmann/CORBIS; **519 R** Steve Helber/AP/Wide World Photos; **522–523** from Great Battles of the Civil War by kind permission of Marshall Editions Ltd; **523 BL** Publisher's Press, Inc.; **523 BR** Collection of Picture Research Consultants, Inc. Photo © Collection of David and Kevin Kyle; **524** © Bettmann/CORBIS; **525** Collection of the personal papers of General Robert H. Milroy, Courtesy of the Jasper County Public Library, Rensselaer, Indiana (detail); **526** AP/Wide World Photos; **528** The Granger Collection, New York; **529** The Granger Collection, New York; **530 R** The Granger Collection, New York; **530 L** Getty Images Inc.—Hulton Archive Photos; **532** AP/Wide World Photos; **533** SuperStock, Inc.; **535** Courtesy of the Library of Congress; **541** The Granger Collection, New York; **542–543** © CORBIS; **544 R** Medford Historical Society Collection; **544 L** The Granger Collection, New York; **545 L** © Corbis/Bettmann; **545 R** The Granger Collection, New York; **546** Smithsonian American Art Museum, Washington, DC/Art Resource, NY; **547** © CORBIS/BETTMANN; **548 R** © CORBIS/BETTMANN; **548 L** Getty Images—Hulton Archive Photos; **550 M** Alamy Images; **550 B** The Granger Collection, New York; **550 T** Dave King/Dorling Kindersley © Confederate Memorial Hall, New Orleans; **551 TL** Copyright © North Wind/North Wind Picture Archives—All rights reserved.; **551 M** Douglas Mudd, National Numismatic Collection, The Smithsonian Institution; **551 TR** neg. #86-113-74, Rudolf Eickmeyer, National Museum of American History, Smithsonian Institution; **551 B** The Museum of the Confederacy, Richmond, Virginia, Photography by KATHERINE WETZEL; **552** Courtesy of the Library of Congress; **553 L** The Granger Collection, New York; **553 R** Courtesy of the Library of Congress; **554 (2)** Courtesy of the Library of Congress; **555** The Granger Collection, New York; **556** The Granger Collection, New York; **557 T** Old Court House Museum, Vicksburg, Photo by Bob Pickett; **557 B** Collection of Mississippi State Historical Museum/Mississippi Department of Archives and History; **558** © Bettmann/CORBIS; **560 Inset** Courtesy of the Library of Congress; **560–561** © CORBIS; **562** © CORBIS/Bettmann; **563** © CORBIS; **565** © CORBIS; **566** His First Vote, 1868 (oil on canvas), Wood, Thomas Waterman (1823–1903)/Private Collection, Christie's Images/www.bridgeman.co.uk/The Bridgeman Art Library, London/New York; **567** The Granger Collection, New York; **568 L** © North Wind/North Wind Picture Archives—All rights reserved.; **568 R** Library of Congress; **568 T** Library of Congress; **569** Robertstock; **570 T** Abolition of Colonial Slavery Meeting, 1830 (letterpress), English School, (19th century)/Private Collection,/The Bridgeman Art Library; **570 M** The Granger Collection, New York; **570 M** © Bettmann/CORBIS; **570 B** The Granger Collection, New York; **571** © CORBIS; **572 B** Corbis-Bettmann; **572 T** Solomon D. Butcher Collection, Nebraska State Historical Society; **573 B** © NewsCom; **573 T** Copyright © North Wind/North Wind Picture Archives; **573 TR** © NewsCom; **574–575** Buffalo Bill Historical Center, Cody, Wyoming/The Art Archive; **578** The Granger Collection, New York; **579** Pearson Education; **583 ML** Union Pacific Historical Collection; **583 MR** The Granger Collection, New York; **583 T** CORBIS/Bettmann; **584** Getty Images; **585 L** Lynton Gardiner (c) Dorling

Kindersley, Courtesy of The American Museum of Natural History; **585 M** Corel Professional Photos CD-ROM™; **585 R** Robe, possibly Roan Eagle, Oglala Sioux, 1870s, Denver Art Museum Collection: Evans Indian Fund, 1931.28. Photo by the Denver Art Museum. All rights reserved.; **586** Courtesy of the Library of Congress; **588** © Wally McNamee/CORBIS; **590 (2)** The Granger Collection, New York; **592 BL** Panhandle-Plains Historical Museum, Canyon TX; **592 MR** Art Archive/Bill Manns; **592 TL** History Collections, Los Angeles County Natural History Museum; **593** Frederic Remington/SuperStock; **594** Lorie Leigh Lawrence/Alamy; **595** Brown Brothers; **596 L** Solomon D. Butcher Collection, Nebraska State Historical Society; **596 R** The Granger Collection, New York; **597 R** Kansas State Historical Society, Topeka; **597 TL** © Bettmann/CORBIS; **599** Courtesy of the Library of Congress; **603** Solomon D. Butcher Collection, Nebraska State Historical Society; **604–05** © akg-images/Waldemar Abegg/Newscom; **608** Stock Montage/Getty Images; **609** The Trustees of the British Museum/Art Resource, NY; **610 L & M** The Granger Collection, New York; **610 R** Mansell/Mansell/Time & Life Pictures/Getty Images; **610 TL** CORBIS; **611 L** The Granger Collection, New York; **611 M** Lynn Historical Society; **611 R** Hulton-Deutsch Collection/ CORBIS; **611 TR** CORBIS; **612** CORBIS; **614** The Granger Collection, New York; **615** Bettmann/CORBIS; **616** Bettmann/CORBIS; **617** Snark/Art Resource, NY; **618** The Granger Collection, New York; **619** CORBIS/Bettmann; **620** The Granger Collection, New York; **621** Underwood & Underwood/CORBIS; **622** Jessie Tarbox Beals, Room in a Tenement flat, 1910, detail, Reprinted by permission of the Museum of the City of New York, The Jacob A. Riis Collection; **624 B** Christie's Images; **624 T** National Baseball Hall of Fame Library, Cooperstown, N.Y.; **625 B** Photo by John Lei/National Park Service/Ellis Island; **625 T** © Bettmann/CORBIS; **627** Everett Collection, Inc.; **628** The Granger Collection, New York; **629** The Granger Collection, New York; **630 (3)** Bettmann/CORBIS; **631 B** Bettmann/Corbis; **631 T** Hulton Archive/Getty Images; **632 B** The Granger Collection, New York; **632 T** © CORBIS; **634 (2)** The Granger Collection, New York; **635** Syracuse University Library, Department of Special Collections.; **636** The Granger Collection, New York; **637** Bettmann/CORBIS; **640–641** (c) Bettmann/CORBIS; **644** © Bettmann/CORBIS; **645** The Granger Collection, New York; **646** The Granger Collection, New York; **649** © CORBIS/Bettmann; **650–651 L** Katrina Leigh/Shutterstock; **651 R** Courtesy of the Library of Congress; **652** The Granger Collection, New York; **653** Stock Montage, Inc./Historical Pictures Collection; **655 L** CORBIS; **655 R** Chicago Historical Society, G1978.154.4; **656** © David J. & Janice L. Frent Collection/CORBIS; **658** Underwood and Underwood photo. Courtesy of the Library of Congress; **659** Corbis/Bettmann; **660** Corbis/Bettmann; **661 L** Getty Images/Hulton Archive Photos; **661 R** Schomburg Center for Research in Black Culture/Art Resource; **662** Corbis/Bettmann; **663** Courtesy, Los Mineros Photograph Collection, Chicano Research Collection, Arizona State University Libraries; **663 R** UT Institute of Texan Cultures, 98–949; **664** © NewsCom; **666 L** Reprinted by permission of the Museum of the City of New York; **666 R** Courtesy of the Library of Congress; **668** Snark/Art Resource, NY; **670** Image by © Bettmann/CORBIS; **671 TL** Rare Book, Manuscript, and Special Collections Library, 103 Perkins Library, Duke University, Durham, North Carolina; **671 B** © CORBIS; **671 T** Getty Images; **672 T** © Minnesota Historical Society/CORBIS; **672 M** The Granger Collection, New York; **672 B** Getty Images; **673** © Ohio State University; **674–675 B** The Granger Collection, New York; **674 T** CORBIS; **675 B** Courtesy of The Advertising Archives; **675 T** Courtesy National Archives and Records Administration, College Park, Maryland; **676–677** The Granger Collection, New York; **680** © Bettmann/CORBIS; **681** The Granger Collection, New York; **683** The Granger Collection, New York; **684** Courtesy of the Library of Congress; **686** The Art Archive, The Picture Desk/Kobal Collection; **687 B** © Dorling Kindersley; **687 BR** Corel Professional Photos CD-ROM™; **687 M** The Granger Collection, New York; **687 T** 2004 © Anchorage Museum/ AlaskaStock.com; **688** © Bettmann/CORBIS; **689 BL** Collection of The New-York Historical Society, New York City; **689 B** Chicago Historical Society; **689 TL** (c) Collection of The New-York Historical Society; **690** Getty Images Inc.— Hulton Archive Photos; **692** The Granger Collection, New York; **693** © The Mariners' Museum/CORBIS; **695 BL** © Bettmann/CORBIS; **695 BR** © SSPL/The Image Works; **695 T** © CORBIS; **697** Culver Pictures, Inc.; **699** Getty Images Inc.—Hulton Archive Photos; **700** The Granger Collection, New York; **701** The Granger Collection, New York; **702–703** Courtesy National Archives and Records Administration, College Park, Maryland; **704 BR** National Archives; **704 BL** The Granger Collection, New York; **704 TL** The Granger Collection, New York; **704 TR** Library of Congress; **705 BL** Poster by Haskell Coffin;

Image by © CORBIS; **705 BM** Library of Congress; **705 BR** © CORBIS; **705 TL** Art Collection, National Museum of the Marine Corps.; **706** The Granger Collection, New York; **708 L** Getty Images; **708–09 M** Hulton Archive/Getty Images Inc.; **708 R** West Point Museum Collection, United States Military Academy; **709 BR** The Art Archive/Culver Pictures; **709 TR** © Bettmann/CORBIS; **710 L** © Bettmann/CORBIS; **710 R** © SuperStock, Inc; **711** Culver Pictures, Inc.; **712** Time Life Pictures/National Archives/Time Life Pictures/Getty Images; **713** West Point Museum Art Collection, United States Military Academy; **714** Courtesy of the Library of Congress; **716 BL** © Bettmann/CORBIS; **716 TL** © David Pollack/CORBIS; **716 TR** Nebraska State Historical Society Photograph Collections; **717 B** © Schenectady Museum; Hall of Electrical History Foundation/CORBIS; **717 M** American Red Cross 1st World War poster (colour litho), American School, (20th century)/Private Collection, Barbara Singer/Bridgeman Art Library; **717 TL** © Bettmann/CORBIS; **717 TR** © Swim Ink 2, LLC/CORBIS; **718** © CORBIS; **721** © royalty-free/ CORBIS; **722** The Granger Collection, New York; **723** Library of Congress; **724** © Bettmann/CORBIS; **726** Mary Evans Picture Library; **727** Hulton Archive/Getty Images Inc.; **728** CORBIS/Bettmann; **730** © Swim Ink 2, LLC/CORBIS; **731** © Associated Press; **732–733** The Great White Way—Times Square, New York by Howard Thain, 1925; oil on canvas, 30 x 36 inches; accession #1963.150. Collection of The New-York Historical Society, detail; **736** © Bettmann/CORBIS; **737** The Granger Collection, New York; **738** Courtesy of the Library of Congress; **739** Shahn, Ben. Bartolomeo Vanzetti and Nicola Sacco from the Sacco-Vanzeti series of twenty-three paintings. (1931–32). Tempera on paper over composition board, 10 1/2 x 14 1/2 " (26.7 x 36.8 cm). The Museum of Modern Art/Licensed by Scala-Art Resource, NY. Gift of Abby Aldrich Rockefeller. Digital Image. (c) The Museum of Modern Art/Licensed by SCALA/Art Resource, NY. The Museum of Modern Art, New York, N.Y., U.S.A. Art © Estate of Ben Shahn/Licensed by VAGA, New York, NY; **740–742** © Bettmann/CORBIS; **743** © Underwood & Underwood/CORBIS; **744** The Granger Collection, New York; **745** Courtesy of the Library of Congress; **746** © Bettmann/CORBIS; **747** AP/Wide World Photos; **748 B** Bettmann/CORBIS; **748 border** istockphoto.com; **748 ML** Frank Driggs Collection; **748 MR** The Granger Collection, New York; **748 TR** © MaxJazz/Lebrecht; **749** The Granger Collection, New York; **750** Alamy Images; **751 B** Pearson Education/PH School Division; **752** The Granger Collection, New York; **754** The Granger Collection, New York; **755 (2)** Ron Wade Buttons; **758** Shahn, Ben. Bartolomeo Vanzetti and Nicola Sacco from the Sacco-Vanzeti series of twenty-three paintings. (1931–32). Tempera on paper over composition board, 10 1/2 x 14 1/2 " (26.7 x 36.8 cm). The Museum of Modern Art/Licensed by Scala-Art Resource, NY. Gift of Abby Aldrich Rockefeller. Digital Image. (c) The Museum of Modern Art/Licensed by SCALA/Art Resource, NY. The Museum of Modern Art, New York, N.Y., U.S.A.. Art © Estate of Ben Shahn/Licensed by VAGA, New York, NY; **760** CORBIS; **761–762** The Granger Collection, NY; **764–65 B** Walter Sanders/Time Life Pictures/Getty Images; **764 BL** CORBIS; **764 BM** © Bettmann/ CORBIS; **764 T** © CORBIS; **765 T** The Granger Collection, New York; **766–767** Courtesy of the Library of Congress. Art © Estate of Ben Shahn/Licensed by VAGA, New York, NY; **768 T** © CORBIS; **769 BR** Library of Congress; **770** Image by © Horace Bristol/CORBIS; **771 B** UPI/CORBIS-BETTMANN; **771 T** Hulton Archive/Getty Images Inc.; **773 B** CORBIS/Bettmann; **773 TL** AP/Wide World Photos; **773 TR** Popperfoto/Retrofile; **774** Courtesy of the Library of Congress; **776** © Hulton-Deutsch Collection/CORBIS; **777 L** The Granger Collection, New York; **777 R** Courtesy of the Library of Congress; **778 B** © CORBIS; **778 T** © David J. & Janice L. Frent Collection/CORBIS; **780** The Granger Collection, New York; **781** CORBIS; **782** © Bettmann/CORBIS; **783 L** © Underwood & Underwood/CORBIS; **783 M** CORBIS; **783 R** © Bettmann/ CORBIS; **784** Detail. National Portrait Gallery, Smithsonian Institution/Art Resource, NY; **785** © Bettmann/CORBIS; **786** (Detail) National Museum of American Art, Washington, DC, U.S.A./Art Resource, NY; **787** Courtesy Everett Collection; **788 T** © CORBIS; **789 L** © CORBIS; **789 M** Smithsonian American Art Museum, Washington, DC/Art Resource, NY; **790 B** Courtesy of the Library of Congress; **790 R** Associated Press, AP Wide World Photos; **791** CORBIS/ Bettmann; **793** © Bettmann/CORBIS; **794** Unemployed, 1938 (tempera on paper), Shahn, Ben (1898–1969)/Private Collection, Christie's Images;/ Bridgeman Art Library. Art © Estate of Ben Shahn/Licensed by VAGA, New York, NY; **795** © Bettmann/CORBIS; **796** Popperfoto/Retrofile; **798–799** © Bettmann/CORBIS; **802** © CORBIS; **803 L** AKG London Ltd; **803 R** CORBIS/ Bettman; **804** Hulton Archive/Getty Images; **806** Popperfoto/Retrofile; **808 (c)** Judith Miller/Dorling Kindersley/Hope and Glory; **809** © Bettmann/CORBIS;

810 © SuperStock, Inc; 810 T Hulton Archive/Getty Images Inc.; 813 © CORBIS; 815 T Naval Historical Foundation Photo Service; 816 Photo by Hulton Archive/ Getty Images; 817 L Courtesy of the Library of Congress; 817 R © CORBIS; 818 The Art Archive/National Archives Washington DC; 819 Courtesy of the Library of Congress; 820 © Bettmann/CORBIS; 821 National Archives and Records Administration; 822 AP/Wide World Photos/U.S. Army; 824 Hulton Archive/Getty Images Inc.; 826 CORBIS; 827 © Molly Riley/Reuters/CORBIS; 829 © CORBIS; 830 Terra Foundation for American Art, Chicago/Art Resource, NY; 831 Courtesy National Archives; 832–833 Courtesy of the Library of Congress, reproduced with permission from the Marcus Family; 832–833 (background) Richard Ward (c) Dorling Kindersley; 836 Image by © Hulton-Deutsch Collection/CORBIS; 837 © CORBIS/Bettmann; 839 B Walter Sanders/Time Life Pictures/Getty Images; 839 TL Hulton Archive/Getty Images Inc.; 839 TR Courtesy of the Library of Congress; 841 UPI/CORBIS/Bettman; 842 © H. Armstrong Roberts/CORBIS; 843 Time Life Pictures/Getty Images; 844 © CORBIS/Bettmann; 846 L © Associated Press; 846 R H. Armstrong Roberts/ Retrofile; 848 BL Michael Ochs Archives.com; 848 BM © Bettmann/CORBIS; 848 T Lambert/Hulton Archive/Getty Images Inc.; 849 BR Courtesy Everett Collection; 849 T Courtesy Everett Collection; 849 TL Getty Images; 850 The Granger Collection, New York; 853 "It's Okay—We're Hunting Communists". From "Herblock Special Report (W.W. Norton, 1974). Reprinted by permission of the Herb Block Foundation.; 854 AP/Wide World Photos; 855 L Image by © Swim Ink/Corbis; 855 R © Swim Ink/Corbis; 856 NASA; 857 (2) Courtesy of The Peace Corps; 858 B MPI/Hulton Archive/Getty Images Inc.; 858 L © CORBIS/Bettmann; 858 R © CORBIS/Bettmann; 863 © CORBIS/Bettmann; 868–69 B AP/Wide World Photos; 868 T Bettmann/CORBIS; 869 B © Peter Bono/Images.com; 869 TL AP/Wide World Photos; 869 TR David Brauchli/ Reuters/CORBIS; 870–871 © Bettmann/CORBIS; 872 BR © Ted Spiegel/CORBIS; 872 L © Hulton-Deutsch Collection/CORBIS; 872 MR Library of Congress; 873 1 © Bettmann/CORBIS; 2 © courtesy of Gray Panthers—www.graypanthers.org; 3 National Baseball Hall of Fame Library/MLB Photos via Getty Images; 4 Time & Life Pictures/Getty Images; 5 © Bettmann/CORBIS; 6 Consolidated News Pictures/ Hulton Archive/Getty Images Inc.; 874 © Bettmann/CORBIS; 875 L © Bettmann/CORBIS; 875 R © Constantine Manos/Magnum Photos; 876 The Granger Collection, New York; 877 © Bettmann/CORBIS; 878 M Don Cravens/Time Life Pictures/ Getty Images; 878 T&B AP/Wide World Photos; 880 T Courtesy of Detroit Free Press; 881 © Bettmann/CORBIS; 883 L © Walt Cisco/CORBIS; 883 R © Bettmann/CORBIS; 884 Paul S. Conklin/PhotoEdit Inc.; 885 Hulton Archive/ Getty Images Inc.; 886 © Bob Adelman/Magnum Photos; 887 ImageQuest; 888 © Bettmann/CORBIS/Newscom; 888 & 889 AP/Wide World Photos; 890 L © David J. & Janice L. Frent Collection/CORBIS; 890 R AP/Wide World Photos; 892 CORBIS/Bettmann; 893 John Olsen/Time Life Pictures/Getty Images; 895 © Najlah Feanny/CORBIS; 896 B © Bettmann/CORBIS; 896 L AP/Wide World Photos; 896 R Ernst Haas/Hulton Archive/Getty Images Inc.; 900 © Bettmann/ CORBIS; 901 Silver Burdett Ginn; 902–903 © Henri Huet/Bettmann/CORBIS; 904 AP/Wide World Photos; 905 Basset/National Archives and Records Administration; 906 © Bettmann/CORBIS; 908 © Michael S. Yamashita/CORBIS; 909 © Bettmann/CORBIS; 910 © Yoichi Okamoto/CORBIS; 911 Charles Bonnay/Black Star; 912 Robert Ellison/Black Star; 913 © Bettmann/CORBIS; 914 B Hulton Archive/Getty Images Inc.; 914 BR © Leif Skoogfors/CORBIS; 914 ML © David J. & Janice L. Frent Collection/CORBIS; 914 TL © Bettmann/ CORBIS; 914 TR © Wally McNamee/CORBIS; 916 B AP/Wide World Photos; 916 T © Henri Bureau/CORBIS SYGMA; 917 Larry Burrows/Time Life Pictures/ Getty Images; 918 © Bettmann/CORBIS; 920 & 921 © Bettmann/CORBIS; 922 Richard Howard/Time Life Pictures/Getty Images; 923 AP/Wide World Photos; 924 B Getty Images/Blank Archives; 924 T © Bettmann/CORBIS; 925 © CORBIS; 926 CORBIS; 927 Pearson Education/PH School Division; 932–933 Shawn Thew/AFP/Getty Images; 934 T White House Historical Asso.; 934 B White House Photo Office; 936 © Wally McNamee/CORBIS; 937 Jim Berry/NEA INC NORTHERN ELECTRONICS AUTOMATION; 938 L © Wally McNamee/CORBIS; 938 R Courtesy Ronald Reagan Library; 939 The Political Bandwagon; 940 & 942 AP/Wide World Photos; 943 AP/Wide World Photos; 944 EWK, Cartoon Arts International/CWS; 945 © Associated Press; 947 AP/Wide World Photos; 947 T & B David Brauchli/Reuters/CORBIS; 949 AP/Wide World Photos; 950 © Peter Turnley/CORBIS; 952 Time Life Pictures/Getty Images; 953 © Associated Press; 955 © Wally McNamee/CORBIS; 956 T AP/Wide World Photos; 956 B CORBIS/Bettmann; 957 Helene C. Stikkel/U.S. Department of Defense Visual Information Center; 958 Andrew Alvarez/AFP/Getty Images; 959 T Larry Lee/Alamy; 959 B Luciano Corbella/© Dorling Kindersley; 962 AP/Wide World Photos; 964 John Flora/Photographer's Direct; 968 Getty Images; 969 AP/Wide World Photos; 971 © Copyright 2002 Brian Fairrington/ Cagle Cartooons. All rights reserved.; 972 L Wathiq Khuzaie/Getty Images; 972 R © Francoise DeMulder/CORBIS; 974 R Courtesy of the Library of Congress; 974 L AP/Wide World Photos; 975 T AP/Wide World Photos; 975 B Russell Boyce/REUTERS/CORBIS; 975 ML AP/Wide World Photos; 975 MR (c) Reuters NewMedia Inc./Jim Bourg/CORBIS; 976 © Steve Raymer/CORBIS; 978 Alfred Eisenstaedt/Time Life Pictures/Getty Images; 979 AP/Wide World Photos; 981 © NASA/GSFC/NOAA/USGS/Reuters/CORBIS; 982 © GEILERT/G.A.F.F./SIPA; 983 © Jeff Christensen/Reuters/CORBIS; 984 BL Win McNamee/Getty Images; 984 M Erich Schrempp/Photo Researchers, Inc.; 984 ML © Royalty-Free/Corbis; 984 TL © SuperStock, Inc.; 984 TR Jupiter Images.; 986 AP/Wide World Photos; 988 A. Ramey/PhotoEdit Inc.; 989 AP/Wide World Photos; 990 © Tom & Dee Ann McCarthy/CORBIS; 991 Myrleen Ferguson Cate/Photo Edit, Inc.; 993 AP/Wide World Photos; 995 © 2000 The Philadelphia Inquirer. Reprinted with permission of UNIVERSAL PRESS SYNDICATE. All rights reserved.; 1000 Corel Professional Photos CD-ROM™; 1001 Index Stock Imagery, Inc.; 1005 TL (BR, Bkgrd) Shutterstock; Art Resource, NY; TR CORBIS/Bettmann; BL CORBIS/Bettmann; BM CORBIS/Bettmann; 1006 Donovan Reese/Getty Images—Photodisc; 1022 CORBIS Royalty Free; 1028 Photograph by Robin Miller, 2001. Independence National Historical Park; 1029 01 © National Portrait Gallery, Smithsonian Institution/Art Resource, NY; 1029 02 © National Portrait Gallery, Smithsonian Institution/Art Resource, NY; 1029 03 White House Collection, copyright White House Historical Association; 1029 04 © National Portrait Gallery, Smithsonian Institution/Art Resource, NY; 1029 05 © National Portrait Gallery, Smithsonian Institution/Art Resource, NY; 1029 06 National Portrait Gallery, Smithsonian Institution/Art Resource, NY; 1029 07 White House Collection, copyright White House Historical Association; 1029 08 White House Collection, copyright White House Historical Association; 1029 09 © National Portrait Gallery, Smithsonian Institution/Art Resource, NY; 1029 10 © National Portrait Gallery, Smithsonian Institution/Art Resource, NY; 1029 11 White House Collection, copyright White House Historical Association; 1029 12 © National Portrait Gallery, Smithsonian Institution/Art Resource, NY; 1030 13 White House Collection, copyright White House Historical Association; 1030 14 © National Portrait Gallery, Smithsonian Institution/Art Resource, NY; 1030 15 © National Portrait Gallery, Smithsonian Institution/Art Resource, NY; 1030 16 White House Collection, copyright White House Historical Association; 1030 17 White House Collection, copyright White House Historical Association; 1030 18 © National Portrait Gallery, Smithsonian Institution/Art Resource, NY; 1030 19 White House Collection, copyright White House Historical Association; 1030 20 © National Portrait Gallery, Smithsonian Institution/Art Resource, NY; 1030 21 © National Portrait Gallery, Smithsonian Institution/Art Resource, NY; 1030 22 White House Collection, copyright White House Historical Association; 1030 23 White House Collection, copyright White House Historical Association; 1030 24 White House Collection, copyright White House Historical Association; 1031 25 © National Portrait Gallery, Smithsonian Institution/Art Resource, NY; 1031 26 © National Portrait Gallery, Smithsonian Institution/Art Resource, NY; 1031 27 © National Portrait Gallery, Smithsonian Institution/Art Resource, NY; 1031 28 White House Collection, copyright White House Historical Association; 1031 29 White House Collection, copyright White House Historical Association; 1031 30 White House Collection, copyright White House Historical Association; 1031 31 White House Collection, copyright White House Historical Association; 1031 32 White House Collection, copyright White House Historical Association; 1031 33 White House Collection, copyright White House Historical Association; 1031 34 White House Collection, copyright White House Historical Association; 1031 35 © National Portrait Gallery, Smithsonian Institution/Art Resource, NY; 1031 36 White House Collection, copyright White House Historical Association; 1032 37 White House Collection, copyright White House Historical Association; 1032 38 White House Collection, copyright White House Historical Association; 1032 39 White House Collection, copyright White House Historical Association; 1032 40 White House Collection, copyright White House Historical Association; 1032 41 White House Collection, copyright White House Historical Association; 1032 42 White House Historical Association (White House Collection) (6196) (detail); 1032 42 White House Historical Association (White House Collection) (6196) (detail); 1032 43 George W. Bush Presidential Library; 1032 B White House Photo Office; 1036 Lawrence Migdale/Pix; 1037 The Granger Collection, New York; 1040 © Monica Graff/The Image Works; 1048 © North Wind Picture Archives; 1049 Getty Images; 1052 Shutterstock; 1057 Shutterstock

Acknowledgments

Text Credits

Grateful acknowledgment is made to the following for copyrighted material:

Alfred A. Knopf, Inc.
"I, Too" by Langston Hughes from *American Negro Poetry, Revised Edition.* Copyright © 1994 by The Estate of Langston Hughes. Reprinted by permission of Alfred A. Knopf, Inc., a division of Random House, Inc.

Bantam Books, a division of Random House, Inc.
Excerpt from *Dauntless: A Novel of Midway and Guadalcanal* by Barrett Tillman. Copyright © 1995 by Barrett Tillman. Used by permission of Bantam Books, a division of Random House, Inc.

Barrett Tillman
Excerpt from *Dauntless: A Novel of Midway and Guadalcanal* by Barrett Tillman. Copyright © 1992 by Barrett Tillman. Reprinted by permission of the author.

Naomi Long Madgett
"Midway" from *Star by Star* (Harlow, 1965; Evenill, 1970). Copyright © 1958 by Naomi Long Madgett. Reprinted in Connected Islands: New and Selected Poems (Detroit: Lotus Press, 2004). Used by permission.

The Seattle Times Company
Excerpt from "Local Schools Shining Light on Solar Panels" from *The Seattle Times, July 21, 2008* by Jeff Raderstrong. Copyright © The Seattle Times Company. Reprinted by permission.

Note: **Every effort has been made to locate the copyright owner of material reprinted in this book. Omissions brought to our attention will be corrected in subsequent editions.**

UNITED STATES
POLITICAL

Golden Gate Bridge, San Francisco, California

115°W   110°W   105°W   100°W

Seattle
Spokane
Olympia
Washington

Portland
Salem
Eugene

Oregon

Boise
Idaho

Pocatello

Great Falls
Helena
Montana

Billings

Wyoming

Casper

Ogden
Great Salt Lake
Salt Lake City

Reno
Carson City
San Francisco
Sacramento
Oakland
San Jose

Nevada

Utah

Cheyenne

Denver
Colorado
Colorado Springs

California

Las Vegas

Minot
Grand Forks
North Dakota
Bismarck

South Dakota

Rapid City
Pierre
Sioux Falls

Nebraska

Lincoln

Kansas

Wichita

125°W

Los Angeles
Long Beach
San Diego

Salton Sea

PACIFIC OCEAN

30°N

115°W

120°W

Arizona

Phoenix

Tucson

Santa Fe
Albuquerque

New Mexico

Las Cruces
El Paso

110°W

Oklahoma
Oklahoma City

Fort Worth

Texas

Austin

San Antonio

160°W   155°W

Honolulu
Hawaii

PACIFIC OCEAN

20°N

0 km   100
0 miles   100
Mercator Projection

180° 70°N 170°W 160°W 150°W
RUSSIA

Arctic Circle

140°W

130°W

Alaska

Fairbanks

CANADA

MEXICO

Anchorage

Bering Sea

60°N

Gulf of Alaska

Juneau

PACIFIC OCEAN

160°E 170°E 50°N

0 km   400
0 miles   400
Albers Conic Equal-Area Projection

105°W   100°W

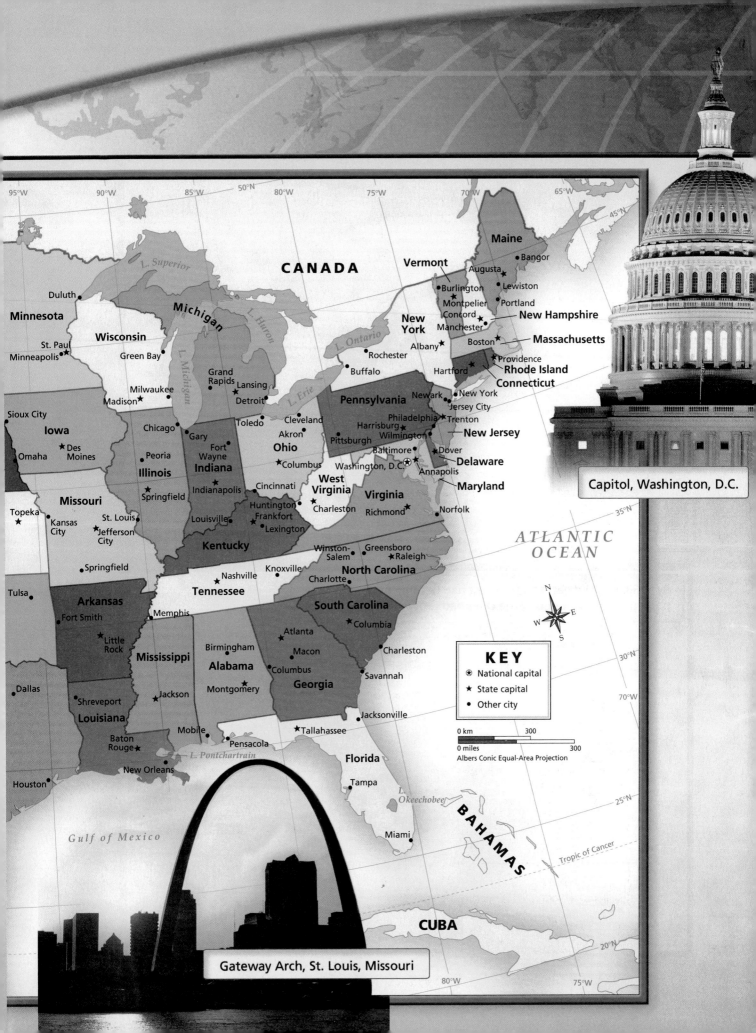

Capitol, Washington, D.C.

Gateway Arch, St. Louis, Missouri

KEY
- ⊛ National capital
- ★ State capital
- • Other city

0 km 300
0 miles 300
Albers Conic Equal-Area Projection

UNITED STATES
POPULATION DENSITY

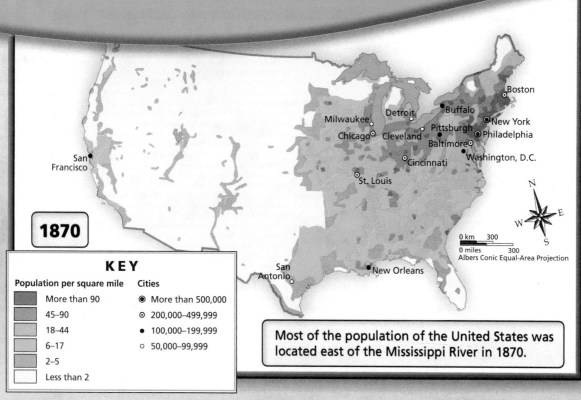

1870

KEY

Population per square mile

	More than 90
	45–90
	18–44
	6–17
	2–5
	Less than 2

Cities

- ◉ More than 500,000
- ◎ 200,000–499,999
- ● 100,000–199,999
- ○ 50,000–99,999

Albers Conic Equal-Area Projection

Most of the population of the United States was located east of the Mississippi River in 1870.

By 1960, the Midwest and the West had become more populated. A number of large cities had grown in these regions.

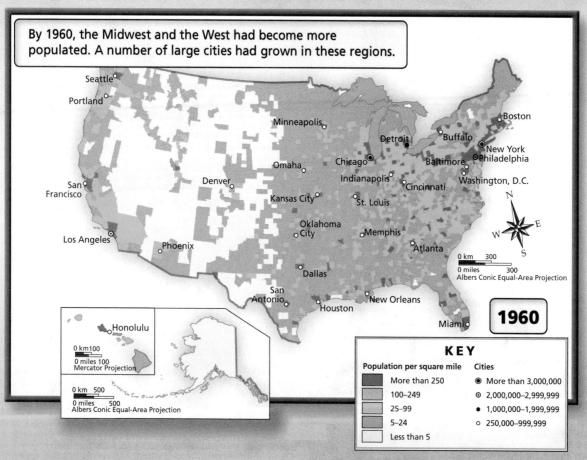

1960

Mercator Projection

Albers Conic Equal-Area Projection

KEY

Population per square mile

	More than 250
	100–249
	25–99
	5–24
	Less than 5

Cities

- ◉ More than 3,000,000
- ◎ 2,000,000–2,999,999
- ● 1,000,000–1,999,999
- ○ 250,000–999,999